HQ XX Corps

1st Div XXI Corps

2d Div III Corps

FULL DRESS
Captain
Artillery

GREAT COAT
All Mounted Men

FULL DRESS
Corporal
Cavalry

3d Div IV Corps

2d Div XI Corps

HQ XXI Corps

THEY FOUGHT FOR THE UNION

BATTLE OF SHILOH

THEY FOUGHT FOR THE UNION

By

Francis A. Lord, Ph. D.

GREENWOOD PRESS, PUBLISHERS
WESTPORT, CONNECTICUT

Library of Congress Cataloging in Publication Data

Lord, Francis Alfred, 1911-
   They fought for the Union.

      Reprint. Originally published: Harrisburg, Pa. :
Stackpole, 1960.
      Bibliography: p.
      Includes index.
      1. United States--History--Civil War, 1861-1865.
2. United States--Armed Forces--History--Civil War,
1861-1865.   I. Title.
[E491.L89 1981]   973.7'41   81-6579
ISBN 0-313-22740-3 (lib. bdg.)   AACR2

The endsheets have been reproduced in black and white in
the Greenwood Press reprint edition.

Reprinted in 1981 by Greenwood Press
A division of Congressional Information Service, Inc.
88 Post Road West, Westport, Connecticut 06881

Printed in the United States of America

10 9 8 7 6 5 4 3 2 1

To the memory of the men who wore the Blue and especially to:

Francis H. Buffum, Color Sergeant
14th N. H. Vols.

Jedediah Buffum, Private
14th N. H. Vols.

Jesse H. Lord, 1st Lieutenant
2nd Conn. Vols.

Foreword

BY MAJOR GENERAL U. S. GRANT III

"Who will tell the story,
Now the Boys in Blue are gone?"

To this refrain of the old song Dr. Lord has made a definitive and full response in THEY FOUGHT FOR THE UNION. It is not an attempt to retell the history of the Civil War, not another account of campaigns and battles fought, or of leaders and the armies they led; but a detailed account of the circumstances surrounding the Union soldiers and their officers, a complete factual background of the war and its impact on those who took part in it. It is made up of information from many various sources which no one could duplicate without devoting years of his life to the search. On many subjects it fills a gap for which "Civil War Buffs" and the general reader interested in the war will be grateful.

Although a compendium of facts, gleaned from innumerable authorities, it is full of human interest giving the soldier's reaction to his surroundings and problems by quotations from diaries and letters. For instance, the reason for a man in the 13th New Hampshire Infantry giving up swearing: "No hard words can possibly do the weather and mud here any degree of justice and he was tired of trying." And in connection with the refusal of the Chief of Ordnance to adopt an improved rifle, and his insistence on continuing the issue of the old muzzle loading musket, this heartfelt statement of a soldier writing to the Army and Navy Journal: "Let them come to the front armed with one Springfield musket, and oppose themselves to an equal number of Rebels armed with repeaters or breechloaders. If they can stand that, let them go to the picket line, and while fumbling for a cap and trying to get it on the cone one of these cold days, offer themselves as a target to some fellow on the other side who has nothing to do but cock his piece and blaze away. If they don't throw down their bungling, slow shooting gun in disgust, they may be excused for indulging in remarks not complimentary to those who compel them to the unequal contest. The objection has been urged that we fire too many shots with our present muzzle-loaders, and consequently it would be folly to add to the waste of ammunition by affording us greater ease or facility in loading. Do our good friends ever reflect that the loss of time in loading is the great cause of haste and consequent inaccuracy in firing?" Certainly no better argument could be advanced for a change to a breech-loading, repeating rifle, such as President Lincoln finally did order to be made and issued.

But the author does not limit himself to views and comments of enlisted men. There is that inimitable exchange of correspondence between Brigadier General H. M. Nagle and Major General E. D. Keyes, in which the former wrote to the latter: "I am most happy to advise you that I have been transferred with my brigade into the Department of North Carolina. It may be equally agreeable and satisfactory to you, as it certainly is to myself, to be assured that the separation will be a permanent one." To this General Keyes replied with equal urbanity: "Your letter of the 15th instant has been received. The happiness you express in your announcement of a permanent separation from me, is, I assure you, most cordially reciprocated. I will add, with the risk of being thought to exaggerate, that I do not believe any one of your previous commanding officers was made more happy at parting with you than I was." Dr. Johnson did not do better in his notorious letter to Lord Chesterfield.

The author justly emphasizes the value of "letters and diaries of enlisted men and company grade officers who usually wrote exactly what they saw, felt, and did." The scope of his book can best be gleaned from the chapter headings and carries the reader from the country's unpreparedness for any such stupendous fight for its existence through the various phases of raising, training, and equipping the armies that finally saved the Union. Necessarily, the similar problems and results in the Confederacy are touched upon when appropriate, but without malice or apparent prejudice. He summarizes the special problems and improvements in the technical services, thereby filling a woeful gap in so many of our popular histories and providing information necessary for the appreciation of the American ingenuity and resourcefulness that made this war unique in military history, the first modern war. Without the telegraph the control of armies in different theaters of operation, widely separated by great ranges of mountains and large rivers, would not have been possible; without the railroads and river steamers the supply of the large forces engaged would not have been practicable, nor would the shifting of large bodies of troops from one theater of operations to another. The innovations in the organization for the removal and care of the wounded, in the use of the field telegraph, observation from the air, map reproduction in the field, wire entanglements, land mines, submarine mines (which then were called torpedoes), booby traps, iron clads, rifled cannon and small arms, etc., are all summarized most interestingly.

The equipment of the soldier, his training, discipline and morale, are equally recorded with appropriate indications of how he felt about them. The author does not avoid the ugly side, the problems and desertion and punishment, the prison camps, and the losses by disease that might have been avoided, if those untrained volunteers and their equally inexperienced officers had known what we know today about sanitation and preventive medicine. But his treatment of these shortcomings is factual and not sensational. They were just part of what the Boys in Blue and those in Gray had to suffer and overcome. Rations, pay, and conditions on the home front are also covered, especially as they affected the soldier and his morale. The author's statements are amply authenticated in footnotes at the end of each chapter, which is a great convenience to the reader in not having to turn constantly to the end of the book for the references. The extent of Dr. Lord's research, as measured by these references and by his bibliography, challenges admiration. Inevitably, there are some omissions which one regrets but which may not have been easily available when the author was doing his background reading: I have looked in vain for Bruce Catton's three volumes, beginning with *Mr. Lincoln's Army* and that so conscientiously researched and thorough history, Kenneth P. Williams's *Lincoln Finds A General*, as well as any one of the two or three books on the part played by the women in the war; although the author does on occasion mention their work. As it was the first time women had been organized nationally to play an important and direct part in a war, and did their duty nobly *in the field*, especially under "Nurses," their organization being "a first" of the Civil War seems to merit more than these passing references.

Some historians will doubtless find some statements about which they will differ with Dr. Lord. Not being a historian, but only a reader of history, I venture to comment on one statement only (page 270) that seems to me inadequately considered, namely: "There was little evidence of generalship on the Federal side and, in fact, the higher command was seen but little in that battle (of the Wilderness)." As to the latter part of this statement it would have been highly improper for either General Meade or General Grant to join with the men in the woods where they would have entirely lost control of the battle situation; but they did visit the various commanders of large units frequently. It was General Grant's primary duty to remain where he and his staff could receive and send messages, "feed the fight," and find means to meet any new attempt of the enemy. That the corps commanders fully did their duty as leaders cannot be doubted. For instance, take General Horace Porter's statement (page 57, in his *Campaigning with Grant*): "I met Hancock on the Orange plank-road, not far from its junction with the Brock road, actively engaged in directing his troops, and restoring the confusion in their alinement caused by the desperate fighting and the difficult character of the ground. All thought of the battle which raged about us was to me for a moment lost in contemplation of the dramatic scene presented in the person of the knightly corps commander. He had just driven the enemy a mile and a half. His face was flushed with the excitement of victory, his eyes were lighted by the fire of battle, his flaxen hair was thrust back from his temples, his right arm was extended to its full length in pointing out certain positions as he gave his orders, and his commanding form towered still higher as he rose in his stirrups to peer through the openings in the woods." There is. no reason to believe that the other corps, division and brigade commanders did not equally lead their men personally. Generals Carroll and Getty were severely wounded and General Alexander Hays was killed.

It was indeed a critical time for the Union cause, perhaps the most critical since Shiloh and Antietam. General Lee's plan was a bold one. Since he had far fewer men than Grant it was folly to fight in the open. His plan was to wait until all Federal divisions had crossed to the south of the Rapidan, and then, when they and their immense trains were entangled in the thickets of the Wilderness, to strike their right flank; to envelop Grant up as he had Hooker, and destroy his army or drive it back in disorder across the river. Of course, General Grant's desire was to get through the Wilderness before General Lee could strike, but his chief objective in the campaign was to bring General Lee to an open battle in the open country; and when he found the attack was coming in the Wilderness, he issued through General Meade such directions as were necessary to meet it. When he found on May 7th that General Lee had withdrawn behind his entrenchments and the attack had finally been repulsed, he moved forward by the left flank in the effort to cut the enemy off from Richmond and bring him to bay in the open country before he could reach shelter behind the fortifications of Richmond and withstand a siege.

Surely it will be conceded that to meet a flank attack successfully while on the march with a very large force without exposing unduly the trains and line of communications was a definite test of the Commander's generalship, and this General Grant did while attacked by a most skillful opponent. Such a withdrawal of a large army and march forward in the face of an active enemy on its flank is generally recognized as an especially difficult maneuver; but it was so directed as to threaten the enemy's communications with Richmond, which forced the latter to retire from his intrenched position and, taking advantage of his interior lines to interpose himself to the forward movement at Spottsylvania. This difficult maneuver was successfully accomplished by General Grant with an army he did not know and to which he was a stranger and in very difficult terrain, his only map of which had many errors. As General Fuller says, "tactically this battle was an indecisive one, strategically the greatest victory yet won in the East; for these two days' fighting satisfied Lee of his inability further to maintain the contest in the field. From the evening of May 6 until his attack on Fort Stedman the following year, never again did he dare assume the offensive. It is true, as we shall see, that he sometimes attacked and often counterattacked; but from now onwards his strategy was purely defensive." And as to the indecisiveness tactically, the attack was definitely repulsed and Lee's army driven back into its entrenchments without renewing the attack on May 7th.

At dinner at the Bohemian Club in San Francisco in the mid 1920's the Chief Engineer of the Southern Pacific Railroad, Mr. Hood, who had been a young soldier in the Army of the Potomac, told a group of us, when asked, that his most tragic recollection of his war experiences was "when after winning the Battle of Gettysburg we had to stand and see General Lee's Army withdraw and safely recross the Potomac River." And then when pressed to tell his most inspiring experience, he said without hesitation, "when we were withdrawn from the Wilderness and coming to the road were turned South towards Richmond!" Chief Hood was a very calm, factual man—he had built the Union Pacific cut-off across the Great Salt Lake and was acknowledged to be quite an engineer—and I am sure he had given us a true account of his feelings as a soldier. Surely, the Battle of the Wilderness cannot be counted as a Union defeat, as Dr. Lord has listed it.

But these are only footnotes to Dr. Lord's excellent book; they are matters of opinion, and to mention them seems almost ingratitude for the great work he has done. The author's understanding reference to the Civil War Centennial Commission and its work is deeply appreciated. I heartily concur in his belief that "the qualities of the Union soldier must be remembered and honored." During the next five years we shall have a special opportunity to join in paying our homage to his memory, to which purpose this book is an important contribution.

Preface

In recent years there has been a constantly increasing number of books published on the Civil War, most of which have been narratives of the war itself or of certain segments, or biographies of leading figures. There has been, too, an occasional reference work, usually of a statistical nature and frequently a reprint of a much earlier study. There has been a lack of reliable information, presented in convenient form, concerning the human resources of both sides, how they were armed, equipped, trained, and employed as individuals. This book is designed to fill that need in an objective and authoritative manner yet in a more palatable form than is supplied by the usual statistical study or reference book. Owing to the tremendous scope of such a project, however, this volume is confined to a treatment of the nature and role of the Northern fighting man and his equipment.

Each chapter deals with a separate phase of the over-all subject, though these necessarily overlap to a certain extent. Great care has been exercised to insure not only thorough, but discriminating documentation throughout. Ample additional information may be found in the voluminous sources listed and described briefly in Chapter 22, *Civil War Bibliography*, which informed critics who have read the manuscript regard as one of the most valuable portions of the book.

Most of the items of equipment illustrated herein are in the author's collection; other photos and drawings are generally from official sources.

Since 1865 the Civil War has furnished a rich field for research, both for historians and collectors. Practically every phase has been investigated by skilled historians both in the United States and abroad. Of recent years numerous writers of renown have bent their efforts in this direction. Unfortunately a great deal of the early writings, and a certain portion of the more recent have been nonobjective and in some instances strongly colored by partisanship. As a result, a certain amount of misinformation, some of it merely erroneous interpretation, some entirely mythical in nature, has become firmly imbedded in the history and lore of the great struggle. One field in which this is true, and which has not received the attention which it merits, is an evaluation of the Federal volunteer. One reason for this is the widely accepted belief that the North won the war only because of its superiority in numbers and its greater material resources. There has been a preponderant admiration for the Southern soldier and a lack of interest in the Federal serviceman *per se*. This attitude is something less than correct, and definitely less than just.

This volume examines the Federal volunteer from his entrance into the service, through the various stages of his military life, until his final discharge or death. Included are motivations for enlistment and continued fighting, training, organization, equipment, weapons, conduct in the field, discipline, morale, welfare, and daily life. There is no attempt to discuss strategy or to narrate the tactical vicissitudes of the campaigns. There is no analysis of the generals and other leading personalities. Statistics are included as need be, but not overemphasized. The account is mainly a description of the Federal soldier, sailor, and marine, and the material things which were furnished for life in camp, in the field, and at sea.

Numerous sources were consulted in preparation of the work, as can be seen, but great care was used in the selection, especially in that of published material. It was felt that many readers needed a bibliography on which they could rely, without subjecting themselves to a time-consuming evaluation of sources. Many private diaries and letters have not previously been cited. Numerous general works which are relished by historians are little used here, for they deal with generalship and units rather than with men. This is particularly true of biographies and autobiographies of noted leaders.

After a lapse of two decades immediately following the war the South became more articulate in expressing itself than it had been during the Reconstruction. The resulting histories and memoirs deal only very lightly with their antagonist, the Northern soldier, as an individual. Contemporary periodicals both in the North and South are also disappointing in this instance, especially in discussing soldier morale. There is one exception, *The Army and Navy Journal*, which has been little exploited by historians. It is used extensively here, however, because it expressed current attitudes and problems, often giving the viewpoints of both sides. One important source, much used by all historians is, of course, the official records, *The War of the Rebellion: A Compilation of the Official Records of the Union and Confederate Armies*, a work of 130 volumes. Also used to some extent was the *Reports of the Committee on the Conduct of the War*. Century Company's old favorite, *Battles and Leaders of the Civil War*, a 4-volume compilation of the writings of various officers on both sides, must never be overlooked by a historian; and another excellent compilation is the 10-volume *Photographic History of the War* which in addition to the hundreds of photographs contains much textual material. Though there are exceptions, the majority of unit histories are replete with local prejudice, gossip, and self-praise. Their chief value was their inclusion of excerpts from soldiers' letters and diaries.

The most revealing and informative sources were the letters and diaries of enlisted men and company grade officers who usually wrote exactly what they saw, felt, and did. Of considerable value, also, were the few autobiographies of those younger officers who rose to high command near the close of the war. Several of these graduated from West Point just prior to the war; others were commissioned from civilian life or rose from the ranks. This type of leader was alert and intelligent, observant of what went around him, capable of retaining in later years an elasticity of mind and honesty of purpose which served to pass on his impressions to posterity. Possibly the most famous of this group is Upton, but Cox, Gibbon, Merritt, and others have left us indebted to them for their objective treatment of the experience of the Federal soldier as seen in the eyes of his comrades and superiors.

In addition to his use of written material the author was born early enough to talk with several Union veterans including his grandfather, men who had served in both the Eastern and Western campaigns of the Civil War. Moreover the author was a professor for a number of years in a college in Mississippi, which gave him an opportunity to become familiar with Southern attitudes toward the war, and above all to learn a great deal concerning the feeling of the Confederate soldiers toward their Northern opponents. And finally, many long conversations with aged Negroes disclosed much interesting and significant information concerning the fighting around Vicksburg, as witnessed by the parents of these people—folk who during the Civil War were slaves on the great plantations in that area.

The author is indebted to many individuals who contributed material for this book. Although these are too numerous to list, I desire to mention especially my colleagues of the Company of Military Collectors and Historians, and specifically Robert L. Miller. Mr. Miller assisted me very substantially, not only with expert advice but, perhaps with what is even more important, constructive criticism. Miss Josephine Cobb of the National Archives aided me in the selection of photographic material. I also owe a great deal to "Bernie" Mitchell, who has helped in the acquisition of many items discussed herein. His interest and concrete assistance are very greatly appreciated. Lastly, but by no means of lesser value, has been the encouragement and hard work of my wife. Only she and I can know what she has done; without her this book could not have been written. "In addition to her other duties" she photographed all the items of my collection which are shown in this book.

The author wishes to express his very sincere appreciation to Colonel Wilbur S. Nye, U.S.A.—Ret. for his assistance.

Permission to use material from their books has been graciously extended by the following publishers and authors:

Francis Bannerman Sons., Inc.: Catalogue 1959.

Benjamin Blied: *Catholics in the Civil War.*

Robert V. Bruce, *Lincoln and the Tools of War.* Bobbs-Merrill Co., Inc.

J. F. C. Fuller, *The Generalship of U. S. Grant.* Indiana University Press. This volume is one in the Civil War Centennial Series.

William B. Hesseltine, University of Wisconsin: *Civil War Prisons.*

Henry Holt and Co., Inc.: Fletcher Pratt, *War on Western Waters.*

Houghton Mifflin Co.: Gamaliel Bradford, *Union Portraits.*

Illinois State Historical Society: *Journal,* Vol. 18, January 1926.

Indiana Magazine of History: Vol. 30, No. 8 (Sept. 1934) "The Fourteenth Indiana in the Valley of Virginia."

The Johns Hopkins Press: E. Stansbury Haydon, *Aeronautics in the Union and Confederate Armies,* Vol. 1.

Little, Brown and Co.: Martha Perry, *Letters from a Surgeon in the Civil War.*

J. B. Lippincott Co.: Victor Robinson, *White Caps—The Story of Nursing.*

Louisiana State University Press, Ella Lonn, *Foreigners in the Union Army and Navy.*

Michigan Historical Commission: Charles Robinson, "My Experiences in the Civil War." *Michigan History Magazine,* Winter 1940 (Vol. XXIV)

Mississippi Valley Historical Review: Letter of Samuel Merrill in the March 2 1928, issue of the *Review.*

National Capitol Publishers, Inc.: Joseph M. Hanson, *Bull Run Remembers.*

W. W. Norton and Co.: Fletcher Pratt, *Stanton-Lincoln's Secretary of War;* Harvey Ford, *Memoirs of a Volunteer.*

Norwegian-American Historical Association: Theodore C. Blegen, *The Civil War Letters of Colonel Hans Christian Heg.*

James G. Randall, *The Civil War and Reconstruction.* D. C. Heath and Co.

Charles Scribner's Sons: George Meade, *Life and Letters of George Meade;* E. P. Alexander, *Military Memoirs of a Confederate;* Charles Blackford, *Letters from Lee's Army.*

Margaret Staton: John Wyeth, *With Saber and Scalpel.*

Viking Press: Material from *The Hidden Civil War* by Wood Gray. Copyright 1942 by Wood Gray. Reprinted by permission of the Viking Press, Inc.

The World Almanac: 1959 edition, published by the New York World-Telegram and Sun.

Yale University Press: James Croushore, *A Volunteer's Adventures.*

FRANCIS A. LORD

Contents

List of Illustrations

The capital letters in parentheses after the titles refer to the sources from which the illustrations were taken, and to which credit is due:

(A) Author's collection
(D) Department of the Army
(F) Edwin Forbes, *An Artist's History of the Great War*, New York, 1890
(H) Harpers Pictorial History, New York, 1868
(L) Library of Congress
(N) National Archives
(S) Smithsonian Institution
(SCW) *Soldier in Our Civil War*, New York, 1885

PRINCIPAL THEATER OF OPERATIONS

CHAPTER 1

Recruiting and Drafting

AT THE outbreak of the Civil War the military forces of the Federal government consisted of a standing army and militia, but neither was prepared for the difficult task of overcoming the resistance of excellent fighting forces operating in an area of roughly one million square miles.

THE ARMY IN 1861

The Regular Army, which had had combat experience in Mexico a decade before, was a well disciplined force dispersed throughout the United States, but chiefly on the western frontier. Numbering only 16,402 men on January 1, 1861, this army was reduced by the resignation and desertion of 313 commissioned officers from the South, or approximately one-fifth the total commissioned strength.[1] Such a force was obviously incapable of crushing a revolt of a determined people who had 401,395 men in the field by the end of the first year of the war.[2] The role of the Regular Army throughout the war was really divided between acting as a token force in the field and serving as an officer pool. Unfortunately it never was permitted to concentrate on either of these roles, so that the contribution of the Regular Army toward winning the war must be found in the higher command echelons. It did not function as a significant training or fighting element.

THE MILITIA

The militia, mostly unorganized and numbering more than 3,000,000,[3] was weak in fighting potential. What little training the militiamen received was antiquated and discipline was poor. With the exception of a few crack units such as were found in the larger cities, the militia regiments were no better than their inglorious predecessors had been at Camden and Bladensburg. The Northern people, who were not military-minded, had never come to appreciate the value of training and discipline for their militia. Only a few of the States had made preparations to get their militia ready before hostilities began. For instance we find that for three months prior to the attack on Fort Sumter the Massachusetts Volunteer Militia, "in anticipation of some great traitorous movement in the South,"[4] drilled almost nightly in their armories. Governor Andrew issued his General

Order No. 4 on January 16, 1861, which placed the militia of his state on a wartime footing. As a result of this order certain companies dropped from their rolles men unfit or unwilling to serve and accepted replacements.[5] Even before these preparations in Massachusetts the New York State Legislature extended to President Lincoln the service of the State militia, to be used as he deemed best "to preserve the Union and enforce the Constitution and laws of the Country."[6] Pennsylvania, Michigan, and Massachusetts were equally prompt.

The reaction in the North to the attack upon Fort Sumter was instantaneous and widespread. Mobs went about New York and elsewhere forcing suspect newspapers and private dwellings to display the Stars and Stripes. The garrison from Sumter met with a hearty reception when it reached New York. Officers and men were carried on the shoulders of crowds wild with enthusiasm. The great city's streets were decked with banners.[7] For a short time dissenters were discreetly silent.

To meet the challenge of insurrection the President called on the States for 75,000 militia for a period of three months. The legal basis for this call of April 15, 1861, was found in two ancient militia acts, those of February 28, 1795, and March 3, 1803. The 1795 act empowered the President to call forth the militia of any State or States "whenever the laws of the United States should be opposed or the operation thereof obstructed in any State, by combinations too powerful to be suppressed by the ordinary course of judicial proceedings, or by the powers vested in the Marshals by this Act."[8] By this act no militiaman could be compelled to serve more than three months in any one year. The 1803 law provided for the calling out of the militia in the District of Columbia for the maintenance of law and order within the District alone.[9] Under this 1803 law the President issued calls in April for three regiments, but many of the men refused to take the oath of allegiance for fear they would thereby become Regular soldiers. However, they were reassured that they were merely militia and were not sent out of the District.[10] It was popularly believed that the war would be of short duration. The Federal government was weak at this period as evidenced by its complete lack of military

1

policy. Secretary of War Simon Cameron, a political appointee, was incapable of administering his office. The States took the lead in the first effort to raise troops since the Regular Army was too small and too greatly dispersed to be of use. Although Regular officers, or former Regulars like Sherman, firmly believed that raw militia troops "never were and never will be fit for invasion," [11] the Northern States, responding enthusiastically to this first call to arms, recruited their militia regiments very rapidly to full strength. Under the call of April 15, 1861, the States raised 91,816 men.[12] Even then, some governors were insisting that the Federal government call many more regiments, and in some cases for longer periods of time than ninety days.[13]

These demands by State governors were backed by a seemingly irresistible advance in the military program of the enemy. In Baltimore the passage of two Northern militia regiments (6th Massachusetts Infantry and 7th Pennsylvania Infantry) was disputed by civilians hostile to the Federal government. Federal forts and arsenals within the Southern lines were seized; railroads and telegraph lines were cut; the Capital was almost in a state of siege, and communication with the outside world was possible only through the medium of private messenger. It seemed as if 1814 was to be repeated.

REGULAR ARMY IS INCREASED

To prevent such a disaster the President on May 3, 1861, issued a proclamation whereby the Regular Army was to be increased by 22,714 officers and men, and the Navy by 18,000 seamen. In addition, he called for 42,834 volunteers. This meant an increase of ten regiments of Regulars and forty regiments of volunteers.[14] Although the call provided for a Regular Army of 42,000 men, enlistments in this force were disappointingly few, so that by December 1861, when the volunteers already totalled 640,000 men, the total of the Regular Army was only 20,334.[15]

VOLUNTEERS

In those early months of the war before Bull Run the Federal government could have accepted a much larger volunteer force, but the war materiel for additional troops was lacking.[16] Hundreds of thousands of volunteers offered their services in 1861 but were turned away because of this unfortunate situation. Not only did the States function as agencies in raising troops, but sometimes individuals tried to raise and proffer regiments or even brigades directly to the President. Usually these individuals were prevented by their respective governors but Daniel Sickles, ex-diplomat and society man, succeeded in raising the famous Excelsior Brigade in New York, took it directly to Washington, and offered it directly to Lincoln. The brigade lost half its men by the vicissitudes of war before the Governor of New York

finally overrode Sickles and the five regiments were credited to New York.[17]

While the volunteers were pouring into State rendezvous camps the three-month militia received their baptism of fire in the Battle of Bull Run, July 21, 1861. The men fought bravely but lost the battle late in the day. These men have never received the credit they deserve; they served for a short period only and saw little action but they did give the Federal government time to catch its breath in the almost impossible task of forming an army out of raw material. Bull Run was the inevitable answer to the clamorous "on to Richmond" cry, but the people were rudely awakened and the fervor of recruiting which so characterized the spring fell off sharply. It is true that the quotas under the 1861 calls were substantially oversubscribed but the distribution was very unequal. Some New England States and such States as Delaware and Maryland failed to fill their quotas.[18]

There was a slight increase in recruiting during the winter of 1861-1862 due to the seasonal slackness of labor in the agricultural regions. But the increase was not sufficient for attaining the goal set by General McClellan, who assumed command after Bull Run, hence it was necessary to resort to special appeals, extraordinary financial inducements, and even covert threats of possible future drafts in order to stir up the laggards. The reasons given for prompt enlistment were: it was a noble cause; the pay was the highest in the world; the rations and supplies were good; and weapons were unsurpassed.[19]

RECRUITING IN 1862

An order of December 3, 1861, placed recruiting in the hands of the War Department. By March 31, 1862, the Army consisted of 23,308 Regulars and 613,818 volunteers.[20] The militia is not included in these figures except in the cases of those militia units which had become "federalized," that is, had come under Federal control. Then they were in the same category as regiments of volunteers raised for service in the war. On April 3, 1862, recruiting for Volunteers was temporarily halted.[21] Officers and men returned to their regiments from their detached duty at recruiting offices; the offices themselves were closed down; and the public property belonging to the volunteer recruiting service was sold to the highest bidders, the proceeds being credited to a fund for collecting, drilling, and organizing volunteers.[22] To replace the men lost by Grant at Shiloh and McClellan on the Peninsula it was necessary to re-establish recruiting, which was done by an order issued June 6, 1862.[23] The shortage of men continued, however, and in May and June special authority was granted to the States of New York, Illinois, and Indiana to furnish men for three months of service. Under this authority New York furnished 8,588 men, Indiana furnished 1,723, and Illinois furnished 4,696.[24] The reinforcement of 15,007 three-month troops would obviously be meager in the light of what was transpiring on the Peninsula and on other fronts. More men were needed at once.

VOLUNTARY ENLISTMENTS

The President and his cabinet were gravely concerned over the military situation in general and that of the Army of the Potomac in particular. Now realizing that a new call was imperative, they reached an agreement which resulted in a War Department

appeared July 15, 1862, the New York *Times* described the situation in many places in the North at that time:

There was a brisker business done at the recruiting offices yesterday than on any day since the issue of the President's requisition . . . The men who are coming forward are far superior, on the average, to those who have filled up the regiments that went from the State last winter. They are mainly men who seem to be acting, not from impulse, or necessity, or in the belief that they will have an easy time of it, but from conscientious motives of patriotism; volunteering freely, under the full comprehension of the serious nature of the work

CIVIL WAR RECRUITING

order published July 2, 1862, calling for 300,000 volunteers.[25] By this call the States raised 421,465 men for three years.[26] The caliber of men responding to this call was exceptionally high. The reason for this high type of volunteer coming forward in response to this call is not difficult to ascertain. He had not enlisted in the spring of 1861 because he was bound by domestic and economic ties that were not as easily severed as were those of the less stable elements that were usually found to predominate in the militia units that responded to the earlier calls. Those who were well established in society and who did try to enlist in 1861 were quite often turned away because the lack of arms and equipment had sharply curtailed the number of regiments permitted each State. Since domestic and foreign sources had largely remedied these deficiencies, the men could now be accepted. In an article entitled "Recruiting in the City," which

they will have to do, and with the determination, by this volunteering, to, if possible, end the struggle quickly and effectually.[27]

The first great outburst of patriotic enthusiasm had subsided. War was no longer romantic. The Federal armies were being depleted by battle casualties and disease; maimed veterans were observed more often in the Northern cities and rural areas. One veteran who responded to this July call pointed out that it required a good deal of courage to enlist in the Federal armies under this call. "The men who responded were not Bohemians, nor mere seekers for a better fortune. They were mostly fixtures in society . . . They were men who could not have been bought from wife, children, and the family home of generations for one hundred or one thousand dollars. And such men were the overwhelming majority of the three-years' volunteers of 1862." [28]

President Lincoln's call of July 2, 1862, for 300,000 three-year troops was a very severe drain on the North. It absorbed the best fighting element, the grand reserve force of the country. After this reserve force had been enlisted in the armed services no later call ever produced men of equal caliber.

STATE QUOTAS ARE ESTABLISHED

As was so often the case throughout the entire war, however, some States were less cooperative in their support of the war effort than others. This was especially true in the raising of men. In some localities volunteering was not as enthusiastic as it should have been. The Federal government finally decided that a draft would be necessary to provide the requisite number of troops. The Southern victories in this stage of the war can be partially attributed to the fact that the Confederate Congress had passed universal conscription as early as April 16, 1862.[29]

The Federal government proceeded slowly along the path of an out-and-out conscription of the manpower of the country. On July 14, 1862, Congress passed a law whereby the President could call out the militia for a period not to exceed nine months with quotas apportioned to each State. By militia was meant all able-bodied male citizens between the ages of eighteen and forty-five.[30] This was merely a revision of the old 1795 militia law and was not a draft administered by the Federal government. States were allowed to draft if they so desired; the main interest of the government was to get the men. The military situation was chaotic; in the East it was becoming obvious that Pope was not going to be able to check Lee, and little was being done in the West. The significance of the Law of July 14, 1862, is that it allowed a draft by the States based on executive interpretation rather than direct legislative sanction. It was also the first step taken by the executive department of the Federal government toward recruiting under authority of this law and the 1795 law.

A PSEUDO DRAFT

The War Department issued a call on August 4, 1862, for 300,000 militia to serve for nine months. This number, which was in addition to the quota of July 2, 1862, stipulated that if any States should fail to meet its quota of the additional 300,000 by August 15th, the deficiency in that State would be made up by a special "draft" from the permanent militia.[31] A general order dated August 9, 1862 listed those who would be automatically exempted, including all telegraph operators and maintenance personnel, engineers, artificers, and workmen employed in any public armory or arsenal, members of Congress, the Vice-President of the United States, customs officials, postal officers, and stage drivers, the merchant marine, and all persons exempted by the laws of the respective States from military duty.[32]

As yet, however, there was no such thing as an actual draft in the North. The detailed provisions for the "draft" by quota were without any direct legal sanction and would have been impossible to enforce in unwilling States due to the lack of sufficient troops at the disposal of the central government. The quota system was not intended as the main source of manpower but rather as a whip to encourage volunteering.[33] It was intended that the system should raise 300,000 militiamen for nine months and that it should round out the quotas of the call of July 2, 1862, in addition to providing replacements for the old regiments. This last provision was authorized by an order appearing August 14, 1862.[34]

As a means of raising men directly, the 1862 quota type of draft was unquestionably a failure. Out of quotas of 334,835 men only 87,588 men can be accounted for by this draft.[35] The draft was valuable, however, in that it acted as a sword of Damocles over certain States, especially in the West, whose leaders in July were dubious about their ability to meet their quotas but who in the end managed to come through with flying colors. The quotas for the calls of July 2 and August 4 totalled 669,670. But the number raised was only 509,053, thus showing a deficiency of about 25 percent.[36] At first glance this deficiency seems quite startling in its implications, but there were about 87,000 three-year volunteers over and above the quota of the first call.[37] That the calls of July and August were so well answered was also due to the fact that the rush season in agricultural regions had passed and there was the usual surplus labor population seeking steady employment. The nine-month call was little more enticing than the three-year call since the majority of the population still believed the war would be of short duration.

In studying the pseudo draft of 1862 one is disappointed to note that the futile system of short terms still prevailed. Nine months was little improvement on three months as far as actual service to the country was concerned. The good features of the experiences of 1862 that carried over and were utilized in 1863 were twofold: Only Federal officers should conduct the draft, and military service should be for a period of at least three years.

BOUNTIES

Two especially vicious practices appeared as a result of this draft law of July 17, 1862, practices that were so to alter the entire Northern recruiting program during the rest of the war that the spendid patriotism of the best type of volunteer has been permanently besmirched as a result. These practices were those of Federal, State, or local bounties and the purchasing of substitutes to serve in place of drafted men. In addition to the hundred-dollar Federal bounty, there were numerous State and local bounties. That the Federal bounty was of material assistance in getting men is proved by the fact that there were many more three-year volunteers than nine-month volunteers. Only the former received the bounty.

Need for Universal Conscription

A widely-read paper of the day, in discussing the bounty question on August 16, 1862, said in part:

The system of indiscriminate bounties for recruits to meet the Presidential requisition for 300,000 men to fill up the National armies, is already and none too early recognized as vicious, wasteful and demoralizing. The mistake of attempting to organize new regiments before the old ones are filled up is also recognized, and the plan abandoned. Let the conscription be just as Heaven, and inexorable as death. All that is worth living for is involved in the issue of the contest in which we are embarked. Let it spare neither high nor low, rich nor poor, but reach all alike.[38]

No better proof of the lack of unity and purpose in the Northern war effort is needed than to study how completely unrealized was the ideal of universal conscription as advanced in this newspaper article. It is difficult today to understand why Northern leadership could not comprehend the necessity of drafting men by a fair system of selection, that is, to force men to serve rather than to permit them to pay substitutes to serve in their stead. That the war might easily be a long one began to dawn on the more thoughtful statesmen when they heard of the sickening slaughter of Burnside's men before the stone wall at Fredericksburg or when they studied the dilatory tactics of Rosecrans at Stone's River.

Only a week after the end of the latter battle, however, Congressman Buffington of the House Committee on Military Affairs read a majority report which urged authorization to raise 20,000 volunteers to serve for *nine months* in Florida. Fortunately the opposition was unable to discern the wisdom of singling out Florida as the theater of operations for these particular men. Nor could the opposition approve nine months as the term of service for these men when "three years or during the war" was becoming accepted as necessary for enlistment.[39] The House Committee was certainly not cognizant of the general military situation.

In the East the morale of the Army of the Potomac was at low ebb owing to Burnside's inept leadership at Fredericksburg. Also responsible for this low morale was the famous Mud March of the following month, when in a torrential rain the Army of the Potomac floundered in impassable roads for a few days and returned to its camp completely demoralized. Resignations and desertions became commonplace.

In the West affairs were little better. An officer writing to his wife on January 22, 1863, commented bitterly on the poor quality of the officers and men, then went on to state that in his opinion:

Nine-tenths of them enlisted just because somebody else was going, and the other tenth was ashamed to stay at home. As they all pretend to be ill whenever there is anything to do, it is impossible to tell whether anything is the matter with a man until he is ready to die. One lover of his country in my company received an honorable discharge who has never done thirteen cents worth of work for the government, on account of feebleness and yet who had never seen a day when he didn't eat his full rations, and when he wasn't able to whip two like myself.[40]

Possibly the largest single factor in this widespread demoralization consisted of the Northern military reverses accompanied by very severe casualties amounting, since the passage of the July 2, 1862 law, to about 75,000 men, killed, wounded, or missing.[41]

The North Lacked a Replacement System

Unlike the Confederates, who had kept their ranks better supplied by a relentless conscription policy, the Northern authorities had not yet supplied an adequate replacement system. The average Confederate regiment was much more efficient than the average Federal regiment, an inevitable result of the pernicious system practiced by the North of raising new regiments instead of keeping the old ones up to strength. Since the spring of 1863 was certain to inaugurate another campaign in which the losses in manpower were to be considerable, a system to replace those losses had to be found.

The Draft

The idea of conscription began to be favorably received by several important legislators, including Aaron A. Sargent of the House and James A. McDougall of the Senate. Even Horace Greeley, who in the spring of 1862 had been incensed by the employment of conscription by the Confederacy, could reason in August of the same year that since the South had started conscription it was honorable for the North to follow its example.[42] As was to be expected, however, the anti-administration Democrats opposed the draft from the start and continued to do so throughout the war. Despite this resistance, Senator Henry Wilson, chairman of the Committee on Military Affairs, introduced a bill to enroll and call out the national forces; this bill was finally passed on March 3, 1863. By "national forces" was meant all able-bodied male citizens of the United States and all aliens who had declared on oath their intention of becoming citizens, between the ages of twenty and forty-five. There were three classes of exemptions: first, those physically or mentally unfit for service and persons convicted of a felony; second, a restricted number of officials including the Vice-President of the United States, Federal judges, cabinet members and State governors; and third, sole supporters of aged or infirm parents or of orphaned children. Those liable to service comprised two classes: first, all men, married or single, between the ages of twenty and thirty-five, and all unmarried men between the ages of thirty-five and forty-five;

and second, married men between the ages of thirty-five and forty-five. This second class was not to be called out until the first class was exhausted.[43] To administer the draft a separate bureau of the War Department, namely, the Provost Marshal General's Department, was set up under the leadership of James B. Fry, an officer of exceptional ability.

The enrollment act itself contained some good provisions. Among these should be mentioned the care taken to arrange for as equitable a distribution of the burden of the draft as possible, with only a few exemptions. The drafted men were to receive the same pay and Federal bounty as did the volunteers. All drafted men were to receive ten days' notice so as to eliminate any possibility of their not knowing that they were to be drafted. The men raised were to be used in organizations where they were needed; the old habit of raising new regiments in order to pay off political debts was to stop. Strict observance of regulations governing medical examinations was ordered, but not followed.

On the debit side of the ledger we must note, first, the inadequacy of the medical examination, which was to prove almost disastrous in the later stages of the war when depleted regiments received as replacements even men who were literally blind, syphilitic, and idiotic. Secondly, there were no provisions for industrial exemptions although it must have been obvious that a great determining factor in the outcome of the war would be the industrialization of the North against the agrarian economy of the South. But probably the worst feature of all in the enrollment law was the system of substitution. For varying sums a man to be drafted could provide a substitute; that is, he could pay another man to go in his place. So great was the demand of substitutes that a familiar element in the war was the substitute broker, who has been defined by James A. Garfield as:

A man who establishes an office and offers to furnish substitutes for different localities. He pays bounties and gathers men in gangs for sale, and when the committees of any town are hard pressed to fill up their quotas they send to the substitute broker and buy his wares at exhorbitant rates. He gets men for comparatively a small bounty and sells them at enormous prices to the districts that are otherwise unable to provide their quotas. The result has been that men in all parts of the United States have been compelled to see their sons bought and sold by these infamous substitute brokers.[44]

As if the substitute feature of the law were not bad enough, the law also permitted men who were to be drafted the privilege of purchasing exemption by paying a commutation fee of three hundred dollars. From this source alone the Federal government received fifteen million dollars in the first draft.[45] It was not without reason that the poor could maintain that the war was a "poor man's fight." Of 292,-441 names drawn in the first draft only 9,881 were

held to personal service. The remainder paid commutation, furnished substitutes, did not report after being drafted, or were exempted for physical defects and similar reasons.[46] Several hundred conscientious objectors, mostly from such religious sects as the Quakers, refused to serve. The exact number cannot be determined because many refused even to pay commutation money.[47]

Under the President's proclamation of June 15, 1863, pertaining to militia to serve for six months, the States furnished 16,361 men.[48] This call was made during Lee's second invasion of the North. The seriousness of those weeks preceding Gettysburg was well expressed when the New York *Herald* pointed out that there could no longer be any doubt that Lee's whole army had crossed the Potomac into Maryland and Pennsylvania, that a grand scheme of invasion of the North was now fully developed, and that a decisive battle could not be long delayed.[49] Interestingly enough, the same paper contained the following notice: "How to avoid the draft—a few more good men wanted for Company H, Eighty-fourth regiment New York State Militia, for thirty days. Headquarters Central Hall, corner of Centre and Grand streets, Cap't. Graham commanding." [50] However, the militia's contribution to the victory at Gettysburg was of little value.

On October 17, 1863, Lincoln called for 300,000 volunteers for three years.[51] This was followed February 1, 1864, by an order for a draft of 500,000, including the calls of 1863, also for three years.[52] These two calls netted 369,380 men.[53] On March 14, 1864 still another call was made, this one for 200,000 men for three years,[54] which resulted in the raising of 292,193 men for the Federal army.[55] Besides the foregoing additions, between April 23 and July 18 there were furnished 83,612 one-hundred-day militia out of a quota of 113,000.[56] All these and more were desperately needed by the armed forces of the nation, especially in the Army of the Potomac where the casualty lists were assuming alarming proportions because of the "fight it out on this line if it takes all summer" tactics of Grant. In the campaign from the Rapidan to the James, Grant's loss was 54,926 men, a number roughly equal to Lee's whole army. To supply these and other losses a call was issued on July 18, 1864 for 500,000 men (reduced by excess of credits on previous calls to 357,152) to serve one, two, and three years. This call was oversubscribed, 386,-461 men being furnished.[57] Although there was the usual poor quality of replacements in this call as in all the 1863 and 1864 drafts, some new regiments of good material were raised. In September Pennsylvania raised a division of six regiments, whose recruits were a "husky, healthy lot of young men, varying in age from 16 to 22 years . . . drawn from professional occupations and trades, and agricultural life . . . men of intelligence and culture." [58] These men performed very capably in action later due to excellent leadership. The last call for troops during the war was made December 19, 1864, when 300,-000 men were called to serve terms of one, two, and three years. By the time military operations ended the following spring, 212,212 men had been raised.[59] When Lee's army surrendered, thousands of recruits were pouring in, and men were being discharged from recruiting station and rendezvous in every State. The national military force on May 1, 1865, numbered 1,000,516 men.[60]

Operation of the Draft

The mode of drafting men was quite similar to that employed in later American wars. Advance public notice of the draft appeared in the local newspapers and civil officers and prominent individuals were invited to be present. A wheel or box was used containing slips of paper with the name of each prospective soldier and his district written thereon. A man, blindfolded, continued to draw out slips until the quota of the district was completed. Then the same drawing would take place for the next district.

The enrollment act was to include "all able-bodied male citizens of the United States, and residents of foreign birth who had declared on oath their intention to become citizens between the age of twenty and forty-five years."[61] There were two classes of men liable to draft: the first class included all men between the ages of 20 and 35 and all unmarried persons above the age of 35 and below 45; the second class included all married persons between the ages of 35 and 45.[62] Drafted men were given the regulation physical examination and appeared before a board of enrollment which consisted of the provost marshal, a commissioner, and surgeon. Each man was examined separately. The board then asked the drafted man his name, age, residence, and whether he claimed exemption. If held to serve he was then asked whether he desired to send a substitute, and if so, what extension of time he desired.

The quality of the substitute was poor. Most of the recruits of this period were called "subs." This nickname was applied to that class of individual who entered the service under the draft act. As one veteran put it: "The word 'sub' is a Latin preposition . . . (meaning) *under* or *below*. How far in that direction it is possible for the human race to go . . . no one can have any adequate conception who never had anything to do with those strange specimens of abnormal humanity that were sent out in the fall and winter of 1863-4 to fill up the skeleton ranks of the old regiments.[63]

When a sufficient number of men had accumulated at the draft rendezvous they were forwarded under guard to the general rendezvous. It may be said that generally the quality of draftees was extremely low. As will be seen later in the discussion of the Union

soldier in combat, the average drafted man was not only of no earthly use to the regiment he joined but was actually a definite liability.

Manpower Procured During the War

We shall now examine more closely the statistics with respect to the total number of men enlisted during the war for the Federal armies, with emphasis on the motivations that prompted them to join the colors and the types of men that went to make up the Federal forces. The aggregate number of men credited to the several calls and put into the service of the Federal Army, Navy, and Marine Corps during the period of April 15, 1861 to April 14, 1865, was 2,656,553.[64] This number does not include the 120,000 emergency men who served periods of two or three weeks during the summer of 1863. The figure of 2,656,553 includes every man mustered into service and does not take into account the fact that the same men in many instances had been discharged and subsequently re-enlisted.[65] It is difficult to arrive at an exact evaluation of the strength of the Federal Army at any one period, because it was constantly discharging veteran organizations and receiving recruits and entirely new regiments as replacements. Accordingly, the figures for the strength of the Army at any given date should be examined. It is obvious that a three-month regiment, although having more men on its rolls than combat-depleted units had, was not to be compared in efficiency to a three-year regiment which had been at the front through several campaigns. The equivalent number for the figure of 1,656,553, which the Secretary of War gave as total enlistments for the war, would be 1,556,678 based on a term of three years.[66] There was the equivalent of 2,050 regiments in the Federal service during the war. This total includes the Regular Army but excludes the Veteran Reserve Corps.[67]

Use of Regular Army Personnel

The Regular Army was the only reliable military entity at the outbreak of the war. Although its commissioned strength was seriously depleted due to so many of its best officers joining the Confederacy, its enlisted personnel remained true to the national government. In the quick, decisive campaign he envisioned in 1861, General Winfield Scott planned to rely solely on Regular troops, by means of which he had won his victories in earlier wars. But the Regular Army was too small to defeat an enemy that was to put approximately a million men in the field before cessation of hostilities. Owing to various causes that will be enumerated later, the Regular Army never was increased to any substantial degree. Most of its best officers had the advantage of a West Point training and long experience, the exceptions being relatively few.

Regular Army Not Used As Cadres

The function of the Regular Army should have been, and was to some extent, to furnish cadres of officers and noncommissioned personnel to the volunteer army that was to bear the brunt of the fighting. Although many of the commissioned officers of the Regular Army were eventually so utilized, the services of the 15,000 privates and noncommissioned officers[68] remaining were not. The latter would have proved valuable as company grade officers and sergeants.

General McClellan wished to break up the Regular Army and distribute its members among the staff and regiments of the volunteer organizations, or if that were not done, at least to build up the Regular Army regiments to their full authorized strength and use them as reserves in critical situations.[69] McClellan's advice was not followed. It is true that there was a grouping of Regular regiments into brigades, but nothing more extensive was attempted. Added to the weakness of the Federal government in the administration of recruiting for the Regular Army was the widespread reluctance of civilians to enter the Regular service. The reasons for this were many: The fact that enlistment in the Regular Army was for a definite period, while the volunteers were to be discharged at the end of the war, which everybody believed would not last three years; the fact that, although both volunteers and Regulars received the same pay, the amount of two dollars per month was withheld from the pay of the Regular soldier but not from that of the volunteer; the fact that the States granted bounties to their volunteers and pensions to their volunteers' families, advantages which the Regular soldier did not have; and lastly, but not least important, the fact that discipline in the Regular units did not appeal to the majority of volunteers.[70]

Discrimination Against Regular Officers

Those officers who remained with the Regular units were discriminated against in comparison with the Regular officers who accepted higher rank and responsibility with volunteer organizations. It was commonplace for two West Point officers of the same former Regular unit to meet on the field, one of whom might be a divisional or corps commander, the other of whom might still be a lieutenant or captain in their old Regular regiment. However, the former received his promotion within the Regular service on the same basis as his less fortunate classmate. This is strikingly illustrated in the postwar reorganization of the Regular Army when generals commanding the higher echelons of the army returned to their old regiments as field and company grade officers. Some ambitious officers of the Regular Army at first hesitated to accept higher rank in the

volunteers, but others sought brief leaves of absence to visit the governors of their respective States to offer their services. William Tecumseh Sherman in writing to his brother John Sherman on May 22, 1861, said: "I shall promptly accept the colonelcy (of a new Regular regiment) when received and I think I can organize and prepare a regiment as quick as anybody. I prefer this to a Brigadier in the militia for I have no political ambition, and have very naturally more confidence in Regulars than Militia."[71]

Often these men were refused leave to accept commissions in State regiments because of General Scott's theory that the Regular Army was to be the main fighting force in the war. Later on, however, the policy of refusing to permit Regular officers to accept commissions in the volunteers was changed. The exception to this is to be found in the Regular artillery regiments, where there was a preponderance of well-trained Regular Army officers, whose presence enabled that branch to contribute so magnificently to the final Union victory. The Regular infantry, on the other hand, was no better than the vounteer infantry due to the fact that the most intelligent, the strongest, the most stable elements refused to join the Regular Army. A large number of foreigners who had no strong State allegiance entered the Regular ranks. Also, in the Regular Army the lower grades among the subalterns were assigned to young men fresh from civil life; thus some of the old regiments and all the regiments created by the act of July 29, 1861, suffered from the same disadvantages as did the newly formed volunteer regiments. "Nevertheless, the 'esprit de corps,' that moral influence which attaches to a word, a number, or a sign, which has the power of transforming men, soon imparted habits of steadiness and discipline to the newcomers who, after the first combats, rivalled their older brethren in courage and sustained the credit of the Regular troops."[72]

At the close of 1862 the Secretary of War appointed a commission to revise the Articles of War and Army Regulations. This commission issued a circular inviting suggestions as to desirable alterations within the military establishment. One of the high ranking officers so solicited urged in vain the need of giving unity to the Army by abolishing the distinction between Regulars and volunteers.[73]

Strength and Losses in the Regular Army

The total number of enlistments for the Regular Army during the war was 67,000.[74] This included a few who enlisted just after the close of the war. At no time during the period of active hostilities did the Regular Army number over 26,000 officers and men.[75] As there were only thirty regiments in the Regular Army, it is apparent that their average numerical strength must have been small, but their losses in action were severe in proportion to their numbers.

The Regular Army lost 2,283 killed in action and 3,515 from disease and other causes during the four years of conflict.[76]

Desertion was exceptionally high in the Regular Army due, in large part, to the types of its enlisted men. A large proportion of the men in the ranks were foreigners, because native-born citizens went with the regiments of their States. Whereas 62.51 per thousand deserted from volunteer units, the Regulars lost 244.25 per thousand.[77] This is partially accounted for by the fact that honorable discharges were far easier to obtain in the volunteer force than in the Regular Army. The volunteer could use the influence of friends, congressmen, and others while such influence was difficult for the foreigner to obtain. The political interest of the State officials in their volunteer regiments was not extended to the Regular soldiers, who had no ties except with the Federal government. Honorable discharges were granted at the rate of 67.24 per thousand to volunteers, 15.08 per thousand to the colored troops, and only 17.88 per thousand to the Regulars.[78] The proportion of discharges for disability was about the same for volunteers and Regulars: 78.81 per thousand for the former and 75.99 for the latter.[79] The better discipline of the Regular Army as compared to that of the volunteers is reflected in the deaths from disease: 42.27 per thousand in the Regular Army but 59.22 per thousand in the volunteers.[80]

MANY SENIOR COMMANDERS WERE REGULARS

An appreciation of the role of the Regular Army in furnishing senior commanders is essential to a complete understanding of the North's war effort. No discussion of the Northern volunteer soldier is complete without a consideration of that source—the "Old Army"—whence he drew many of his regimental and most of his brigade, divisional, corps, and army commanders. The militia, the only other organized military force at the outbreak of the war, is of much less significance personnel-wise, but nevertheless merits attention because of its role as a reserve force during the War.

ROLE OF THE MILITIA

Generally speaking, before formation of the volunteer army, the militia dominated the scene until after Bull Run and then left the stage except for temporary appearances during invasions of the North by Confederate troops. During the first invasion of Northern soil by the Army of Northern Virginia, the Governor of Pennsylvania called out 25,000 militia "for service within the State to repel rebel invasion."[81] These troops, which were not mustered into Federal service but were, nevertheless, recognized and paid by the United States, were discharged and returned to their homes after serving only two weeks. Such, in general, was the nature of the militia

MILITIAMEN IN 1861

"Holiday soldiers" of the 7th New York. Fancy gray uniforms and elaborate equipment were characteristic of "crack" militia units at the beginning of the war. They mostly disappeared after the first hard campaign, such as the Peninsular campaign, following which replacement items were issued. The mess kits fastened to the knapsacks in this picture, for example, saw very little use in the field.

active contribution to the war effort, as differentiated from their status as inactive reserves.

Although the subject will be treated under the chapter on discipline, it is advisable to state here that the militia was not as efficient a training element for officers as had been hoped at the beginning of the war. An act was passed by Congress in 1792 providing for a uniformed militia to be raised in each State which would form a reserve force to be called out in case of invasion or rebellion. However, during the long period of peace the militia organization had been almost wholly neglected. Most of the States had laws for the organization of militia but these laws were little regarded.

STATUS EARLY IN 1861

The commencement of the war found only two or three States with a militia organization sufficiently sound to admit a ready response to the President's proclamation of April 15, 1861. Even those regiments that did respond were filled with volunteers who had no previous training. During the first year of the war most of the States passed militia laws providing for the enrollment of all able-bodied white male citizens (some, for instance Rhode Island and Massachusetts, included colored citizens) between the ages of 18 and 45 with certain specified exceptions. The militia thus organized was divided into two classes, the active and inactive militia. The active milita included the voluntary companies organized into a given

PERMISSION TO ENLIST
Written consent of Milton Van Ness for his son Whitfield to enlist in the Army. Young Van Ness became a member of the 104th N. Y. Infantry.

number of regiments and recruited to full strength by a draft from the enrolled men between the ages of 18 and 30. The inactive militia comprised all men between the ages of 30 and 45 who were required under penalty of a dollar fine per year to appear on a specified day to answer to their names. The active militia was fully officered and equipped and was called out once or twice a year for a few days' drill.

It had been a prevalent idea among the militiamen that they could not be required to serve outside their State nor could they be retained in Federal service for more than three months. This led to certain militia regiments marching to the rear at the sound of the enemy's cannon during the Bull Run campaign. But the act of July 17, 1862 authorized the President to call out the militia for nine months instead of three.

STRENGTH OF THE MILITIA

It is impossible to give more than an approximation of the number of militia enrolled though it was probably over 3,000,000 by 1862.[82] Of the 77,875 three-month troops called out in the spring of 1861 a little more than half were militia; of the 30,000 or 40,000 called out in the summer of 1862, all or nearly all were militia. There were also some militia regiments among the nine-month force raised under the call of August 9, 1862.[83] Some militia regiments offered their services for longer periods and enlisted as a unit in the service of the Federal government. Among these was the famous 55th New York Infantry, which filled its vacancies and enlisted in the Federal service for three years or the war "and the Fifty-Fifth *militia* [became] the Fifty-Fifth *volunteers* . . ."[84] The militia law, nevertheless, left the men solely in the control of the States until they were sworn in the service of the national government. Thus the appointment of all officers was the privilege of the State and the opportunity was not overlooked in the paying off of political debts to favorites.

By the summer of 1863 the military authorities had learned that they must depend on the volunteers, not on the militia, even during invasions of Northern territory. As General-in-Chief Halleck reported November 15, 1863, with reference to the operations of the Gettysburg campaign: "Lee's army was supposed to be advancing against Harrisburg, which was garrisoned by raw militia, upon which little reliance could be placed."[85]

VOLUNTEER TROOPS

It was the volunteer troops who bore the brunt of the fighting and suffered the losses that were the price of Union victory. It is impracticable to analyze the various motivating factors that caused over two million men to enter the military service of the Federal government. Dealing with exact figures is much easier and more accurate than attempting to evaluate human emotions. In studying letters and diaries of the Civil War period one finds that some factors occurred more frequently than others. Certainly one of the most compelling reasons was the desire for excitement. This mania to "see something" before the war was over affected the younger elements more than the others. It persisted throughout the entire war and was just as strong in one section as in another. Many minors who were refused permission by their parents solved their dilemma by running away and enlisting. Boys of this type were to be found in every unit. As one described it: "The war fever seized me in 1863. All the summer and fall I had fretted and burned to be off. That winter, and before I was sixteen years old, I ran away from my father's farm and enlisted in the Eleventh New York Battery, then at the front in Virginia."[86] Although there were few "boy regiments" or "boy companies" in the Federal army there were thousands of soldiers in the ranks whose recorded ages were sixteen and seventeen. Probably 200,000 recruits overstated their ages a year or more, many others understated it.[87] Often boys in their teens were prompted to enlist by the news that a unit from their State had participated in a great battle, whereupon the boys were seized with the desire to emulate their more fortunate friends who were getting all the glory. Such was the case with 97 Iowa youths who enlisted after hearing of the part played by the First Iowa Infantry at Wilson's Creek. The average age of the 97 was less than twenty years.[88]

Women Also Served

In addition to the men and boys, there were many women who served in various capacities in the Federal Army. Some went as nurses and laundresses. Among the incidents of the Battle of Chancellorsville worthy of special mention was the heroic conduct of Anne Etheridge, who was known and respected by every soldier of Kearny's fighting division. This young and attractive girl was one of the laundresses of the 3rd Michigan Infantry. When the regiment was ordered to the front, the other laundresses returned to their homes, but Anne accompanied the regiment, marching and camping with the men through all their campaigns and engagements. She soon became a favorite of all, and woe to the soldier of any other unit who uttered a disrespectful word in her presence. At the Battle of Williamsburg, while dressing wounds under fire, she had attracted the attention of General Phil Kearny, who presented her with sergeant's chevrons and ordered the quartermaster to provide her with a horse and saddle in order that she could more efficiently perform her services.[89]

Some women went to the front posing as men. Private Franklin Thompson, 2d Michigan, turned out to be a woman. She fought in several battles and had a good record.[90]

Laundresses were allowed to accompany the troops, and were furnished with certificates. Regulation decreed that no woman of "bad character" be permitted to follow the army.[91] Fox makes no mention of the number and distribution of laundresses.[92]

Why Men Volunteered

Though many youths waited impatiently until they could get their parents' consent to enlist or took matters in their own hands and ran away to join any unit that was available, the majority of the volunteers offered themselves to their country primarily from a sense of duty. In the North there was very little enthusiastic sentiment about military life, especially in the Eastern and Middle states. It is true that the West responded with more unanimity and probably with more alacrity to the often repeated summonses to leave peaceful pursuits and take the field. This was due rather to the comparative newness of the civilization in the West than to any specific martial characteristic in the population. The

truth is that the Northern people were busy, preoccupied, full of schemes for the development of the country. The poetry of war hardly entered the mind of the Northern volunteer whose course was determined by a sense of duty. He regarded the Southerners as completely to blame and was determined to put them down, cost what it might. The war was all weary work to him, a distasteful job that had to be done, "a sort of anachronism."[93]

The history of recruiting during the Civil War is the story of a steadily decreasing willingness on the part of the North to offer freely its manpower as soldiers and a resulting steady increase in the necessity for inducements to overcome the unwillingness. From the beginning of the War the press and pulpit played their parts in prodding the laggards, while in town meetings and "rallies" local orators proclaimed undying devotion to the Union. One soldier who reacted favorably to a politician's harangue later observed that although the speaker to whom he listened declared that life must be cheapened, the effusive orator never "helped on the work experimentally."[94]

Group Enlistment

Up to the commencement of drafting, the recruiting of troops was either by individual or group en-

A YOUNG SOLDIER

Sergeant John L. Clem, 22d Michigan Infantry, who enlisted at the age of nine. After serving as a drummer boy he became a mounted orderly to Maj. Gen. George H. Thomas. Clem remained in the Army after the war, eventually attaining the rank of major general.

listments. In the case of individuals enlisting it was
often necessary for them to join a regiment from
another county or even State; especially was this
true in the early months of the war when the Federal government was not accepting many of the regiments already formed.

The 40th New York Infantry (Mozart Regiment)
was an example of this. Four companies of this regiment were raised in Massachusetts, but the quota
of that State being full, these companies joined the
40th New York.[95]

Group enlistments functioned as follows: a group
of men would go in a body to some recruiting station and signify their readiness to enlist in a certain
regiment provided a designated member of their
number would be commissioned captain. That the
war was unnecessarily prolonged because of the
"town meeting" attitude there can be no doubt.

In 1861 it was common for an individual who had
been in the Regular Army or militia, or who had
served with a volunteer unit in the Mexican War,
to take the initiative in recruiting for his district
and circulate an enlistment paper for signatures. Because of his active interest, his chances were pretty
good to obtain a commission as captain; the men
who had materially assisted him in his work would
secure lieutenancies. On the return of the three-
month troops some of the companies immediately re-
enlisted in a body for three years, sometimes under
their old officers. In 1862 the recruiting offices increased greatly in number and functioned in processing recruits both for old units already in the field
and for new organizations. Unquestionably at this
time the latter were more popular. The lot of a recruit
in an old company was, at the best, not an enviable
one, and sometimes was made very disagreeable,
because of the large bounty the recruit received,
amounting in some cases to a thousand dollars.[96]
Later on in the war when the notorious "bounty
jumper" made his appearance in the ranks of the
veteran regiments and openly boasted that Uncle
Sam would never get him to the front, the smug
tolerance of the veteran toward the recruit turned
into bitter hatred and disgust.[97]

RECRUITING CAMPAIGNS

Flaming advertisements and billboard posters were
used with considerable effect in getting the men to
the recruiting stations. One such poster for the purpose of getting recruits for a regiment already in the
field informed the prospective soldiers that although
"the regiment (2d Massachusetts Infantry) is second
in number, (it) is second to none in regard to discipline and efficiency, and is in the healthiest and
most delightful country."[98] War meetings, held in-
doors or outdoors according to the clemency of the
weather, were used to stir lagging enthusiasm. Often
bands and choirs regaled the audiences with "Red,
White, and Blue" and "Rally 'round the Flag." Vet-

erans of 1812 and 1848 were called upon to urge
the younger men to give themselves to the cause.
Often there was a patriotic maiden lady in the
gathering who kept a flag or a handkerchief waving,
declaring she "would go in a minute if she were a
man." In addition there was usually a man who
would make one of fifty (or some other safe number) to enlist, when he well knew that no such
number could be obtained. Often there was one
present who, when challenged to sign the enlistment
roll would agree to do so, if certain wealthy men
would also put down their names.[99]

There were many amusing repercussions from the
blatant patriotism of some of the orators at these
war meetings when later on they were called upon
to fulfill their promises of heroic conduct on the
battlefields. Illustrative of the many incidents of this
sort was that of a man who, by virtue of his promise
"to be found where the bullets were thickest" was
elected captain of his company. His promise was
literally fulfilled, for during the first engagement of
his regiment he was found hiding under an ammunition chest.[100]

Despite the name-calling and town politics prevalent in many of these meetings, they were usually a
success and once the first man had signed the enlistment roll, he would be followed by others. Often
towards the end of the meeting a stampede would
set in to fill the town's quota. Local pride played a
large part in filling the ranks of the Army prior to
the enrollment act of March 3, 1863. The strenuous
efforts made by the towns, cities, and States to fill
their quotas plus the very liberal bounties offered by
the various localities were effective enough so that
there was very little drafting before the spring of
1863. Up to February 1, 1863, there were probably
not more than 10,000 drafted men in the Army.[101]

VETERAN VOLUNTEERS

As the war wore on, any continuance of the Federal armies in the field depended not only on insuring
a continual supply of replacements by draft but also
on re-enlisting those well-trained veterans already
in the field, many of whose terms of service were
about to expire. Accordingly, the War Department
issued a general order[102] June 25, 1863, which permitted the volunteers already in the service to re-
enlist for a period of three years or the war. A furlough of at least thirty days was granted to officers
and men of the organizations re-enlisting under this
order. Where a large proportion re-enlisted, the regiment was to be sent home in a body at government expense; and during its stay to be reorganized and to recruit its ranks. Every soldier received a
bounty of four hundred dollars for re-enlisting, which
he retained even though the government did not
require his services for the complete three years.
The date of rank for the officers was made continuous
from the date of original muster. The force thus re-

organized was termed "veteran volunteers" and, as an honorable distinction, service chevrons were authorized for it by the War Department.[103]

It is difficult to ascertain why some regiments re-enlisted almost in a body while others had very few men "sign over." Local conditions were responsible in many of the units. For example, the 6th Connecticut Infantry left the Petersburg front for home with very few re-enlistments, due, in large part, to war weariness.[104] The 2d New Hampshire Infantry was a fighting regiment, but when it received worthless conscripts as replacements it resented their pres-

ence so much that few cared to serve out the war with these new men.[105] On the other hand, other regiments with high morale usually re-enlisted because there was great pride in preserving the regimental organization. In one regiment in the Western theater there were only fifteen men who did not re-enlist and these were the physically disabled and malcontents.[106] If a regiment had a popular colonel it would very often follow his urging and "see the thing through" because of confidence in him.[107] In some units the feeling against those men who refused to re-enlist was quite strong and in the 25th Indiana

THE CALL TO ARMS

Recruiting posters of this type were posted in towns throughout the North. This one was displayed in 1862 to raise troops for the 105th Ohio Infantry, which fought in the armies of Grant and Sherman.

Infantry, at least, they were termed "rounders" as a title of opprobrium.[108] Many men who had put down their names took them off the re-enlistment list when new recruits were made noncoms while they (the old men) had been in the field on hard service for two years.

After the men who had not re-enlisted had gone, the remaining personnel was almost entirely new. In some cavalry squadrons there was not six percent of the original men who enlisted in 1861.[109]

Over 136,000 veterans re-enlisted, however, and their contribution to the defeat of the South may be considered decisive. Organizations which would have been lost to the service were preserved and recruited. Capable and experienced officers were retained in command. "The force thus organized and retained . . . performed an essential part in the great campaign of 1864, and its importance to the Country cannot be overestimated."[110] One soldier considered the re-enlisting of the three-year men in the field to be the most patriotic event of the war. As he put it, these men knew what war was, had seen their regiments and companies swept away until only a remnant remained. They did not have the excitement of the war meetings to urge them on, but "with a full knowledge of the duties required and the probability that many would fall before their term expired, with uncovered heads and uplifted hands they swore to stand by the flag until the last armed foe surrendered."[111] All recruiting and enlisting of volunteers ceased April 29, 1865.[112]

MEDICAL EXAMINATIONS

After the enlistment roll had been filled in sufficiently for the town quota, a local physician conducted the medical examination of the recruits. In too many cases this examination was a mere formality. The men who passed were then taken to a recruiting station where they signed the roll of the company or regiment into which they were going. This roll included a description of the men as to height, complexion, and occupation. A guard then conducted them to the examining surgeon, who was detailed for the purpose by the War Department. The surgeon examined the volunteers for dissimulated or concealed diseases; after the draft was in operation, however, he had to detect simulated or feigned diseases and ailments. Because of the general enthusiasm early in the war, large numbers of men entered the ranks with concealed infirmities which early required their discharge. In his report covering the period August 12, 1861, to March 17, 1862, the Medical Director of the Army of the Potomac said in part: "It seemed as if the army called out to defend the life of the nation had been made use of as a grand eleemosynary institution for the reception of the aged and infirm, the blind, and the deaf, where they might be housed, fed, paid, clothed, and pensioned, and their townships relieved of the burden of their support."[113]

PHYSICAL CRITERIA

Under the volunteer system large numbers of boys from fourteen to eighteen years of age, immature and feeble, were admitted into the volunteer regiments, with the result that soon they found their way into the hospitals. Equally unfit for active duty were many men of advanced age, some of sixty years and upwards.[114] Of the men accepted in the years 1861 and 1862, a large part, nearly 200,000, were soon found to be unfit for service and were discharged.[115] In 1863 the requirements for enlistment were made much more stringent. The minimum age was 18; the maximum age was 45. No man was to be accepted who was under the height of 5 feet 3 inches and although there was no maximum limit, the rule of practice was for the examining surgeon to reject very tall men (6 feet 3 inches and up), especially those whose chests were narrow and contracted, whose muscular systems were imperfectly developed, and who betrayed a tendency to hernia or to varicose condition of the veins. The weight extremes were set at 110 to 220 pounds.[116] Due to the use of the paper cartridge which required being torn open by the teeth before use in the musket, men were rejected who lacked a "sufficient number" of teeth for that purpose. In most respects the physical requirements for enlistment were substantially as they are today. Disqualifying mental infirmities were: manifest imbecility or insanity, senile dementia, monomania, and melancholia. Men convicted of a felony were disqualified by the regulations as were habitual drunkards and men with venereal diseases.[117]

OTHER REQUIREMENTS

The volunteer was required to sign a "volunteer enlistment" form in which he declared his desire to serve for a specified period of time. This form was signed by the examining surgeon who certified, on honor, that he had carefully examined the volunteer and that in his opinion he was "free from all bodily defects and mental infirmity which might disqualify him from performing the duties of a soldier."[118] The recruiting officer, likewise certified on honor that he had "minutely inspected" the volunteer and that he was "entirely sober when enlisted," of lawful age and qualified to perform the duties of a soldier.[119] The volunteer enlistment form also provided for the father's consent in case the volunteer was a minor. No later than six days after enlistment the soldier took the oath of allegiance which could be administered by a civil magistrate or an officer of the Regular Army, but preferably by the latter.[120] The oath was as follows:[121]

I, A—B—, do solemnly swear or affirm (as the case may be) that I will bear true allegiance to the United States of America, and that I will serve them honestly and faithfully against all their enemies or opposers whatsoever, and observe and obey the orders of the President of the United States, and the orders of the officers appointed over me, according to the rules and articles for the government of the armies of the United States.

MUSTERING IN

In the case of men joining old regiments the oath was administered to the men, whereupon they were sent at once to join their units in the field. Hundreds of men who enlisted under the call issued by President Lincoln on July 2, 1862, were killed or wounded before they had been in the field a week. On the other hand, the new regiments were usually kept in their camps for several weeks before being sent to the front. A committee appointed by the Secretary of War examined more than 200 regiments during September and October, 1861, and discovered that the average time occupied in recruiting each of these regiments was six weeks.[122] Often the new regiments were mustered in as a unit and all the men took the oath of allegiance together. After muster-in the men were trained in their camp until the regiment was forwarded to the seat of war. When one-half a company had been mustered into service, the 1st lieutenant thereof could also be mustered in; and when the organization of the company was completed, the captain and 2nd lieutenant could be mustered in.[123] The major was mustered in after the muster of six companies; the lieutenant colonel after the muster of four companies; but the colonel, chaplain, surgeon, adjutant, assistant surgeon, and quartermaster had to wait until the entire regiment was mustered in.[124] Aliens were not required to take the oath of allegiance to the government because it conflicted "with the duty they owe to their own sovereigns," but military commanders were directed to adopt, "in lieu thereof . . . such other restraints of the character indicated as they shall find necessary, convenient, and effectual, for the public safety."[125]

EFFECT OF MILITARY REVERSES

The almost complete collapse of morale in the first three months of 1863 was due to the military disasters incurred during the preceding year in the Peninsular Campaign, in the Second Bull Run Campaign, and at Fredericksburg. Civilians and soldiers alike were affected. Desertion in the Federal army was rife and volunteering came to a standstill. By March, 1863, nearly 400,000 recruits were required to bring the regiments up to the legal and necessary standard.[126] The military disasters had been followed by an equally demoralizing inactivity; the safety of the country depended on a speedy and continued re-enforcement of the Army. In addition to the casualties of war and the extraordinary rate of desertion, there was the loss of thousands of men whose terms of service had expired. The enrollment act of March 3, 1863, was passed to provide a complete inventory of the military resources of the North in men. This act provided for the appointment of James B. Fry as Provost Marshal General. Under his leadership the draft was put into operation and continued to function to the end of the war. The office of Provost Marshal General was charged with the duties of arresting deserters, enrolling the national forces for draft, and enlisting soldiers.

FOREIGNERS IN THE SERVICE

Lincoln's call for volunteers for the task of preserving the Union met with a stirring response through all the North, among immigrants as well as among native-born. Men of Scandinavian blood joined the colors with enthusiasm in Wisconsin, Minnesota, Iowa, Illinois, and other States in which they had but recently settled. The 9th Wisconsin Infantry was organized as a German immigrant regiment, and the 11th Wisconsin Infantry was preponderantly Irish. The 15th Wisconsin Infantry was a Scandinavian unit; its colonel (Heg) fell at Chickamauga.[127]

An analysis of the racial composition of the Federal Army is extremely difficult to make due to inadequacies of the national government records. Such an attempt was made shortly after the war but was reluctantly abandoned owing to lack of an adequate clerical force and to the different system of returns instituted after the war.[128] Unquestionably there were hundreds of thousands of foreigners in the Federal ranks. This is readily understood when one examines the census figures of the forty years preceding the war. During those four decades immigration from Europe, but more especially from England, Ireland, and Germany, was heavy. The following table tells

A DRUMMER BOY

Gilbert J. Marbury, Company H, 22d New York Infantry, photographed by the trail of a Napoleon field piece near Harpers Ferry in 1862.

the result of famine and revolution in those countries more graphically than words:[129]

Country where born	Number of Immigrants	Years
England	302,665	1820 to 1860
	247,125	1841 to 1850
	32,092	1851 to 1860
Ireland	967,366	1820 to 1860
	162,332	1841 to 1850
	748,740	1851 to 1860
Germany	1,486,044	1820 to 1860
	422,477	1841 to 1850
	907,780	1851 to 1860

During the war the American Emigrant Company imported both skilled and unskilled laborers upon order of employers who advanced the necessary travel expenses and who paid a small commission for the service. These immigrants were under a contract to work for these employers. When substitute brokers were able to lure the newly-arrived foreigners into military service, the employers immediately countermanded orders already made for more immigrants. In other words, the emigration company was sincerely interested in functioning as a provider of labor for northern industry. A bill was submitted in the Senate by John Sherman which had as its purpose the prevention of enlistment of newly-arrived immigrants.[130] It was also proposed that any immigrant who broke his contract for repayment of emigration expenses would be liable for double the amount that should remain unpaid of these expenses, and if such money were not paid it would be the duty of the person, or persons, who enlisted him in the Federal service to make such payment. By a Senate resolution adopted May 24, 1864,[131] the President was requested to state:

If any authority has been given any one, either in this country or elsewhere, to obtain recruits in Ireland and Canada for our army or navy; and whether any such recruits have been obtained, or whether to the knowledge of the Government, Irishmen or Canadians have been induced to emigrate to this Country in order to be recruited; and if so, what measure, if any, has been adopted in order to arrest such conduct.

Lincoln referred this resolution to the Secretary of State who replied that no authority to recruit abroad had been given by the Government and that applications for such authority had been invariably rejected. He admitted that the Federal army included not only Canadians and Irishmen but also many subjects of continental European powers, maintaining, however, that these persons were voluntary immigrants into the North and had enlisted after their arrival of their own accord.[132]

In considering the efficiency of the Federal soldier as a combat man one must not differentiate between these foreigners and native-born Americans. We now know that many foreigners fought well and many native Americans did not. However, during the war many native-born Americans thought that the majority of foreigners in the Federal ranks were worthless. Army officers of both sides and thousands of disgusted enlisted men agreed with Meade when he alluded to the "worthless foreigners, who are daily deserting to the enemy," and Breckinridge when he spoke of the men, "chiefly foreigners" who had come into his lines.[133] It was inevitable that a force as large as the Federal army would include practically every race and nationality. Although the effort to enlist Mexicans was just as much a failure for the North as it was for the South,[134] the effort to secure the services of American Indians was somewhat more sucessful and 3,530 were enlisted, of whom 1,018 gave their lives.[135] At least one Oriental served in the Federal Army.[136] Between five and six thousand Jews served in the Union Army. A total of seven thousand served on both sides[137] out of a total Jewish population of 100,000-150,000 in the United States in 1861. General O. O. Howard spoke well of the Jews under his command and the records show that seven Jews received the Congressional Medal of Honor during the war.[138]

War literature is replete with humorous incidents involving foreigners in the Federal Army. This was especially true of the Irish whose proverbial humor was expressed on many occasions. At Cold Harbor the color bearer, an Irishman, of the 19th Massachusetts was captured. When asked how he came to lose the colors, this brave soldier (Mike Scannell) replied: "I'll tell you. We lay in the pit dug for us, and the first we knew the rebels came rushing over and said, 'you damned Yankee, give me that flag!' 'Well', I said, 'it is twenty years since I came to this country, and you are the first man who ever called me a Yankee. You can take the flag for the compliment.' "[139]

Another instance of the ready wit of the Irish soldier occurred in the same regiment when another Irishman was put on guard and detailed at headquarters. He spent the night pacing his beat in a driving rain in front of the colonel's tent. By morning the guard was wet to the skin. When the colonel emerged from his tent, the Irishman said: "Colonel, will you allow me to speak a word with you?" "What is it?" said the colonel. "Well, Colonel, I wish you believed as you did before the war. Then you believed in putting none but Americans on guard and here I am, an Irishman, wet to the skin, having been on guard all night." The colonel laughed and retired. (Colonel Hincks had edited a "Know-Nothing" paper whose motto was: "Put none but Americans on guard."[140]

PERCENTAGES BY RACE OR NATIONALITY

Despite the observations of many Southern writers and foreigners, especially English, who were inimical to the Northern cause, the oft-repeated assertion that the Federal army was composed in the main of Hessians, Irishmen, and Negroes is unfair and false. The muster rolls stated the birthplaces of the men. From these rolls it appears that, in round numbers, out of 2,000,000 men, three-fourths were native Americans. Of these 2,000,000 soldiers, Germany furnished 175,000; Ireland, 150,000; England, 50,000; British America, 50,000; other countries, 75,000.[141] The Committee of Inquiry,[142] appointed by the Secretary of War June 9, 1861, discovered that of the 200 regiments it inspected in September and October of 1861, the New England States furnished 37, the Western States 62, and the Middle States 101. In 76.5% of these regiments native Americans were found to constitute the majority; in 6.5% the majority of men were Germans; in 5.5% the majority were Irish, and in 5.5% the regiments were half foreign and half native-born. Although admitting that its findings were not conclusive the committee considered it to be near the truth to state that about two-thirds of the volunteer soldiers were American born, and nine-tenths, citizens, educated under the laws of the Union and in the English tongue.[143] This committee investigated these regiments in the first year of the war, but its findings are indicative of the composition of those regiments which, enlisting with sincere patriotism in 1861 and 1863, kept their patriotism throughout the long, bitter struggle that followed. The contribution of these men in winning the war was decisive. The colored troops were comparatively few in number; only a few regiments were brought into action at all and their losses were negligible.

NEGROES

During the war there were enlisted 186,097 colored troops,[144] of whom 2,532 were killed or died of wounds.[145] The proportion of officers, all of whom were white, who were killed in action while serving in colored regiments was considerably higher than among the colored enlisted men. To the lack of civilian training and experience which hampered the Negro in his development into a good combat soldier, must be added the fact that the quality of Negro obtained was often not the best. Substitute brokers did not hesitate to procure the services of colored men confined in jails within the national capital itself.[146] On February 6, 1864 a Federal soldier noted

that "the colored men enlist very freely. They often choose the arm of service which they enter from their fancy for certain colors; some preferring one color, some another—choosing the infantry for its blue, the artillery for its red, the cavalry for its yellow. When a young Negro has enlisted, and returns in full regimentals to bid his friends goodbye, he struts like a turkey cock . . . while the old men and women throw up their hands with a hundred benedictions, the girls languish for a glance of his eye, and the children run after him in wonder with their mouths and eyes wide open."[147] This description, while exaggerated so far as the Negro's motivation for enlisting, does express the enthusiasm of the colored people for the Union.

SOUTHERNERS IN THE FEDERAL SERVICE

The enemy also supplied men to the Union cause. As it became obvious that their cause was lost, some Confederate prisoners of war enlisted in the Federal service. This was true also of many deserters from the enemy. These ex-Confederates were termed "Galvanized" or "Company Q" men, and were, in most cases, assigned to units sent West to fight Indians.[148] This was done so that there would be no chance of fighting their own kin or friends, nor would there be any temptation to return to their old allegiance.

THE "AVERAGE" FEDERAL SOLDIER

The "average" Federal soldier was: race, white; nationality, native-born; age 25; height, 5 feet 8¼ inches; and weight, 143½ pounds. When classed by ages, the largest class is that of 18 years, from which the classes decrease regularly to that of 45 years, beyond which age no enlistment was legally accepted. Of 1,012,273 recorded ages taken from the rolls, there were 133,475 at 18 years; 90,215 at 19 years and so on. The number at 25 years of age was 46,626; and at 44 years, 16,070. The general average size would have been greater had it not included the measurements of recruits from 17 to 20 years of age, who evidently had not attained their full stature when their measurement was recorded. The tallest man, a captain in the 27th Indiana Infantry, was 6 feet 10½ inches in height; the shortest was a soldier in the 192d Ohio Infantry who, at 24 years of age, was only 40 inches tall. In both cases the regimental commanders attested to the ability of these two extremes to endure fatigue.[149]

NOTES CHAPTER 1

1. Report of Provost Marshal General, *House Executive Documents*, 39 Cong. 1 Sess., Part I, Document 1, pp. 6-7.

2. Livermore, T. L., *Numbers and Losses in the Civil War in America 1861-65*, p. 47. Hereafter this work will be cited as *Numbers and Losses*.

3. Upton, Emory, *The Military Policy of the United States*, p. 225.

4. Adjutant General of Massachusetts, *Annual Report*, 1861, p. 6.

5. Commonplace early in the war.

6. Victor, O. J., *A History of the Southern Rebellion*, Vol. I, p. 161.

7. Doubleday, Abner, *Battles and Leaders of the Civil War*, Vol. 1, pp. 48-49. Hereafter, this work will be cited as *Battles and Leaders*. The garrison's commander, Major Robert Anderson, was promoted to brigadier general a month later.

8. Peters, Richard, (editor), *The Public Statutes at Large of the United States of America*, Vol. 1, p. 424. Hereafter cited as *Statutes at Large*.

9. *Ibid.*, Vol. 2, pp. 215-225.

10. *The War of the Rebellion: A Compilation of the Official Records of the Union and Confederate Armies*, First Series, Vol. 51, Part 1, pp. 322-323. Hereafter, cited as *Official Records*.

11. Thorndike, R. S. (editor), *The Sherman Letters*, p. 111.

12. *Official Records*, Third Series, Vol. 4, p. 1264.

13. *Ibid.*, Vol. 1, pp. 93-144.

14. *Ibid.*, pp. 145-146.

15. *Ibid.*, p. 154.

16. Nicolay and Hay, *Abraham Lincoln*, Vol. 4, pp. 77-78.

17. Comte de Paris, *History of the Civil War in America*, Vol. 1, pp. 175-176.

18. *Official Records*, Third Series, Vol. 4, p. 1264.

19. Appeal of large bounties came later.

20. Phisterer, Frederick, *Statistical Record of the Armies of the United States*, p. 62.

21. U. S. War Department, "General Order No. 33," April 3, 1862. *General Orders for 1862.*

22. *Ibid.*

23. *Official Records*, Third Series, Vol. 2, p. 109.

24. Phisterer, p. 4.

25. *Official Records*, Third Series, Vol. 2, pp. 180-188.

26. *Ibid.*, Vol. 4, p. 1265.

27. New York *Times*, July 15, 1862, p. 1.

28. Buffum, F. H., *A Memorial of the Great Rebellion*, (History of the 14 New Hampshire Vols,), pp. 1-3.

29. Upton, pp. 466-467.

30. Sanger (editor), *Public Laws of the United States of America* (1862), p. 597. Hereafter cited as *Public Laws*.

31. *Official Records*, Third Series, Vol. 2, pp. 291-292.

32. *Ibid.*, pp. 333-335.

33. Many localities wanted to avoid the stigma of draft.

34. *Official Records*, Third Series, Vol. 2, pp. 380-381.

35. *Ibid.*, Vol. 4, p. 1265.

36. *Ibid.*

37. *Ibid.*

38. *Frank Leslie's Illustrated Newspaper*, Vol. 14 (August 16, 1862), p. 321.

39. *House Reports*, 37 Cong., 2 Sess., Report 5, January 9, 1863.

40. Samuel Merrill, 70th Indiana Infantry, to wife, January 22, 1863. *Mississippi Valley Historical Review*, Vol. 14, March, 1928, p. 510.

41. Livermore, pp. 87-97.

42. *New York Tribune*, Aug. 9, 1862.

43. *Public Laws*, 1863, pp. 731-737.

44. *Congressional Globe*, 38 Cong., 2d Sess., p. 1075.

45. *Official Records*, Third Series, Vol. 3, p. 1178.

46. *Ibid.*, Vol. 5, p. 732.

47. *Ibid.*, Vol. 4, 932-33.

48. Phisterer, p. 5.

49. New York *Herald*, June 30, 1863, p. 6.

50. *Ibid*, p. 8.

51. *Official Records*, Third Series, Vol. 3, p. 892.

52. *Ibid.*, Vol. 4, p. 59.

53. *Ibid.*, p. 1266.

54. *Ibid.*, p. 181.

55. *Ibid.*, p. 1266.

56. *Ibid.*, p. 1267.

57. *Ibid.*

58. Embick, M. A., *Military History of the Third Division, Ninth Corps*, p. 1.

59. *Official Records*, Third Series, Vol. 4, p. 1268.

60. Report of Secretary of War, *House Executive Documents*, 39 Cong. 1 Sess., Document 1, Vol. 1, p. 1.

61. Report of Provost Marshal General, House Executive Document, 39 Cong., 1 Sess., Doc. 1, p. 54.

62. *Ibid.*

63. Bartlett, A. W., *History of the Twelfth Regiment, New Hampshire Volunteers*, p. 151.

64. Report of Secretary of War, *House Executive Documents*, 39 Cong., 1 Sess., Document 1, Vol. 1, p. 31.

65. *Ibid.* Livermore (p. 1) gives the enlistments as 2,-898,304 but includes some militia who were never mustered into the United States service.

66. Livermore, p. 50.

67. Phisterer, p. 23.

68. *Official Records*, Third Series, Vol. 1, p. 22.

69. McClellan, G. B., *McClellan's Own Story*, p. 97.

70. Comte de Paris, Vol. 1, pp. 287-288.

71. Thorndike, p. 121.

72. Comte de Paris, Vol. 1, p. 289.

73. Cox, J. D., *Military Reminiscenses of the Civil War*, Vol. 1, pp. 438-440.

74. Fox, W. F., *Regimental Losses in the American Civil War*, pp. 527-528.

75. *Ibid.*, This includes both present and absent.

76. *Ibid.*

77. Report of the Provost Marshal General, *House Executive Documents*, 39 Cong., 1 Sess., Document 1, pp. 76-77.

78. *Ibid.*, p. 77.

79. *Ibid.*, pp. 76-77.

80. *Ibid.*

81. *Ibid.*, p. 53.

82. *American Annual Cyclopedia and Register of Important Events of the Year 1862*, Vol. 2, p. 17. Hereafter cited as *Annual Cyclopedia*.

83. *Ibid.*

84. DeTrobriand, Regis, *Four Years in the Army of the Potomac*, p. 73.

85. Report of the General-in-Chief, November 15, 1863, *House Executive Documents*, 38 Cong., 1 Sess., Document 1, p. 19.

86. Wilkeson, Frank, *Recollections of a Private Soldier in the Army of the Potomac*, p. 1.

87. Many were younger than they stated.

88. Clark O., (ed) *Downing's Civil War Diary*, pp. 3-4. Downing served in Co. "E" 11th Iowa Infantry.

89. Hays, G. A., *Under the Red Patch* (History of 63rd Penn. Infantry), pp. 185-186.

90. Fox, p. 60.

91. *Revised Regulations*, U.S. Army, 1861, p. 112.

92. Fox, *passim*.

93. Ropes, J. C., *The Story of the Civil War,* Vol. 1, pp. 105-106.

94. Goss, W. L., *Battles and Leaders,* Vol. 1, p. 149.

95. Fox, p. 192.

96. Billings, John, *Hardtack and Coffee,* p. 202.

97. Blanding, S. F., *In the Defenses of Washington,* p. 6.

98. Billings, p. 37.

99. *Ibid.,* p. 38.

100. Related to the author by Color Sergeant Francis H. Buffum, 14th New Hampshire Infantry.

101. *Annual Cyclopedia,* 1863, Vol. 3, p. 18.

102. United States War Department, "General Order No. 191," June 25, 1863.

103. Report of Provost Marshal General, *House Executive Documents,* 39 Cong., 1 Sess., Document 1, p. 57.

104. Entry for September 12, 1864, Diary of Frederick Stearns, Co. "L" 1 N. Y. Engineers.

105. Haynes, M. A., *A History of the Second Regiment New Hampshire Volunteer Infantry in the War of the Rebellion,* p. 206-207.

106. Cox, Vol. 2, p. 92.

107. Entry for February 2, 1865, Diary of 1st Lt. Frederick Frank, Co. "K" 11th Indiana Infantry.

108. *Harpers New Monthly Magazine,* Vol. 30 (December 1864), p. 128.

109. Crowninshield, B. W., *A History of the First Regiment of Massachusetts Cavalry Volunteers,* p. 199, 201.

110. Report of Provost Marshal General, *House Executive Documents,* 39 Cong., 1 Sess., Document 1, Appendix to Sec. of War's report, Part 2, p. 58.

111. Adams, John, G. B., *Reminiscences of the Nineteenth Massachusetts Regiment,* p. 80.

112. Report of Provost Marshal General, *House Executive Documents* 39 Cong., 1 Sess., Document 1, Appendix to Sec. of War's report, part 2, p. 127.

113. *Official Records,* First Series, Vol. 5, p. 82.

114. Bartholow, Roberts, *A Manual of Instructions for Enlisting and Discharging Soldiers, passim.*

115. Report of Secretary of War, *House Executive Documents,* 32 Cong., 2 Sess., Document 83, p. 55.

116. Bartholow, pp. 34-54.

117. *Ibid.,* pp. 16-24.

118. Billings, p. 200.

119. *Ibid.*

120. United States War Department, "General Order No. 61," August 19, 1861, *General Orders Affecting the Volunteer Force 1861,* p. 27.

121. United States War Department, *Revised Regulations for the Army of the United States 1861,* Section 935, p. 131.

122. *Annual Cyclopedia,* 1861, Vol. 1, p. 37.

123. United States War Department, "General Order No. 61," August 19, 1861, *General Orders for 1861,* p. 27.

124. *Ibid.,* p. 28.

125. United States War Department, "General Order No. 82," July 21, 1862, *General Orders for 1862,* pp. 58-59.

126. Report of the Provost Marshal General, *House Executive Documents,* 39 Cong., 1 Sess., Document 1, p. 1.

127. *O.R.,* 1st Ser., Vol 30, Pt. 1, 528-531.

128. *The Medical and Surgical History of the War of the Rebellion,* Part 1, Medical History 1, p. 22.

129. *House Executive Documents,* 37 Cong., 2 Sess., Document 116, p. 18. "Preliminary Report on the Eighth Census."

130. *Senate Misc. Documents,* 38 Cong., 2 Sess., Document 13, pp. 6-7.

131. *Annual Cyclopedia* 1865, Vol. 5, p. 35.

132. *Ibid.,* p. 36.

133. It is unfair to generalize, however.

134. A few served in both armies.

135. Fox, p. 533.

136. Page, V. D., *History of the Fourteenth Regiment Connecticut Vol. Infantry,* p. 131. Since this man, a Chinese, bore the name of Joseph Pierce, there may well have been others whose race is hidden under an Anglicized or assumed name.

137. Wolf, Simon, *The American Jew as Patriot, Soldier and Citizen,* p. 424.

138. *Ibid.,* 106-08.

139. Adams (19th Massachusetts Infantry), p. 105.

140. *Ibid.,* p. 15.

141. Fox, p. 62.

142. *Annual Cyclopedia,* 1861, Vol. 1, p. 37.

143. *Ibid.,* That this proportion of native-born volunteers may even have been greater is suggested in the fact that the U. S. Census of 1890 showed that 82% of all surviving Union veterans were native-born and 18% foreign born. (John Bigelow, Jr., *Campaign of Chancellorsville,* p. 17).

144. Phisterer, p. 11.

145. *Ibid.,* p. 69.

146. *House Reports,* 38 Cong., 2 Sess., Report 23, pp. 1-11.

147. Thompson, S. M., *Thirteenth Regiment of New Hampshire Voluntter Infantry,* p. 234.

148. *Official Records,* Third Series, Vol. 4, p. 1232; Second Series, Vol. 6, p. 808; First Series, Vol. 41, Part 2, p. 465; Vol. 48, Part 1, p. 455.

149. Fox, p. 62.

CHAPTER 2

Training

INDIVIDUAL and unit training received far less attention during the Civil War than it does today. There was little or no planning or programming, no branch or general service schools, no prescribed training standards or systems of inspection to insure combat-readiness. Although some improvement is noticeable as the war went along the overall picture is a dismal one. The Nation paid in blood for the inadequate preparation of its soldiers for battle.

STATE TRAINING

The training of volunteer regiments remained the States' responsibility until arrival at the seat of war when the new units came under Federal supervision. In the home camps there were usually a few old soldiers or militiamen in each regiment capable of giving instruction in simple parade ground maneuvers. The period of drill was short because the majority of regiments left for the front shortly after their organization.

QUALITY OF TRAINING DEPENDED ON THE COLONEL

Throughout the entire war the War Department never possessed a genuine training program, nor did the States. The whole question of the caliber and degree of training to which any individual regiment was subjected can be answered by an examination of the efficiency of field officers and especially the regimental commander. A good colonel could "make" a regiment; a bad one could and did ruin one. In this connection the value of professional training should not be overlooked. Very often in the Civil War a State would send out several regiments composed of the same type of material and, theoretically at least, with equal chances of becoming efficient fighting regiments. Whereas some would serve with conspicuous gallantry and enviable steadiness in combat, others would show a consistently high percentage of desertion and would be unreliable in battle. The explanation is to be found in the quality of the higher officers of the regiment and, as mentioned before, especially that of the regimental commander who was responsible for training and discipline. An examination of nearly three hundred rolls of volunteer regiments from four States disclosed that ap-

proximately one-half of the regimental commanders of those regiments lacked sufficient ability or patriotism to serve until the war was won. The four states, New Hampshire, Connecticut, Ohio, and Michigan, were chosen because an opportunity to examine troops from both Eastern and Western States was thus afforded. Of the 298 colonels who left their States at the heads of their regiments: 21 were killed or died in service; 142 served through the war; and 135 either resigned or were dismissed prior to April 1865. These figures are even more significant when one realizes that 112 of these regiments were in service for one year or less; Ohio, alone, having 42 "Hundred-Day" regiments. Of the 13 cavalry regiments from Ohio only 4 regimental commanders who left the State served to the end. The other 9 resigned.[1] Most of the colonels who left the service did so during their very first year with their regiments. The implication with respect to training is obvious; many Federal regiments, possibly 50% of them, were trained by incompetents. Practically all regiments in the Federal Army that saw active service did so less than twelve months after being mustered in to the service and once at the front their training was at best sporadic and impractical.

REGULAR ARMY IMPROPERLY EMPLOYED

There were few men in the North who were so farseeing as to forecast the gigantic strain on the reserve of skilled officers at the disposal of the Federal government in 1861. The statement of a foreign writer that "when the rupture came, it was to her West Point men that the North had exclusive recourse for forming her army"[2] is only partially correct. Several vitally important commands were entrusted to politicians who had had no military service at West Point or anywhere else. The Regular force never was permitted to function in the role that common sense dictated it should; the Regular Army should have been expanded and utilized as a training school for officers. It could easily have supplied trained officers to instruct the newly forming volunteer units, at least down to the brigade level. But unfortunately the Federal government was forced to give too much initiative to the States at the beginning of the war. Later, when it wished to revoke that initiative, it was then too late, as the States refused to relinquish control over their own troops until those troops had left the States' confines. The militia law left the citizen soldiers solely in the control of the States until they were sworn into the service of the United States, and this control was absolute, including the function of training. Regiments left their States soon after muster into the service.

The Regular Army was kept intact throughout the war and never was used as an officer pool, but it did furnish most of the higher commanders of the Federal Army. Two small classes of West Point cadets were hurriedly graduated in May and June, 1861, "brave boys just out of their bell-buttoned coatees, and were set in saddle and hard at work drilling whole battalions of raw lads from the shops and farms, whose elected officers were to the full as untaught as their men." [3] Other Regular officers served throughout the entire war as mustering officers at State rendezvous camps because of the necessity of checking on inefficient or dishonest examining surgeons. Such employment of trained officers was unfortunate but probably necessary in the light of the large number of men who were discharged earlier in the war due to inadequate physical examinations.

What was even more disastrous was the decision to follow General Scott's advice which resulted in keeping some six hundred junior Regular officers with their regiments. Only a very few Regulars, except the general officers and some colonels, served with volunteer troops. The War Department was so persistent in maintaining both a Regular and a volunteer force that it was exceedingly difficult for a Regular Army officer to transfer to the volunteer service.

Those Regular officers that did serve with volun-

teers justified, in most cases, the investment their country had made in them. As one volunteer officer said: "On the whole, no regiments in the field made progress so rapid, or held their own so well as those placed under regular officers." [4] Those regular officers, graduates of West Point, who remained loyal to the Federal government were well qualified to drill regiments and command them in battle. Experience demonstrated that a volunteer regiment could in a very few weeks be converted into an efficient and thoroughly reliable force in battle by a single young officer of the Regular Army. This fact is strikingly proven in the history of the famous Vermont Brigade which, out of more than two hundred brigades in the Federal Army, suffered the greatest loss in casualties. In making a brilliant record on the battlefield, this brigade of five Vermont regiments lost 973 men killed, 774 men by disease and death in Southern prisons, and 2,328 wounded out of a total enrollment of 8,817 officers and men. [5] All but one of the regiments of this brigade were commanded by West Point graduates; the other was commanded by an officer with previous combat experience. [6] A Federal general believed that "by a judicious use of the small body of officers whom the country had educated at so great expense, a fine army of 500,000 men, or more, could have been called into service, organized, disciplined, and put into the field by August 1, 1861." [7] This would not have interfered with the militia which, of course, would have acted on the defensive until an adequate army was raised.

Regular regiments did their own recruiting and this was a further drain on personnel. Officers appointed from civil life to positions in the new Regular regiments created by Lincoln's proclamation of May 4, 1861, were assigned to this recruit-

REGIMENTAL GUARD MOUNT
The guard detail is at *parade rest* while the fife and drum corps "sounds off." There was far more preoccupation with this sort of thing than with preparation for combat.

ing while Regular officers appointed to the new Regular regiments received assignment to field duty with their new units.[8] On March 3, 1862, in the nineteen old Regular regiments, there were 261 officers who were recent appointments, and who could have been available for duty with the regiments. Of this number, 21 were general officers, and 29 were field officers of volunteers.[9]

NO PLAN TO USE PROFESSIONAL INSTRUCTORS

The War Department possessed no deliberate plan for utilizing its professional soldiers in the war. If a civilian, who had been a Regular officer, was fortunate enough to be well known in his community, he was sometimes commissioned but, just as often, he was ignored completely. A notable example was Grant whose early attempts to be permitted to serve his country in some capacity were in vain. The Regular officers who had not, prior to the war, resigned their commissions as did Grant, Sherman, McClellan, and others, were more than likely to serve in modest capacities while grocers and bankers led regiments into combat. Although over 300 Regular officers were "submerged," of those trained officers who did have a chance, 51 became major generals, 91 brigadier generals, and 106 colonels.[10] Since there were 2,047 regiments[11] in the Federal Army it is plain to see that the majority of them were led by amateur soldiers. The rank and file of the volunteers needed only capable, intelligent, and enterprising officers to make them good soldiers. As a department commander wrote McClellan late in 1861, the training of this material should have been entrusted to "subaltern officers—lieutenants capable of instructing the rank and file in the drill and maneuvers of the piece."[12] Although he applied repeatedly to General Scott for such officers his applications were not noticed.

While unquestionably the best source for training the volunteers was to be found in the Regular service it can not be assumed that all Regular officers were prepared for the war in which they were destined to be the leaders. Many of these were merely professional soldiers who had failed completely to overcome the rigidity of mind fostered by life on an army post. Even the successful generals of the Civil War did very little reading in the field of military science after graduation from the Military Academy. It was before the days of post libraries and books of any sort were a rarity at the garrisons. When a general of volunteers expressed surprise to a general of Regulars at finding how little most line officers had added to their theoretic reading after graduation, the Regular replied: "What could you expect of men who have had to spend their lives at a two-company post, where there was nothing to do when off duty but play draw-poker and drink whiskey at the sutler's shop?"[13] A Regular artillery officer[14] testify-

ing before the Committee on the Conduct of the War displayed surprising ignorance of his own branch of service as it had functioned in such significant periods of military history as the Napoleonic era. When Grant was asked after the war what military books he then owned, he replied that he possessed none and never had any except West Point textbooks.[15] Sherman admitted that as late as the fall of 1861 he had to learn the evolutions of the line, which were new to him.[16] Perhaps no further study for men like Grant and Sherman was better than to have had so much as to have dwarfed their minds into an imitation of former commanders. The ablest Federal commanders were men like Grant and Sherman, who had been educated at West Point, and who had "breathed the atmosphere of war in Mexico. They were men of no formal school, no fixed doctrine, and of no set ideas, they were men who in many cases . . . had left the army years before the war, and in place of being asphyxiated by mess life had gained independence in struggle for existence."[17]

Regular officers possessed a knowledge of army organization, regulations, methods and forms for making out returns and conducting business with the ordnance office and quartermaster department. This routine of army paper work and drill had to be learned by all new officers. But there was a marked conservatism as to military methods and arms in Regular Army circles. American inventors had produced several excellent breech-loading repeating rifles, yet the war was fought almost entirely by muzzle-loading percussion rifles and muskets. Until Grant and Sherman were leading the Federal armies there was far too much of foreign adventurers, French uniforms, and sieges conducted according to Crimean methods. Throughout the entire war there were too many Regular officers who would see disaster occur for lack of a little spontaneity on their part and yet would be able to show that they literally had obeyed every order received. One corps commander has reported the following incident which illustrates this:

> I was once ordered to support with my command a movement to be made by another. It was an important juncture in a campaign. Wondering at delay, I rode forward and found the general officer I was to support. I told him I was ordered to support him in doing what we both saw was needing to be done; but he had no explicit orders to begin the movement. I said that my orders to support him were sufficient to authorize his action, and it was plain that it would be unfortunate if the thing were not done at once. He answered cynically, "If you had been in the army as long as I have, you would be content to do the things that are ordered, without hunting up others."[18]

In addition to Regular officers who left the service before the outbreak of the war and were thereby free to develop initiative, some of the younger officers graduated close enough to the war so that they, too, were not "spoiled." Men of this type, Merritt, Custer, Kilpatrick, Porter, Upton, combined professional training with flexibility of mind and, as a result, rendered brilliant service to their country. But these men came into their own no earlier than 1863. An Englishman in 1862, in commenting on the Northerners as "energetic, fearless, ingenious, resourceful, beyond any other nation of the earth" was amazed that a "people who individually are proverbial for their readiness in surmounting obstacles that seem to others hopeless, should as a nation have made the most ignominious failure the world has ever seen . . ." and could only find an explanation in the fact that they were "infamously led." [19]

MILITIA OFFICERS FILLED THE GAP

The militia regiments were sources for officers, poorly trained as most of those units were. The officers of the organized militia regiments did what the Regular regiments should have done in that the militia officers departed from their original commands and, being distributed throughout the new army, were active in organizing the new volunteer regiments. Some of these militia regiments, especially Ellsworth's Zouaves of Chicago and the 7th New York Infantry were just about as good as West Point in the regimental and company drill maneuvers. The 7th New York furnished 700 officers for the newly organizing regiments, Regular and volunteer, after itself being mustered out of service as a regiment.[20] It was to the militia that the government turned after the fall of Fort Sumter. In the call for 75,000 three-month militia the Secretary of War designated one to three cities in each State to be places of rendezvous for the regiments.[21] These cities were selected more to get the militia assembled at easy points to transportation than to prepare for any definite training. The abbreviated term of service allowed little time for instruction of any sort, but that it was sorely needed there can be no doubt. As a good many soldiers discovered, some of their officers, even regimental commanders, were as green as their men. A few officers attempted to overcome this by cramming from text books.[22] In at least one case a colonel failed to show the men how to unload their pieces. As a result one soldier was wounded at drill.[23] Later this Regular officer was promoted to the command of a corps and by refusing to listen to reports of volunteer officers was directly responsible for the disintegration of the Federal flank at Chancellorsville.

INITIAL RESULTS OF INADEQUATE TRAINING

In the skirmish at Big Bethel which took place two months before Bull Run, Federal regiments fired into each other due to lack of training in reconnaissance. At Bull Run the militiamen formed lines slowly and badly under fire. The rear ranks were almost as deadly to friend as to enemy. Field officers had great difficulty in getting company and squad leaders to keep their men under control. As a result,

it was necessary for the higher commanders to expose themselves more than customary under such conditions and their losses were disproportionately excessive. The want of discipline in these regiments was so great that many men would run from fifty to several hundred yards to the rear and continue to fire—fortunately for the braver ones, very high in the air, and compelling those in front to retreat.[24] The three-month troops were inferior to the three-year men. That some were patriotic there can be no doubt, but many were drawn directly from the scum of the larger cities, and represented the unemployed class who wanted a three-month outing at government expense.[25] It is notorious that in the Bull Run campaign two of these militia units left when their time was up and refused to participate in the battle.[26] The blame, however, should not rest entirely on the militiamen. Many of Patterson's regiments refused to remain in service beyond their three months because of lack of such essentials as shoes, clothing, and pay.[27] The Federal commander in testifying to the Joint Committee on the Conduct of the War commented on the short-sighted policy of the high command before Bull Run:

> I had no opportunity to test my machinery; to move it around and see whether it would work smoothly or not. In fact, such was the feeling, that when I had one body of eight regiments of troops reviewed together, the general [Scott] censured me for it, as if I was trying to make some show. I did not think so.[28]

It is generally admitted that there was no lack of courage among most of the raw levies who received their baptism of fire at Bull Run. The defeat there has been ascribed to lack of training and in large part this is true. Many men who did everything wrong at Bull Run did everything right at Gettysburg and in the Wilderness.

TRAINING CAMPS INSTITUTED

Realizing that the three-month troops could not be depended upon to re-enlist after their term of service expired, the President issued May 3, 1861, his call for troops to serve for three years. Three weeks later the Secretary of war circularized the governors of the States informing them that as soon as their three-year regiments raised under the May 3, 1861 call were organized and equipped, they would be assembled at camps of instruction. These camps, the Secretary urged, would be best located in close proximity to wood, water, and subsistence. He pointed out that a rolling terrain or a terrain with porous soil was best for camp sites. Each camp was to be the rendezvous of four or eight regiments and the Secretary pointed out that since some of these regiments probably would not be called into activity much before frost they would have "ample time to acquire discipline, habits of obedience and tactical instruction . . . ."[29]

Thus far the training of the volunteers was exclusively a State affair. The departure of the three-month militia for home left a vacuum in the key points in the central zone of the North, hence it was necessary to forward the three-year regiments to these areas as rapidly as possible. Camps for the reception of these troops were set up at such places as New York, Elmira, Harrisburg, and Cincinnati with Regular officers in charge.[30] This is the first instance of the Regular Army being utilized in a training program other than isolated cases of individuals or small groups of cadets. Unfortunately this attempt like the previous ones failed because of friction over the old question of States' rights in conflict with the Federal government. Troops sent to these camps were few in number because the only troops sent were those *recruited directly* by the Federal government.

For those troops, and they were in the great majority, who had enlisted for specific organizations, there was no Federal supervision of training at all until these regiments arrived at the headquarters of the field armies or units where camps of concentration had been established. The largest of these were located at Washington, Cairo, and St. Louis. Many regiments even skipped this rung in the training ladder and went directly to the front. These concentration camps compare in size with the cantonments of the two world wars of a later period in American military experience. The men were quartered in wooden barracks twenty by fifty feet and, more rarely, twenty by eighty feet. Each camp was located for quick and easy transportation and was more of a staging area than a training camp. Troops poured into them; some remained but a short while, and were sent right on to the front; others remained for somewhat longer periods. Benton Barracks in St. Louis was reported by one diarist as containing 40,000 men at one time.[31]

Camp Defiance in Cairo was at first under the control of an exceedingly able officer.[32] The reports of this camp indicate that the men were in splendid physical condition and well drilled. It was from this camp that Grant took the troops that distinguished themselves at Fort Donelson. The Eastern regiments received their training in the "hundred circling camps" around the nation's capital. Here it was that McClellan fashioned out of raw material the instrument known as the Army of the Potomac whose "courage, discipline, and efficiency finally brought the war to a close."[33] Such a claim cannot be discussed here because the question is one of strategy, but there can be no dispute as to McClellan's genius for organization nor for the admiration and respect he commanded from his men.

Some Regiments Were of Inferior Material

Even some of these early regiments were of varying quality. An officer who had much to do with recruitment and organization of New York units has stated that city regiments from his state were composed of much poorer material than from rural areas. It was computed that over one-half of the total desertions from the men recruited in New York State prior to October 1862, occurred in New York City and Brooklyn. This was "attributable not only to the inferior class of recruits, but the ease of secretion in large cities." To cope with the problem, a reward of five dollars was offered in these cities for the apprehension of a deserter, and the police did arrest some. But not only were some of the men of inferior quality, their officers also were often of comparable low value. While a New York infantry regiment was encamped in New York city, an official visit revealed that at the guardhouse there was "a very large collection of bottles of liquor" which recruits and their friends had attempted to smuggle into camp. The example of poor discipline was set by the regiment's colonel, who had been cashiered from another unit, the 1st New York Infantry. This regiment had been a "distinctively New York City regiment, composed of what were known in those days as Bowery Boys!" The official who inspected this regiment was presented with a bill for audit; the bill was for "medical stores" for the regiment, and was composed only of the following items: 120 gallons of bourbon whiskey, 42 gallons of pale sherry, 21½ gallons of pale Otard brandy, 40 gallons of cabinet gin, and 24 dozen allsop East India ale. There was nothing else on this list which the regimental commander seriously expected the inspector to honor. The inspector, however, refused to honor "such an extraordinary array of drugs which, without doubt, never went into any hospital, but enlivened the officers' mess [however] this was a fair indication of the character of the regiment . . . [which] went to the field, was disbanded in a year, and the men incorporated in other regiments." The officers were discharged from the service.[34]

The great failure of the North in its training camp program was the complete lack of a system of regimental depots. These depots should have been located at natural places for the arming, equipping, and instructing of recruits in all the details of the school of the soldier. There should have been at least two per congressional district with depot cadres of at least 24 officers and noncommissioned officers from each regiment in the field. These men would have been "in sympathy with the community, proud of their regiments, and subject to the direct orders of the government, who would always have been on the alert to enlist recruits and to bring deserters to justice."[35]

In lieu of this sound principle of regimental depots, which failed because politicians wanted new regiments and the attendant patronage opportunities, the War Department provided for territorial recruitment on a much more restricted scale. In a general order

INFANTRY TRAINING CAMP

Not much activity in evidence here. For hundreds of years soldiers have suffered more loss of morale from idleness and boredom than from hard work.

dated August 28, 1861, the Department authorized all commanding officers of volunteer regiments to "detail from time to time, as required, one commissioned officer, or two if necessary, with one or two noncommissioned officers or privates, to recruit in the districts in which the regiments or companies were raised." [36] Such authorization was to be subject to the approval of the regimental, brigade, division, and corps or department commanders. The realization of the imperative necessity for a recruiting system and a training program under the supervision of Regular Army officers was expressed in the order of December 3, 1861, when it was directed that a Regular officer was to be general superintendent of the recruiting program in each State with headquarters in the largest or most central city.[37] On the requisition of the superintendents, a suitable number of volunteer officers, noncommissioned officers and privates were to be detailed for duty in the staff departments and as drill masters at the depots. But the great advantage of enlisting a man for a regiment from the man's own locality did not exist in this plan. The men recruited under this system were sent in small squads from the regimental rendezvous to the general depots upon which commanders of volunteer regiments, batteries, and independent companies made their requisitions for men. The State thus again became the territorial limit, instead of a regimental or congressional district. However, by a

later general order,[38] officers were directed to recruit for their own regiments instead of for the general service. By the time [39] the government returned to the system which had been abolished by the stopping of recruiting in April 1862, it was too late because individual volunteering for the old regiments had practically ceased by then. Because of this haphazard method of recruiting men and the ever-pressing demand for re-enforcements, the great majority of regiments went into action with inadequate training.

INDIVIDUAL INSTRUCTION—BASIC TRAINING

The amount of instruction received by the volunteers before leaving the State usually did not amount to much. Many of them continued the ordinary duties of home life for days and even weeks after enlistment. Then, in squads or even individually, they reported to the local rendezvous camp for drill. Very often the camp was situated on the fair grounds and the men either lived in town or were quartered in government barracks. The first instruction was in the facings. Usually the men were without uniforms and drilled without arms. An old Mexican War veteran or ex-militiaman would instruct them in the position of the soldier and endeavor to teach them the difference between their left foot and right foot. After all the men had finally arrived at the camp the tempo was stepped up and drill began in earnest, often continuing six or eight hours a day.[40] The men were

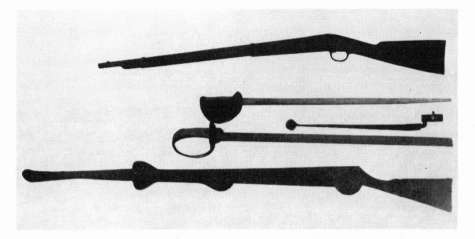

DRILL WEAPONS MADE
OF WOOD

In each of our wars new troops
have had to drill with wooden
rifles and cannon. It will be different next time; the war will have
been decided before there is time
to make wooden guns.

usually a good natured, chaotic mass of volunteers,
retaining sufficient independence in some of the
squads to declare that "they would not go into certain
companies or even in that regiment, unless they were
guaranteed their 'rights'!"[41] The field officers and
some of the company officers generally reported at
the camp a little later than the men and there would
then ensue a kind of anomalous, tentative period
before the officers were clad in their authority. When
that was accomplished a great many members of the
regiment would see many things in a different light
from that of a few weeks or even days before. The
efficiency of a regiment in combat was in direct
ratio to the degree to which the men were disciplined
and often it was that a Federal defeat could be
directly attributed to bad training which actually
meant poor discipline.

"When it was so easy to march with less rapidity
than the rest, personal courage could not be displayed to the same extent by all; if a single man
hesitated or was allowed to hesitate with impunity,
it was enough to render the hesitation contagious,
causing the bravest soldier to lose his dash, and the
most resolute chief all his daring."[42]

No Instruction in Personal Hygiene

Apart from his heightened vulnerability in battle
due to lack of combat experience, the recruit was an
easy prey to disease unless he was gradually conditioned to the hardships of military life. It would
have been a much better system that would have permitted the recruits to have become gradually inured
to their new life in camps of instruction until they
had acquired the training and physical condition
essential for combat.

Weapons Instruction

As soon as uniforms, equipments, and weapons
arrived, the men began to feel and look more like
soldiers. Generally the weapons were condemned
muskets or inferior European discards but their arrival inaugurated instruction in the manual of the

piece. Instruction was given in loading the piece
which included: extracting the paper cartridge from
the cartridge box; biting off the end of the cartridge;
inserting it in the gun barrel; drawing the ramrod;
ramming the cartridge home; returning the ramrod;
and placing the percussion cap on the nipple of the
musket. All this required much practice and was
especially difficult for the shorter men, due to the excessive length of the muskets. Since the musket had
to rest on the ground exactly perpendicular and immediately in front of the soldier, the drawing of the
ramrod was awkward even for tall men. The officers
of the line directed the drill in the manual of arms
and often took muskets in order to familiarize themselves with the drill which played so prominent a
part in the instruction for the volunteers.

It was a fortunate company, like Company "C" of
the 4th Connecticut Infantry, which had an ex-Regu-
lar in its ranks to advise the others.[43] But more often
the best-informed soldier was some ambitious man,
sometimes a college student,[44] or a man with previous military experience earlier in the war, who
instructed the officers and men. Private R. N. Pearson,
Company K, 31st Illinois Infantry, had served in
the three-month troops and was a competent drill
master. He taught the officers of his regiment the
manual of arms and himself later commanded the
regiment as colonel.[45] Sometimes however, the men
with previous military experience were worse than
useless, for they knew altogether too much to learn
themselves and too little to instruct others correctly.

The volunteers possessed too much individuality to
fit at once into the military machine without question.
Sergeants and corporals were regarded as in some
way necessary to facilitate drill, and when they requested the men to do anything which recommended
itself to the men's judgment the men obeyed but
not otherwise. One recruit while being drilled for
the first time and becoming tired of doing the same
things over and over, went up to the drill sergeant
and said: "Let's stop this fooling and go over to the
grocery." The sergeant's reply was addressed to the

corporal of the recruit's squad and, although unprintable, resulted in an unusually extended course of instruction for the already bored volunteer.[46]

There was little instruction in the use of the bayonet although the fact that there was some is evidenced by occasional references to such instruction in general histories.[47] The French manual [48] of the bayonet was followed in drill but the value of the bayonet in combat was more psychological than actual. Few men were killed or wounded by the bayonet; however, some commanders insisted on bayonet drill for their men. Much of this drill was conducted in open order formation so as to facilitate corrections by the officers. For example, on December 8, 1863, the 13th New Hampshire had an hour of bayonet drill—"bayonet exercise"—for the whole brigade; for this the 13th alone required a field of many acres. The space occupied by each man in this drill was necessarily as wide as the man with his musket and attached bayonet could reach out in every direction. At a distance a body of men drilling with the bayonet, looked "like a line of beings made up about equally of the frog, the sand-hill crane, the sentinel crab, and the grasshopper; all of them rapidly jumping, thrusting, swinging, striking, jerking every way, and all gone stark mad." [49]

Marksmanship

Most of the volunteers were bad marksmen when they enlisted and the first muskets which were issued to them were so defective as to preclude any opportunity for target practice. The pistols and revolvers were in better shape, most of them being brand new, and as a result the officers could practice where often their men could not. If not obvious at the time of issue, the defective nature of the muskets was discovered at the regimental target practice and resulted in the irate colonel appealing to his superiors for better weapons.[50] The old smooth-bore muskets were possibly more dangerous at the breech than at the muzzle, for from the latter nothing was found to be hit, while from the former a victim cringed at every shot. "Quite a number of the men had never fired a gun in their lives; and several of them, when commanded to fire, would shut their eyes, turn their heads in the opposite direction, and blaze away." [51]

Some regiments used blank cartridges in their exercises in firing the piece. Many of the regiments used "buck and ball" as ammunition, a round ounce ball in a paper cartridge with three large buckshot secured to it. This made a heavy charge, and, if the soldier did not hug his musket tightly to his shoulder while firing, he was knocked down by the "kick." [52]

Some of the volunteer regiments were drilled in firing by file and by company, to the front, to the right oblique, to the left oblique, and to the rear. To assist regimental commanders in teaching their men to shoot, the War Department republished Willard's *System of Target Practice* in 1862. This called for practice in shooting at ranges of 150 yards (target 6 feet high and 22 inches wide), and up to 1,000 yards (target 6 feet high and 264 inches wide). The instruction called for aiming exercises; use of blank cartridges in sighting and aiming; ball cartridges in firing individually, by platoon, and by company. As an incentive, prizes could be offered in a competition which called for ten shots at a white target, 3 feet in diameter, with a black bullseye. The prizes were: Company prize—a brass stadia (i.e. an instrument for measuring distance); regimental prize—a silver stadia; Army prize—a silver medal 2½ inches in diameter. An interesting provision of the instructions was that calling for guards to have target practice when going off duty. This was because muzzle loaders could not be unloaded safely. The old guard simply discharged their pieces at a target.

Target practice would be for a three-month period commencing on January 1; the ranges would be the

BAYONET DRILL IN A TYPICAL TRAINING CAMP.

ISSUING AMMUNITION

Sergeant Thomas Lawrence, Company F, 22d New York Infantry (left) and an assistant, preparing to issue blank ammunition for the caliber .577 Enfield rifle-musket. Specimens of these ammunition boxes are in private collections today. Similar boxes were used for artillery fuzes.

following, in yards: 150-225; 250-300; 325-350; 400-450.[53] Some of the regiments soon had opportunity to practice shooting at targets under permission granted by the War Department, whereby each soldier could expend ten rounds a week. In the 98th New York it was found that even this restricted practice enabled the men to estimate distances and to fire with more precision. At first but one shot in five or six hit the target of the size of a man at 150 yards. Later on the men improved, but the best firing did not give over one-third hits, which was probably the average in other regiments.[54]

From the available records it would appear that men from the West, especially the frontier areas, were better marksmen than those from the East. However, Berdan's sharpshooters came from both east and west. All were equally good marksmen.[55] However, some Western regiments were as poor at rifle shooting as many Eastern units. On Christmas Day, 1861, the 4th Illinois Cavalry held a target shooting contest. The target, a life-size image of a man (called Jeff Davis by the men), painted on a board, was 200 yards away. Each captain detailed 30 of his best shots and allowed each man to choose his own way of firing, i.e. standing, kneeling, sitting, or prone. First to fire was Company "A," which fired by volley and missed the board completely. The other companies of the First Battalion then fired in turn, but the best record of any company was six shots (out of 30), not one of which would have hit in a vital spot. The next day (December 26th) the Second Battalion tried their luck and registered seven hits.

Later, the Third Battalion did a little better because its members had fired their muskets a few times previously. However, some companies of the regiment had never fired a shot until the target competition began.[56]

Despite practice in shooting at targets, or lack of any practice at all (the case with many regiments), a large proportion of men in combat fired at everything or anything, if they fired at all. Through fear or excitement, many men promptly forgot the little training they had received, and either inserted the cartridge wrong, failed to put the percussion cap on the nipple, or forgot to press the trigger. One of the most frequently quoted evidences of excitement in battle was the sight of soldiers shooting their ramrods at the enemy. When the soldier forgot to withdraw his ramrod after ramming the cartridge down his musket barrel, he was amazed to see the ramrod quivering in a tree or the body of an enemy soldier.

The evidence is conclusive that only a small proportion of the soldiers were effective marksmen in combat. An examination of muskets picked up at random after the battle of Gettysburg would certainly indicate that the Army of the Potomac received wretched training in loading and firing. Of the 24,000 loaded muskets examined, only 6,000 were properly loaded. There were double charges in 12,000 muskets; in the remaining 6,000 the examiners found from three to ten charges. In some muskets six balls to a single charge of powder were found; others contained six cartridges, one on top of the other without having been opened. In one musket twenty-three complete charges were inserted while in another there were found "confusedly jumbled together twenty-two balls, sixty-two buckshot, with a proportionate quantity of powder."[57]

COMPANY TRAINING

After individual instruction for the volunteer came the school of the company. The officers, if diligent, kept a couple of jumps ahead of the men by cramming *Tactics* (now called drill regulations), *Army Regulations*, and the *Articles of War*. Studious officers read Wilcox's *Evolutions of the Line*, (a translation of an Austrian book) and Holabird's translation of Jomini's *Treatise on Grand Military Operations*. Other widely used works were Scott's *Military Dictionary* and Cullum's translation of Duparcq's *Elements of Military Art and History*.

At the first company drill the men would be serene in their ignorance of drill movements, while their officers, who had crammed Casey for a week or so, were in a vertebral cold-shiver temperature. The officers were very familiar with Casey—in a book—but soon realized there was a difference between tactics on paper and tactics on the drill ground.[58] In the better regiments schools were held for the company officers where the mistakes of the day were

INFANTRY COMPANY IN TRAINING—SHOWING AVERAGE STRENGTH, AND FRONTAGE WHEN IN LINE.

discussed and instruction given in outpost duty and other advanced subjects. In the 5th New Hampshire Infantry, a school of this type was conducted by the lieutenant colonel for the company officers while the colonel took the first sergeants and heard their lessons in drill maneuvers and Army Regulations. He met with them two evenings every week with a view to making good officers of them in the future. This, an unusual practice for any volunteer regiment, really paid rich dividends. The 5th New Hampshire became one of the very best volunteer regiments in the entire service; it was an extremely dependable unit, and lost the greatest number in combat of all Federal infantry regiments.[59]

REGIMENTAL TRAINING

Regimental drill followed company drill in normal sequence and here it became obvious to everyone how unfortunate had been the selections made by the governors, many of the appointments having been made for political reasons only. Even potentially good regimental commanders had their embarrassing moments; as, for example, the colonel of a Western regiment (5th Wisconsin Infantry) whose horse shied when the band played and a shower of small paper slips was seen flying about. The colonel halted his command but was forced to call his officers to him and have them march their units back to camp. Without his notes he was helpless.[60]

Most regimental schedules included a dress parade in the evening which was often attended by the "beauty and fashion" of the surrounding district. Each company was formed in its own camp area by the first sergeant. The tallest men formed on the right of the company and so on down to the shortest men on the left. The men then counted off into ones and twos, so that each man would know his place. Then the order to right face and march by the flank would be given. The band would strike up some lively tune and each company would march out to the drill field in full dress. When aligned correctly, the regiment would present arms on command of the adjutant (a first lieutenant), who in turn would transmit the salute to the colonel. The colonel would then drill the regiment in the manual of arms although often this was omitted in the early stages of a regiment's training due to the lack of training of the regimental commander. The first sergeants then reported those absent in their companies after which the officers executed a "front and

THE REGIMENT

A regiment passing in review. Note the white gloves and new clean uniforms, always the subject of derisive comments from field soldiers.

center" and after halting a few paces in front of the colonel, saluted him and received any instructions he might have to give. After the parade the companies were marched back to their quarters.

At one of these dress parades the regiment would receive its colors from wealthy friends. Presentation speeches were made by the governor or his representative to which the commander of the regiment replied with "fitting words," pledging that the colors would never be sullied by an act of dishonor on the part of his regiment. The colors, carried by a color sergeant and color corporal, were very expensive affairs. The State flag of the 10th Massachusetts Infantry was made of rich blue silk trimmed with yellow silk fringe and mounted with gold cord and tassels. The State motto was written in a scroll with the words, "Tenth Regiment Massachusetts Volunteers" in gilt beneath; the State coat of arms was also on the flag, which measured 6 by 6½ feet and cost $275.00.[61]

CAMP POLICE

Meanwhile the men were learning that soldiering included camp police although some original attitudes underwent partial revision in the process. In one case an officer was informed by one of his men that he had "enlisted to put down the Rebellion, not to pick up garbage, sweep streets, clean out sinks [latrines], and mow brush."[62] Inspections were frequent, often taking the form of knapsack drill, where the men, without previous warning, were marched out on the drill field with loaded knapsacks. There they formed in columns of companies and were told to "unsling knapsacks." This done, the colonel, major, and company commander would inspect each man's knapsack, discovering such items as unclean underclothing, Bibles, whiskey bottles, novels, cards, love letters, photographs, revolvers, knives, and stationery.[63] Another type of inspection was made either in quarters or outside in which the arms and accoutrements were examined. While still in the State the men were presented with many articles of dubious value which will be discussed in detail under the heading of equipment. Much advice was given to the recruit not only by ex-militiamen who had never "smelled powder" themselves but also by the press. A Washington paper under the heading "A Few Hints to Volunteers" said in part:

When the recruit goes into quarters if they should happen to have been previously occupied by troops, his first object should be to see that they are free from vermin or noxious insects. If his investigations discover anything of this kind, he should immediately report to his captain, and if the matter is not attended to his only remedy is to take an "outside seat" until something is done.[64]

Another widely-read journal advised the recruit that on arrival at camp he eat at once and go right to sleep, while to the recruit on sentry duty was given the welcome news that "a little pepper in your mouth will prevent you from falling asleep on your post."[65]

MOUNTED INSTRUCTION

Since the non-arrival of horses and equipment precluded drill, artillery and cavalry units generally drilled on foot until after arrival at the camps of instruction outside of the State. Artillery used the manual *Instruction for Field Artillery* which first appeared in 1860 and with slight modification was used throughout the war. It was written by a board of Regular officers, each member of whom attained high rank in the war.[66] The cavalry used the "41 Tactics" or "Poinsett Tactics" (authorized by the Hon. J. R. Poinsett, Secretary of War, February 10, 1841) which was mainly a translation of the French cavalry manual. Also using the French drill was McClellan's system of cavalry drill. This drill system called for a double rank formation. With the exception of the 1st Maine Cavalry, all the regiments in the Army of the Potomac used the same drill.[67] These 1841 "Tactics" were used by the Eastern cavalry during the entire war and by the Western cavalry units until the fall of 1864 when they began to use the "Cooke tactics," written by Colonel Philip St. George Cooke and officially adopted by the War Department November 1, 1861. A general work which was in fairly common usage was Roemer's *Cavalry; Its History, Management, and Uses in War.*

The cavalry branch was popular with the Easterners who, forgetting that the mounted man is the slave of his horse, thought that because they could perform the day's march on horseback, less labor would be required on their part. Cavalry drill was difficult in those regiments that had no intermediate field officer between the colonel and his captains. These regiments were composed of ten companies (now called "troops") and numbered one thousand men. The front of such a regiment was too extended for the flanks to hear the colonel's words of command in drill. Neither the Eastern nor the Western States had men who were "natural" cavalrymen; in the East the buggy had long since replaced the saddle horse, while in the West the farmer was more of a husbandman than a stockraiser. Owing to ignorance of the care necessary to preserve the animals, the volunteers found themselves dismounted after a few days' campaign, and many cavalry regiments were even obliged to leave the field and go into cantonments. One colonel took his new cavalry regiment 850 miles in December 1861 by boat and train and so negligent were he and his subordinates in the fundamentals of care of the horses that on arrival at his destination only 41 out of 1,000 animals were fit for duty.[68]

STAGING AREAS

For each regiment, infantry, cavalry, or artillery, the receipt by the colonel of orders from the War Department to take his regiment to the seat of war was invariably received with great enthusiasm by officers and men. The fear that "the war will be over before we get there" was sensibly diminished by travelling orders and for several days the men were busy preparing for the long rail or boat trip. As there was no such thing as military secrecy the relatives and friends for miles around thronged to the camp to witness the departure. Usually the men marched to the railroad depot with their band leading the way. "It was an interesting spectacle— to see a thousand soldiers, but yesterday in civil life, marching away from their homes and dearest objects of existence to venture every hardship that a colossal struggle, covering a thousand battle-fields, involved, with a risk of life that amounted to a certainty of death for a large number." [69]

In most regiments the men were loaded down with so much impedimenta that they literally staggered; hence the short march to the depot was a fatiguing exercise. In the fitting out of the individual kits of a volunteer regiment for active service, neither the State nor the National Government appeared to exercise much control. First came the family friends with several scores of "absolutely indispensable articles," such as thimble, scissors, paper of pins, a needle-book with all sizes of needles, several spools of thread, a big ball of yarn for darning—some went so far as to put in a bundle of patches—buttons, bandages—these were a few of the motherly, wifely, or sisterly tokens, tucked away in the soldier's knapsack. Then outside friends brought their offerings, among them cases of medicine for self-doctoring; tourniquets for the stoppage of blood flow; havelocks; handkerchiefs, etc. Masculine admirers, who had a sanguinary idea of soldiering—for others—contributed their addition to the outfit in the shape of enormous pocket knives containing a complete kit of tools; dirks; revolvers with bullet mold and powder flask. A knife-fork-spoon contrivance was a trophy for the more favored ones. Yet this was only a beginning.

While in camp, money obtained easily from home was expended lavishly. Innumerable knick-knacks, as useless as numerous, were laid in store. One of the favorite articles of outfit was the steel-plated vest, a garment into which a pair of heavy iron breast-plates were to be slipped when going into action, at other times to be carried in the knapsack.[70] Many of the new soldiers had their pictures taken before leaving the State. A member of the 19th Massachusetts Infantry, anxious that his best girl should see him in the full garb of a warrior, arrayed himself in heavy marching order and went to an "ambrotype saloon" to have his picture taken. The soldier was disappointed because in this ambrotype everything was reversed, so that his musket was at his left shoulder, his haversack and canteen on the wrong side—"in fact I was wrong end to in every respect." This soldier's regiment soon went by rail to New York City where the men were marched to a barrack and given some thin soup and a Testament. "I had already two Testaments in my knapsack, but I took this, although I wished they had put a little more money [into a better] soup and [omitted] the Testament." [71]

Some regiments, especially in the Western States, made their trip by boat, but for most regiments the journey was by rail. In any case, there were many soldiers who had never been on either a steamboat or a train. When one regiment was loaded into perfectly clean box cars it indignantly demanded: "Are we cattle, to be used in this way? Do they think because we are so far from home they can use us like hogs?" [72] A few months later they considered themselves lucky beyond measure when they were permitted to ride on open flat cars in a driving rain. At this stage of their military career many soldiers still retained definite ideas of their "rights." En route for the South one soldier jumped from the train to pick blackberries but his corporal at once ordered him back on the train. To this the soldier paid no heed until the command had been repeated several times whereupon he looked at his squad leader significantly and said: "Corporal S., you are forgetting yourself, sir." [37] He was not disturbed further.

REGIMENTAL MASCOTS

Accompanying many of the regiments to the South were regimental mascots. Certainly one of the most unusual was that of the 12th Wisconsin Infantry— a young bear, about one-third grown. While in camp at Camp Randall, Madison, this bear was tied to a 12-foot post. When the regiment moved to the front by rail, the bear slept most of the way to Chicago. In that city, before a large crowd of spectators, the bear marched at the head of the regiment and, very naturally, attracted attention along the entire marching route. The regiment kept this mascot for some time; he liked to wrestle and ate hardtack as well as the rest of the regiment. But when a long march into the field was coming up, his owner sold him.[74]

Present with the 35th Ohio Infantry was their mascot, a dog, who saw action at Mill Spring, Shiloh, Perryville, Chickamauga, and Missionary Ridge. "Jack" knew every man and beast in the regiment and had a friendly recognition for them whenever and wherever encountered. Soldiering agreed with him very well for he was not sick a day during his term of service, and always reported for his rations! [75] The most famous mascot of all was unquestionably "Old Abe," the eagle of the 8th Wisconsin Infantry. This mascot was entrusted to a soldier who had no other job but under strict orders was to care for the bird. Old Abe was carried on an elaborately constructed perch with heart-shaped shield on which was inscribed the Stars and Stripes and, along the base, "8th Reg. W. V." When the

"FIELD TRAINING"
The 22d New York Infantry paraded in full field equipment at Maryland Heights, across the Potomac from Harpers Ferry.

regiment was in line, Old Abe always rode on the left of the color bearer, out in front of the regiment. In battle or on the march, the eagle was carried in the same manner as the colors. The bearer of Old Abe wore a belt to which was attached a socket to receive the end of a five-foot staff which supported the perch. A leather ring was fastened to one of Old Abe's legs; attached to the ring was a strong hemp cord about 20 feet long. Old Abe survived all the battles of his regiment, which was called the "Eagle Regiment" by other units.[76]

CAMPS OF INSTRUCTION

The immediate destination of the troops was one of the camps of instruction located near large cities sufficiently removed from the actual combat zone to permit training and organization to be completed without interference from enemy troops. The largest and most important training center was located in and around Washington which, when first viewed by the Federal volunteer impressed him with its "negro cabins, an army of aimless curly-heads, long winding trains of army wagons, big warehouses of quartermaster's stores, immense stacks of commissary supplies, strolling soldiers, a provost-guard, groups of furloughed officers, barracks, camps, hospitals, parks of artillery, all the varied and indescribable paraphernalia of war."[77] Here the new levies of infantry were formed into provisional brigades and placed in camp in the suburbs of the city for equipment, instruction, and discipline.

As soon as regiments were in a fit condition for transfer to the forces confronting the enemy they were so assigned. General Fitz John Porter was at first assigned to the charge of this training program; he was succeeded by General Ambrose E. Burnside who, however, was soon relieved by General Silas Casey who was peculiarly fitted for the task. Although a great many of the troops were raw, Casey believed that because of the excellent material in the volunteer forces they could be made superior to Regulars. "The difficulty with them is their officers . . . very frequently there are men in the ranks

better fitted to command than the officers themselves. You have to find them out by trying. That is the great difficulty in the whole of this army."[78] Under Casey, this "day nursery" as it was called, processed over 100,000 men before the Army of the Potomac left for the Peninsula in March and April 1862. Casey accompanied as a divisional commander the forces he had trained and another camp of instruction was ordered to be organized at Annapolis, Maryland, under the command of Major General Wool.[79] This camp was to train 50,000 men at a time with the three branches of service, infantry, cavalry, and artillery to receive training under its own training chief. The Chief of Ordnance, Quartermaster General, Commissary General, Surgeon General, and Paymaster General were each to designate an experienced Regular officer to be chief of his respective department at the camp. General Wool was to handle all details for brigading, equipping, drilling, and disciplining this "Reserve Corps d'Armee."

The whole project was impracticable from the beginning. The very magnitude of the objective was sufficient to make it difficult to achieve. It was not merely a question of assembling 50,000 men; the demand for re-enforcements was so great, due to the losses on the Peninsula, that no body of troops, even as few as 5,000, could be permitted to remain together for the sole purpose of training. Raw regiments, as well as individual recruits, had to be sent at once to the front, where the only opportunities for training were offered during the suspension of active operations. Thus the Annapolis project was a failure; on his return from the Peninsula (where he had failed as a division commander), Casey was again assigned as chief of training in the Washington area.

The new regiments were pouring in to the camps almost daily when Casey re-assumed his old position. Drill commenced at 7 a.m. and often lasted until 8 p.m. with breaks for fatigue details and work on the fortifications constituting the defenses of Washington. In one brigade the closing event one day was a dress parade conducted entirely by privates and noncommissioned officers, one of whom, a corporal, acted as colonel. The corporal's "charge to the acting officers could not be excelled by any Colonel in the Brigade." [80]

TRAINING LACKED REALISM

The fact that many regiments became proficient in close order drill and parade evolutions was admirable, but that this type of training might not be the best to prepare troops for combat never occurred to the high command. That there were some misgivings on this all important question is evidenced by an article which appeared in the *Army and Navy Journal:*

The commonly received idea of military training extends no further than the daily monotonous routine of squad, company, and battalion [regimental] drill, the excellence of which has for its measure the mathematical precision with which each movement is executed. [This precision takes a long time and involves laborious practice] . . . The condition of troops on the field of battle does not admit of the preservation of perfect unbroken order, nor or perfect mathematical precision of movement. It is not likely that troops so taught will, when placed in circumstances requiring a departure from their preconceived ideas, be apt to consider all deviations from the precision of parade as evidence of mismanagement and failure? [81]

Later on in the war the *Army and Navy Journal* reiterated the need for practical training. It pointed out that "it is very useful to let volunteers, and indeed all soldiers, understand what is about to be done. Instead of confining himself to the drill as laid down in the tactics the . . . [regimental] commander should imagine an enemy, and manoeuvre over a rough country and through woods, as if the enemy were there, explaining to the men the why and wherefore." [82]

It was Hooker's boast that in the course of his reorganization of the Army of the Potomac he instituted practical instruction. There is no evidence, however, to show that field exercises were performed; the "practical instruction" apparently consisted solely of company, regimental, and brigade drills. There was no training at all for the divisional and corps commanders and their staffs under conditions of battle; no maneuvering of large units in the presence of a simulated enemy. Nor was there any appreciable emphasis placed on training in musketry. The sharpshooter regiments were an exception. They had target practice daily under the supervision of their commander, Colonel Hiram Berdan, himself a noted rifleman. The colonel's units were great copy for newspapers, who commented in detail on the excellent shooting done by these experts with the rifle. President Lincoln and General McClellan were wont to visit the sharpshooters and try their skill with them. [83]

COMBINED ARMS TRAINING

Grouping of infantry, cavalry, and artillery in the same area often afforded an opportunity for sham battles; occasionally the infantry practiced forming hollow squares against cavalry. [84] Each arm had its own camp. The newly arriving artillery troops reported to Brigadier General William F. Barry, the Chief of Artillery of the Army of the Potomac. As the regiments and batteries arrived they were assigned to the artillery reserve, while some of the heavy artillery regiments were formed into a permanent garrison in the defenses of Washington. These units were drilled by Colonel R. O. Tyler, 1st Connecticut Heavy Artillery, but later went to the front as infantry to serve in Grant's 1864 campaign.

BERDAN'S SHARPSHOOTERS
Demonstration for Gen. McClellan near Washington, September 20, 1861.

ARTILLERY TRAINING

Heavy artillery underwent more types of drill than the volunteers of any other branch of the military service. For example, the 4th New York Heavy Artillery was drilled in infantry movements and the use of muskets, the Enfield rifle being the gun used. The companies were required to drill two hours a day as artillery and two hours as infantry. In some companies Belgian rifles were used in the infantry drill, the artillery drill being chiefly performed with 8-inch siege guns mounted on barbette carriages. At Fort Greble the target was usually a buoy anchored in the river. Also used were targets of heavy timber which were set up at various ranges of from 200 to 2,000 yards. Not infrequently these latter targets were completely demolished in one day of practice.[85]

The field artillery batteries likewise had target practice but in their case the targets were usually not specially constructed for artillery practice but rather some prominent object such as a tree or old building which had been deserted by its former inhabitants. Occasionally articles of condemned equipment were set up. On March 19, 1864, the batteries of the Second Corps went up to headquarters for target practice, where across a ravine some old shelter tents had been set up. At these tents the various batteries of the corps fired solid shot, shell, and spherical case shot; the various types of projectiles were fired in rotation so as to enable the men to observe the effects of each type. At the close of the practice there were no tents standing and many were torn in shreds.

Battery "B" 1st Rhode Island Light Artillery fired about 20 rounds from each piece, and was credited with making the best shots with shell and spherical case shot.[86] In the 10th Massachusetts Battery the practice was to take either the whole or part of the battery out for target practice "once in a while." Apparently some battery commanders believed more in practice in actual firing the guns than did others. On one occasion the 10th Massachusetts used a distant pig pen as a target. But "immediately after a well-directed shot, the occupant, who it seemed, was at home, issued forth very promptly, attended by her family, unharmed, but amazingly astonished."[87] However, sometimes the target practice of a new battery almost led to tragic results, as, for instance, when the 5th Massachusetts Battery, firing at a large tree on top of a hill, some 1,000 yards away, set their sights at 1,300 and 1,600 yards, and almost killed the inhabitants of a village on the other side of a hill. This was the first time anyone in the battery had ever fired the guns; the battery later was much more accurate in combat.[88] These volunteer batteries were composed of excellent men and they learned their business fast.

A Regular officer in one of the artillery camps had, in addition to his own Regular battery, three volunteer batteries to instruct. The first marked feature he noted with these volunteers was their quick intelligence. "In a few weeks they were well set up, neatly dressed, and soldierly looking and in their knowledge of the details of the duties of artillerists quite as well informed as many of the old soldiers of the battery."[89] The Federal artillery contribution to winning the war was possibly the greatest of any of the combat arms. It is a matter of record that the artillery saved the day on many vital occasions, but it could have accomplished even more had its training been more along the lines of combat conditions. While drilling in anticipation of Grant's 1864 campaign, the artillery of the Army of the Potomac continued to perform displayful evolutions. One artilleryman has written that:

Teams were hitched to the guns almost daily, and they were whirled over comparative dry ground in a highly bewildering and exceedingly useless manner. Every enlisted man in the army knew that we were to fight in a rugged wooded country where the clearings were surrounded by heavy forest, and where deep shrubs and timber-clad ravines hazed the air, and where practice and practice and still more practice in estimating distances was required, if we were to fire accurately and effectively. Did the artillery officers zealously practice us in estimating distance? Never, to my knowledge . . . Never, while I was in the artillery camp, did I see the guns unlimber for target practice.[90]

However, a former member of the 10th Massachusetts Battery described in detail the practical drill received by his battery in gun drill, estimating ranges, cutting fuses, and mounting and dismounting the gun. Gun crews vied with each other in these drills and parade drill was at a reasonable minimum. This apparent contradiction is probably explained by the fact that Billings' battery was commanded by an exceptionally efficient and imaginative officer, Brevet-Major J. Henry Sleeper.[91]

CAVALRY TRAINING

Cavalry arriving in the Washington area reported to Brigadier General George Stoneman, the chief of cavalry for the Army of the Potomac. There was also a cavalry training and recruiting depot located at Carlisle Barracks, Pennsylvania.[92] Cavalry is a most difficult force to organize, arm, equip, and train. Many months of patient training, dismounted and mounted, are necessary before cavalry is qualified to take the field. It was not until Hooker assumed command that for the first time the difference between Regulars and volunteers ceased to exist so far as this arm of the service was concerned. In the Regular cavalry service it was a common statement that a cavalryman was of little real value until he had had two years of service.[93]

TRAINING IMPROVES

While some foreign observers deplored the lack of smartness of the Federal volunteers, the evidence is overwhelming that by 1863, "in every essential for good conduct and ready manoeuvre on the field of battle, or for heroic efforts in the crisis of a desperate engagement [the volunteer regiment] . . . could not be excelled if its officers had been reasonably competent and faithful.[94] At Chancellorsville and Gettysburg and for the remainder of the war the Federal Army consistently displayed those military capacities which a Swiss observer maintained were "equal to those of the best troops in the world." [95]

General Meade writing to his wife two days after Gettysburg said: "The men behaved splendidly. I really think they are becoming soldiers. They endured long marches, short rations, and stood one of the most terrific cannonadings I ever witnessed." [96] At the same time Grant was similarly impressed by his troops around Vicksburg. "The close of the siege of Vicksburg found us with an army unsurpassed in proportion to its numbers, taken as a whole of officers and men." [97]

TRAINING AT THE FRONT

A regiment at the front continued its training in the lulls between battles or campaigns. Usually this training was limited in scope and embraced a continuance of the close order drill which it had practiced earlier in its career. Just as often as not, however, a regiment's training would be restricted entirely to what it learned on the battlefield. The soldier was forced to acquire experience on the battlefield, often at his own expense. The cost of tuition for such a course was high; for example, regiments were put into action at Antietam "without even an hour's practice in file-firing, and . . . stood their ground . . . manfully, though helplessly, the merest food for cannon." [98] In the West the situation was the same. A non-commissioned officer of the 12th Iowa Infantry was approached by a recruit from a regiment which had just arrived at the front who asked him if he "would kindly show him which end of the bullet should be put into the gun first . . ." Although the recruit's entire regiment was equally ill-prepared, one week later it was marched to the front and met the attack on the morning of April 6, 1862, at Shiloh.[99] The *Atlantic Monthly* urged its readers to start daily target practice because "when called upon to send an army into the field, we find that more than half of its members have never fired a gun." [100]

Sometimes the men were better drilled than their colonel and partially compensated for his ignorance by deploying themselves. In a battle in Louisiana the 8th New Hampshire Infantry lost patience with its colonel, "who knew so little of drill that he tried to deploy from column into line by inversion and kept bawling helplessly, 'deploy!' . . . and [ignoring him] hurried forward in squads, or singly, to skirmish with the enemy." [101]

Fortunate was the regiment which was brigaded with veterans, because the new men profited by the experience of the older battle-tested units. More often, however, each regiment had to learn by bitter experience involving a weeding-out process whereby incompetent officers were eliminated. The process was a costly one if the elimination did not take place before an active campaign. Costly also, was the incredible carelessness of many soldiers in their handling of weapons and projectiles both in camp and at the front. There is hardly a regimental history which does not record an example of soldiers killed or maimed through stupid carelessness, either on their own part or that of a comrade. For example, while the 11th Ohio Infantry was in camp (June 12, 1863), one of its members found a 12-pound shell and brought it into the quarters of Company "A". While the soldier was picking with his bayonet at the shell, it exploded, killing two and severely wounding two others. One of the killed was the soldier who was using his bayonet on the shell.[102] Carelessness in the handling of their muskets cost the 14th Connecticut at least two of its men in the regiment's first battle.[103]

In quiet sectors, reviews and drills were held when possible. The sham battles were particularly exhilarating and entertaining to the men, sometimes a whole corps (numbering 15,000 to 25,000 men) would participate. The troops were issued blank cartridges and permitted to use them without stint.[104] While units as large as a corps were frequently reviewed, it was extremely rare that such a unit was drilled in a body. One such exercise was held for the diversion of some English officers who were visiting the Army of the Potomac after Gettysburg. The corps commander stood on a hill and through the medium of mounted staff officers drilled his three divisions on a plain below. The drill closed with a charge against the hill and it happened very comically that the Irish brigade came up just opposite the general's staff and the English officers on the hill, and incited to the mischief, probably by the English uniforms, charged down on the group and dispersed the dignified assembly with hilarious cheers.[105]

The following letter written by a soldier of the 18th Massachusetts at Camp Barnes near Washington, described a review in November 1861:

Dear Sister:

Wednesday that Grand Review of which before this you have had an account and probably more of an one than I could give you for, of course, a spectator would have a better chance to see than one taking part in the same. Old *Abe, McClellan,* Seward and Cameron and the big folks were there and rode around and reviewed us. After which the whole of the troops marched by them. There were about seventy-five thousand soldiers (quite a muster, wasn't it) there. It made a splendid show I assure you. Porter's Division had many compliments, and the 18th had some alone to themselves. The 18th was the only Reg't. I saw that wore their overcoats. They were worn to cover up our homely uniforms I suppose. We started from camp about eight a.m. and did not get back until about dark.[106]

REPLACEMENT TRAINING

Replacements received most of their training after joining their regiments. There was no provision made for replacements at all in the first few months of the war due to the prevalent belief that the war would be of short duration. From the Battle of Bull Run until the 1863 draft new regiments were formed while the older units became skeletonized at the front for lack of replacements. Between the inception of the draft and the end of the war "twenty-one depots . . . [were] established in the principal states for collecting and forwarding to regiments volunteers and substitutes, and also drafted men . . . There were, [in addition], six special depots for recruits enlisted in rebel states by agents from loyal states."[107] These depots, however, were not fundamentally training centers and made no pretense or turning out well-trained men. When General Sherman in a communication to Grant requested re-enforcements "he was perfectly willing to take raw troops then being raised in the North-west, saying that he could teach them more soldiering in one day among his troops than they would learn in a week in a camp of instruction."[108] Despite Sherman's contention, if the replacements arrived only a few days before their regiment went into combat the casualties were unduly increased with both old and new men alike. When officers had to stop the advance of their men in order to instruct raw recruits in the fundamentals of loading and firing,[109] an important attack could be jeopardized. The men realized this fact. A lieutenant in the 8th United States Colored Troops wrote to his father, complaining that his regiment has been drilled too much for dress parade and too little for the field. They march well, he said but they cannot shoot rapidly or with effect. Some of them can, but the greater part cannot. Colonel Fribley had applied time and again for permission to practice his regiment in target firing, and been always refused. The result was that the regiment suffered very heavily while inflicting but slight loss on the enemy.[110]

ENGINEER TRAINING

The Federal engineer units received their training from the small Regular company of Engineers which was enlarged on August 3, 1861, to a force of 49 officers and 600 men.[111] Several excellent volunteer regiments of engineers were raised especially in New York and Michigan. They were officered by a large and educated class of civil engineers. Enlisted men were selected with regard to their fitness for the nature of the work to be done. These men, artisans, road workers, and lumbermen were given a brief course of basic military training[112] and then sent to build fortifications in front areas. In the defenses of Washington these engineers were assisted by heavy details from infantry regiments. Large entrenched camps were also constructed in the vicinity of Louis-ville, Paducah, and St. Louis. After assuring the security of these localities the engineer units took the field and performed noteworthy service throughout the war. Mahan, professor of military and civil engineering at the United States Military Academy, and Duane, chief engineer of the Army of the Potomac, wrote training manuals for engineers.

INSTRUCTION OF SERVICE TROOPS

The remaining arms and services of the Federal Army received very little training of any description. The United States Military Railroads were officered by ex-civilians who had had previous railroad experience and manned by inexpert labor. The United States Military Telegraph Corps was in reality a civilian bureau attached to the Quartermaster Department in which a few of its favored members received commissions. The men in the field were mere employees—kept that way by Stanton because he wished to avoid their being given a military status which would have placed them under the orders of superior officers. The Signal Corps had a camp of instruction at Fort Monroe, Virginia, to which officers and men were detailed from volunteer infantry regiments. This camp was superseded by one at Georgetown, District of Columbia, which was opened August 29, 1861. Officers and men from various regiments of the Pennsylvania Reserve Corps were assigned to the Signal Corps at this camp and received instruction in flag signalling, the telescope, reconnaissance, torch signalling at night, signal flares, rockets, and the electric telegraph.[113] The camp commander was Albert J. Myer who had been appointed Signal officer of the Army June 27, 1860. The balloon corps of the Federal Army was composed entirely of civilians under the leadership of Professor T. S. C. Lowe, a prominent aeronaut. Ground crews to assist the balloonists were detailed from regiments in the immediate vicinity of the balloon.[114] These crews, untrained in their work, had to be instructed by the aeronauts, a process that was repeated whenever the balloon moved its base of operations. The services, quartermaster, commissary, paymaster, ordnance, intelligence, adjutant general's department and judge advocate's department drew their personnel from the civilians who possessed abilities that peculiarly fitted them for the specialized work they would have to perform. Investigation has not disclosed any specific training having been given to any of these special categories. The Medical Department was officered by doctors, most of whom had received some training in medicine and surgery before entering the service. No special training in removing wounded seems to have been given the musicians who acted as stretcher bearers in combat, but the Ambulance Corps which was an integral part of the military organization was drilled in removing wounded from the field.[115]

NOTES—CHAPTER 2

1. Waite, Otis, *New Hampshire in the War, passim;* Reid, Whitelaw, *Ohio in the War,* Vols. 1 & 2, *passim;* Robertson, Jno., *Michigan in the War, passim;* Croffutt and Morris, *The Military and Civil History of Connecticut During the War of 1861-1865, passim.*

2. *Fraser's Magazine for Town and Country,* Vol. 71, (Apr. 1865), p. 424.

3. Miller, F. T., *Photographic History of the Civil War,* Vol. 8, p. 76. (Hereafter cited as Photographic History). There is a photograph of some of these West Pointers in *Photographic History,* Vol. 8, p. 185.

4. *The Atlantic Monthly,* Vol. 14 (September 1864), p. 349.

5. Fox, p. 116.

6. Benedict, G. G., *Vermont in the Civil War,* Vol. 1, *passim.*

7. Schofield, J. M., *Forty-Six Years in the Army,* p. 515.

8. Adjutant General's Report (March 3, 1862), *House Executive Documents,* 37 Cong., 2 Sess., Document 65, pp. 2-3.

9. *Ibid.*

10. See Upton, pp. 258-61.

11. Phisterer, p. 23.

12. Wool to McClellan, November 11, 1861, *Official Records,* First Series, Vol. 4, pp. 629-630.

13. Cox, Vol. 1, p. 175.

14. Joint Committee on the Conduct of the War, *Report,* Vol. 4, p. 444.

15. Schofield, pp. 523-524.

16. Sherman, W. T., *Personal Memoirs,* Vol. 1, pp. 219-220.

17. Fuller, J. F. C., *The Generalship of Ulysses S. Grant,* p. 5.

18. Cox, Vol. 1, p. 184.

19. *The London Quarterly Review,* Vol. 224 (October 1862), p. 287.

20. *Photographic History,* Vol. 8, p. 70.

21. *Official Records,* Third Series, Vol. 1, pp. 68-69.

22. Initially this was fairly common in volunteer units.

23. This officer was Colonel O. O. Howard.

24. Report of Colonel Samuel Heintzelman, commanding the 3rd Division at Bull Run, *Official Records,* First Series, Vol. 2, p. 403.

25. Comte de Paris, Vol. 1, pp. 176, 178.

26. They were the 4th Pennsylvania Infantry and Varian's New York Battery. These regiments were derided in a cartoon in *Harper's Weekly: A Journal of Civilization,* Vol. 5 (September 7, 1861), p. 576.

27. Joint Committee on the Conduct of the War, *Report,* First Series, Vol. 2, pp. 138-139.

28. *Ibid.,* p. 38.

29. *Official Records,* Third Series, Vol. 1, pp. 229-230.

30. United States War Department, "General Order No. 58," August 15, 1861, *General Orders for 1861.*

31. Clark, p. 19.

32. Brigadier General Benjamin M. Prentiss (afterwards distinguished at Shiloh).

33. McClellan, George B., *McClellan's Own Story,* p. 98.

34. Burt, Silas W. (Col.), *My Memoirs of the Military History of the State of New York . . . 1861-1865,* pp. 137-139.

35. Upton, p. 426.

36. United States War Department, "General Order No. 69," August 28, 1861, *General Orders for 1861.*

37. *Ibid.,* "General Order No. 105," December 3, 1861.

38. United States War Department, "General Order No. 3," January 11, 1862, *General Orders for 1862.*

39. June 6, 1862. *Ibid.,* "General Order No. 60." This was in the middle of the Peninsular Campaign.

40. *Photographic History,* Vol. 8, p. 182. The author of this article was in the 32nd Illinois Infantry, but there is ample evidence of such concentrated drilling in most diaries, journals, and unit histories.

41. Buffum, p. 44.

42. Comte de Paris, Vol. 1, p. 191.

43. Andrews, E. B., *A Private's Reminiscences of the First Year of the War,* p. 23, Andrews records how the officer commanding the company would lean over and, in a whisper, ask: "Pat, Pat, what's the next order to give?"

44. Many college students were commissioned at once.

45. Morris, W. S., *History 31st Regiment Illinois Volunteers,* p. 19.

46. *Battles and Leaders,* Vol. 1, p. 153.

47. In *Photographic History,* Vol. 8, p. 183, appears a photograph of the 40th Massachusetts Infantry drilling with the bayonet.

48. McClellan, George B., *Manual of Bayonet Exercise.* This was mainly a translation of the manual by the fencing expert, M. Gomard.

49. Thompson, p. 221.

50. Entry for October 29, 1862, diary of Col. Oliver L. Spaulding, 23d Michigan Infantry.

51. Buffum, p. 70.

52. Smith, W. B., *On Wheels and How I Came There,* p. 55. Smith was a member of Co. "K" 14th Illinois Infantry.

53. United States War Department, *A System of Target Practice,* 1862, *passim.*

54. Kreutzer, William, *Service with the Ninety-Eighth N. Y. Volunteers,* p, 109.

55. Eight states were represented, 3 from West.

56. Avery, P. O., *History of the Fourth Illinois Cavalry Regiment,* pp. 47-48.

57. Muskets often burst because of the soldier's carelessness.

58. Buffum, p. 45.

59. Fox, p. 139.

60. Jones, Evan R., *Four Years in the Army of the Potomac,* p. 45.

61. Roe, Alfred S., *The Tenth Regiment Massachusetts Volunteer Infantry 1861-1864,* p. 21.

62. Buffum, p. 47.

63. These items usually disappeared after the first march.

64. Washington *National Republican,* Vol. 2, (August 22, 1862), p. 1.

65. "Items for Soldiers," *Frank Leslie's Illustrated Newspaper,* Vol. 16, (April 18, 1863), p. 50.

66. These men were Major William H. French, First Artillery; Captain William F. Barry, Second Artillery; Major Henry J. Hunt, Second Artillery.

67. Crowninshield, (1st Massachusetts Cavalry), p. 297.

68. *House Executive Documents,* 37 Cong., 2 Sess., Document 60, p. 31. This regiment, the 7th Pennsylvania Cavalry, soon had a new colonel.

69. Buffum, p. 55.

70. *Ibid.,* p. 53.

71. Adams, p. 89.

72. Buffum, p. 61.

73. Jones, p. 46.

74. *Story of the Service of Company "E" . . . 12th Wisconsin Regiment . . . in the War of the Rebellion,* pp. 104-105.

75. Keil, F. W., *Thirty-Fifth Ohio,* pp. 223, 225.

76. Barrett, J. O., *"Old Abe": The Live War-Eagle of Wisconsin,* pp. 24-25.

77. Buffum, p. 59.

78. Testimony of General Silas Casey, January 8, 1862, Joint Committee on the Conduct of the War, *Report,* First Series, Vol. 1, p. 216. See also *Official Records,* First Series, Vol. 5, p. 12.

79. United States War Department, "General Order No. 59," June 5, 1862, *General Orders for 1862*.

80. Sometimes the men would burlesque their officers' mistakes.

81. "Military Training," *The United States Army and Navy Journal and Gazette of the Regular and Volunteer Forces*, Vol. 1 (October 10, 1863), p. 98. (Hereafter cited as *Army and Navy Journal*).

82. *Ibid.*, Vol. 2, (February 25, 1865), p. 419.

83. Stevens, *Berdan's United States Sharpshooters in the Army of the Potomac*, p. 9.

84. Buffum, p. 79.

85. Kirk, Hyland C., *Heavy Guns and Light* (4th N. Y. Heavy Artillery), pp. 47-48.

86. Rhodes, John H., *The History of Battery "B" First Regiment, Rhode Island Light Artillery*, p. 267.

87. Billings, John D., *The History of the Tenth Massachusetts Battery of Light Artillery*, pp. 52, 55.

88. *History of the Fifth Massachusetts Battery*, pp. 139-142.

89. Gibbon, John, *Personal Recollections of the Civil War*, p. 14. These volunteer batteries were from Rhode Island, New Hampshire, and Pennsylvania.

90. Wilkeson, pp. 21-22.

91. Billings, *Hardtack and Coffee*, p. 182.

92. *Photographic History*, Vol. 4, p. 2 shows a picture of guard mount at this famous cavalry training center.

93. *Ibid.*, p. 48.

94. Cox, Vol. 1, pp. 166-167.

95. Le Comte, Ferdinand, *The War in the United States*, pp. 53-54.

96. Meade, G. G., (ed.), *The Life and Letters of George Gordon Meade*, Vol. 2, p. 125.

97. Grant, U. S., *Personal Memoirs*, Vol. 1, p. 573.

98. Lawrence, G. A., *Border and Bastille*, p. 28.

99. *Glimpses of the Nation's Struggle*, Third Series, pp. 30-31. See also Keifer, Joseph W., *Slavery and Four Years of War*, Vol. 1, p. 252.

100. *The Atlantic Monthly*, Vol. 9, (March 1862), p. 305.

101. Croushore, James H., (ed.), *A Volunteer's Adventures*, p. 66.

102. Horton and Teverbaugh, *A History of the Eleventh Regiment (Ohio Volunteer Infantry)*, p. 95.

103. Page, (14th Connecticut Infantry), p. 44.

104. Sumner, George C., *Battery "D" First Rhode Island Light Artillery in the Civil War*, p. 5.

105. Livermore, *Days and Events*, p. 289. See photograph of a divisional sham battle in *Photographic History*, Vol. 8, p. 205. This division, part of the Fourth Army Corps, was photographed near Missionary Ridge in 1863.

106. Lettter from Camp Barnes, Halls Hill, Virginia, November 25, 1861.

107. Annual Report of Secretary of War, (March 1, 1865), *House Executive Documents*, 38 Cong., 2 Sess., Document 83, p. 4.

108. Grant, Vol. 2, pp. 322-323.

109. Buffum, p. 219. This happened to the 14th New Hampshire Infantry at Winchester, September 19, 1864, but is by no means a unique instance.

110. Norton, O. W., *Army Letters*, (1861-1865), March 1, 1864, pp. 201-202. The regiment went into the battle of Olustee, Florida with 554 officers and men; of these 319 were killed or disabled by serious wounds. Many others were slightly wounded but remained on duty.

111. *Photographic History*, Vol. 5, p. 223.

112. In a letter dated February 10, 1862, Alexandria, Virginia, William H. Westervelt, Co. "E" 1st New York Engineers, said that men of his regiment were receiving drill in pontoon bridge laying and the construction of gabions and fascines.

113. Brown, J. W., *The Signal Corps U. S. A. In the War of the Rebellion*, p. 55.

114. Haydon, F. S., *Aeronautics in the Union and Confederate Armies*, Vol. 1, p. 274.

115. Photographs of such drill are found in *Photographic History*, Vol. 8, pp. 297, 305.

CHAPTER 3

Manuals and Training Literature

OF THE FEW remaining "neglected fields" of research in the Civil War period, one of the most surprisingly fertile and rewarding is in the field of manuals and books of instruction. The war literature itself is already replete with general histories, biographies, and, to a lesser extent, unit histories. However, practically nothing has been written about the manuals which were used to instruct officers and men in such essentials as the school of the soldier, the manual of the piece, and the complicated maneuvers required of higher units in battle deployment.

MANY UNOFFICIAL MANUALS USED

These manuals were used in great numbers and were of almost infinite variety. Men of all grades and ability wrote manuals. The mere fact that the Secretary of War authorized a particular drill system to be used did not prevent unit commanders from using another system which they considered superior! By the end of the first year of the war this tendency had given way to a reasonable uniformity but various systems were experimented with from time to time and the result is an astonishingly large number of manuals and books of instructions, both official and unofficial which appeared from 1861 to 1865. The more widely used ones are listed in the accompanying bibliography but it must be assumed that others exist which have escaped notice and which perhaps some reader possesses or has seen elsewhere.

FRENCH INFLUENCE DOMINANT

In examining Civil War manuals and military books, one is struck by the persistent influence of French military doctrine and tactics. This influence extended from the Napoleonic period to the Crimean War and is sharply reflected in most American military authors from Winfield Scott to George B. McClellan. Both of these officers observed French troops in Europe and both wrote manuals based on the French system. Several young Regular Army officers translated French manuals and military memoirs for American readers; some translations were especially well done, particularly Halleck's

four-volume work on Jomini's *Napoleon,* Benet's work on Waterloo, and Holabird's translation of Jomini's *Treatise on Grand Military Operations.* During this period there was little use made of British military experience. Some of this lack of interest was doubtless due to the traditional hostility of the United States for Great Britain during this period.

Perhaps the most determining factor, however, was the favorable impression made on American military observers and soldiers of fortune who served in the French army. Doubtless the best known of the military adventurers was Philip Kearny, who fought in Algiers where the French had adopted the Zouave system in 1830. Although a few officers (notably Scott) had been sent to Europe as individual observers, it was not until the Crimean War that the War Department inaugurated the policy of sending teams of carefully selected young professional officers to study first hand the various foreign military systems. Among those who went to the Crimea was Captain George B. McClellan, who stated in his report that he considered the French Zouaves to be the best troops he had ever seen and that to defeat such troops would be the greatest honor of all.

As a result of the report of McClellan and other enthusiastic writers, the Zouave system became very popular with the American public, which was only too well aware of the obvious defects of the militia system. Among the "converts" was young Elmer E. Ellsworth who decided to organize his own unit which would be radically different from the other militia units, most of which put social convivialty first and military efficiency last. Noting that the French Zouaves were "selected for their fine physique and tried courage," Ellsworth carefully recruited for his "U. S. Zouave Cadets," trained them in the Zouave drill, and, in 1859, challenged to competitive drill "any company of the militia or Regular Army of the United States or Canada." The Zouave drill emphasized open order drill and skirmishing. In contrast to the ponderous and unimaginative movements prescribed by Scott or Hardee, this new organization of Ellsworth's used a drill system

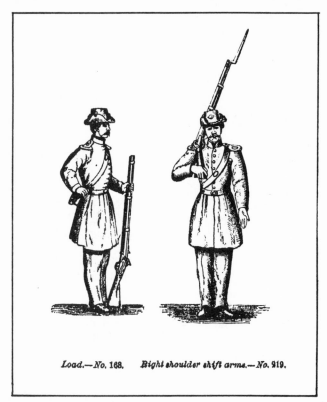

Load.—No. 168.   Right shoulder shift arms.—No. 219.

ILLUSTRATION FROM OLD DRILL MANUAL

which, while difficult to master, did result after prolonged training in a spectacular demonstration of intricate timing and machine-like precision. To Ellsworth the French Zouaves appeared to be the realization of what an armed body of men ought to be, and he prepared a drill manual for his Zouave Cadets which was used in his sensational victories in the drill competitions of 1859-1860.

Although killed early in the war, Ellsworth lived long enough to see his Zouave system used or imitated by many militia and volunteer regiments both East and West.

Old Drill Manuals Resurrected

The books of "tactics," or drill regulations as they are termed today, varied greatly in content and degree of simplicity. Some of the texts describing the older systems of tactics were resurrected decades after their original appearance, often unrevised, and were offered for sale primarily because their authors were household names. Often these older manuals, although reprinted in 1861, contained the original text and explanatory plates applicable to the flintlock musket which had been superseded two decades before the war began! Manuals written by erstwhile United States Regular Army officers (like Cooper and Hardee) were reprinted, sometimes without any indication of authorship after the authors themselves had joined the C. S. Army. Many of these officers attained high rank in the Confederate service,

especially Cadmus M. Wilcox, Henry Heth, and, of course, W. J. Hardee. Nor did the Confederate authorities fail to use a good thing when they had it; they appropriated for their own use such works as the U. S. Ordnance Manual, Mahan's works on engineering, and Cooke's Cavalry Tactics.

Official Publications

Although the Government Printing Office printed various manuals and books of instructions, it did not do so on a large scale until about 1863. Meanwhile several well-known publishing houses, such as Harpers, Lippincott, and Van Nostrand, tended to dominate the field. Lippincott concentrated heavily on medical manuals while Van Nostrand covered a wide variety of military and naval subjects. Even before 1861, David Van Nostrand had gone into the publishing of military and naval books in earnest. When the war broke out, his friendship with such men as Brigadier General J. G. Barnard and others was continued and these men prepared some excellent professional monographs and books which were published by Van Nostrand who became the "official publisher for the United States Army and Navy." His business cards, preserved in the publishing company's archives, carry that phrase. Two books are particularly noteworthy: Captain S. B. Luce's Seamanship, which was published in 1861 and was the official naval textbook of the U. S. Naval Academy and the U. S. Navy until 1898. At the outbreak of the war, the U. S. Army was lacking a satisfactory system of infantry drill; this need was supplied by Brigadier General Silas Casey, whose system of "tactics," published in 1862 by Van Nostrand, was adopted as the standard guide for training the Union Army. It was also reproduced in Richmond and used by the C. S. Army.

In addition to the manuals and books of instruction, there is a wealth of detailed information for the historian and collector in the General Orders and Army Regulations issued to troops during the war. The General Orders, as promulgated by the Adjutant General's Office (and even by armies, corps, and divisions), contain many examples of specific instructions for the information of the lower units. Also, from 1861 to 1863, the General Orders contained the reports of findings by general courts martial. A study of these is eminently worthwhile because in them one gets an almost contemporaneous insight into the Army, with its varied types of rugged individualism and the resulting problems in maintenance of discipline. Fortunately, the charges and specifications of the individual court martial report usually contain the exact words which the undisciplined farmer boy used when expressing his personal opinion of the company commander! Such reports make very interesting reading and convince us that very little change has taken place in the vocabulary which the American soldier uses during times of stress. Early in 1864 reports of court martial findings were issued separately from the *General Orders,* not through any special desire to avoid publicity but because the number of such trials increased greatly with the influx of drafted men after the middle of 1863. Valuable, also, are the 1857, 1861, and 1863 editions of the *Army Regulations* since they governed so closely the officers and soldiers during service. Such details as uniforms, equipment, and organization are readily located in the *Regulations.*

The services of the Union Army differed widely in the extent to which they supplied their members with manuals of instruction. In addition to an almost daily issuance of general orders, the Adjutant General's Department supplied its clerks with detailed instructions in printed form, company commanders with examples how to maintain the company records, and instructions to recruiting officers. Because of the excellent works by Benet and DeHart, there was considerable uniformity in preparation and reporting of court martial cases, all of which came eventually for review to the Judge Advocate General's Department. In the field of international law, Francis Lieber's book on rules of land warfare, written in 1863, has become a classic.

As one would expect, some of the best and most professional manuals were written by engineer officers. Long before the war, young and professionally competent engineers were publishing excellent technical studies on various aspects of civil and military engineering.

During the war the Federal engineer units received their training from the small regular company of engineers which was enlarged August 3, 1861, to a force of 49 officers and 600 men. Volunteer regiments of engineers were raised and received a large and educated class of civil engineers who were commissioned as officers. The enlisted personnel, drawn from artisans, road workers, and lumbermen, were given a brief course in basic military training and then additional military engineering training. The manuals in general use by engineer units were: D. H. Mahan's *Treatise on Field Fortifications* (originally appeared in 1836 and revised a third time in 1863); and J. C. Duane's *Manual for Engineer Troops* which appeared during the war. Mahan was professor of military and civil engineering at the United States Military Academy, while Duane was chief engineer of the Army of the Potomac.

The services, quartermaster, commissary, paymaster, ordnance, intelligence, adjutant general's department, and judge advocate's department, drew their personnel from the civilians who possessed abilities that peculiarly fitted them for the specialized work they would have to perform. There is no evidence that the services gave any specific training to their personnel, although training manuals were used in some cases, especially by members of such

services who served with line units. In addition to some small pamphlets published by the U. S. Sanitary Commission there were several technical medical manuals available for doctors assigned as surgeons or assistant surgeons in base hospitals or with line units.

INFANTRY DRILL REGULATIONS

Although there were several systems of drill regulations for the infantry, the most commonly used early in the war were Scott's *Tactics* (3 volumes) and William J. Hardee's *Tactics* (2 volumes). Scott's system was reprinted in 1861 with no changes from the first edition of 1835. The infantry company drilled in two ranks and loaded "in twelve times (movements)." Hardee's tactics prescribed a manual of loading in nine "times."

In 1862 it was found necessary to discard both Scott and Hardee due to lack of uniformity in the two drill systems, and 3-volume set of tactics ap-

A

SYSTEM

OF

TARGET PRACTICE.

FOR THE USE OF TROOPS

WHEN ARMED WITH THE MUSKET, RIFLE-MUSKET, RIFLE, OR CARBINE.

PREPARED PRINCIPALLY FROM THE FRENCH.

PUBLISHED BY ORDER OF THE WAR DEPARTMENT.

WASHINGTON:
GOVERNMENT PRINTING OFFICE.
1862.

MANUAL FOR TARGET PRACTISE

peared. The new system, like Scott's and Hardee's, was based on the French system. This new set of tactics, prepared by Brigadier General Silas Casey, was officially prescribed for regulars, volunteers, and militia. Casey kept the double rank formation but increased the intervals between regiments and brigades. The brigade became the tactical unit in deployment, which, in general, was to be made upon the heads of columns. This was considered to be the safest and most rapid means of forming line of battle. The "direct step" was to be 28 inches in length at the rate of 90 a minute; the "double quick step" was to be 33 inches in length at the rate of 165 a minute. Loading was to be done "in eight or nine times," according to whether the soldier was using the Maynard primer or the percussion cap type of rifle musket. Casey himself, who was not too sold on his system, told the War Department at the time he submitted his *Tactics* that "most undoubtedly there are still improvements to be made." The exigencies of war prevented much change but by 1864 the merits and demerits of Casey's system had been subjected to the test of combat.

EMORY UPTON'S SYSTEM

A brilliant young professional soldier, General Emory Upton, had meanwhile been formulating his ideas on tactical deployment in battle and was convinced that changes were necessary. Using a battalion of the Second Connecticut Heavy Artillery (serving, however, as infantry), he gave a demonstration of his projected drill system to some distinguished general officers a few days before the battle of Winchester. The reaction was encouraging but unfortunately Upton was wounded in the battle.

On recovery from his wound he sought service in the cavalry in order to familiarize himself with that branch of service. Active service in the Selma Campaign, in which the cavalry, armed with the Spencer carbine, acted mostly as mounted infantry, was of the greatest value to Upton. Tactics became the theme of his daily conversation. The war soon ended but in January, 1866 Upton submitted his ideas to the Army and they were officially adopted in August, 1867.

These tactics were a fundamental change from the old French system; they reduced the number of commands and were much simpler and easier to understand. The old facings were abolished. Wheeling was now to be by fours, thereby permitting a column of fours to form directly to the right, left, front, or rear. Upton's system permitted a unit commander to form line in any direction easily because no cognizance had to be taken of inversions. The reader will recall many instances where units in the Civil War lost invaluable time because of the necessity of "getting straightened out" from approach march in column before forming line in presence of the enemy.

CAVALRY DRILL REGULATIONS

Civil War cavalry "tactics" date back to 1826 when a board of officers was convened to report "a complete system of cavalry tactics." Major General Scott was president of the board whose tactics were published in 1834 and were thereafter known as the "Scott's Tactics." The system was a double rank deployment, in which two troops, side by side, each in double rank, constituted a squadron, and four squadrons a regiment. In 1841, while J. R. Poinsett was Secretary of War, these tactics were modified, with the main change being that now a regiment would consist of 10 companies or 5 squadrons. These new drill regulations, like Scott's, were mainly a translation from the French. They were called the *'41 Tactics* or *Poinsett Tactics* and, despite various attempts to improve them, were in use by the Eastern armies throughout the war. The Western cavalry used the *'41 Tactics* until 1864 when it began to use a system prepared by Colonel Philip St. George Cooke. Cooke's system was officially adopted by the War Department November 1, 1861 but was little used although the War Department stated that "all additions or departures from the exercises and maneuvers laid down are positively forbidden."

The principles of the Cooke *Tactics* differed materially from any preceding them. The single rank formation for cavalry was here introduced. In 1857 the War Department published McClellan's famous report on foreign armies. In this report, McClellan recommended that the single rank formation be adopted. Cooke acknowledged getting his ideas from conversations with McClellan. Actually, the British had tested the single rank formation in Portugal in 1833-1834 and had found that it greatly simplified all cavalry movements. In the Western armies of the Confederacy, the single rank formation began to be used early in the war. Morgan used it from the start, and soon Nathan B. Forrest and Joseph Wheeler also began to use it due to the conditions under which they were operating. Wheeler wrote a system of cavalry tactics which were adopted by the Army of the Tennessee, February 17, 1864.

ARTILLERY DRILL REGULATIONS

In contrast with the infantry and cavalry branches of the service, the tactics for the Federal artillery were uniformly accepted from the very begining of the war. This fact did not prevent various proponents of new systems from attempting to get their manuals adopted by the War Department, but despite the excellence of some of these, especially Roberts' and Gibbon's, the field artillery tactics of 1860 and the heavy artillery tactics of 1862 remained the officially accepted systems for the Federal artillery. John Gibbon's excellent *Artillerist's Manual*, written in 1860, was reprinted during the war but never adopted by the War Department. When Gibbon first met Lincoln, May 1862, the President indicated he would ask Stanton about the possibility of adopting the manual but apparently with no success.

Tactics for the United States artillery, as for other branches of service, went back some three decades and can be definitely traced to French sources. A board was convened in October 1826, with Scott as president, to prepare a system of instruction for field artillery. In December of that year the board recommended the *Manual of the Garde Royale,* which had been translated by Lieutenant Daniel Tyler, 1st U. S. Artillery. This was subsequently published. In 1839 another system of French artillery tactics appeared in Captain Robert Anderson's translation of the French *Instruction for Field Artillery, Horse and Foot,* adapted to the U. S. service. However, some dissatisfaction arose from American military circles who believed the British system to be superior. The two factions compromised, the result being the manual *Instruction for Field Artillery, Horse and Foot,* adopted by the War Department, March 6, 1845. This was followed, December 5, 1850, with the adoption of a system for mountain artillery, and on May 10, 1851 with a system for heavy artillery.

The instructions of 1845 were excellent as far as they went but they included only service of the piece and maneuvers limbered for a battery. Proper organization and management in the field of artillery were almost completely neglected. In 1858, a board of officers convened to correct these deficiencies. The board prepared the manual *Instruction for Field Artillery* which was adopted by the War Department March 6, 1860. The appearance of this manual, only a year before the outbreak of war, was extremely fortunate for the Union cause. As is well known, the excellent Regular and volunteer batteries of the Federal army made a decisive difference in several critical battles of the war. Certainly some of the credit for their brilliant combat record must go to the excellent training they received, a training based on the 1860 manual.

This new system embodied the instruction of 1845 but went much further; in fact, it exceeded in coverage and completeness of execution any system of tactics which had been prepared up to that time for the artillery arm. So well-written was this manual that the volunteer batteries were enabled to prepare systematically and thoroughly for field service in the least possible time and the most efficient manner. At the same time these new instructions were approved, the War Department adopted a helpful supplement, *Evolutions of Field Batteries,* translated from the French by Robert Anderson (now promoted to major), and including essentially the maneuvers involved in "School of the Battalion."

The heavy artillery tactics of 1851 included only the manual of the piece, a few maneuvers, and the nomenclature of siege, seacoast, and garrison artil-lery. Just enough instruction for dismounted detachments was included to enable the cannoneers to be marched to and from their pieces. The 1862 manual was an improvement in that it called for the ma-neuvering of detachments as provided for in field artillery units, and also contained material on the service of rifled guns.

Mountain artillery has never existed as an inde-pendent branch in the U. S. Army. The 1860 field artillery manual divided artillery personnel into field and foot—the former serving mounted in horse bat-teries—the latter serving as mountain, rocket, siege, garrison, and seacoast batteries.

NAVAL MANUALS

For the student of Naval tactics there is an unex-pectedly long list of manuals and books of instruc-tions. In contrast with the Army, there was much less competition between various "systems" but rather one finds more or less definitive and authoritative manuals for specific phases of Naval ordnance, ships, tactics, and seamanship. There appears to be little duplication and many of the manuals are written for rather restricted and technical subjects. As a result of the limited scope of these manuals, they were generally rather brief and, for reasons unknown to this author, are comparatively hard to find today. Perhaps this is due to the relatively small number of men in the Navy during the war, and to the great growing interest and competition among collectors in American naval history. Apparently the Marine Corps used naval manuals appropriate to its service.

OTHER BOOKS

In addition to the military and naval manuals pub-lished during the war, there were also used a very great many religious tracts, Bibles (especially pocket Testaments in various languages), and such miscel-laneous items as guide books for men on leave, re-prints of Hoyle on card playing, and similar works. A representative collection of the books carried by officers and men during the Civil War is much more complete (and interesting!), if one has some ex-amples of these lesser-known types. They were really used!

LIST OF CIVIL WAR MANUALS

Government libraries and archives have been con-sulted as well as many other sources, and it is be-lieved that there is no one definitive list or reposi-tory of Civil War manuals and text books. The list which follows is a beginning; the author and pub-lisher would welcome additional information, so that eventually a relatively complete enumeration may be compiled.

Works marked with an asterisk are not in the author's collection and therefore he is unable to comment on their contents with the desired degree of confidence. However, every book which is marked with an asterisk was actually published and copies do exist. The author wishes to express his special thanks to the D. Van Nostrand Company. He is indebted for their assistance in details on that famous publishing house, and for permission to use material in their book *A Century of Book Publishing*, from which came the data on the role of the Company in publishing manuals during the Civil War. Vice President Adrian N. Clark of the Van Nostrand Company was especially cooperative. Likewise, the staffs of the National Archives, Library of Congress, and Army War College Library were interested and courteously helpful. From conversations with these staffs the author is convinced that no complete collection of Civil War manuals exists, at least in repositories of the United States Government. This is probably also true for non-Government libraries and for private collections.

I. GENERAL MILITARY WORKS

A. *Military Strategy or The Art of War:*

1. Foreign Systems

Anonymous, *Reminiscences of an Officer of Zouaves,* 317 pp. D. Appleton, N.Y. 1860
Translated from the French and includes an excerpt from McClellan's Report of the U. S. Military Commission in Europe, 1855-1856.

Benet, S. V., Capt., Ordnance Dept., U. S. Army (Translator), *The Political and Military History of the Campaign of Waterloo,* 227 pp. 3rd Ed., Van Nostrand, N. Y., 1864
The first edition appeared in 1853. This book is smaller than most works of this type.

Coppee, Henry (Translator), *Spirit of Military Institutions* (by Marmont), Lippincott, Phila., 1862, 272 pp.

Craighill, William P. (Translator), *Strategy and Tactics,* 400 pp. Van Nostrand, N. Y., 1864
This is a translation of the work by General G. H. Dufour; it is small but contains 29 diagrams and has a military design on the cover.

Cullum, George W. (Translator and Editor), *Elements of Military Art and History,* (Ed. de la Barre Duparcq, French Army), 456 pp., Van Nostrand, N. Y. 1863.
This book, beautifully designed with military symbols on the cover, is mainly a history of branches of service, (infantry, cavalry, etc.) and discusses convoys, river crossings, terrain, etc.

Delafield, Richard, Major, Corps of Engineers, U. S. Army, *Report on the Art of War in Europe,* 287 pp. and many plates. George W. Bowman, Washington, D. C. 1860.
This book, issued as Senate Executive Document 59, 36 Congress, 1 Session, was written from notes made by Delafield while a member of the "Military Commission to the Theater of War in Europe."

Halleck, Henry W., Major General, U. S. Army (Translator), *Military and Political Life of the Emperor Napoleon,* (Jomini), 4 vols. and atlas, Van Nostrand, N. Y. 1864.

Holabird, S. B., Colonel, U. S. Army (Translator), *Treatise on Grand Military Operations* (Jomini), 2 vols. and atlas, Van Nostrand, N. Y., 1865.

Lendy, Capt. (Translator), *Maxims, Advice, and Instructions on the Art of War,* (from the French), Van Nostrand, N. Y., 1862; 212 pp; also Lippincott, Phila.

McClellan, George B., Maj. Gen'l, U. S. Army, *European Cavalry,* Lippincott, Philadelphia, 1861.
The Armies of Europe, 499 pp., Lippincott, Phila. 1861.
This book embodies McClellan's report of his observations on the Crimean War.

McClellan, George B., Major General, U. S. Army, *Report . . . (on the) . . . War in Europe in 1855 and 1856,* 360 pp. and many plates, A. O. P. Nicholson, Washington, D. C. 1857.

Mendel, G. H., Capt., Topographical Engineers, U. S. Army, and Craighill, William P., Lt., Corps of Engineers, U. S. Army, (Translators), *The Art of War,* 410 pp. and maps. (Jomini), Lippincott, Phila. 1862. Inscribed on inside cover "Col. C. E. Pratt, 31st Reg't N. Y. S. Y., February 10th, 1862." This same work of Jomini's also translated by two other American officers (Major O. F. Winship and Lt. E. E. McLean) and published by G. P. Putnam & Co. in 1854, but contains only 353 pp., and no maps at all. However, it is a better translation and includes more critical notes and philosophy of war.

Mordecai, Alfred, Major, Ordnance Dept. U. S. Army, *Military Commission to Europe,* 232 pp. and many excellent plates, G. W. Bowman, Wash. D. C. 1860. This report appeared as Senate Executive Document 60, 36 Congress, 1 Session. It is invaluable as a source book for European ordnance, much of which was used by both sides in the Civil War.

"An Army Officer" (Prime, Frederick E., Lt. Corps of Engineers) *Siege of Bomarsund 1854,* 56 pp. and plates. D. Van Nostrand Co., N. Y. 1856.
A journal of the operations of artillery and engineers during the siege.

Roemer, J. (Army of the Netherlands), *Cavalry: Its History, Management, and Uses in War,* 515 pp. many illustrations, Van Nostrand, N. Y. 1863.

Russell, William Howard, *General Todleben's Defense of Sebastapol 1854-1855,* 274 pp. Van Nostrand, N. Y., 1865.

Wilcox, C. M., Lt. 7th U. S. Infantry, *Evolutions of the Line as Practiced by The Austrian Infantry,* 132 pp. and plates, Van Nostrand, N. Y. 1860.

2. American Systems

Anonymous, "An Officer of the United States Army," *Cadet Life at West Point,* T. O. H. P. Burnham, Boston, 1862.

Barnard, J. G., Brig. Gen'l, U. S. Army and Barry, W. F., Brig. Gen'l, U. S. Army, *Report of the Engineer and Artillery Operations of the Army of the Potomac from its Organization to the Close of the Peninsular Campaign,* 230 pp. and 18 maps and diagrams, Van Nostrand, N. Y. 1864.
Barnard was Chief Engineer and Barry Chief of Artillery of the Army of the Potomac on the Peninsula. This is a truly professional study, well illustrated, and has an attractive castle and cannon design on the cover.

Anonymous, *The Soldier's Guide,* 63 pp. *Known also as "The Volunteer's Text Book" and is an adaptation of Scott's tactics for volunteers, militia, and home guard. T. B. Peterson & Bros., Philadelphia, 1861.

Boynton, Edward C., Capt. U. S. Army, *History of West Point,* 391 pp. with plates. Van Nostrand, N. Y. 1863.
A splendidly bound book with military symbols on cover and back strip.

Gillmore, Q. A., Brig. Gen'l, U. S. Army, *Official Report . . . of the Siege and Reduction of Fort Pulaski*, (Papers on Practical Engineering No. 8), 96 pp. and numerous maps and plates, Van Nostrand, N. Y. 1862.
Engineer and Artillery Operations Against the Defenses of Charleston Harbor in 1863, 354 pp. and 76 plates. Van Nostrand, N. Y. 1865.
This excellent professional study was written in 1864; a supplement was added in 1868.

Halleck, Henry W., *Elements of Military Art and Science*, 449 pp. and plates. 2nd Ed., D. Appleton, N. Y. 1860.
This second edition contains notes on the Mexican and Crimean Wars which occurred after the appearance of the first edition (1846). A third edition appeared in 1862 with no changes from the second edition.

Lendy, Captain, *A Comprehensive Encyclopedia of Military Science, Art and History*, Lippincott, Phila.

Schalk, Emil, *Summary of the Art of War*, 182 pp. and maps, Lippincott, Phila. 1863. The first edition appeared in 1862.
Campaigns of 1862 and 1863 Illustrating the Principles of Strategy, 252 pp. and maps, Lippincott, Phila. 1863.

Szabad, Emeric, Capt. U. S. Army, *Modern War: Its Theory and Practice*, 284 pp. and maps. Harper & Bros. N. Y. 1863.

B. *Manuals For Use Of All Branches Of The United States Military Forces*

Andrews, C. C. Capt. 3 Minn. Vol., *Hints to Company Officers on Their Military Duties*, 68 pp., Van Nostrand, N. Y. 1863. This excellent little book was written while the author was a prisoner of war in Georgia. It contains about as complete a definition of the characteristics necessary for an efficient unit commander as can be found anywhere.

Anonymous, *Instructions For Officers and Non-Commissioned Officers on Outpost and Patrol Duty and Troops in Campaign*, 88 pp., Gov't Printing Office, Wash. D. C. 1863.
Secretary of War Stanton approved this book March 25, 1862 and ordered it to be distributed to regiments in the field. The section on troops in campaign is a reprint of Article 36 of the 1861 Army Regulations.
Instructions for Making Muster-Rolls, Mustering Into Service, Periodical Payments and Discharging From Service of Volunteers and Militia, 46 pp. and numerous examples of forms to accompany the text, Gov't Printing Office, Wash. D. C. 1862.
On September 30, 1862, Secretary of War Stanton approved and authorized the use of these instructions which are divided into 109 sections. These instructions were revised in 1863 to include the new material under the 1863 Enrolment Act. The new version was entitled *Instructions for Mustering Officers and Other Kindred Duties*, included 124 sections (51 pp.), and was authorized for adoption by Secretary of War Stanton November 20, 1863.

Berriman, M. W. Capt., U. S. Army, *The Militiaman's Manual and Sword-Play*, 107 pp. and plates. 2nd Ed., Van Nostrand, N. Y., 1861.
This book includes not only a manual of the sword and rapier, but also infantry and cavalry drill. (1st Ed. 1858).

Cooke, *The Handy-Book For the United States Soldier*, 128 pp. and illustrations, Lippincott, Phila., 1861.
Written for the recruit who had just been mustered into service, and intended to be an introduction to the authorized U. S. Infantry Tactics.

Cooper, Samuel, Adj. Gen'l U. S. Army, *A Concise System of Instructions and Regulations for the Militia and Volunteers of the United States*, New Edition, Charles Desilver, Phila. 1861. Part I, Infantry Tactics, 130 pp. and plates; Part II, Cavalry Tactics, 44 pp. and plates; Part III, Artillery Tactics, 42 pp. and plates; Part IV, Regulations, 91 pp.
This work is a revision of Cooper's 1836 edition.

Craighill, William P., 1st Lt. U. S. Corps of Engineers, *The Army Officer's Pocket Companion*, 314 pp., Van Nostrand Co., N. Y. 1863.
As the title indicates, this little book is small enough to put in one's pocket. It was written for use of staff officers in the field.

Gilham, William Major, Commandant of Cadets, VMI, *Manual of Instruction for the Volunteers and Militia of the United States*, 743 pp. and many diagrams, Charles Desilver, Phila. 1861.
One of the best known manuals; to the collector this book included about everything for all branches of service. However, it was too bulky to be easily carried on the person.

Grafton, Henry D. Capt. 1st U. S. Artillery, *A Treatise on the Camp and March . . . For Use of Volunteers and Militia in the United States*, 83 pp. and plates, Van Nostrand Co., N. Y. 1861.
Includes in addition to tips on camping and marching such material as construction of field works, military bridges, and also contains a list of ranges of artillery pieces. A handy book which was used by both Eastern and Western regiments. Originally published in 1854 by Fetridge and Co., Boston.

Hammond, Pinkney J. Chaplain U. S. Army, *The Army Chaplain's Manual*, 286 pp. Lippincott & Co., Philadelphia 1863.
Designed as a help to chaplains, this book includes "all the laws and regulations in regard to chaplains . . . (and) the proper steps to be taken to secure a chaplain's appointment."

Heth, Henry, *A System of Target Practice for the Use of Troops When Armed With the Musket, Rifle-Musket, Rifle, or Carbine*, 48 pp., Henry Carey Baird, Phila. 1858.
Published by order of the War Department. In 1862 this work was republished by the Government Printing Office but with Heth's name omitted since he had joined the Confederate Army.

Jebb, *Treatises on Attack and Defence**, Lippincott, Phila.

Kautz, August V., Brig. Gen. U. S. Army, *Customs of Service for Non-Commissioned Officers and Soldiers*, 303 pp. Lippincott, Phila. 1864. This small, compact book contains a wealth of information including such rarely discussed subjects as "Special enlistments," duties of corporals and sergeants, and how a soldier should conduct himself in battle.
The Company Clerk, 142 pp. Lippincott, Phila. 1864. This handy book is all that the title implies. Excellent for reference on the forms used in company administration during the war.

Kelton, J. C., Lt. 6th U. S. Infantry, *A New Manual of the Bayonet for the Army and Militia of the United States*, 108 pp. and 30 excellent folding plates, Van Nostrand, N. Y. 1861.
*New Manual of Sword and Sabre Exercise**, Van Nostrand, N. Y.

LeGal, Eugene Col. 55 N. Y. Infantry, *School of the Guides*, 60 pp. and diagrams, Van Nostrand, N. Y. 1862. One of the smallest Civil War manuals, this little work was designed for the use of the Militia of the United States.

Lippitt, Frances, *A Treatise on the Tactical Use of the Three Arms: Infantry, Artillery, and Cavalry.** D. Van Nostrand, New York, 1865.

Mahan, D. H., Professor U. S. M. A., *Advanced-Guard, Out-Post and Detachment Service* of Troops, 305 pp. and 12 plates, John Wiley, New Edition, N. Y. 1864. The first edition of this little manual appeared in 1847; it was revised in 1861 as *An Elementary Treatise on Advanced-Guard, Out-Post and Detachment Service* of Troops, with 168 pp. and 6 plates. The 1864 edition contains much additional material in two new chapters on "strategy and tactics" and "Organization of the U. S. Military Forces."

McClellan, George B. Capt. 1st U. S. Cavalry, *Manual of Bayonet Exercise*, 106 pp. 24 full-page plates, Lippincott, Phila. 1852. Printed by Order of the War Department. In 1865 this manual was reprinted and again in 1862, this time with McClellan's rank given as "Commander-in-Chief, U. S. Army."

Quincy, Samuel, Col., *A Manual of Camp and Garrison Duty,** 43 pp. New Orleans, 1865.

Sanderson, James M., *Camp Fires and Camp Cooking,*" Washington D. C. 1862. Issued by Headquarters, Army of the Potomac, January 1862.

Scott, H. L. Col. and Inspector-General, U. S. Army, *Military Dictionary*, 674 pp. and many illustrations, Van Nostrand, N. Y. 1864. The first edition appeared in 1861. Scott's work is unusual in that it includes a bibliography of the Amercan and foreign works used by the author in preparing this dictionary.

Swaine, P. T. Lt., 10th U. S. Infantry, *U. S. Volunteer: A Book of Instructions For Officers and Soldiers*, 145 pp. and one plate. S. C. Perkins, Boston, 1861. This is one of the rarest Civil War manuals. It includes the principles of target practice, dress parade, guard duty, and inspections. Bound with this book is another by the same author entitled *A Manual for Colt's Revolving Rifle*, which consists of 25 pp. and one plate. It was published by Wrightson and Co., Cincinnati, Ohio 1861.

Viele, Egbert L. Capt. 7 N. Y. National Guard, *Handbook for Active Service*, 252 pp. Van Nostrand, N. Y. 1861.
Used extensively by soldiers in the East and West, this book discusses everything from the school of the soldier to field fortifications.

Wayne, Henry C. Brevet Maj. U. S. Army, *The Sword Exercise Arranged for Military Instruction*, 62 pp. and 11 plates. Gideon & Co., Wash., D. C. 1850.
Published by authority of the War Department. In the same volume is Wayne's *Exercise for the Broadsword, Sabre, Cut and Thrust, and Stick*, 43 pp. and 12 plates. This work, also published by authority of the War Department, was published by Gideon & Co. in 1849.

Wilcox, C. M. Lt. 7th U. S. Infantry, *Rifles and Rifle Practice*, 276 pp. and plates on ammunition which are invaluable to the collector. Van Nostrand, N. Y. 1859. In addition to being a treatise on rifle marksmanship, this manual contains descriptions of the infantry long arms of Europe and the United States and the ammunition of those weapons.

Willard, *Manual of Target Practice for the United States Army,** Lippincott, Phila. 1862, 80 pp.

Worthington, Thomas, *The Volunteer's Manual**, co-authored by Major Sidney Burbank and Lt. P. T. Swaine, Applegate & Co. Cincinnati, 1861.

II. INSTRUCTIONS AND REGULATIONS FOR MILITARY DEPARTMENTS AND ARMS OF SERVICE

A. *General Orders and Circulars of the War Department, Military Divisions, and Field Armies*

(Adjutant General's Office, War Department), *General Orders (for) 1861 (to) 1865*, Government Printing Office, Wash., D. C. 1861 to 1865.
General orders for 1861, 1862 and 1863 included the findings of general courts-martial. In 1864 and 1865 these court marital findings were published separately (two volumes each for both years). Military divisions geographical areas) and such field units as the Army of the Potomac also issued their own general orders and circulars. Also, general orders applying only to the volunteers and militia units in the Federal service were published separately from 1861 to 1864.

B. *Regulations*
1. United States Army

(War Department), *Regulations for the Army of the United States, 1857*, Harper & Bro., N. Y. Approved January 1, 1857 by Jefferson Davis, Secretary of War. These regulations were widely used in early days of the war. Author's copy belonged to Richard Yates, war governor of Illinois.
Regulations for the Army of the United States, 1861, 457 pp. and a 21 page appendix containing the Articles of War. Harper & Bro., N. Y.
These regulations were approved May 1, 1861, and like the 1857 regulations were published (so far as can be determined) only by Harper. Inscribed copy in author's possession: Captain M. C. Meigs, 13 June 1861.
Revised Regulations for the Army of the United States, 1861, 559 pp. Adopted by the War Department August 10, 1861. These regulations are larger in size and content than the May 1, 1861 Regulations, are beautifully bound in blue, green, or brown with lettering and eagle design in gold. Several publishers put out these regulations, including Lippincott, George W. Childs of Phila., and also the Government Printing Office. On June 25, 1863, a revised version appeared with 594 pp., the increase in size over the Revised 1861 Regulations being due to an appendix which incorporated the changes since August 10, 1861.

2. Militia, National Guard, Cadets

Anonymous, *Infantry Tactics for Schools*, 180 pp. and 29 plates, A. S. Barnes & Burr, N. Y., 1863.
General Regulations for the Military Forces of the State of New York, 352 pp. and plates, Weed, Parsons & Co., Albany, 1858.
This is an extremely attractive book and contains excellent plates on swords and insignia. The author has a copy presented to Major E. E. Ellsworth by the Adjutant General of New York.

Carrington, Henry B. (compiler), *General Regulations for the Military Forces of Ohio,** 469 pp. Richard Nevins, Columbus, Ohio. 2nd Ed. 1861.
Published by Order of the General Assembly. The introduction states that the "organization of this force, based on the Prussian method . . . will afford a school for military training." The copy examined by the author belonged to Capt. S. K. Williams, Co. "E" 22nd Ohio Infantry.

Pinckney, Stephen R. Col. 95 Reg. N. Y. N. G., *National Guard Manual*, 281 pp. and plates. Frank McElroy, N. Y. 1864.
Written in catechism style; the first edition was published in 1862.

C. Adjutant General's Department

(War Department), *Official Army Register for 1861 (to) 1865*, published by Order of the Secretary of War. *Regulations for the Recruiting Service of the Army of the United States. Both Regular and Volunteer*, 99 pp. G. P. O. Wash., D. C. 1862. Approved Dec. 1, 1862. *Rules for Keeping the Principal Record Books Used at Department and General Headquarters and at the Adjutant General's Office*, 88 pp. and many forms. G. P. O., Wash., D. C., 1864.

Due to the inclusion of so many varied types of administrative forms in this book, it is an excellent source of reference, especially for those interested in unit record keeping.

D. Judge Advocate General's Department: Bureau of Military Justice

Anonymous, *Digest of Opinions of the Judge Advocate General*, 138 pp., G. P. O. Wash. D. C., 1865.
Issued by the Bureau of Military Justice, War Department.

Benet, S. V. Capt. Ordnance Dept. U. S. Army, *A Treatise on Military Law and the Practice of Courts-Martial*, 377 pp. Van Nostrand, N. Y. 1862.
A much used book; in 1864 appeared a 4th edition of 389 pp. In 1863 a 2nd edition of 607 pp. was published by George W. Childs, Phila. The new edition included all recent congressional legislation in regard to the Army, volunteers, militia, bounties, and pensions.

Callan, John F., *The Military Laws of the United States*, 484 pp., John Murphy & Co., Baltimore, 1858. Covers the period 1776-1858.

Coppee, Henry Capt. U. S. Army, *Field Manual of Courts-Martial*, 160 pp. Lippincott, Phila. 1863.
A small, excellently bound usable book for field service.

DeHart, William C., *Observations on Military Law and the Constitution and Practice of Courts Martial*, 433 pp., Wiley & Putnam, N. Y. 1846.
Used during the Mexican War and re-issued with no change by D. Appleton & Co. during the Civil War.

Halleck, Henry W. Maj. Gen'l U. S. Army, *International Law*,* Van Nostrand, N. Y. 1861.

Lieber, Francis, *Instructions for the Government of Armies of the U. S. in the Field*,* Van Nostrand, N. Y. 1863.
Guerilla Parties Considered with Reference to the Laws and Usages of War, 22 pp., Van Nostrand, N. Y. 1862.

Scott, R. N., Maj. U. S. Army (compiler), *Military Laws of the United States of America Affecting the Regular Army*, 65 pp., Adjutant General's Office, Wash., D. C. 1865.

E. Provost Marshal General's Department

Anonymous, *Regulations for the Government of the Bureau of the Provost Marshal General*, 57 pp., G. P. O., Wash., D. C. 1863.
These regulations were approved April 21, 1863 or about one month after the establishment of the Bureau. On September 1, 1864 a revised version of these regulations was approved; the new regulations manual consisted of 84 pp. and was used the rest of the war.

F. Quartermaster General's Department

Anonymous, *General Orders, Quartermaster General's Office*, 1863-1865, General Orders were issued prior to January 1, 1863 but this volume includes those issued in the period January 1863 to December 1865. The number of general orders issued by the Quartermaster General's Department were: 1863-24; 1864-62; 1865-82.

Rules and Regulations for the Government of Employees of the Quartermaster's Department at the Washington Depot, 74 pp., Philp and Solomons, Wash., D. C. 1863.

Anonymous, *Instructions for Transport and Erection of Military Wire Suspension-Bridge Equipage*, 24 pages and 10 excellent folding plates. Government Printing Office, Washington, D. C., 1862.
These instructions were approved May 13, 1862 by the Quartermaster's Department and the author's copy was the personal property of Meigs.

Brinkerhoff, Roeliff, Captain and Assistant Quartermaster, U. S. Vols. *The Volunteer Quartermaster*, 289 pages and plates, D. Van Nostrand Co., New York, 1865.
The excellent plates in this manual on barracks, officers' quarters, etc. are difficult to find elsewhere.

Case, Theodore S., Colonel and Quartermaster General of Missouri, *The Quartermaster's Guide*, 310 pages. P. M. Pinckard, St. Louis, 1865.
Intended primarily to be a book for ready experience, it contains everything from the 1863 Army Regulations and General Orders of the War Department which was in any way connected with the Quartermaster's Department. A copy in possession of the author was a presentation from Colonel Case to Quartermaster General Meigs.

Hunter, R. F. Captain, late of the U. S. Army, *Manual For Quartermasters and Commissaries*,* D. Van Nostrand Co., New York, 1863.

Patten, George, *Army Manual*, 306 pages and plates, J. W. Fortune, 4th edition. New York, 1864. 1st edition 268 pp., appeared in 1861. Although a "catch-all," this book was written mainly for quartermasters and commissaries of subsistence.

G. Subsistence Department

Anonymous, *Circulars from the Commissary General of Subsistence*, Washington, D. C., 1865.
Bread and Bread Making, 49 pages, Washington, D. C., 1864.

H. Pay Department

Anonymous, *The Army Paymaster's Manual*, 172 pages, Government Printing Office, Washington, D. C., 1866.
Prepared for officers of the Pay Department and including supplements for 1863-64-65 bound together.

Webb, Ezra (Compiler), *Army Pay Digest and Ready Calculator*,* D. Van Nostrand, New York.

I. Medical Department

Bartholow, Roberts, *A Manual of Instructions for Enlisting and Discharging Soldiers*, 276 pages, J. B. Lippincott & Co., Philadelphia, 1864. Adopted by the Surgeon-General for issue to Army Medical officers. Much emphasis is placed on the initial examination of recruits and means of detecting feigned diseases. Stamped on the cover is the medical shield and "U. S. Army Medical Department."

Dalton, John C., Dr., *A Treatise on Human Physiology*, 690 pages. Blanchard and Lea, 2nd edition, Philadelphia, 1861. First edition of this well-illustrated book appeared in 1859. Copy in the author's possession was the personal copy of William A. Hammond, Surgeon General, U. S. Army.

Grace, William, *The Army Surgeon's Manual*, 225 pp.,* 2nd Ed., Bailliere, N. Y. 1861.

Gray, Henry, *Anatomy, Descriptive and Surgical*, 816 pages, Blanchard and Lea, Philadelphia, 1862. Stamped on the cover is: "USA Hospital Department." This is the second American edition form, revised and enlarged from an original London printing in 1858.

Greenleaf, Charles R., Assistant Surgeon, U. S. Army, *A Manual for the Medical Officers of the United States Army*, 199 pages, J. B. Lippincott, Philadelphia, 1864. Excellent for medical officers concerned with administrative duties; the book contains examples of forms required by regulations in medical reports.

Gross, S. D., *A Manual of Military Surgery*, 186 pages, J. B. Lippincott, Philadelphia, 1862. This small compact manual first appeared in 1861.

Guthrie, G. T., *Commentaries on the Surgery of the War . . . 1808 to 1815 . . . and in the Crimea in 1854-1855*, 614 pages, J. B. Lippincott & Co., 6th edition, Philadelphia, 1862. Stamped on the cover is: "U. S. Army Medical Department."

Hamilton, Frank Hastings, *A Treatise on Military Surgery and Hygiene*, 648 pages and 127 illustrations, Bailliere Brothers, New York, 1865. Appearing a few months before the end of the war, this book is a gold mine for the student of Civil War medical material. The book contains good drawings of litters, ambulances, hospital trains, and, in addition, cites actual case histories.
A Practical Treatise on Military Surgery, 232 pages and several illustrations, Bailliere Brothers, New York, 1861. Designed primarily for newly-appointed military surgeons.

Hammond, William A., Surgeon General, U. S. Army, *A Treatise on Hygiene with Special Reference to the Military Service*, 596 pages, J. B. Lippincott & Co., Philadelphia, 1863. Stamped on cover the medical shield and: "U. S. Army Medical Department."

Henderson, Thomas, Assistant Surgeon, U. S. Army, *Hints on the Medical Examination of Recruits for the Army and on the Discharge of Soldiers . . .* °, J. B. Lippincott, Philadelphia. 211 pp. 1st Ed. 1840.

Hough, Franklin B. (Translator) *Baudens' Military and Camp Hospitals, and the Health of Troops in the Field*°, Bailliere Bros., N. Y.

Longmore, Thomas, *A Treatise on Gunshot Wounds*, 132 pages, J. B. Lippincott, Philadelphia, 1862. Stamped on cover: "U. S. Army Hospital Department."

MacLeod, George H. B., *Notes on the Surgery . . . in the Crimea with Remarks on the Treatment of Gunshot Wounds*, 403 pages, J. B. Lippincott, Philadelphia, 1862. Stamped on the cover is: "U. S. Army Hospital Detachment."

Nightingale, Florence, *Notes on Nursing: What it is, and What it is not*, 140 pages, D. Appleton and Company, New York, 1861.

Ordronaux, John, *Hints on the Preservation of Health in Armies for the Use of Volunteer Officers and Soldiers*, 142 pages, D. Appleton and Company, New York, 1861. Small, compact, easily carried in the pocket. A new edition appeared in 1864 with Van Nostrand as the publisher.
Manual of Instructions for Military Surgeons on the Examination of Recruits and Discharge of Soldiers, 238 pages. Prepared at the request of the U. S. Sanitary Commission, D. Van Nostrand Co., New York, 1863.

Packard, J. H., *Manual of Minor Surgery*, J. B. Lippincott, Philadelphia, 1863. 288 pp. and 145 ill. Authorized by Surgeon Gen'l of U. S. Army.

Peaslee, E. R., *Human Histology*, 616 pages, Blanchard and Lea, Philadelphia, 1857. Inscribed inside front cover: "Dr. Head, U. S. Army, May, 1861."

Power, John Hatch, *Anatomy of the Arteries of the Human Body*, 401 pages, J. B. Lippincott, Philadelphia, 1863. "Authorized and adopted by the Surgeon-General of the United States Army for use in Field and General Hospitals." Stamped on Cover: "U. S. Army Medical Department."

Smith, Stephen, Hand-Book of Surgical Operations, 279 pp. and 257 illustrations. Prepared for the military surgeon who previously "had no small and convenient work suitable for a pocket companion . . . (and who had to) either encumber himself with the large treatises . . . or rely upon his unaided memory . . .", Bailliere, N. Y., 1862.

Stromeyer and Esmarch, *Gunshot Injuries*°, J. B. Lippincott, Philadelphia.

Tripler, Charles S. and Blackman, George C., *Handbook for the Military Surgeon*°, Cincinnati, 1861, 2nd edition, 163 pages.

J. *Ordnance Department*

Anonymous, *Report of Experiments with Small Arms for the Militia Service*, 35 pages. A. O. P. Nicholson, Washington, D. C., 1856.
The Ordnance Manual for the Use of Officers of the United States Army, 475 pages and 18 plates, Gideon and Company, Washington, D. C., 1850. This second edition of the *Ordnance Manual* was revised and prepared by Captain A. Mordecai, Ordnance Department. In 1862 a third edition of 559 pages and 33 plates appeared. This edition was approved November 4, 1861; it was revised by Captain T. S. Laidley, Ordnance Department, and published by Lippincott.
Regulations for the Government of the Ordnance Department, 140 pages, Gideon and Company, Washington, D. C., 1852.
Instructions for Making Quarterly Returns of Ordnance and Ordnance Stores, 140 pages. Government Printing Office, Washington, D. C., 1863. These instructions, called "Ordnance Memoranda No. 1," were prepared by the Ordnance Bureau and were approved February 10, 1863. An extremely helpful book for the collector or historian of ordnance equipment of the Civil War. The copy in the author's possession was the property of General George H. Thomas. In 1865 a revised version containing 208 pages was published.

Holley, Alexander L., *European Ordnance and Iron-Clad Defenses*°, D. Van Nostrand, New York.
Ordnance and Armor, 900 pages and 493 illustrations, D. Van Nostrand, New York, 1865. Written in 1864, this book was an encyclopedia of modern American and European ordnance, especially cannon, projectiles, heavy ordnance and its effect on armor plating.

Thomas, Lynall, *Rifled Ordnance*°, D. Van Nostrand, New York, 5th edition, 1864.

Wiard, Norman, Memorial to the Senate and House of Representatives: (Senate Miscellaneous Document 47, 38 Congress, 2 Session, Volume 1.)°, Holman, New York, 2nd edition, 1863. Some of the pamphlets which accompanied Wiard's "Memorial" were also used as manuals of instruction, especially the ones on field artillery and marine artillery.

K. *Corps of Engineers*

Barnard, J. G., Major, Corps of Engineers, U. S. Army, *The Dangers and Defenses of New York*, D. Van Nostrand Co., New York, 1859.

Cullum, George W., Brigadier General, U. S. Army, *Systems of Military Bridges in Use by the United States Army*°, D. Van Nostrand Co., New York, 1863. Originally appeared in 1849 as No. 4 of *Papers on Practical Engineering*.

Duane, J. C., Captain, Corps of Engineers, U. S. Army, *Manual for Engineer Troops*, 275 pages and several excellent plates, D. Van Nostrand Co., 3rd edition, New York, 1864. Consists of 5 parts: (1) Panton Drill; (2) Rules for Conducting a Siege; (3) School of the

Sap; (4) Military Mining; (5) Construction of Batteries. The first edition of this excellent manual appeared in 1861.

Engineer Department, *Papers on Practical Engineering*, were written by various officers of the Corps of Engineers and Corps of Topographical Engineers. The first paper appeared in 1841. These *Papers* appeared from time to time up into the war period. They are on specialized subjects and reflect a high degree of professional capacity on the part of the engineer officers who prepared them.

Head, George Edward, *System of Fortifications**, D. Van Nostrand Co., New York.

Kimber, *Vauban's First System, The Modern System, and Field-Works**, D. Van Nostrand Co., New York. Each of these three books was supplemented with a model of the fortifications discussed in the book. An early pioneer in the idea of the table model for military instructions! First appeared in 1852.

Mahan, D. H., Professor, U. S. Military Academy, *An Elementary Course In Civil Engineering for the Use of Cadets of the United States Military Academy*, 401 pages and many illustrations, Wiley and Halsted, 6th edition, New York, 1857.
A Treatise on Field Fortifications, 168 pages and plates, John Wiley, 3rd edition, New York, 1861. The first edition of this handy little manual appeared in 1836. It also was published in 1863.

Mendell, G. H., Captain, Corps of Engineers, *A Treatise on Military Surveying**, D. Van Nostrand Co., New York, 1865. 193 pp.

L. *Corps of Topographical Engineers*

Lee, T. J., Captain, Corps of Topographical Engineers, *Tables and Formulae*, 242 pages, Gideon and Company, 2nd edition, Washington, D. C., 1853. The first edition appeared in 1849. This book was prepared expressly for the use of the Corps of Topographical Enginers.

M. *Signal Corps*

Myer, Albert J., Brigadier General and Chief Signal Officer, U. S. Army, A Manual of *Signals*, 457 pages and many illustrations, D. Van Nostrand Co., New York, 1868. Although this manual was printed after 1865, it contains much material from the wartime manual which was "hastily prepared, printed upon an office press, and issued to the officers of the Signal Corps of the Army . . . in the field in the midst of the War of the Rebellion." The earlier work was intended to be a manual of instruction but was incomplete.

N. *United States Military Railroads*

Haupt, Hermann, Brigadier General and Chief, U. S. Military Railroads, *Military Bridges*, 310 pages and 69 lithographic engravings, D. Van Nostrand Co., New York, 1864. An excellent professional treatment of the subject by one of the most neglected figures of the Civil War.

O. *United States Military Telegraph Corps*

This author knows of no manuals which were prepared specifically for this branch of the service. However, in 1872, the Government Printing Office published *A Manual of Military Telegraphy* (100 pages) which contains material written in the form of instructions for use during the war.

P. *Military Balloon Corps*

All available information indicates that no manuals were prepared for members of the Federal balloon service.

Q. *Infantry*

Anonymous, *U. S. Infantry Tactics for . . . Colored Troops . . .**, D. Van Nostrand Co., New York. Approved March 9, 1863.
Rules for the Management and Cleaning of the Rifle Musket, Model 1863 for the Use of Soldiers, 25 pages. Excellent descriptive illustrations on almost every page. It was officially approved April 28, 1863. Some of the earlier models of Civil War Springfield riflemusket also had books of instruction similar to this manual.

Baxter, D. W. C., Lt. Colonel, 2 Regiment, National Guard, *Baxter's Volunteers Manual* or "Right Guide for the Soldier in the U. S. Army,"* 137 pages and plates, King and Baird, Philadelphia, 1861. Contains the "school of the company" and one of the best sets of instructions for the manual of the percussion musket. Bound in the same volume and also printed by King and Baird in 1861—Ellsworth's: *Light Infantry Drill Arranged for the U. S. Zouave Cadets* (72 pages); and the *Zouave Drill Book* of 72 pages, which includes bayonet and skirmishes drills.

Brewerton, G. Douglas, U. S. Army, *The Automaton Company**, D. Van Nostrand Co., New York, 1863.
The Automaton Regiment*, D. Van Nostrand Co., New York, 1862.

Butterfield, Daniel, Major General, U. S. Army, *Camp and Outpost Duty for Infantry*, 119 pages, Harper and Brothers, New York, 1863. A small, handy little book which was much used. A copy in the author's collection is inscribed: C. V. Petteys Co. "H," 9th, New York, H. A. "in front of Petersburgh," March 25, 1865.

Cairns, John T., Captain (not Regular Army, probably Militia), *The Recruit*, 172 pages, Lewis H. Embree, 18th ediition, New York, 1861. Written for infantry and riflemen and "respectfully dedicated to the recruits of the United States." First edition appeared in 1844 and the text and plates were written for the flintlock musket. The 1861 edition contained no changes and since the flintlock musket drill was obsolete this manual was not used very extensively.

Casey, Silas, Brigadier General, U. S. Army, *Infantry Tactics*, 3 volumes, D. Van Nostrand Co., New York, 1862. Casey's *Tactics* were the most-used drill maneuvers of any system in the war. On August 11, 1862, this system was approved by the President and adopted for instructions of infantry of armies of the U. S. "whether Regular, Volunteer, or Militia." The 3-volume set consists of: Vol. I—School of the Soldier and Company (279 pages); Vol. II—School of the Battalion [Regiment] (279 pages); Vol. III—Evolutions of a Brigade and Corps D'Armee (183 pages). Each volume contained explanatory plates.

Coppee, Henry, Captain, U. S. Army, *The Field Manual of Evolutions of the Line*, 144 pages, J. B. Lippincott Co., Philadelphia, 1862. First edition appeared in 1861. This small, excellently bound little volume is filed with drawings to show the various evolutions.
The Field Manual for Battalion Drill, 152 pages and many drawings, J. B. Lippincott Co., Philadelphia, 1862. Similar in Size and binding to Coppee's other manuals. First edition in 1861; also was reprinted in 1863.

Duffield, William W., Colonel, 9th Michigan Infantry, *School of the Brigade . . .* or, Rules for the Exercise and Manoeuvres of Brigades and Division, 242 pages. Designed as a sequel to the U. S. Infantry Tactics adopted May 1, 1862 and in the same format and binding as Coppee's manuals, J. B. Lippincott Co., Philadelphia, 1862.

Duryee, Abram, Colonel, & N. Y. N. G. *Standing Orders for the Seventh Regiment, National Guard**, D. Van Nostrand Co., New York.

"Government," *Rhymed Tactics,* 144 pages and plates, D. Van Nostrand Co., New York, 1862. This very unique manual has two unusual features; the drill instructions are written as poetry; and the explanatory plates showing the various positions are actual photographs of line officers of the 31st New York Infantry.

Hardee, W. J., Lieutenant Colonel, U. S. Army, *Rifle and Light Infantry Tactics,* 2 volumes, J. B. Lippincott Co., Philadelphia, 1863. Vol. 1—Schools of the Soldier and Company's Instructions for skirmishes, 250 pages and plates.
Vol. 2—School of the Battalions, 232 pages and plates. Hardee's *Tactics* were adopted March 29, 1855 and were first published that year by Lippincott, Grambo and Company, Philadelphia. On May 1, 1861, they were authorized for the use of the United States Army by the Secretary of War. Lippincott published a 1-volume edition of Hardee's tactics in 1861, 1862, 1863, but without the author's name (Hardee had been commissioned a Lieutenant General in the C. S. Army.) This new edition contained 450 pages and many plates and was titled: *U. S. Infantry Tactics.* An abbreviated edition of 240 pages was compiled during the war by Colonel W. H. Allen and sold by John Bradburn of New York for 37½ cents a copy! Hardee's *Tactics* were widely used by the C. S. Army throughout the war and by the U. S. Army until the fall of 1862.

Monroe, J., Colonel, 22d New York State Militia, *Company Drill and Bayonet Fencing**, D. Van Nostrand Co., New York, 1862.

Morris, William H., Brigadier General, U. S. Army, *Infantry Tactics,* 2 volumes*, D. Van Nostrand Co., New York, 1864.
Field Tactics for Infantry, 146 pp., D. Van Nostrand Co., New York, 1864.

Patten, George, *Infantry Tactics,* 149 pages (paper covers), J. W. Fortune, New York, 1861. This is the third edition of 10,000 copies, containing excellent illustrations on the various operations in loading the musket, stacking arms, and similar instructions which are usually not shown in such manuals. General McClellan strongly recommended its use by volunteer officers.

Scott, Winfield, Lieutenant General, U. S. Army, *Infantry Tactics,* 3 volumes, Harper and Brothers, New York, 1840. Scott's *Tactics* were adopted April 10, 1835 and revised in 1840. There were many reprints including an edition in 1861.
Vol. 1—School of the Soldier and Company, 246 pages and 14 plates.
Vol. 2—School of the Battalion, 300 pages and 23 plates.
Vol. 3—Evolutions of the Line, 267 pages and 26 plates.
The 1861 *Tactics* were somewhat larger than the earlier editions. Also, in 1861, Moss Brothers and Company of Philadelphia published a 138 page *Abstract of* (Scott's) *Infantry Tactics,* but this manual reproduced the old plates and text applicable to the flintlock musket!

Steffen, William, *Digest of the United States Tactics,* 121 pp. Loring, Boston, 1862. These tactics are unusual because they were written expressly for a particular regiment (44th Mass. Inf.), in which the author, a Prussian Artillery officer, had served as an instructor.

R. Cavalry

Anonymous, *Cavalry Tactics,* 3 Vols. J. B. Lippincott, Phila. 1861. These tactics, mainly a translation from French sources were adopted February 10, 1841 while J. R. Poinsett was Secretary of War and accordingly are known as the "Poinsett Tactics" or " '41 Tactics." Vol. 1, Dismounted Drill, 200 pp. Vol. 2, Mounted Drill, 287 pp. Vol. 3, Evolution of a Regiment, 111 pp. Volume 3 also contains the manual of the Colt's revolver. This 3-volume set was reprinted as late as 1864. In that year a one-volume edition was printed by order of the War Department. This edition contains 450 pp., many fine folding plates, and was printed by the Government Printing Office 1865.

Congdon, J. A., *Cavalry Compendium**, J. B. Lippincott, Co., Phila., 1864.

Cooke, Philip St. George, Col. 2d U. S. Cavalry, *Cavalry Tactics,* 2 vols. Lippincott, Phila., 1862. Adopted by the War Department November 1, 1861. Vol. 1, School of the Trooper, platoon, squadron, 217 pp. Vol. 2, Evolutions of a regiment and of the line, 108 pp. This same set appeared again in 1864. The volumes are easy to carry in the pocket (like Casey's *Infantry Tactics*). As early as 1861 the Government Printing Office also issued a 2-volume set of Cooke's *Tactics* but the volumes are larger than Lippincott's and not as well printed. A 1-volume edition was published by J. W. Fortune, New York, in 1862. It contains 294 pp. and 60 ill. drawn by Lt. Col. George Patten "late of the U. S. A."

Garrard, Kenner, Capt. 5th U. S. Cavalry, *Nolan's System for Training Cavalry Horses,* 114 pp.* D. Van Nostrand, New York, 1862. Includes a chapter on "Rarey's Method of Taming Horses" and a chapter on "Horseshoeing."

McClellan, George B., Maj. Gen. U. S. Army, *Regulations for the Feild Service of Cavalry in Time of War,* 216 pp. and plates. Lippincott, Phila. 1862. Includes instructions for outpost and patrol duty, cavalry skirmish drill, and the taming and use of horses. A revised edition of 106 pp. was published by Philp and Solomons, Washington, D. C., 1863.

Patten, George, *Cavalry Drill**, Von Nostrand, New York, 1863.

S. Artillery

Anderson, Robert, Brig. Gen. U. S. Army, *Instructions for Field Artillery,* 122 plates, Van Nostrand, New York. *Evolutions of Field Batteries of Artillery,* 179 pp. 32 pates.* Van Nostrand, New York 1861, 2nd edition. 1st edition 1860.

Anonymous, *Ranges of Parrott Guns,* 29 pp. Van Nostrand, New York 1863. A compact, handy little book.

Barnard, J. G. Maj. Corps of Engineers, *Notes on Sea-Coast Defence,* 110 pp. and 1 plate. Van Nostrand, New York, 1861.

Benton, J. G. Capt. U. S. Army, *Course of Instruction in Ordnance and Gunnery . . . For the Use of the Cadets of the* (U. S.) . . . *Military Academy,* 518 pp. and drawings, D. Van Nostrand, New York, 1861. Encyclopedic in content. A revised edition of 550 pp. appeared in 1862.

Board of Artillery Officers, *Instruction for Field Artillery,* 348 pp. and 88 plates, Lippincott, Phila. 1860. This manual replaced the 1845 artillery tactics. The three officers who comprised the board—Capt. William H. French, 1st U. S. Artillery, Capt. William F. Barry and Capt. Henry J. Hunt, 2d U. S. Artillery—all became general officers during the War. These tactics, approved by the War Department, March 6, 1860 were reprinted in 1861 and 1863, but the editions appearing during the war were inferior in quality of paper and clarity of the plates. A revised edition of 229 pp. and 89 plates was approved March 1, 1863 and was printed by the Government Printing Office the same year.

Instruction for Heavy Artillery, 261 pp. and 39 plates. Approved October 20, 1862, and printed by the Government Printing Office in 1863. This manual replaced the 1851 edition of 270 pp. and 39 plates. Apparently the *Instruction for Mountain Artillery* which was published in 1851 was not used to any appreciable extent during the war, nor was it revised since mountain artillery was not employed during the period 1861-1865.

Brewerton, G. Douglas, *The Automaton Battery*°, Van Nostrand, New York, 1863.

Gibbon, John Brig. Gen. U. S. Army, *The Artillerist's Manual*, °568 pp. and numerous illustrations. Van Nostrand, New York, 1860. This is an extremely fine artillery manual. A second edition appeared in 1863 but the manual was never officially adopted.

Patten, George, *Artillery Drill*, 180 pp. and numerous plates. (Paper covers) J. W. Fortune, New York, 1863. Appeared originally in November 1861.

Roberts, Joseph Col. 3d Pa. Artillery. *The Hand-Book of Artillery for the* Service of the United States, 250 pp. Van Nostrand, 5th Ed. New York, 1863. This very handy reference book was compiled largely from Gibbon's *Artillerist Manual*, *Heavy Artillery Tactics*, and the *Ordnance Manual*. It was widely used both because of its content and its compact size.

Wiard, Norman, *Memorial . . . to the Senate and House of Representatives*°, Holman, 2nd Ed. New York, 1863. This "Memorial" included 8 pamphlets, most of them directly related to artillery, and many of them published separately as manuals of instructions. These pamphlets were: 1. Great Guns, 2. Field Artillery, 3. Marine Artillery, 4. Small Arms, 5. Ships, Rams, and Forts, 6. Proposals, 7. Experiences of a Contractor, 8. Review of the Report of the Chief of Navy Ordnance Bureau, 1862.

III. NAVAL REGULATIONS, MANUALS, AND BOOKS ON INSTRUCTION

A. General Orders, Regulations, and Laws Affecting the U. S. Navy

Anonymous, *General Orders and Circulars Issued by the Navy Department From 1863 to 1887*, 353 pp. Government Printing Office, Washington, D. C. 1887. General orders and circulars were not regularly distributed prior to January 10, 1863. Until that date the *Code of Regulations* contained in the 1858 Annual Report of the Secretary of the Navy was used.

Regulations for the Government of the United States Navy 1865, 344 pp. Government Printing Office, Washington, D. C. 1865. These regulations, approved April 18, 1865, were probably collected for the first time in this edition. Apparently earlier regulations were issued at irregular intervals and were not widely distributed.

Regulations, Circulars, Orders, and Decisions Relating to the U. S. Naval Engineer Corps from its Organization until March 1865, 75 pp. Government Printing Office, Washington, D. C. 1865.

Circulars of the Bureau of Ordnance, U. S. Navy, 55 pp. No publisher given but circulars from 1861 to November 16, 1863 are bound in one volume. Many circulars issued during this period are omitted because they had become obsolete by the end of 1863.

Allowances Established for Vessels of the United States Navy 1864, 164 pp. Government Printing Office, Washington, D. C. 1865. Issued by the Navy Department and invaluable for its information on naval equipment. This book includes everything from 5-ton anchors to the number of flutes allowed each naval band!

Harwood, A. A., U. S. Navy, *The Practice of Naval Summary Courts-Martial*, 29 pp. Franck Taylor, Washington, D. C. 1863.

Levy, U. P. Capt. U. S. Navy, *Manual of Internal Rules and Regulations for Men-Of-War*,° 70 pp. Van Nostrand, 2nd Edition, New York, 1861. The next year (1862) a third edition of 88 pp. appeared. This included a section by A. C. Stimers on rules and regulations for the Engineer Department of the Navy.

B. Navigation and Naval Tactics

Anonymous, *Navigation and Nautical Astronomy*, 170 pp. Printed for the U. S. Naval Academy in 1863 by: Welch, Bigelow, and Co., Cambridge, Mass. This manual ran through at least five editions and was later published by Van Nostrand.

Barrett, Edward, Lt. U. S. Navy, *Temporary Fortifications Prepared for the Naval Service*, 14 pp. Printed for the author, New York, 1863.

King, W. R. *U. S. Navy, Lessons and Practical Notes on Steam*°, 3rd Edition Van Nostrand Co., New York.

Luce, S. B., Lt. U. S. Navy, *Seamanship*°, Van Nostrand, 2nd Ed., New York, 1863.

Murphy, John M. and Jeffers, W. N., U. S. Navy, *Nautical Routine and Stowage*°, Van Nostrand, New York, 1861.

Parker, Foxhall A., Commander, U. S. Navy, *Squadron Tactics Under Steam*, 172 pp. and 77 plates. Van Nostrand, New York, 1864. Issued by authority of the Navy Department.

Walker, W. H., Captain, U. S. Navy, *Notes on Screw Propulsion*°, Van Nostrand, New York, 1861.

Ward, James H., Commander, U. S. Navy, *A Manual of Naval Tactics*, 208 pp. and illustrations. Appleton, New York, 1859.

C. Ordnance and Gunnery

Anonymous, *Hotchkiss Rifle Projectiles*, 13 pp. and drawings. No publisher given. Issued by the Bureau of Ordnance and Hydrography, Navy Dept. January 1, 1862.

Ordnance Instructions for the United States Navy, 213 pp. and plates, C. Alexander, Washington, D. C. 1852. In 1860 the 2nd edition of this valuable source book appeared with 171 pp. of text and 59 pp. of appendices. The publisher was George W. Bowman of Washington D. C. The excellent drawings explain such varied subjects as "preparation of vessels of war for battle, duties of officers and men when at quarters, ordnance and ordnance stores, and gunnery." On December 31, 1863, the Navy Department approved a third edition of 192 pp. which was published by the Government Printing Office in 1864. This and a 4th edition (1866) also contain excellent plates and explanatory text.

Barrett, Edward, Lt. U. S. Navy, *Gunnery Instructions, Simplified for the Volunteer Officers of the U. S. Navy*, 88 pp. and excellent descriptive plates. Van Nostrand, New York, 1862. Includes descriptions of ordnance, gun carriages, lists of gun ranges, powder types, weights of projectiles.

Brandt, J. D., *Gunnery Catechism*°, 197 pp. Van Nostrand, New York, 1865.

Buckner, W. P. Lt. U. S. Navy, *Calculated Tables of Ranges for Navy and Army Guns*, 79 pp. Van Nostrand New York, 1865. Approved by the Ordnance Bureau, Navy Department.

Dahlgren, J. A. Lt. U. S. Navy, *Naval Percussion Locks and Primers,* 125 pp. and plates. A. Hart, Philadelphia, 1853.

System of Boat Armament in the United States Navy, 122 pp. and plates. A. Hart, Philadelpha, 1852. In 1856 this was republished as *Boat Armament of the United States Navy,* with 212 pp. which contain additional material on rifle muskets. The front plate is in color and depicts the Dahlgren boat howitzer being landed with Perry's men in Japan, 1854.

Lockwood, Henry H., *Exercises in Small-Arms and Field Artillery Arranged for The Naval Service,* 168 pp. and 103 plates. T. K. and P. G. Collins, Philadelphia, 1852. Published by order of the Bureau of Ordnance and Hydrography, Navy Department and consisted of: Part 1. Small-arms, company exercises; Part 2. Small-arms, battalion exercises; Part 3. Field artillery without horse; Part 4. Small and broadsword exercise. Copy in the author's possession contains the inscription: "Yardley, U. S. Frigate *Powhatan* off Charleston, April 30, '63."

Luce, S. B., Lt. U. S. Navy, *Instructions for Naval Light Artillery Afloat and Ashore,* 120 pp. and 21 plates. Van Nostrand, New York, 1862. This second edition is a revision of Lt. William H. Parker's original manual, prepared for the U. S. Naval Academy.

Simpson, Edward, Lt. U. S. Navy, *A Treatise on Ordnance and Naval Gunnery,* 493 pp. and excellent plates, some in color. Van Nostrand, 2nd Ed. New York, 1862. The 1st edition of this Naval Academy textbook was published in 1859.

Thomas, Lynall, *Rifled Ordnance,* 200 pp. Van Nostrand, New York, 1864.

D. Miscellaneous

Dickerson, Edward N., *The Navy of the United States,* 80 pp. John A. Gray and Green, New York, 1864.

Marshall, Edward C., *History of the United States Naval Academy,* 156 pp. Van Nostrand, New York, 1862.

Osbon, *Hand-Book of the United States Navy,** Van Nostrand, New York, 1864. Gives the history of every vessel of the U. S. Navy from April 1861 to May 1864.

Totten, B. J., Commander, U. S. Navy, *Naval Text-Book and Dictionary*,* 2nd ed. Van Nostrand, New York, 1863.

IV. TYPES OF NON-REGULATION MANUALS AND HANDBOOKS USED BY MEMBERS OF THE UNITED STATES ARMED FORCES IN THE WAR

A. Religious Books

(American Bible Society), *New Testament,* American Bible Society, New York, 1861. Plate inside cover has American flag and "New York Bible Society." Such New Testaments were also printed in German for German-speaking troops in the Union Army.

(American Tract Society), *Soldiers' Hymns and Psalms,* 94 pp. American Tract Society, New York. Printed for the Army Committee, YMCA.

Hymns and Tunes of the Army and Navy, 128 pp., American Tract Society, New York. Copies of this collection of religious hymns and songs were presented to soldiers by the U. S. Christian Commission.

Anonymous, *The Heavy Knapsack,* 64 pp. Perkinpinet and Higgins, Phila. 1864. This religious tract was written "by a Chaplain of the U. S. A."

Forman, J. G., Chaplain, 3d Missouri Infantry, *The Soldier's Manual of Devotion or Book of Common Prayer . . . (and) Hymns and National Songs,* L. A. Parks, Alton, Illinois, 1861. Apparently Chaplain Forman presented his manual to other members of the regiment. The copy in the author's possession was carried by Capt. D. B. Greene, 3d Missouri Inf. who was killed January 11, 1863 at Arkansas Post.

(Protestant Episcopal Bible Society), *The Soldier's Prayer Book,* 64 pp., Protestant Episcopal Bible Society, Phila. 1861.

(Reformed Protestant Dutch Church), *Army Life or Incidents from the Prayer Meeting and the Field,* 179 pp. Reformed Protestant Dutch Church, New York, 1863.

Waterbury, J. B., DD., *Something for the Knapsack,* 48 pp. American Tract Society, New York.

B. Song Books (non-religious)

Moore, Frank (ed.) *Songs of the Soldiers,* 312 pp., Putnam, New York, 1864.

Lyrics of Loyalty, 336 pp., Putnam, New York, 1864. *Rebel Rymes and Rhapsodies,* 299 pp. Putnam, New York, 1864.

C. Guide Books

Anonymous, *The Stranger's Guide in Philadelphia,* 272 pp., Lindsay and Blakiston, Philadelphia, 1864. Printed for the Great Central Fair of the U. S. Sanitary Commission in Philadelphia, June 1864.

Bohn, Casimir, *Hand-Book of Washington,* 134 pp., Casimir Bohn, Washington, D. C., 1861.

Philp, James, *Washington Described,* 239 pp., Rudd and Carleton, New York, 1861. Edited by William D. Haley. Includes advertisements for such items as Remington revolvers, rifles, carbines, and muskets.

CHAPTER 4

Organization

THE ORGANIZING of the Federal forces went on simultaneously with the training of troops. It was only in the last year of the war that the organization of the arms and services became fixed. In addition to inevitable change in organization due to accumulated experience as the war progressed, should be mentioned the fact that the lack of a general staff corps was keenly felt by the Federal high command.

THE WAR DEPARTMENT

By constitutional provision President Lincoln was commander in chief of the armed forces of the United States. Lincoln who lacked professional military training himself, to a large extent relied on his commanders to conduct campaigns. He hesitated to dictate policy, but at times he found it necessary to be commander in fact as well as in name. One such occasion was that of January 27, 1862, when his "General War Order No. 1" directed all the armies of the Republic to take the field the same day (February 22, 1862) in honor of Washington's birthday. In general, however, Lincoln left the conduct of military operations to his generals.

The first War Secretary, Simon Cameron, who had been connected with the Pennsylvania Railroad, took as Assistant Secretary of War the capable railroad manager, Thomas A. Scott.[1] Unfortunately for his country, Cameron was more of a politician than a statesman. As Secretary of War in 1861 he was given the rare opportunity of serving the nation in the darkest days since its creation, but he cast the opportunity aside. "He began his Secretaryship with the distribution of offices and ended it with the distribution of contracts." On January 15, 1862, Cameron was removed and his office filled by Edwin McMasters Stanton.

Scott's position was not legalized until August 10, 1861, when Congress authorized the President to appoint "by and with the advise, and consent of the Senate, an officer in the War Department, to be called the Assistant Secretary of War . . . who shall perform all such duties in the office of the Secretary of War, belonging to that department, as shall be prescribed by the Secretary of War, or as may be required by law."[2]

Scott resigned June 1, 1862, and after three unimportant incumbents had succeeded him in turn, the office was very capably held by Charles A. Dana until the end of the war. Dana served from January 18, 1864, to July 31, 1865, and his *Recollections of the Civil War* (1898) are invaluable to a study of the period.

An Army officer has said that on the day the new Secretary (Stanton) was sworn in, the War Department resembled "a great lunatic asylum more than anything else."[3] Stanton's first move was to close his Department Tuesdays, Wednesdays, Thursdays and Fridays against all business except that relating to military affairs. Saturdays were given over to the business of Senators and Representatives, and Mondays to the business of the public. Although the war had produced 660,000 soldiers, they were not yet organized into a national fighting force. It is true that McClellan was organizing one element of the land forces of the nation, the famous Army of the Potomac, but what was needed was a unified control and direction of all the armies both in preparation and eventual employment.

The Army swarmed with incapable and good-for-nothing officers. At Stanton's wish Congress passed a law authorizing summary dismissal of officers by the President at discretion.[4] Stanton had the confidence and support of Congress, and under him the bureaus of the War Department were expanded to handle all war business in the proper way. He was the man the country had been waiting for, a man of great firmness of resolution and unimpeachable honesty of character. His arrival was the "shot in the arm" for the War Department. At times he was brusque, tactless, and perhaps unjust. General Hitchcock, who acted as a military adviser to the government for a while, has stated that he was offensive to his subordinates, especially the Chief of Engineers (Brigadier General Joseph G. Totten) and Quartermaster General (Brigadier General Montgomery C. Meigs).[5] On one occasion a general and sergeant were delegated to present to the

Secretary eight enemy battle flags which they had materially assisted in capturing but Stanton would not receive the delegation because of pressure of business.[6] Despite this and similar instances of tactlessness, the Secretary conducted his office with efficiency and rendered invaluable service to the Federal war effort. Since neither he nor the President was a military man, it was necessary for them to be advised on questions of a military nature. They were greatly handicapped by the fact that there was no general staff to assist them.[7]

The commander in chief of the Army at the outset of the war was Brevet Lieutenant General Winfield Scott who had held this office since July 5, 1841. Scott had served with distinction in the War of 1812 and the Mexican War, but was too old to be of much help in this new crisis. He was supplanted November 6, 1861 by Major General George B. McClellan, whose successful campaign in West Virginia was overrated owing to its sharp contrast to the Bull Run debacle. The dilatoriness of the "Young Napoleon" was too much for Lincoln and Stanton, however. On March 11, 1862 McClellan was relieved as commander in chief and his control limited to the command of the Army of the Potomac. The following month he led this army on the Peninsula, where "he always saw double when he looked rebelward." McClellan never solved his staff problem. He selected his father-in-law, Brigadier General Randolph B. Marcy, as his chief of staff, but due to McClellan's refusal to regularly delegate his powers to the chief of staff, Marcy did not dare to act definitely in his name. The result was a complete paralysis at headquarters when McClellan was absent.

The office of commander-in-chief remained vacant over four months but was filled July 11, 1862, by the appointment of Major General Henry Wager Halleck to the post. Halleck was nominally in command of all the Federal armies; actually he was only the military adviser to the President. There was a fatal lack of co-ordination among the various Federal armies in the first three years of the war. Large Federal forces were dissipated in the pursuit of a dozen different plans. There was no common objective. The commander of the Army of the Potomac had the largest army under his control and although he confronted the best led and most efficient enemy force, he had no control over the movements of the other Federal armies in the theater of operations. The commanders of Eastern and Western armies went their own gait without effective co-ordination until Grant came to supreme military command, March 12, 1864. Grant was given genuine control of all the Federal armies, was permitted to select his own field army commanders, and with his headquarters with the main Federal army, the Army of the Potomac, he fought the war to a finish.

General George G. Meade was retained as nominal commander of the Army of the Potomac, but Grant actually directed it in person while synchronizing the movements of the other Federal armies.

RANK OF HIGHER COMMANDERS

Along with the appointment of Grant as commander in chief of the Army went the commission of lieutenant general. This ended an evil that had plagued the Army since the beginning of the war. Unlike their adversaries, the commanders of the Federal armies had no rank higher than that of major general. With the exception of Scott, the commander in chief, commanders of armies and corps all had had the same rank, that is, major general. This was partly due to a distrust of high military rank and partly to the large number of officers of high rank who performed unimportant and nominal duty in the rear echelons while "their work in the active armies was done by men of lower grade, to whom the appropriate rank had to be refused." Some military men found nothing wrong in this, however, believing that that assignment by the President of a major general to the command of an army or corps gave him a temporary precedence over other major-generals who, when relieved, lost the precedence temporary rank created giving a flexibility to the grade of major-general." [8] If only the feelings of a comparatively few regular officers had been wounded the results might not have been significant, but when professional pride and jealousy resulted in lack of cooperation in battle, disaster often resulted. When Pope replaced McClellan in an endeavor to defeat an advancing enemy, his position was embarrassed by the fact that he was called from another army and a different field of duty to command an army of which the corps commanders were all his seniors in rank.[9] At Gettysburg the Army of the Potomac consisted of 7 army corps containing a total of 19 infantry divisions, which were in turn subdivided into 51 brigades. The army and army corps were commanded by major generals; 3 of the divisions were commanded by major generals but 16 were commanded by brigadier generals. Of the 51 brigades, 22 were led by brigadier generals, and 29 by colonels.[10] Even after Grant assumed chief command of the Army he fared little better than had his predecessors in this regard. Although Grant wanted Buell for a command, the latter refused to serve, maintaining that it would be a degradation to accept the assignment because he ranked both officers (Sherman and Canby) under whom he would have to serve. All three of them ranked Grant in the "old army" who said very truly that "the worst excuse a soldier can make for declining service is that he once ranked the commander he is ordered to report to." [11] There was far too much of Buell's attitude among some of the other high Federal commanders in the war.

ORGANIZATION BY GEOGRAPHICAL AREA

The military organization of the country on a geographical basis was the division of the States and territories into military divisions, military departments and districts. The divisions, established by order of the President, were as follows: The Geographical Division, which embraced the Departments of Washington and Northeastern Virginia, was assigned to General McClellan, with headquarters at Washington;[12] the Military Division of the Mississippi, which embraced the Departments of the Ohio, Cumberland, and Tennessee, was assigned to General Grant, October 16, 1863;[13] the Military Division of West Mississippi, which embraced the Departments of Arkansas, and the Gulf, was assigned to General E. R. S. Canby, May 7, 1864;[14] and the Middle Military Division, which embraced the Middle Department and the Departments of Washington, the Susquehanna, and West Virginia, was assigned to General Sheridan, August 7, 1864.[15] There were other military divisions but they came into existence after the conclusion of the war. One department functioned for a brief period as a division. This was the Department of the Mississippi, which, in the spring of 1862, brought together the Armies of the Ohio and Tennessee under Major General Halleck for combined operations.

The several states and territories of the United States were in turn subdivided into 44 Military Departments. This continued subdivision of Military Divisions into Departments was constantly fluctuating. When Grant assumed supreme command in March, 1864, there were but 19 departments,[16] some of the more important being: Department of the East, Department of New England, Department of the Potomac, Western Department, and Department of the Shenandoah.[17]

THE FIELD ARMY

The forces called for by the President were organized first into armies, and later into army corps and armies. The troops sent to a military department were usually called the Army of the Department in which they operated or were located; the corps were designated by numbers, and were part of the army of a department, or sometimes constituted that army.

The largest military unit in the Federal forces was the "army" of which there were eleven at one time or another during the war. With the exception of the army that fought at Bull Run, all the Federal armies were divided into corps. The Bull Run force, termed the Army of Northeastern Virginia, was divided into five divisions. It is interesting to note that the commanding general (Irvin McDowell) was a West Point graduate, as were all the commanders of the four divisions that participated in the battle. Of the 11 brigades at Bull Run, 8 were led by West Point men. The more important Federal armies were: the Army of the Potomac, Army of Virginia, Army of the James, Army of the Ohio, Army of the Cumberland, and Army of the Tennessee. The other armies were in existence for short periods only and were soon merged into larger units.

There were two attempts to group corps within an army into "grand divisions" under separate generals, all of whom were subordinate to the army commander. Neither of these attempts was successful. In his Fredericksburg campaign, Burnside divided the Army of the Potomac into four grand divisions,[18] but due to lack of harmony among the commanders the organization broke down. Hooker abolished the grand divisions because he distrusted their leaders. In the West, Sherman organized his army into three grand divisions for his march to the sea. In this case the grand divisions were "armies" but these armies were no stronger numerically than had been Burnside's grand divisions, hence the comparison is a fair one. Here the organization and not the leadership was to blame for the failure of the grand division system to work effectively. Sherman's organization was faulty in that the three grand divisions were very unequal in strength, one (the Army of the Cumberland) having nearly five times the infantry strength of the Army of the Ohio, and more than twice that of the Army of the Tennessee. This faulty organization continued to the end of the Atlanta campaign and, was according to Gen. Schofield, one of the causes of many of the partial failures or imperfect successes that characterized operations.[19]

In addition to these two instances of organization of an army into grand divisions, it can be said that strategically speaking the Union Army, as commanded by General Grant from March 9, 1864 to April 1865, was composed of grand divisions. The center division was the Army of the Potomac, and all west to Memphis, along the line described as the Federal position at the time, and north of it, was the right wing; the Army of the James, under General Butler, was the left wing.[20]

The commander of a Federal field army was invariably a major general. In most cases his corps commanders were also major generals, a situation which resulted in friction, jealousy, and lack of cooperation. The appointment of all generals, their aides-de-camp, and all the officers and employees of the administrative departments, belonged to the President, subject to the confirmation of the Senate. In the staffs of the Federal armies the chiefs of the different services were Regular officers invested with a rank commensurate with the importance of their functions. They served at the general headquarters of the Army of the Potomac and the armies of the West as the Chiefs of Cavalry, Artillery, Engineers, and Topographical Engineers. These chiefs were ranked as brigadier generals as were the Assistant

Adjutant-General and the Quartermaster General in the administrative departments. The Assistant Adjutant General was the center of the formal organization of the army, keeping its records, carrying on its correspondence, and formulating the orders of his chief. An Inspector General was in charge of discipline and training in the army, and was the superintendent of the outpost and picket duty. If there was no special organization in an army for an intelligence function, that too, was entrusted to The Inspector General. When the Army of the Potomac took the field in the spring of 1862, McClellan created the office of Commandant of General Headquarters, which was given to a Regular Army major. This officer's responsibilities were in the nature of guard and police duty, for which he was assigned six companies of infantry.[21]

A major general was permitted to nominate his own aides-de-camp. These aides held ranks inferior to the various chiefs of the arms and services mentioned above. Among the more important aides were the Chief of Ordnance, the Commissary of Subsistence, and The Inspector General. Quite often they were volunteer officers detailed from the line. A general officer's aides were usually his most intimate associates in the military family and were sometimes selected with too much regard for their social qualities. It would have been advisable to have had general officers as chiefs of staff who outranked every other officer of their grade in the unit in which they functioned.

Too often staff officers were untrained and not well posted in such essentials as tactics, capabilities of the different arms of the service, military engineering, map reading; and above all, they did not possess the rare gift of seeing no more and no less than what was really and distinctly before them.[22] Nevertheless, it was said, the general officer who sought for sober, zealous, and bright young soldiers for his staff could always find them.[23] One observer reported that General Butler's staff formed a body of young men of whose courtesy, refinement, and soldierly qualities, any country might be proud. They were brave to a fault, being all very young: a colonel, the chief of the staff, was not more than thirty.[42]

Each army headquarters was designated by its own distinctive flag. The flag of the Army of the Potomac was adopted by General Meade, who chose solferino as the color surrounding a golden eagle in a silver wreath.[25] When General Grant first saw this showy standard unfurled as the army broke camp for the Wilderness Campaign, he exclaimed, "What's this! Is Imperial Caesar anywhere about here?"[26]

THE ARMY CORPS

Federal armies were composed of corps commanded by major generals. As mentioned above, the exception to this was the Army of Northeastern Virginia, which was a grouping of divisions only. When McClellan organized the Army of the Potomac he delayed the corps formation because he believed that the Army should be in the field for a while in order to enable the general officers to acquire the requisite experience as division commanders. McClellan also maintained that he would be in a better position to select his corps commanders after actually testing them in action. This care and deliberation were characteristic of McClellan. It was not until March 8, 1862, that the corps formation was introduced in the Army of the Potomac. Late in 1862, in a private letter, Brigadier General J. G. Barnard, the former Chief Engineer of the Army of the Potomac, wrote to W. H. Hurlbert: "The Army of Genl. McClellan was no sooner pushed into the field than it was divided under five different commanders, each independent of the other. If we have seen no indication as yet of that commanding ability and force of will which would, if left untrammelled, create unity of action and give room for skill in execution (qualities, certainly possessed by the head of the rebel government), we should at least remember Napoleon's aphorism that one bad general is better than two good ones independent of each other and acting in the same theatre of war."[27]

In the Western armies the corps formation was not used until October 1862. The Federal forces fought piecemeal at Shiloh due to lack of compactness in organization; corps organization would have helped to avert this. The introduction of the corps into the Army of the Potomac was made by the President himself. The division commanders whose names had become familiar to the army, thanks to Bull Run and sundry reviews, were advanced in position but not in grade. McDowell, Sumner, Heintzelman, Keyes, and Banks were the first five corps commanders. This action by Lincoln was confirmed in a general order [28] which stated that the President was authorized to establish and organize army corps according to his discretion. By this order each corps staff was to consist of one Assistant Adjutant General, one Quartermaster, one Commissary of Subsistence, one Assistant Inspector General—each to be a lieutenant colonel to be selected by the President from the regular or volunteer forces. Each corps commander was also allowed a major and two captains as aides-de-camp to be appointed by the President on the recommendation of the corps commander. Confirmation by the Senate was required.

The army corps organization worked out quite well in practice. Usually the corps were given to West Point graduates [29] and would have functioned better if they had had West Pointers also as Chiefs of Staff in every instance.[30] Among the advantages of the corps organization were: the provision for separate action, the relief of army headquarters "of great labors," the utilization of the highest talent of gifted generals which would have been wasted to some extent upon small divisions, the *esprit de corps* in a larger body which removed regimental or brigade bickerings. The corps was to the Federal soldier what the division was to the American soldier of 1917 and 1941. Such titles as the "Fighting Second," the "Bloody Sixth," and the "Gallant Fifth" indicate the pride the members of those corps felt in their organizations.

The average corps in the Army of the Potomac in 1863 numbered 16,000 men.[31] Corps were consolidated in the latter stages of war. Before consolidation a corps numbered 19,000 to 20,000 men. Grant consolidated the five corps of the Army of the Potomac into three, thereby increasing their average strength from 15,646 to 26,077 officers and men available for duty.[32] The Eleventh Army Corps had acquired a bad reputation at Chancellorsville and Gettysburg and was transferred West; some thought that such a corps should be broken up and not permitted to retain its organization.[33] There were twenty-five army corps in the Federal Army. Some of these corps were abolished and new ones organized under the old numbers. Corps numbering One through Eighteen were organized in 1862; Nineteen through Twenty-Three in 1863; and Twenty-Four and Twenty-Five in 1864.[34] The Twenty-Fifth Army Corps, the last one organized, was a Negro unit. The histories of these corps have been sketched but only a few have been thoroughly covered by historians.

In the Army of the Potomac each corps headquarters was designated by a headquarters flag.[35] In the West, General Rosecrans established a different system [36] of corps flags but in general the provisions regarding flags to designate corps headquarters were not generally adopted. Some corps headquarters carried their flags in combat with them as, for instance, the Nineteenth Army Corps, where a mounted sergeant carried the flag through every engagement in which the corps took part.[37]

To increase *esprit de corps* and for a ready recognition of corps and divisions in the various armies, a system of badges for the various corps was adopted. The idea first originated with General Philip Kearny, who had the soldiers of his division wear a red patch to distinguish them from other troops. The idea of corps badges to be worn throughout the Army of the Potomac was suggested to Hooker by his Chief of Staff, General Daniel Butterfield, who devised the badges in detail. Butterfield's biographer has related how the different badges came to be selected.[38] The design for the First Army Corps was a disc, "the first thing thought of." A patch or lozenge was reserved for the Third Army Corps, as Kearny's division was of that corps. For the Second

Army Corps the trefoil was chosen, as a sort of shamrock, there being many troops of Irish origin in that corps. The order for the first corps badges (Army of the Potomac, March 21, 1863) was prompted by the need of ready recognition of corps and divisions to prevent injustice by reports of straggling and misconduct through mistakes as to their organization. The Chief Quartermaster was directed to furnish without delay the badges to officers and men.[39]

The idea of corps badges was taken to the Western armies by the transfer of the Eleventh and Twelfth Army Corps from the Army of the Potomac to Tennessee in 1863. When these corps arrived at Chattanooga they were wearing their corps badges. Rivalry between them and the Western corps was strong and the contrast in neatness of dress between the two sections was marked. One of the Easterners asked an Irishman of the Western troops what his corps badge was. The Westerner slapped his cartridge box and replied, "This is my corps badge." As a result of this, his unit, the Fifteenth Army Corps, adopted the cartridge box with the words "Forty Rounds" as their corps badge.[40] Only two (Thirteenth and Twenty-First) of the twenty-five corps failed to adopt badges.

The badges were cloth and were worn either on the cap or left side of the hat. There appears to have been no continuous government issue of these badges; the men bought them from sutlers or made them from the lining cloth of their overcoats. The corps emblems were used everywhere—being painted on ambulances, wagons, and other materiel, as well as worn by the men. Most of the metal corps badges were sold by sutlers. In addition to brass and tin, silver badges, engraved with the soldier's name, company, and regiment were popular. These fancy badges were widely advertised in *Harper's Weekly*, *Leslie's*, and *The Army and Navy Journal*. One soldier considered his corps badge as possessing the power to protect him from all reb missiles.[41] A rather unusual use of the corps emblem was that made by men of the Fifth Army Corps, who delighted in showing the enemy that their corps had destroyed part of the Weldon Railroad. In August 1864, men of this corps took rails, heated them; and then twisted one rail over another, thus forming a Maltese cross, their corps badge. However, men of the Second Corps "Could hardly do this as the rails could not be twisted into the shape of the trefoil." [42] In the last two years of the war they were well known to friend and foe alike. When Confederate prisoners were brought into the lines of the 2d Division of the Second Corps at Bristoe Station, and saw the white trefoil of their captors, they recognized their old antagonists of Gettysburg and exclaimed: "Those damned white clubs again!" [43]

Sometimes corps badges were a disadvantage,

especially to wounded men who, in some cases, were treated only at their own corps hospital.[44] This happened to a First Army Corps soldier who sought treatment at an Eleventh Army Corps field hospital at Gettysburg. His corps badge identified him but the surgeon later relented and treated him. A suggestion for a badge for Regular officers was never acted upon due to the termination of the war.[45]

Corps differed widely in degrees of combat efficiency. Probably the best of them all was the Second Army Corps under "Hancock the Superb." This fighting corps could boast up to 1864 that it had never lost a gun or color. It efficiency fell off noticeably after the influx of the worthless replacement material it received in the last year of the war. An order was issued to fill this corps to 50,000 men early in 1864, but this was never done. Proof of the fighting done by this corps is the fact that of the hundred regiments in the Federal Army which lost the most men in battle, the Second Army Corps contributed thirty-five.[46] In an article entitled "The Second Army Corps." the *Army and Navy Journal* said: "Its list of casualties in action swells far beyond that of any other corps in the army, reaching the large number of 25,000. Its trophies of guns and colors captured on the field are perhaps as numerous as those of any other organizations."[47]

Another fine unit was the Third Army Corps, which lost its identity March 23, 1864, at the time of the reorganization of the Army of the Potomac. The loss in morale resulting from this act was quite serious and the resentment never ended until the death of the last survivor of the corps. During the remainder of the war the disappointment at the dissolution of this, the oldest corps in the Army, was shared alike by officers and men. To emphasize their strong feeling on this subject, some of the members of the corps secured some boards from a "secesh" picket fence and placed them around an enclosure which they called a cemetery. In this "cemetery" they erected a board grave marker on which they inscribed: "Sacred to the memory of the old 3d Corps. Killed by General Order No. 9, March 1864. Actuated by Personal Malice, Spite and Jealousy. 'How Sleep the Brave.'"[48]

There was much healthy rivalry between the various army corps, but the attitude towards the Eleventh Army Corps was something else, it was a complete lack of respect. This feeling resulted from the disintegration of that corps when attacked by Jackson at Chancellorsville, which "was something curious and wonderful to behold . . . never, before or since, [had the narrator seen] thousands of men actuated seemingly by the same unreasoning fear that takes possession of a herd of animals. Many of them ran right through [the] line of battle and picket line, and into the enemy's line! The only reply one could get to argument or entreaty was 'all ist ver-

loren; wo ist der pontoon bruecke?'"[49] Little respect was felt for troops of this corps and they met with taunts and jeers from the other corps.[50] An officer in a private letter of March 1, 1863, thought the Eleventh Corps "disgracefully undisciplined" and stated that its former commander, General Franz Sigel, was "pretty generally regarded as a humbug in the Army of the Potomac." According to this officer, Sigel's men were marauders and not believed in as fighters.[51] Some of this contempt was perhaps undeserved but had existed ever since the corps had come up in the rear at Fredericksburg. "To 'fight mit Sigel' had so long been a current jest that the troops were hardly disposed to do justice."[52]

A keen observer's comment about the Eighteenth Army Corps could well be used to explain why some corps were not as efficient as others. The Eighteenth Corps, he said, "was not a body of men of the same military habits, like the Second and Sixth Corps, which had been schooled as a body for thirty months by a succession of commanders, each of whom had imbibed the notions of discipline which actuated his predecessor."[53]

THE DIVISION

The various corps were organized, for the most part, into three divisions. Sometimes a corps would have four divisions, but this was exceptional. Normally the division commander was a major general [54] and, here again, the multiplicity of major generals led to friction and lack of cooperation. There was no gradation of rank among the commanders of armies, corps, and divisions! Schofield, in speaking of the refusal of a division commander to support him in an important maneuver of Sherman's in 1864, said he believed the other's commission was anterior to his own and, therefore, the other general would not cooperate.[55]

While the division was a necessary organizational element, we do not find any marked divisional *esprit de corps* on the part of the Federal soldier. To him the significant units were his regiment and corps. An order of August 3, 1861 authorized divisions of three brigades each.[56]

In the fall of 1861 Major General Benjamin F. Butler received authority to raise for special service a division consisting of one regiment from each New England State.[57] Although this project failed to materialize, there were a few successful attempts to organize unique divisions. One of these divisions was the famous Pennsylvania Reserves, which consisted of thirteen regiments of infantry, a regiment of cavalry, and one of artillery. These troops were all from Pennsylvania, numbering more than 15,000 men. This division was recruited with the express understanding that the unity of the command should be maintained throughout its three years of service.[58]

In the Army of the Potomac there were only two

divisions in which the infantry was all from the same state.[59] The average Federal division comprised about 6,200 infantry. At Fredericksburg, Hancock's division numbered 4,834 of whom 219 were killed, 1,581 were wounded, and 229 were missing—a casualty percentage of 41.9. Nearly all the missing soldiers were killed in front of the stone wall at Marye's Heights, their bodies being unidentified. Previous to Fredericksburg this division had already lost 3,290 men on the Peninsula and at Antietam. Over 14,000 men were killed or wounded in this division during the war; yet it never numbered 8,000 muskets, and often could muster only half of that.[60]

Another excellent division was the "Regular Division" which was composed of two Regular brigades of infantry. The regiments of this division were small, seldom having more than eight companies and often only three. The division was first commanded by Sykes and later by Ayres. In the Wilderness it lost one-fourth its number in thirty minutes, an experience which a war correspondent could well label "a stern initiation to a campaign which 80 days have not ended." [61] A War Department order [62] had originally called for two Regular divisons but apart from Ayres' division, the only other large Regular organization was a Regular brigade of four infantry regiments which served in the West.[63] Thus the Regular Army had its token forces in the field; it was represented by a division with the Army of the Potomac in the East, and by a brigade with the Army of the Cumberland in the West.

THE BRIGADE

The Federal brigade was composed of from four to five regiments.[64] In some cases, due to depletion of regiments, brigades contained more than five regiments. In the Atlanta campaign some brigades in the Fourth Army Corps and Fourteenth Army Corps had nine regiments.[65] By War Department order, brigades were to be under brigadier generals, but it was just as common, if not more so, to have a colonel in command. Owing to the paucity of brigadier generals, resulting from casualties, it often happened that one brigadier general would be subordinate to another with the resulting friction that so unhappily characterized the relationship between many professional soldiers in the Civil War. In one important military operation and efficient brigadier general had to be promoted to silence the political friends of another brigadier general who demanded that their friend be permitted to command.[66]

In the Eastern armies, brigades were numbered serially in their own divisions: for example, 1st Brigade, 2d Brigade, 3d Brigade, 4th Brigade of 2d Division, and so on. However, in the Western armies the brigades were numbered without any reference to their divisions at all; hence in the roster of the Army of the Ohio at Shiloh we find that the 4th Division was composed of the 10th, 19th, and 22d Brigades. This lack of system was changed in 1863, when the organization of all Federal armies became uniform.[67]

Brigades sometimes had small detachments of artillery and cavalry more or less temporarily attached to them, but normally these arms either functioned as independent units or were attached to divisions and corps. After the abolishment of regimental bands each brigade of volunteers was allowed a 16 piece band.[68]

Unlike their enemy, the Federal armies had few "State brigades" because the policy of the War Department was to form brigades of regiments from different States. There were a few noteworthy exceptions to this rule, however, for we do find such States as New York, Pennsylvania, New Jersey, and Vermont with "State brigades."[69] The famous Irish Brigade, composed of regiments from three different States, fought with conspicuous gallantry in the Army of the Potomac. Its original New York regiments chose numbers corresponding to those of certain famous Irish regiments in the British Army. Although the average brigade in the Army of the Potomac consisted of 4.7 regiments aggregating about 2,000 effectives,[70] this Irish Brigade of 5 small regiments lost over 4,000 men in killed and wounded during its service.[71]

Another brigade of five regiments that achieved immortal fame was the Iron Brigade, or Black Hat Brigade, which also served with the Army of the Potomac although composed of Western regiments. It continued to wear black hats long after the other units of the Eastern Armies had discarded theirs, and as a result was well known to the Confederates. The Iron Brigade suffered 61% in casualties at Gettysburg; it was truly a fighting brigade in a fighting division and a fighting corps, all commanded by fighting generals. At Gettysburg the brigade lost 1,153 out of 1,883 engaged. There were 162 killed, 724 wounded, and 267 missing. This was the 4th Brigade (Meredith), 1st Division (Wadsworth), First Army Corps (Reynolds).[72] After Reynolds fell, the I Corps was under Doubleday, then Newton.

THE REGIMENT

The regiment was the most important organizational element of the Federal Army. When a Federal soldier would be asked to name his unit he would almost invariably name his regiment. The pride he felt for his State was expressed in the title of the regiment itself. While there are only a few corps, division, and brigade histories of the Civil War there are literally hundreds of regimental histories, about 500 in all. It is obvious that this is partly due to the fact that there were naturally many more regiments than any of the larger organizations, but it is also indicative of where the Federal soldier placed his loyalty.

SOLDIERS FROM THE WOLVERINE STATE

On the right, holding a musician's sword, is musician F. D. Barnes, Company F, 4th Michigan Infantry. The sword and the bowie knife worn by his companion were popular early in the war but were soon discarded. The 4th Michigan served from 1861 through 1864. At Gettysburg it fought in the Wheatfield.

The organization of the Federal regiment was largely determined by an informal board consisting of the Secretary of the Treasury and two Regular officers. The Secretary of War was completely overwhelmed with the task of providing arms and supplies and so the problem of organizing of the Regulars and volunteers was passed to the Secretary of the Treasury![73] Both officials recommended for all the troops a regimental organization of three battalions, two of which were to be kept in the field, the third to remain in depot for the purpose of drilling and recruiting. As a result, the three battalion organization was accepted for the Regulars, but rejected for the volunteers on the ground that it was inexpedient to abandon an organization with which the militia units were already familiar. Separate tables of organization for the Regulars and volunteers were established and adopted by Congress in the laws of July 22, 25, and 29, 1861.[74] Various modifications were made in the regimental organization, but by September, 1862, reasonable uniformity had been reached in the organization of all Federal regiments.[75]

REGIMENTAL STRENGTHS

The regular infantry regiment consisted of two or more battalions each, with eight companies to a battalion. Each company was authorized 100 men; a battalion's maximum strength was 807. The total strength of a regular regiment was 2,020 as a minimum, or 2,452 as a maximum. The regiment was commanded by a colonel; each battalion by a major. There were also a regimental and battalion adjutant, and regimental and battalion quartermaster and commissary officers.[76] A lieutenant colonel was second in command of the regiment. The Regular infantry regiments went into combat with only a fraction of their authorized strength due to the fact that their companies were constantly absent on detached service. The bands originally authorized for the Regular regiments were abolished in 1862.

The volunteer infantry regiment consisted of ten companies; each company was officered by a captain, a first lieutenant, and a second lieutenant. There was no battalion organization but each regiment was authorized one major in addition to the lieutenant colonel who was second in command to the colonel.[77] The average volunteer infantry regiment numbered 1,000 men on leaving the State and during its service received 300 replacements.[78] Late in the war the average strength of a regiment, according to the entire returns of the Army, was 872, of which there were 91 constantly sick and 781 ready for duty. Also, of each regiment, 35 were commissioned officers and 837 were enlisted men; the latter included noncommissioned officers and privates. Thus, officers constituted 4 percent and the enlisted men 96 percent of the entire strength of a regiment. This strength was almost the minimum prescribed by the July 22, 1861 Act of Congress, which called for 38 commissioned officers and from 854 to 1034 enlisted men per regiment.[79] The average effective strengths of the various types of regiments were as follows:[80]

	Absent	Sick in Hospital	Total	Effective Strength
Regulars	226	64	290	710
Volunteers ..	265	89	354	646
White	264	86	350	650
Colored	158	46	204	796

The militia regiments were organized in similar fashion to the volunteers.[81] Regimental bands were abolished July 27, 1862[82] in favor of fifers and drummers. As mentioned earlier, the order abolishing bands for the regiments authorized brigade bands and it was one of these that Horace Porter noticed playing "Nellie Bly" under heavy fire at Five Forks.[83] Although one foreign observer[84] considered the music execrable, there is ample evidence to show that the soldiers missed its morale effect and questioned whether it was a wise policy which deprived them of a great deal of comfort.[85]

In numbering its regiments each State had its own system. Usually the practice was to number each arm of service consecutively and when the term of service of a regiment expired its number was not used again. Illinois was so proud of the record of the State's six regiments in the Mexican War that it started numbering with 7 in the Civil War. The 2d Pennsylvania Heavy Artillery had 3,200 men and when two regiments were made out of it, both kept the original regimental number. One, however, added the word "Provisional." Pennsylvania was also unique in that she numbered her regiments consecutively as fast as they were organized irrespective of the arm of service.

Within all regiments the companies were lettered according to the seniority of the original captains, with Companies "A" and "B" on the flanks; "A" on the right and "B" on the left. "A" was given the post of honor because in marching by the right flank it would be ahead and would meet danger first. "B" was given the next most honorable position because in marching by the left flank it would be in the lead.[86] There was a great advantage in being the lead company due to the jamming up which invariably occurred in the companies when a marching column was halted. On parade and in combat colors were carried by a color guard composed of noncommissioned officers selected for their courage. The guard in some regiments enjoyed exemption from guard, picket duty, roll call, and company drill.[87] The colors and guard took position in the center of the regiment. In most cases these color guards protected the colors and standards with great devotion and valor. To enhance morale General McClellan ordered that there should be inscribed upon the colors or guidons of all regiments and batteries the names of the battles in which they had borne a meritorious part. There was no official action taken on this order with the result that regiments and batteries of their own accord put the names of battles in which they were engaged on their colors, "which led to great abuse."[88] General Meade sought to remedy this by appointing boards to investigate each individual case.

The nature of the war waged by the North entailed the diversion of large numbers of troops to protect communications (road and rail lines, depots, arsenals, etc.,) and to garrison conquered territory. As a result there were over three hundred regiments in the Federal army that never saw action with as many more which were under fire only a few times.[89] However, forty-five regiments each lost over two hundred men in killed or mortally wounded. Of these 45 regiments, 31 were Eastern regiments, 13 were Western regiments, and 1 was a Regular army regiment.[90] The infantry regiment sustaining the greatest loss in battle was the 5th New Hampshire Infantry, which lost 17.9 percent of its original enrollment in killed alone. In 1864 this fine regiment was "dis-

graced" by being filled with drafted men, 420 of whom deserted before joining the command.[91]

REGIMENTS WITH DISTINCTIVE NAMES

Nationality groups tended to enlist together; as a result we find French, German, Scottish, and Irish regiments in the Federal army. The Lafayette Guards (55th New York Infantry), a French regiment, was armed and equipped by the French residents of New York City. Several of its noncommissioned officers had seen service in the Crimea, Algeria, and Italy.[92] The 46th New York Infantry was a German regiment, which used German commands at drill.[93] The 79th New York "Highlanders," composed principally of men of Scottish birth, soon discarded their kilts but wore Cameron tartan trousers at Bull Run.[94] Both the 9th Massachusetts and 9th Connecticut Regiments of Infantry were Irish regiments. But whereas the 9th Massachusetts lost 204 killed and mortally wounded during its three years of service, the 9th Connecticut lost only 10 men killed in four years of service. The 9th Massachusetts saw heavier fighting, but some of the discrepancy was due to the poor leadership and discipline of the Connecticut regiment.[95]

Other groups who seemed more willing to submerge their nationalistic tendencies enlisted in those regiments most conveniently located to their homes. Sometimes men of the same profession would form a regiment. For example, the 48th New York Infantry, which was officered to some extent by ministers, was promptly nicknamed "Perry's Saints" in honor of its colonel "who left the pulpit to take up the sword."[96]

The 33d Illinois Infantry, the "Teachers Regiment," attracted to its ranks teachers and students from all parts of the State. This regiment was derisively termed the "Brain Regiment." By some it was maintained that this unit would not obey an order unless it was absolutely correct in syntax and orthography, while others stated that "the men of the regiment that were discharged for mental incapacity at once secured situations as officers in other regiments."[97]. The 100th Indiana was known as the "Persimmon Regiment" because of the propensity of its members to fall out of ranks and gather the ripe persimmons along the line of march.[98] Iowa raised an unusual regiment, known as the "Iowa Temperance Regiment," which was composed of men "who touch not, taste not, handle not spirituous or malt liquor, wine, or cider." We are told that if the men later on in their service adopted other principles or habits "it has only been at such times as they were under the overruling power of military necessity."[99] Another unusual Iowa unit was the 37th Iowa Infantry, which well merited its cognomen, the "Graybeard Regiment," since nearly all its officers and men were over forty-five years of age; three-fourths of them were greyheaded and many wore long, white beards.[100] The opposite extreme was "Birney's Zouaves," a Pennsylvania regiment, the membership of which had an average age of nineteen years. This regiment left the State with a 36-piece band, a 30-piece drum corps, and two vivandieres who remained with the regiment until the latter part of 1861 when they left for home.[101] Other unusual regiments were: "Duryea Zouaves" (5th New York Infantry); "Mozart Regiment" (40th New York Infantry); "Tamany Regiment" (42nd New York Infantry—organized by the Tamany General Committee); "Ellsworth's Avengers" (44th New York Infantry—whose requirements for its members were that they be unmarried, able-bodied, not over 30 years of age, not under 5 feet 8 inches in height, and of good moral character); "California Regiment" (61st Pennsylvania Infantry); "Roundheads" (100th Pennsylvania Infantry, recruited in a section of the State settled by English Roundheads and Scotch-Irish Covenanters); "Corn Exchange Regiment" (118th Pennsylvania Infantry, raised under the auspices of the Philadelphia Corn Exchange); and the "Railroad Regiment" (89th Illinois Infantry, organized in Chicago by the railroad companies in Illinois).[102]

Perhaps the most unique of them all were the famous Berdan's Sharpshooters, known officially as the 1st and 2nd United States Sharpshooters. These two regiments killed more men than any other two regiments in the service. They were United States troops, not State troops; each company, however, was furnished entirely by some one State. To be eligible for enlistment in the sharpshooter units each recruit had to fire ten consecutive shots whose aggregate distance from the center of the target would "string less than fifty inches, an average of less than five inches for each shot. The distance was 600 feet at a rest or 300 feet standing. At the latter distance many of the men could put all ten shots in the bullseye.[103] These men were extensively employed in skirmishing and sniping. At Yorktown their special rifles, equipped with telescopic sights, rendered the enemy batteries practically useless. Both regiments lost over 10 percent

SHARPSHOOTER
Note the telescopic sight.

in killed; the 1st U.S. S.S. lost 546 killed and wounded while the 2nd U.S. S.S. lost 462 killed and wounded.[104] Their weapons will be described in more detail in a later chapter.

CONSOLIDATION OF REGIMENTS

By the early part of 1863 many regiments had become so depleted through battle casualties and the discharge of men for disability that it was necessary to provide for consolidation of such regiments. Accordingly, a general order[105] was issued January 7, 1863, which provided for the consolidation of all volunteer regiments that had been reduced to one-half the maximum number prescribed by law. Only regiments of the same arm and from the same State could be so consolidated. No company was to be formed which should exceed the authorized maximum strength; with such regimental consolidation would be a corresponding reduction in the number of officers. A later order[106] directed that each infantry regiment to be consolidated would be consolidated into five or a less number of companies with the colonel, major, and one assistant surgeon to be mustered out of the service. The companies to be formed by consolidation were to be of the authorized strength and organization and the lettering of those companies would be changed so as to insure a consecutive alphabetical system beginning with the letter "A". It was further directed that division and corps commanders were to select the officers to be retained in the service, allowing the less efficient ones to be mustered out. It was ordered that those infantry regiments that had been reduced below the minimum strength allowed by law, but were above half the maximum strength, should lose their colonel and one assistant surgeon, while their companies should each lose a second lieutenant.[107]

This consolidation met with strong opposition from all classes of the Army. Sherman believed that the depleted regiments should be filled with replacements. On April 23, 1863, he wrote his brother, Senator John Sherman, asking him to use his influence to stop this consolidation of regiments and to fill all the regiments with conscripts.[108] The only State which acted on this sensible plan and did keep its veteran regiments up to strength without constantly forming new ones was Wisconsin. There was a positive loss to the service by the withdrawal of numerous competent officers. The opposition among meritorious officers was so strong that the Army of the Potomac's corps commanders unanimously requested the commander in chief to take no action in the matter until the bad effect of such a step should be laid before the President. As a result the power was used sparingly and only where the discharge of officers proved advantageous to the regiment concerned and to the service in general. Recruiting was used in many cases to bring the depleted regiments up to strength. Some

NEGRO INFANTRY
Company E, 4th U. S. Colored Infantry in front of their barracks at Fort Lincoln, part of the defenses of Washington.

regiments were not recruited up to strength after their original three-year men had been discharged; those of its membership who re-enlisted were continued in their old organization which was now entitled "battalion." This battalion retained its same position in the brigade, division, and corps as had the former regiment.[109] During the war the Federal Government raised a total of 2,047 regiments, of which 78 were artillery, 272 were cavalry, and 1696 were infantry. Of the 2,047 regiments, 30 were regular army units and 120 were colored units.[110]

VETERAN VOLUNTEER CORPS

While discharged soldiers were exempt from the draft, an attempt was made late in the war to raise a corps from veterans who had been honorably discharged but due to disgust or war weariness had refused to re-enlist. Herein lay the difference between this veteran corps and the force called "Veteran Volunteers," who re-enlisted in their old regiments during the winter of 1863-1864 for a period of three years.[111] On November 26, 1864, Stanton proposed to General Hancock, then commanding the 2nd Army Corps under Grant, that he should resign the command of the corps and, returning to the North at a season when active operations would be largely prohibited by stress of weather, should undertake the organization of this new corps which was to be composed entirely of veteran soldiers. Hancock was selected because of his great popularity and prestige. He was well known as a fighting general who, enjoying the devotion of his veterans, would be the ideal choice for a corps that would act as a shock troop force in the coming campaign. A special boun-

ty[112] was authorized November 28, 1864, and recruiting for the corps began.

A Philadelphia recruiting poster for Hancock's "Army Corps of Veterans" called for: "aid in furnishing Veterans to serve under the gallant Hancock and enable him to do his part in putting down the accursed Rebellion. Remember, that every Veteran who shoulders his musket and returns to the scenes in which he has so long participated, is worth a cartload of raw recruits, or a wagon-load of bounty-jumpers. Help to fill the quota." As the poster pointed out, there were in Pennsylvania more than 40,000 discharged soldiers who had served honorably more than two years. The majority of them wanted to return "to see the thing out" and only hesitated in order to see with whom they would go. The poster pointed out that the total of a year's pay and bounties (Federal, City of Philadelphia, and ward) would come to $1,131.00. A final appeal was made to veterans everywhere. "Come and join us, whether you live in Maine or Michigan, New Jersey, Delaware, or Iowa. At the recruiting depot you can see the rifle which fires 16 shots per minute and which you can keep at the expiration of your term of service." This rifle was the famous Henry rifle. The poster quoted is in the author's possession.

The recruiting hit a snag because of the provision that no recruit could be credited to any district other than the one to which he owed liability to draft. The bounty brokers were too powerful and did not permit this restriction to their profits to function adequately. These brokers controlled five-sixths of the recruiting. Another reason for the lack of success in raising the corps was the refusal of the Government to permit

Hancock to select officers from active units in the field. Although the idea was an excellent one and there were probably at least 100,000 men of this class physically able to serve again,[113] the total number raised by April 30, 1865, was only 4,422 officers and men.[114] Despite the granting to States' governors[115] the right to raise regiments for Hancock's force, it was a dismal failure.

INVALID CORPS

Paradoxically enough, while the attempt to secure the services of able-bodied veterans in an elite corps was a failure, the attempt to utilize the services of semi-crippled veterans was fairly encouraging. During the first year of the war there was an indiscriminate granting of discharges for disability but the War Department finally realized that certain maimed and enfeebled soldiers were able to perform light duty and thus could release able-bodied men for field duty. Accordingly, on April 7, 1862, authority was given the chief medical officer in each city to employ as cooks, nurses, and attendants, any convalescent, wounded, or feeble men who could perform such duites, instead of giving them discharges.[116]

Later these feeble and wounded men who were unfit for field duty were organized into Invalid Detachments with military commanders who used them as guards, clerks, hospital attendants, nurses, cooks, and other extra-duty men. These men were not dropped from the rolls of their original regiments, but were carried as being on detached service. As soon as a man became fit for duty he was immediately sent back to his regiment.[117] These detachments were eventually organized into an Invalid Corps which recruited its membership not only from men then under the control of the Medical Department in the hospitals and convalescent camps, but also from those officers and men who had already been honorably discharged on account of wounds or disease and who desired to re-enter the service.[118] A special uniform was prescribed which consisted of a jacket of sky blue kersey with dark blue trimmings cut like the United States cavalry jacket. Trousers were to be sky blue and the regulation forage cap was authorized. Officers were authorized to wear a frock coat of sky blue cloth with dark blue velvet collar and cuffs. Shoulder straps were to be of regulation size but worked on dark blue velvet. Their trousers were similar to those of the enlisted men but had a double stripe of dark blue cloth down the outer seam.[119] One veteran described the color as a "sickly blue," while the Confederates termed its wearers "condemned Yankees."[120] The men enlisted in the Invalid Corps did not receive any pension or bounty for their enlistment in the corps. They received the pay and allowances of United States infantrymen and were enlisted for a period of three years.[121]

The preliminary organization of this corps was that of companies divided into two types of battalions. The first type of battalion included the most efficient and able-bodied men who were able to perform guard duty and light marching. These battalions acted as provost guards and were armed with muskets. The second type of battalion included those men with a lesser degree of physical efficiency and those who possessed special qualifications as cooks, nurses, and clerks. These men served in the hopitals and public buildings and were armed with side arms only.[122] The original idea was to form regiments having one each of both types of battalions so that they would be able to furnish proper details at any point where they might be stationed for garrison and hospital duty.[123] After trial of these regiments it was found advisable to have separate organizations, and as a result, a regimental organization was authorized for the first type of battalion. This regiment was composed of six companies of the first class while the second battalion companies were separated from the regiments and on March 21, 1865, were turned over to the Medical Department "for which they had always been mainly intended.[124]

VETERAN RESERVE CORPS

Meanwhile, the name was changed from Invalid Corps to Veteran Reserve Corps, a name that was much more popular than the old one.[125] On October 1, 1864, the corps consisted of 764 officers and 28,738 men, organized into 24 complete infantry regiments of the first battalion and 153 unassigned companies of the second battalion.[126] More than 60,000 men served in the corps during the war, escorting prisoners of war, recruits, and conscripts. Their discipline was good and they rendered valuable service. The officers[127] were experienced, and all personnel were completely loyal to the Northern war effort, and were thoroughly dependable in conducting unwilling replacements to their depots.

The Veteran Reserve Corps would have been even more of a success than it was, had it offered a bounty to compete with the extraordinary bounties paid by the Government, especially to those who had previously seen service.[128] The high wages paid for all kinds of manual labor incident to the withdrawal of vast numbers of men from agriculture and industry naturally tended to discourage veterans from entering a corps which offered no special financial inducements at all. Another reason for lack of enthusiasm for the Veteran Reserve Corps was "the causeless and senseless jealousy and dislike manifested towards the corps by soldiers of active regiments in the field."[129] While it is difficult to appreciate the logic that condemns a man for continuing to serve his country after having been wounded in battle, it is nevertheless true that this animosity was communicated to many who had been discharged for disability and would have been proper candidates for the corps.

CORPS OF ENGINEERS

Aside from the infantry, the other arms in the Federal army that possessed at least a regimental organization were the engineers, artillery, and cavalry. The Corps of Engineers, although small in contrast with the other arms, was very important in its influence over all the branches of the Army. It had the charge and superintendency of the Military Academy from March 16, 1802, to July 13, 1866. Every Regular officer who had attended the Academy had followed a curriculum of study prepared, and in part administered, by the Corps of Engineers. The Corps itself was small at the outbreak of the Civil War, consisting of one company of engineers that had been organized during the Mexican War. By act of Congress this was increased August 10, 1861, and as re-organized the Corps consisted of 49 commissioned officers and 600 enlisted men formed into a battalion of four companies.[130] Three of these companies served in the East with the Army of the Potomac but there was no regular engineer unit in the Western Theater.

The Corps of Topographical Engineers was separate from the Corps of Engineers and by the Act of August 10, 1861, was constituted with 42 commissioned officers and one company. On March 31, 1863, the Corps of Engineers absorbed the smaller corps by consolidation and the re-organized Corps of Engineers[131] comprised a "Battalion of Sappers, Miners, and Pontoniers" consisting of five companies.[132] Chiefs of Engineers during the war were: Joseph G. Totten until his death April 22, 1864; Brigadier General Richard Delafield, April 22, 1864 to end of the war. Chief of Topographical Engineers were: Colonel John J. Albert until his retirement September 9, 1861; Colonel Stephen H. Long, September 9, 1861 until the office was merged into the Corps of Engineers March 3, 1863. At the end of the war the Corps had a total of 105 commissioned officers and 752 enlisted men. To supplement this small engineer corps it was found necessary to raise five volunteer regiments. These were organized on a twelve-company basis. McClellan took two infantry regiments which comprised an unusual number of sailors and mechanics in their ranks and formed them into an engineer brigade.[133]

Brigadier General J. G. Barnard was appointed Chief Engineer of the Army of the Potomac.[134] Under Barnard the engineer force on the Peninsula consisted of a battalion (three companies) of regular engineers commanded by Captain J. C. Duane and the brigade of volunteer engineers under Brigadier General D. P. Woodbury.[135] In the Army of the Potomac the engineer forces were divided into three parts, all attached to Headquarters: the Topographical Engineers (commanded by Brigadier General G. K. Warren), the Engineer Battalion, and the Engineer Brigade. These separate branches had no common head, a fact which led to the consolidation of March 31, 1863.

The Western Theater was served by seventeen regular engineer officers and two volunteer engineer regiments, not brigaded. The Chief Engineer in the West was Captain (later Brigadier General) O. M. Poe.[136] In addition to these organized engineer units each regiment normally had its corps of pioneers or axemen, whose work it was to open up and corduroy roads, to clear or "slash" the front of a position, and to construct or repair bridges, barricades, and log works.[137]

ARTILLERY AND CAVALRY

In addition to infantry and engineers there were artillery and cavalry regiments in the Federal Army; in the case of the artillery the units usually functioned on a battery basis in combat while the cavalry operated by regiments, brigades, divisions, and even corps. At Bull Run the Regular artillery distinguished itself; the small Regular cavalry force does not appear to have done much of importance. Both arms, however, developed greatly in efficiency in the course of the war. The artillery was an excellent combat arm from the beginning but the cavalry did not "find itself" until Hooker's reorganization in 1863. Because of the fact that the artillery played so important a role from Fort Sumter to Appomattox it will be discussed first.

ARTILLERY

Men volunteered readily for the artillery because it had a glamour and dash not associated with the plodding infantry. With the exception of coast artillery most of the artillery was horse-drawn, and this fact, coupled with the mechanical nature of the arm, combined to cause volunteer batteries to spring up in small hamlet and city alike. The interest in raising artillery units was not confined to any one section, although the Eastern States had a head start due to the superiority of its militia artillery batteries in 1861.

When McClellan inventoried his artillery four days after Bull Run, he found only 9 imperfectly equipped batteries of 30 guns, 650 men, and 400 horses.[138] None of these batteries was attached to an infantry regiment, a fact which astonished a foreign observer who believed that the morale effect of having artillery distributed among the inexperienced foot soldiers would encourage them to fight better.[139] Using the Regular artillery as a training force under the direction of Brigadier General William F. Barry, the Federal commander proceeded to organize the new Regular artillery regiment authorized by Congress[140] and the volunteer artillery batteries and regiments that poured into the artillery camps. A Regular artillery regiment consisted of 8 or 12 batteries, each battery having a minimum of 80 or a maximum of 156 officers and men. Thus a twelve-battery regiment (including the colonel, lieutenant colonel, three majors, and staff) would total either 997 or 1,909 men.[141] A 24-

piece band was later abolished (1862). The organization of the volunteer artillery regiment was finally fixed as a twelve-battery organization, each battery consisting of 144 officers and men.[142] Since volunteer artillery was usually called for and received by batteries, it was forbidden to muster in the field officers, chaplain, and regimental staff without special authority from the War Department.[143] In addition to this regimental organization, there were many light batteries raised that operated independently and were known by their commanders' names.[144]

McClellan followed definite principles in his organization of the artillery of the Army of the Potomac. He started with the principle that artillery strength should be in the proportion of 2½ pieces to every 1000 men in his army; this proportion was to be later increased, if possible, to 3 pieces per 1000 men. His emphasis was on the employment of the smoothbore 12-pounder gun of the model of 1857, variously called the "gun-howitzer," the "light twelve-pounder," or the "Napoleon." It was hoped that each field battery should have 6 guns and no battery was to have less than 4; the guns of each battery were to be of uniform caliber. The general endeavored to have his field batteries assigned to divisions, *not* to brigades, in proportion of four to each division (one Regular and three volunteer batteries) to be commanded by the Regular battery captain. If the divisions formed a corps, at least half the divisional artillery was to constitute the reserve artillery of the corps.[145]

When the Army of the Potomac entered on the Peninsular Campaign in March 1862, its artillery was divided into 92 batteries of 520 guns with a total strength of 12,500 men and 11,000 horses. Of the whole force, 30 batteries were Regulars and 62 batteries were volunteers.[146] William F. Barry had been promoted to brigadier general and commanded the field force, while the reserve artillery was under the command of Brigadier General H. J. Hunt. Hunt succeeded Barry as Chief of Artillery of the Army of the Potomac, and served as such throughout the war. The office of Chief of Artillery under McClellan was merely administrative but under Pope it became a command function,[147] and continued to be such under Burnside, Hooker, and Meade.

Despite McClellan's wishes, batteries were at first attached to infantry brigades, one battery to each brigade. This was soon changed and batteries were assigned to infantry divisions, two or three batteries to each division. The spectacular success resulting from the massing or grouping of artillery caused a complete change in artillery organization under Hooker, who grouped his artillery into brigades attached to corps headquarters. The artillery brigade was a distinct organization commanded by the senior officer of artillery of each army corps who acted as chief of artillery at the corps headquarters.[148] However there

was no effort made to keep batteries of the same artillery regiment together, Regular or volunteer. A battery was generally known in the army by the name of its captain.

For the defences of such vital areas as Washington and coastal cities the North raised 32 regiments of heavy artillery. These regiments were organized on a twelve-company basis, with 150 men per company. Each regiment thus totalled 1800 men and was divided into 3 battalions of 4 companies each.[149] Most of these heavy artillery regiments remained in the forts and defences to which they were originally assigned, but some of them took the field in the spring of 1864 and served at the front as infantry. A notable exception was the 1st Connecticut Heavy Artillery, which served in the field with the Army of the Potomac as siege artillery. One of these heavy artillery regiments, the 1st Maine Heavy Artillery, sustained the greatest loss of any regimental organization in the entire Federal Army, this entire loss occurring in the brief span of ten months. Of a total enrollment of 2,202 it lost 423 killed (19.2%), 260 by disease, and 860 wounded. At the Petersburg assault of June 18, 1864, the regiment, with 900 men engaged, lost 632 in killed and wounded; 13 officers were killed and 12 wounded.[150] This frightful loss in officer personnel is especially significant. In sharp contrast, another heavy artillery regiment which was poorly disciplined and led, allowed its supporting battery to be annihilated during an engagement while the loss of this regiment in the action was 13 killed, 32 wounded, and 330 missing.[151]

Consolidation of an artillery regiment took place when it had six or less batteries; such a regiment lost its colonel, two majors, and an assistant surgeon. The batteries formed by consolidation were of authorized maximum strength and were relettered in order to achieve a consecutive alphabetical sequence.[152] For any artillery regiment that had become reduced below the minimum strength allowed by law but was above half the maximum strength, it was ordered that it lose its colonel, one major, one assistant surgeon, and all additional officers who had been authorized to be added to it at the President's discretion.[153]

CAVALRY

The cavalry at the outbreak of the war consisted of the following regiments of Regulars: First and Second Dragoons, First Mounted Rifles, and the First and Second Cavalry Regiments. All these units had ten companies each. (In the Civil War the element now termed a "troop' was almost invariably called a "company"). The Regular cavalry force was increased by one regiment on May 4, 1861. This regiment consisted of three battalions each of two squadrons, with each squadron comprising two companies. The new regiment was authorized a minimum strength of 997 men and a maximum strength of 1,189.[154] In the fall of 1861,[155] the War Department merged the two regiments of dragoons, the regiment of mounted rifles, and the two regiments of cavalry under a common denomination, to be known respectively as the First, Second, Third, Fourth, and Fifth Cavalry. These regiments had 10 companies each; the Sixth Cavalry raised under the May 4th order had 12 companies.

In May 1861, the War Department reluctantly authorized the organization of a volunteer cavalry regiment. The leading figure in the organization of this regiment, the 1st New York Cavalry, was Carl Schurz. It was originally intended to be a German-American regiment. This regiment, known as the Lincoln Cavalry, served through the war. The regiment was composed of 4, 5, or 6 squadrons of 2 companies each, with a minimum of 79 and a maximum of 95 men per company. It was officered by a colonel, a lieutenant colonel, and a major, plus the necessary complement of company officers and regimental staff.[156] In July 1862, the authorization for additional company officers and enlisted men raised the strength of each company to 104.[157]

There was one regiment of lancers in the Federal Army. This regiment, the 6th Pennsylvania Cavalry, known as Rush's Lancers after its colonel, carried the lance from December 1861 to May 1863, when it discarded the awkward weapon as unsuited for the wooded country of Virginia.[158]

The average cavalry regiment numbered 1,200 men at original muster and gained 600 men as replacements. Although the cavalry lost proportionately fewer in killed and wounded than did the infantry, it lost heavily in men who were captured while foraging, on outpost duty, and on raids inside the enemy lines. The Federal cavalry regiment that lost most heavily in the war was the 1st Maine Cavalry. This twelve-company regiment had a total enrollment of 2,895 and lost 174 in killed and mortally wounded, while 145 more died while in Confederate prisons. The cavalry of the Federal armies lost 10,596 killed and 26,490 wounded in the war.[159] In the consolidation order of April 2, 1863, it was directed that each cavalry regiment consolidated into six or less companies would lose its colonel, two majors, and one assistant surgeon.[160] Later, it was ordered that when a cavalry regiment was reduced below the minimum strength allowed by law but was still above half the maximum strength it should lose its colonel, one major, one assistant surgeon, and each company a second lieutenant.[161]

The seven companies of Regular cavalry that served at Bull Run were attached to the various divisions in a rather haphazard fashion. In his organization of the Army of the Potomac, McClellan planned at first to assign at least one regiment of cavalry to each division of the active army, and to form a cavalry reserve from the Regular regiments and some picked regiments of volunteer cavalry.[162] McClellan failed to carry out his plan, however, and the cavalry force on the Peninsula was used for provost duty, courier service, and fruitless patrolling. In addition to this unwise employment of cavalry, which continued throughout the first two years of the war, must be added the fact that great difficulty existed in obtaining mounts for those regiments already in the field. In the Federal cavalry of 1861-1862, there were 82 regiments of cavalry, which, fully recruited and mounted, would have exceeded 98,000 troopers, but so difficult was it to get horses that less than five hundred men were fit for effective service during the campaign of the Second Bull Run.[163] Throughout this period, the chief of cavalry of the Army of the Potomac, Major General George Stoneman, functioned in an administrative capacity only.[164]

There was no independent cavalry force before Hooker's time, the cavalry having been attached to divisions, corps, and grand divisions. In April 1863, Hooker organized the cavalry of the Army of the Potomac into a corps and intrusted its command to Stoneman. This corps, consisting of 11,402 men,[165] was divided into three cavalry divisions. The pusillanimous nature of Stoneman's leadership of the cavalry corps during the Chancellorsville campaign was partially responsible for Hooker's defeat. Dispatched early in the campaign to cut Lee's communications, Stoneman advanced at a snail-like pace and accomplished little for his commander. Hooker replaced him with Major General Alfred Pleasonton.

The War Department, nevertheless, which had confidence in Stoneman's administrative ability, placed him at the head of the Cavalry Bureau which was attached to the War Department. This new bureau was given complete control of the organization and equipment of the cavalry forces of the Army. It was charged with providing all mounts and remounts to the Army and had supervision of the purchase of all animals. The purchases themselves continued to be made by the Quartermaster's Department. Inspection of all horses was made by cavalry officers only.[166] It was designed that the entire management of everything pertaining to a cavalryman or cavalry horse should pass through this bureau.[167] The Cavalry Bureau not only built immense yards, stables,[168] and equipment depots, but improved the training of the Federal cavalry so much that this arm played an increasingly important part in the last two year of the war. The bureau is significant in that it was the first of the bureaus of the combat arms in the United States service that the lessons of 1917-18 showed were as essential to efficiency and morale of the combat arms, but which the Army abandoned in 1942, though retaining bureaus for the services.

In the reorganization of the Army of the Potomac in April 1864, Major General Philip H. Sheridan was given command of its cavalry corps which then amounted to 12,424 men organized into 32 regiments.[169] This corps was divided into three divisions of two brigades each. Attached to the corps were 12 batteries of horse artillery. There was also a reserve brigade in the 1st Division. Each brigade averaged 4 cavalry regiments. The leadership of the cavalry at this stage of the war is significant. The corps commander, Sheridan, was a graduate of West Point (1853); the 1st Division was commanded by Alfred T. A. Torbert (West Point 1855); the 2d Division was commanded by David McM. Gregg (West Point 1855); the 3d Division was commanded by James H. Wilson (West Point 1860). Five of the seven brigade commanders were West Point graduates. This corps was led by youthful but well-trained officers; its record was outstanding.[170]

The Federal cavalry forces in the West had no corps organization until almost at the end of the war. They operated as divisions until a cavalry corps of 7 divisions[171] was formed in December 1864, and given to Major General J. H. Wilson, who at the age of 27 years led his corps in the Tennessee, Alabama, and Georgia campaigns. Federal cavalry in the West operated in relatively small detachments before the Sherman march to the sea, largely because of the nature of the opposition encountered by Federal forces in that area. This opposition took the form of enemy cavalry raids and sudden attacks on vulnerable spots in the widely-extended Federal lines of communications.

Further details on organization for the combat arms and services will appear later in chapters 5-8.

NOTES CHAPTER 4

1. Ingersoll, L. D., *History of the War Department*, p. 345.
2. United States War Department, "General Order No. 54," August 10, 1861, *General Orders for 1861*.
3. Macartney, Clarence, *Lincoln and His Cabinet*, p. 320.
4. United States War Department, "General Order No. 91," July 29, 1862, *General Orders for 1862*.
5. Croffut, W. A., *Fifty Years in Camp and Field*, pp. 441-442.
6. *Battles and Leaders*, Vol. 4, pp. 88-89.
7. The *Army and Navy Journal* stressed the need for such an agency and ascribed much of the lack of success to inadequate staff work on all levels. "Staff Work," Vol. 1 (October 3, 1863) pp. 84, 89; "Responsibilities of the Staff," Vol. 1 (February 13, 1864), pp. 392-393.
8. Cox, Vol. 1, pp. 437-438.
9. *Battles and Leaders*, Vol. 2, p. 450.
10. *Ibid.*, Vol. 3, pp. 258-259.
11. *Ibid.*, Vol. 4, p. 99.
12. United States War Department, "General Order No. 47," July 25, 1861, *General Orders for 1861*.
13. *Ibid.*, "General Order No. 337," October 16, 1863, *General Orders for 1863*. Grant was succeeded in command of this division by General W. T. Sherman, March 12, 1864.
14. *Ibid.*, "General Order No. 192," May 7, 1864. *General Orders for 1864*.
15. *Ibid.*, "General Order No. 240," August 7, 1864, *General Orders for 1864*.
16. *Battles and Leaders*, Vol. 4, p. 102.
17. Phisterer, pp. 25-49.
18. These were: "Right Grand Division" (2nd and 9th Corps); "Center Grand Division (3rd and 5th Corps); "Left Grand Divisions" (1st and 6th Corps); "Grand Reserve Division" (11th and 12th Corps). Approximately 2 brigades of cavalry and 1 battery of horse artillery were attached to each guard division.
19. Schofield, pp. 122-123. The reason for the excessive size of the Army of the Cumberland was that General Thomas, its commander, was "disinclined to part with any of his troops, and the troops did not wish to be separated from the old army in which they had won so much honor, nor from the commander whom they revered . . .*Ibid.*
20. *Battles and Leaders*, Vol. 4, p. 102.
21. McClellan, pp. 133-134.

22. "Responsibilities of the Staff," *Army and Navy Journal*, Vol. 1 (February 13, 1864), pp. 392-393. In an earlier issue the Journal recommended that the chiefs of staff for brigadier general, divisional commander, and corps commander be respectively a colonel, a brigadier general, and a major general. "Staff Work," *Ibid.*, Vol. 1 (October 3, 1863), p. 89.
23. Cox, Vol. 2, p. 300.
24. "A visit to General Butler and the Army of the James," *Fraser's Magazine for Town and Country*, Vol. 71 (April 1865), p. 443.
25. See Quartermaster General, United States Army, (Director of Compilation), *Flags of the Army of the United States Carried during the War of the Rebellion*, where all the army, corps, division, and other authorized flags of the Federal forces are reproduced. The flags of the Army of the Potomac are presented in full. See Beale, *The Battle Flags of the Army of the Potomac at Gettysburg, Penna.*
26. *Battles and Leaders*, Vol. 4, p. 97.
27. J. G. Barnard to W. H. Hurlbert, December 1862. Hurlbert was the translator of Prince de Joinville's *The Army of the Potomac*.
28. United States War Department, "General Order No. 91," July 29, 1862, *General Orders for 1862*.
29. In the Spring of 1863, 71% of the corps commanders in the Army of the Potomac, 63% of the division commanders, and 32% of the brigade commanders were West Point graduates.
30. Upton, p. 337.
31. Bigelow, p. 27.
32. *Ibid.*, p. 40.
33. *Army and Navy Journal*, Vol. 1, (October 24, 1863), pp. 136-137.
34. Phisterer, pp. 55-61.
35. This applied to divisions and brigades and was by order of General McClellan, March 24, 1862. The flag was 5 by 6 feet; 1st Division's color was red, 2d Division's color was blue, 3d Division's color was red and blue. Billings, *Hardtack and Coffee*, p. 257.
36. Rosecrans used a system in which the color denoted the corps, the number of stars on the flag denoted the division, while the figure in the star denoted the brigade. *Army and Navy Journal*, Vol. 1 (September 5, 1863), p. 31.
37. Irwin, Richard B., History of the *Nineteenth Army*

Corps, p. 103. Near the end of the war this corps adopted a new set of flags with the corps badge on them. *Ibid.*, p. 440. It had no flag at all until February, 1864.

38. Bigelow, p. 48;

39. Circular, Headquarters, Army of the Potomac, March 21, 1863.

40. Billings, *Hardtack and Coffee*, p. 262.

41. Buffum to author.

42. Page, (14th Connecticut Infantry), p. 302.

43. Rhodes, *Battery B, 1st R.I. Light Artillery*, p. 249.

44. Some corps had their own hospitals, e.g. at Gettysburg.

45. *Army and Navy Journal*, Vol. 2, (March 25, 1865), p. 486.

46. Fox, p. 67.

47. *Army and Navy Journal*, Vol. 1, (February 6, 1864), p. 371.

48. Hays, (63d Penn. Vols.), pp. 223-224.

49. Walker, Francis A. (Quoting General Morgan, an eye witness), *History of the Second Army Corps*, pp. 228-229.

50. *Glimpses of the Nation's Struggle*, Third Series, p. 47.

51. Bigelow, p. 491.

52. Walker, pp. 229-230.

53. Livermore, *Days and Events*, p. 381.

54. But in January 1863, 13 divisions (and 3 army corps!) were commanded by brigadier generals.

55. Schofield, p. 131.

56. United States War Department, "General Order No. 49," August 3, 1861, *General Orders for 1861*. An earlier order ("General Order No. 15," May 4, 1861) had authorized divisions of volunteers, each division to consist of three or four brigades.

57. *Ibid.*, "General Order No. 86," October 1, 1861. See also Croushore, James H., *A Volunteer's Adventures*, p. XI.

58. Fox, p. 114.

59. The divisions of Doubleday and Humphreys. Both divisions were from Pennsylvania.

60. Fox, pp. 35, 115.

61. Letter dated July 26, 1864 from Charles A. Page, war correspondent, New York *Tribune*, Gilmore, p. 185.

62. United States War Department, "General Order No. 16," May 4, 1861, *General Orders for 1861*.

63. *Glimpses of the Nation's Struggle*, Third Series, p. 125.

64. *United States War Department*, "General Order No. 49," August 3, 1861, *General Orders for 1861*. This order authorized four or more regiments. McClellan customarily formed 4-regiment brigades. Fox (p. 64) gives the number as five.

65. Fox, p. 64.

66. During the siege of Charleston in 1863, Lincoln promoted Brigadier General Gilmore (who was conducting the siege) over Brigadier General Saxton who demanded that he, as ranking officer, should command although "perfectly willing the General Gilmore should carry out all plans and operations."

67. Fox, p. 65.

68. United States War Department, "General Order No. 91," July 29, 1862, *General Orders for 1862*.

69. 1st and 2nd Excelsior Brigades were New York units; Pennsylvania had a "Philadelphia Brigade" and the famous "Bucktail Brigade" (so named because its members wore buck tails in their hats. See Thomson and Rauch, *History of the Bucktails*, pp. 139-140). There was an "Iowa Brigade" in the West.

70. Bigelow, p. 27. These figures are for April 1863.

71. Fox, p. 118. The regiments, with one exception, numbered only 800 men each on leaving their States. The three New York regiments became so reduced in numbers that at Gettysburg they were consolidated into units of 2 companies each.

72. Curtis, O. B., *History of the Twenty-Fourth Michigan of the Iron Brigade*, p. 66.

73. Upton, p. 233.

74. United States War Department, "General Order No. 15," May 4, 1861; "General Order No. 16," May 4, 1861; "General Order No. 48," July 13, 1861; "General Order No. 49," August 3, 1861, *General Orders for 1861*.

75. *Official Records*, Third Series, Vol. 2, pp. 518-520.

76. Adjutants, quartermasters, and commissary officers were all lieutenants.

77. Other officers were: an adjutant (lieutenant), a quartermaster (lieutenant), 1 surgeon and 2 assistant surgeons, and a chaplain.

78. Fox, p. 466.

79. Bulletin No. 46, United States Sanitary Commission, pp. 10-11.

80. Phisterer, p. 63.

81. Such oddities as Company "J" and ensigns soon disappeared from regimental organizations.

82. United States War Department, "General Order No. 91," July 29, 1862, *General Orders for 1862*.

83. *Battles and Leaders*, Vol. 4, p. 711.

84. Lecomte, p. 60.

85. *Army and Navy Journal*, Vol. 2 (December 31, 1864), p. 292.

86. Their captains were the ranking company officers.

87. The turnover was rapid.

88. Bigelow, p. 496.

89. Fox, p. 555; Livermore, *Numbers and Losses*, p. 66.

90. Fox, p. 3.

91. *Ibid.*, p. 2. It should be noted in an evaluation of these figures that the average regiment of Federal infantry in 1863 had 433 officers and men present for duty on the battle line.

92. DeTrobriand, Vol. 1, pp. 73-76.

93. *Battles and Leaders*, Vol. 2, p. 8.

94. Todd, pp. 1, 5.

95. Fox, pp. 470, 473.

96. See the regimental history.

97. Elliott, p. 8.

98. At first the men did not know that only the "old" ones were edible.

99. Ingersoll, L. D., *Iowa and the Rebellion*, pp. 501, 513. This regiment was also known as the "Methodist Regiment," after its colonel who was a Methodist clergyman.

100. Moore, Frank, *The Rebellion Record*, Vol. 8, p. 7. Many of these men had sons in the military service.

101. *History of the Twenty-third Pennsylvania Volunteer Infantry*, pp. 32-33. This regiment originally had 15 companies but Companies "L," "O," "P," and "R" were later transferred to the 61st Pennsylvania Infantry. *Ibid.*, p. 248.

102. Fox, pp. 195, 261, 278, 288, 373.

103. Fox, pp. 418-419; Stevens, *Passim*.

104. Fox, pp. 418-419.

105. United States War Department, "General Order No. 7," January 7, 1863, *General Orders for 1863*.

106. *Ibid.*, "General Order No. 86," April 2, 1863.

107. *Ibid.*, "General Order No. 182," June 20, 1863.

108. Thorndike, p. 200.

109. For instance, the 5th New Hampshire Infantry became the "5th New Hampshire Battalion" after the discharge of its original three-year men. However, many regiments were consolidated. Child, William, *A History of the Fifth Regiment New Hampshire Volunteers . . . 1861-1865*, p. 289.

110. Phisterer, pp. 22-23.

111. This "Veteran Volunteer Force" comprised over 136,-000 re-enlistments and should not be confused with "Hancock's Veteran Corps" or with the "Veteran Reserve Corps."

112. *Official Records*, First Series, Vol. 42, Part 3, p. 728; Third Series, Vol. 4, pp. 970-971.

113. This is only a rough estimate.

114. *Official Records,* Third Series, Vol. 4, pp. 1088-1089, 1283.

115. For example, Governor Morton of Indiana received authority to raise two regiments. *Ibid.,* p. 1263.

116. United States War Department, "General Order No. 36," April 7, 1862, *General Orders for 1862.*

117. *Ibid.,* "General Order No. 69," March 20, 1863, *General Orders for 1863.*

118. *Ibid.,* "General Order No. 105," April 28, 1863.

119. *Ibid.,* "General Order No. 124," May 15, 1863; "General Order No. 158," May 29, 1863.

120. Wilkeson, pp. 212-213.

121. United States War Department, "General Order No. 130," May 15, 1863, *General Orders for 1863.*

122. *Ibid.,* "General Order No. 212," July 9, 1863.

123. Report of the Provost Marshal General, *House Executive Documents* 39 Cong., 1 Sess., Document 1, Part 1, pp. 92-93.

124. *Ibid.,* p. 93.

125. United States War Department, "General Order No. 111," March 18, 1864, *General Orders for 1864.*

126. Report of the Provost Marshal General, *House Executive Documents*, 39 Cong., 1 Sess., Document 1, Part 1, p. 93.

127. Of every 100 officers in the Veteran Reserve Corps, 82 had been disabled by wounds, 13 incapacitated by disease, and 5 rendered unfit for field duty by accident injuries. *Ibid.*

128. *Ibid.,* Part 2, pp. 15-16.

129. *Ibid.*

130. There were: 1 colonel, 2 lieutenant colonels, 4 majors, 12 captains, 15 first lieutenants, 15 second lieutenants, 40 sergeants, 40 corporals, 8 musicians, 256 artificers, and 256 privates. United States War Department, "General Order No. 54," August 10, 1861, *General Orders for 1861*

131. The new tables of organization called for a Chief Engineer with the rank of brigadier general (Joseph G. Totten), 4 colonels, 10 lieutenant colonels, 20 majors, 29 captains, and 17 first lieutenants. United States War Department, "General Order No. 79," March 31, 1863, *General Orders for 1863.*

132. The fifth company (Company "E") was formerly the company of topographical engineers.

133. These were the 15th and 50th New York Engineers.

134. Barnard had earlier served McDowell in the same capacity in the Bull Run campaign.

135. Barnard and Barry; *Report of the Engineer and Artillery Operations of the Army of the Potomac from its Organization to the Close of the Peninsular Campaign,* p. 13.

136. The Western engineer regiments were: 1st Michigan and 1st Missouri Engineers. The fifth engineer regiment, the 1st New York Engineers, served in the East.

137. Some were enlisted to serve as pioneers.

138. *Official Records,* First Series, Vol. 5, p. 68.

139. Gurowski, Adam, *Diary from March 4, 1861 to November 12, 1862,* pp. 99-100. Gurowski was an opinionated "military expert" whose adverse comments on the Northern war effort and leaders were widely read. However, his suggestion here appears to have had some validity.

140. United States War Department, "General Order No. 16," May 4, 1861, *General Orders for 1861.*

141. *Ibid.*

142. *Ibid.,* "General Order No. 126," September 26, 1862, *General Orders for 1862.*

143. *Ibid.* The field officers were: 1 colonel, 1 lieutenant colonel, 1 major for every four batteries. Provision was also made "at the President's discretion" for 1 first lieutenant, 1 second lieutenant, 2 sergeants, and 4 corporals to each battery.

144. These were often 6-gun batteries with a strength of 250 men. Fox, p. 466.

145. McClellan, pp. 114-115.

146. *Official Records,* First Series, Vol. 5, p. 68.

147. Hunt's service was outstanding throughout the war.

148. The corps chief of artillery had been authorized by "General Order No. 91," War Department, July 29, 1862, but the artillery brigade appeared first in May 1863.

149. The commissioned personnel included a colonel, a lieutenant colonel, three majors (1 per battalion), and one captain and four lieutenants for each company. With replacements, each regiment averaged 2200 men as total membership in the War. Fox, p. 466.

150. Fox, p. 125. The 5th New Hampshire Infantry suffered the greatest loss of any infantry regiment in the war. The 1st Maine Heavy artillery was serving as infantry when it incurred the casualties cited here. However, any comparison of the two as to relative battle losses is impracticable because of the great different in size between these two excellent regiments.

151. Billings, (10th Massachusetts Battery), pp. 320-321. The artillery regiment was the 4th New York Heavy Artillery. A Confederate describing this action stated that the Federal support "didn't kill any of our men. We never saw such queer shooting. They all pointed their guns up into the air and shot far above us." *Ibid.,* p. 317.

152. United States War Department, "General Order No. 86," April 2, 1863, *General Orders for 1863.*

153. *Ibid.,* "General Order No. 182," June 20, 1863.

154. *Ibid.,* "General Order No. 16," May 4, 1861, *General Orders for 1861.* Each company was allowed a minimum of 79 and a maximum of 95 men.

155. *Ibid.,* "General Order No. 54," August 10, 1861.

156. *Ibid.,* "General Order No. 16," May 4, 1861.

157. *Ibid.,* "General Order No. 91," July 29, 1862, *General Orders for 1862.*

158. In *Photographic History,* Vol. 4, p. 25, there is shown a group of men of this unique regiment. A lance in the author's collection and probably used by the regiment is about 9 feet long. It is marked with U. S. Ordnance stampings and is definitely a regulation lance. Another lance, probably imported, used in the war, is slightly over 8 feet in length.

159. Fox, pp. 6, 112, 124, 466.

160. United States War Department, "General Order No. 86," April 2, 1863, *General Orders for 1863.*

161. *Ibid.,* "General Order No. 182," June 20, 1863.

162. *Official Records,* First Series, Vol. 5, pp. 13-14.

163. July-August 1862. Upton, p. 438.

164. "General Order No. 110," Headquarters, Army of the Potomac, March 26, 1862.

165. Fox, p. 113.

166. United States War Department, "General Order No. 236," July 28, 1863, *General Orders for 1863.*

167. *Army and Navy Journal,* Vol. 1 (August 29, 1863), p. 3.

168. Excellent photographs of some of these appear in *Photographic History,* Vol. 4, pp. 325, 333.

169. Fox, p. 113.

170. Sheridan, P. H., *Personal Memoirs,* Vol. 1, pp. 349-353.

171. Fox, p. 113. Only three full divisions and one brigade of a fourth participated in the campaign. The rest were utilized elsewhere. Cox, J. D., *The March to the Sea: Franklin and Nashville,* pp. 226-227.

CHAPTER 5

The Combat Arms

THE PRINCIPAL combat arms in the Civil War were the Infantry, Cavalry, and Artillery. Also included in this chapter are the Corps of Engineers, which was a combat arm as well as a technical and supply service; and the Balloon Corps, or Corps of Military Aeronauts, which was not actually an arm, being rather a special agency. But it had purely combat functions, acting in direct support of the combat arms.

INFANTRY

Details on infantry organization and experience in combat and on the march are given elsewhere in this volume. However, because infantry regiments formed the bulk of the Federal Army, a brief summary of this combat arm is advisable.

ORGANIZATION

Each infantry regiment consisted of 10 companies of foot, and the Field and Staff. The latter were mounted, and consisted of the colonel and such officers as were not attached to the company formations. Newly recruited regiments ranged in numbers from 845 to 1025. Nominally an infantry regiment consisted of 1000 men, less the depletion incidental to its service, the actual number of effectives being far below the nominal one. The average regiment of infantry in the Army of the Potomac in April 1863 numbered 433 present for duty, equipped.

FRONTAGES AND DEPTHS

Exact figures on frontages and distances of infantry units during the war are difficult to determine. The following principles were laid down in a manual which was published in 1862, for the use of staff officers in the field.[1] The frontage for a regiment would be equal to the number of files (front and rear men in double rank) multiplied by 20 inches which was the front allowed to a man. For example: if a company numbered 100 men and the company was developed in double rank formation (the normal formation for combat) the frontage of the company would equal 1000 inches or 27.7 yards. A regiment of ten companies would have a frontage of approximately 277 yards. The depth of a column depended first, upon the space occupied from front to rear by

a man, i.e., 19 inches; second, the interval of 13 inches between the ranks; and third, upon the variable interval between the subdivisions of the column. The depth of a column of 8 companies, closed in echelon by division, was 13 yards. The interval between deployed regiments was about 20 yards, but in closed column this interval was reduced to 7.5 yards. Brigades were separated by intervals of 25 yards; divisions by intervals of 40-50 yards.

FIRE EFFECTIVENESS

A foot soldier in ranks could fire three times a minute. The accuracy of the ordinary individual musket was uncertain beyond 200 yards; but when enemy troops were in masses, the fire was effective

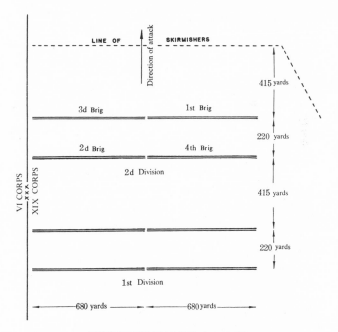

INFANTRY IN THE ATTACK

The attack of the 19th Corps in the Battle of Opequon (Winchester) September 19, 1864—showing frontages and depths. In this particular action this corps of two divisions attacked in column of divisions. The assaulting division advanced in two lines, with two brigades in each line. The attack was launched when the skirmishers were about 415 yards from the enemy. The depths and frontages, though typical, will not apply to every case. Note that the skirmish line on the right is refused for protection against a threat on that flank.

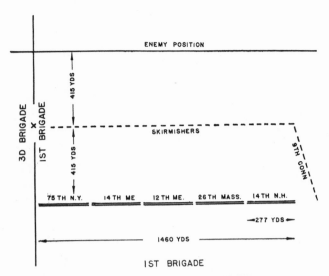

A BRIGADE IN THE ATTACK

This is the same situation as shown in the preceding illustration. Here we see the formation of the 1st Brigade, which contained six regiments. One regiment was employed as skirmishers to protect the right flank against a threat from that direction. The skirmishers in front of the brigade consisted of one company from each regiment. The distances shown here are based on the assumption, not necessarily true, that each regiment had ten companies with about 60 men per company, or 600 to a regiment. Some regiments, of course, had fewer men, some more. But it may be seen that a brigade deployed in a single line (2 ranks) as shown here, occupied about three quarters of a mile of frontage. On many occasions an attack was made in a massed, or column formation.

beyond that distance. At 250 yards the musket ball was still deadly, and instances were known where men were killed or wounded at even greater distances. The maximum effective range of the rifled spherical bullet was over 400 yards; that of the Minié bullet was 1000 yards. A foot soldier traveled in one minute:

in "common time"—90 steps= 70 yards
in "quick time"—110 steps=86 yards
in "double quick time"—140 steps=109 yards

From these figures it is possible to compute the number of discharges a body of infantry would receive from a defending body of infantry. It is likewise possible to calculate the number of discharges received by cavalry while charging. A horse at a walk passes over 100 yards in 1 minute; at a trot, 200 yards; at a gallop, 400 yards.

RATE OF MARCH

The chief of staff always prepared a description of the march, indicating the mission, the composition of the columns—that of the advance guard, rear guard, and flankers. This march order contained special instructions for each column, and designated, on the preceding evening, the position of each unit in the column. March orders also specified for each day's march the dates, halting-places, and instruc-

tions for camps or bivouacs, as well as steps to be taken in the event of a retreat by the advance guard, including action of the supports in case of an attack. Successive locations of headquarters were clearly designated.

The distances to be covered in a day can not be as long in the presence of the enemy as when no hostile action is anticipated. "It is considered very good work, if a considerable corps travels ten or twelve miles a day. If it attempts more, it loses many men, and forced marches soon become as murderous as a battle, especially with young troops." A column of infantry marched about 2½ miles an hour at route step, including halts; a column of cavalry alternating walking and trotting would make about 6 miles an hour. In route marching the interval between the ranks of infantry and cavalry, and between pieces and carriages, would be about 1 yard.

MARCH DISTANCES

A division of infantry of 12 regiments of 700 to 800 men each, marching in close column by company and at route step, occupied a road-space of 700-800 yards. Two batteries of artillery, with caissons, marching in double column, occupied 350-400 yards. A corps of 25,000 men in similar order occupied a road-space of about 2½ miles and would need a little over 1 hour to deploy by either flank, and about a half hour to deploy on the center. A division of cavalry of 24 squadrons of 48 files each, marching by platoons, made a column 1300 yards long. This division could deploy by either flank in 8 minutes, at a trot; in 4 minutes on the center if the ground was free from obstacles.

POSITIONS

Troops took positions to make or receive an attack; a position is a portion of ground offering some advantage either for attack or defense and usually is an elongated rectangle or a succession of rectangles in a broken line.

In addition to good fields of fire and communication between units a position should have: 300 yards between the lines and 200 yards from the first line to the front; a usual allowance is 120 yards front to 1,000 men of all arms, and a total depth of 600 yards.

FORMATION OF INFANTRY IN THE ATTACK

When approaching the enemy, the army is drawn up in four or five lines consisting of: an advance guard, a battle corps in two lines, a reserve, and a rear guard. The infantry of the battle corps marches in front with its organizational artillery. If the ground permits, a detachment of cavalry precedes the head of the column to support the advance guard and cover the deployment. The mounted artillery follows immediately after the leading infantry regiment, so that, on signal, the artillery can take up position. After the infantry comes the main body of the cavalry and the reserve, followed by the trains. The rearguard brings up the rear.

On encountering the enemy, the commanding general, forewarned by the advance guard which is distant from the main body about a half day's march, hastens forward to the place of encounter. The advance guard takes a defensive position, and holds the enemy in check by a determined fire fight, while the main body is deploying for battle. The commanding general conducts a personal reconnaissance of the enemy and the terrain, and dispatches members of his staff to the heads of the columns to give the generals instructions for their deployment.

The cavalry deploys on the flanks. Infantry first deploys by regiments en masse, in two lines 300 yards apart (which is a proper interval since it insures that the second line is beyond musket range of the enemy's lines and will not be cut up if the first line is smashed, but is still sufficiently close to be well in hand.)

The masses are then deployed, either to move against the enemy in this order, preceded by skirmishers, or to form double columns at deployment distance, a formation always taken by the second line, the center of its regiments being opposite the intervals of the first.

The action is begun by skirmishers, who halt as soon as they are within good range of the enemy's skirmishers, and hold them in check. The main body halts at the same time, and being soon unmasked by the skirmishers, the first line opens fire. The attack is launched by the second line, which passes through the intervals of the first line. The first line then forms in double columns and is ready to assist the second line which is now in close contact with the enemy.

INFANTRY IN THE DEFENSE

In defensive action the advance guard forms a line of advanced posts with supports, and fights in open order, while falling back by echelon or checkerwise, to join the reserve. At the same time the main body has formed in two lines. In the defense as in offensive action, the second line is in double columns, and is responsible for flank protection for the main body.

EXAMPLES OF INFANTRY DEPLOYMENT

Employment of infantry in battle depended, according to the 1861 Regulations, "on the number, kind, and quality of the troops opposed, on the ground, and on the objects of the war." However, from the myriad of personal and official accounts, it is obvious that no single principle of attack was adhered to by unit commanders. Federals attacked in mass formations even through 1864, when it was obvious that such attacks were extremely costly and usually futile due to the extensive defensive

positions constructed by the enemy. The mistakes made early in the war were repeated time and again through 1862, 1863, and 1864. For example:

At Antietam Sedgwick's division of Sumner's corps attacked with "very little" distance between the lines. According to the recollections of the survivors it ranged from 16 to 25 yards. Because no regiment was in column there was absolutely no preparation for facing to the right or left in case either of the exposed flanks should be attacked. The lines were so close together that the projectiles that went over the heads of the first line hit in the second or third. And yet, as late as June 1864, infantry units charged across open fields in close formations, which could only result in extremely heavy casualties, and usually terminated with the surviving Federals streaming to the rear, heavily shaken in morale. At Petersburg, the 1st Maine Heavy Artillery, serving as infantry, lost 115 killed, 489 wounded, 23 missing out of 632— and this loss occurred in a space of ten minutes. Eventually veteran troops refused to press home their assault unless there was some hope of success.

The fire of lines of battle usually commenced at a range of 300 yards, although skirmishers and sharpshooters would frequently try their skill at 500 and even 1000 yards. The attacking formations would then move forward at the double quick in order to seize the enemy's position with a minimum of casualties. As the war wore on, the use of entrenched positions tended to change the war from one of movement to one of position, especially in the Army of the Potomac after Cold Harbor. This was also true for Sherman's army in the West until Joe Johnston was replaced by Hood. Nevertheless, many Federal units were decimated because commanding officers continued to attempt frontal assaults on powerful defensive positions occupied by resolute veterans of the Confederate army.

CAVALRY

In marked contrast to the artillery, which performed very capably from the beginning, the cavalry did not really find itself until shortly before Gettysburg. One of the reasons for this slow start was that Lieutenant General Scott refused to accept the mounted arm because in 1861 he and others in authority believed that cavalry would be of no use in the wooded country in which the war was to be fought.[2] Scott believed that the Regular cavalry would be sufficient, and that no volunteer cavalry should be raised. The Regular cavalry consisted of five regiments in January 1861, and a sixth was added in April of that year. At first these units were pushed into the field by companies. Reorganized later, the troopers were so largely used as orderlies and headquarters guards as to seriously impair the efficiency of the arm. Regiments were not brigaded until 1863, and even then only as small units. They should have been filled up to the maximum and formed as a division of three brigades of two regiments each; which should have held in check, if it did not destroy, the Confederate cavalry. In the early days of the War, the Federal volunteer cavalry regiments were no match for that of the enemy.

The Federal cavalry was recruited from offices, mines, and workshops; many of the men had never been on a horse or handled a firearm. Probably the would-be trooper enlisted because he thought he would prefer riding to walking, with perhaps an idea that at the end of a march his horse would be put up at some livery stable. Certainly no one had any definite idea of the duties involved in training and caring for mounts. The men were enlisted from all ranks of life with no reference to previous occupation and capability. No selection was even made according to size and weight. The men ranged from pigmies to giants, and there was never any authority for transferring them, after enlistment, to other branches of the service, according to fitness. Even later in the war, when experience should have taught better, whole regiments were recruited after the same ideas; and as late as 1864 perfectly inexperienced company officers were put over equally green men, and in some cases even the field officers were totally ignorant of cavalry technique.[3]

The North was rich in men, money, and draft horses, but poor in riding horses, riders, and marksmen.[4] Russell describes the Federal cavalry in 1861 as "a few scarecrow—men who would dissolve partnership with their steeds at the first serious combined movement."[5] In the Regular cavalry, three years had been considered as necessary to transform a recruit into a good cavalryman, but as late as the Peninsular campaign of 1862, where fourteen regiments of cavalry were employed by the Federals, considerably over half of this force was composed of volunteers who had been in service about six months.[6]

At the beginning of the war it was impossible to properly train cavalry before putting it into the field, and consequently whole regiments of exquisite greenness were thrust into the Virginia mud in winter, there to try to learn, practically without a teacher, from books and hard knocks, in a few weeks or months at best, what in Europe in the best schools, under chosen instructors and on trained horses, could be accomplished only in years.[7]

Another obstacle was the enormous expense of equipping and maintaining cavalry. The equipments for a regiment of 1200 men alone cost nearly $300,000, the officers pay was greater than that of the infantry, and a larger number of artificers was necessary. It cost in favorable times probably fifty cents a day to feed each horse, and in remote places three or four times that. There was probably only one regiment in the Army of the Potomac where the soldiers owned their horses, the 3rd Pennsylvania cavalry.[8]

In the Army of the Potomac in 1863 there were about 40 regiments of cavalry[9] originally, of 1200 men and horses each. In 1864, there were about 42 regiments, but due to the fact that losses were not replaced in these regiments, they usually numbered 300 men or less.[10]

ORGANIZATIONAL CHANGES

In the spring of 1863 there came a great change for the Federal cavalry. Under Hooker the cavalry of the Army of the Potomac was divided into divisions and brigades, and better officered than before. Discipline was good and the regiments were well drilled. In the Gettysburg campaign the Federal cavalry acquitted itself well, and was especially valuable in fighting a delaying action on the first day of the battle until infantry could come up. Just before the campaign of 1864 opened, Sheridan took command of the cavalry corps of the Army of the Potomac, and when they met Stuart's cavalry they invariably won. In the Shenandoah Valley campaign the Federal cavalry was extensively employed. The terrain was ideal for cavalry operations and here the supremacy of the Federal cavalry was especially marked. Here, for the first time, the cavalry attacked Confederate infantry in line on a large scale. At the Battle of Winchester, the Confederate division of General Wharton was ridden over in perfectly open country by the Federal cavalry, and almost the entire division, a small one, was captured. After the battle, Wharton's position was marked by piles of muskets, windrows of them, which had been dropped when the Federal cavalry struck. The plain across which the cavalry had charged was dotted with dead horses and many dead cavalry soldiers.

The enemy cavalry in this campaign was reinforced by another brigade under Rosser, but his squadrons were ridden over at Woodstock and hotly pursued for 26 miles. Rosser's entire artillery was captured—guns, horses, men, and even officers. At Five Forks the Federal cavalry fought infantry and what was left of the Confederate cavalry.[11]

CAVALRY EQUIPMENT-MOUNTS

The Federal cavalry used the Morgan and Canadian breeds of horse which, while not large, possessed good endurance. Many of these animals purchased in 1861 were still giving good service in 1865.[12] Nevertheless, many of the horses passed by dishonest inspectors had nearly every disease and unsoundness that injures horseflesh. Complaint was lodged that the horses approved by inspectors were blind, spavined, ring-boned, and broken-winded. Some had the poll-evil; some were so old as to be utterly worthless; many were colts and unable to endure service.[13] In 1863 the contract system of purchasing horses was abolished and at the same time the Government increased the prices paid for horses. The horses had to be able to pass a rigid inspection.[14] That a rigid inspection was necessary can be readily seen when one realizes that in the period from June 30, 1861 to September 30, 1862, the Government purchased 146,453 horses.[15]

Care of the horses in the winter was faulty. The animals were compelled to stand in the open air all winter because there was neither timber nor lumber to build sheds for them.[16] The efficiency of the cavalry until 1863 in the field was further restricted by the failure of the men to unsaddle and groom their mounts at reasonable intervals. Irregular watering and feeding contributed to the reduction of Pleasonton's cavalry force from 10,000 to 5,000 serviceable horses during the Chancellorsville campaign.[17] Each company of cavalry had its own farrier who was also supposed to be a skilled veterinarian. After August 1, 1863, these "veterinary surgeons" were selected by the Chief of the Cavalry Bureau upon the nomination of the regimental commanders.[18]

The Cavalry Bureau, established July 28, 1863,[19] provided for monthly inspection of all cavalry units. Commanders submitted to the Bureau reports on the condition of the mounts in their commands, the number of miles traveled, the character of service rendered, the treatment of the horses, and the quality and character of rations. These reports divided cavalry horses into four classes: horses unfit for any use whatever in any branch; horses unfit for cavalry but fit for draft service; horses that could be made serviceable by care and treatment in depots; and serviceable horses.[20]

The largest cavalry depot was at Giesboro in the Defences of Washington. All dismounted men from the Army of the Potomac were sent to this depot to be remounted, and then to return to their regiments in the field. Such a camp, however, offered many kinds of dissipation and demoralization to men temporarily in it. Many good cavalry soldiers deteriorated so greatly as never to be good for anything again, while not a few never rejoined their regiments, procuring, frequently by dishonest means, a discharge or special detail. No doubt this camp was better than nothing, but was very far from what it should have been.[21]

Despite the improvement achieved by the Cavalry Bureau, as late as the spring of 1864 Sheridan's cavalry was composed of horses that were thin and worn down by unnecessary picket duty. This situation was remedied only when the cavalry corps was permitted to function independently and not as a mere line of pickets for the infantry.[22]

CAVALRY UNIFORMS AND WEAPONS

The uniform of the cavalryman was similar to that of the artillery except that the distinguishing color was yellow, and he wore crossed sabers on his cap or hat. The cavalry trooper's trousers were reinforced and he wore boots and spurs. He wore a belt carrying a cartridge box, a cartridge cap box, saber, and revolver; and across his shoulder was a wide black leather sling to which was attached the carbine. At first some troopers had no carbines; [23] McClellan organized the 6th Pennsylvania Cavalry as lancers due to lack of arms.[24] The lance was disliked by the men of this regiment as being too cumbersome.[25] Then single-loading carbines were used at first, but in the latter part of the war many were exchanged for repeating carbines. The most commonly used single-loading carbines were the Smith, Merrill, Burnside, Sharps, and Ballard, while the repeating carbines were the Colt revolving carbine, the Henry, and the Spencer. The Colt revolver was generally carried,[26] but other makes were also used in some regiments. Michigan cavalry regiments were considered to be among the best in the service [27] and in recognition of that fact they were among the very first to receive the Spencer carbine. The saddle used was the famous McClellan saddle which was light and comfortable and did not hurt the withers of the animal. It was equipped with wooden hooded stirrups. While some claim that it was merely a modification of the Mexican or Texan saddle, [28] a member of the Army board which adopted the saddle for the United States service shortly before the war maintained that it was copied by McClellan from the Cossack saddle.[29] Officers saddles were of the flat French or English type with iron stirrups, or the regulation McClellan saddle. A curb bridle was used by both officers and men.

LOADING AND PACKING

Until late in the war Federal cavalry horses were generally overloaded. Each trooper carried three days' subsistence for himself and his horse, forty rounds of carbine and twenty rounds of pistol ammunition, his haversack, canteen, tin cup, coffee pot, shelter tent, lariat, picket pin, extra shoes and nails, curry comb, brush, gun tools, and cleaning materials. Saddle bags and pommel bags were attached to the saddle.[30] The load of the horse, without the trooper, must have weighed about 110 pounds, and with trooper—equipped as he was with carbine, saber, and pistol—at least 270 pounds.[31] A new type of equipment which combined the cartridge box, pistol box, and cap box into one unit enabled the trooper to carry more than double the ammunition of the three old boxes, and transferred the weight from the trooper's waist to his shoulders by two broad belts.[32] But this new type of container was never generally adopted and many cavalrymen suffered rupture, hemorrhoids, weak-back, and diarrhea from the weight of ammunition and heavy side arms attached to the waist.[33]

One of the main problems, in addition to overloading the horses with unnecessary equipment, was the complete unfamiliarity of many of the men with horsemanship and care of horses. Typical of this was a company of the 10th New York Cavalry which was ordered to escort a general officer very early in its service. This company had drawn everything "on the list" in the way of equipment. As the company commander reported later:

My company had been mustered into the service only about six weeks before and had received horses less than a month prior to this march . . .
[We started out]. Such a rattling, jingling, jerking, scrabbling, cursing, I never before heard. Green horses— some of them had never been ridden—turned round and round, backed against each other, jumped up or stood up like trained circus horses. Some of the boys had a pile in front, on their saddles, and one in the rear, so high and heavy it took two men to saddle one horse and two men to help the fellow into his place . . . .
[The general] went like greased lightning . . . . In less than ten minutes Tenth New York Cavalrymen might have been seen on every hill for two miles rearward . . . Blankets slipped from under saddles and hung by one corner; saddles slid back until they were on the rumps of the horses; others turned and were on the under side of the animals; horses running and kicking; tin pans, mess-kettles, patent sheet-iron camp stoves . . . flying through the air . . . [I ordered the men to close up] but they couldn't . . . Their eyes stuck out like maniacs. We went only a few miles, but the boys didn't all get up till noon.[34]

Yet from this raw material was developed a regiment which earned a place on the list of "fighting regiments" of the Federal Army, losing 102 killed while serving in the Cavalry Corps of the Army of the Potomac. As the troopers gained experience, they reduced the load of the horse to an absolute minimum and their horses were packed so lightly that the carbine was the biggest part of the load. The troopers were well repaid for any personal discomfort in the resulting good condition of their mounts and their confident reliance on them.

EMPLOYMENT OF CAVALRY

In combat the cavalry used mounted saber and revolver charges, dismounted attacks, and combinations of mounted and dismounted attacks. Federal cavalry did not use their carbines while mounted but fought on foot with one-fourth of their number acting as horse holders. To a great extent the Federal cavalry was mainly used in scouting and skirmishing in the early part of the war. Stoneman complained to the Adjutant General of the Army of the Potomac that his force of 13,875 horses had to guard a line almost 100 miles in length. The condition of the roads was such at the time of Stoneman's complaint (February 28, 1863) that the horses were out at least half the time, either on patrol or picket duty.[35] This complaint resulted in a shortening of the Federal picket line and a more frequent use of reconnaissance patrols.

Hooker was the first commander in the East to permit his cavalry to fight together as a corps. He told Averell to go out and defeat the Confederate cavalry leader Fitzhugh Lee, remarking that there had not been many dead cavalrymen lying around lately.[36] This more aggressive policy, which must be the role played by cavalry if it is to justify itself, was in evidence in the cavalry fights of Middleburg and Upperville in June 1863, where the enemy commented on the improved fighting of the Federal cavalry.[37] The troopers themselves had performed capably earlier in the year in the first purely cavalry fight in the Eastern theater (Kelly's Ford, March 17, 1863), but while the Federal regiments had demonstrated battle tactics and discipline probably equal to their opponents, their commander (Averell) had lacked the aggressiveness essential to an effective cavalry commander.

With the assignment of young, aggressive leaders to brigade and division commands, the cavalry force of the Army of the Potomac became an effective fighting unit and performed well in its contacts with enemy horse in the Gettysburg campaign. At Brandy Station, June 9, 1863, Federal troopers learned that they could successfully compete with the enemy and this awareness of their own capabilities never left them. At Gettysburg, dismounted cavalry under Buford fought Confederate infantry in a delaying action on Seminary Ridge that permitted Federal infantry to come up during the morning of July 1, while on the third day Federal mounted attacks checked Stuart's attempts to get in the Federal rear during Pickett's charge.

Much of the employment of Federal cavalry in the war was in dismounted actions where repeating carbines made the Northern force equal to much larger enemy cavalry forces. Federal cavalry units used their horses to move them rapidly to an important sector where, as at Cold Harbor, Virginia, their superior fire power was used with great effect.[38] Mounted charges were also frequently employed, especially to exploit breakthroughs made by the infantry. At Five Forks, Virginia, as noted previously, in a mounted charge Federal cavalry assisted in the capturing of 5,000 Confederate prisoners, at a loss of 800 cavalry and 300 infantry. The cavalry pursued the enemy until nightfall constantly picking up groups of Confederates trying in vain to escape.[39] At Cedar Creek the cavalry, lining the stone walls with dismounted troopers, held the Confederate infantry at bay for hours. Mounted cavalry encouraged the broken infantry to reform and stopped hundreds of fugitives by driving them back to their colors.[40]

Due to lack of weapons and equipment, cavalry in the West was kept inactive long after its organization was completed. As in the East, its strength was dissipated by its being split up into small detachments which were incapable of defeating the large raiding columns of Morgan, Forrest, Chalmers, and Wheeler. The excessive demands on the cavalry for guides, orderlies, and grooms for staff officers further

FEDERAL ARTILLERY IN ACTION

Battery B, 1st Pennsylvania Light Artillery in action during the siege of Petersburg, June 17, 1864. The noted Civil War photographer, Mathew Brady, may be seen in the center, with his hands in his coat pockets.

weakened the Federal cavalry forces in the West. Buell in writing to Halleck, July 23, 1862, emphasized the urgent importance of a larger cavalry force, pointing out that the enemy was throwing large cavalry forces on the 400 miles of railroad communication on which his army was dependent for supplies.[41] The Government responded favorably to this and other appeals with the result that at the Battle of Stone's River, December 31, 1862–January 2, 1863, Rosecrans' cavalry force of 4,000 troopers successfully repulsed enemy cavalry which attacked the Federal rear in the hope of destroying supplies and cutting communications. A few months later Federal cavalry forces were stabbing deep into enemy territory on daring raids. The tactics were similar to those employed in the East. Here again, the superior fire power of the Federal cavalry was in evidence. On November 3, 1863, at Collierville, Tennessee, an enemy brigade attacked a dismounted Federal cavalry regiment armed with revolving rifles. The regiment (2nd Iowa Cavalry), lying on the ground, waited until the advancing brigade was 50 yards away, sprang to its feet, and delivered such a murderous fire that only a few men reached the Federal line.[42] The cavalry forces in the West operated as brigades and divisions until the end of 1864, when General Wilson, as their new chief of cavalry, organized them into a cavalry corps.

ARTILLERY

Cooperating closely with the infantry in both offensive and defensive operations, and making a very significant contribution to final victory was the Federal artillery. The uniform of this arm was similar to that of the infantry except in the piping and insignia. The color for artillery was scarlet which was worn on the short blue jackets and along the seams of the blue trousers. The hat or cap insignia was crossed cannons.

In the early part of the war some foot artillerymen were equipped with a short Roman-type sword,[43]

while mounted artillerymen carried long, excessively-curved sabers. Neither of these weapons was effective in the hand-to-hand fighting that so often resulted from the attempts of Confederate infantry to capture Federal batteries. The revolver was found to be the best weapon for repelling the enemy once they had arrived in the gun positions themselves. After several batteries had been run over and captured, our slow-going ordnance authorities decided to issue revolvers to the cannoneers, but even then many batteries never were so armed.[44] Some field artillery units may have been equipped with a short musket but artillerymen in the defenses of Washington used the regulation-length musket.

The troops of the artillery were divided into two kinds; heavy artillery, and light or field artillery. To the heavy artillery belonged the service of siege, seacoast, and garrison artillery. Railway artillery was also used to a limited extent.

The field artillery contained the batteries which supported the infantry on the field of battle. It consisted of two types: horse artillery, in which all personnel were mounted, and which operated with the cavalry; and horse-drawn artillery, which supported the infantry, the cannoneers either marching at the sides of their pieces, or riding on the caissons and limbers.[45]

Organization of the artillery arm proceeded slowly. In their march to First Bull Run, the batteries not belonging to regiments were attached to brigades. No attempt was made to provide an artillery reserve. One of the batteries, borrowed from the Navy, was hauled by drag-ropes, as were the guns at Bunker Hill in 1775. Elsewhere the Federal forces distributed their artillery in brigades also. In August 1861, General Lyon's army in Missouri was organized into brigades, each of which had its battery; so also with Grant's troops in the Cairo area in October 1861.

On August 23, 1861, the Chief of Artillery, Army of the Potomac, wrote McClellan: "To insure success, it is of vital importance that the army should have an overwhelming force of field artillery. To render this the more effective, the field batteries should, as far as possible, consist of regular troops." McClellan therefore urged that the whole of the Regular artillery be ordered to Washington excepting those batteries absolutely necessary elsewhere. This request resulted in bringing to the Army of the Potomac half the Regular artillery of the United States. When McClellan assumed command of the Army, July 27, 1861, it embraced about 50,000 infantry, less than 1,000 cavalry, and 650 artillerymen manning 9 incomplete batteries aggregating only 30 guns.

In his re-organization, McClellan laid down some basic principles for the artillery arm:

1. Proportion of artillery—2.5-3 pieces per 1000 men.

2. Each field battery to be composed of 4-6 guns, those of each battery to be of uniform caliber.

3. Field batteries to be assigned to divisions (not brigades), in the proportion of 4 batteries per division, one of which should be a Regular battery, the rest volunteers. The captain of the Regulars to command the rest of the division's batteries.

4. The reserve artillery of the whole army to consist of 100 guns.

5. Amount of ammunition to accompany each gun —at least 400 rounds.

6. Provision of a siege train of 50 guns (13-inch seacoast mortars and 100-pounder and 200-pounder Parrotts).

When the three corps embarked on the Peninsular Campaign they were accompanied by 49 batteries aggregating 299 guns of which 100 were in the artillery reserve. Of the 49 batteries, 20 were Regular. At Antietam there were 6 infantry corps and 1 cavalry division—to this total of 19 divisions there were attached 62 batteries, of which 22 were Regulars. At the close of the Peninsular Campaign, General Barry was appointed Inspector of Artillery, and his position as Chief of Artillery, Army of the Potomac, was filled by Henry J. Hunt, who continued in the position to the end of the war. At Fredericksburg, Burnside had 6 corps and 2 cavalry divisions, supported by 67 batteries, of which 26 were Regulars. At Chancellorsville, Hooker had 7 infantry corps and 1 cavalry corps. He had 71 batteries, of which 21 were Regulars.

When the Army of the Potomac took the field in 1864, by an extensive reorganization it had been reduced to 4 infantry corps and 50 batteries of field artillery. This artillery was never in better condition than at the beginning of the Wilderness campaign. The batteries were excellently equipped in personnel and materiel. Due to the nature of the terrain, however, Grant sent most of his field artillery back to Washington. Nevertheless, in place of field artillery,

much siege artillery and many Coehorn mortars were used.

In the Federal armies, other than that of the Potomac, there was not the completeness of organization inaugurated by McClellan; hence in few of them is there found any trace of an artillery reserve. In the Army of the Ohio such an organization was not deemed necessary by either Buell or Rosecrans; but General Thomas, who relieved the latter October 19, 1863, distributed 18 of his batteries to divisions, while a general reserve embraced 12 more including the 6 Regular batteries with that army.[46]

ARTILLERY MATERIEL

The types of artillery pieces used in the land service of the United States were: guns, howitzers, Columbiads, and mortars. Classified as to employment these pieces were termed sea-coast, garrison, siege, and field artillery. "Guns" were long cannon. Smoothbore guns were denominated by the weight of their respective projectiles, while rifled guns were denominated by their bore in inches. "Howitzers" were chambered pieces, of larger caliber than a gun of like weight, and mounted in similar manner. The "Columbiads," guns of much larger caliber than the ordinary gun, were used for throwing solid shot, shells, spherical case, or canister. "Mortars" were the shortest pieces in the service; they were used for high-angle fire, throwing shells, fire-balls, and carcasses (spherical shells with holes and specially designed with a burning composition).[47]

At the outbreak of the war, the entire artillery branch of the United States Army in active service consisted of seven batteries, each of four guns, eighty men, and from forty to sixty horses.[48] The guns were smoothbore six-pounders and twelve-pounder howitzers. There was not a single rifled piece in the service. As late as July 25, 1861, the artillery pieces were of various and in some cases unserviceable calibers.[49] In time the old type of smoothbore guns were replaced by the Napoleon or light twelve-pounder gun-howitzer of about 1200 pounds weight. This gun had a bore diameter of 4.62 inches and fired a spherical projectile with a time fuse. The projectiles were solid shot, case-shot, shell, and canister. For ranges up to 1500 yards this gun was the best type in use; and with case-shot at 800 yards, or canister at 200 yards, it was extremely effective against infantry.

The rifled field guns used extensively in the war were the Parrott ten-pounder and the regulation wrought-iron 3-inch gun. The former weighed 900 pounds, had a bore of 2.9 inches in diameter, and was made of cast-iron, reinforced at the seat of the charge with a wrought-iron jacket which was shrunk on. Some critics claimed this feature to be one of the main defects of the Parrott guns; they frequently broke off just forward of the wrought-iron reinforcing and sometimes blew up with fatal results to their crews.[50] However, some observers believed the fault to lie with the ammunition. The regulation wrought-iron 3-inch gun weighing 820 pounds was built up of sheets of boiler iron wrapped around a central tube or core. The charge of powder for both the Parrott and 3-inch gun was one pound; the projectiles used in them were all elongated and consisted of solid shot, case-shot, shell, and canister. Each of these different types of projectiles weighed about ten pounds. The range of all these rifled field guns at about 12° (the greatest elevation their respective carriages would admit) was from 3000 to 3500 yards, or about 1¾ to 2 miles. With higher elevations, readily procured by the simple improvisation familiar to every artillerist of the day, (that of digging in the trail) ranges of 4000, 5000, or even 6000 yards were obtained.[51] Horse artillery, known also as flying artillery, was usually equipped with 10-pounder rifled guns.[52]

The 1st Connecticut Artillery acted as railway artillery in the Petersburg campaign where they served a 17,000 pound mortar which was mounted on a flatcar pushed by a locomotive. On one occasion, to avoid the tell-tale smoke emitted by a puffing locomotive, the Federals mounted a field gun on a flat car, armored the area around the gun with iron-platting backed by massive beams, and propelled the flatcar with its load by manpower.[53] In loading, a very short sponge staff was used, at one end of which was attached a rammer head. After first swabbing out the bore, the charge, thirty-five pounds of powder, was inserted and rammed down. Then four men, by means of a pair of tongs made for the purpose, lifted the shell and placed it in the muzzle of the mortar; a sharp pointed wire was inserted into the vent to make a hole in the cartridge bag, and next

the primer was inserted into the hole, to which the lanyard was attached by means of a hook to the looped wire in the top of the primer tube. At the command READY the man drew the lanyard tight, and at the command FIRE gave the lanyard a quick pull by throwing his hand and arm down behind him. This drew out the wire in the primer, causing friction which ignited the powder in the tube and cartridge. *Boom* would ring out from the mouth of the mortar, sending on its aerial flight the messengers of death and destruction.[54] The 200-pound exploding shell, which went nearly two miles, would crush and explode any ordinary field magazine, terrorizing the Confederate gunners, and silencing their enfilading batteries on Chesterfield Heights.[55]

Siege artillery before the war consisted of cast-iron 12-, 18-, and 24-pounders weighing respectively 3600, 4900, and 5800 pounds; 8-inch howitzers; and 8- and 10-inch mortars. Their maximum range was 1¼ miles.[56] These guns could not breach beyond 1000 yards. Siege guns were use at Fort Pulaski, Fort Mason, Yorktown, Richmond, and Corinth that effectively breached at ranges of 1700 to 2000 yards. The difference is explained by the better type of rifled guns used during the war by Federal siege artillery. Some of the principal[57] siege guns were: the 12-, 18-, and 24-pounder guns; the 8-inch and 24-pounder howitzers; and 8- and 10-inch Columbiads; and the 8- and 10-inch mortars. The landing, transporting, mounting, and service of pieces of such immense weight (the lightest weighing more than 9000 pounds and the heaviest about 17000 pounds)[58] was of course attended with considerable difficulty.

Not a single member of the 1st Connecticut, except the colonel, had any prior experience. They learned their new duties, managed to displace their massive

RAILWAY ARTILLERY
In front of Petersburg, 1864. Showing "Dictator," the 13-inch mortar that was able to destroy hostile field pieces at a range of nearly two miles, using 200-lb. projectiles.

weapon during all the movements of the army, and served it with great ability during the retreat from the Peninsula and later at Fredericksburg.

At Malvern Hill the field artillery saved the army. The Confederate attacks were smashed by sixty pieces massed in rear of the Federal infantry. At Fredericksburg the siege artillery supported the infantry assaults but were unable to achieve the effective counterbattery work that was desired. Unfortunately many Federal infantrymen were killed by premature bursts from shells with defective fuzes fired by the siege artillery.[59] By 1864, the danger of using defective fuses or making wrong range estimates was minimized as the officers gained skill, and, in the case of siege artillery, solid shot was used as it did not explode and hence was safer at long ranges.[60] In connection with its operations, siege artillery at times used calcium searchlights that were effective to about 3000 yards.[61]

Seacoast artillery used 8-, 10-, 13-, and 15-inch smoothbore guns weighing from 9240 to 49000 pounds, whose projectiles weighed from 65 to 430 pounds. Parrott rifles used as seacoast artillery were 100-, 200-, and 300-pounders the weights of which ranged from 9600 to 25000 pounds; mortars used were of 10- and 13-inch weighing 9500 and 17000 pounds respectively. An experimental gun with a 20-inch bore diameter, weighing 116,000 pounds and throwing a solid shot of 1,000 pounds, was cast [62] but little use of it was made during the war. A new method of hollow casting and internal cooling was invented and perfected by Major T. J. Rodman of the Ordnance Department which greatly reduced the danger of flaws from cooling in the manufacture of large guns.[63]

Although the Confederates used some Whitworth breech-loading cannon, the Federals used muzzle-loading guns almost exclusively.

Further information on material is given in Chapter 10.

ARTILLERY AMMUNITION

The projectiles were used to secure effects according to their special capabilities. Solid shot was employed at long range and against troops in column because of its greater accuracy and penetrating power. Shells or case-shot were used against cavalry in column and was effective because of the disorder caused by their bursting among the horses. Canister, shrapnel, or grape were used only at short ranges.[64] Grapeshot was employed against infantry lines because of the wide dispersive effect of the balls. This type of projectile generally contained nine balls, arranged in layers of three each and kept in position by a series of plates which were held together by a vertical rod secured by nuts on each end. At discharge of the projectile from the piece these balls

CIVIL WAR LOGISTICS
Some of Grant's replacement artillery and ammunition at City Point, Virginia, 1864.

fanned out, producing a horizontal cone of balls very effective against the frontal attack of a line of infantry though somewhat less effective against an oblique attack. Similar in principle was the canister projectile which consisted of a large number of iron or leaden balls in a cylinder of tin which was torn asunder at the discharge of the gun. When the exigency of the battle warranted, double and even triple canister were used.[65] Shrapnel projectiles were shells filled with musket balls which were packed into a mass of sulphur and resin. A charge of powder fitted into their base of the cylinder, ignited by either a time fuze, propelled the balls out the front end like a giant shotgun. But it was effective only with air bursts, properly adjusted. Very extensively used also were shells that exploded either by percussion or time fuse, the shell breaking up in irregular but substantial fragments.

Further information on ammunition is given in Chapter 10.

ANIMAL TRANSPORT

The problem of training horses for the field artillery was aggravated by the lack of good horses early in the war. In 1861 this defect was due in some degree to the lack of adequate care of those horses already acquired by the Government. In December 1861 the Washington depot consisted of half-open sheds where the horses were tied to mangers without straw or other bedding and so closely packed together that it was impossible for them to lie down. Of the 4,000 horses at this depot there was not one that was actually fit for artillery service.[66]

The process of teaching correct care of horses was a long one for many of the volunteer batteries. Campaigning always took a heavy toll of artillery horses both in killed and disabled. Most of the artillery and cavalry horses of the Army of the Potomac were disabled by *thrush*, a rotting of the hoof caused by prolonged standing in mud, during Burnside's campaign. In the Second Army Corps one battery alone had to turn in 60 unserviceable horses. Many guns were sent back to Washington because they lacked serviceable animals to pull them. Strangely enough, no mules were affected by this hoof disease.[67] After Hooker took command of the Army of the Potomac there was a noticeable improvement in the care of animals in all branches of the service and at a review held in September 1863, "the artillery looked even more serviceable than the infantry, and, independent of the large number of guns, was well horsed and well manned."[68]

EMPLOYMENT OF ARTILLERY

In combat the guns were generally placed in either the second or third line of defense to support the infantry in the front line.[69] Professor Lowe and some of his assistant aeronauts directed artillery fire from balloons on the Peninsula and in the West.[70] It was customary to protect artillery batteries from capture by assigning infantry companies to their defense; the two branches were mutually supporting. Federal artillerymen defended their guns with commendable tenacity, and cases are on record where guns were limbered up and brought away when the enemy was already within the battery position.[71]

The original expectation of creating a field artillery overwhelmingly stronger than that of the enemy was never realized. The Confederates were equally alive to the importance of this measure, meeting gun for gun the artillery of the Federal Army. At Antietam the total number of guns on each side was probably about the same. At Gettysburg, Meade's 67 batteries were opposed by 68 Confederate. When preparing for the final struggle in the campaign of 1865, the Army of Northern Virginia contained 81 batteries.[72]

Federal artillery distinguished itself in every battle from Bull Run to Appomattox, and while it is impracticable to compare it with the other arms in the Federal service, its excellent fighting ability materially raised the fighting morale of Federal infantry in many closely-contested struggles.

ENGINEERS

The contribution of the engineers toward military operations was exceedingly significant and much of the credit belongs to the Engineer troops of the Regular Army. Although these troops consisted of a single company at the outbreak of war, they were later expanded by recruiting to a battalion of four companies.[73] This battalion, with the 16th and 50th New York Volunteer Engineers, comprised the engineer troops of the Army of the Potomac. Another New York Volunteer Engineer Regiment, the 1st, served in South Carolina and built the longest pontoon bridge of the war at Richmond, Virginia, May 1865. A colored regiment, the 1st Louisiana Engineers, served at Port Hudson, in the Red River campaign, and at the siege of Mobile.

In the West, the 1st United States Veteran Volunteer Engineer Regiment served with the Army of the Cumberland, while the 1st Missouri Engineers served at New Madrid, Corinth, Holly Springs, in the Vicksburg campaign, and before Atlanta. The 1st Michigan Engineers was composed almost entirely of mechanics and engineers. Like the other engineer units it was a large regiment—1800 strong—containing 12 companies of 150 men each. In repairing the damaged railroads along the lines of communications these men built bridges and trestles whose combined length could be measured by the mile, and erected blockhouses by the score. The construction of some of these bridges, their size and height, and the speed with which they were rebuilt, constituted some of the most impressive feats of military engineering. This regiment could fight also; one detachment won distinction by its brilliant and

ENGINEERS IN ACTION
Upper wharf at Belle Plain, erected by Corps of Engineers, May 15, 1864.

successful defense of the army trains which were attacked by Wheeler's cavalry during the battle of Stone's River.[74] During active operations the engineers worked well in advance of the army. In general, the Corps' duties related to the construction of permanent and field fortifications and the construction of works for the attack and defense of places. It was responsible for preparation of passage of rivers, for the movements and operations of armies in the field, and the necessary reconnaissances and surveys for the execution of these functions.[75] In addition to its service in the field, the Corps was responsible for the seacoast and lake defenses and the preservation and repair of the Atlantic harbors and seawalls.[76]

Until March 31, 1863,[77] the Corps of Topographical Engineers was responsible for all the topographic, geodetic, and hydrographic works.[78] The need for accurate military maps was urgent both in the East and West. The Topographical Engineers were very busy on the Peninsula and their commander, Brigadier General A. A. Humphreys, was forced to use civilians to supplement the small staff allotted him. These civilians were furnished by the Superintendent of the Coast Survey, Professor Bache, and from other civilian sources.[79] Owing to the entire absence of reliable topographical maps, the labor of this Corps were difficult and arduous in the extreme; the men frequently obtained their information under fire and casualties were not infrequent. During the Peninsular Campaign it was found impractical to draw a distinct line of demarkation between the duties of the two corps of engineers, so that reconnaissance of roads, lines of intrenchment, fields of battle, and of the position of the enemy as well as the constrution of siege and defensive works, were habitually performed by details from either corps, as the convenience of the service demanded. During the Antietam campaign General McClellan united the two corps and this consolidation was made permanent for all engineer forces in the Army the following March. The Topographical Engineers in the West were attached to brigade, division, and corps staffs, and the highest engineer and department headquarters. This resulted in a much greater dispersion of map experts than McClellan had on the Peninsula where he tended to keep them all concentrated at army headquarters.

The Western armies were too far from Washington to be able to count on assistance from there and it was essential that each large unit have a complete map establishment of its own. The office of the chief topographical engineer in the West had a printing press, two lithographic presses, and one photographic establishment with complete arrangements for map mounting and a full corps of draftsmen and assistants. During the first year of the war, maps were reproduced by photograph, but unless a very fine and expensive lens was used the various sheets were distorted at the borders which prevented the sections from being joined accurately. Other disadvantages of the photographic maps were that they faded when exposed to sun light and copies could not be made at night or in the rain. Much superior were the maps reproduced from lithographic stones and presses which were, however, too heavy for transportation in an active campaign and were used only in the rear echelon.

The best device used was a photo-printing outfit which used a system of chemical baths. The printing was done by tracing the required map on thin paper and laying it over a sheet coated with nitrate of silver. The sun's rays passing through the tissue paper blackened the prepared paper except under the ink lines, thus making a white map on a black ground. As new information came in the maps were altered; occasionally there would be several editions of the same map in a day. Data for maps were obtained by interrogation of refugees, spies, prisoners and "any and all persons familiar with the country in front of us."[80] Copies for the cavalry were printed directly on muslin, as such maps could be washed clean whenever soiled and could not be injured by hard service. Many officers sent handkerchiefs to the topographical engineer office and had maps printed on them. The Corps of Engineers took over the function of map making after its absorption of the Corps of Topographical Engineers; the latter became the topographical branch of the Corps of Engineers. The number of sheets of maps furnished during the last year of the war by the topographical branch to the armies in the field was 20,938.[81]

EMPLOYMENT

The Corps of Engineers planned and laid out the permanent fortifications which protected Washington and other important centers. In the field they designed and supervised the construction of defensive fortifications; their siege works, whether at Yorktown or at Petersburg, were of high order. Although some of their positions on the Petersburg front were laid out at night, no corrections in their general line of fortifications were necessary. "Slashing" was necessary in building a line of works through forests. In this work the engineers were aided by infantry details who drew their tools from wagons maintained by the Quartermaster's Department. In the defense of railroads and vital road junctions the engineers constructed blockhouses of rectangular or octagonal shape. While a few of these blockhouses were built around Washington, they were most generally found protecting the long lines of railroad communications in the West where Confederate raiders were especially active. In one of his raids the Confederate Forrest used Greek fire to burn a bridge defended by a blockhouse.[82] General Sherman was favorably impressed with the blockhouse type of railroad defense.[83]

The engineers were responsible for making roads passable for the army; this was done by corduroying sloughs, building trestle bridges across small streams, and laying pontoon bridges over large streams and rivers. Some of the largest trestle bridges were built in the West, while pontoons found more general use in the East. The bridge equipage for the Army of the Potomac on the Peninsula consisted of bateaux with the anchors and flooring material (French model), trestles, and engineer's tools, with the necessary wagons for their transportation.[84] In August 1862, troops, including artillery, crossed the Chickahominy on a pontoon bridge which was about 1400 feet in length and was built under direction of officers of the 50th New York Engineers.[85] The engineers under Pope used rough timbers and improvised derricks,[86] in addition to the pontoons, while Burnside's pontoon bridges over the Rappahannock River before Fredericksburg were more elaborate.[87] In the Chancellorsville campaign, the engineers laid a 390-foot bridge in 70 minutes. The bridge, train, wagons, and boats had been masked in dense woods a mile from the river to be crossed and the entire operation was smoothly and rapidly accomplished.[88] One of the most spectacular engineering feats in the East was the construction of a 2,000 foot pontoon bridge in deep water (in some places as deep as 85 feet) with a very strong current. This was in the midst of Grant's 1864 campaign and the bridge carried about all the Army of the Potomac with its trains and artillery.[89] The total number of pontoon bridges built in Grant's 1864 campaign in the East was 38; their aggregate length was 6,458 feet. Pontoon trains were modelled after the French wooden trains and the Russian canvas trains. The light canvas boats were efficient and worked quite well in the terrain in which they were used during the war [90] but were found not to be as durable as the wooden boats. However, their light weight was a great advantage in transportation and was no hindrance in bearing heavy weight. Canvas pontoon boats were also used individually for secret crossings of streams when the building of pontoon bridges would have been slow and vulnerable to enemy observation. These canvas boats could carry infantry with full field equipment, and artillery pieces and caissons; they were ideally adapted for use as landing barges.[91]

The services of Federal engineer troops were ceaseless; although their losses were small in killed and wounded, as compared with the "fighting infantry," yet every engineer organization was recruited more

PONTOON BRIDGE OVER THE JAMES

than twice over the make up for the losses due to plain wear and tear. They were put in line of battle at various times, acting as infantry, and were just as likely as the other troops to see action. However, they suffered mainly from the fire of sharpshooters while performing their normal duties, without arms and often without infantry support. Troops crossed bridges, were guided along freshly cleared roads, and their officers used maps—all without any thought as to who made all this possible.[92]

CORPS OF MILITARY AERONAUTS

Enjoying the same quasi-military status as the telegraphers were the military aeronauts of the Federal balloon corps. These aeronauts were all rated as civilian employees and had no command functions of a military nature. Their families received no pensions and the aeronauts themselves were probably liable to summary execution as spies in the event of capture. They wore ordinary civilian clothes that were suitable for field service. A few attempted to wear "B.C." (Balloon Corps) or "A.D." (Aeronautic Department) as insignia on their headgear but these insignia were not official. The aeronauts soon discarded them as they only provoked amusement.[93]

In the decade of the fifties ballooning had become widely known in the United States. Aeronauts gave exhibition flights and made ascensions at numerous county fairs and urban gatherings throughout the country, and constant publicity in the press soon popularized their work far and wide.[94] Several of this ballooning fraternity who offered their services to the government during the war served on various fronts, both East and West. The sight of the huge gas bags with their baskets rising slowly above the ground, often subject to enemy fire, soon became commonplace to Federal ground forces in many areas. One of the most interested observers was Count Ferdinand Von Zeppelin of the Prussian Army who visited America to study the Federal employment of balloons in warfare.[95]

Although there were several military aeronauts in the Federal service, the chief of them all was T. S. C. Lowe who missed participation in the first battle at Bull Run because he was unable to procure men, transportation, and means for inflation of his balloon.[96] Shortly afterwards, another aeronaut ascended 3,000 feet from the deck of a tugboat in Hampton Roads and observed the enemy beyond Newport News.[97] Most of the balloons operated in the East, where at first they were assigned to the Corps of Topographical Engineers,[98] and thus came under the control of the Chief Topographical Engineer of McClellan's staff.[99] In the long inaction of the Army of the Potomac around Washington from July 1861 to March 1862, the balloon corps under Lowe operated two balloons, making ascensions above the lines to observe the enemy camps where often the ob-

server could estimate almost down to a platoon th size of the Confederate forces by the camp fire Often these ascensions were rendered doubly perilou because "some stupid sentinel, ignorant whether th aerial voyager was friend or enemy, would be sur to fire at the indiscreet individual who thus hovere over their heads."[100] Such incidents convinced th aeronauts of the advisability of clearly identifyin their aircraft. Accordingly, some balloons or baske were marked with red, white, and blue buntin the "Constitution" was decorated with a large po trait of George Washington; the "Union" had gigantic spread eagle and the Stars and Stripe while the "Intrepid" bore its name conspicuously o its side.[101] By January 1862, Lowe had seven balloon in operation.[102] On the Peninsula the balloon cor under Lowe used mobile field generators that func tioned efficiently most of the time, but during th Battle of Fair Oaks it was necessary to transfer ga from one balloon to another to save time.

McClellan permitted the addition of a telegraphi train to the aeronautic establishment, thus relievin it of dependence upon the Military Telegraph Corp for telegraphic equipment. At those times whe aerial telegraph was used, operators were borrowe from the Telegraph Corps or from the headquarter of various high commands. When it was impractica to use the aerial telegraph, written messages, wit a stone or other weight wrapped up in them, wer dropped to an officer below, who sent them b courier to their destinations.[103] By means of th telegraph, Lowe participated in the first artiller fire direction with aerial observation in America history. A telegraph line was run from the balloo car to the gun positions and the effect of each sho was communicated to a general officer more tha three miles distant from the point of observation.[10] Flags were also used instead of telegraph fo artillery fire direction. However, observation, not fir direction, was Lowe's main function and his con stant surveillance of the enemy lines and position was of definite informational value.[105] After th Peninsular Campaign, Lowe designed a new system of long distance visual signalling by means o small balloons, which bore conspicuous markings fo day communication and different colored flares fo night operations. He also constructed a powerfu oxyhydrogen or calcium light apparatus to facilitat night operations of the balloonists when secrecy o position was not essential.[106] When Lowe was take ill shortly before the battle of Malvern Hill, anothe aeronaut[107] assumed charge of the balloon corps and remained its acting head until the army was with drawn from the Peninsula. Again, he became chie of the Corps after the Chancellorsville disaster, and kept this rank until the balloon train was disbande during the march to Gettysburg.[108]

The history of the Corps was indeed a checkere

MILITARY AERONAUTS
Inflating the balloon *Intrepid* during the Battle of Fair Oaks. Professor Lowe is in civilian clothes with his right hand on the balloon.

one. Beginning its existence under the Corps of Topographical Engineers, it enjoyed its greatest prosperity under Brigadier General A. A. Humphreys, Chief Topographical Engineer on McClellan's staff. After the Peninsular Campaign, it came under the control of General Ingalls, Chief Quartermaster of the Army of the Potomac. On April 7, 1863, the Balloon Corps was transferred from the immediate supervision of the Quartermaster's Department and placed under the Corps of Engineers, subject to the direction of Captain Cyrus B. Comstock, Chief Engineer of the Army of the Potomac. Comstock disliked Lowe's freedom and found much to criticize in the civilian's conduct of purchasing supplies. There appears to be no question here of Lowe's honesty, but at times the pressure of time forced him to make purchases of balloon supplies without going through official channels. Comstock was later superseded as

Chief Engineer by Brigadier General G. K. Warren. During the movement north to intercept Lee's invasion of Pennsylvania, General Hooker ordered the Signal Corps to take over the Balloon Corps and its administration but Colonel Myer protested that he had neither the men nor the appropriation with which to operate the additional branch of the service. Thereupon the balloon train was ordered back to Washington and disbanded.[109] It is interesting to conjecture what might have happened at Gettysburg and later if the Balloon Corps had been permitted to operate throughout the remainder of the war. At least one Confederate general never could understand why the North abandoned balloons early in 1863. "Even if the observers never saw anything, they would have been worth all they cost for the annoyance and delays they caused us in trying to keep our movements out of sight." [110]

NOTES CHAPTER 5

1. Craighill, William P., *The Army Officer's Pocket Companion, Passim.*
2. Russell, Vol. 2, pp. 129, 139.
3. Crowninshield, pp. 9-10.
4. In the West the situation was somewhat better.
5. Russell, Vol. 2, p. 157.
6. *Battles and Leaders*, Vol. 2, p. 429.
7. Crowninshield, p. 6.
8. *Ibid.*
9. Organization of Regiments and Companies of the Volunteer Army of the United States. "General Order No. 126," War Department, September 6, 1862, *Regiment of Cavalry—*

12 companies or troops
1 colonel
1 lieutenant colonel
3 majors
1 surgeon
1 assistant surgeon
1 regimental adjutant (an extra lt.)
1 regimental quartermaster (an extra lt.)
1 regimental commissary (an extra lt.)
1 chaplain
1 sergeant major
1 quartermaster sergeant
1 commissary sergeant
2 hospital stewards
1 saddler sergeant
1 chief farrier or blacksmith

Company or Troop of Cavalry
1 captain
1 first lieutenant
1 second lieutenant
1 first sergeant
1 quartermaster sergeant
1 commissary sergeant
5 sergeants
8 corporals
2 teamsters
2 farriers or blacksmiths
1 saddler
1 wagoner
78 privates.

(There being no bands allowed, and no musicians authorized for companies, 2 musicians may be enlisted for each company. They will be rated and paid as privates)

Regiment of Artillery—12 Batteries
1 colonel
1 lieutenant colonel
1 major for every 4 batteries
1 adjutant (not an extra lt.)
1 quartermaster (not an extra lt.)
1 chaplain
1 sergeant major
1 quartermaster sergeant
1 commissary sergeant
1 hospital steward
Battery of Artillery
1 captain
1 first lieutenant
1 second lieutenant
1 first sergeant
1 quartermaster sergeant
4 sergeants
8 corporals
2 musicians
2 artificers

1 wagoner
122 privates

(As a general rule, artillery will be called for, and received, by batteries, thus rendering the field and staff unnecessary.)

10. Crowninshield, p. 31.
11. *Ibid.*, pp. 16-30.
12. Denison, Frederic, *Sabres and Spurs: The First Regiment Rhode Island Cavalry in the Civil War*, p. 31.
13. *House Executive Documents*, 37 Cong., 2 Sess., Document 60, p. 27.
14. *Army and Navy Journal*, Vol. 1 (August 29, 1863), p. 3.
15. Report of Secretary of War, December 1, 1862, *House Executive Documents*, 37 Cong., 3 Sess., Document 1, p. 72.
16. *Army and Navy Journal*, Vol. 1 (August 29, 1863), p. 3.
17. Report of Secretary of War, March 1, 1865, *House Executive Documents*, 38 Cong., 2 Sess., Document 83, p. 167.
18. United States War Department, "General Order No. 259," August 1, 1863, *General Orders for 1863.*
19. *Ibid.*, General Order No. 236," July 28, 1863.
20. *Ibid.*, "General Order No. 237," July 28, 1863.
21. Crowninshield, pp. 121-122.
22. *Official Records*, First Series, Vol. 36, Part 1, p. 787.
23. *Ibid.*, First Series, Vol. 5, p. 13.
24. McClellan, p. 118.
25. *Army and Navy Journal*, Vol. 1 (November 14, 1863), p. 185.
26. The Remington was about as popular.
27. Halleck to Governor Blair, August 8, 1863. Manuscript letter in Burton Historical Collection.
28. *Photographic History*, Vol. 4, p. 58.
29. Maury, Dabney, *Recollections of a Virginian*, p. 107.
30. *Photographic History*, Vol. 4, p. 62.
31. Bigelow, p. 488.
32. *Army and Navy Journal*, Vol. 1 (December 5, 1863), p. 229. This was the cavalry model of the Mann patent.
33. *Ibid.* See also *Medical and Surgical History of the War of the Rebellion*, Part 3, Medical Volume, p. 872.
34. Preston, N. D., *History of the Tenth Regiment of Cavalry New York State Volunteers*, pp. 54-56.
35. Bigelow, p. 72.
36. *Ibid.*, pp. 73-74.
37. Many Southern writers so commented after the war.
38. *Official Records*, First Series, Vol. 36, Part 1, p. 794.
39. Page, C. A., *Letters of a War Correspondent*, pp. 295-296.
40. *Official Records*, First Series, Vol. 43, Part 1, p. 449.
41. Van Horne, Vol. 1, p. 163.
42. *Official Records*, First Series, Vol. 31, Part 1, p. 245.
43. Cowles, p. 386.
44. Buell, Augustus, *The Cannoneer*, p. 58.
45. Board of Artillery Officers, *Instruction for Field Artillery*, 1860, p. 1. A battery of mountain howitzers were used in 1861. Saunier, pp. 13-14.
46. Berkheimer, William E., *Historical Sketch of the Artillery, United States Army*, pp. 79-103.
47. Roberts, Joseph, Colonel, *Hand-Book of Artillery* (1863) pp. 10, 28-37. See Weller, Jac. "The Field Artillery of the Civil War," Journal of Military Collector and Historian, Vol. 5, No. 2 (June 1953); No. 3 (September 1953).
48. *Army and Navy Journal*, Vol. 1 (September 12, 1863) p. 39.
49. *Official Records*, First Series, Vol. 5, p. 67.
50. Buell, p. 147. Buell said that "if anything could justify desertion by a cannoneer, it would be assignment to a Par

ott battery!" See also Cowles, p. 128; *Senate Miscellaneous Documents*, 38 Cong., 2 Sess., Document 47, pp. 1-32; Plates to 34 in Gillmore.

51. *Army and Navy Journal*, Vol. 1 (September 12, 1863), p. 39.

52. *Photographic History*, Vol. 5, p. 33. See also: Benjamin F. Taylor, *Pictures of Life in Camp and Field*, pp. 8-9. 3rd Edition, Chicago, 1884).

53. *Ibid.*, Vol. 3, pp. 184-187, p. 199.

54. Rhodes, (Battery "B" 1st Rhode Island Light Artillery), pp. 313-314.

55. *Photographic History*, Vol. 5, p. 51.

56. *Army and Navy Journal*, Vol. 1 (September 19, 1863), p. 51.

57. A complete classification and list is given in *Instructions for Heavy Artillery*, 1860.

58. *Photographic History*, Vol. 5, pp. 23, 25.

59. Cowles, p. 499.

60. At Petersburg siege artillery sometimes fired at ranges of 1700 yards.

61. *Frank Leslie's Illustrated Weekly*, Vol. 12 (July 6, 1861), p. 117; *Battles and Leaders*, Vol. 4, p. 25.

62. *Army and Navy Journal*, Vol. 1 (September 26, 1863), p. 68.

63. *Ibid. Official Records*, Third Series, Vol. 5, p. 1042. There was a total of 7,892 cannon issued from 1861 to 1866. *Ibid.*

64. United States War Department, "General Order No. 45," February 16, 1863, *General Orders for 1863*.

65. Double canister was fairly common. It consisted of loading the cannon with two canister projectiles instead of one. At Gettysburg some batteries used triple loads. Buell, p. 76.

66. Cowles, pp. 117-118.

67. Walker, p. 139.

68. Agassiz, p. 11.

69. *Ibid.*, p. 202.

70. Haydon, F. S., *Aeronautics in the Union and Confederate Armies*, Vol. 1, p. 213.

71. *Civil War Papers*, Vol. 1, p. 207.

72. Berkheimer, p. 93.

73. These 4 companies were from Regular Army.

74. Fox, pp. 511-512.

75. United States War Department *Revised Regulations for the Army of the United States* 1861, Article 46.

76. Report of the Secretary of War, (November 22, 1865), Vol. 1, *House Executive Documents*, 39 Cong., 1 Sess., Document 1, pp. 913-942.

77. The date it became an integral part of the Corps of Engineers. United States War Department, "General Order No. 79," March 31, 1863. *General Orders for 1863*.

78. Comte de Paris, Vol. 1, p. 26.

79. *Official Records*, First Series. Vol. 5, p. 25.

80. Van Horne, Thomas, *History of the Army of the Cumberland*, Vol. 2, pp. 456-458.

81. Annual Report of the Secretary of War, March 1, 1865, *House Executive Documents*, 38 Cong., 2 Sess., Document 83, p. 31.

82. Van Horne, Vol. 2, pp. 439-458.

83. Sherman, Vol. 2, pp. 146, 398.

84. *Official Records*, First Series, Vol. 5, p. 25.

85. Rhodes, (Battery "B" 1st Rhode Island Light Artillery), p. 113.

86. *Photographic History*, Vol. 2, pp. 18-19.

87. *Ibid.*, p. 91.

88. *Ibid.*, Vol. 5, p. 223.

89. Report of Secretary of War, March 1, 1865, *House Executive Documents*, 38 Cong., 2 Sess., Document 83, p. 34.

90. *Ibid.*, November 22, 1865, *House Executive Documents*, 39 Cong., 1 Sess., Document 1, Vol. 1, pp. 943-944.

91. *Photographic History*, Vol. 5, p. 235; Vol. 3, p. 121.

92. Thompson, Gilbert, p. 100.

93. Haydon, Vol. 1, pp. 269, 279. Their chief, "Colonel" T. S. C. Lowe, was so addressed by courtesy; he never held a commission.

94. *Ibid.*, p. 33.

95. *Photographic History*, Vol. 1, p. 113.

96. *Official Records*, Third Series, Vol. 3, pp. 256-257.

97. La Mountain, who made this ascent August 10, 1861. *Annual Cyclopedia*, 1862, p. 184.

98. *Official Records*, Third Series, Vol. 3, p. 259.

99. Haydon, Vol. 1, p. 230.

100. Comte de Paris, Vol. 1, pp. 261, 282.

101. *Photographic History*, Vol. 8, p. 377.

102. Haydon, Vol. 1, p. 233.

103. Bigelow, p. 20.

104. This first took place on September 24, 1861. *Official Records*, Third Series, Vol. 3, pp. 262-263.

105. *Ibid.*, First Series, Vol. 5, p. 32.

106. *Ibid.*, Third Series, Vol. 3, p. 293.

107. James Allen. Haydon, Vol. 1, p. 55.

108. *Ibid.* Three balloons were in operation in the Chancellorsville campaign. Bigelow, p. 20.

109. Haydon, Vol. 1, pp. 291-292.

110. Alexander, E. P. (Brigadier General C.S.A.), *Battles and Leaders*, Vol. 3, p. 358 (note).

CHAPTER 6

The Technical Services

IN THIS chapter are grouped, somewhat arbitrarily, a number of branches and semi-military agencies which today would be called technical services. These are the Signal Corps, the Military Telegraph Service, the U. S. Military Railroads, the Ordnance Department, and the Medical Department. Today the Signal Corps, the Ordnance Department, and the Medical Department also have supply responsibilities, but in 1861-65 their functions, except for the Ordnance Department, were almost entirely of a service nature. The Ordnance Department was also responsible for design, procurement, and issue of various weapons and items of materiel.

SIGNAL CORPS

There was no Signal Corps in the Federal army in 1861. The entire signal force consisted of one officer, Major Albert J. Myer, who had been appointed Signal Officer of the Army June 27, 1860. Myer, a former Army surgeon, had used torch and flag signals in minor Indian combats with some success. He served on McDowell's staff at Bull Run.[1] Up to 1863, Myer remained the only officer actually commissioned in the signal service; all others were simply *acting* signal officers on detached service from their regiments. In the interim between Bull Run and the Peninsular campaign, Myer tried in vain to get electric field telegraphs and other equipment and it was only when the army was fairly in the field that the plans began to receive favorable attention.[2] One signal train, partially completed, was the first movable telegraphic train of which there is record. McClellan gives Myer credit for first using a successful signal system in large operations.[3] Myer stated that an appropriation of $42,450.00 for signal equipment and expenses would be necessary for the fiscal year ending June 30, 1863,[4] but it was not until March 24, 1863, that the Signal Corps was organized.[5] The impetus for the organization of a Signal Corps resulted from the appearance of Major Myer before the Military Committee of the Senate. Myer stressed the fact that the Confederate Congress had already organized a signal service while the Federal army needed a definite organization for the acting signal corps which had already been serving for eighteen months.[6]

ORGANIZATION

The Signal Corps as organized consisted of one Chief Signal Officer of the Army (a colonel), one lieutenant colonel, two majors to act as inspectors, and one captain assisted by a number of lieutenants[7] for each army corps or military department. For each officer of the Signal Corps there were to be enlisted or detailed one sergeant and six privates who were to receive the pay of similar grades of engineer troops. No officer or enlisted man could serve in the Corps until he had been examined and approved by a military board to be convened for that purpose by the Secretary of War.[8] Boards were set up April 28, 1863, to examine officer candidates in the three R's, elementary chemistry, elementary natural philosophy, surveying, topography, field signals, field telegraphs, and the conduct of signal communications in the field.[9] By a general order of May 18, 1863, incompetent or inexperienced officers were prohibited from transmitting signal messages under any authority whatsoever, and signal communications were to be treated as confidential at all times.[10]

The office of Chief Signal Officer of the Army was three-fold in character. It was the headquarters of the Signal Corps; it collected, completed, and filed its records. Acting as advisory superintendent and controlling authority of the special duties of the corps, it assigned officers and men to signal duty. A second important function of the office was in the purchase and disbursement of office supplies and signal equipment to the various detachments of the corps in the field. Lastly, the office examined signal accounts and returns of signal equipment held by officers responsible to the Government for such property. Myer was appointed Chief Signal Officer on September 18, 1863, his appointment to date from March 3, 1863. Because of difficulty over the military telegraph with Secretary of War Stanton he was relieved November 10, 1863. His successor, Lieutenant Colonel W. J. L. Nicodemus, was relieved

December 26, 1864, for publishing documents without the knowledge or sanction of the Secretary of War.[11] The third incumbent of the office, Colonel B. F. Fisher, served to the end of the war.

The Corps developed rather slowly; the average number of officers on duty in December 1863, was but 198. In his report of that month, the Secretary of War admitted that the full capacity of the Corps had not yet been developed because of the different opinions entertained by commanding officers as to its value. Most of these officers conceded that the Corps had been useful in combined land and naval operations while commanding officers of Western armies commended it favorably.[12] On November 1, 1864, the Corps numbered 168 officers and 1,350 enlisted men, distributed in detachments among the armies in the field and the military departments.[13] These detachments consisted usually of four officers and eight enlisted men for each division of infantry.

EMPLOYMENT

Signal flags were used by day and torches by night; when possible signal towers were erected to increase the range of observation. Code and cipher were used. The code was given to the officers only and when they had memorized the characters it was destroyed.[14] Cipher discs were also used; the cipher itself was changed daily, sometimes oftener. In sending a long message it would be changed a number of times.[15] Lines of flag and torch communication were established from one part of the army to another, often 20 or 30 miles long, and were maintained day and night for weeks and even months. Repeating stations operated along the line at necessary intervals while the telescopes in the stations were manned by reliefs. At each station enlisted men worked the flags or torches while an officer would call out the numbers indicating the letters

SIGNAL STATION ON ELK RIDGE NEAR THE ANTIETAM

of the message. Signal flares were also used. The use of the telegraph by the Corps created much friction with the Military Telegraph Service and was kept at a minimum. This friction resulted in the relief of Colonel Myer from his position as Chief Signal Officer nor was he restored to that position until after the war.

MILITARY TELEGRAPH SERVICE

Entirely independent of the Signal Corps was the United States Military Telegraph Service which, while nominally a branch of the Quartermaster's Department, was in reality a separate organization

SIGNAL STATION ON STONY MOUNTAIN

At the beginning of the Wilderness campaign Meade had a signal station on this low hill 5 miles south of Brandy Station. In the distance is Clark's Mountain, where Lee had a similar installation.

which reported directly to and received orders directly from the Secretary of War.[16] Comprising all the telegraph lines and offices in the United States this Corps enabled the War Department to be in direct communication with every arsenal, general military depot, military prison, barracks, rendezvous, camp, and fort in the Union. Every message to and from them passed through Stanton's office and was deciphered there. The War Department had controlled the telegraph in Washington from the beginning of the war; militia on its orders took over the telegraph in that city on April 19, 1861.[17] At the same time President Lincoln called on Thomas A. Scott (who also acted as assistant to the Secretary of War) to restore the Capital's communications that had been cut at Baltimore. Assisting Scott was Andrew Carnegie.[18] During 1861, these two men rendered valuable service in keeping the telegraphic communication between Washington and other points in operation. Early the next year the President by virtue of Congressional act took military possession of all telegraph lines in the United States. At this time E. S. Sanford was appointed military supervisor of all telegraphic messages throughout the country while Anson Stager was made military superintendent of all telegraphic lines and offices in the United States.[19] On April 8, 1862, Stager was commissioned a colonel and assistant quartermaster and appointed as military superintendent of telegraph lines throughout the United States.[20]

The field service of the Military Telegraph Service was functioning well as early as June 1861, when McDowell's headquarters were very rapidly connected with the lesser units by telegraph lines of insulated wire which when on the ground, would not be cut by heavy artillery traffic.[21] However, there was no telegraphic communication from the War Department during the critical days of the Bull Run campaign and Patterson later claimed that the first information he received of McDowell's retreat was in a Philadelphia paper three days after the battle.[22] The telegraphic operations of the Army of the Potomac on the Peninsula and in Maryland were superintended by Major Thomas T. Eckert and were under the immediate direction of a civilian, who, with a corps of operators, was attached to McClellan's headquarters. From the organization of the Army of the Potomac up to November 1, 1862, including the Peninsular and Maryland campaigns, upwards of 1,200 miles of military telegraph lines were constructed in connection with the army's operations, and the number of operators and builders employed was about 200.[23] During 1863 the Military Telegraph Service constructed 1,755 miles of land and submarine telegraph making a total number of 5,326 miles of land and submarine military telegraph lines in operation during the year. At least 1,200,000 telegrams were sent and received over the military lines in operation during the fiscal year ending July 30, 1863, being at the rate of 3,000 a day. The messages, most of them urgent, varied in length from 10 to 1,000 words.[24] The following year, 1864, the telegraph service was still further expanded. During that year about 1,000 persons were constantly employed in the service which operated 6,500 miles of military telegraph. In that last year of the war there were transmitted 1,800,000 messages. By the end of the war there were 76 miles of submarine tele-

MILITARY TELEGRAPH SERVICE IN THE FIELD

FIELD TELEGRAPH STATION

One of Grant's field telegraph sets used for transmitting messages to his corps. Note wire reel on wagon, used for laying wire.

graph in operation.[25] The expenditure upon the military telegraph during the war was $2,655,500.00. From May 1, 1861, to December 31, 1863, the construction and maintenance of United States Military Telegraph systems cost $22,000.00 a month; in the year 1863, the cost was $38,500.00 a month; and in 1864, it was $93,500.00 a month.[26]

One great advantage of the telegraph over other signal devices was that it was unaffected by heavy fog or mist. Communication between two forts was greatly improved when a submarine telegraph supplanted the flag and torch method of visual signalling which had been in operation previously[27]. The field telegraph system was devised by Major Eckert. It consisted of reels of insulated cable strong enough to resist cannon wheels. These reels, carried on the backs of mules, played out the wire over the field, where it was raised on lances or on trees.[28] Compact portable electric batteries were at times transported in ambulances, called "Battery wagons," constructed for the purpose, but more often were set up under tent flies in close proximity to the commanding general's headquarters.[29]

The tapping of wires was done whenever possible by both sides in the war. An order of January 1, 1864 provided that the cipher books issued by the Super-

ERECTING TELEGRAPH LINE
IN FIELD
Sketched by A. R. Waud during
the Battle of Fredericksburg.

intendent of Military Telegraphs should be entrusted only to the care of telegraph experts selected by the Superintendent and approved and appointed by the Secretary of War.[30] As a result of this order, headquarters in the field could only use plain language or a cipher which neither the commanders nor their staff could decipher. The result was that valuable time was often lost. When Grant was commanding the Federal armies he had a message deciphered, without the above august approval. As a result, the cipher operator was removed but was later restored at Grant's request. The general had no intention of running counter to his superior's instructions on telegraphic regulations and apparently there were no further incidents of this nature.[31]

Except for the few quartermasters in the Military Telegraph Service, all the personnel were civilians and hence not authorized a uniform but some wore officers' uniforms without insignia of rank.[32] This was advisable in many cases because of the ill feeling felt by some Army personnel toward the telegraphers, who were well paid and exempt from military draft.

U.S. MILITARY RAILROADS

Another semi-military unit was the organization known as the United States Military Railroads. Although this organization was under the Quartermaster's Department,[33] it actually functioned as a separate branch in the field and is entitled to separate treatment.

The great railroad development, which began during the second quarter of the century, so interested the United States Government that about 1837 the Government began the policy of lending to railroad companies Army officers who had made a scientific study of this new means of transportation.[34] The nature of the Civil War was to be such that the part the railroads were to play in strictly military operations was hardly second to that of the Navy. Our experience was probably the basis upon which the Prussians built their system, who in 1866 for the first time in Europe made effective war-use of railroads.[35]

The greatest and most important single obstacle to efficient railroad operation lay in the use of several different gauges of tracks. In the Northern states alone more than ten different widths were in everyday use. In the South, a 5-foot width was favored, but not exclusively. In the border states, where the Civil War would be fought, all possible gauges were used and a maximum of confusion existed. Between Philadelphia and Charleston, for example, passengers and freight had to change cars eight times because of variations in gauge. These differences of gauge were inconvenient enough in peacetime, but in wartime they became of paramount importance, for they precluded the transfer of rolling stock from one road to another as military necessity might dictate. Frequent large troop concentrations required unusually

large shipments of freight just when demands on railroads throughout the Union were at a maximum, so at best there was a constant shortage of rolling stock. To these initial difficulties were often added those caused by Confederate raiding parties. As early as mid-summer of 1861 *Harper's Weekly* declared that no less than fifty of the finest locomotives of the Baltimore and Ohio had been destroyed in Virginia. By early 1862, the situation had become critical.[36]

In 1861 and part of 1862, the War Department was run by ex-railroad men, Cameron and Thomas Scott, while General McClellan, who commanded the Army during most of this period, had been a railroad executive. Scott, while Assistant Secretary of War, also kept close supervision of the railroads. Resigning June 1, 1862, he nevertheless was used by the War Department on special missions and in 1863 saved Rosecrans' army from defeat and thwarted the efforts of the Confederates to force the Federal evacuation of Tennessee. He accomplished this by building roads and bridges for the rail line which was necessary for the rapid movement of two army corps from the Army of the Potomac to Rosecrans' relief in Chattanooga. The entire force, numbering 23,000 men arrived at its destination 3½ days less than earlier estimates.[37] During Scott's incumbency as Assistant Secretary of War, large sums of money were paid to private railroad companies for the transportation of men and war materiel.[38]

Shortly after the beginning of the Peninsular campaign, Secretary Stanton called Herman Haupt to be Chief of Construction and Transportation, United States Military Railroads.[39] Haupt was nominally in charge of all the military railroads of the United States, but really confined his activities to those used by the Army of the Potomac. A very efficient construction corps was organized by the new chief who was soon commissioned a colonel and later promoted to brigadier general. As the personnel of the Corps were civilians, they did not wear uniforms. Rolling stock and other equipment was marked "U.S.M.R.R." Haupt had differences with General Pope who was opposed to the military railroads being independent and wished to bring them completely under the control of the Quartermaster's Department. Haupt was supported, however, by the Secretary of War, and his command retained its freedom of action. He invented a torpedo for quickly wrecking wooden bridges and discovered a most effective way of destroying enemy locomotives by firing a cannon ball through the boiler which necessitated removal of all the flues before repair could be commenced. The versatile general perfected a modern-appearing rubber float and a large raft of blanket boats capable of ferrying infantry across large rivers. Box cars with their locomotive were loaded in floats and transported considerable distances by water, arriving safely at their destination with no breakage of bulk in the cargo.[40]

Haupt's bridge over Potomac Creek was an unprecedented accomplishment, especially remarkable in that it was built by an untrained crew without waste of time. During the campaigns of Napoleon trestle bridges of more than one story had been considered impracticable, but Haupt chose to ignore tradition. Using round sticks cut from the neighboring woods and not shorn of their bark, he built a structure 80 feet in height comprising four stories, three of which were trestles and one crib-work. . . . [Lincoln said that he] had "seen the most remarkable structure that human eyes ever rested upon. "That man Haupt had built a bridge across Potomac Creek, about 400 feet long and nearly 100 feet high, over which loaded trains are running every hour and upon my word . . . there is nothing in it but beanpoles and cornstalks." This bridge, completed in nine working days, consisted of more than two million feet of lumber. Nine months had been spent in building the former structure on the same site.

Haupt also developed a procedure by which any rail not bent into a curve of less than a foot radius could be straightened without even heating. He invented a portable contrivance, consisting of blocks of wood, and, by using 12-16 men at each end, could straighten the rail almost perfectly in 2-3 minutes. Workmen would then re-lay and spike it back into place. "Although not perfectly formed, the finished product was straight enough for trains to run over it; and such reconstructed rails could be aligned more precisely at leisure." Rails which were too bent to be straightened while cold were piled along the way and collected later. They, too, could be straightened in furnaces which were of simple construction and portable.

Haupt also used interchangeable parts in bridge construction. For the first time in history trusses 400 feet long, and in three spans, were raised in a day and a half. The new type of truss was adapted to any span or location—all the parts were alike and interchangeable; any piece of timber in the bridge could be reversed and it would fit equally well. Sixty-foot spans were prepared well behind the lines, loaded on flat cars and transported to rail-end, then hauled by oxen to the river's edge. No parts had to be put together until the construction gang arrived to the appointed spot, yet they could be assembled in record time.[41]

The work of the Corps in the East was greatly handicapped by the lack of a permanent force; details of common soldiers, all unskilled and many useless, were assigned to Haupt. These details were changed every day. The situation in the West was better because E. C. Smeed, Haupt's counterpart in that section, had a well-trained corps of veterans in bridge construction.[42]

The role played by the railroads in Virginia and Maryland was a very significant one although, since for the most part they were single-track lines, their carrying capacity was not as great as it might have been.[43] On September 14, 1863, General Haupt was relieved from further duty with the War Department and turned over his duties to Colonel (later Major General) D. C. McCallum who was appointed Superintendent of Military Railroads.[44] Earlier in the War (February 11, 1862) McCallum had been appointed

HAUPT'S BEANPOLE BRIDGE

This improvised bridge over Potomac Creek was characterized by Lincoln as "the most remarkable structure that human eyes ever rested upon."

RAILROAD MATERIAL AT ALEXANDRIA

superintendent of railroads in the United States "with authority to enter upon, take possession of, hold and use all railroads, engines, cars, locomotives, equipments, appendages, and appurtenances, that . . . [might] be required for the transport of troops, arms, ammunition, and military supplies of the United States . . ."[45] After taking over Haupt's duties he followed the Army of the Potomac and greatly assisted the operations of the army by the reconstruction and operation of railroads which the enemy destroyed in its retrograde movements after Gettysburg.

With few exceptions, the operations of military railroads were conducted under orders issued by the Secretary of War or by army commanders in or out of the field.[46] By special order,[47] the War Department had directed the commanding officers of troops along the United States Military Railroads to give all facilities to the officers of the roads and the quartermasters, for unloading cars so as to prevent any delay. On arrival at depots, whether in the day or night, the cars were to be unloaded at once and working parties sufficient for the task were to be on hand. Commanding officers were charged with guarding the track, sidings, wood, water tanks, and other equipment within their commands and were held responsible for the result. Any military officer who neglected his duty in this respect was subject to dismissal from the service as was any officer who interfered with the operation of the railroad. This order was necessary because several attempts were made by army or department commanders to operate railroads, which had, without an exception, proved signal failures, disorganizing in tendency, and destructive of all discipline.[48]

The guarding of these installations and equipment was facilitated by the construction of blockhouses. In the West, Major General Grenville Dodge hit upon a plan of building blockhouses and stockades at all the bridges and stations. A single infantry com-

pany, so fortified, could hold off a regiment, because Forrest's fast-moving cavalry seldom had any artillery to train against this form of defense. Later, when Grant came to command in western Tennessee, he was greatly impressed with this unique railroad defense and ordered all bridges and stations to be fortified in like manner. Grant considered Dodge to be the ablest army railroad builder in the West.[49] In the East, blockhouses were less effective because cavalry troops under such Confederate cavalry leaders as Stuart and Hampton generally had artillery with them.

The difficulty of procuring a sufficient force of competent railroad men, especially in the East, for the construction and transportation departments, was almost insurmountable. Owing to the peculiar nature of the service and the rapid expansion of the railroad system, the supply of railroad operatives had always been limited. Many railroad men had entered the army in various positions while the stimulus imparted by the war to the business of Northern railroads had greatly enhanced the value of the services of those who remained at their posts, thus rendering the home demand for skillful labor far in excess of the supply. Certain of this skilled personnel was draft exempt. When the large number of men necessary to equip the military lines was sought for, it was extremely difficult to induce those who were really valuable to leave secure positions and enter upon a new and untried field of action. Nor was this new field of action without its danger. The men on the United States Military Railroads were continually exposed to great danger from the regular forces of the enemy, guerillas, and scouting parties. It was by no means unusual for men to be out with their trains for five to ten days, without sleep, except what could be snatched upon their engines and cars while the same were standing to be loaded or unloaded. Often the rations were scanty or nonexistent, and, with little sleep and limited rations, the men were continually occupied in a manner to keep every faculty strained to its utmost. The greatest number of men employed at any one time was 24,964; these men operated 419 locomotives and 6,330 cars on 2,105 miles of track.[50] The members of the Construction Corps were well paid, receiving $2.00 a day and double pay for overtime. One member noted on August 23, 1863, that he had earned $85.00 the previous month and much preferred to be in the Corps than earn $100.00 a month as a clerk in Washington.[51]

A good example of their work is found in Sherman's campaign in October, 1864. Hood, with substantial infantry and artillery forces, got in the rear of Sherman's army and, first at Big Shanty and later north of Resaca, destroyed 35½ miles of track and 455 linear feet of bridges, killing a large number of railroad men. Fortunately, however, the detachments of the construction corps which escaped were so distributed that even before Hood had left the road two strong working parties were at work, one on each side of the breach at Big Shanty, and this gap of 10 miles was closed. The 25 miles of track north of Resaca were laid in 7½ days although the men had to cut the cross ties and carry them by hand, while it was necessary to send a distance of nearly 200 miles for the rails. Throughout the war the economy so essential in the management of civil railroads was compelled to give way to the lavish expenditure of war and the question to be answered was not, "How much will it cost?" but rather "Can it be done at all at any cost?"

By executive order of August 8, 1865, the United States Military Railroads were returned to the original owners.[52]

The Federal war effort was rendered incalculable service by civilian and military railroads. Particularly noteworthy was the progress made in adapting the railway to front-line military use. Early in the war, P. H. Watson, Assistant Secretary of War, sent Haupt an armor-clad, bullet-proof car mounting a cannon. Haupt had no use for it, however, and it was finally side-tracked in the yards at Alexandria. However, before the end of the war a much more practicable railway gun mount was designed. At least one armored train, consisting of two cars, was used in the operations around Richmond in 1864.

Credit for the first modern ambulance train belongs to the Medical Director of the Department of Washington. In 1863 he ordered the construction of several complete trains equipped with special cars for the surgeon and his staff, for the apothecary and his storeroom, for a kitchen, and for ten ward cars, each of which carried thirty patients. Many of these trains were built during the war, and three of them ran on a regular schedule during Sherman's campaigns around Atlanta. One officer reported "that men on hospital trains are often as comfortable and better fed than in many permanent hospitals." Throughout the war, locomotives of hospital trains had their stacks and hood painted a brilliant scarlet; at night three red lanterns were hung in a row under the headlight. As a result, the Confederates never molested one of them; on the contrary, even the "ferocious" Nathan Bedford Forrest went out of his way to warn hospital trains whenever a stretch of track was to be obstructed or torn up.

In the course of the campaigns, certain deficiencies showed up. For example, military railroads were constantly hampered by two practices of the Quartermaster Department: the practice of ordering too great quantities of stores taken up to the front; and inefficiency in unloading supply trains. Each quartermaster in the field acted independently, and all of them tended to stock up for any contingency; as a result every time the armies retreated carloads of goods were returned unused to base supply depots, or destroyed. Lack of promptness in unloading and returning cars added to the confusion. Instead of unloading an entire train as soon as it arrived, one or two cars would be unloaded and the rest run on a siding to remain there, sometimes for weeks. As a result of his experiences, Haupt laid down three fundamental rules for military railway management, to be followed by all subordinates insofar as possible: First, Do not allow supplies to be forwarded to the advanced terminus until they are actually required and only in such quantities as can be promptly removed; second, insist on the prompt unloading and return of cars; and, lastly, permit no delays of trains beyond the time fixed for starting, but when necessary and practicable, furnish extras, if the proper accommodation of business requires them.

The North discovered that the fighting power of her armies was increased by the strategic use of railways. The early arrival of reinforcements at threatened points, which was made possible by the railroads, gave strategic advantages otherwise unattainable. Expeditions were undertaken at distances from bases of supplies which would have been impossible without the use of the rail lines to bring up supplies.[53]

ORDNANCE DEPARTMENT

Munitions of war were furnished by the Ordnance Department whose first chief, Colonel Henry K. Craig, was relieved April 23, 1861 and replaced by Colonel (later brigadier general) James W. Ripley. On September 15, 1863 Ripley was succeeded by Brigadier General George D. Ramsay who, in turn, on September 12, 1864 was succeeded by Brigadier General Alexander B. Dyer. General Dyer served until the end of the war. To the small Ordnance Department, which was in existence at the outbreak of war, was added, August 10, 1861,[54] one colonel and one lieutenant colonel selected from the Regular Army, and six second lieutenants selected from graduates of the Military Academy or from the Corps of Engineers, Corps of Topographical Engineers, or from the Artillery. The Chief of Ordnance had the rank, pay, and emoluments equivalent to that of the Quartermaster General of the Army (brigadier general). The Department as finally constituted consisted of one brigadier general, two colonels, two lieutenant colonels, four majors, sixteen captains, twelve first lieutenants, and twelve second lieutenants.[55]

FIELD DUTIES

The field duties of the Ordnance Department were performed mostly by officers detailed from the volunteers. Every armory was under the superintendence of a Regular officer of the Department. Assisting the officers in the field were the unit commanders who were required to make quarterly statements of ordnance materiel in their commands. The Department was represented on the Peninsula by Captain C. P. Kingsbury until July 1862, and thereafter until the end of the campaign by First Lieutenant Thomas G. Baylor.[56] Many of the officers were busy continually during the autumn and winter of 1861, testing the relative merits of new arms and projectiles.

On May 18, 1863, the War Department prescribed the rules to be observed by boards in examining men to be commissioned as company grade officers in the Ordnance Department. In addition to proficiency in orthography and composition, they had to be able to give prompt and intelligent answers to any questions in relation to geography, physical and political, forms of government, chemistry, mathematical rules and formulae; and have a fair knowledge of and skill in mechanical and architectural drawing. Good health, loyalty, and sound groundwork in military subjects were essential.[57] A later order, December 9, 1863, defined the requirements more exactly and set the maximum age limit of applicants at 28 years.[58]

ARMORIES

The first source of arms for the greatly expanded army was in the Federal armories. There were two of these at the time of the attack on Fort Sumter, but that at Harper's Ferry was burned April 19, 1861 in order to prevent it falling into enemy hands. About 15,000 muskets were thus destroyed. The Government took possession of the Rock Island arsenal under the act of July 19, 1864 but the war was over before this source proved of much value.[59] The government was forced to expand the productive capacity of its armory at Springfield, which had an annual capacity of 25,000 muskets at the beginning of the war. At the end of the year (1861) it was producing 8,400 muskets monthly.[60] By 1863, the Springfield Armory was producing muskets for about $9.00 each as compared to $20.00 charged by the private contractors, whose product was equal, however, to the Government standard in every respect.[61] The Armory also duplicated many parts for the foreign arms, especially the Enfield and German muskets. In his report of December 5, 1863, the Secretary of War said that the excellence of arms and munitions of American manufacture supplied by the Ordnance Department to the Army was so obvious that the soldiers were no longer willing to use those which had been imported from other countries.[62] On March 4, 1861, the Federal Government had on hand in "loyal arsenals" the following fabricated weapons: 437,433 muskets and rifles; 4,076 carbines; 27,192 pistols; and 16,933 sabers and swords.[63]

PURCHASES

The initial demand for weapons was so great that in the summer of 1861, the Government sent Colonel George L. Schuyler to Europe to purchase 100,000 rifled muskets, 10,000 revolvers, and 10,000 carbines.

Many of these weapons were found to be useless. A suggestion in the spring that 50,000 to 100,000 arms be purchased abroad had been vetoed by Secretary of War Cameron, who believed the home market should be patronized. With the increase in the productive capacity of Springfield Armory went the employment of every known private manufactory of arms in the country.[64] Up to December 31, 1861, these private contractors had delivered: 30,727 muskets; 6,971 carbines; and 24,815 sabers and swords. During the same period there had been purchased in the market: 236,167 muskets; 14,180 carbines; and 63,718 sabers and swords.[65] The strength of the Army at this time was 527,804.[66] Although the various States had their representatives purchasing arms abroad, the governors were in constant friction with General Ripley over arms deliveries. Secretary of War Cameron asked the governors to withdraw their agents because the competition was highly detrimental to the public service.[67] One writer explains the unsatisfactory situation of the ordnance supply by the statement that the bureau chief, General Ripley, "appears never to have had the energy, resourcefulness and administrative capacity which the youthful Quartermaster General Meigs so consistently displayed."[68]

Much of the friction lay in the type of weapons purchased abroad. By June 30, 1862, more than $10,000,000 had been expended in the purchase of nearly 738,000 rifles, muskets, and carbines of which number only 116,740 were Enfields.[69] The Enfield was the best of the foreign arms; most of the others purchased were of little value. The Belgian muskets, for example, were very generally disliked. An Illinois colonel claimed that with his men armed with the Belgian musket he could tell how many pieces had been fired. "How can I tell that? Oh, I count the men on the ground; it never deceives me. It is fire and fall flat." The Belgian muskets kicked like a mule and burst with the greatest facility. Several soldiers in Illinois regiments were killed in this way.

The bayonet, too, was a novelty—a soft iron affair, apparently designed to coil around the enemy as it came in contact, thus taking him prisoner.[70]

Some of the artillery equipment, especially the gun carriages, manufactured by contractors was of inferior construction.[71] In some cases the gun contractors received large orders through the friendship of Congressmen while the prices fixed by many of them were "beyond necessity or reason."

In October 1861, the firm of E. Remington and Sons solicited an order for the manufacture of their revolver—"acknowledged to be in all respects equal to Colt's army revolver"—at $15.00, but could get a contract for only 5,000. At the same time an order was given to Colt's company for an indefinite number of his revolvers at $25.00 and under this order the company had delivered 31,000 by June 9, 1862.[72] In another case the Government paid $8.50 for sabers that were selling elsewhere for $4.12. The purchasing of arms in the West by General Fremont was found to be very irregular. To rectify an admittedly bad situation a Commission on Ordnance and Ordnance Stores consisting of Joseph Holt, Robert Dale, and Major P. V. Hagner was appointed to audit and adjust all contracts, orders, and claims on the War Department in respect to ordnance, arms, and ammunition.[73] Its report was made July 1, 1862, and the disclosures were so startling that a more stringent regulation of all contracts took place which resulted in a savings to the government of nearly $17,000,-000.[74]

The Ordnance Department reached its highest efficiency in the last year of the war. The Secretary of War reported[75] on March 1, 1865, that in the past fiscal year there had been produced:

    1,750 pieces of ordnance
    2,361 artillery carriages and caissons
  802,525 small arms
  794,055 sets of accouterments and harness
  1,674,244 projectiles for cannon
 12,740,146 pounds of bullets and lead
  8,409,400 pounds of gunpowder
169,490,029 cartridges for small arms.

At the end of the war a total of 1,195,572 rifles and muskets remained unissued by the Ordnance Department in addition to all the weapons in hands of troops.[76]

BREECH-LOADING WEAPONS

In one respect, especially, was the Ordnance Department censured. The initial refusal of General Ripley to approve the universal arming of the Federal Army with breech-loading weapons is perfectly understandable. The simplest and quickest methods of arming the new regiments was by giving them the weapons on hand, or by purchasing weapons already fabricated, or by using the machinery located at Springfield and in the private manufactories to continue the production of the type of weapon for which they were best adapted at the time. But this position need not have been held indefinitely. In the words of an able Confederate general, "There is reason to believe that had the Federal infantry been armed from the first with even the breech-loaders available in 1861 the war would have been terminated within a year.[77] The older generals in the North preferred muzzle-loaders; they could not see that the difficulty of ammunition supply, upon which their opposition was mainly based, was completely outbalanced by the enormous advantage of being able to load when in a prone position.[78] In December 1864, the Chief of the Ordnance Department admitted that "the experience of the war has shown that breech-loading arms are greatly superior to muzzle loaders for infan-

try as well as for cavalry."[79] At the outbreak of war the only large state that had extensively adopted the breech-loader for its military service was Prussia. This country had adopted the famous "needle-gun" (Zuendnadel Gewehr), a weapon well known to American ordnance officers.[80] During the years 1860, 1861, 1862, and 1863, there were granted 119 patents for inventions of breech-loading cannon and 244 patents for improvements in small arms of which a large proportion were for improvement in breech-loading arrangements.[81] The service journal gave increased publicity to breech-loading weapons. One contributor writing under the heading "Breech-Loading Rifles" said in part:[82]

If those in authority have any doubts as to the propriety of thus adding to our efficiency (i.e. by giving them breech loaders) let them come to the front armed with one Springfield musket, and oppose themselves to an equal number of Rebs armed with repeaters or breech-loaders.

RAPID-FIRE WEAPONS

A general of Volunteers has related that models of automatic rapid-fire and repeating field pieces were familiar objects "at the rear" but he never saw any of them in action in any army in which he served. This officer was even ordered to send his rifled cannon to the rear and keep his smooth bores although the rifled guns had a longer range, were lighter, and equally effective at close range with cannister. "We could subdue our adversaries' fire with them, when their smooth bores could not reach us. Yet we were ordered to throw away our advantages and reduce ourselves to our enemy's condition upon the obstinate prejudice of a worthy man who had had all flexibility drilled out of him by routine."[83] Up to June 30, 1862, only 8,271 breech-loading rifles were listed out of a total of over 700,000 guns purchased.

In September 1863, the Department came under the head of a man who believed in the superiority of the breech-loading weapons. In his report of August 1864, this new chief (Brigadier General Ramsay) could report the purchase of 33,652 repeating rifles and carbines (mostly Spencers) and 15,051 single-shot breech loaders since January 1, 1864.[84] The Secretary of War in March 1865, recommended the adoption of breech-loading arms for the military service generally,[85] but the war was over a month later. Nevertheless, the fact still remains, that breech-loading weapons had been available from the outbreak of hostilities.

MEDICAL DEPARTMENT

A very important service which expanded remarkably in the course of the war was the Medical Department.

ORGANIZATION AND PERSONNEL

At the outbreak of hostilities, this Department consisted of a Surgeon General with the rank of colonel, thirty Surgeons with rank of major, and

FIRST AID
Treatment of wounded in th[e]
field during the Seven Days[,]
June 1862.

eighty-four Assistant Surgeons with rank of captain or
first lieutenant.[86] To this Regular force there were
soon added ten Surgeons and twenty Assistant Surgeons; the increase of Surgeons was by promotion and
the new Assistant Surgeons were appointed after
examination from civil life.[87] Five days later the War
Department ordered that each volunteer regiment
should have one Surgeon and one Assistant Surgeon
to be appointed by the governors of the States.[88]
Many of those appointed were country physicians
with little practice in their profession and no idea
of military medical administration. Some volunteers
received appointments as Brigade Surgeons.

The medical officer, the regimental surgeon, and
the assistant surgeon brought to their new positions
the professional attainments of civil life, and they
had only to apply their medical and surgical knowledge to the military surroundings. Some fresh details,
it is true, they had to acquire, but with a little experience, and by careful study of the Army regulations supplemented by a reasonable share of common
sense, they became fitted for their duties.

Brigade Surgeon

The brigade surgeon had more to learn, for his
higher grade placed nim in a broader field. He most
frequently found himself in charge of general hospitals in the larger cities, or of great division and
corps hospitals with armies in the field. In many instances, however, he advanced at once to the grade
of "medical director" of a division or corps, or even
of an army itself. In these instances he was on the
staff of the general, who depended upon him in
no slight degree for information as to the health

of the command, and as to its general availability f[or]
active operations. His suggestions were usual[ly]
listened to and orders touching the hygiene of troo[ps]
and camps were often issued at his instance. Th[e]
greater the general and the more liberal his view[s]
the more was he disposed to listen to the words o[f]
his medical director. The duties of a medical direct[or]
of a District, Department, or army were both arduou[s]
and delicate. It was his duty to see to the health o[f]
every man in the command, to so provide that a be[d]
should be ready for every sick or wounded soldi[er]
whenever and wherever it might be called fo[r,]
to see that medicines and medical supplies shoul[d]
be on hand at every depot, or with every column, an[d]
to anticipate all future demands by bringing fres[h]
supplies from the central stores. Then too the medica[l]
director had to think of the medical officers ove[r]
whom he was placed. He was a sort of bishop to h[is]
military flock; his duty was to help the diffiden[t,]
overworked, or lagging; to encourage by advice o[r]
instructions those who might be perplexed or weary[;]
to restrain and hold in check the overzealous.

Regimental Surgeon

Regimental surgeons were often perplexed in th[e]
early days of the war because of their ignoranc[e]
of Army Regulations, which they regarded as fetter[s;]
these men often denounced all systems as "re[d]
tape." These officers were civilians at heart and fel[t]
deeply for the sick and wounded of their individua[l]
commands; they naturally wished to procure in[-]
stantly for the men those things of which they stoo[d]
in need and they disliked the formality of requisi[-]
tions, which they deemed unnecessary. They wer[e]

impatient of delay, and yet they did not know how to make haste; they hurried to the office of the medical director for information, and he often knew little, if any more, than his questioners.

CONTRACT SURGEONS

One of the earliest difficulties, and one of the most pressing, was a scarcity of medical men, especially of young medical men, who possessed the slightest pretensions to decent medical attainments. The regimental officers were efficient enough but more than these were wanted to supply the depot hospitals which were being established at various points. The men who supplied most of these subordinate medical positions were known as "contract physicians" or "doctors," to use the common phase, in the true military parlance of the Surgeon General's office "acting assistant surgeon." These gentlemen held no commissions, but signed a contract with the medical director, which contract would be approved by the Surgeon General in Washington. The pay was usually from eighty to one hundred dollars per month, and was charged to the medical appropriation expended under the orders of the Surgeon General.

The grade of medical men who at this time, early in the War, held these positions, was often low. Many ignorant physicians, or those who had been long out of practice, if indeed they ever had any, obtained contracts.

Not infrequently it happened that charlatans and imposters succeeded in forcing themselves into these appointments, and the soldier, as would naturally be supposed, suffered in consequence. This condition of affairs obtained probably to a greater extent in the western armies than elsewhere.[89] However, a member of the 63rd Pennsylvania Infantry believed that inefficient doctors were far too commonly encountered. He said in part: "While there were some noble, humane and self-sacrificing physicians in the army, who were an ornament to the class and a God-send to the poor, broken down, fever-stricken or wounded soldier, unfortunately they formed a minority to the unskilled quacks whose ignorance and brutality made them objects of detestation to the soldier. Many of these fellows, if compelled to depend upon their profession in civil life, would have starved, but having, through the influence of political friends, been appointed army surgeons, as soon as they donned the shoulder straps, blossomed out into miserable tyrants. Brutal as well as ignorant and careless of the poor soldiers placed in their care, they helped to fill many graves where our army marched. After awhile, when a large number of these would-be doctors had been kicked out of the army, the service improved."[90]

During the war there were 40 surgeons killed and 73 wounded while in the performance of their duty.[91]

SURGEON GENERAL'S OFFICE

The Surgeon General, Colonel Thomas Lawson, died May 15, 1861, and was succeeded by Colonel Clement A. Finley, the senior medical officer on the Army List. At the time of his appointment Finley was 64 years of age; his 43 years of service included the Black Hawk and Mexican Wars. On April 23, 1862,[92] he was placed on the retired list and his place taken by William A. Hammond[93] who was promoted from the rank of first lieutenant to the position. Hammond had served twelve years in the Army but in 1860 had resigned to take a professorship at the University of Maryland. Although but 35 years of age, he had already attained an enviable professional and scientific reputation.[94]

Meanwhile the Department had been increased by ten Surgeons and twenty Assistant Surgeons in addition to the number authorized by existing laws. A corps of fifty medical cadets to act as dressers in the general hospitals and as ambulance attendants in the field was authorized; the cadets were to receive the same pay and rank as cadets at the Military Academy. These medical cadets were students of medicine, between the ages of 18 and 23, and had been reading medicine for two years and had attended at least one course of lectures in a medical college. Female nurses were permitted to be used as substitutes for soldiers in general or permanent hospitals.[95] Further additions to the Department were made April 19, 1862, including as many Hospital Stewards as the Surgeon General deemed necessary; one Assistant Surgeon General; one Medical Inspector General of Hospitals; eight Medical Inspectors; and some medical purveyors.[96] In May, 1862, the Medical Inspector General and all Medical Inspectors were given absolute power to discharge on their own certificate without superior approval, any man whose physical disability made it "disadvantageous to the service that he be retained therein."[97] A few days later six medical storekeepers were added who functioned as skilled apothecaries.[98]

In July the President was empowered to appoint 40 Surgeons and 120 Assistant Surgeons of Volunteers who should be examined by a military board convened by the Secretary of War. Vacancies in the grade of Surgeon were to be filled from the grade of Assistant Surgeon on the ground of merit only; the title of Brigade Surgeon was abolished and its stead the holders of that title were designated as Surgeons of Volunteers. An additional Assistant Surgeon was alloted to each volunteer regiment.[99] Since all of these additional assistant surgeons, more than 1,000 in all, were appointed by the governors, there was no qualifying examination for them. "The ablest as well as the most ignorant practitioners in the land were eligible for appointment. Such as came into the army without receiving a previous license or diploma were permitted to experiment with the lives and health of their patients until found incompetent; or, detected in malpractice, they were at last brought before a board and dismissed from service." [100] The organization of the Medical Department as it finally evolved was: [101]

Regular establishment: 1 Surgeon-General, 1 Assistant Surgeon-General, 1 Medical Inspector-General, 16 Medical Inspectors, 170 Surgeons and Assistant Surgeons.

Volunteers: 547 Surgeons and Assistant Surgeons, 2109 Regimental Surgeons, 3882 Regimental Assistant Surgeons.

Contract: 85 Acting Staff Surgeons, 5532 Acting Assistant-Surgeons.

The Medical Department became so thoroughly systematized that wounded and sick men were cared for better than they had ever been in an army before. This was due in large part to the efficient medical director Dr. Letterman, to whom must be given credit for the ambulance system which was adopted by Congress after its year of trial in the Army of the Potomac.

EVACUATION AND HOSPITALIZATION

At the front, the ambulances of each corps were under command of a captain who acted under direction from the medical director of the corps. A first lieutenant commanded the ambulances of a division, and second lieutenant those of a brigade. To each ambulance was assigned a driver and two stretcher bearers and to three ambulances a sergeant, mounted. The ambulances of a division always went together, behind the division, and on the march were attended by a surgeon, an assistant surgeon, a hospital steward, a cook, and three or more nurses, who were to attend to the wants of the sick and wounded in the ambulances, supplying them with tents and food. In

an engagement the stretcher bearers of each regiment with the sergeant, reported to the assistant surgeon of the regiment. When a man was wounded, he was brought to the medical officer, put into an ambulance, and taken to the division hospital. In this way, normally, every man was carried to the hospital of his own division.

Under this new system the division hospital was the basic medical unit. From the division, a medical officer of good executive ability was selected, to whom was assigned the general supervision of the hospital. He was assisted by operating surgeons to whom were assigned assistants, also known to be skillful men, who were surgeons and assistant surgeons. This team of surgeons decided when to operate.

From each brigade an assistant surgeon was detailed to provide food and shelter for the wounded. His duty was to erect hospital tents before a battle and to have hot coffee and rations ready; and a supply of clothing, bedding and rations.

Another assistant surgeon from each brigade was detailed to the division medical team to keep the records; take the name and type of wound for each casualty, with the operation performed; list the deaths; and record the place of burial. An assistant surgeon was to remain with each regiment to see that the wounded from the field were put into ambulances, and to supply emergency first aid. [102]

Before the outbreak of war the sick of the Army had been cared for in post hospitals which were small units established at each garrison. When the volunteers went into camp they established regimental hospitals which cared for the sick of their own regiments. It was found necessary to establish general hospitals near the base of operations as perma-

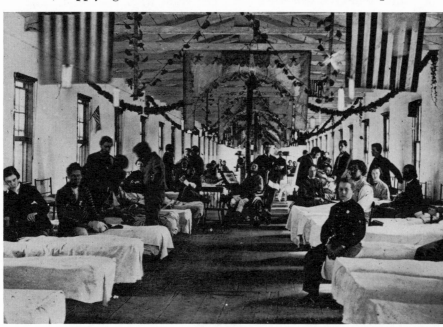

GENERAL HOSPITAL

nent agencies to take care of the sick left behind by the regiments when they moved to the front.[103] During the war, 204 general hospitals with a capacity of 136,894 beds treated 1,057,423 cases with a mortality rate of 8 percent.[104] In the field the Medical Department operated field hospitals while regimental medical officers served at the very front.

Early in January 1864 the War Department established hospital and ambulance flags for the Army as follows: [105]

For general hospitals, yellow bunting 9 by 5 feet, with the letter H, 24 inches long, of green bunting, in the center.

For post and field hospitals, yellow bunting, 6 by 4 feet, with letter 24 inches long, of green bunting in the center.

For ambulances and guidons to mark the way to field hospitals, yellow bunting 14 by 28 inches, with a border, one inch deep of green.

The surgeon at the front line was equipped with a case called the "Surgeon's field companion" while

AMBULANCE

his orderly carried medical supplies in a bulky 20-pound knapsack.[106] Surgeons usually wore a green sash to distinguish them from line officers and some wore a special surgeon's sword. Hospital stewards wore arm bands with the design of the mercurian double-snake,[107] while in combat surgeons and stretcher bearers often wore white arm bands.

Wounded were evacuated from the front line by stretchers similar to those used today.[108] As soon as possible the more severely wounded were placed in ambulances of which the most common type was the two-horse. This ambulance was a stout spring wagon with two stuffed, leather-covered seats the whole length. Hinged to the inner sides of these seats was a third leather-covered seat which could be let down so that men could sit facing each other or three men could lie down lengthwise. In the rear of each

ambulance, under each seat was a water keg, and in front under the driver's seat was a supply of beef stock and hospital stores. On each side of the ambulance was hung a canvas-covered stretcher. The whole ambulance was neatly covered with white canvas on bows.[109]

During the second session of the 37th Congress a bill was introduced to organize a special ambulance corps but was defeated because it was believed inexpedient to change the existing system which employed 4,000 ambulances, 10,000 horses, and 10,000 carefully picked men.[110] Much of the efficiency of the slowly-developed system depended on the personnel of the ambulance trains.

FLAWS IN THE SYSTEM

Much attention was aroused by a pamphlet which appeared in 1863; written by a professor of clinical medicine at Harvard, whose son had just died from wounds received at Kelly's Ford. The doctor described how his son, after receiving his wound, lay helpless on the ground but "no one connected with an ambulance corps ever approached him there." Finally a cavalryman assisted his son (a cavalry officer) into the saddle "and he rode off, leaning over the neck of the animal—a terrible mode of proceedings, considering his severe wound in the abdomen. All this happened when he was in the rear of our victorious army, or, in other words, at just the place and time, at which a thorough ambulance corps should have been busily at work, *seeking out,* and relieving with every means *a great Government should have had at its disposal,* the wretched, and perhaps dying sufferers. But what in reality does the Government do to meet such an emergency! It provides a carriage, which a perfectly healthy man would find exceedingly uncomfortable to drive in, even for a few miles, and one driver, sometimes not the most humane."

This doctor visited the front at the time of Second Bull Run. There was great complaint about the laziness and brutality of the ambulance driver. "On arriving at our place of destination, lying about on the grass or in an old house and its out houses, we found about one hundred and fifty soldiers, suffering from gunshot wounds of every description, inflicted five or six days before. Four surgeons of the army were in attendance; but from want of food and sleep they were nearly exhausted; and being unable to perform but little duty, they requested me to remove some limbs . . . In the afternoon we loaded the ambulances with the wounded and . . . started for Washington, which after a night of horror, made such by the cries and groans of the sufferers, the drunkenness, profanity, and inhumanity of the drivers, we reached about four o'clock the next morning. The men were deposited in the various hospitals in the city." [111]

AMBULANCE TRAINS

The ambulance trains were manned by officers and men detailed from the line. Each corps had its own ambulance train; in 1863 each corps in the Army of the Potomac had three trains (one per division); each train was equipped with 40 two-horse ambulances. The ratio of distribution of ambulances was about three per regiment. The forage and rations for the ambulance train were carried in

HOSPITAL CAR

four-horse wagons. Enlisted men were selected for the ambulance duty proportionately from the regiments. Each ambulance and wagon had a driver and two stretcher bearers. In addition, each train had several blacksmiths and supernumeraries. The total force of the ambulance corps for an army corps was 13 officers and from 350 to 400 men, commanded by a captain. Each division train was commanded by a first lieutenant, assisted by a small number of second lieutenants and sergeants. All were mounted. In some corps a few of the older type of four-horse ambulances would be found.[112] The majority of wounded who had to travel by rail went in coaches or flat cars, but hospital cars were used with greater frequency as the war went on. The use of hospital boats[113] was limited to four of the sea-going type[114] although many smaller hospital craft operated on the inland lakes and rivers.

STATE AND PRIVATE MEDICAL CARE

In 1861, when the States were responsible for the recruiting and subsistence of their troops, they naturally took care of their sick at the same time. State and private hospitals sprang up in the most of the large cities. The Government allowed the soldiers in these hospitals a definite ration allowance[115] but the States soon found their hospitals a burden to maintain and in the summer they were transferred to the Government. However, State agents under the various war governors were permitted for some time to send home to their States the sick and wounded men.

SICKNESS AND SICK RATES

The rate of sickness in the Army was a problem of grave concern. The sickness ratio was highest among white troops in August 1861, when it was 364 cases per thousand.[116] Most of the men were fresh levies, all from civil life and many from agricultural districts. In fact, as far as their health was concerned, they might almost have been looked upon as children. The men from the country had often not passed through the ordinary diseases of child life, and no sooner were they brought together in camps, than measles and other children's diseases showed themselves, and spread rapidly. The malarial influences of the rivers, too, produced an adverse effect upon men brought from higher regions and other more healthy surroundings. Violent remittent, intermittent, and low typhoid fevers invaded the camps, and many men died.

According to Brinton, general hygiene was bad, the company and regimental officers did not know how to care for their men, and the men themselves seemed to be perfectly helpless. This inability to care for themselves seemed to be one of the strangest peculiarities of the volunteers at the beginning of the war. And here it must be remembered that (in 1861 and 1862) men volunteered willingly for the war, were young men of good families, and often of education and attainments. In many instances, farmers eagerly became soldiers, leaving their families, their farms, and their business without hesitation. These men had been accustomed to think and act for themselves, and yet as soon as they entered the ranks and became soldiers, it seemed as if all individualism was lost; they ceased to think for themselves, and became incapable of self-protection. And there was difficulty, too, in regard to their caretakers, for the men who suddenly found themselves officers and who were the national guardians, as it were, of the rank and file, were utterly inexperienced, and in every way unaccustomed to take charge of others. The Commissary of Subsistence, whose duty it was to feed the troops, was, if he were a volunteer, ignorant of the details of his office. So also was the Quartermaster, and yet on the efficiency of these officers much of the comfort of the private soldier depended.[117]

Much of the sickness was due to the faulty eating habits. An assistant surgeon of the 24th New York Infantry had to keep away from camp for weeks or he would have been mobbed by men who had gotten sick due to their own gluttony. On one occasion nine thousand eggs disappeared before less than two thousand of these men, who would then blame the assistant surgeon for their subsequent stomach disorders.[118]

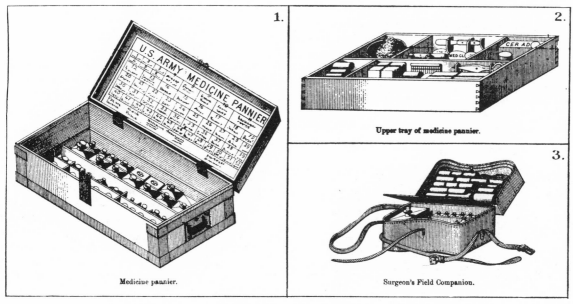

SURGEON'S FIELD KITS

Sickness in the Army of the Potomac was probably most prevalent in the weeks just after Fredericksburg. Many regiments were in no better shape than the 13th New Hampshire Infantry which could turn out only a fraction of its men for regimental drill. Without question, the condition of the Army of the Potomac at Falmouth during the winter of 1862-1863 was very comparable to the situation at Valley Forge in the Revolutionary War. As one of the 13th described it:

It is fearful to wake at night, and to hear the sounds made by the men about you. All night long the sounds go up of men coughing, breathing, heavy and hoarse with half-choked throats, moaning and groaning with acute pain, a great deal of sickness and suffering on all sides, and little help here, near or in the future. This camp of 100,000 men is practically a vast hospital. The experience of the 13th New Hampshire was typical of many other regiments. It had left the State less than three months before, had lost a total of 42 men at Fredericksburg, but out of its enrollment of 1,040 men on October 1st, it had in December less than 400 effectives, and few of them were really well men. An average of 250 men attended sick call, besides the sick in hospital.[119]

First among the causes assigned for the numbers sick was the recklessness with which the men had been enlisted. Apparently the order [120] that required the regimental surgeon and assistant surgeon to minutely inspect their men received very little attention.[121] These inexperienced officers were in turn obstructed in the performance of their duties by the line officers which resulted in confusion and conflict of authority.

A commission appointed June 9, 1861, with no power beyond that of inquiry and advice in respect of the sanitary interests of the United States forces, examined over two hundred regiments in the fall of 1861. The commission found that camp sites were generally selected for military reasons alone, and with very little if any regard to sanitary considerations. The regimental surgeon was seldom consulted. In many instances disease was directly traceable to this omission. One-fourth of the regiments were found encamped on sites which had been previously occupied by others. Artificial drainage was usually very poor while about 20 percent of the privies were not attended to properly. Tents were not ventilated at night.[122] The number of sick in the Army of the Potomac decreased slightly in the period from September, 1861 to February, 1862,[123] but had increased to about 20 percent at the end of the Peninsular Campaign. The lack of system in the treatment of the sick and wounded was sharply criticized [124] and all the remarkable energy and ability of Surgeon Letterman was required to restore the efficiency of his department by improving the supply, ambulance, and field hospital service.[125]

DEATH RATE

The net result of the conditions at Falmouth and other camps, both East and West, in the Federal Army during the war, was that five men died of disease for every two who died of wounds received in battle. Of the 359,528 deaths in the Federal Army, 249,468 were from causes other than the enemies' bullets, and nearly all of them were from disease.[126] Of those who died from diseases, one-fourth died of fever, principally typhoid; one-fourth died of diarrhea, or other forms of bowel complaint; nearly one-fourth died from inflamation of the lungs, or consumption, principally the former; the remaining fourth died of such diseases as smallpox and measles. The following table shows the greatest percentage of losses by disease to be in the colored units, followed by the white volunteers, with the regulars showing the best record of the three classes.

	Enrolled	Died— All Causes	Died— Disease	Percent All Causes	Percent Disease
White volunteers	2,067,175	316,883	167,510	15.3	8.1
Regulars	67,000	5,798	2,552	8.6	3.8
Colored Troops	186,097	36,847	29,658	19.7	15.9

The number of deaths was more than double the number from battle. Part of this extraordinary loss was due to the severity of the campaigns. Men from the woods of Maine encamped two thousand miles distant along the bayous of Louisiana. And, yet, some of the greatest losses by disease occurred in regiments that were not subject to the exposure of active service; these were regiments which performed garrison duty only, and were provided with comfortable quarters and good food. The greatest loss by disease occurred in some Negro regiments which were doing garrison duty, and were stationed in the same district from which they had been recruited and where they had lived all their lives. The Vermont Brigade (composed of only white personnel), while encamped in Virginia, in 1861, lost scores of men by disease, while the regiments in adjoining camps were entirely exempt; and, yet, these Vermonters excelled in physique, cleanliness and intelligence. The most striking feature of the statistics is that the regiments which incurred the greatest loss in battle, were the ones which suffered least from disease. One-fifth of the deaths from disease occurred in regiments that never were in battle.[127]

GROWTH OF MEDICAL DEPARTMENT

The Medical Department expanded steadily and, in 1863, there were 182 General Hospitals with a capacity of 84,472. The number of patients in general hospitals June 30, 1863, was 9.1 percent, and in the field 4.4 percent of the entire mean strength of the Army, of whom 11 percent were sick and 2.5 percent wounded. The Medical Inspectors added materially to the efficiency of the Department by their thorough inspections.[128] In September 1863, Surgeon General Hammond incurred the displeasure of the Secretary of War and on a technicality was convicted by a court-martial of certain charges and dismissed from the service.[129] His place was taken by Joseph K. Barnes (promoted brigadier general August 22, 1864) who served to the end of the war. The same year, 1863, witnessed other important changes in the Medical Department. A Medical In-

spector General, under the direction of the Surgeon General, was given "supervision of all that relates to the sanitary condition of the army, whether in transports, quarters, or camps, the hygiene, police, discipline, and efficiency of field and general hospitals, and the assignment of duties to Medical Inspectors."[130] Medical Inspectors carried out inspections and reported to the Medical Inspector General.

NURSES

Under the exclusive control of the senior medical officer, the employment of women nurses in general hospitals was permitted.[131] The need for good nurses was great; some of the nurses in the earlier part of the war had been inefficient and irresponsible. General Haupt was hindered in his evacuation of troops during Second Bull Run by a drunken rabble who came out as nurses by permission of the War Department.[132]

To the credit of the female nurses, however, more than 2,000 of them served in the Civil War and their

HOSPITAL TENT

record is all the more impressive because of the appalling conditions under which they worked. Many of the hospitals were hastily improvised with the essential equipment unobtainable. The nurses worked by the dim light of candle stubs or army lanterns, sometimes in thick dust, sometimes in frost. The nurses endured inhuman hardships, their chief reward being the gratitude of sick and wounded men. The soldiers welcomed the nurses, cheered them, and loved them for what they did. The coming of the female nurse meant change of linen and bandages, it meant hot soup and good coffee. She was the link with life at home; she was the promise of the future.[133] Nurses were assisted in the hospitals by members of the Auxiliary Relief Corps which was organized May 1, 1864 by the Sanitary Commission. The Corps, consisting of 35 men, worked in Base or "Depot Field Hospitals" where they ran reading rooms, issued supplies, wrote letters for the patients, and ran special diet kitchens.[134]

MILITARY HOSPITALS IMPROVE

In time the military hospitals became thoroughly organized. One doctor was assigned to every two wards, each of 50 beds. Each hospital had a medical officer of the day. The administration of the hospital was divided into three main sections, each presided over by a hospital steward. The general steward had charge of all the wards, clothing, and condition of the patient, the commissary steward had charge of the food, while the dispensing steward issued drugs, medicines, and hospital stores.[135] In 1864 it was found necessary to establish additional hospitals and increase the capacity of those nearest the scene of active operations. During the year the health of the Army was believed good considering the nature of the campaign of 1864. The number of sick and wounded both with their commands and in general hospitals was less than 16 percent of the strength of the Army.[136] The food was generally good; one wounded soldier recorded in his diary on Christmas Day that "the tables were set around the circular corridor, one-half mi. in length, [and] nearly 3000 sat at the table. All had enough."[137]

SURGERY

While some primary and even a few plastic surgical operations[138] were performed at the general hospitals, most of the surgery was performed either at the firing line or, more frequently, at the field hospitals located a short distance to the rear. In the last year of the War the field casualties of the Federal armies were reported with much completeness and accuracy. A total of 106,846 cases of shot wounds were recorded, of which only 30.7 percent were of the lower extremities, indicating the nature of the fighting, which was frequently in entrenched posi-

tions. For anesthetics the Federal surgeons used chloroform, ether, opium, and a mixture of chloroform and ether.[139] Handkerchiefs were used over and over again as masks, but there were several hundred major operations reported during the war in which no anesthetic at all was used. "Much of the battlefield surgery during the war was, in all probability, not only unnecessary but harmful. The rate of mortality after operation 14.2 percent: . . .was inevitable owing to the defective knowledge at the time as to surgical cleanliness."[140]

After arrival at the general hospitals the wounded had a good chance of survival. The difficulty lay in getting them there alive. At the field hospitals "when the wounded came in by cords, overwhelming the weary surgeons, amputation or neglect were alternative, and the latter generally meant death."[141] A war correspondent of the *New York Tribune* reported May 17, 1864 that Doctor Morton, one of the first discoverers of ether, had administered ether to over 2,000 cases in a week during the Wilderness Campaign.[142] In the same campaign a surgeon wrote to his wife that he had been operating for four days upon men who had been wounded in a battle which lasted only two hours.[143] After the Battle of Gettysburg the wounded men were taken very quickly to the field hospitals. One of these hospitals had a long table around which gathered the surgeons and attendants. "This was the operating table, and for seven days it literally ran blood. A wagon stood near rapidly filling with amputated legs and arms; when wholly filled, this gruesome spectacle withdrew from sight and returned as soon as possible for another load.[144] The amputee cases were discharged for dis-

MEDICAL SUPPLIES

A round tin can for pills, a square can marked *Pilutae Quiniae Sulphatis* and *U. S. A. Medical Purveying Depot, Astoria, L. I.* In addition to the two tourniquets there is a glass used by medical personnel at the Battle of Antietam.

ability as soon as possible and most of them received treatment by civilian doctors after leaving the Army, but the Medical Department issued 1,388 artificial legs and 1,121 artificial arms during the year 1865.[145]

The Sanitary Commission, a volunteer civilian agency, was very zealous in its work in the hospitals and on the battlefield, and at times, was critical of the efficiency of the work of the Medical Department of the Army. Although it continued to call attention to specific failures it claimed to recognize, "as few others can, the immense labor which devolves upon the Medical Department in times like these, and the immense work which is done." The Commission has left one of the best descriptions extant of the problems confronting the Medical Department during Grant's 1864 campaign. As the Commission pointed out in its *Bulletin* of June 15, 1864:

[The Commission] realizes as others may not, that the transporting of twenty-five thousand wounded men from the battlefield to distant hospitals, involves unavoidable delays and suffering, especially when, as now, the Army is moving rapidly forward, with as frequent change of base, compelling as a military necessity, the instant transportation of wounded from the vicinity of previously occupied fields to general hospitals, no matter how severe may be the wounds or how impassable the roads, or how deficient the means of transportation at command. . . . Sometimes at a single wharf, as was the case at Belle Plain, a business equal to that of a city of fifty thousand inhabitants has to be carried on. There are the Quartermasters and Commissaries with their crowds of boats and immense stores, wagons in trains a mile long pushing in

HOSPITAL MESS HALL
Decorated for a holiday dinner.

CONVALESCENT CAMP AT ALEXANDRIA, VA.
Despite its unusually good appearance, this hospital's condition was unsatisfactory. The wards were dirty and poorly ventilated, the grounds inadequately drained, and the death rate high.

from the shore, and impatiently waiting to be loaded; reinforcement, five to ten thousand men in one single day, arriving to be disembarked and moved forward to the battlefield; prisoners by the thousands also, to be brought down to the boats under guard; and meanwhile, with it all, at this same wharf must place and time be found for receiving the wounded as they are brought in, two or three hundred ambulances, and wagons at once, followed immediately by as many more—with a crowd of those men, who with wounds less severe, have walked in with slow steps from corps and division hospitals. [Sometimes wounded arrive unexpectedly; at others] the slow, cautious handling upon stretchers, borne down in long file, of men with amputated limbs or terrible wounds; the feeding of the hungry and trying to alleviate their suffering—all this continued by night the same as by day, through the darkness and the rain.[146]

DENTAL SERVICE

Apparently the Medical Department gave dental service to the soldiers, as one diarist has recorded that his major was "indisposed and in his tent most of the day" due to having had ten teeth extracted under chloroform.[147] Sometimes students of dentistry and doctors wishing to get some experience in their profession would visit the army for a while and practice on the teeth of some command with whom they had friends or from whose commander they had obtained permission.[148]

NOTES CHAPTER 6

1. The Federals did not use signals extensively.

2. *Official Records*, First Series, Vol. 5, p. 71.

3. *Ibid.*, p. 31.

4. *House Executive Documents*, 37 Cong., 2 Sess., Document 96, p. 2.

5. United States War Department, "General Order No. 73," March 24, 1863, *General Orders for 1863.*

6. Brown, J. W., *The Signal Corps, U. S. A. in the War of the Rebellion*, pp. 144-145.

7. Not to exceed 8. United States War Department, "General Order No. 73," March 24, 1863, *General Orders for 1863.*

8. *Ibid.*

9. *Ibid.*, "General Order No. 106," April 28, 1863.

10. *Ibid.*, "General Order No. 139," May 18, 1863.

11. Brown, J. W., pp. 164, 180-181.

12. Report of Secretary of War, December 5, 1863. *House Executive Documents*, 38 Cong., 1 Sess., Document 1, p. 13.

13. Report of Secretary of War, November 22, 1865, *House Executive Documents*, 39 Cong., 1 Sess., Document 1, Part 1, p. 44.

14. Bigelow, p. 20.

15. *Ibid.* See also *Photographic History*, Vol. 8, p. 316. According to modern crypto analytic methods this cipher system was not very secure. While serving in the Office of the Chief Signal Officer in Washington early in 1942, the author often saw trained cryptoanalysts "break" it in a few minutes.

16. About a dozen quartermasters were included in it for the receipt and disbursement of funds. Bigelow, p. 19.

17. Plum, William R., *The Military Telegraph During the Civil War in the United States*, Vol. 1, pp. 64-65.

18. This was soon done.

19. Meneely, p. 251. Stanton's order of February 25, 1862. Earlier (November 25, 1861) Stager had been named general manager of the Military telegraph lines only. (Special Order No. 313; *Official Records*, Third Series, Col. 1, p. 672.) The Assistant Secretary of War retained nominal control of the whole system.

20. United States War Department, "General Order No. 38," April 8, 1862, *General Orders for 1862.*

21. Moore, *Rebellion Record*, Vol. 2, p. 4.

22. Plum, Vol. 1, p. 74.

23. *Official Records*, First Series, Vol. 5, p. 31.

24. *Annual Cyclopedia*, 1863, p. 30.

25. Report of Secretary of War, March 1, 1865, *House Executive Documents*, 38 Cong., 2 Sess., Document 83, p. 130.

26. Report of Secretary of War, November 22, 1865, *House Executive Documents*, 39 Cong., 1 Sess., Document 1, part 1, p. 44.

27. Entry for January 16, 1865, journal of Major Harrison Soule, 6th Michigan Heavy Artillery. Manuscript in Michigan Historical Collection.

28. Comte de Paris, Vol. 1, p. 280. A photograph of the stringing of wire in the field can be seen in *Photographic History*, Vol. 8, p. 349.

29. *Photographic History*, Vol. 8, pp. 349, 359.

30. Generals were to report any violations.

31. *Official Records*, First Series, Vol. 32, Part 2, pp. 150, 159, 161, 172-173, 323-324, 361.

32. Plum, Vol. 2, pp. 110-111.

33. Report of Secretary of War, November 22, 1865, *House Executive Documents*, 39 Cong., 1 Sess., Document 1, Part 1, p. 37.

34. *Photographic History*, Vol. 5, p. 274.

35. Even more significant was their use in the Franco-Prussian War.

36. Many were destroyed by guerrillas.

37. *Photographic History*, Vol. 5, p. 296 gives credit for this operation to D. C. McCallum. The two corps, accompanied by their artillery, trains, baggage, and animals accomplished the distance of 1192 miles in 7 days. Report of Secretary of War, November 22, 1865, *House Executive Documents*, 39 Cong., 1 Sess., Document 1, Part 1, p. 36.

38. The gross amount paid for the transportation by railroad companies during the second half of 1861 was: men—$1,551,514.44; horses—$86,249.65; supplies—$375,944.52. *House Executive Documents*, 37 Cong., 2 Sess., Document 114, p. 42.

39. Haupt, Herman, *Reminiscences*, p. 43. The date was April 22, 1862. Haupt was a graduate of West Point (1835) but resigned soon after leaving the Academy to enter the railroad business.

40. *Ibid.*, 69, 101, 142, 149, 224, 257, 283.

41. Many details of Haupt's principles can be seen in his manual.

42. Haupt, p. 291.

43. Comte de Paris, Vol. 1, p. 208.

44. *Photographic History*, Vol. 5, p. 289.

45. *House Executive Documents*, 39 Cong., 1 Sess., Document 1, p. 5.

46. *Ibid.*, p. 33.

47. "Special Order No. 337," War Department, November 10, 1862.

48. *House Executive Documents*, 39 Cong., 1 Sess., Document 1, p. 34.

49. Grant, Vol. 2, p. 352.

50. *House Executive Documents*, 39 Cong., 1 Sess., Document 1, pp. 36-37.

51. Most soldiers got much less.

52. *House Executive Documents*, 39 Cong., 1 Sess., Document 1, pp. 36, 38.

53. Railroads were especially useful in weather which slowed down wagon movements.

54. United States War Department, "General Order No. 54," August 10, 1861, *General Orders for 1861*.

55. Upton, p. 254.

56. *Official Records*, First Series, Vol. 5, p. 29.

57. United States War Department, "General Order No. 138," May 18, 1863, *General Orders for 1863*.

58. *Ibid.*, "General Order No. 393," December 9, 1863, *General Orders for 1863*.

59. Report of Secretary of War, November 22, 1865, *House Executive Documents*, 39 Cong., 1 Sess., Document 1, Part 1, p. 43.

60. *House Reports*, 37 Cong., 2 Sess., Report 43 (February 28, 1862), p. 13.

61. *The Atlantic Monthly*, Vol. 12, (October, 1863), p. 450.

62. Report of Secretary of War, December 5, 1863, House Executive Documents, 38 Cong., 1 Sess., Document 1, p. 10.

63. House Reports, 37 Cong., 2 Sess., Report 43 (February 28, 1862), p. 12.

64. *Official Records,* Third Series, Vol. 1, pp. 278-279, 355, 475-476, 544; Vol. 2, p. 190.

65. *House Reports*, 37 Cong., 2 Sess., Report 43, p. 12.

66. *Official Records*, Third Series, Vol. 1, p. 775. There were but 477, 193 present for duty.

67. *Ibid.*, 469-470; 491, 572, 675-676.

68. Ripley had no imagination.

69. *Official Records*, Third Series, Vol. 2, pp. 855-856.

70. Peterson, Harold, "The Illinois Soluier and the Belgian Musket," Journal of the Military Collectors and Historians, Vol. 2, No. 1, March 1950.

71. *Official Records*, First Series, Vol. 5, pp. 67-68.

72. Senate Executive Documents, 37 Cong., 2 Sess., Document 64, *Passim;* Document 72, p. 14, 16.

73. Offical Records, Third Series, Vol. 1, pp. 538-539, 927; Vol. 2, p. 192.

74. *House Report* No. 2, 37th Cong., 2d Sess.

75. Annual Report of Secretary of War, March 1, 1865, *House Executive Documents*, 38 Cong., 2 Sess., Document 83, p. 5.

76. *Official Records*, Third Series, Vol. 5, p. 145.

77. Alexander, p. 53.

78. Fuller, J. F. C., *The Generalship of Ulysses S. Grant*, p. 52.

79. *Official Records*, Third Series, Vol. 4, pp. 971-972.

80. *Senate Executive Documents*, 36 Cong., 1 Sess., Document 60, pp. 172-173, 192-195.

81. *Army and Navy Journal*, Vol. 1 (May 7, 1864), p. 617.

82. *Ibid.*, Vol. 2 (December 24, 1864), p. 278.

83. Cox, Vol. 1, pp. 182-183.

84. *Official Records*, Third Series, Vol. 2, p. 855; Vol. 4, p. 593.

85. Annual Report of Secretary of War, March 1, 1865, *House Executive Documents*, 38 Cong., 2 Sess., Document 83, p. 6.

86. *Medical and Surgical History of the War of the Rebellion*, Part 3, Surgical Volume, p. 899.

87. United States War Department, "General Order No. 20," May 14, 1861, *General Order for 1861*.

88. *Ibid.*, "General Order No. 25," May 25, 1861.

89. Brinton, John H., *Personal Memories*, pp. 62-66.

90. Hays, Gilbert A., *Under the Red Patch* (63rd Pennsylvania Infantry), pp. 70-71.

91. Fox, p. 43.

92. United States War Department, "General Order No. 46," April 23, 1862, *General Orders for 1862.*

93. *Ibid.*, "General Order No. 48," April 28, 1862.

94. *Photographic History*, Vol. 7, pp. 347-348.

95. United States War Department, "General Order No. 54," August 10, 1861, *General Order for 1861*.

96. *Ibid.*, "General Order No. 43," April 19, 1862, *General Orders for 1862.*

97. *Ibid.*, "General Order No. 53," May 16, 1862.

98. *Ibid.*, "General Order No. 55," May 24, 1862.

99. *Ibid.*, "General Order No. 79," July 15, 1862.

100. Upton, p. 432.

101. Photographic History, Vol. 7, p. 5. The custom was well established on both sides of releasing captured medical personnel. *Official Records,* First Series, Vol. 35, Part 2, pp. 170, 175, 176, 200, 210.

102. Stevens, *Three Years in the Sixth Corps,* pp. 180-182.

103. *Medical and Surgical History*, Introduction to Part 1, Medical Volume, p. XXV.

104. Report of Secretary of War, November 22, 1865, *House Executive Documents*, 39 Cong., 1 Sess., Document 1, Part 1, p. 35. A photograph of a general hospital is shown in Photographic History, Vol. 7, p. 214.

105. United States War Department, "General Order No. 9," January 4, 1864, *General Orders for 1864.*

106. Pictures of this equipment can be seen in *Medical and Surgical History*, Part 3, Surgical Volume, pp. 915-916.

107. *Photographic History*, Vol. 7, p. 217.

108. *Medical and Surgical History*, Part 3, Surgical Volume, pp. 923-927. For pictures of Civil War ambulances see *Ibid.*, pp. 945-956.

109. *Photographic History*, Vol. 7.

110. *Annual Cyclopedia* (1863), pp. 29-30.

111. Bowditch, Henry I., *A Brief Plea For An Ambulance System For The Army of The United States* (1863), pp. 7, 20-21.

112. *Army and Navy Journal*, Vol. 1, (December 26, 1863), p. 280.

113. *Medical and Surgical History*, Part 3, Surgical Volume, pp. 958, 960-970, 977-979, 982-983 and Plate 174 of the atlas to *Official Records* contain pictures of these cars and boats.

114. Report of Secretary of War, November 22, 1865, *House Executive Documents*, 39 Cong., 1 Sess., Document 1, Part 1, p. 35.

115. United States War Department, "General Order No. 47," April 26, 1862, *General Orders for 1862*.

116. *Medical and Surgical History*, Part 3, Medical Volume, p. 23.

117. Brinton, pp. 61-62.

118. MacFarlane, Doctor C., *Reminiscence of an Army Surgeon*, pp. 4-5.

119. Thompson, p. 93.

120. United States War Department, "General Order No. 51," August 3, 1861, *General Orders for 1861.*

121. *Official Records*, First Series, Vol. 5, p. 81.

122. Annual Cyclopedia (1861), pp. 36-41; *The Atlantic Monthly*, Vol. 8 (November 1861), pp. 571-580; *Ibid.*, Vol 10 (October 1862), 463-497.

123. From 7% to 6.18%. McClellan, pp. 126-128.

124. Washington *National Republican*, Vol. 2 (July 22, 1862); p. 2. *The United States Sanitary Commission* (1863), pp. 83-84.

125. McClellan, pp. 127-128. Doctor Jonathan Letterman, medical Director, Army of the Potomac.

126. *Official Records*, Third Series, Vol. 5, pp. 664-665.

127. Fox, pp. 49-50.

128. Report of Secretary of War, December 5, 1863, *House Executive Documents*, 38 Cong., 1 Sess., Document 1, p. 13.

129. *Photographic History*, Vol. 7, p. 348.

130. United States War Department, "General Order No. 308," September 12, 1863, *General Orders for 1863*.

131. *Ibid.*, "General Order No. 351," September 12, 1863, *General Order for 1863*.

132. The medical service was probably at its worst during this campaign.

133. Robinson, Victor, *White Caps—the Story of Nursing*, pp. 153-154.

134. Sanitary Commission *Bulletin*, February 15, 1865.

135. *Harper's New Monthly Magazine*, Vol. 29 (August 1864), pp. 310-312.

136. Report of Secretary of War, March 1, 1865, *House Executive Document*, 38 Cong., 2 Sess., Document 83, pp. 11-12.

137. Entry for December 25, 1864, diary of Color Sergeant Francis H. Buffum, 14th New Hampshire Infantry. Manuscript in author's possession. The hospital was at Chestnut Hill, Philadelphia.

138. Out of about 10,000 recorded cases of gunshot injuries of the face, 32 attempts at plastic surgery were made but without very good results. *Medical and Surgical History*, Part 1, Surgical Volume, pp. 368-380.

139. *Ibid.*, Part 3, Surgical Volume, pp. 3, 887. Chloroform was used most frequently.

140. *Photographic History*, Vol. 7, p. 232.

141. Buffum, p. 320.

142. Letter of Charles A. Page, May 17, 1864, Gilmore, p. 67.

143. Letter of Surgeon John G. Perry, 20th Massachusetts Infantry, Cold Harbor, Va., June 4, 1864. Perry (editor), *Letters from a Surgeon in the Civil War*, p. 187.

144. At Fredericksburg blankets were used instead of wagons.

145. Report of Secretary of War, November 22, 1865, *House Executive Documents*, 39 Cong., 1 Sess., Document 1, Part 2, p. 895.

146. Sanitary Commission *Bulletin*, June 15, 1864.

147. Entry for October 30, 1862, diary of Colonel Oliver L. Spaulding, 23rd Michigan Infantry. Manuscript in Michigan Historical Collection.

148. Very little data is available on the practice of dentistry.

CHAPTER 7

The Administrative and Supply Services

PLAYING perhaps a less spectacular role than the combat arms, but a role whose importance cannot be overestimated, were the various services of the Federal armed forces. The functions of a general staff were divided among what is now termed the special staff, that is, the chiefs of the different service departments. Especially was this true of the Adjutant General's Quartermaster's, Subsistence, and Ordnance departments which were represented on the staff of each army, army corps, and division. These officers, while subject to the authority of the chiefs of the combat units to which they were assigned, continued nevertheless to maintain direct relations with their respective departments.

The vital problem of supply of food, clothing, weapons, and equipment was entrusted to Regular officers assisted by the addition of volunteer officers commissioned by the President. There was no sudden expansion in such service organizations as the Quartermaster General's Department, but with each new brigade that Department was increased by a captain. This officer could look for instruction from chief quartermasters, chief commissaries, or depot commissaries, who, at the beginning of the war, were exclusively selected from the Regular Army. Three or four months sufficed to qualify brigade and division quartermasters and commissaries for efficient discharge of their duties[1] since integrity and business capacity were the only qualifications required.

THE ADJUTANT GENERAL'S DEPARTMENT

The personnel of all of these services, however, always tended to be insufficient for the task of providing for the support and management of large armies which were being augmented at irregular intervals by substantial increments of recruits. "There was constantly occasion to regret the absence of a general staff, such as is to be found in European armies, serving as a direct medium between the chief and all the subordinate agents placed under his command."[2] The functions of the office of chief of staff had not existed in the small peace establishment and, so far as they had been exercised, they had been

included in the Adjutant General's Department. Because this Department was seriously depleted early in the war by many of its personnel being employed elsewhere, commanding generals were obliged to resort to other branches of service.[3]

THE ADJUTANT GENERAL

Shortly before the outbreak of war, the Adjutant General of the Army, Colonel Samuel Cooper, resigned and his place was taken by Assistant Adjutant General Lorenzo Thomas[4] who, as colonel and later as brigadier general, held the office until the end of hostilities. On March 25, 1863, Thomas was ordered to superintend the recruiting of Negroes in the West[5] and his duties in Washington were performed by Colonel Edward D. Townsend. The Adjutant General was assisted by two classes of subordinates, administrative officers and staff officers serving with generals in the field. These subordinates ranged in rank from captain to colonel. By a general order of August 10, 1861, the Adjutant General's Department was to consist of: one Adjutant General with rank of brigadier general; one Assistant Adjutant General with rank of colonel; two Assistant Adjutant Generals with rank of major; and twelve Assistant Adjutant Generals with rank of captain.[6] About a year later it was ordered that there should be added to the Department by regular promotion of its officers then in service, one colonel, two lieutenant colonels, and nine majors. The grade of captain in the Department was abolished and all vacancies occurring in the grade of major were filled by selection from among the captains of the Regular Army.[7]

Administrative officers served in the Department's headquarters in Washington from which the regulations, orders, and much of the military correspondence of the Secretary of War and General-in-Chief of the Army issued. It was the place of deposit for the purely military records such as muster rolls, which contained the military history of every soldier of the Army; returns which showed the actual condition of each corps, division, brigade, and regiment from month to month; files of enlistments and certificates of discharge of enlisted men. Here were made out the commissions of all military officers appointed by the President, and all commissions as well as resignations and casualties affecting such officers were here recorded. The *Annual Army Register,* containing the military history of all officers so commissioned was also made up, printed, and distributed under supervision of this Department. From here the various manuals of instruction, so liberally furnished by the Government to its troops, and all the blanks used by the Army, except in the disbursing departments of the staff, were distributed.[8] All correspondence with bodies of troops in the field was conducted by the Department under the Adjutant General who transmitted the orders of the President, Secretary of War, and General-in-Chief to the generals in command and they addressed all their reports to him. The recruiting service for the Regular Army and the muster in and muster out of volunteer regiments was regulated and supervised by the Department.[9] Information involving pension claims was constantly being sought to settle claims in behalf of officers and enlisted men; reports were made to questions of soldiers' relatives "residing in all parts of the civilized world" and similar administrative functions were performed by the Department in Washington.[10]

The appointment branch of the Adjutant General's Department was a very important place in 1861, and its chief was in close contact with the Secretary of War and the President, who, realizing the hopelessness of making all the important appointments himself, soon turned most of them over to the branch for processing. Final action on these appointments was taken by the Secretary of War in combination with the President.[11]

Adjutant General's Field Service

The field service of the Department was handled by the assistant adjutant generals who were attached to the staffs of the various armies, corps, divisions, and brigades of the Federal Army. In a letter on the reorganization of the Adjutant General's Department, Adjutant General Lorenzo Thomas informed Congress that "the assistant adjutant general of every army, army corps, division, and brigade is, by the very nature of his office, chief of the staff on which he serves. Under the commanding officer, he directs the service of all other departments of the staff, and of the whole command."[12] The regimental adjutants were in direct communication with the brigade assistant adjutant generals. These field representatives prepared, classified, received, and transmitted all the reports and records of their commands. In addition, the assistant adjutant generals were assigned to such special duties as the organization of new regiments. The part played by officers of the Adjutant General's Department in the organization of the Army of the

Potomac during the fall and winter of 1861 was commended by its commander who characterized their management of the affairs of the Department as excellent.[13] While the number of Regular officers serving in the Department in 1864, was but twenty, they were assisted by over three hundred volunteer officers, most of whom were captains.[14]

JUDGE ADVOCATE GENERAL

The legal department of the War Department in 1861 centered in the person of the Judge Advocate, Brevet Major John F. Lee, who had held the position since March 2, 1849. His function was primarily that of acting as prosecutor at courts-martial. The tremendous increase of the Army after Sumter necessitated an expansion in Lee's bureau. In 1862 Congress ordered that the President should appoint, with Senate approval, a judge advocate general with the rank, pay, and emoluments of a colonel of cavalry, to whose office should be returned for revision the records and proceedings of all courts-martial and military commissions and where a record should be kept of all proceedings had thereupon.[15] Colonel Joseph Holt was selected as Judge Advocate General on September 3, 1862, and in that capacity served until the end of the war. In addition, the President, with approval of the Senate, was permitted to appoint for each army in the field a judge advocate with the rank, pay, and emoluments of a major of cavalry who should perform the duties of judge advocate for the army to which they respectively were assigned, under the direction of the Judge Advocate General.

Courts-Martial

Courts-martial were "military courts instituted for the investigation and punishment of all offenses committed by officers, soldiers, settlers, retainers to the camp, and persons serving with the army, in violation of military law, and the customs of war. Their powers and duties are laid down in general terms in the Articles of War . . . Commissioned officers clothed with military rank, and entitled to command, are the only persons in the United States service who are eligible as members of courts-martial; this excludes all paymasters, surgeons, and assistant-surgeons, whose rank is only assimilated."

Courts-martial were of three kinds, *General, Regimental,* and *Garrison.*[16] A general court-martial was competent to take jurisdiction over any military offense, but in practice generally confined itself to certain serious offenses and all offenses involving commissioned officers. Regimental or garrison courts-martial handled crimes which comprised all those which infracted the ordinary properties of military service, as irregularities and disorders which were not of a grave and serious description; besides such specific offenses as were named in the Articles of War which were subject to their authority.[17] A regimental court-martial was assembled on the regimental commander's order and consisted of three commissioned officers. A like number comprised a garrison court-martial which could be appointed by the commanding officer of a garrison, fort, barracks, or other places where the troops consisted of mixed branches of the service.[18] In July, 1862, the following changes and additions were made with respect to regimental and garrison courts-martial.

Each offender punishable by a regimental or garrison court-martial was tried before a field officer of his regiment who was detailed for that purpose. This field officer heard and determined the offense and ordered the punishment to be inflicted. He also made a record of his proceedings and submitted the same to his brigade commander, who, upon the approval of the proceedings of such field officer, ordered the same to be executed. The punishment in such cases was limited to the punishment authorized to be inflicted by a regimental or garrison court-martial. If there was no brigade commander, the proceedings were submitted to the post commander.[19]

A general court-martial had jurisdiction in cases:

(1) Which involved the trial of a commissioned officer.

(2) Beginning, exciting, causing, or joining in any mutiny. This included knowing of, and not giving information of an intended mutiny or not trying to suppress the same.

(3) Striking, or drawing or lifting up any weapon, or offering violence to a superior office in the execution of his duty.

(4) Deserting the service.

(5) Enlisting in any other regiment, troop, or company before being regularly discharged.

(6) Persuading to desert.

(7) Disobedience of an order, or drawing sword upon an inferior officer, in case of quarrels, frays, etc.

(8) Selling, losing, or spoiling through neglect, horse, arms, accouterments.

(9) Sentinel sleeping upon post.

(10) Offering violence to persons bringing provisions or necessities to camp, out of the United States.

(11) Misbehaving before the enemy, abandoning post, throwing away arms, quitting the colors to plunder and pillage.

(12) Making known the watch-word to any not entitled to receive it, or giving a different parole on watch-word from that received.

(13) Forcing a safe-guard in foreign ports.

(14) Relieving the enemy, or harboring and protecting an enemy.

(15) Holding correspondence with, or giving intelligence to the enemy.

(16) Compelling a commander to surrender.

(17) Persons not citizens of, or owing allegiance to the United States in time of war, who are found lurking as spies in or about fortifications or encampments of the United States.[20]

The legal punishment for soldiers by sentence of a court-martial, depending on the offense and the jurisdiction of the court were: death, confinement; confinement on bread and water; solitary confinement; hard labor; ball and chain; forfeiture of pay and allowances; discharge from the service; reprimands; and, if noncommissioned officers, reduction to the ranks. Ordnance sergeants and hospital stewards, however, though liable to discharge, could not be reduced, nor could they be tried by regimental or garrison courts-martial except by special permission of the department commander. Solitary confinement, or confinement on bread and water, was not to exceed 14 days at any one time, with intervals between the periods of such confinement not less than such periods, and no person should undergo such confinement for more than a total of 84 days in any one year.[21]

ARTICLES OF WAR

Courts-martial were governed by the military code known as the "Articles of War." These Articles were drawn up by Congress in 1806 and constituted the entire code of laws in force in 1861 for the Government of the armies of the United States; and by its provisions alone, courts-martial were made the proper and sole tribunals for the trial of military offenses. "A court-martial is a lawful tribunal, existing by the same authority that any other court exists by, and the law military is a branch of law as valid as any other, and it differs from the general law of the land in authority only in this, that it applies to officers and soldiers of the army, but not to other members of the body politic, and that it is limited to breaches of military duty. Courts-martial are regulated by the Articles of War, the general regulations of the army, and by the orders of the President relating thereto, and extant at that time; their practice is moreover regulated, in points where the written law is silent, by the custom of war, by which expression, as here applied, must be understood the customs and usages of the United States Army."[22]

While courts-martial tried cases where jurisdiction was conferred and defined by statute, military commissions tried individuals not subject to courts-martial. This limitation on the jurisdiction of courts-martial had existed from the beginning of the war but had been codified by Francis Lieber in 1863.[23] Courts-martial tried all offenses committed by commissioned officers, certain crimes and offenses of enlisted men, and fraud or wilful neglect of duty by contractors for supplies for the Army of the United States, sutlers, and camp retainers. Spies could be tried by either courts-martial or military commissions.

A court-martial numbered from five to thirteen members, all commissioned officers, and could be appointed by the President, any general officer commanding an army, a commander of a division or separate brigade, or a colonel commanding a separate department. In courts-martial, Regulars were tried by Regulars and volunteers by volunteers. Each court-martial was attended by a judge advocate who furnished the accused with a copy of the charges and specifications, the detail of the court, and the list of witnesses for the prosecution. A clerk recorded the proceedings and in important cases a shorthand expert was present.[24] The trial was a solemn affair; the court and witnesses appeared in full uniform. In proposing a sentence, each member would write out one and hand it to the judge advocate, who beginning with the mildest, would put them successively to a vote. The first vote that was carried was the final one.[25] The judge advocate would then forward the findings to the officer who appointed the court.

A concurrence of two-thirds of the members of a general court-martial was necessary for a sentence of death. Flogging up to fifty lashes was permitted in cases involving desertion,[26] but this form of punishment was abolished in the first year of the war.[27] A year later it was ordered that no sentence of death or imprisonment in the penitentiary should be carried into execution until the same should have been approved by the President.[28]

Under Burnside the problem of desertion became so acute that his successor, General Hooker, was able to get Lincoln to relinquish his right to review the sentences of courts-martial. Deserters were arrested, promptly tried, sentenced, and punished accordingly. "The spectacle of a few of them shot to death in the presence of the troops produced a most salutary effect."[29] The President could still be appealed to in cases involving a general officer, persons sentenced to imprisonment in penitentiaries, and persons sentenced to death for any crime other than for being a spy, deserter, or for mutiny or murder.[30]

In 1870 the Adjutant General reported that 121 men were executed during the war—a very insignificant fraction of those who, by military law, were liable to the death penalty.[31]

BUREAU OF MILITARY JUSTICE

The wagoners and train rabble and stragglers continued to commit great outrages in the rear of the armies. There appeared to exist a situation where "no one could be executed but poor friendless wretches who had none to intercede for them."[32] To improve this situation there was attached to and made a part of The War Department, a bureau known as the Bureau of Military Justice to which should be returned for revision the records and proceedings of all the courts-martial, courts of inquiry, and military commissions of the armies of the United States.[33]

Courts of inquiry were courts which could be ordered by a general or commanding officer to examine into the nature of any transaction, accusation, or imputation against any officer or soldier. These courts, numbering from one to three officers and a judge advocate, differed from courts-martial in that the witnesses did not give their opinions on the merits of the case unless specially required.[34]

The Judge Advocate General, Colonel Joseph Holt, was promoted to brigadier general and placed at the head of the bureau. He was assisted by an Assistant Judge Advocate General with the rank of colonel. All questions of military justice or the proceedings of military courts and commissions were forwarded promptly to the Judge Advocate General as chief of the Bureau of Military Justice. Judge advocates were required to forward to their chief at the end of each month a list of all cases tried and to be tried within their jurisdiction.[35] From March 2, 1865 to November 22, 1865, the Bureau received, reviewed, and filed 16,591 records of general courts-martial and military commissions; and 6,123 special reports were made as to the regularity of proceedings, the pardon of military offenders, the remission or commutation of sentences, and upon numerous miscellaneous subjects and questions referred for opinion. The "Digest of Opinions of the Judge Advocate General," commenced in January, 1865, came into extensive use and "proved of considerable advantage to the service in continuing to establish a uniformity of decision and action in the administration of military justice."[36]

The important codification of the rules of land warfare known as "Instructions for the Government of armies of the United States in the field," prepared by Francis Lieber, appeared as a War Department general order April 24, 1863.[37] These instructions were intended to embody the general principles of the laws of war by which the commanders of armies, departments, and districts were to be governed in their treatment of the inhabitants of the country militarily occupied. The application of these principles in particular situations was left to the good judgment and discretion of the commanders whose knowledge of the circumstances in each case it was presumed best qualified them to decide.[38]

INSPECTOR GENERAL'S DEPARTMENT

Formal inspection of the armed forces of the Army was performed by officers of the Inspector General's Department, whose first chief was Colonel Sylvester Churchill. The entire Department from the beginning of the war to August 10, 1861, consisted of Churchill and one other Regular Army colonel. To assist these two officers the President was authorized to appoint, with the consent of the Senate, five assistant inspector generals with the rank and pay of majors of cavalry.[39] At this time Churchill was retired and his place taken by Colonel (later Brigadier General) Randolph B. Marcy who served until the end of the war.

While he was in command of the Army of the Potomac, McClellan was greatly assisted in his organization of that army by Colonel D. B. Sacket and Major N. H. Davis of the Inspector General's Department.[40] The Inspector General's inspections were for the purpose of examining the condition of the men, animals, and materiel of the various units of the army. The inspections proper were followed by the troops passing in review.[41]

The Department constituted a board of officers to prepare a list of sutlers' supplies and provided for inspections of sutlers' merchandise and prices.[42]

The small force of two colonels and five majors proved too small to function efficiently and accordingly it was ordered July 29, 1862, that each army corps should have as an assistant inspector general, a lieutenant colonel, to be appointed from the Regular Army or the volunteer force. These officers were to be on the staffs of the corps commanders.[43] They were appointed by the Inspector General and were permanently assigned to the army corps where they served irrespective of changes in the corps commanders, unless otherwise assigned by the President.[44] Line officers were appointed division and brigade inspectors; they were assigned the duty of making inspections of the troops and forwarding reports to corps headquarters. Here the corps assistant inspector general consolidated them and in turn sent them on to the army inspector general.[45]

In the Army of the Potomac the Department began to function efficiently early in 1863 and under Hooker was not so much reorganized as created.[46] Vacancies in the Department were filled by competent officers. Colonel E. Schriver was announced as Inspector General of the Army. Infantry officers were named as inspectors of infantry, cavalry officers as inspectors of cavalry, and artillery officers as inspectors of artillery. These inspectors themselves were thoroughly organized under the command of the inspector general of the Army of the Potomac. There were frequent formal inspections of regiments and these inspections extended to the outposts and pickets. Regiments were announced in army general orders as either satisfactory or unsatisfactory; poor regiments were deprived of leaves and furloughs for officers and men, while good regiments were granted increases in their allowances of leaves and furloughs.[47]

QUARTERMASTER GENERAL'S DEPARTMENT

One of the most important of the services was the Quartermaster General's Department, which supplied the armies' uniforms and equipments, provided transportation by land and water, and constructed housing for men and animals. The Quartermaster General at the outbreak of war was Brigadier General Joseph E. Johnston, who resigned April 22, 1861, to join the Confederate Army. His place was taken by Major E. S. Sibley who served from May 15, 1861 to the end of the war. Colonel Montgomery C. Meigs served as Quartermaster General of the Army with rank of brigadier general.[48] Meigs was on inspection duty from August 1863 to January 1864, during which time Colonel Charles Thomas was acting Quartermaster General. At the time of his appointment as Quartermaster General, Meigs was 45 years of age. After graduation from the Military Academy in 1836, he had entered the Corps of Engineers where he worked on such important projects as the Potomac Aqueduct, the iron dome of the Capitol, and the extension to the Post Office.

The Quartermaster Department was increased in August 1861 by one colonel, two lieutenant colonels, four majors, and twenty captains. All these officers were Regulars and their new commissions were with the rank, pay, and emoluments of cavalry. This same order provided for promotion to major of any Regular captain when he should have had 14 years of continuous service. There were to be as many master wagoners with the pay and allowances of sergeants of cavalry, and as many wagoners with the pay and allowances of corporals of cavalry as the military service, in the President's judgment, might deem necessary.[49] The Department was further increased with the result that in 1864 the regular establishment consisted of: 1 brigadier general, 3 colonels, 4 lieutenant colonels, 11 majors, 46 captains, and 12 storekeepers; while the volunteer establishment consisted of 465 captains.[50]

GRAFT

In 1862, one of these captains had attracted attention by his "expose" of corruption in connection with the Department. His book bore the intriguing title, *Nine Months in the Quartermaster's Department on the Chance of Making a Million!* As the author expressed it:

"The man who enters (the Quartermaster) Department with the expectation of living an easy life, and who intrusts his business to his employees, it matters not how trustworthy they may be, or how much they may enjoy his confidence, will, ere three months pass over his head, find himself irrevocably involved."

The captain's complaint would have been more sympathetically received if he had not lost his commission on the ground that he "had a million of dollars unaccounted for." Accounting to the captain, his loss of the commission "afforded infinite satisfaction to the Shylocks, sharks, and thieves, who, for nine months, had tried to get their hands into the public treasury, but failed."[51] On the whole, however, the great majority of the personnel were trustworthy and efficient although there were serious deficiencies while Cameron was Secretary of War. Unwise purchases by men like General Fremont also initiated investigations by committees of Congress from time to time.

On July 1, 1864, the War Department ordered that every Quartermaster and Assistant Quartermaster should appear for examination as to his qualifications before a board to be composed of three staff officers of the Quartermaster General's Department, of whom at least two should be from the volunteers. Such boards were convened under the direction of the Secretary of War by the Quartermaster General. It was ordered that those officers examined who displayed lack of sufficient business ability to serve in the Department were to be dismissed from the service with one months' pay while those who failed due to intemperance, gambling, or immorality were to be dismissed from the service with no pay.[52] Shortly after this order appeared, another order was issued which provided for the regulations covering the examinations, and set up the boards to examine the officers. The boards were conducted in similar fashion to courts-martial; witnesses were heard and papers presented. An officer had to satisfy his examining board as to his moral character, his ability to read and write English with facility, his performance of ordinary problems in arithmetic, and his comprehension of the rules and regulations of the Army with special reference to the Quartermaster General's De-

partment. His general intelligence and aptitude for business had to be good.[53]

FIELD ORGANIZATION

The field organization by August 1864 consisted of: For each regiment, Regimental Quartermaster (lieutenant); each brigade, Quartermaster (captain); each division, Quartermaster or Division Quartermaster (major); each army corps, Chief Quartermaster (lieutenant colonel); each army, Chief Quartermaster (colonel).[54]

RESPONSIBILITIES

The Department was responsible for many tasks that were extremely specialized in nature. It purchased and distributed among the army corps all equipments (except ordnance and food), tents, tools, camp furniture, and cooking utensils. The Department was responsible for all transportation of troops whether by land or water. It administered all telegraph lines and railways that had been taken possession of by the Army, and contracted with rail-

MAJOR SUPPLY BASE
Part of McClellan's base at White House, Va., during the Peninsular campaign.

SUPPLY IN THE FIELD
Part of Mead's Great Trains at Brandy Station just before the Wilderness campaign.

way companies for further transportation. The construction and distribution of all wagons, field forges, ambulances, and harness was its responsibility as was the purchase of all animals and the distribution of all fuel and forage. It constructed all barracks, hospitals, stables, and wharves.[55]

Because of the obvious need for a division of labor, late in the war the Department was organized into nine divisions. Each division, responsible for one particular phase of the Department's activities, was commanded by a colonel who acted as chief of his division. These divisions were to remain in existence "during the present rebellion and one year thereafter" and their functions were as follows:[56]

Procurement and disposition of horses and mules for cavalry, artillery, wagon and ambulance trains, and all other purposes for which horses or mules may be procured for the armies of the United States.

Procurement, storage, and disposition of cloth and clothing, knapsacks, camp and garrison equipage, and all accouterments of the soldier which are provided by the Quartermaster Department.

Purchase, charter hire and maintenance of all vessels used in the transportation of the Army, and of prisoners of war, excepting river steam vessels and barges upon the Western rivers.

Purchase or charter of all transportation for the Army and its supplies by land and upon the Western rivers, including all railroad and telegraph lines operated by the United States for military purposes.

Procurement and issue of forage and straw for the Army.

Erection, procurement, and maintenance, etc., of all barracks, hospital buildings, storehouses, stables, bridges (other than railroad bridges), wharves, etc.

Procurement and issue of all wagons, ambulances, traveling forges, and harness (except such as are furnished by the Ordnance Department), heating and cooking stoves, etc.

Inspections of the Quartermaster Department.

Correspondence, returns, reports, and records pertaining to the Department.

Six additional colonels were assigned the duty of inspectors. A number of colonels were assigned the duty of inspectors. A number of colonels (not exceeding 10) were serving as Chief Quartermasters at depots, while each army of more than one corps in the field was represented by one colonel who acted as Chief Quartermaster. It was ordered that two-thirds of each of the above grades were to be taken from among the quartermasters in the Volunteer Service.[57] By previous law, the Chief Quartermaster of each army corps held the rank of lieutenant colonel.

In his organization of the Army of the Potomac, General McClellan appointed Captain (later brigadier general) S. Van Vliet as Chief Quartermaster of the Army of the Potomac. Van Vliet organized his department, collected stores, and established supply depots. The principal depot for supplies in Washington was under Colonel D. H. Rucker, Assistant Quartermaster, and the principal depot on the south side of the Potomac was under Lieutenant Colonel Rufus Ingalls. On July 10, 1862, Van Vliet at his own request was relieved from duty with the Army of the Potomac and Ingalls took his place, serving through the Peninsular and Maryland Campaigns.[58] General Ingalls served as Chief Quartermaster of the Army of the Potomac through the rest of the war. His work received the hearty commendation of General Grant who said: "There never was a corps better organized than was the quartermaster's corps with the Army of the Potomac in 1864."[59]

PROCUREMENT OF SUPPLIES

The problem of supplying the Federal Army was not fairly in hand until past the middle of the war. The supply of clothing was aided by Soldiers' Aid Societies, contributions by soldiers' relatives and friends, and the knitting of socks by patriotic women in the North. American manufacturers and contractors in the fall of 1861 objected strenuously to the Government purchase of $800,000 worth of uniforms abroad although the uniforms themselves were of good material.[60]

In October 1861, the Quartermaster General noted that it was a remarkable thing that men should volunteer so rapidly that the resources of the country were unable to provide the material for clothing them as fast as they came forward. At the time Meigs was writing, the Government was in debt to contractors at all the principal points of purchase, and he feared would remain so for some time to come, but expressed the hope that if the troops could once be equipped, the great stimulus to manufacturing at home and the importations from abroad would enable the Department to keep the men from suffering.[61] Some of the suffering could have been avoided if the men had husbanded carefully that which they did have. In addition to the clothing lost in battle and discarded on the march, much clothing was sent home by the soldiers. The Quartermaster General would have been astonished had he seen the thousands of boxes of military clothing sent home in the earlier part of the war. Later this was interdicted, and ceased mostly during the last years of service.[62]

In the fiscal year ending June 30, 1862 the Department purchased: [63]

Overcoats	$ 1,281,522
Uniform coats	1,446,811
Trousers	3,039,286
Blankets	1,458,808
Boots and shoes	3,446,520
Sibley tents	42,392
Wall tents	24,500
Hospital tents	5,518
Common tents	70,735
Shelter tents	80,656

The clothing made in the last year of the war was of excellent quality, durable, strong, and of domestic manufacture.[64] The main Quartermaster depots were located at New York, Cincinnati, St. Louis, Alton (Illinois), and Steubenville, Ohio.

From June 30, 1861, to September 30, 1862, the Department purchased 146,453 horses and 101,135 mules; while in the fiscal year ending June 30, 1862, the Department had purchased 2,500 ambulances and over 200,000 wagons.[65] The lack of barracks for the new regiments in the winter of 1861-1862 explains the large number of large tents issued to the troops. The wall tents (10 feet square with 3-foot walls) were issued to officers; the wedge tents (6 feet square) were issued to non-commissoned officers and privates; while the Sibley tents (a cone, 16 feet in diameter at the base) were issued to the enlisted men. Each Sibley tent held 16 men.[66] One soldier in writing home that winter complained of lack of room in his tent but admitted that it was warm enough.[67]

The Quartermaster General's Department was responsible for the wagon trains. At first these trains were excessively cumbersome; one officer reports that in July 1861, McClellan had about 15 four-horse or six-mule teams to carry the personal outfit of himself and his staff, while brigade headquarters (there were no corps of divisions) had only a proportionately smaller number of teams.[68] McClellan himself reduced the size of supply trains and amounts of tentage and officers' baggage in August 1862, near the end of his active service with the Army of the Potomac.[69] The amount of transportation in the army was further reduced in 1863.[70]

The Chief Quartermaster of the Army of the Potomac marked on each wagon the corps badge with the division color and the number of the brigade. The particular brigade to which any wagon belonged could be told at a glance. Each wagon was also marked as to its contents: if ammunition, whether for artillery or infantry; if forage, whether for grain or hay; if rations, whether bread, pork, beans, rice, sugar, coffee, etc. Empty wagons were never allowed to follow the army or stay in camp but would return to the base of supply for a load of precisely the same article that had been taken from it. Empty trains were obliged to leave the roads free for loaded ones.[71] Over 4,000 heavy wagons were used in Grant's 1864 campaign.[72] And, at the same time Sherman's transportation was about 5,180 wagons, 860 ambulances, 28,300 horses, and 32,600 mules.[73]

The Quartermaster General's Department administered the captured railroad lines in the West in the early part of the war,[74] but later on the United States Military Railroads under General McCallum, although technically under the Department, actually functioned independently. It was the duty of the Quartermaster General's Department to load all material upon the cars, to direct where such material should be taken, and to direct to whom the material should be delivered.[75]

The Department furnished all the supplies for the construction and operation of the military railroads and made all the disbursements of moneys for their maintenance. All employees were carried and paid on the rolls of the Quartermaster Department.[76]

The Department was charged with the duty of burying the dead, and excluding those buried by soldiers and others on the battlefield the Department records showed the interment in cemeteries of 116,148 persons, of whom 98,827 were loyal, 12,596 disloyal, and of whom 95,803 were whites and 20,345 colored persons.[77]

COMMISSARY GENERAL OF SUBSISTENCE

The supplying of food to the Army was the responsibility of the bureau headed by the Commissary General of Subsistence, who, in April 1861, was Colonel George Gibson. The Subsistence Department at

MESS HALL

Army mess at a semi-permanent installation such as a base camp or hospital.

the commencement of the war contained but twelve officers of all grades but subsequently this number was increased to twenty-nine.[78] Colonel Gibson died September 29, 1861; he was succeeded by Colonel Joseph P. Taylor who died June 29, 1864 (Taylor was promoted to brigadier general the year of his death); while the last incumbent, Brigadier General Amos B. Eaton served from June 29, 1864 to the end of the war. Each regiment had a commissary officer (a lieutenant) and a regimental commissary sergeant. A chief commissary was provided for in the organization of the Army of the Potomac under McClellan, who selected Colonel H. F. Clark on August 1, 1861, as his Chief Commissary.[79] At the same time the Department was increased by the addition of four Commissaries of Subsistence with the rank, pay, and emoluments of majors of cavalry; and the addition of eight Commissaries of Subsistence with the rank, pay, and emoluments of captains of cavalry. These officers were to be taken from the line of the Army, either Regulars or volunteers.[80] In February 1863, there were further authorized: one Brigadier General to be Commissary General of Subsistence; and by regular promotion, one colonel, one lieutenant colonel, and two majors, all these three grades to be Assistant Commissaries of Subsistence.[81]

In 1864 it was ordered that every Commissary and Assistant Commissary of Subsistence should appear for examination as to his qualifications before a board to be composed of three staff officers of the Subsistence Department of whom two at least should be volunteers. Such boards were convened under the direction of the Secretary of War by the Commissary General of Subsistence. All officers lacking business ability were discharged with one month's pay while those found to be intemperate or immoral were dismissed from the service with no pay.[82] Shortly afterwards, the regulations were set up for these boards which examined the officers on the following: occupation of the officer previous to entry into service; length of time in service and the manner in which he performed his duties; business and official correspondence; arithmetic; business qualifications; and physical and moral qualities.[83]

Several men left the service under a cloud.

One Commissary of Subsistence, in a small volume written after the war, has explained why he decided to go back into a combat arm. "The matter of offering presents, commissions, bribes, or whatever you please to call them, had become common, and I began to doubt the wisdom of remaining on such duty." [84]

Despite its small number the Department was an important one. The Commissary General of Subsistence during the whole war drew upon the Treasury for over $369,000,000.[85] The Department, especially in the early part of the war, advertised for food in the cities of Boston, New York, Philadelphia, St. Louis, and San Francisco.

RATIONS

Fresh beef was generally supplied on the hoof to the armies in the field and in larger proportion of the ration to marching columns, to lessen as far as possible, the quantity of transportation required. The troops on the coast of the Carolinas and at the Gulf posts, including New Orleans, received their fresh beef by shipment from New York.[86] Fresh beef was generally obtained by contract but most other commissary supplies were procured by advertising for bids, the lowest being the one taken.[87] Instructions were given to the generals operating in enemy territory to subsist their armies so far as possible upon the country, receipting and accounting for everything taken, so that all persons of proved loyalty could be remunerated for their losses. But it was discovered that the adoption of the policy early in the war of carrying nearly all supplies with the army in the field made it very difficult to effect a radical change, although some reduction in trains was made in 1863.[88] As indicated above there was still greater reduction in 1864. In a petition of some fifty regiments to be allowed to use an extract of coffee with sugar and milk combined, in lieu of the normal coffee and sugar ration, it was pointed out that the latter ration for 100,000 men for 20 days weighed a total of 250 tons, "one half of which would be saved . . . an important item on a march or advance, reducing the number of wagons for this ration half." [89]

In November 1863, men in the Army of the Potomac were pleased to learn that henceforth they would have to carry no more than 5-days rations at any one time. "They had despaired of seeing any change; they had seen the 8-days, the 10-days, and, in one or two instances, the 11-days mule burden piled on the men's backs over and over again, cruelly, wastefully, and uselessly. Never once accomplishing the purpose, never in any single instance lasting over six days."[90]

The Count of Paris while observing the Federal army on the Peninsula was surprised at the amount of food consumed by the American soldier, He estimated that 2,000 wagons, drawn by 12,000 animals were strictly necessary to victual an army of 100,000 men and 16,000 horses at only two days' march from its base of operations.[91] Food for most of the early volunteers was abundant. One State Quartermaster General[92] instructed the colonel of a new regiment to advertise for bids to supply his regiment with daily cooked rations which included:

Breakfast: Fresh meat, fish, or ham; potatoes, bread and butter, coffee, with milk and sugar; pickles, salt, pepper, vinegar.

Dinner: Fresh beef or mutton; potatoes; ordinary vegetables of the season; bread and butter; stewed dried apples; pickles, pepper, salt, vinegar, boiled rice, mush, or Indian pudding and molasses. And, as often as three times a week, in addition to the foregoing, pork and baked beans, and bean or vegetable soup.

Supper: Cold meats, fish, bread and butter; stewed dried apples, coffee or tea with milk and sugar.

Such a fare contrasted markedly with that of the men in the 11th Indiana Infantry who, in the Shenandoah Valley three years later, were "living on green bark, green apples and fresh beef without salt.[93] In this case the lack of food was due to the rapid advance of Sheridan's army which left the commissary wagons miles in the rear. After Cedar Creek the 12th Connecticut Infantry and some other regiments "were at the point of starvation." [94]

PREPARATION OF FOOD

The main difficulty, however, was not lack of food but rather the almost universal ignorance of the men as to what to eat and how to prepare the rations issued them. Much quaint and useless advice was given to the men of the new regiments. For example, the *Soldiers' Health Companion* advised its readers to avoid strong coffee and, at the same time, outlined the recipes for 37 soldier's dishes which were especially nutritious, including Turkish Falaff (a stew), semi-citric lemonade, and macaroni pudding.[95] Nevertheless, certain dishes which were practicable (and indigestible) became favorites. Some men made pancakes (commonly called "slapjacks") by mixing flour with water and frying it in grease. "If a feller is hungry (as we generally are) they taste a little better than hard bread, as does most anything else." [96] However hardtack was used in a dish which became popular. It was prepared as follows:[97]

Hardtack would be broken up into small pieces and wet with water; then the soldier would take his half canteen [split canteen], put in his salt pork, and fry it over the fire, and would add to it the wet broken cracker, cook the whole together a little while with judicious stirring to properly mix the fat, and before serving put some sugar on top. This dish received among the cavalry a designation unsuited to ears polite . . . it was the standard food of both

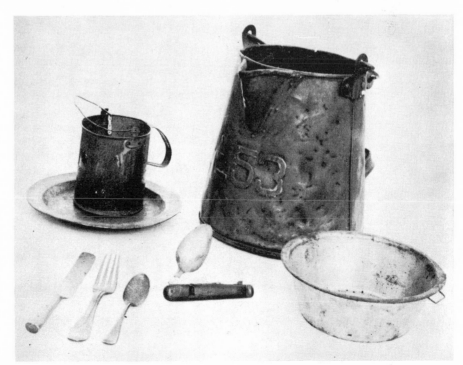

MESS EQUIPMENT

Copper coffee pot used by Company E, 53d Pennsylvania Infantry; and a tin basin, cup, and plate used by Private Peter J. Keck, Company E, 115th New York Infantry. The knife-fork-spoon combination was picked up on the Wilderness battlefield. The knife in the left foreground has a wooden handle, the fork is of tin, and the pewter spoon was used at Libby prison.

cavalry and infantry in the Army of the Potomac.

Some considered the pig to have been the most important contribution to the Southern food supply and at times the pig was "the principal commissary department of the cavalry."[98]

LIQUOR

Although beer and wine were sold by sutlers and peddlers in the camps, the only government liquor issue was that of whiskey by the Commissary Department. Commissary whiskey was stored in large quantities at depots and, in the early part of the war, was of good quality. But when this supply was out, age did not form an element of the article supplied. "It was new and fiery, rough and nasty to take . . . Various devices were in vogue to take off the ragged edge . . . One was to put it over the fire and let it simmer, another to set it afire and let it burn awhile. What disappeared was popularly supposed to be the worst part. Some called it the fusel oil. There was a tradition, probably baseless, that no commissary or quartermaster ever paid anything for his own whiskey, but that water enough was turned into the barrels to keep his account square."[99]

RATIONS

The Army rations were of two kinds, a camp ration and a marching ration. The camp ration consisted of: 22 ounces of bread or flour, or 1 pound of hard bread (hardtack); fresh beef as often as the commanding officer or regiments required it, and when practicable in place of salt meat; beans and rice or hominy, and one pound of potatoes per man to be issued at least three times a week; and "some other proper food" of equivalent value when these articles were not available. A ration of tea could be substituted for a ration of coffee upon the requisition of the proper officer. In hospitals fresh or preserved fruits, milk or butter, and eggs were issued when possible.[100] The marching ration consisted of: 1 pound of hardtack; ¾ pound of salt pork, or 1¼ pounds of fresh meat; sugar, coffee, and salt.[101] The camp ration was somewhat reduced June 22, 1864,[102] and shortly thereafter desiccated potatoes and desiccated vegetables were permitted to be substituted in the ration for beans, peas, rice, or hominy.[103] These desiccated vegetables came in sheets like pressed hops and were used as an antiscorbutic. They were not very satisfactory and the men soon began to call them "desecrated vegetables." [104] Those issued early in 1863 were "dirty, sandy, mouldy, and utterly uneatable. The men received them on their plates in liberal quantities, and after one taste threw them away in disgust, not caring where they fell— the camp was paved with them."[105]

But the desiccated vegetables were being foisted on the men whether they like them or not. In August, 1863 a soldier described them as square cakes an inch thick and apparently consisting of potatoes, carrots, turnips, onions, cabbage, and red peppers. These ingredients had been scalded and then pressed and dried. Although the men who received these desiccated vegetables were hungry for vegetables in any form, no one could cook them. The trouble seemed to be that each vegetable had lost its individual flavor in the cooking and were all "blended together in a nondescript sort of a dish that isn't good a bit.[106]

FOOD DEFICIENCIES

That some of the food supplied by the contractors was bad there is no doubt. "For sugar . . . [the Gov-

FALL IN FOR SOUP
Mess in the field—winter quarters.

rnment] often got sand; for coffee, rye; . . ." [107] Raw
roops in unhealthy climates soon became casualties
y eating too much of this poor food, which often as
ot, was poorly cooked. Often there was too much
alt meat and an insufficiency of vegetables, which
ed to scurvy.

Rations were issued uncooked and were cooked
ither by the individual soldiers themselves or by
ompany cooks. The company cook generally knew
ess about cooking than any man in the com-
any. "Not being able to learn to drill, and too dirty
o appear on inspection, he is sent to the cook house
o get him out of the ranks. We were not sorry when
he cook house was abolished."[108]

Such civilian agencies as the United States Sani-
ary Commission sent large quantities of onions and
anned fruits to the field forces in 1864 to overcome
he deficiency of anti scorbutic items. Some states
ent shipments of food to their regiments. For ex-
mple, the vessel *Helen and Elizabeth* arrived at
Aquia Creek in March 1863, completely loaded with
vegetables for the Rhode Island troops, and boxes
or individuals from thoughtful friends. The cargo
f vegetables was in good condition and made a
velcome addition to camp fare. One battery of artil-
ery received eight barrels of potatoes, onions, and
pples and quite a number of boxes for the men;
hey appreciated the many tokens of remembrance
nd shared with those tent mates who were not so
ortunate as themselves.[109] Much of the problem of
upplying the troops with rations over extended
eriods was that new troops tended to consume all
heir rations the first day or two. In addition to sup-
lying food to the Federal armies, the Subsistence
Department was responsible for the feeding of pris-
ners of war who, by 1865, were held in thirty-two
orts, prison-barracks, camps, and hospitals.[110]

In general it would appear that much of the trouble
ver rations was due to the exigencies of war, as
or example, in the case of the 5th Michigan Infantry
n the Peninsula where the men went two weeks
vithout access to their wagons.[111] But at the very
ime the 5th Michigan Infantry was without adequate food, another Michigan regiment (the 16th
Michigan Infantry), also on the Peninsula, was well
ed; the rations consisted of hard bread, coffee, sugar,
alt, and fresh beef while on the march. In camp
he men had beans, rice, and desiccated vegetables,
vhile they could buy cheese, lemons, ginger cakes,
nd condensed milk of the sutler, and even a little
utter at times. The rations furnished them, were
nore than abundant.[112]

On the whole the food appears to have been suffi-
ient in quantity but was deficient in such essentials
s vegetables, fruits, and dairy products. Such a
ormality as having an officer taste the soup was
oon abandoned.[113] Soldiers' rations were supple-
nented by food sold by sutlers who had a sort of

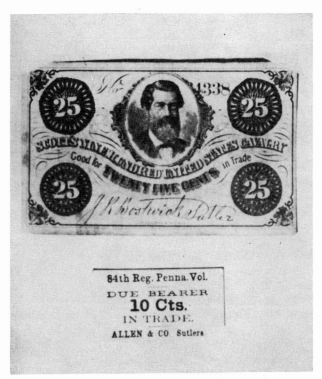

SUTLER CURRENCY

The 25¢ fractional currency was used by the 11th New
York Cavalry. The 10¢ sutler chit was used by the 84th
Pennsylvania Infantry. Sutlers used these notes and chits as
tokens.

semi-official concession with the regiments. The concession was usually secured through political influence in their States.[114] The men grumbled at the ex-
orbitant prices demanded by the sutlers, but nevertheless indulged in such luxuries as molasses cookies,
ten for a quarter; butter and cheese, sixty to eighty
cents a pound, and invariably a very small pound,
while condensed milk was fifty cents per pound
can.[115] In December 1864, sutler prices at City Point,
Virginia, included such prices as:[116] Can of fruit,
$1.00 to $1.25; sweet potatoes, .15 per pound; cheese,
.60 per pound; onions, .15 per pound; butter, .85 per
pound. Sutler prices in the West were roughly comparable.

Large Government bakeries were established near
permanent camps, and in 1864-1865 the Army was
using mobile bake-ovens on wheels.[117] Often units below strength saved on their ration allowance by bak-
ing with flour instead of drawing their bread ration,
with the result that they were paid the difference
which was put into a Company Fund. One regiment
of Sickles' brigade saved thirteen hundred dollars in
less than two months in this way.[118] A company on
the march did not draw the beans, rice, soap, and
candles that it was entitled to while in camp, and
company commanders were permitted to receive the
equivalent of these missing items of the ration in cash
to distribute among the company, although some did
not avail themselves of the opportunity.

PAY DEPARTMENT

The responsibility of paying the troops was solely in the hands of the Pay Department under the head of the Paymaster General of the Army. This was the only department which did not require a special Congressional law for its expansion. The Act of July 5, 1838 granted the President, whenever volunteers or Regulars should be called into the service of the United States, the authority to appoint additional paymasters at the rate of one to every two regiments, the paymasters to remain in service only so long as needed to pay to new troops. The highest number of additional paymasters was 447 in 1865 when the large Federal armies were being demobilized.[119] The Paymaster General at the beginning of the war, Colonel Benjamin F. Larned, had held his commission since July 20, 1854. On his death, September 6, 1862, he was succeeded by Lieutenant Colonel Timothy B. Andrews, who, after being placed on the retired list November 14, 1862,[120] served until November 29, 1864. He was then succeeded by Colonel Benjamin W. Brice[121] who served until the end of the war. The Paymaster General was assisted by two Deputy Paymasters General with rank of lieutenant colonel, and twenty-five Paymasters with the rank of major. These officers, with the Additional Paymasters that were added as necessity required, were considered sufficient in number for the performance of all the duties of the Pay Department.[122]

On March 13, 1863, it was ordered by the War Department that all persons who received appointments as Additional Paymasters should, before being commissioned, appear before a board of examiners to be appointed by the Secretary of War. This board would examine them as to their physical, mental, and moral fitness. Those who had already been commissioned were to appear also; all officers found unfit were to be mustered out of the service.[123] The following year more definite criteria of examining were laid down this time to include both Additional Paymasters and Paymasters. These officers were required to demonstrate their ability to write good business letters, to solve arithmetical problems quickly and accurately, and to perform the routine peculiar to the Pay Department. They were examined on their moral and business habits and their physical capacity to travel and endure the vicissitudes of climates.[124]

METHOD OF PAYMENTS

It was required by army regulations that all payments were to be made by paymasters of the Regular Army. This included all Additional Paymasters but excluded militia or volunteer officers. The troops were paid in such a manner that the arrears at no time ex-

PAY DAY
If this drawing is accurate, the officers present are permitting a gross disrespect to the National flag.

ceeded two months unless circumstances made a longer interim unavoidable, in which case the paymaster charged with the payment was required to report the situation promptly to the Paymaster General. By Army Regulations, troops were to be paid on the last day of February, April, June, August, October, and December. Pay rolls were made out in quadruplicate; one copy was sent to the Adjutant General in Washington, two to the Paymaster General, and the fourth was kept at the regiment.[125] In 1861, some militia regiments rioted due to their failure to be paid promptly[126] while others were mustered out without receiving their pay before arrival home, a fact which tended to discourage re-enlistments.[127]

The Paymaster, as a rule, waited for months for the army to be ready for a march to a battle. On the eve of the army's departure, he would appear and pay off the troops.[128] Such delays in pay day had a very real effect on the men's morale. In January 1863, the Government owed officers and men in the 1st Massachusetts Cavalry more than $200,000 and some men who had not been paid for 7-9 months received urgent letters from their families who were in serious distresss for lack of money.[129] At this period of the war, right after Fredericksburg, one of the main causes of discontent which was almost ruining the Army of the Potomac was this failure of "major cash" to make his appearance on time. Many letters were sent home from the Army with this written on the envelope:

Soldiers' letter and na-ray a red, hard-tack in place of bread;
Postmaster, please pass it through, Na-ray a red, but four months due.

Others had the following inscription: "Please pass free. Dead broke and 1,000 miles from home, and no pay from Uncle Sam in six months." The failure of the Pay Department caused the number of desertions to increase very substantially.[130]

Irregular payments affected the officers to a greater extent than the enlisted men, since they were not issued rations. If an officer's pay was withheld for six or twelve months as was frequently the case, he was forced to allow his servant to forage for him or starve. If he foraged, the men followed his example, although not driven by the same necessity, inasmuch as they were provided with food and clothing. The result was extensive straggling and much serious plundering.[131] The Commissary in many cases would not extend credit and the officers were forced to pay the sutlers on credit at excessive prices.[132] Often there were no sutlers available. Also, a "duty" of 3% on the excess over $600 would be deducted from all salaries of officers or payments to persons in the civil, military, naval, or other employment or service of the United States. Paymasters and disbursing officers

were ordered to make the deductions when making any payments to the officers concerned.[133]

Troops were "paraded" for payment by companies; company commanders were required to attend at the pay table. The officers were paid first, then the noncommissioned officers, and finally the privates in alphabetical order. If any one was out of camp, on detail, and not able to be present, the officer in command generally signed for the absent soldiers and received the money, which he turned over to the owner on his return to camp.[134] As soon as the men were paid the camp would be full of "sutlers and soldier robbers (who) had everything you could think of to sell to a soldier and 3 prices for everything and plenty of whiskey and plenty of drunken men.[135]

PAY AND ALLOWANCES

The pay of officers per month was as follows:

Lieutenant general	$270.00
Major general	220.00
Brigadier general	124.00
Colonel (Engineers, Topographical Engineers, Cavalry, Ordnance)	110.00
Colonel (Infantry, Artillery)	95.00
Lieutenant colonel (Engineers, Topographical Engineers, Cavalry, Ordnance)	95.00
Lieutenant colonel (Infantry, Artillery)	80.00
Major (Engineers, Topographical Engineers, Cavalry, Artillery)	80.00
Major (Infantry, Artillery)	70.00
Captain (Engineers, Topographical Engineers, Cavalry, Ordnance)	70.00
Captain (Infantry, Artillery)	60.00
Lieutenants (Engineers, Topographical Engineers, Cavalry, Ordnance)	53.33
First lieutenants (Infantry, Artillery)	50.00
Second lieutenant (Infantry, Artillery)	45.00

In addition to their base pay, lieutenants serving as regimental quartermasters or adjutants received an additional $10.00 a month. Certain officers were allowed varying numbers of rations and those serving mounted were allowed a specified number of horses with forage allowances.[136] Officers were allowed to employ soldiers as servants but were required to deduct from their own monthly pay the full amount paid to or expended by the Government per month on account of their servants.[137] There were frequent complaints by the officers that their pay scale was insufficient due to the increase in the cost of living as the war went on, and, in the case of married officers, the necessity of maintaining two establishments. Officers circulated a petition for a pay raise among their members in the 3rd Division, Tenth Army Corps, and the feeling was general that if Congress did not "act reasonably" many of them would resign.[138]

In 1861 the monthly pay for enlisted men was as follows:

Sergeant-Major	$21.00
Quartermaster-Sergeant	21.00
Chief Bugler	21.00
First Sergeant	20.00
Sergeant	17.00
Corporal	14.00
Private	13.00

Certain specialists in the Corps of Engineers, Corps of Topographical Engineers, Ordnance, Cavalry, and bands received somewhat higher pay than enlisted men of the line.[139] Up to August 10, 1861, the pay for cavalry privates was $12.00, all others $11.00 a month; from August 10, 1861,[140] to June 22, 1864, it was $13.00 a month; from June 22, 1864 to the end of the war it was $16.00 a month.[141] With the increases in privates' pay went corresponding increases in the pay of non-commissioned officers and specialists. Each enlisted man in the cavalry who furnished his own horse and horse equipments received 50¢ a day in addition to his base pay.[142] This allowance was soon dropped to 40¢ a day,[143] and although still in effect as late as August 1861, eventually disappeared as the Government procured sufficient horses to amount all the cavalry units. Colored troops received $7.00 a month with an additional $3.00 a month for clothing[144] until June 22, 1864, when they were placed on an equal pay footing with the whites.[145] Early in 1862, it was ordered that all Federal soldiers who were prisoners of war should receive the same pay during their imprisonment as though they were doing active duty.[146]

Apparently the men of some units were supplied with counterfeit Confederate currency, specimens of which are in collectors' hands today. The enemy did not hesitate to accept this bogus money, sometimes in lieu of Federal currency. While the 1st New Hampshire Battery was in camp near Sharpsburg, a peddler visited the men, "selling writing paper, maps of Virginia, and facsimiles of Confederate money, printed in Philadelphia." These imitation notes had been bought in considerable quantities at five and ten cents apiece by the men in anticipation of an opportunity to use them. Some of the native Virginians had no interest in "useless Northern script" but readily accepted the counterfeit money.[147]

ALLOTMENTS

A general order of August 3, 1861,[148] provided that the Secretary of War should devise a system of allotment tickets by which the family of the volunteer could draw such portions of his pay as he might request. This system was established the following month.[149] Each man signed an Allotment Roll, alloting a definite sum to his parents or anyone whom he chose. This roll was endorsed by the company commander and turned over to the paymaster who

sent it to the State Treasurer, and he, in turn, sent it to the city or town treasurer who notified the donee. The donee himself had to call and get the money. The system insured safety and saved the cost of paying the express rates involved in sending the money by mail.[150] Many men took advantage of this system. One major recorded that two-thirds of the pay of his regiment was sent home.[151] Sometimes, when a Governor visited troops from his State, he would be accompanied by an allotment commissioner to whom would be entrusted the funds of those men who wished to send money home.[152]

BENEFITS

On August 3, 1861, the Government provided that any volunteer who was wounded or otherwise disabled in the service should be entitled to the same benefits "which have been or may be conferred on persons disabled in the Regular service; and the widow, if there be one, and if not, the legal heirs of such as die, or may be killed in service" should receive $100.00 in addition to all arrears of pay and allowances.[153] On July 29, 1862, it was ordered [154] that all officers and enlisted men of Regulars, volunteers, and militia who had been totally disabled by wound or disease since March 4, 1861, should receive the following monthly pensions:

Lieutenant colonels and higher	$30.00
Majors	25.00
Captains	20.00
First lieutenants	17.00
Second lieutenants	15.00
Enlisted men	8.00

In case of death the pension was to be made payable to the widow, or if no widow existed, then to the children—subject to the condition that the pension continue to the widow during her widowhood, or to the children until they severally reached the age of sixteen. There were lesser scales of pensions for lesser disabilities.

FINAL PAYMENTS

The Pay Department was largest in number after the war was over when more personnel were necessary in making final payments to the troops at muster out. From June to October, 1865, the Department made final payment to more than 800,000 officers and men. This was "an extraordinary exhibit of work performed chiefly within the three months of June, July, and August—two hundred and seventy millions of money paid to eight hundred thousand individual men." Each man's account had to be separately computed in the items of pay, clothing allowance, bounty, and deductions. The final amount in each case had to be stated and the signature of each officer and man appended in duplicate to the receipt rolls. The total of money disbursed by the Department from July 1, 1861, to October 31, 1865 was $1,029,239,000.[155]

PROVOST MARSHAL

Military police duty in the Federal Army was performed by the Provost Marshal Department, which only came into being in March 1863. Up to that time police duty was done by army provost marshals and their guards consisting of line units detailed for the purpose.

MILITARY POLICE IN WASHINGTON

Immediately after assuming command of the troops in and around Washington, General McClellan appointed Colonel Andrew Porter, 16th Infantry, as Provost Marshal of Washington.[156] Porter was fairly effective in suppressing gambling houses, drinking houses, brothels, and preserving order in general.[157] He soon cleared the streets of Washington and Georgetown of all the vagrant soldiery who had daily congregated in those cities but had no proper business there.[158]

Provost Marshal Porter countersigned enemy safeguards and issued passes to citizens. These passes were examined at important points of ingress and egress around the city.[159] He accompanied the Army of the Potomac to the Peninsula where his provost guard, consisting of the 2d Cavalry and companies from the 8th and 17th Infantry Regiments, was engaged to a great extent in preventing straggling on the march. When in towns and cities the provost guard was split up in small groups of about six men each, to prevent looting.[160] After the Peninsular Campaign, Porter was relieved by Major W. H. Wood, 17th Infantry, who served through the Maryland Campaign.

It soon became evident that the Department would have to be expanded in scope so as to assume new responsibilities. One of these was the checking of desertion which in the fall of 1862, became a serious problem to the Government. In September 24, 1862, the War Department published an order[161] respecting Special Provost Marshals and defining their duties. It was ordered that in addition to a Provost Marshal General of the War Department with headquarters at Washington, there would be assigned one or more Special Provost Marshals for each State whose duty it would be to arrest all deserters, whether Regular, volunteers, or militiamen, and send them to the nearest military commander or post. The deserters would then be sent forward to their respective regiments. These special marshals were given authority to arrest disloyal persons and to investigate treasonable practices. This order, however, was not sufficient to check desertion nor to insure the success of the draft that was to take place the following spring.

APPREHENSION OF DESERTERS AND DRAFT DODGERS

It was decided to include in the Enrollment Act of March 3, 1863 the formation of a separate department to be known as the Provost Marshal Bureau. At its head was placed Colonel James B. Fry, Assistant Adjutant General, United States Army.[162] The situation when Fry assumed office was grave indeed. Nearly 400,000 recruits were required to bring the regiments then in service up to the necessary strength. The Government, through the Bureau, assumed direct control of the business of recruiting which had heretofore been transacted mainly by the State governments. The Provost Marshals of the several Congressional districts, aided by a commissioner and surgeon in each, were made recruiting officers. Thus the principal duties of the Bureau came to include the arrest of deserters, the enrollment of the national forces for draft, and the enlistment of volunteers.[163] To check desertion it was ordered that all commanders of regiments and independent detachments, all surgeons in charge of hospitals or detachments, and all commanders of troops on detached service should send monthly descriptive list of all deserters in their commands to the Provost Marshal General.[164] Between October 1, 1863 and October 1, 1864, the Provost Marshals arrested 39,392 stragglers and deserters.[165] Although about 200,000 men[166] deserted from the Federal Army during the war, the Provost Marshal's Bureau arrested and returned 76,526 of them between March 1863, and the end of the war.[167]

In enforcing the Enrollment Act and the subsequent drafts that followed, the Provost Marshal General was assisted by Acting Assistant Provost Marshals (captains) in each State, and by Boards of Enrollment in each Congressional district. These boards consisted of clerks, deputy provost marshals, surgeons, and special agents (usually three per district) for the detection and arrest of deserters. The districts, comprising towns, townships, and wards, had one enrolling officer each.[168]

These men met with much resistance in certain sections. The Acting Assistant Provost Marshal General for Illinois was concerned about the flight from his State of persons subject to military duty. On March 8, 1864, he reported to Colonel Fry that "at least 1,000 young and able-bodied men intend to leave this district [Ninth District] for California, Idaho, and other places with a view of escaping the draft . . . The copperheads are the ones who intend to leave . . ."[169] On October 2, 1864, an uprising in Orange and Crawford counties in Indiana threatened to become general when 500 well armed men, after taking horses and money from citizens and home guards, dispatched runners for reenforcements.[170] In these and other States many supporters of Vallandigham and other obstructionists joined draft protective associations, which, under arrangements with the provost marshals, were permitted to furnish substitutes in proportion to their numbers. Local districts even made efforts to enlist runaway Southern Negroes, Confederate prisoners, and convicts.[171] In one case a Navy officer, while waiting in a railroad station was drugged and "drafted" into the Army.[172]

Despite opposition in many quarters, the Provost Marshal General and his subordinates appear to have performed their duties well. The worthless material that appeared too often in the form of replacements during the last years of the war was more the result of faulty legislation than the execution of their legislation. Fry's bureau provided the Government with a complete inventory of the military resources of the loyal States in men, an inventory which showed an aggregate number of 2,254,063 not including 1,000,516 soldiers actually under arms when hostilities ceases. The Bureau raised 1,120,621 men at a cost per man of $9.84 while the cost of recruiting the 1,356,593 men raised prior to the organization of the Bureau was $34.01 per man.[173]

POSTAL SERVICE

Among the semi-military functions which were very important to the soldier was the postal service which, in some units, was very efficiently organized and administered. The Federal soldier was either an inveterate letter writer at the time of his enlistment, or he soon became one. "Clumsy fingers, which hadn't uncorked an ink-bottle since the owners' last one was shied out of the schoolhouse window years before, wrestled with exasperating pen, delusive ink, and intractable paper."[174] Realizing the morale value to the soldiers of an inexpensive postal service, the Government passes an order August 3, 1861, which permitted all letters written by soldiers to be transmitted through the mails without prepayment of postage.

The postage, however, had to be paid by the recipient.[175] However, generally the soldiers used stamps when they had them, in order to save their families the expense of paying on the other end. In the early months of the war gold and silver money disappeared, as it commanded a premium, so that change became scarce. As a result, stamps were used as money for making change. This was before scrip was used by the Federal Government to take the place of silver; and although the use of stamps as change was not authorized by the Government, everybody took them, and the soldiers about to leave for the war carried large quantities with them. Many of these stamps were in poor condition because they had passed through so many hands. They were passed about in small envelopes, containing 25 and 50 cents in value. The soldiers were often greatly disgusted to find that their stamps were just about ruined either from rain, perspiration, or compression, as they attempted, after a hot march, to get one for a letter. If they could split off one from a welded mass of a hundred or more, they counted themselves fortunate. Later the Postmaster General issued an order allowing soldiers to send letters without pre-payment by merely writing "Soldier's Letter" on the envelope. There was a large number of fanciful envelopes made during the war; one young man after the war had a collection of over 7,000 of these envelopes, all of them of different design.[176]

A system of receipt vouchers for registered letter was arranged whereby the soldier could send valuable enclosures through the mail by paying a registering fee of five cents plus the regular postage. A trustworthy agent to receive such letters was appointed by the commanding officers of regiments o brigades.[177] For the regular mail a carpet bag wa hung up against the adjutant's tent of each regiment. In permanent camps and behind the front it wa often necessary to empty the bag twice a day. From its camp near Washington the 11th Massachusett Infantry, 863 officers and men, sent an average o 4500 letters weekly.[178]

The postal service of the Army of the Potomac wa very completely organized. Each regiment had a post-boy who carried the letters to his command t brigade headquarters where the mails of the differen regiments were placed in one pouch and set up t division headquarters. From division headquarter the mail went through corps headquarters to army depots and finally to GHQ.

Cases for the letters were made of rough board which on a march were packed away in the bottom of an Army wagon.[179] One wagon was sufficient t carry the whole mail equipment, boxes, tent, anc furniture. Usually the post-boys were selected from among the younger enlisted men. In the 2nd Michigan Infantry one of these post "boys" turned out to be a girl who had been handling the mail for a brigade in the Ninth Army Corps. She was discovered, but shortly thereafter deserted.[180] The postal service was the medium by which the soldiers received newspapers from their home town. Usually however, they obtained the big dailies by purchase from newsboys who brought them by boat and train from the North. Soldiers on the Petersburg fron read accounts of Sheridan's victory at Opequon, Virginia, four days after it occurred, but knew about it as early as one day after the battle. "When a victory is gained and telegraphed to Grant, we hear of it the same day, but if it is a reverse, we have to read of it in the papers. We now get the Washington Chronicle, the Philadelphia Enquirer, Free Press and the New York World."[181] Soldiers in the Army of the Potomac bought their newspapers from agents who were selected from the highest bidders among discharged and disabled soldiers.[182]

As soon as a regiment was reasonably certain that is was not going to move for a while, its members notified their friends and relatives in the North, who sent the soldiers food, clothing, as well as all kinds of non-essentials, in boxes by means of the Adams Express Company which became a household word during the war. One foreign observer named this company one of the two institutions (the other was the telegraph) which practically followed the skirmishers. "At the same time, with the first tent generally grew up a shanty with the firm of Adams Express, which conveyed parcels of every size to the army and throughout the Union . . ."[183] One of the largest boxes on record was a box weighing nearly 400 pounds sent to twenty members of 6th Wisconsin Battery. One member alone received thirty pounds of baked chickens, pies, small and big cakes.[184]

NOTES CHAPTER 7

1. Upton, p. 262.
2. Comte de Paris, Vol. 1, p. 265.
3. *Official Records*, First Series, Vol. 5, p. 23.
4. United States War Department, "General Order No. 7," March 20, 1861, *General Orders for 1861*.
5. *Official Records*, Third Series, Vol. 5, pp. 118-124.
6. United States War Department, "General Order No. 54," August 10, 1861, *General Orders for 1861*. All commissions were in the cavalry branch, with corresponding pay and enrolments.
7. *Ibid.*, "General Order No. 91," July 29, 1862, *General Orders for 1862*. This order affected the permanent establishment only and had no reference to temporary volunteer appointments.
8. *House Executive Documents*, 37 Cong., 3 Sess., Document 1, p. 41.
9. *Ibid.*, p. 42.
10. *Ibid.*
11. Fry, James B., *Military Miscellanies*, pp. 280-281.
12. *House Miscellaneous Documents*, 37 Cong., 2 Sess., Document 73, p. 2.
13. McClellan, p. 122.
14. United States War Department, Adjutant General's Office, *Official Army Register for 1864*. The Regular officers were: 1 brigadier general, 2 colonels, 4 lieutenant colonels, 13 majors. The volunteer officers were 60 majors and 249 captains.
15. United States War Department, "General Order No. 91," July 29, 1862, *General Orders for 1862*.
16. Gilham, William, *Manual of Instruction for the Volunteers and Militia of the United States* (1861), pp. 701-702.
17. De Hart, William C., *Observations on Military Law, and the Constitution and Practice of Courts Martial* (1861), p. 62.
18. Gilham, p. 702.
19. United States War Department, "General Order No. 91," July 29, 1862, *General Orders for 1862*.
20. DeHart, pp. 62-64.
21. United States War Department, *Revised Regulations for the Army of the United States 1861*, Section 895.
22. Benet, S. V., *A Treatise on Military Law*, p. 8.
23. United States War Department, "General Order No. 100," April 24, 1863. *General Orders for 1863*.
24. *Army and Navy Journal*, Vol. 1, (March 19, 1864), pp. 507-508.
25. Croushore, pp. 44-45. All but the accused wore side arms. *Ibid.*
26. Eighty-Seventh Article of War. United States War Department, *Revised Regulations for the Army of the United States 1861*, pp. 512-513.
27. United States War Department, "General Order No. 54," August 10, 1861, *General Orders for 1861*.
28. *Ibid.*, "General Order No. 91," July 29, 1862, *General Orders for 1862*.
29. Comte de Paris, Vol. 3, pp. 3-4; *Official Records*, First series, Vol. 25, Part 1, p. 137.
30. *Army and Navy Journal* Vol. 1 (March 19, 1864), pp. 507-508.
31. Billings, *Hardtack and Coffee*, p. 163.

32. Letter of Colonel Theodore Lyman of Meade's staff, May 17, 1864. Agassiz, p. 117.
33. United States War Department. "General Order No. 216," June 22, 1864, *General Orders for 1864*.
34. Ninety-First and Ninety-Second Articles of War, United States War Department, *Revised Regulations for the Army of the United States 1861*, p. 513-514.
35. United States War Department, "General Order No. 270," October 11, 1864, *General Orders for 1864*.
36. Report of Secretary of War, November 22, 1865, *House Executive Documents*, 39 Cong., 1 Sess., Document 1, Part 1, pp. 45-46.
37. United States War Department, "General Order No. 100," April 24, 1863, *General Orders for 1863*.
38. Scott, Robert, *An Analytical Digest of the Military Laws of the United States*, p. 441 (Note).
39. United States War Department, "General Order No. 54," August 10, 1861, *General Orders for 1861*.
40. *Official Records*, First Series, Vol. 5, p. 24.
41. United States War Department. *Revised Regulations for the Army of the United States 1861*, Section 241.
42. United States War Department, "General Order No. 27," March 21, 1862. *General Orders for 1862*.
43. *Ibid.*, "General Order No. 91," July 29, 1862, *General Orders for 1862*.
44. *Ibid.*, "General Order No. 212," December 23, 1862, *General Orders for 1862*.
45. Line officers liked such assignments.
46. Walker, Francis A., *History of the Second Army Corps*, pp. 202-203.
47. This practice should have been tried much earlier.
48. United States War Department, "General Order No. 64," August 22, 1861, *General Orders for 1861*. This order dated Meigs' commission as being in effect from May 15, 1861.
49. *Ibid.*, "General Order No. 54," August 10, 1861, *General Orders for 1861*.
50. *Ibid.*, Adjutant General's Office, *Official Army Register for 1864*, pp. 5, 74-75.
51. Leib, Charles, *Nine Months in the Quartermaster's Department or the Chance of Making a Million*, pp. 171, 186-187.
52. United States War Department, "General Order No. 221," July 1, 1864, *General Orders for 1864*.
53. *Ibid.*, "General Order No. 252," August 31, 1864, *General Orders for 1864*.
54. Annual Report of Secretary of War, March 1, 1865, *House Executive Documents*, 38 Cong., 2 Sess., Document 83, p. 138.
55. Comte de Paris, Vol. 1, pp. 631-632.
56. Quartermaster General's Office, "General Order No. 30," July 30, 1864.
57. United States War Department, "General Order No. 231," July 18, 1864, *General Orders for 1864*.
58. *Official Records*, First Series. Vol. 5, pp. 27-28.
59. Grant, Vol. 2, p. 188.
60. *Official Records*, Third Series, Vol. 1, pp. 582-586.
61. *Ibid.*, p. 570.
62. Buffum, p. 178.
63. Report of Secretary of War, December 1, 1862, *House Executive Documents*, 37 Cong., 3 Sess., Document 1, p. 76.

64. Annual Report of Secretary of War, March 1, 1865, *House Executive Documents*, 38 Cong., 2 Sess., Document 83, p. 131.

65. Report of Secretary of War, December 1, 1862, *House Executive Documents*, 37 Cong., 3 Sess., Document 1, pp. 72-73.

66. Comte de Paris, Vol. 1, p. 293.

67. Letter of Corporal Moses W. Jewett, Co. "B" 6th Connecticut Infantry, Hilton Head, Port Royal, S. C. January 8, 1862. Manuscript in author's possession.

68. Keifer, Vol. 1, p. 185.

69. Headquarters, Army of the Potomac, "General Order No. 153," August 10, 1862.

70. United States War Department. "General Order No. 274," August 7 1863, *General Orders for 1863*.

71. Grant, Vol. 2, pp. 188-190. A good photograph of a corps wagon train is shown in *Photographic History*, Vol. 4, pp. 100-101.

72. Annual Report of Secretary of War, March 1, 1865, *House Executive Documents*, 38 Cong., 2 Sess., Document 83, p. 146.

73. Major, Duncan K., and Fitch, Roger S., *Supply of Serman's Army during the Atlanta Campaign*, p. 102.

74. Report of Secretary of War, December 1, 1862. *House Executive Documents*, 37 Cong., 3 Sess., Document 1, p. 68.

75. *Ibid.*, 39 Cong., 1 Sess., Document 1, p. 38.

76. Major and Fitch, p. 29.

77. Annual Report of Secretary of War, November 22, 1865, *House Executive Documents*, 39 Cong., 1 Sess., Document 1, Part 1, pp. 37, 39.

78. *Ibid.*, Part 2, p. 893.

79. *Official Records*, First Series, Vol. 5, pp. 28-29.

80. United States War Department. "General Order No. 54," August 10, 1861, *General Order for 1861*.

81. *Ibid.*, "General Order No. 40," February 11, 1863, *General Order for 1863*.

82. *Ibid.*, "General Order No. 221," July 1, 1864, *General Order for 1864*.

83. *Ibid.*, "General Order No. 252," August 31, 1864, *General Order for 1864*.

84. Symonds, H. C. (Major, Commissary of Subsistence), *Report of a Commissary of Subsistence, 1861-1865*, p. 90.

85. *Official Records*, Third Series, Vol. 5, p. 1039.

86. Report of Secretary of War, Dec. 1, 1862, House Executive Documents, 37 Cong., 3 Sess., Document 1, pp. 12-13.

87. *Ibid.*, December 5, 1863, *House Executive Documents*, 38 Cong., 1 Sess., Document 1, p. 12.

88. *Ibid.*, p. 43. (Report of the General-in-Chief, November 15, 1863).

89. *Senate Executive Documents*, 37 Cong., 2 Sess., Document 16, p. 2. The ration remained unchanged.

90. Page (14th Connecticut Infantry), pp. 198-199.

91. Comte de Paris, Vol. 1, p. 212.

92. Quartermaster General H. H. Fomtan, Michigan Militia, to Colonel Dwight A. Woodbury, May 20, 1861. Manuscript letter in Michigan Historical Collection.

93. Entry for August 20, 1864, diary of First Lieutenant Frederick Frank, Co. "K" 11th Indiana Infantry. Manuscript in author's possession.

94. Croushore, p. 230.

95. *Soldier's Health Companion* (1861) pp. 29, 75-90.

96. Shannon, F. A. (editor), *The Civil War Letters of Sergeant Onley Andrus*, p. 30. Entry for November 27, 1862. (Andrus was in the 95th Illinois Infantry).

97. Crowninshield, p. 99.

98. *Ibid.*, p. 303.

99. *Ibid.*, pp. 298-299.

100. United States War Department, "General Order No. 54," August 10, 1861, *General Orders for 1861*.

101. Billings, *Hardtack and Coffee*, p. 112.

102. United States War Department, "General Order No. 216," June 22, 1864, *General Orders for 1864*.

103. *Ibid.*, "General Order No. 226," July 8, 1864, *General Orders for 1864*.

104. Several sources report the use of this term.

105. Thompson, (13th New Hampshire Infantry), p. 101.

106. Norton, *Army Letters*, pp. 175-176. Letter written home from 83rd Pennsylvania Infantry. August 22, 1863.

107. *Harpers New Monthly Magazine*, Vol. 29 (July 1864), p. 228.

108. Adams (19th Massachusetts Infantry), p. 27.

109. Rhodes (Battery "B" 1st Rhode Island Light Artillery), p. 157.

110. Report of Secretary of War, November 22, 1865, *House Executive Documents*, 39 Cong., 1 Sess., Document 1, Part 1, p. 34.

111. Letter of Lieutenant Charles H. Hutchins, 5th Michigan Infantry, near Fair Oaks, Virginia, May 28, 1862. Manuscript in Burton Historical Collection.

112. Letter of Second Lieutenant Francis D. Keeler, Co. "E" 16th Michigan Infantry, Fair Oaks, Virginia, May 20, 1862. Keeler, *War Letters Written During the Rebellion*, pp. 46-47.

113. A photograph of an officer of the 31st Pennsylvania Infantry tasting the soup of his command is shown in *Photographic History*, Vol. 8, p. 83.

114. Joinville, De. Prince, *The Army of the Potomac*, p. 14.

115. Rhodes, (Battery "B" 1st Rhode Island Light Artilley), p. 126.

116. *Harper's Weekly*, Vol. 8, (December 10, 1864), p. 787.

117. *Photographic History*, Vol. 8, p. 49.

118. Comte de Paris, Vol. 1, pp. 297-298.

119. Report of Secretary of War, November 22, 1865, *House Executive Documents*, 39 Cong., 1 Sess., Document 1, Part 1, p. 33. The number of additional paymasters was: 110 in 1862; 171 in 1862; 210 in 1863; 319 in 1864. Ingersoll, *A History of the War Department . . .* , p. 262.

120. United States War Department, "General Order No. 185," November 14, 1862, *General Orders for 1862*.

121. *Ibid.*, *Official Army Register for 1865*, p. 12. Shannon (Vol. 2, 265) says that Major C. H. Fry served July 15, 1862 to December 10, 1862 as acting Paymaster General.

122. Report of Secretary of War, December 5, 1863, *House Executive Documents*, 38 Cong., 1 Sess., Document 1, p. 74.

123. United States War Department, "General Order No. 61," March 13, 1863, *General Orders for 1863*.

124. *Ibid.*, "General Order No. 252," August 31, 1864, *General Orders for 1864*.

125. *Ibid.*, *Revised Regulations for the Army of the United States 1861*, Sections 327, 341, 1646.

126. *Official Records*, Third Series, Vol. 1, p. 359.

127. *Ibid.*, p. 415. See also *Ibid.*, pp. 395, 416-417; 512-513; First Series, Vol. 46, Part 2, pp. 561-562.

128. Thompson (13th New Hampshire Infantry), p. 274.

129. Crowninshield, p. 109.

130. Rhodes (Battery "B" 1st Rhode Island Light Artillery), p. 151.

131. Croushore, pp. 97-98.

132. *Army and Navy Journal*, Vol. 2 (January 14, 1865), p. 326.

133. Act of Congress, July 1, 1862, quoted in "General Order No. 9," Quartermastetr General's Office," February 17, 1864.

134. Rhodes (Battery "B" 1st Rhode Island Light Artillery), p. 183.

135. Diary of Lt. Henry J. Waltz Co. "I" 93d Pennsylvania Infantry. July 25, 1864. Manuscript in author's possession.

136. United States War Department, *Revised Regulations for the Army of the United States 1861*, Section 1310.

137. *Ibid.*, "General Order No. 91," July 29, 1862, *General Orders for 1862.*

138. *Army and Navy Journal*, Vol. 2, (September 10, 1864), pp. 35-36; (October 1, 1864), pp. 85-86; (November 19, 1864), p. 196; (December 3, 1864), p. 228.

139. United States War Department, *Revised Regulations for the Army of the United States 1861*, pp. 350-353.

140. *Ibid.*, "General Order No. 54," August 10, 1861, *General Orders for 1861.*

141. *Ibid.*, "General Order No. 216," June 22, 1864, *General Orders for 1864.*

142. *Ibid.*, "General Order No. 15," May 4, 1861, *General Order for 1861.*

143. *Ibid.*, "General Order No. 25," May 25, 1861, *General Orders for 1861.*

144. Militia Act of July 17, 1862.

145. United States War Department, "General Order No. 216," June 22, 1864, *General Orders for 1864.*

146. *Ibid.*, "General Orders No. 9," February 1, 1862, *General Orders for 1862.*

147. *1st New Hampshire Battery*, pp. 22-23.

148. United States War Department, "General Order No. August 3, 1861, *General Orders for 1861.*

149. *Ibid.*, "General Order No. 81," September 19, 1861, *General Orders for 1861.*

150. Cowles, p. 231.

151. Entry for October 26, 1863, Journal of Major Harrison Soule, 6th Michigan Heavy Artillery, Michigan Historical Collections.

152. Rhodes (Battery "B" First Rhode Island Light Artillery), p. 80.

153. United States War Department, "General Order No. 49," August 3, 1861. *General Orders for 1861.*

154. *Ibid.*, "General Order No. 91," July 29, 1862, *General Orders for 1862.*

155. Report of Secretary of War, November 22, 1865, *House Executive Documents*, 39 Cong., 1 Sess., Document 1, Part 2, pp. 898, 901.

156. *Official Records*, First Series, Vol. 5, p. 30.

157. See photograph of a provost detail destroying a house in Alexandria from which liquor had been sold to soldiers. *Photographic History*, Vol. 5, p. 189.

158. The problem was never completely solved.

159. A photograph of a provost guard examining passes at a bridge is shown in *Photographic History*, Vol. 8, p. 81.

160. Cowles, p. 241.

161. United States War Department, "General Order No. 140," September 24, 1862, *General Orders for 1862.*

162. *Ibid.*, "General Order No. 67," March 17, 1863, *General Orders for 1863.*

163. *House Executive Documents*, 39 Cong., 1 Sess., Document 1, p. 1. Fry was promoted brigadier general April 21, 1864.

164. United States War Department, "General Order No. 72," March 24, 1863. *General Orders for 1863.*

165. Report of Secretary of War, March 1, 1865, *House Executive Documents*, 38 Cong., 2 Sess., Document 83, p. 13.

166. Actual number difficult to determine, because of faulty records.

167. *House Executive Documents*, 39 Cong., 1 Sess., Document 1, p. 2.

168. *Ibid.*, p. 13.

169. *Official Records*, Third Series, Vol. 4, p. 159.

170. *Ibid.*, p. 752.

171. Gray, Wood, *The Hidden Civil War*, p. 209.

172. Trumbull, H. Clay, *War Memories of an Army Chaplain*, pp. 199-200.

173. *House Executive Documents*, 39 Cong., 1 Sess., Document 1, pp. 1-2. The figure of $9.84 is exclusive of bounties.

174. Buffum, p. 168.

175. United States War Department, "General Order No. 49," August 3, 1861. *General Orders for 1861.*

176. Billings, *Hardtack and Coffee*, pp. 63-64.

177. *United States War Department*, "General Order No. 23," March 3, 1862., *General Orders for 1862.*

178. Comte de Paris, Vol. 1, p. 285.

179. See photographs of the four-horse team and wagon for army mail, Army of the Potomac, and a corps mail wagon and army post office, *Photographic History*, Vol. 8, pp. 33, 35-36.

180. Entry for April 22, 1862, diary of Corporal William Boston, Co. "H" 20th Michigan Infantry. Manuscript in Michigan Historical Collections.

181. *Ibid.*, entry for September 23, 1862.

182. New York *Herald*, No. 9760, (June 5, 1863), p. 1.

183. Salm Salm, Princess Felix, *Ten Years of My Life*, p. 42.

184. Jones, Jenkin L., *An Artilleryman's Diary*, p. 292.

CHAPTER 8

Special Agencies

IN ADDITION to the various combat and administrative branches, the Federal Army was served by a number of unrelated special agencies. Some of these were composed of individual civilians or groups of citizens. For example, there was the camp sutler, the forerunner of today's post exchange; and several civilian welfare agencies such as the Sanitary Commission. The Civil War also saw the genesis of today's intelligence service, now a staff and command function and purely military in character. In 1861 it was started, under McClellan, as a civilian detective agency.

THE SUTLER

In addition to the shanty set up in each camp by the Adams Express Company, there was the inevitable sutler's hut or tent, which also followed or even accompanied the troops into the field. Each regiment was allowed one sutler, who, in some cases, was appointed by the brigade commander on the recommendation of the commissioned officers of the regiment. In other cases, however, State governors appointed sutlers, often in payment of past or future political debts. The sutler was a civilian and his prices were set by a board of officers detailed from the brigade of which his regiment was a part. As mentioned previously, the Inspector General's Department was responsible for preparing a list of sutlers' stores and inspecting merchandise and prices. Sutlers were allowed a lien upon the pay of the officers and enlisted men of the regiment for which he was chosen. This lien was not to exceed one-sixth of a man's monthly pay. The list of items permitted to be sold by sutlers was a long one. Some of them were: fruits, dairy products, newspapers, books, tobacco, shoe cleaning equipment, combs, razors, scissors, emery, and crocus.[1] On February 7, 1863, this list was enlarged to include: canned meats, oysters, condiments, pickles, fish, tin plates, cups, cutlery, twine, wrapping paper, uniform clothing for officers, socks, shirts, drawers, and shoes.[2]

It was not long before the sutlers had no competition because their prices were fixed and peddlers in many regiments were not allowed in the camp area.

As one soldier expressed it, the men bought of the sutlers or went without. Occasionally a sutler used cards instead of money for charge. These cards were marked by the sutler and could only be used at his tent and nowhere else.[3] Complaints were frequent that the sutlers' prices were too high or that the weights were inaccurate. The result was that often the sutler would witness a raid on his establishment by an infuriated soldiery which was rarely interfered with by superior officers.[4] Major William B. Hicks of the 14th Connecticut Infantry recorded in his diary, June 19, 1863 how soldiers went about cleaning out a sutler—"a not uncommon event." The victim was usually, though not always, one who had inspired general indignation by excessively high prices for his goods. "The manner of his punishment is on this wise. The guy-ropes that hold up his large store tent are secretly cut; the tent, of course, collapses, and in the general confusion the numerous and often apparently sympathizing bystanders help themselves to all the plunder they can conveniently lay hands on. This, of course, is sheer robbery, yet the sutler's business in many instances is not much better. The proper remedy would be for the Government to employ a man to furnish the troops at cost or a reasonable profit such articles as stationery, tobacco, underclothing, etc. Perhaps some of the Chaplains could be made useful in this way.[5]"

This would have been a better arrangement, since the sutlers tended to appear only when there was no danger from enemy action. As a soldier of the 14th Indiana Infantry put it: "Our sutler has 'played out', [we] fancy, as we have seen nothing of that individual for some two months. 'Twould perhaps be a fine thing for the regiment if 'twas so, as these gentlemen sutlers skin the soldiers unmercifully."[6] Perhaps there wasn't too much exaggeration in the statement of the trooper of the 1st Massachusetts Cavalry who said that it is doubtful if the sutler in his regiment realized more than three hundred percent profit.[7]

General Halleck believed that the entire abolition of the sutler system would "rid the army of the incumbrance of sutler-wagons on the march, and the nuisance of sutler-stalls and booths in camp; it would relieve officers and soldiers of much of their present expenses, and would improve the discipline and efficiency of the troops in many ways, and particularly by removing from camps the prolific evils of drunkeness." The General believed that the Quartermaster and Commissary Departments could have provided all articles legitimately supplied by sutlers at a much less price; he resented the partial freedom from military authority enjoyed by the sutlers; and he regretted their peculiar opportunity to act as spies, informers, smugglers, and contraband traders.[8] The sutler often timed his arrival with that of the paymaster. At City Point and Bermuda Hundred in the fall of 1864, a war correspondent noted the heaps of fruit and vegetables; he marveled at the fresh fish, figs, jellies, and wines. Soldiers could purchase the latest novel for twice the sale price printed on the cover while copies of *Harpers* or the *Atlantic Monthly* cost 50¢ each.[9]

Welfare Agencies

The supplies furnished by the Government and sutlers were supplemented by donations from individuals and agencies in the North who not only provided supplies but also sent agents to distribute them. One Indiana soldier has recorded that Governor Morton visited his regiment bringing such items as combs, handkerchiefs, and soap. In addition he took a lot of extras to patients in the hospital, causing the other regiments to think that Indiana had the finest governor in any State.[10] Ladies Aid Societies gathered contributions of clothing and hospital supplies and dispatched them where they were most needed. Local YMCA organizations sent supplies and money to regiments from their areas.

The two corps of Hooker, sent by rail from the Army of the Potomac in 1863 to reenforce Rosecrans' force in Tennessee, were provided in one town enroute with delicious food and hot coffee. The ringing of the courthouse bell, the signal of the arrival of each train, gave ample notice to the farmers who, laden with fruits and melons, would hasten to town and join the citizens in serving the swarming soldiers, who, as this was their first experience of the kind since they had left Harrisburg, were puzzled to know on what terms they were being fed.[11] Very widely known and appreciated was the Cooper Shop Refreshment Saloon which, located in Philadelphia within five minutes' walk of the railway depot, fed a total of 600,000 men during the war.[12] The food, building, and services were donated by public-spirited citizens of the city. Several States had organizations similar to the "New England Soldiers' Relief Association" which cared for wounded, furloughed, and transient soldiers. A similar agency in New York City was established by the State military authorities to protect the sick and wounded soldiers who were preyed upon by sharpers in going to the city from Washington. Couriers were appointed to travel on the trains with the soldiers in order to attend to their interests and keep outsiders from interfering with them.[13]

Sanitary Commission

Cutting across State boundaries and confining their activities to no particular State or district were the Sanitary and Christian Commissions. The first of these, the United States Sanitary Commission, was organized June 9, 1861,[14] in imitation of the commissions that followed the Crimean War and Indian Rebellion. Elisha Harris, who helped to establish the Commission, wrote medical monographs for use in the field, and originated a system of recording deaths and burials of soldiers. The hospital car he designed for use in the war won an award in the 1867 Paris Exposition and was used by the Prussian Army in the Franco-Prussian War.[15] The Sanitary Commission was organized into five departments as follows: Sanitary Inspection which investigated the condition in the different camps of the widely-extended armies; General Relief which supplied food, clothing, hospital

UNITED STATES SANITARY COMMISSION

In the field near Petersburg in 1864. The officer to the left of the door resembles Gen. Sedgwick, but Sedgwick was killed at Spotsylvania.

stores to all soldiers but especially the sick and wounded; Special Relief which maintained "Homes" where recruits, soldiers on furlough, and strays could obtain shelter, food, and medical care; Field Relief units, which, equipped with wagons and tents, worked from corps down to brigades; and an Auxiliary Relief Corps which worked in hospitals and among the wounded on the field.[16]

The Commission aided soldiers in correcting any irregularities in their papers which prevented them from receiving their pay, bounties, or pensions. A very helpful contribution was the compilation of a hospital directory which enabled friends and relatives to locate soldiers in hospitals. Funds for the Commission were raised by voluntary subscription and "Sanitary Fairs" in the larger cities.[17] The receipts of the Commission during the period June 27, 1861-July 1, 1865, amounted to $4,813,750.64 of which it disbursed $4,530,774.92.[18] In addition to the money raised, the Commission sent more than $15,-000,000 worth of supplies to the hospitals, camps, and front line.[19] A soldier at the front described the activities of the Sanitary Commission in his area as follows:

An agent or employee of the Commission would sometimes go along the line of our works with a haversack full of navy tobacco, little circular pincushions, and writing paper and envelopes, carrying a knife in one hand and a large plug of navy tobacco in the other. When he found a man who used the weed, he would cut him off a very small chew, while to everyone who did not use it he generally presented a pin-cushion about as large as an old "bungtown" cent, or if they preferred, a few sheets of writing paper and as many envelopes, all of which were necessaries, and were gladly received by the men. At first some of the men would ask the privilege of cutting off their own chews of tobacco, and would then cut off a chew and tender it to the agent, quietly marching away with the remainder of the plug. But after this trick was played a few times, the agents did their own cutting and delivering, and would often appear along the line with the tobacco already cut into nice little chews ready to be given away.[20]

Christian Commission

The United States Christian Commission was organized at a convention of the Young Men's Christian Association held in New York, November 16, 1861. A group of ministers under the leadership of George H. Stuart of Philadelphia officered the Commission, which, as might be expected, placed its main emphasis on ministering to the religious needs of the troops. The Commission had a home and field organization. The Government gave free transportation to the Christian Commission delegates who carried their Bibles, Testaments, tracts, and books to troops in all the battle areas. One delegate in a few months distributed "106 Hymn Books, 379 Soldier's Books of various kinds, 94 copies of parts of the Scripture, 1773 Religious Papers, 3,652 pages of tracts."[21] The Commission aggregated $4,030,441.80 in receipts for the three years ending January 1, 1865. During 186— alone the Commission distributed 569,794 Bibles and Testaments; 4,815,923 Hymns and Psalm books; and 13,681,342 pages of tracts.[22]

Union Commission

A third organization, the United States Union Commission, was organized in June 1864, to care for war refugees in Cairo, Louisville, St. Louis, Cincinnati, and other points. This Commission handled nearly 100,000 displaced persons in a period of seven to eight months.[23] Its aims were to return the evacuees to their homes, to start up schools again, and to furnish the necessary seed and agricultural implements whereby the impoverished farm areas could be made to produce again.

Some Western States as Indiana, Illinois and Wisconsin had "Sanitary Commissions," while the Western Sanitary Commission furnished hospitals and nurses for sick and wounded men in several of the Western States. The Western Sanitary Commission was entirely distinct from the United States Sanitary Commission.[24]

Intelligence Service

In their interrogation of civilians, refugees, contrabands, and prisoners of war, the provost guards were enabled to obtain information of a military value. Eventually a line officer was made head of an intelligence bureau with the title of Deputy Provost Marshal General. Such an intelligence service did not come into existence, however, until early in 1863 and then only in the Army of the Potomac.

Secret Service

The gathering and evaluation of intelligence data in the first part of the war was haphazard and often completely unreliable. The Federal Secret Service in the Army of the Potomac was first entrusted to Allen Pinkerton, a personal friend of General McClellan. Pinkerton was conducting a detective agency in Chicago when McClellan summoned him to be chief detective in the Department of the Ohio.[25] Immediately after McClellan was assigned to command in Washington he organized a secret service force and placed Pinkerton at its head.[26] Pinkerton was known to the Army as "Major E. J. Allen." The War Department also had special agents who reported directly to the Secretary of War. Among these were Colonel Lafayette C. Baker who investigated the fraudulent practices of contractors and bounty jumping and similar cases. Some information was obtained by William P. Wood, Superintendent of Old Capitol Prison, in his contacts with military prisoners. Pinkerton's force consisted of spies and scouts; the ormer were usually civilians who remained more or less permanently behind the enemy's lines, while the latter were usually regularly enlisted men of the Federal Army who donned the enemy's uniform and crossed their lines in order to deceive their pickets and capture them so that the main body could be surprised and defeated. Federal scouts dressed in Confederate uniform were often successful in their conversations with enemy civilians who unwittingly divulged much information of military value.[28]

On December 16, 1861, in a circular to the army, McClellan ordered that all deserters, spies, prisoners of war, and contrabands brought within the Federal lines from Virginia should be brought immediately to the commander of the division within whose lines they came. They were not to be interrogated by any person until arrival at division headquarters where either the divisional commander or one of his staff should question them. This order was soon altered to the extent that such persons entering the Federal lines were to be taken at once to the Provost Marshal of the division who would interrogate them in the presence of the divisional commander or a member of his staff. At the conclusion of the interrogation they were to be then forwarded to the Provost Marshal General and finally to the chief of staff of the Army of the Potomac.

Although McClellan maintained that the examination of spies, deserters, and prisoners of war enabled him to estimate with "considerable accuracy" the strength of the enemy in front of him,[29] the evidence is decidedly to the contrary. "The fiction as to [the strength of] Lee's forces is the most remarkable in the history of modern wars. Whether McClellan was the victim or an accomplice of the inventions of his 'secret service', we cannot tell. It is almost incredible that he should be deceived, except willingly."[30] One of the Federal Secret Service operators in the Confederate commissariat at Yorktown reported 119,000 rations issued daily[31] while the enemy never had half that number in the defenses of the place.[32] Throughout the entire Peninsular Campaign McClellan accepted such gross exaggerations at their face value. On June 26, 1862, he believed that the arrival of Jackson would swell Lee's forces to 160,000 men at a time when both forces totaled less than 100,000 men.[33] The total Confederate forces (Army of the Northern Virginia including Ewell's and Jackson's divisions) numbered 95,481 (Livermore's estimate) or possibly as low as 75,769 (Confederate reports).[34] At one time McClellan believed the enemy to have had 200,000 men opposing him on the Peninsula.[35] In an endeavor to arrive at as accurate an estimate of the enemy's strength as possible, General Meigs in Washington compiled the Confederate order of battle from the regiments and brigades mentioned in enemy newspapers that got through the lines. Meigs found 90 regiments of infantry, 1 regiment of cavalry,

and 5 batteries of artillery designated by name in the Confederate reports of the Seven Days Battles. By comparing this data with other sources he concluded that Lee had about 150 regiments. These regiments at 700 men each would total 105,000 or at 400 (which he found to be a full average) the total of the infantry would be 60,000.[36] When the other arms of the Confederate Army are added to this total the estimation is fairly accurate[37] but McClellan held Meigs as a personal enemy and refused to accept the latter's estimate. Pinkerton left the Army of the Potomac when his commander was removed from its command.

For a while the Secret Service was practically nonexistent except for a few spies inside the Confederacy. When Hooker assumed command there was not a record or document of any kind at the headquarters of the Army of the Potomac that gave any information at all in regard to the enemy. "There was no means, no organization, and no apparent effort, to obtain such information, and we were almost as ignorant of the enemy in our immediate front as if they had been in China."[38]

Bureau of Military Information

An efficient intelligence organization was established and Hooker called to headquarters Colonel G. H. Sharpe, commander 120th New York Infantry, and put him in charge of it as a Deputy Provost Marshal General.[39] This organization was known as the Bureau of Military Information.

In the Chancellorsville Campaign that soon followed, one of Hooker's cavalry generals (General Averell), was completely fooled by two Confederate prisoners who exaggerated the strength of their forces to such an extent that Averell advanced his mounted force of 4,000 sabres only twenty-eight miles from April 29th to May 4th. In removing Averell from command, Hooker said his purpose "in detaching him from this army . . . has been to prevent an active and powerful column from being paralyzed by his presence."[40] Such credulity on the part of Federal commanders and the inexperience of scouts and spies in approximating the numbers of large masses of troops were less apparent in the latter stages of the war. Incompetent generals were removed while the scouts and spies learned through experience. Colonel Sharpe remained the head of the Bureau of Military Information until the end of the war and supervised the secret service work in the East. He had some excellent subordinates, one of whom, Lieutenant H. B. Smith, was chief detective of the Middle Department (Maryland, Delaware, and part of Virginia). Smiths' force of about forty soldiers and civilians gathered an immense amount of significant information as to the plans and movements of important citizens which was forwarded to the Provost Marshal's office.[41] Another valuable assistant was Major H. H.

Young, whose force of about thirty or forty scouts operated chiefly in the Shenandoah Valley where they earned the official appreciation of Sheridan by "cheerfully going wherever ordered, to obtain that great essential of success, information . . ." Ten of these men lost their lives.[42]

Sometimes an embittered "poor white" acted as a spy for the Federals. The Army of the Potomac was materially assisted when on picket by a shrewd poor white who knew the country thoroughly. "On account of some injury received from some of the wealthy rebels, he regarded them with a most deadly hatred and did all in his power to injure them out of revenge. He knew every road and bridle path, and his services as a spy and scout were invaluable."[43] Another source of information for the army was the engineer officer at headquarters whose duty it was to ascertain the topography of every new region the army was to occupy. This involved making surveys and interrogating natives, deserters, and prisoners. By such means the maps were prepared with all possible information as to terrain, roads, bridges, and fords included. Federal armies on all fronts used the information gathered by their engineer officers at headquarters.[44]

Prisoners of war interrogation was often a fruitful source of information for the Federal Army. Even when the captured soldier would reveal nothing he was bound to conceal, enough was known to enable a diligent provost marshal to construct in a short time a reasonably complete roster of the enemy.[45] The dispatch of Early's corps to the Shenandoah Valley in 1864 was ascertained in all its essential details in one afternoon's interrogation of prisoners who "all told the same story and stated that they belonged to various regiments, brigades and divisions of Early's corps; had left Lee's army June 13th, and had arrived by rail at Lynchburg on the day before the battle."[46]

In the West a substantial secret service organization was built up for General Grant by General Dodge but their names were carefully guarded and very little was ever revealed about any of them.[47] This body of scouts was organized in the fall of 1861 to aid Fremont in clearing up the many rumors that were rampant as to the enemy's intentions. It appears that fiction and not fact played the greater role in military circles west of the Mississippi in the first year of the war. Dodge's force was recruited from a western Tennessee regiment under Colonel Hurst. These men were great fighters and invaluable in securing information; some of them could tell a company, regiment, brigade, or division by the space occupied in the field or along the road. Exaggerations of the size of enemy forces diminished.[48] Out of this scouting force emerged a spy system and the spies finally were organized into a trained group of secret service men. These spies stayed within the enemy lines for months at a time, sending out their information by women who got permission to visit relatives among the refugees who had fled to the safety of the Federal lines. Dodge's secret service force broke up shortly after Grant went East to command the Federal Army but a few of the outstanding spies attached themselves to the Sixteenth Army Corps which Dodge commanded up to the time he was wounded before Atlanta.

Sherman as a G-2

In marked contrast to such commanders as McClellan, Sherman possessed the ability to judge very accurately the force of the enemy opposing him. In fact, he generally preferred his own estimate, arrived at by general reasoning, to that of information procured for him by spies or vouchsafed by deserters. A great deal of information came from the Negroes who seemed to know everything. These people told the Federals where such items as enemy field guns and hidden weapons were stored. The Negroes had a very effective intelligence net operating for General Sherman. Colored men of this informal organization would carry information about 20 miles each night and the information was always reliable. They never moved during the day. Every one of the net knew every other member within a radius of 10 miles. The "net" was actually a system of overlapping circles. No passwords were used; no regular places of meeting were ever utilized. The colored preachers were the guiding forces behind the movement. No Federal soldier was ever betrayed by this organization;[49] in fact the same can be said, almost with no exceptions, for all Negroes in the South.

Counterintelligence and Censorship

The prevention of military information reaching the enemy was never achieved by the Federal Government. That such prevention was essential was realized by many Federal commanders who sought to control the sources from which Confederate generals were obtaining invaluable data concerning troop movements, order of battle, and campaign plans. On August 21, 1861, the War Department prohibited all communication by any means whatsoever, respecting military operations or installations, whereby intelligence might be directly or indirectly given to the enemy.[50] One of the most fruitful sources of information for the enemy was to be found in the private letters written home by officers and men. On May 18, 1862, in enjoining circumspection in letter writing, the commander of the Army of the Potomac pointed out that to communicate precise intelligence of the strength, position, or movements of the army in private letters not designed for publication, was itself highly improper, but when such intelligence was allowed to pass into the public prints, it amounted to giving information to the enemy.[51]

During the Fredericksburg campaign there was a

temporary censorship which prevented the dispatch of all letters and telegrams from the camps.[52] An examination of letters written home by officers and men of the Federal Army shows that, generally speaking, they wrote about what they wished with very little concern as to what might happen if their letters were intercepted by the enemy. The following was written by a colonel whose regiment formed a part of the forces he described in the following detail:[53] "These forces consist of the 19th, 24th Ill.–37th, 38th Ind.–18th Ohio, 78th Pa., 1st Mich. and 9th Mich. 1 Ky. Cavalry–7th Pa. Cavalry, Hewets Bat., and Stewarts Bat.–making nearly 10,000 troops . . ."

The telegraphic censorship of the press in Washington imposed February 26, 1862, met with so much opposition from Congress that the matter was referred to a committee which reported March 20, 1862 that it did not object to censorship of military operations, but dispatches of a political or general character were not to be supressed.[54]

There was no effective governmental restraint on the newspapers of the North which, though deserving of admiration, undoubtedly did the national case serious injury by continually revealing military information. "It is doubtful whether any war has ever been as fully 'covered' as the Civil War . . . Usually the correspondents were accorded the most liberal privileges. Government passes were put into their hands; they had the use of government horses and wagons; they were given transportation with baggage privileges on government steamers and military trains . . ."[55] Unlike such generals as Rosecrans who went so far as to give intimations of his plans to the press, General Sherman blamed the press as being responsible for a constant disclosure of secret movements against the enemy.[56] There is no doubt that Confederate generals used the Northern papers to great advantage. General Lee, especially, constantly perused the columns of the Northern journals with the eye of a military expert on the lookout for information as to developments within the lines of the Army of the Potomac.[57] Probably there were less serious disclosures of information on the part of the Southern press because they perhaps exercised greater discretion and also because they were under stricter control, while the sum total of their activity was far less.[58]

There is no evidence to indicate that Federal prisoners did not divulge information as readily as did their opponents. Those Federals who talked freely to their captors would certainly not record the fact, but according to their own testimony, some Federals refused to answer questions of military nature when interrogated by the enemy. A major captured on the Petersburg front was questioned by General Mahone as to his corps, artillery, and cavalry forces, and whether the commanding general was in that sector. On telling the general that he was too good an officer to expect to receive correct answers to such questions the major was released from further questioning.[59]

Counterintelligence work by the Federal services was never as effective as the military and naval authorities wished it to be. It was probably best effective in such occupied States as Missouri where apparently "a great number of persons within . . . [the Federal] lines . . . [were] carrying on treasonable correspondence with the enemy, rendering him all the aid and comfort in their power, and themselves amenable to the articles of war as spies." It was believed, also, that "Numerous regularly employed spies of the enemy . . . [frequented Federal] camps and cities."[60] The activities of the hostile population in Missouri became so injurious to the Federal military operatons in that State that on April 22, 1863 a set of laws of war was prescribed for judge advocates and military courts in their handling of offenses by the inhabitants against the Federal occupation forces. In doing so, there was drawn up a series of definitions of such terms as "spy," "guerrilla," "partisan," "brigand," and "military insurgents."[61] Two days later the War Department issued, as "General Order No. 100," its famous "Instructions for the Government of Armies of the United States in the Field." This work, prepared by Francis Lieber, defined for military occupation forces everything from martial law to rebellion and treason.[62] Lieber's work was not only used in the Civil War, it was also used in later wars and occupations by United States forces after 1865.

NOTES CHAPTER 8

1. United States War Department, "General Order No. 27," March 21, 1862, *General Orders for 1862.*

2. *Ibid.*, "General Order No. 35," February 7, 1863, *General Orders for 1863.* The 47th Ohio Infantry assessed their sutler 5% per month on his average business. Saunier, p. 179.

3. Metal tokens were also used.

4. Blanding, pp. 46-49.

5. Page, (14th Connecticut Infantry), pp. 131-132.

6. "The Fourteenth Indiana in the Valley of Virginia," *Indiana Magazine of History*, Vol. 30, No. 3, (September 1934).

7. Crowninshield, p. 106.

8. Annual Report of the General-in-Chief, November 15, 1863, *House Executive Documents*, 38 Cong., 1 Sess., Document 1, pp. 43-44.

9. Letter of Charles A. Page, Headquarters of General Butler, September 2, 1864, Gilmore, pp. 243-244.

10. State preference was marked.

11. Johnson, Robert Underwood, *Remembered Yesterdays*, p. 55. Johnson says that much correspondence, numerous

friendships and some marriages" resulted from the twenty minutes' stay of these trains.

12. Moore, James, *History of the Cooper Shop Volunteer Refreshment Saloon*, pp. 129-207.

13. New York *Herald*, No. 9740 (May 16, 1863), p. 4.

14. *Annual Cyclopedia* (1864), p. 734. Reverend Henry W. Bellows was elected president.

15. These hospital trains were widely publicized at international fairs.

16. *Annual Cyclopedia*, (1864), pp. 736-738; *Photographic History*, Vol. 7, p. 324; Gilmore, p. 180.

17. A good description of the New York fair held in April 1864, is given in *Harper's New Monthly Magazine*, Vol. 29 (June 1864) pp. 131-132.

18. *Battles and Leaders*, Vol. 4, p. 90.

19. *Photographic History*, Vol. 7, p. 324.

20. Little, Henry F. W., *The Seventh Regiment New Hampshire Volunteers in the War of the Rebellion*, p. 338.

21. From notes at the end of a manuscript diary of Rev. R. S. Goodman, Delegate of the Christian Commission from La Parte, Indiana, Manuscript in William L. Clements Library.

22. *Annual Cyclopedia* (1864), p. 803.

23. *Ibid.*, p. 804.

24. *Ibid.*, pp. 739-740.

25. *Photographic History*, Vol. 8, p. 262.

26. *Official Records*, First Series, Vol. 5, pp. 51-52.

27. *Photographic History*, Vol. 8, pp. 280-284.

28. *Photographic History*, Vol. 8, p. 284.

29. *Official Records*, First Series, Vol. 5, pp. 52-53.

30. Cox, Vol. 1, p. 250.

31. Pinkerton's report, *Official Records*, First Series, Vol. 11, Part 1, p. 251.

32. McClellan accepted the figures.

33. Comte de Paris, Vol. 2, p. 83.

34. Livermore, *Numbers and Losses*, p. 86.

35. Battles and Leaders, Vol. 2, p. 438. See also Allan, William, *The Army of Northern Virginia in 1862*, p. 78.

36. *Official Records*, First Series, Vol. 11, Part 3, pp. 340-341.

37. Livermore, Numbers and Losses, p. 86.

38. Testimony of Major General Daniel Butterfield, March 28, 1863, *Report*, Committee on the Conduct of the War, Second Series (1865), Vol. 1, p. 74.

39. *Photographic History*, Vol. 8, p. 264; Bigelow, p. 47.

40. But Hooker was also inept.

41. *Photographic History*, Vol. 8, p. 276.

42. *Official Records*, First Series, Vol. 46, Part 1, p. 481.

43. Hays, *Under the Red Patch*, p. 48. After the war this man attended a house raising, and some Confederate veterans who knew of what he had done for the North "killed him in cold blood." *Ibid.*

44. Van Horne, Vol. 2, p. 457.

45. Cox. Vol. 1, p, 252. Cox kept up the enemy order of battle in his memorandum book throughout the Atlanta Campaign. *Ibid.*

46. Dupont, H. A., *The Campaign of 1864 in the Valley of Virginia and the Expedition to Lynchburg*, p. 79.

47. More publicity was given Eastern personnel.

48. This could come only with experience.

49. *Glimpses of the Nation's Struggle*, Second Series, pp. 314-321.

50. United States War Department, "General Order No. 67," August 26, 1861, *General Orders for 1861*. Any communication of intelligence value had to have the authority and sanction of the general in command.

51. "General Order No. 125," May 18, 1862, Headquarters, Army of the Potomac.

52. Meade, Vol. 1, p. 339.

53. Letter of Colonel John G. Parkhurst, 9th Michigan Infantry, one mile south of Fayetteville, Ky., June 1, 1862. Manuscript in Historical Collections.

54. *Annual Cyclopedia* (1861), pp. 480-481.

55. Randall, J. G., "The Newspaper Problem in its Bearing upon Military Secrecy during the Civil War," *American Historical Review*, Vol. 23 (January 1918), pp. 306-307.

56. Thorndike, p. 191.

57. Randall, pp. 311-312.

58. *Ibid.*, p. 313.

59. This was an exception.

60. "General Order No. 12," February 7, 1863, Headquarters, Department of the Missouri.

61. *Ibid.*, "General Order No. 30," April 22, 1863.

62. United States War Department, "General Order No. 100," April 24, 1863, *General Orders for 1863*.

CHAPTER 9

Equipment

THIS CHAPTER deals with individual and organizational equipment, with emphasis on that issued to the infantry or branches generally equipped as infantry. This includes a description of infantry weapons, a subject which is continued in further detail in Chapter 10. The latter also covers heavier ordnance and ammunition.

INDIVIDUAL EQUIPMENT

This topic deals chiefly with clothing and weapons pertaining to the individual infantryman.

CLOTHING

Further details and specifications of uniforms and insignia are contained in Chapter 11.

Wide extremes existed in the quality and abundance of clothing issued in different departments, corps, divisions, and even in regiments from the same State. There was often a wide diversity between parts of the same outfit; for instance, often the overcoat would be good and the blanket poor, or vice versa.[1] At first the clothing allowance was $2.50 a month for infantry and $3.00 a month for cavalry[2] but this was raised May 25, 1861, to $3.50 a month to soldiers of all branches.[3] Normally this latter sum was sufficient if the soldier exercised reasonable care, because the quality of the clothing improved greatly as the war progressed. After August 1862, careful provisions were made for the prompt supply of all necessary clothing to soldiers immediately on their entrance to service.[4] The soldier was permitted to turn in worn-out items for new ones. If he overdrew his yearly clothing allowance of $42.00 the difference was deducted from his pay; on the other hand, if he was careful of the clothing issued him, he generally managed to refrain from drawing the whole amount of his allowance and the Government paid him the difference. By a joint resolution of Congress, approved July 12, 1862, the Secretary of War was authorized to furnish extra clothing to sick, wounded, and other soldiers who should lose items of clothing by the casualties of war.[5] The Quartermaster General of the Army was greatly concerned over the improvidence of the inexperienced troops which resulted in an extraordinary destruction and loss of clothing and other supplies.[6] The wastage was greatly increased by the soldiers trading or selling their clothing and equipment for food, whiskey, and money. The Government found it necessary to make it a criminal offense for any person to receive or purchase articles of clothing or equipment from a soldier.[7] Vast amounts of clothing were lost in battle when knapsacks were piled, blankets, overcoats, and other clothing thrown off. Whether victorious or defeated, the regiments seldom recovered the property thus laid aside.[8] Grant was impressed by the wagon-loads of new blankets and overcoats thrown away by the troops to lighten their knapsacks as they set out on the first day's march in the Wilderness campaign.[9]

The militia regiments in answering Lincoln's first call for troops wore their traditional uniforms, many of which were utterly unsuited for active field duty. Several Federal regiments fought in gray uniforms at Bull Run;[10] in the West other troops gave up their gray State uniforms only a month before Shiloh.[11] Militia regiments vied with each other in the variety of their uniforms. The 79th New York Highlanders wore the kilt (replaced later by tartan trousers); the Garibaldi Guards wore the garb of the Italian light infantry;[12] while both French and non-French regiments quite often appeared in Zouave uniforms. Although these fancy uniforms furnished by the States were withdrawn after issue of the regulation outfit,[13] many Zouave regiments kept their uniforms all through their term of service.[14] While some regiments wore a modified Zouave uniform,[15] others like Duryea's New York Zouaves wore the complete outfit, often with ludicrous effect. A foreign correspondent approaching this regiment at parade noticed with amusement the discoloured napkins tied around their heads, without any fez cap beneath, so that the hair sometimes stuck up through the folds. The ill-made jackets, the loose bags of red calico hanging from their loins and the long gaiters of white cotton made them appear such "military scarecrows" that he could scarcely refrain from laughing outright.[16] A taciturn Vermont general, noted for his disgust for display and sham, on meeting a young officer in fantastic Zouave uniform asked him who he was. The officer answered that he was an officer in a Zouave regiment. "An

MISCELLANEOUS EQUIPMENTS

Shaving equipment—pocket mirror in embossed case, tin shaving cup, razor strap, and razor.

Field optical equipment—naval telescope used at Mobile Bay; Army telescope (left) from South Mountain battlefield; small brass telescope; binoculars made in France and marked "U. S. Army Signal Glass."

Lighting equipment—candle lantern; candlesticks with cover; and candle holder made of a bayonet.

Today these are true relics, for in 1940 the U. S. Army, discovering that electricity was here to stay, stopped issuing candle lanterns.

officer!" said the general, "I thought you were a circus clown."[17] This impractical uniform was worn on the Peninsula where an observer thought the "red breeches and white turbans altogether too conspicuous a uniform for comfort in war."[18] It was worn at Second Bull Run;[19] and even as late as the siege of Petersburg.[20]

The majority of the soldiers, however, both East and West, wore the regulation uniform as prescribed for the Regular Army.[21] This uniform consisted of a blue forage cap or a black hat; a dark blue frock coat, blouse, or jacket; sky blue trousers; a sky blue overcoat or poncho.

INSIGNIA

Branches of service were indicated by insignia on the cap or hat, trimming on the coat, and piping on the trousers. These were: Scarlet for Artillery; sky-blue for Infantry; yellow for Cavalry and Engineers. The insignia worn on the cap or hat were: crossed cannons for Artillery; a bugle for Infantry; crossed sabres for Cavalry; a turreted castle for Engineers; a shield with the letters "T.E." in old English characters for Topographical Engineers; and crossed flags for the Signal Corps. Soldiers also wore their regimental number and company letter on their headgear; later in the war their corps badges (1863-1865) tended to displace all other insignia on hats and caps.[22]

Rank was indicated by the bars, leaves, eagles, and stars on the shoulder straps exactly as in the United States Army of today except that second lieutenants wore blank shoulder straps. In addition to the shoulder straps or epaulets, rank was also indicated by the spacing of the two rows of coat buttons for general officers. Field officers also wore double rows of buttons but company grade officers wore single rows of buttons on their coats. The braid on the sleeve cuffs of officers' overcoats used early in the war to designate rank was not extensively worn. All commissioned officers wore either epaulets or shoulder straps while the noncommissioned officers wore chevrons. The wearer's branch of service was indicated by the color of cloth of his shoulder strap. Epaulets were clumsy and soon disappeared in active service. Late in the war the War Department issued an order permitting officers in the field to dispense with shoulder straps. The designation of rank, however, was to be worn. Officers also were permitted by this order to wear overcoats of the same color and shape of those of the enlisted men of their command. No ornaments were required to be worn on the overcoats, hats, or forage caps, nor were sashes or epaulets required to be worn in the future.[23] This sensible order unquestionably saved some lives; it would have saved a great many more had it been promulgated earlier in the War.

Some officers and many soldiers wore a forage cap, copied after the French kepi which was as "shapeless as a feed bag,"[24] with a leather visor which curled up when dry and drooped when wet. Nevertheless, this unattractive headgear was roomy enough in the top for a wet sponge, green leaves, a handkerchief, or some other protection against the sun.[25] In general, the forage cap appears to have been more popular in the East than in the West where the hat was widely worn. The dress hat was heavy, hot, stiff and ill-looking. Many regiments refused to draw them while others got rid of them as soon as possible. These hats were decorated with black feathers and were looped up on one side by a brass eagle. The men did not like them mainly because of their awkard size and Pilgrim Father appearance. The headgear worn by the Western troops was not this dress hat but one resembling the civilian hat of the day. One of the few units in the Army of the Potomac which clung to the hat throughout its service was the Iron Brigade. Its commander had the men wear the hats as a mark of identification for the brigade.[26] Searching for comfort on the Peninsula, the 16th New York Infantry was issued straw hats in June 1862,[27] but such a case was exceptional. Some troops were issued helmets with visors before and behind which kept the rain off the men's necks but these hats were so sweltering in summer that they were discarded.[28]

The men wore frock coats for dress; the four-button blouse or short jacket was normally worn in the field. The blouse was loose-fitting enough to allow the soldier freedom of movement. It was considered by some as too thick for summer and too thin for winter,[29] but others appeared to consider it the most practical item of uniform issued them.[30] The quality of overcoats varied greatly; those examined by the author appear well made though not especially attractive in appearance. One soldier tells us that his overcoat made him feel "like a little nubbin of corn in a large preponderance of husk."[31]

Soldiers took what clothing was handed them and hoped to effect exchanges with their comrades later. The trousers were substantial and comfortable, often a little roomy in the seat and wide round the waist for youngsters, but the recruits grew out to them in time. The canvas leggins issued early in the war appear to have been unpopular because of the time necessary to adjust them;[32] they usually were kicked loose on the first march. The custom of rolling the trousers snugly at the ankle and hauling the gray woolen sock, leggin-wise, over them became fairly universal. The socks themselves were well made, but many men preferred those knitted at home, principally, because "the Government socks were evidently modelled for a race of gorillas."[33] Long socks were best for long marching. Generally, the "bootees" or shoes issued to the troops wore better than civilian socks and shoes. These bootees, also called "mud-scows" and "gunboats" by the men, were low-cut, stitched, very light, and often the soles were very cheap, very broad, and the heels broad and low.[34]

Although the quality of shoes varied, the average life of a pair of contractor's shoes was from twenty to thirty days.[35] Some paper-soled shoes were issued, while others were so thin that they were only good on dry ground.[36] The shoes worn by the Federal troops were square-toed[37] as were the boots worn by many officers and most mounted men.

Flannel shirts were issued the men, generally three a year. The underwear was usually of good quality, consisting of "mud-colored shirts and drawers"[38] of flannel material. Early in the war the men had to wear leather collars to force them to hold their heads

INFANTRY PRIVATE FULLY EQUIPPED

This photo of a Castro-like model was made for the Quartermaster in 1862. It shows an infantryman in heavy marching order. The haversack, however, was usually worn on the left side under the canteen, with its carrying strap over the right shoulder. Veterans usually dispensed with the knapsack, and wore the blanket as a long roll slung over the shoulder. Many soldiers threw away the eagle ornament on the crossbelt of the cartridge box, being convinced that it made them too distinct a target for enemy marksmen.

erect. These "dog collars," as the men named them, were pieces of stiff upper leather, about two inches wide in the middle and tapering to one inch at the ends, which were fastened by buckles. They soon disappeared as did most of the havelocks given the early volunteers.[39]

Another item of uniform that did not survive the tests of combat was the shoulder scale. Intended to be a protection against saber strokes of cavalry, this was a metal epaulet to be worn by all enlisted men. Eventually, however, it became an article for dress occasions only, since its bright finish rendered it too conspicuous at the front. The heavy artillery regiments which garrisoned Washington wore their shoulder scales into action at Spotsylvania but soon discarded them.[40]

In fact, all regiments went through a shaking down process until they carried only the equipment really necessary for fighting and living in the field. The contrast between the appearance of a veteran regiment and a brand new one was always significant, amusing, and pathetic. The experience of the 15th New Jersey Infantry in this respect was shared by many others. While encamped near Washington in September 1862, this new regiment found itself surrounded by the bivouacs of the troops recalled from the Peninsula. "The contrast was very great between their equipment and our own. They were destitute of almost everything. Many were shoeless, and with hardly clothing to cover themselves, presented a ragged and untidy appearance. But their arms and accoutrements were in splendid order. They were bronzed with the summer's sun, and thin, and worn to bare muscle, from privations and fatigue."[41]

No Summer Uniform

The absence of a light uniform for summer wear was much criticized. One disgusted Federal in the Department of the Gulf failed to see why the Navy could be in white uniforms while he and his regiment were dressed in heavy, dark-blue coats, thick trousers, and thick, black felt hats.[42] Another criticism was that many of the uniforms fabricated in the early part of the war were made of shoddy material. Because of inferior uniforms that soon fell apart, the 2d New York Infantry appeared on parade at Fort Monroe with blankets wrapped about them while their sentinels were barefoot.[43] A similar situation in the 16th Maine Infantry increased the sick list to frightful proportions because the shortage continued into the inclement November weather.[44] Sometimes deficiencies were made good by wealthy officers as, for example, the donation of a pair of warm woolen gloves to every man in his brigade by General Wadsworth.[45] The Government issue of clothing was functioning efficiently by 1863 and the Secretary of War's report that the clothing issued in 1864 was of excellent quality, durable, and strong was undoubtedly correct.[46]

Rifles

Federal infantrymen were armed mainly with the Springfield Rifle Musket, Model 1861. This was a percussion rifle 58½ inches long, muzzle-loading, caliber .58. The rifle barrel was 40 inches long; the pitch in the rifling was one turn in 6 feet; there were 3 grooves each 3/10 of an inch wide, .005 of an inch deep at the muzzle, increasing regularly in depth to .15 at the breech. This rifle, with its 18 inch socket bayonet, weighed 9.75 pounds. The ammunition used was a hollow based cylindroconical bullet of 500 grains; muzzle velocity was 950 foot seconds.[47] Including the bayonet and ramrod and other appendages there were 84 pieces in this weapon, which in 1861 cost $14.93 to manufacture.[48] All parts were interchangeable. From 1861 to 1865 Springfield Armory produced 793,434 and private contractors 882,561 of these arms. In 1863 and 1864 slight improvements were made but the Model 1861 rifle musket remained, practically unchanged, as the basic infantry weapon of the war. The Ordnance Department thought it equal to the best in the world, especially to the Enfield Rifle Musket, which was also very extensively used by the Federal army as well as their adversaries.[49]

The Enfield rifle was one of the best of the foreign arms. It was made chiefly at the government armory at Enfield, England where, shortly before the war, machinery had been installed which was a direct copy of that in the United States armory at Springfield, Massachusetts. The Enfield rifle was one-hundredth of an inch smaller in caliber than the Springfield (caliber .58); the difference was small enough so as not to prevent the use of caliber .57 ammunition in the Springfield rifle.[50] The Enfield was sighted to 1100 yards but it was believed by at least one observer that this sighting was excessive since the Enfield was not accurate beyond 700 yards.[51]

Springfield Armory was the only government armory in operation after the burning of the arsenal at Harper's Ferry in April 1861. The output of the armory at Springfield was so meager that it was necessary to arm the volunteers of 1861 and 1862 with older models of United States weapons. The best of these were the model 1855 rifle, model 1855 rifle musket, model 1841 rifle, and model 1842 musket. All of these were percussion weapons. The model 1855 arms were caliber .58; the model 1841 rifle (also known as the Mississippi Rifle, Windsor Rifle, Jager Rifle) was caliber .54; the model 1842 musket was caliber .69. The 1816 and 1835 models of flintlock muskets that were converted to percussion shortly before[52] and during the war to meet the pressing need for arms were also caliber .69 weapons.

To supplement domestic weapons the Government and the various States made extensive purchases of foreign weapons. Probably the most widely used of these, next to the Enfield, which has already been mentioned, were the Belgian muskets. These guns were of uneven caliber and crooked barrels. The recoil was fearful[53] and the men detested them. They soon gained the nickname of "European stovepipes" by men who found them unreliable in battle.[54] The English and Belgian sources were insufficient and agents purchased from the little German States all their old-fashioned arms, which those States hastened to get rid of at a price which enabled them to replace their obsolete weapons with the new breechloading needle guns. In short, the refuse of all Europe passed into the hands of the American volunteers.[55] Included in this debris were thousands of Austrian and Prussian muskets. These weapons were heavy, clumsy, and slow of fire. An examination of a shipment of 3,000 Austrian guns by the Adjutant General of the Army revealed that only 500 could be used.[56] Illustrative of the varied models and calibers of weapons issued to volunteer regiment is the following list[57] of the muskets and rifles issued New York regiments in 1861 and 1862. The list shows that 136 different regiments received 16 different models of weapons, varying in caliber from .71 down to .54.

Model	Caliber	No. of Regt's to whom issued
Long Enfield	.577	57
1842 Musket	.69	31
French Vincennes, sword bayonet	.69	11
U.S. Rifle Musket	.58	11
Austrian Rifle	.54	7
1840 Altered smoothbore Musket	.69	7
Austrian Rifle	.58	4
Austrian Rifle	.55	3
French Rifle Musket	.69	3
Short Enfield, sword bayonet	.577	3
Remington Rifle, sword bayonet .	.54	3
1822 altered musket	.69	3
Prussian smoothbore musket	.71	2
Short Austrian rifle musket	.69	2
French Liege rifle, sword bayonet	.58	1
Prussian altered musket	.69	1

At least one Western regiment, perhaps more, was armed with Russian muskets, caliber .72.[58] In fact it appears that the Western units were discriminated against in the procuring of the better models of weapons, although McClellan wrote the Secretary of War in October 1861 that his infantry regiments were to a considerable extent armed with unserviceable weapons. McClellan maintained that many good arms intended for the Army of the Potomac had gone elsewhere.[59] The general did not specify where these weapons were sent. Apparently they did not get to the Department of the Missouri as we find General Sherman complaining of the old condemned muskets with which he was forced to arm his men.[60] At Vicksburg the Federals captured 60,000 muskets that were so far superior to their own that their altered flintlocks and Belgian muskets were exchanged for the better weapons. Most of these were Enfields that had been brought to the Confederacy via the blockade.[61] Some Western troops carried antiquated weapons until after Chickamauga.[62]

Breechloading rifles were issued by the Government to some regiments late in the war, but only after the Chief of Ordnance, Brigadier General Ripley, had been replaced by an officer who realized the advantages of the breechloader over the muzzleloading rifle. Previous to Ripley's removal some States had equipped a few of their regiments with breechloading weapons. The best of the single shot breechloaders were the Ballard, Merrill, and Sharps rifles. All were excellent weapons and the Sharps especially was in the great demand. It was used by Berdan's sharpshooters in the Army of the Potomac[63] and was issued to the flank companies of the Connecticut regiments[64] as well as to other State units. At Cold Harbor in June 1864, a soldier using a Sharps rifle hit a Confederate at a distance of 800 yards after vainly trying to accomplish this with the regulation Springfield musket, which was not very accurate at that distance.[65]

Three types of breechloading repeating rifles were in use by volunteer infantry regiments 1863, 1864 and 1865. The most generally used of these was the Spencer rifle which had excellent range and accuracy. The Spencer was a seven-shooter and because of the amount of ammunition it consumed in action received an unfavorable report from the Chief of Ordnance in 1861.[66] Each man had to carry 100 rounds of Spencer ammunition instead of 40 rounds, and "it is to be feared that sometimes the bundles of cartridges were surreptitiously lightened."[67] This rifle, however, fully justified itself in combat. In actual service the Spencer was a great improvement on the muzzle loader, especially in tight places, and the men of the 37th Massachusetts were flattered that they were the first in the 6th Corps to be armed with this rifle.[68] The 10th New Hampshire and 118th New York Infantry Regiments were also armed with the Spencer but members of these regiments were cursed by the enemy for using "that infernal Yankee gun that shoots seven times at once."[69] The members of the 7th Illinois Infantry supplied themselves with these rifles at their own expense; the cost was $51.00 per gun.[70] Men in the 97th Indiana had to pay $45.00 for theirs. Soldiers armed with muzzle loaders envied the men who had these breechloaders, such as the Spencer or Henry, because the repeaters were "good shooters" and soldiers possessing them had the confidence in combat of having many shots in reserve.

Another repeater that was very effective but was used mainly in the last year of the war was the

Henry sixteen-shot repeater. This weapon was found most extensively in the West where the men purchased their own at the cost of about three months' pay.[71] Another type of repeating rifle, although used in fewer numbers than either the Spencer or Henry, was the Colt revolving rifle. This weapon, like the Colt revolver, was made with either five or six chambers. The bullet was forced into seven grooves which formed a spiral and which became steadily more contracted as it approached the muzzle of the rifle. The result was a long range rifle which was formidable in practical hands but considerable time was required in reloading.[72] Some complaint was made that all the chambers had a tendency to go off at once. General Rosecrans believed in the Colt rifle, however, and in 1863 asked for 5,000 of them, believing that five or six chambers were better than one.[73] The inventor of this rifle, Samuel Colt, was commissioned colonel in May 1861, and ordered to raise a regiment to be known as the 1st Connecticut Revolving Rifles. Colt's regiment was to be armed with his revolving rifles; each man was to be over six feet tall and a good marksman. The regiment was disbanded in a few weeks over administrative questions.[74] The cost of the Colt rifle was $45.00 while such foreign weapons as the Belgian, Austrian, and Prussian muskets, were $6.00 or $10.00 depending on whether they were smoothbore or rifled.[75]

Some new types of guns didn't work out well in battle. In September 1864 a gun of strange construction was issued to a portion of the 16th Michigan Infantry to be tested in the first engagement. The piece had two triggers. Each trigger exploded a separate cartridge; the one farthest from the breech first, the other afterwards. At least that is what it was intended to do. As a fact, the explosion of the first cartridge always ignited the second and sometimes exploded the barrel. Such was the result of the test at Preble's Farm, and the men of the 16th Michigan who had been so unfortunate as to be allotted the new guns were seen moving along the dead and wounded replacing them with a weapon they knew all about.[76] This was the Lindsay rifle.

AMMUNITION

With such a variety of calibers for weapons the problem of ammunition supply was extremely difficult. The caliber .69 muskets used a round ball, or a round ball with three buckshot called "buck and ball." This was effective only up to 200 yards and the Minie bullet was used in its stead when available and soon as the smoothbores could be rifled. The Minie bullet was of the usual elongated shape but was hollowed at its base for about one-third of its length. When fired, the gasses forced the lead into the riflings of the barrel. This bullet was also more effective than the old caliber .69 ammunition because instead of the soldier having to insert the

powder and ball separately into the barrel, the Minie bullet and powder were encased together in a paper cover and were inserted into the barrel at one count. The Minie bullet was also used in caliber .58 and .69 rifles. Minie bullets had tremendous smashing power. At Cold Harbor, Virginia the first sergeant of Company "A," 2nd New Hampshire Infantry was wounded in the right arm by a Minie bullet which shattered the bone into 23 pieces.[77] Ordnance officers discouraged as much as possible any variation from the use of caliber .58 rifles for the infantry. An officer who had purchased a small number of repeating rifles was informed by an ordnance officer that .58 was the smallest effective caliber for an infantry rifle.[78]

The records of the Ordnance Office show that 33,350 explosive bullets were issued to the troops in the early part of the war.[79] About 10,000 of these were not shipped to the front but that the others were used there can be no doubt. On June 8, 1863, each soldier in the 2nd New Hampshire Infantry was issued 40 rounds of these "musket shells" as they were called. This fact seemed to be known to the Confederates, who accused their opponents of using explosive bullets. But the Confederates also used them.[80] The explosive bullet was of a conical shape and contained a small copper shell arranged on the principle of a fuse and calculated to explode a short time after it had left the rifle. Such a bullet inflicted terrible laceration in the area of its entrance into a man's body.

With the exception of such rifles as the Spencer which used a metallic cartridge, all rifles and muskets were fired with either a percussion cap or the famous Maynard primer. The percussion caps were carried in the cap box on the soldier's belt. Loading was slow with these small caps, as they were easily dropped while being placed on the nipple of the gun. To increase the rate of fire of percussion weapons a dentist, Doctor Maynard, had invented a primer tape some twenty years before the war. Model 1855 weapons were manufactured with the intent of using his primer. The principle was good; with each cocking of the gun a fresh primer was pushed up over the nipple of the gun in position for use. But the primers frequently failed to explode the cartridge,[81] and percussion caps were resorted to again and used throughout the war. In December 1864, the 116th New York Infantry, as the best regiment in the Nineteenth Corps, was selected to try out the Seely "gun capper." However, the colonel soon reported that the men did not want them and considered them worthless, an opinion concurred in by General Sheridan.[82]

In 1861 and 1862 soldiers were frequently ordered to carry 60, 80, or even 100 rounds of ammunition into combat with them. As their cartridge boxes would only hold 40 rounds, it was necessary to carry the extra cartridges in their pockets where they were easily blown up by loose matches or in the haversacks where the paper cartridges would break open, allowing the powder to mix with the coffee or sugar.[83] As the volunteers became veterans and learned to shoot more carefully, they began to husband their ammunition and the overloading of the men with surplus ammunition became less necessary. In a prolonged battle, however, the question of adequate ammunition was an ever-pressing one.

BAYONETS AND KNIVES

Depending on the model and make, each rifle or musket was equipped with a socket or saber bayonet. The socket bayonet was the type used on all United States regulation muskets and rifles except the model 1841 rifle, 1855 rifle, and Remington 1863 rifle. The Plymouth rifle used a saber bayonet but this weapon was issued to the Navy only. The non-regulation Merrill and Sharps rifles also were equipped with saber bayonets. Most troops disliked the saber bayonet because they were too cumbersome [84] and their employment in the war limited. A correspondent of the *Army and Navy Journal* recommended the adoption of a knife bayonet with a blade about 10 or 12 inches long; a weapon of that size could be used either as a bayonet or a knife.[85]

Early in the war many recruits were presented with bowie knives of various lengths. On one occasion the local pastor made the presentation speech in donating these bowie knives to a group of Western volunteers. To emphasize his remarks the doctor of divinity drew one of the knives from its sheath and held it up before the "tearful and shuddering audience," exhorting the men to "Strike! till the last armed foe expires." Although one of the volunteers made a lurid speech in response, assuring the donors that those blades should never be dishonored, they were never used "except to saw slices of bacon, chop off chickens' heads, or cut sticks to hold the coffee pots over the fire."[86]

CARE OF WEAPONS

Volunteers were inclined to be careless in the use of firearms until the deaths of a few comrades and tightening discipline had impressed them sufficiently to exercise the necessary caution in the handling of their weapons. The war correspondent, William H. Russell, while riding through the Federal camps near Washington in 1861, noticed the occasional discharge of the men's muskets. In answer to his looks of inquiry, an officer informed him that the discharge of muskets was "volunteers shooting themselves."[87] Newspapers in those early months of the war carried daily accounts of deaths and wounds caused by the discharge of firearms in the tents.[88]

Unit commanders were charged with enforcing proper care of weapons by their men. The barrel and other metal parts of the Springfield rifle musket were required to be kept shiny.[89] This meant constant care and most of the men preferred the Enfield, Spencer, or Sharps rifles because these weapons were either blued or browned and hence easier to keep clean as well as much less conspicuous in combat. Clean guns were an indication of good discipline. After their heavy losses at Cold Harbor, the troops of the Sixth Army Corps suffered in morale, and discipline became lax with the result that they allowed their rifles to rust badly.[90] Recruits often failed to use the wood or cork tompions issued to keep in the muzzles of the guns when not in use; others soon lost the leather gun slings; and many regiment commanders failed to enforce the regulations requiring the men to clean their weapons after firing. Efficient regimental commanders had frequent and thorough inspection of arms. The cleanliness of muzzle loading weapons was tested by tossing the rifle with the iron ramrod in the barrel. A clean gun would give a clear ringing sound. The nipple and vent were also inspected and the rifle examined to see that its exterior was all polished.[91]

On October 24, 1862, all commanding officers of detachments, regiments, and posts were required to render a report to the Chief of Ordnance of the number, make, caliber, and condition of both smooth and rifled arms in their units.[92] This inventory was followed by an order requiring each regimental commander to detail a competent and skillful mechanic to act as armorer to repair the arms of the regiment.[93] By the end of 1863 most of the Eastern and Western troops were equipped with the Springfield rifle musket and the foreign arms were discarded with the exception of the Enfield rifle. Some fortunate commanders of regiments managed to secure breechloading weapons for their men.

SWORDS AND REVOLVERS

All commissioned officers wore swords both behind the lines and at the front. A straight sword was authorized for sergeants and musicians but these weapons were extremely awkward and saw little use. Much more practical were the large holster revolvers worn by all officers and the small pocket revolvers carried by many of the men. The holster revolvers were either five or six chamber weapons and cost from $13.00 to $25.00 each.[94] With the exception of the La Faucheux, a French weapon, these revolvers used a paper or linen-cased cartridge. The more commonly used revolvers were the Colt, Remington, Allen, Savage, Starr, and Whitney. The Colt, of both caliber .36 and .44, was an excellent shooting weapon. The Remington, Whitney, and Allen were about as good but the others were too large to handle easily.

MACHINE GUNS

At least three different types of machine guns were actually used in combat in the war. One of these, the Requa rifle battery, was invented by Requa and Billinghurst, gunsmiths of New York City. This weapon consisted of 25 rifled barrels arranged horizontally on a plane, the entire apparatus resting on a light field carriage. In tests this gun was impressive because of its accuracy, rapidity, and range. The effective range was 1½ miles.[95] In the operations against Charleston this gun proved its worth; it fired 175 shots per minute without fouling at ranges up to 1,200 yards.[96] The Requa battery was served by a four-man crew. A second type of machine gun, also tested in combat, was called the "Coffee Mill" and worked on a different principle from the Requa gun. The Coffee Mill used the principle of an open breech surmounted by a funnel or hopper which was filled with cartridges; these cartridges were composed of solid steel tubes containing the charge, which were successively dropped into the open space of the breech by means of a crank. A hammer, moved by this crank, struck a percussion cap placed at the bottom of the cartridge and caused the discharge. After this discharge the tube fell into a box, from which it was taken to reload. This gun fired 100 shots a minute, and threw ounce balls with great precision to a distance of seven or eight hundred meters.[97] A better gun, the invention of Richard Gatling, appeared in 1862 and was used by General Butler in the East,[98] and on some river boats late in the war.[99] The Gatling gun fired 250-300 shots a minute but was not adopted by the United States Government until after the war was over. The Comte de Paris claimed that Lincoln recommended the adoption of the "Coffee Mill" and even tried it out himself.[100] That the Government and State authorities were hesitant in adopting unusually novel weapons is more readily appreciated when one realizes that all sorts of cranks were constantly besieging them with inventions of questionable merit. One such crank, in writing to Governor Blair of Michigan two weeks after the fall of Fort Sumter, claimed that his weapon "worked on scientific and mechanical principles . . . (and would) deliver the balls on an exact range say 1 foot apart or any other distance desired at any range the barrels are capable of projecting them . . ." This was a type of machine gun which its inventor claimed was "more efficient than 120 men with any other small arms."[101]

GRENADES

Hand grenades were used fairly extensively in siege operations by both sides. At Vicksburg the Confederates filled glass bottles with powder and balls with fuses in the ends[102] while at the siege of Port Hudson, Federal soldiers improvised hand grenades out of 6-pounder shells.[103] The most common type of hand grenade used by Federal troops was the Ketchum 1-pound hand grenade.[104] One Confederate source would indicate that the Federals used hand grenades freely but with not too great effect.[105]

SHARPSHOOTERS AND SNIPERS

All infantry regiments had much skirmishing to do and individuals who possessed unusual ability with the rifle were often detailed to act as snipers. In the East, when circumstances permitted, this type of work was assigned to companies of Berdan's two regiments of sharpshooters. These units wore a special uniform, consisting of a dark green coat and cap with black plume, light blue trousers (later exchanged for green ones) and leather leggings. The regiments, known as the Green Coats, presented a striking contrast to the regular blue of the infantry. Each man was equipped with a knapsack of hair-covered calf skin with cooking kit attached, a durable complete outfit much superior to the infantry knapsack.[106] As few men as possible were accepted for the sharpshooters who were over 35 years of age.[107]

A few companies were armed with target rifles weighing from 15 to 34 pounds. These rifles, equipped with telescopic sights, were fired from a rest and were effective at ranges well over a mile. One Confederate had seen a Berdan sharpshooter kill a man at such a distance that the report of the rifle could not be heard. The distance was estimated at about a mile.[108] Although the heavy target rifles were exceedingly cumbersome to carry on the march, they were especially valuable in siege operations where they were used against artillerymen and officers with deadly effect. The telescopic sight was "an instrument which . . . (reduced) the art of aiming to a point of mathematical certainty."[109] These sharpshooters operated with deadly efficiency. At Chancellorsville a Confederate sharpshooter killed a colonel just in rear of the 1st New Hampshire Light Battery. Accordingly one of Berdan's sharpshooters was summoned to "fix the rebel." Members of the battery watched curiously at his manner of going to work. First, "he took off his cap and showed it over the earthwork. Of course, Johnnie Reb let go at it, thinking to kill the careless man under it. His bullet struck into the bank, and instantly our sharpshooter ran his ramrod down the hole made by the Johnnie's ball, then lay on his back and sighted along the ramrod. He accordingly perceived from the direction that his game was in the top of a thick bushy elm tree about one hundred yards in front. It was then the work of less than a second to aim his long telescope rifle at that tree and crack she went. Down tumbled Mr. Johnnie like a great crow out of his nest and we had no more trouble from that source."[110]

The chief of the Ordnance Department wished to have Berdan's men equipped with muzzle-loading Springfield rifles and he was strongly supported in this desire by General Scott and the Assistant Secretary of War, Thomas Scott. When Colonel Berdan made a requisition for the Sharps breechloading rifles to equip those companies not outfitted with the target rifles, General Ripley went so far as to say he preferred the old smoothbore with "buck and ball" while General Scott said that breechloaders would spoil the command.[111] Eventually Berdan won his point

BODY ARMOR

and his men were issued Colt five-shot revolving rifles; later Sharps rifles replaced the Colts. Berdan's sharpshooters in the East had their counterpart in the West where Birge's sharpshooters, equipped with the Henry rifle, acted as skirmishers and snipers. They performed unusually effective service at the siege of Fort Donelson.[112]

Body Armor

Although the Government never issued armor of any sort, sutlers and private dealers sold iron vests to many recruits. One dealer sold over 200 of these "iron-clad life preservers" in a single day to members of the 15th Connecticut Infantry. "The track of the command from Washington to Arlington Heights was marked by these abandoned armor plates, the largest quantity being hurled from Long Bridge into the Potomac when the regiment was about to step on 'sacred soil,' as an offering to the gods."[113] Another regiment, perhaps less religiously-motivated than the Connecticut unit, threw their armor into the gutter in front of the White House;[114] still another regiment waited until they got to their camping area when they either threw the breastplates away or used them for frying pans with cleft sticks for handles.[115] These vests were so heavy that they were soon thrown away and in the few cases where they were tried in battle they failed to live up to expectations. One such breastplate (probably discarded by a Confederate soldier) was worn by a Federal soldier until he was severely wounded. He then gave it to a comrade who was killed by a Minie ball which struck the breastplate near its lower border and passed through it carrying pieces of the plate into the abdomen.[116] A typical advertisement for one of these soldiers bulletproof vests stressed that it had been "repeatedly and thoroughly tested with pistol bullets at 10 paces, rifle bullets at 40 rods, by many army officers and approved and worn by them." Simple and light, it was guaranteed to save thousands.[117]

The breastplates worn by Federal soldiers were of two principal types. The most popular type, the "Soldier's Bullet Proof Vest," was manufactured by G. and D. Cook and Co. of New Haven, Connecticut. It consisted of a regular black military vest, containing pockets into which were inserted two thin pieces of spring steel, one on either side of the chest. When the vest was buttoned, the plates overlapped in the center. The standard infantry vest weighed 3½ pounds, while a slightly heavier model for cavalry and artillery weighed 6 pounds. The second most popular type of breastplate was made by still another New Haven firm, the Atwater Armor Company. It was a far more complicated product than the Soldiers' Bullet Proof Vest and cost about twice as much. The main body of the armor consisted of four large plates held together by a keyhole and rivet system. To the button of the cuirass formed by these plates were attached hinged tassets of two leaves each. Many lives were

Metal plates from soldier's bullet-proof vest, taken from body of Union private near Kinston, N. C. Photo courtesy of Confederate Museum, Richmond and Harold L. Peterson.

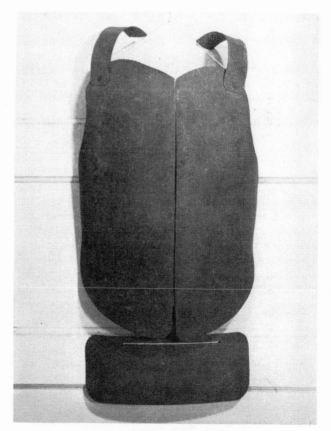

Breastplate taken from the body of a Union officer at Gaines' Mill battlefield. Courtesy of Washington Light Infantry, Charleston and Harold L. Peterson.

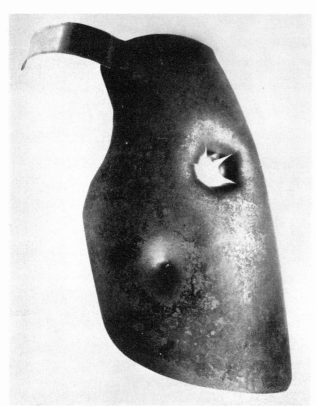

One of the plates worn by Colonel William P. Rogers, 2d Texas Infantry when he was killed at Corinth, 1862. Courtesy of Wisconsin State Historical Society and Harold L. Peterson.

saved by these armored vests but they passed out of use after 1862 due mainly to their bulk and weight, and the ridicule to which the wearers were subjected. There were several standing jokes about the "man in the iron stove" which never seemed to grow stale.[118]

INDIVIDUAL EQUIPMENT OF INFANTRYMAN

The equipment of an infantry soldier consisted of a knapsack, haversack, canteen, cartridge box, cap box, belt, and bayonet scabbard. The knapsacks, worn on the back, were made of painted canvas resembling huge non-porous plasters, and were attached by straps which closely bound all clothing closely about the chest and shoulders—a most vicious combination for hard marching in hot weather. Many knapsacks had wooden frames; the top boards pressed directly on the shoulder blades. Rubber-covered knapsacks protected their contents from moisture but were even more uncomfortable than canvas under a hot sun. Observers commented on the baggy appearance of the knapsacks and the fact that they slipped down too far toward the small of the back. One observer commented that "the hardiest packhorses in the world would break down under the heavy, sagging, illy-adjusted loads borne by our soldiers!"[119] Some men stencilled their company letter and regiment on the backs of their knapsacks.[120]

Much of the difficulty with the regulation knapsacks could have been avoided if the men had packed

them only with those items necessary for their comfort. These included a double wool blanket, half a shelter tent, and a rubber blanket. Some units, like the 4th New Jersey Infantry, late in the war turned in their knapsacks, cartridge boxes, and belts and received in exchange the Colonel Mann accouterment.[121] The designer of these accouterment, Colonel William D. Mann, resigned his commission in the 7th Michigan Cavalry and went to Washington early in 1864 where he persuaded the Ordnance Department of the worth of his improved system of cavalry and infantry accouterment. The Government soon gave large orders for their manufacture and most of the regiments which used them apparently liked them, mainly because the suspenders arrange-

GUM BLANKETS

The rubber poncho, or "gum blanket" as it was called, was one of the most useful and popular items of issue. Sherman during his long marches, threw one of these on the ground at night for his bed, with another over a fence rail for a tent. But the other senior commanders did not march as light as did Sherman.

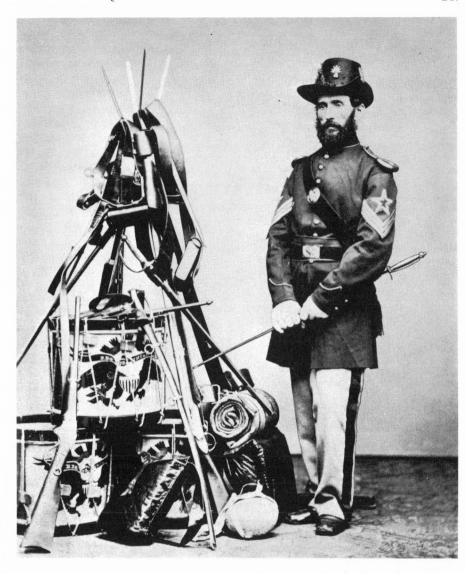

SOLDIERS' EQUIPMENT
Ordnance sergeant with display of stacked muskets, infantry drums, a Spencer carbine, pistol, artillery saber, noncom's sword, cartridge boxes and belts, haversack, canteen, knapsack, and blanket roll.

ment kept the weight of the accouterment off their loins or kidneys.[122]

Even after many of the non-essentials had been eliminated, the soldiers were still burdened with the superfluously loaded knapsacks. In the Chancellorsville campaign many troops carried both overcoat and blanket although it was intended that only one or the other should be taken. One Confederate divisional commander reported that "the enemy abandoned such a large number of knapsacks in retreating to his works that when this division began its homeward march in the rain it was thoroughly equipped with oil cloths and shelter-tents of the best quality."[123]

The rubber blanket was about 6½ feet long and 3½ feet wide with eyelet holes in the sides and ends. Two of them could be laced together at the sides and with forked sticks be made into a tent if the shelter tent was lost.

The experience gained at Chancellorsville convinced the Quartermaster General and corps com-

manders of the Army of the Potomac that the knapsack was an unnecessary incumbrance which should be replaced by the blanket roll. At Chancellorsville the Army of the Potomac lost about 25 percent of its knapsacks. In the Fifth Corps it was about 30 percent; in the Eleventh and Twelfth Corps it was about 50 percent.[124] Even though knapsacks were carried by some regiments in the field all through the war, they were usually stored before setting out on an active campaign and their place taken by a blanket. This blanket, with a change of underclothing in it, was rolled into a cylinder and slung across the left shoulder and, crossing to the right hip, was tied together by a string.[125]

When troops were in the field and wagons were used only for transportation of ammunition, the soldier carried his own ammunition and rations. The total weight carried by each soldier was forty-five pounds. It consisted of his knapsack, haversack, subsistence, and change of underclothing; overcoat or blanket, arms and accouterments, and one half of a shelter tent. Eight days' short rations were carried on the person, stowed as follows: five days' in the knapsack, and three days' in the haversack. Forty rounds of ammunition were carried in the cartridge boxes, and twenty rounds in the pockets of the man's clothing.[126]

The soldier's rations were carried in a canvas haversack slung over the right shoulder and resting on the left hip. Many officers carried large leather haversacks of more elaborate design. The regulation haversacks were marked with the number and name of the regiment, the company letter, and the soldier's company number.[127] The Government haversack was better than those made by private firms; the regulation type had an inside lining which kept the rations from contact with the canvas, but usually these linings soon disappeared as the men cut them up for gun cleaners.[128] Coffee and sugar rations were sometimes issued in small cotton bags and the haversack soon became quite odorous with its mixture of stale parts of rations.[129] A tin ration container, apparently of Government issue, appeared during the war, but the author has been unable to ascertain the extent of its use by troops in the field.[130] The tin canteen, covered with cloth, in shape much "like a ball that has been stepped on and flattened down,"[131] was carried by all officers and men. The canteen was carried on the outside of the haversack, suspended from the right shoulder by a string or narrow strap of cloth or leather. Its capacity was three pints[132] and to supplement this supply of water, recruits often purchased worthless water filters that were soon discarded. Knives, forks, tin cups, and tin plates were also issued, usually by the State before the regiments arrived in Federal camps or forts. However, the cost for these articles was borne by the Federal Government.[133]

A set of rifle accouterments completed the infantry soldier's equipment. A black leather cartridge box, capable of holding forty rounds of ammunition, was carried at the rear of the right hip by a wide cross belt that was suspended from the soldier's left shoulder. Attached to this cross belt and almost directly over the heart was a brass eagle ornament that was dressy but, due to its shiny surface, very noticeable. One observer found it "puzzling to explain the necessity of the breast-plate, except it be to furnish a conspicuous target for the enemy."[134] The cartridge box was decorated with a brass oval shield stamped with the letters "U.S." Cartridge boxes made late in the war are without this brass plate; they merely have the letters "U.S." stamped into the leather. The interior of the cartridge box was divided into tin compartments which made it somewhat difficult for recruits to get out the cartridges in the excitement of combat.

Some regiments in the field and many regiments in garrison dispensed with the cross belt. A full load of ammunition produced an undue weight on the loins.[135] In some units soldiers were forbidden under penalty of a fine to wear the cartridge box on the waist belt.[136]

The waist belt was of black leather fastened by an oval belt plate similar in appearance to the plate on the cartridge box. The regulation belt plate for enlisted men was of brass, oval in shape, with "U.S." in large block letters in the middle. Some of the regiments wore their State letters for a while, as for example, New York soldiers had "S.N.Y." on their buckles. Noncommissioned officers wore a belt similar to the commissioned officers. This belt had a square belt plate with a large American eagle and floral designs on the border. Carried on the waist belt were the cap box and bayonet scabbard. The cap box, containing percussion caps, was of black leather and was worn between the belt plate and the right hip.

The bayonet scabbard, also of black leather, was suspended from the waist belt on the left side of the body. There were two main types; those for the triangular bayonet and those for the saber bayonets. The ends of both were protected with brass tips. Regulations forbade the cutting of any of the belts without the captain's permission.[137] In the early part of the war, those men who cut their waist belts to get a better fit were often charged with new ones; and if a man wore his cartridge box on his waist belt (instead of using the cross belt), he was fined as much as one-fifth a month's pay. Later on many veterans wore their cartridge boxes this way.[138] As the 150th Pennsylvania Infantry marched towards Chancellorsville a few of its members were caught in the act of removing the metallic eagle from the cross belt, "but a threat of punishment put a stop to this unwarranted scheme."[139]

Spit and Polish

The insistence on "spit and polish" plagued many soldiers so long as they remained in rear areas. In the 19th Massachusetts "dress coats with brass shoulder scales and leather neck-stocks were issued, and when not in line or on guard, our spare moments were spent in cleaning brasses. If any men ever earned thirteen dollars a month we did."[140] It is not surprising that some men refused to wear the brass ornamentation or to keep them shiny. In January 1863 a serious disturbance, amounting almost to mutiny, arose in the 13th New Hampshire over wearing brasses, "a miserable, old-fashioned piece of regular army foolishness." The 13th solved the problem by burying "the entire mess of stuff" in one deep hole at midnight. As the men put it: "We came down here to put down the rebellion; not to garnish ourselves with old brass, and poor at that, and spend hour after hour in polishing it."[141] Leather equipment was kept polished with blacking. Service at the front however, caused many units to present a very nonuniform appearance. Soldiers replaced lost or damaged articles of uniform and equipment with the first available item that came along. This applied even to weapons.[142]

"Dog Tags" Not Issued

Identification of Federal soldiers killed in combat was rendered very difficult at times because there was no issue of identification discs by the Government or State agencies. At Cold Harbor a member of Grant's staff noticed the men, in preparation for what was obviously to be a desperate assault, calmly writing their names and home addresses on slips of paper, and pinning them on the backs of their coats, so that their dead bodies might be recognized upon the field.[143] Some soldiers purchased identification discs from private manufactures. A more extensively used item purchased by the soldiers was the identification disc. One type of disc was brass, about the size of a quarter, stamped "War of 1861" on one side, while the soldier's name company, and regiment were stamped on the other.[144] However, many items were of no value and only served to overload the soldiers.

Soldiers' Handbooks

In 1861, many soldiers were presented with a copy of the Soldier's Pocket Health Companion, a book which listed 25 different items every soldier should have. Among these were:

6 linen pocket handkerchiefs
2-6 yards of white flannel
1 yard linen or muslin
1 pair slippers
1 dozen court-plaster
1 small box of lard
1 small bottle Laudanum for diarrhea
1 small bottle brandy
1 small bottle peppermint
1 small bottle camphor
1 paper cayenne pepper

"Let every soldier provide himself with them and store them away in one corner of his knapsack—they will occupy but little room."(!)[145]

Cost of Individual Equipment

The cost of outfitting the officer or soldier varied according to time and place but the initial outlay for the former was always considerable. One lieutenant of General Pope's division in May, 1862, listed his outlay as amounting to nearly five hundred dollars.[146] Almost half of this amount, however, was spent on horses, an expense normally incurred in infantry regiments only by field officers. One of the expensive items of officer equipment was the sword, which, in the case of the colonel of the 15th Wisconsin,[147] for example, cost $125.00. This was a very handsome specimen and most swords cost less. However, these weapons were always an expensive item

and newly-commissioned officers appreciated the thoughtfulness of relatives or friends who gave swords as going-away presents. Some officers wore cavalry sabers as issued by the Government. Saddles cost the officers as much as $65.00.[148] The initial outfit of an enlisted man was about thirty dollars[149], exclusive of arms and equipment. Downing, in his diary, November 1861, listed the cost as follows.[150] Coat $6.71; overcoat 7.20; pants 3.03; shoes 1.96; 2 shirts 1.76; hat 1.55; blanket 2.96; 2 pr drawers 1.00; 2 pr socks .52; cap .60; leather collar .14; total, $27.43.

Two years later the cost was slightly more although some items were not included. A corporal in the 124th Indiana recorded the following costs in his diary:[151] Coat $7.00; overcoat 7.50; pants 3.50; 3 shirts 4.20; blanket 3.50; 2 pr drawers 1.80; 2 pr socks .70; cap .70; total, $28.90.

Even this reduced list was cut down later on. Active service also eliminated the officers' fancy trappings. The glittering epaulet had no place within the range of a Whitworth rifle equipped with a telescopic sight; the humid heat of a Chickahominy June day took the starch out of the last collar and made the buttoned-up coat ridiculous. The sash was soon discarded and the costly shoulder-straps of gold embroidery gave way to ones of metal.

ORGANIZATIONAL EQUIPMENT

Trains

In the early months of the War the Federal Army was handicapped in its movements by unnecessarily cumbersome wagon trains and elaborate camp equipage. Even the infantry regiment[152] was characterized by this weakness. In 1861 the 1st New Hampshire Infantry left for the war with 116 horses and 16 baggage wagons![153] However, combat conditions resulted in a sharp curtailment of such impedimenta. On October 18, 1862, the War Department limited each full infantry regiment to six wagons.[154] Later on such hard-marching generals as Grant and Sherman reduced the number of wagons to an absolute minimum for all branches of the service. Due to the nature of the terrain, however, and the long supply lines essential for an invading army, there always was an inescapable dependence on such trains as ammunition, ambulance, and, to a lesser extent, supply trains as well. As an officer of the Sixth Corps expressed it: "No one who has not seen the train of an army in motion, can form any just conception of its magnitude, and of the difficulties attending its movements. It was said that the train of the Army of the Potomac, including artillery (just before Gettysburg), if placed in a single line, the teams at the distance necessary for the march, would extend over 70 miles."[155]

Camp Equipage

Before leaving their respective States, troops were quartered in private dwellings or local barracks of

ESCORT WAGON

Used for hauling supplies and ammunition. Traditional means of Army transportation until about 1940, when the horse and mule virtually became extinct in the military service.

SIBLEY TENT

Forerunner of the pyramidal squad tent more familiar in recent times.

varied types; on arrival at Federal camps they were housed in government barracks or tents. The barracks were standardized by the Quartermaster General's office in 1864 with original specifications drawn up in 1860. Enlisted men's barracks were 24 by 128 feet and were equipped with air shafts and ventilators. A very common structure was the two-company barracks; the first floor contained the mess rooms, kitchens, and company officers' quarters, while the men slept on the second floor. Field officers were quartered in separate barracks.[156]

The tent equipment of units before arrival at the front was often excessive. While encamped in the Washington area, De Trobriand's 55th New York Infantry was equipped with 250 wedge tents (1 per 4 men) and 32 wall tents plus 2 hospital tents.[157] Another type of tent in common use during the war was the A-tent. This type of tent was often used as roofing over log walls about three feet high. Bunks

were made on each side and across the back end. Beds were then made by spreading boughs on stakes driven into the ground. After a soldier's blankets were spread on the boughs the result was a "springy, elastic and easy bed fit for the warrior god . . . or the Union soldier."[158]

The A-tent and the Sibley tent were both large enough for stoves. Sibley tents, too large for the field, were used when troops were in permanent or semi-permanent quarters. During the war the Federal

SIBLEY STOVE

Efficient heater for tent or hut. Burned wood, coal, coke. Replaced during World War II by an oil-burning stove.

Army used 43,958 of them and about 16,000 of the stoves specially designed to be used in them. The Sibley tent stove was an airtight cylinder 30 inches tall, with an 1 8inch base diameter, five sections of pipe tapering from 5 to 4 inches and resting in one section, a hinge or slide door 8 inches high, 6 inches wide and 8 inches from the bottom. This model weighed 30 pounds. There were also specifications for 25 and 18-pound models.[159]

The October 1862 order to restrict the size of regimental trains likewise limited the tentage allowed each regiment to three wall tents for the field officers and staff. Company officers and men were allowed shelter tents. The company officers were allowed one complete shelter tent each, but the men slept two to a tent, each man carrying half. Officers' baggage was also limited by this order to a small valise or carpet bag and a mess kit.[160] Over 300,000 of these shelter tents were issued during the first year of the war. These were soon improved by the use of rubber cloth and gradually were supplemented by the waterproof poncho. That useful article was a square piece of cloth with a hole in the center for the head. It could be used as a raincape during the day and at night it formed the floor of the shelter tent. Some 40,000 of these were used in 1861 and about 1,500,000 in 1864.[161]

MESSING FACILITIES

While the troops were in barracks and permanent or semipermanent camps, it was customary to have the company cooks prepare the meals in the unit kitchens. On the march and at the front, men either cooked in small groups or individually. Sometimes two men from each company would cook for the men of their own company, but the consequences were waste, crudity, and unwholesomeness. "There is hardly ever enough, because so much is spoiled and wasted in the cooking, and what is eaten is generally not fit for dogs."[162] Members of each mess carried coffee pots,[163] fying pans, and small kettles to cook their rations. In addition to his tin cup and plate, each soldier was issued a knife, fork, and spoon. Many soldiers were presented with knife-fork-spoon combinations before leaving their States for the seat of war.

NOTES CHAPTER 9

1. *Army and Navy Journal*, Vol. 1 (November 14, 1863), p. 180.

2. *Official Records*, Third Series, Vol. 1, p. 153.

3. *Ibid.*, p. 234.

4. *Ibid.*, Vol. 2, pp. 882, 934. Drafted men were to be put at once into uniform. Circular issued May 23, 1863, *Ibid.*, pp. 482-484.

5. United States War Department, "General Order No. 85," July 23, 1862, *General Orders for 1862.*

6. Report of the Quartermaster General, November 18, 1862, *House Executive Documents*, 37 Cong., 3 Sess., Document 1, pp. 76-77.

7. United States War Department, "General Order No. 73," March 24, 1863, *General Orders for 1863.*

8. *Official Records*, Third Series, Vol. 2, p. 805.

9. Grant, Vol. 2, pp. 190-191. Grant claimed he had never seen such waste in his previous service.

10. Haynes, p. 7. The reserve division (Blenker's) was completely attired in gray. *Photographic History*, Vol. 8, p. 78.

11. Among these was the 23rd Indiana Infantry, which donned the blue with reluctance.

12. This uniform was of a dark greenish-blue color, with a flat-brimmed round-top hat set off with cock's feathers. *Glimpse of the Nation's Struggle*, Third Series, p. 96.

13. *Official Records*, Third Series, Vol. 2, p. 803.

14. Among these was Hawkins' 9th New York Infantry. One brigade (140th and 146th New York Infantry), known as the "Zou Zou Brigade," wore this uniform.

15. These include Lew Wallace's 11th Indiana Infantry; also the 14th New York Infantry.

16. Russell, W. H., *My Diary North and South*, Vol. 2, pp. 176-177.

17. Carpenter, G. N., *History of the Eighth Regiment Vermont Volunteers*, p. 30.

18. Cowles, Luther E., *History of the Fifth Massachusetts Battery*, p. 218.

19. Jackman, Lyman, *History of the Sixth New Hampshire Regiment in the War for the Union*, p. 78.

20. Clark, Walter (editor), *Histories of the Several Regiments and Battalions from North Carolina in the Great War 1861-65*, Vol. 2, p. 265. (Hereafter, this work will be cited as *North Carolina Regiments*.)

21. United States War Department, *Revised Regulations for the Army of the United States*, 1861, pp. 476-488; Plate 172 of the atlas to the *Official Records*.

22. *Ibid.*, Sections 1454, 1455, 1485-1488, 1528.

23. United States War Department, "General Order No. 286," November 22, 1864, *General Orders for 1864.*

24. The men preferred hats.

25. *Army and Navy Journal*, Vol. 1 (November 14, 1863), p. 180.

26. A unique honor, and one of which the men were proud.

27. Ellis Thomas, *Leaves from the Diary of an Army Surgeon*, p. 110, The name of the regiment was printed on the black band.

28. The author has not seen one of these helmets.

29. *Army and Navy Journal*, Vol. 1 (November 14, 1863), p. 180.

30. *Battles and Leaders*, Vol. 1, p. 152.

31. *Ibid.*

32. *Army and Navy Journal*, Vol. 1 (November 14, 1863), p. 180.

33. *Ibid.*

34. *Ibid.*

35. De Trobriand, 136.

36. Thompson (13th New Hampshire Infantry), p. 31, See also Stevens, pp. 211-212.

37. Confederates used this fact in identifying footprints left by unknown troops. Wyeth, John A., *With Sabre and Scalpel*, p. 279.

38. Among the scarcest of Civil War items.

39. Named after the English general who designed them for use in India during the 1857 rebellion. Made of white cloth and covering the head and neck they were considered valuable in averting sunstroke. Croffut and Morris, p. 65.

40. Wilkerson, p. 83.

41. Haines, A. A., *History of the Fifteenth Regiment New Jersey Volunteers*, p. 14.

42. *Army and Navy Journal*, Vol. 1 (July 9, 1864), p. 758.

43. *Battles and Leaders*, Vol. 2, p. 145. See also Russell, Vol. 2, p. 168.

44. This unit lost 240 men from disease.

45. Vail, p. 41.

46. Annual Report of Secretary of War, March 1, 1865, *House Executive Documents*, 38 Cong., 2 Sess., Document 83, p. 131. Specimens of these uniforms of these later contracts in private collections and museums are of fine material and show excellent workmanship.

47. See chap. 22.

48. *Annual Cyclopedia* 1861, pp. 28-29.

49. *Official Records*, Third Series, Vol 1, p. 264.

50. Belknap, C. E., *History of the Michigan Organizations at Chickamauga, Chattanooga, and Missionary Ridge 1863*, p. 117.

51. New York *Times*, Vol. 11 (April 9, 1862), p. 10.

52. There were still over 24,000 unaltered by 1859. *Official Records*, Third Series, Vol. 1, p. 1.

53. Many regimental histories attest to this.

54. Jones, pp. 66-67.

55. Comte de Paris, Vol. 1, pp. 298-299.

56. *Official Records*, Third Series, Vol. 2, p. 430.

57. *Annual Report*, Adjutant General of New York, January 27, 1863, pp. 1028-1106.

58. The 101st Illinois Infantry. Haskell, (editor), "Diary of Colonel William Camm 1861 to 1865," *Journal of the Illinois State Historical Society*, Vol. 18, (January 1926), p. 934).

59. *Official Records*, First Series, Vol. 5, p. 10.

60. Thorndike, p. 135.

61. *Battles and Leaders*, Vol. 3, p. 537.

62. Royse, Isaac, *History of the 115th Regiment Illinois Volunteer Infantry*, p. 26.

63. Stevens, p. 236. This rifle could be fired 10 times a minute by a man in a prone position. *Ibid.*, p. 119.

64. Croffut and Morris, p. 67.

65. Page, (14th Connecticut Infantry), pp. 284-285.

66. *Official Records*, Third Series, Vol. 1, pp. 733-734.

67. Bowen, James L., *History of the Thirty-seventh Regiment Mass. Volunteers in the Civil War of 1861-1865*, p. 355.

68. *Ibid.*

69. Thompson (13th New Hampshire Infantry), p. 459.

70. Hedley, F. Y., *Marching through Georgia*, pp. 216-217.

71. The usual price was about $50 per gun.

72. Comte de Paris, Vol. 1, p. 300.

73. "W. D. B." *Rosecrans' Campaigns with the Fourteenth Army Corps*, p. 25.

74. Croffut and Morris, p. 73.

75. Kautz, A. V., *The Company Clerk*, p. 71. The principal weapons used by the Federal Army are shown on Plate 173 of the Atlas to the *Official Records*.

76. Smith, J. L., *History of the 118th Pennsylvania Volunteers*, pp. 520-521.

77. Haynes, p. 232, Amputation was performed within an hour.

78. Keifer, J. W., *Slavery and Four Years of War*, Vol. 1, p. 183, Keifer had purchased a few repeating rifles whose caliber was .44.

79. *Medical and Surgical History of the War of the Rebellion*, Part 3, Surgical Volume, p. 701.

80. Haynes, p. 159. For use of explosive bullets by the enemy see: Billings, (10th Mass. Battery), p. 253; Hays, 470; *Medical and Surgical History*, Part 3, Surgical Volume, pp. 702-704.

81. Stevens, p. 252.

82. Clark, Orton S., *The One Hundred and Sixteenth Regiment of New York State Volunteers*, pp. 258-259.

83. Page (14th Connecticut Infantry), p. 34.

84. Hyde, T. W. *Following the Greek Cross*, p. 14; Stevens, p. 39.

85. *Army and Navy Journal*, Vol. 2, (November 12, 1864), p. 180.

86. Hinman, W. F., *The Story of the Sherman Brigade*, p. 37.

87. Russell, Vol. 1, p. 147.

88. *Ibid.*

89. Hosmer, J. K., *The Color Guard*, p. 17.

90. Croushore, p. 165.

91. Copp, E., *Reminiscence of the War of the Rebellion*, pp. 39-40.

92. United States War Department, "General Order No. 167," October 24, 1862, *General Orders for 1862*.

93. *Ibid*, "General Order No. 189," November 18, 1862.

94. Kautz, p. 71.

95. "A Novel Rifle-Battery," *New York Times*, Vol. 11 (July 26, 1862), p. 3.

96. The gun was called the "Death Provider." Gillmore, Q. A., *Engineer and Artillery Operations Against the Defenses of Charleston Harbor in 1863*, pp. 254-255.

97. Comte de Paris, Vol. 1, pp. 305-306. One of these guns was probably the one recaptured by Federal forces on the Peninsula. Cowles, pp. 355-356.

98. Butler was quite receptive to new ideas.

99. Used by the Navy after 1862.

100. Comte de Paris, Vol. 1, p. 306.

101. Stephen Bowerman to Governor Austin Blair, April 27, 1861. Manuscript letter in Burton Historical Collection.

102. Wells, S. J., *The Diary of Seth J. Wells*, p. 83.

103. Irwin, Richard, *History of the Nineteenth Army Corps*, p. 196.

104. Specimens are marked "Patent of August 20, 1861." A diagram of this grenade appears in *Medical and Surgical History of the War of the Rebellion*, Part 3, Surgical Volume, p. 699.

105. Clark (editor), *Histories of the Several Regiments and Battalions from North Carolina in the Great War 1861-65*, Vol. 1, p. 321.

106. Stevens, p. 5.

107. Captain Benjamin Giroux to Colonel Hiram Berdan, 1st USSR, January 9, 1862. Manuscript letter in Burton Historical Collection.

108. Stevens, p. 463.

109. *The Atlantic Monthly*, Vol. 9, (March 1862), pp. 304-305. A picture of one of these target rifles with its telescopic sight is shown in Stevens, p. 460.

110. *Names and Records . . . First N. H. Battery of Light Artillery during the Late Rebellion*, p. 25.

111. Stevens, p. 7.

112. *Battles and Leaders*, Vol. 1, p. 407.

113. Thorpe, Sheldon B., *The History of the Fifteenth Connecticut Volunteers*, p. 15.

114. Buffum, pp. 66-67.

115. Thompson (13th New Hampshire Infantry), p. 27.

116. *Medical and Surgical History of the War of the Rebellion*, Part 3, Surgical Vol. p. 713. Some said they were no better against bayonets. Haynes, p. 78.

117. *Frank Leslie's Illustrated Newspaper*, Vol. 13 (April 26, 1862), pp. 416. A private's vest coat $5.00; an officer's vest $7.00.

118. Peterson, Harold L., "Body Armor in the American Civil War," *Journal of the Society of Military Collectors and Historians*.

119. *Frank Leslie's Illustrated Newspaper*, Vol. 15, (October 4, 1862), p. 18. A serious weakness was the lack of entrenching tools. Only a few shovels and picks were issued each regiment. In the siege of Petersburg the men used coffee pots, bayonets, their hands, and shovels whittled from hardtack boxes. Vail, pp. 73-74.

120. Examples can be seen in collections today.

121. Baquet, Camille, *History of the First Brigade, New Jersey Volunteers*, p. 363.

122. Isham, Asa B., *An Historical Sketch of the Seventh Regiment Michigan Volunteer Cavalry*, p. 37. An exception was the 2nd Connecticut Heavy Artillery which called them "belly trunks." Vail, p. 139. An excellent source for equipment is Wilbur F. Hinman's *Corporal Si Klegg and His Pard* (Cleveland, 1887).

123. *Official Records*, First Series, Vol. 25, Part 1, p. 945.

124. Bigelow, p. 487.

125. *Medical and Surgical History of the War of the Rebellion*, Part 3, Medical Volume, p. 871; *Photographic History*, Vol. 3, p. 272.

126. Report of the Chief Quartermaster, Army of the Potomac, May 29, 1863, in *House Executive Documents*, Document 83, 38, Cong., 2nd Sess., p. 165.

127. United States War Department, *Regulations for the Army of the United States* 1861, Section 112.

128. *Army and Navy Journal*, Vol. 1 (November 28, 1863), p. 213.

129. Therefore new haversacks were often filched from recruits.

130. Author's collection. See *Army and Navy Journal*, Vol. 1 (November 28, 1863), p. 213.

131. The cloth could be soaked in water to produce coolness by evaporation.

132. Thompson, p. 35.

133. United States War Department, "General Order No. 70," September 3, 1861, *Geenral Orders for 1861*.

134. *Army and Navy Journal*, Vol. 1 (November 28, 1863), p. 213.

135. *Ibid*. See also *Medical and Surgical History of the War of the Rebellion*, Part 3, Medical Volume, p. 871.

136. Page, (14th Connecticut Infantry), pp. 59-60.

137. United States War Department, *Regulations for the Army of the United States*, Section 103.

138. Page (14th Connecticut Infantry), pp. 59-60.

139. Chamberlin, Thomas, *History of the 150th Pennsylvania Volunteers*, p. 87.

140. Adams, (19th Massachusetts Infantry), p. 13.

141. Thompson, p. 105.

142. In this connection see the photograph of Federal troops in *Photographic History*, Vol. 8, p. 203. No two men are uniformed and equipped alike. Some wear corps badges on their caps; some wear boots, others shoes; privates are wearing noncommissioned officer's belts; some wear cross belts, others do not; some have removed the eagle ornament from the cross belts they are wearing; while some men have Enfield rifles, others are carrying Springfields of different models.

143. Porter, Horace, *Campaigning with Grant*, p. 174.

144. Specimen in the author's collection.

145. *Soldier's Pocket Health Companion*, p. 27.

146. Letter of Lieutenant William C. Stevens, 3rd Michigan Cavalry, May 1862. Manuscript in Michigan Historical Collections.

147. Heg, p. 56.

148. *Ibid*., p. 65.

149. *Official Records*, Third Series, Vol. 5, p. 286.

150. Clark, pp. 16, 90.

151. Diary of Corporal James Brown, Co. "K" 124 Indiana Infantry. Manuscript in author's possession.

152. Organization of regiments and companies of the Volunteer *Army of the United States*:
("General Order No. 126," War Department, September 6, 1862).

Regiment of Infantry—10 Companies

1 colonel
1 lieutenant colonel
1 major
1 adjutant (an extra lt.)
1 quartermaster (an extra lt.)
1 surgeon
2 assistant surgeons
1 chaplain
1 sergeant major
1 regimental quartermaster sergeant
1 regimental commissary sergeant
1 hospital steward

Company of Infantry

1 captain
1 first lieutenant
1 second lieutenant
1 first sergeant
4 sergeants
8 corporals
2 musicians
1 wagoner
and 64 privates, minimum; 82 privates, maximum

153. Abbott, Stephen G., *The First Regiment New Hampshire Volunteers* in the Great Rebellion, p. 118. The 2nd New Hampshire Infantry also left the State with 16 wagons (4 horse), but had to turn them in to the Quartermaster pool on arrival in Washington. Hayes, p. 7.

154. United States War Department, "General Order No. 160," October 18, 1862, *General Orders for 1862*. This order also fixed the number of wagons for a corps headquarters train at 4, for a division on brigade headquarters train at 3, and for a light battery or squadron of cavalry at 3.

155. Stevens, George T., *Three Years in The Sixth Corps*, p. 223.

156. U. S. War Department, Quartermaster General's Office, "General Order No. 17," April 27, 1864. *General Orders for 1864*.

157. De Trobriand, p. 79.

158. Thompson, p. 124.

159. Some of these were used as late as World War II.

160. United States War Department, "General Order No. 160," October 18, 1862. *General Orders for 1862*.

161. Comte de Paris, Vol. 1, p. 293. Specifications for the various types of tents in use in 1864 were laid down in General Order No. 60, Quartermaster General's Office, December 12, 1864.

162. *Soldier's Pocket Health Companion* (New York, 1861), p. 16.

163. A specimen in the author's collection is made of copper and was used by troops of the 53d Pennsylvania Infantry. It is labelled with the company letter and regimental number.

CHAPTER 10

Weapons and Munitions

BECAUSE THE Civil War marked a definite transition in military science it also witnessed the appearance of new techniques and weapons of war. It is doubtful if any war in history had so many "firsts" as did the conflict of 1861-1865. The variety and number of weapons employed are almost endless, and the amounts of war materiel used were enormous. The United States Government purchased (1861-1865), exclusive of those made at Springfield, 1,912,360 muskets and rifles, 407,923 carbines, and 373,971 pistols and revolvers. This represents 69 different makes of weapons, the majority of which required special cartridges. Up to June 30, 1862, there were purchased 726,705 muskets and 28,364 carbines and pistols. These muskets and rifles varied in caliber from .54 to .72.

Since it is beyond the scope of this book to include a complete list of all the weapons used by Federal forces in the war, the author has listed the more common types as determined by available literature and from consultation with collectors and experts in the field. The reader is referred also to Chapters 5 and 17. For those who wish to read more intensively on specific phases, a list of books, by subject, is included in the bibliography, Chapter 22. Especially valuable for additional research are the service manuals described in Chapter 3.

Throughout the war, inventors were constantly trying to interest the Government and Ordnance Departments in their wares. Lincoln's indulgence toward inventors did not proceed merely from caprice or a desire for amusement. He fully appreciated the weight of weapons in the scales of war; and he soon came to realize that if he did not encourage the development and use of better weapons, no one would. Lincoln's concern for the tools of war was a distinct phase of his role as commander in chief.

But Lincoln got no thanks from the Ordnance bureaus for his pains. "What does Lincoln know about a gun?" one functionary growled. "We're bothered to death with these inventors running here all the time." To the bureaucratic way of thinking, Lincoln should have left such matters strictly to their proper arbiters: the chiefs of the two Ordnance bureaus. But

Lincoln was no respecter of red tape. "He did despise forms and almost hated those that loved them," wrote his former law partner Herndon.

BREECHLOADERS VS. MUZZLE LOADERS

Lincoln knew his own technical limitations. He also knew that Captain Hardwood of the Navy Ordnance Bureau was a stopgap administrator, not an ordnance expert, and that Ripley, Chief of Army Ordnance "combatted all new ideas in the fabrication of firearms, artillery, and projectiles."[1] Ripley fought off adoption of repeating rifles by the Army, claiming that men with breechloaders used up ammunition too fast and recklessly. But men with muzzle-loaders forgot to put on percussion caps and probably half the guns in battle were not discharged or failed to go off, due to excitement or carelessness. Men with muzzle-loaders were notoriously apt to fire wildly. It does not appear that men with breechloaders were any more careless; probably they were much more deliberate in their firing. As a soldier wrote to the *Army and Navy Journal*: (Vol. 2, December 24, 1864, p. 278)

Let them come to the front armed with one Springveld musket, and oppose themselves to an equal number of Rebs armed with repeaters or breechloaders. If they can stand that, let them go to the picket line, and while fumbling for a cap and trying to get it on the cone one of these cold days, offer themselves as a target to some fellow on the other side who has nothing to do but cock his piece and blaze away. If they don't throw down their bungling, slow-shooting gun in disgust, they may be excused for indulging in remarks not complimentary to those who compel them to the unequal contest. The objection has been urged that we fire too many shots with our present muzzle-loaders, and consequently it would be folly to add to the waste of ammunition by affording us greater ease or facility in loading. Do our good friends ever reflect that the loss of time in loading is the great *cause* of haste, and consequent inaccuracy in firing?

Lincoln was well acquainted with the tedious process a soldier had to go through to load and fire the regulation Springfield muzzle-loading rifle. Reaching into his cartridge pouch, the soldier took out a paper cartridge containing the powder charge and the bullet. Holding this between his thumb and forefinger, he tore it open with his teeth. Next he emptied the powder into the barrel and disengaged the bullet with his right hand and the thumb and two fingers of the left. Inserting the bullet point up into the bore, he pressed it down with his right thumb. Then he drew his ramrod, which meant pulling it halfway out, steadying it, grasping it again, and cleaning it. He rammed the ball halfway down, took hold of the ramrod again, and drove the ball home. He then drew the ramrod out and returned it to its tube, each movement again in two stages. Next he primed the piece by raising it, half cocking it, taking off the old cap, taking a new one out of the pouch and pressing it down on the nipple. At last he cocked the gun, aimed it and fired. And if he had a particular target in mind, which was unlikely in all the excitement, he probably missed it clean.

An experienced man with steady nerves could fire three rounds per minute at the most. Choked by fear and battle smoke, unnerved by the shrieking of shells and the whining of bullets, rattled by the screams of dying men and the wolfish yipping of the charging enemy, not many soldiers did so well. And entirely apart from speed, a lot could go wrong if a man got overexcited. He might ram the bullet into the barrel before he poured in the powder. He might leave the ramrod in the barrel and then fire it off, past retrieving. He might load the cartridge, paper and all, without breaking it open. If he made any of these easy mistakes, his gun was useless; he had to find another. If any conclusions can be drawn from the 24,000 muskets and rifles examined after Gettysburg, only about 25 percent of the men in combat were effective in loading and firing correctly the muzzle-loading musket. The obvious solution was a gun which could be loaded at the breech. The soldier with a breechloader could not, even if he tried, put in more than one load at a time. He would not have to worry about a ramrod in loading. The ramrod was stuck in the ground while the soldier discharged his piece and often the ramrod would be left behind when the soldier's unit moved forward. He could lie prone and load just as rapidly and easily as when he was standing, thereby creating less of a target for the enemy. Not only would loading be infinitely simple, but some breech-loading rifles would be better than muzzle-loaders in range and accuracy also, since tighter-fitting bullets could be used. And with such advantages would come the priceless asset of confidence, especially in the face of an enemy armed only with muzzle-loaders. In retrospect, the dependence of the Federal Army on muzzle-loaders seems inexcusable.[2]

Breech-loading rifles proved their worth time and again during the war. It was tragic that the red tape and mediocrity of a few unimaginative individuals prevented their adoption early and in substantial numbers. For example, the Sharps had been invented before the war began. Companies and regiments were armed with Sharps by their State Governments or at their own expense. The gun was safe for its users. "I never knew of an accident occurring by premature discharge of a Sharps rifle" wrote the historian of Berdan's Sharpshooters after the war. It consistently outdid the Springfield rifle in range. Although the Sharps was sighted only up to a thousand yards, some of Berdan's men experimented with whittled sights at Todd's Tavern, Virginia, in 1864 and managed to fire with fair accuracy at fifteen hundred yards. The tighter-fitting breechloader bullets came out of the muzzle with greater speed than those of muzzle-loaders. Rebels opposite the Sharpshooters in the Petersburg trenches could tell the "forced balls" by their sound and the fact that they hit before the report of the gun came along; and, said one Confederate, "You can just bet your boots we were mighty careful how we got in their way." The Sharps were accurate. At Kelly's Ford on the Rappahannock in November 1863, two Sharpshooters in different companies aimed at and hit the same retreating rebel at seven hundred yards.[3] And the Sharps could be fired 8-10 times a minute as compared with 3 times a minute with the muzzle-loading musket.

HEAVY ORDNANCE

The United States began intensive experimentation with rifled cannon late in the 1850's, and a few rifled pieces were made by the South Boston Iron Foundry and also by the West Point Foundry at Cold Spring, New York. The first appearance of rifled cannon in any quantity, however, was near the outbreak of hostilities, when the Federal artillery was equipped with 300 wrought-iron 3-inch guns. This "12-pounder," which fired a 10-pound projectile, was made by wrapping sheets of boiler iron around a mandrel. The cylinder thus formed was heated and passed through the rolls for welding, then cooled, bored, turned, and rifled. It remained in service until 1900. Another rifle giving good results was the cast-iron 4.5-inch siege gun. This piece was cast solid, then bored, turned, and rifled. Uncertainty of strength, a characteristic of cast iron, caused its later abandonment.

The United States rifle that was most effective in siege work was the invention of Robert P. Parrott. His cast-iron guns, many of which are seen today in the battlefield parks, are easily recognized by the heavy wrought-iron jacket reinforcing the breech. The jacket was made by coiling a bar over the mandrel in a spiral, then hammering the coils into a welded cylinder. The cylinder was bored and shrunk on the gun. Parrotts were founded in 10-, 20-, 60-, 100-, 200-, and 300-pounder calibers, one foundry making 1,700 of them during the Civil War.

Like other nations, the United States had large stocks of smoothbores on hand just before the war. The Ordnance Board believed that conversion of these to rifled cannon simply involved cutting grooves in

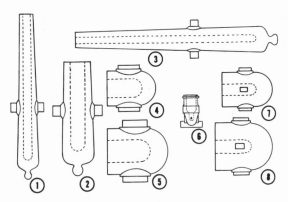

GUNS AND MORTARS

1. 3-inch field gun, rifled. 2. Siege howitzer. 3. 4½-inch siege gun, rifled. 4. 8-inch siege mortar. 5. 10-inch siege mortar. 6. Coehorn mortar. 7. 10-inch seacoast mortar. 8. 13-inch seacoast mortar.

the bore, right at the forts or arsenals where the guns were. In 1860, half of the United States artillery was scheduled for conversion. As a result, a number of old smoothbores were rebored to fire rifle projectiles of the various patents which preceded the modern copper rotating band. Under the James patent, the weight of metal thrown by a cannon was virtually doubled; converted 24-, 32-, and 42-pounders fired elongated shot classed respectively as 48-, 64-, and 84-pound projectiles. After the siege of Fort Pulaski, General Q. A. Gillmore praised the 84-pounder and declared "no better piece for breaching can be desired;" but experience soon proved the heavier projectiles caused increased pressures which converted guns could not long withstand.

The early United States rifles had a muzzle velocity about the same as the smoothbore, but whereas the round shot of the smoothbore lost speed so rapidly that at 2,000 yards its striking velocity was only about one-third of the muzzle velocity, the more streamlined rifle projectile lost speed very slowly. But the rifle had to be served more carefully than the smoothbore. Rifling grooves were cleaned with a moist sponge, and sometimes oiled with another sponge. Lead-coated projectiles like the James, which tended to foul the grooves of the piece, made it necessary to scrape the rifle grooves after every half dozen shots, although guns using brass-banded projectiles did not require the extra operation. With all muzzle-loading rifles, the projectile had to be pushed close home to the powder charge; otherwise, the blast would not fully expand its rotating band, the projectile would not take the grooves, and would "tumble" after leaving the gun, to the utter loss of range and accuracy.

When the U. S. Ordnance Board recommended the conversion to rifles, it also recommended that all large caliber iron guns be manufactured on the method perfected by Captain T. J. Rodman, which involved casting the gun around a water-cooled core.

The inner walls of the gun thus solidified first, were compressed by the contraction of the outer metal as it cooled down more slowly, and had much greater strength to resist explosion of the charge. The Rodman smoothbore, founded in 8-, 10-, 15-, and 20-inch calibers, was the best cast-iron ordnance of its time. The 20-inch gun, produced in 1864, fired a 1,080-pound shot. The 15-inch gun was retained in service through the rest of the century, and these monsters are still to be seen at Fort McHenry National Monument and Historic Shrine or at Fort Jefferson in the national monument of that name in the Dry Tortugas Islands.[4]

According to the *Ordnance Manual*, U. S. Army (1862) all ordnance for the land service was made by private contractors under the direction of officers of the Ordnance Department. The kinds and calibers used were as follows:

Type	Caliber	Material	Model
"Gun" (field)	3 inch, rifled	Iron or steel	1861
	6-pounder	Bronze	1841
	12-pounder	Bronze	1841
	12-pounder	Bronze	1857
"Gun" (Siege & garrison)	4.5 inch, rifled	Cast iron	1861
	12-pounder	Cast iron	1839
	18-pounder	Cast iron	1839
	24-pounder	Cast iron	1839
"Gun" (seacoast)	32-pounder	Cast iron	1841
	42-pounder	Cast iron	1841
"Columbiad"	8 inch	Cast iron	1844
	8 inch	Cast iron	1861
	10 inch	Cast iron	1844
	10 inch	Cast iron	1861
	15 inch	Cast iron	1861
"Howitzer" (mountain)	12-pounder	Bronze	1841
"Howitzer" (field)	12-pounder	Bronze	1841
	24-pounder	Bronze	1844
	32-pounder	Bronze	1844
"Howitzer" (siege & garrison)	24-pounder	Cast iron	1841
	8 inch	Cast iron	1841
	8 inch	Cast iron	1861
"Howitzer" (seacoast)	8 inch	Cast iron	1841
	10 inch	Cast iron	1841
"Mortar" (siege)	8 inch	Cast iron	1841
	8 inch	Cast iron	1861
	10 inch	Cast iron	1841
	10 inch	Cast iron	1861
"Mortar" (seacoast)	10 inch	Cast iron	1844
	10 inch	Cast iron	1861
	13 inch	Cast iron	1841
	13 inch	Cast iron	1861
"Mortar" (Coehorn)	24-pounder	Bronze	1841

Guns and howitzers took their denominations from the weights of their solid shot in round numbers, including the 42-pounder; larger pieces, rifle guns, and mortars, from the diameter of the bore. In the early period of the war, there were in some of the forts guns of older models than the above. The 42-pounder gun, and the 8- and 10-inch sea-coast howitzers were "suppressed" by order of February 9, 1861. Some additional models appeared during the war.

It was in siege operations that the rifles forced a new era. As the smoke cleared after the historic bombardment of Fort Sumter in 1861, military men were already speculating on the possibilities of the

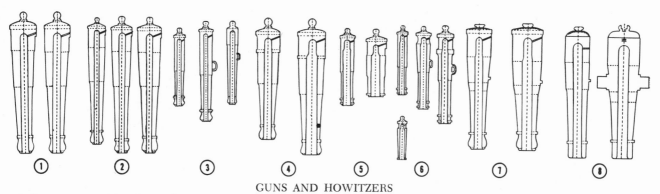

GUNS AND HOWITZERS

1. Seacoast guns, 32 and 42 pdrs. 2. Siege and garrison guns, 12, 18, and 24 pdrs. 3. Field guns, 6 and 12 pdrs. 4. Seacoast howitzers, 8 and 10 inch. 5. Siege and garrison howitzers, 24 pdr. 6. Field howitzers, 12, 24 and 32 pdrs. 7. Columbiads, 8 and 10 inch. 8. New Columbiads, 8 and 10 inch (128 and 64 pdrs.).

new-fangled weapon. The first really effective use of the rifles in siege operations was at Fort Pulaski, 1862. Using 10 rifles and 26 smoothbores, General Gillmore breached the 7½-foot-thick brick walls in little more than 24 hours. Yet his batteries were a mile away from the target! The heavier rifles were converted smoothbores, firing 48-, 64-, and 84-pound James projectiles that drove into the fort wall from 19 to 26 inches at each fair shot. A year later, Gillmore used 100-, 200-, and 300-pounder Parrott rifles against Fort Sumter. The big guns, firing from positions some two miles away and far beyond the range of the fort guns, reduced Sumter to a smoking mass of rubble. The range and accuracy of these rifles startled the world. A 30-pounder (4.2 inch) Parrott had an amazing carry of 8,453 yards with 80-pound hollow shot. But strangely enough, neither rifles nor smoothbores could destroy earthworks.

Another type of heavy ordnance which was extensively used in siege operations by the Federals was the mortar. Mortar projectiles were quite formidable; the 13-inch mortar of the 1860's fired a 200-pound shell. These large projectiles had to be taken to the muzzle with block and tackle. During the siege of Petersburg, the Federal piece used against Petersburg was "The Dictator" which had special wrought-iron beds with a pair of rollers. In spite of their high trajectory, mortars could range well over a mile, as shown by these figures for United States mortars of the 1860's, firing at 45-degrees elevation: [5]

Caliber	Weight of projectile	Range in yards
8-inch siege	45	1837
10-inch siege	90	2100
12-inch seacoast	200	4625
13-inch seacoast	200	4325

There was also a 24-pounder Coehorn mortar used primarily against personnel at comparatively short ranges. Reports of this weapon indicate that its tactical use was similar to the Stokes mortar of World War I or the infantry mortars of World War II.

FIELD ARTILLERY [6]

Ammunition for smoothbore field artillery consisted of five basic types of projectiles. For long range work, solid shot, explosive shell, and spherical case were used, and solid shot was employed more often than not. There was always the chance that a projectile of this type might sweep down a line of men or hit a column head on. Shell, because of its black powder bursting charge, did not shatter; sometimes there were only two fragments. The most effective long range projectile was spherical case if its fuze worked properly. When the small bursting charge could be exploded a few yards in front of and above the target, the individual balls would hit in a fairly dense pattern. However, all fuzes of that day were poor; those of the Confederates particularly so.

In theory, guns fired solid shot, while howitzers used shell and spherical case. In practice, this procedure was not observed, particularly after the Napoleon had become almost the only active smoothbore field piece. The ammunition for this weapon consisted of all three long-range types.

For close work a tin can of iron or lead balls called "canister" was the ultimate in effectiveness. In fact, from a casualty producing point of view in the war, it was the only truly satisfactory ammunition. The maximum range for canister before the war was supposed to be about 300 yards; however, Federal canister in particular, because of its lead balls, would do damage at a much greater distance. Grape shot, larger than canister, was effective at 700 yards and beyond. In theory, each bore-size had its proper size of grape, so designed that a layer of three shots would exactly fill the bore. There were three layers, each separated by rings, an iron plate at top and bottom, and supposedly a stem holding everything together until discharge.

Rifled field pieces had seen but little use before the

war; but in 1861 dozens of inventors appeared with ideas and even model weapons. There was, of course, no doubt that the rifle could shoot farther and more accurately than the smoothbore, for a similar charge in small arms had just achieved astonishing results. Yet only three of the many field pieces suggested and tried were ever officially adopted. Bronze, the best material for smoothbore field pieces, would not do, since the lands in a bronze barrel could not stand up under the firing of rifle projectiles. Iron or steel was necessary for rifles; all three of the really successful field pieces were made of this material.

The 20-pounder Parrott rifle was the largest piece used regularly in the field. All things considered, the rifle was superior to the smoothbore at medium range, having better accuracy and greater sustained velocity. Above 2,000 yards—a long range during the war—the smoothbores were useless. At short range, however, the rifle was inherently at a great disadvantage. It could not fire canister effectively for the same reason that one cannot effectively use shot cartridges in a sporting rifle. A Napoleon would send its short thick charge (4.5 inches in diameter by 3.5 inches long, weighing about 12 pounds) out to about 300 yards in a fairly even pattern, about 20 yards across.

The basic difference between Civil War artillery and that of the 20th Century lay in the absence of smokeless propellants, high-explosive bursting charges, recoil mechanisms, breechloading guns, fixed ammunition, built-up steel barrels, and steel carriages. Yet all of these innovations were known to the Ordnance Department.

Even more important than the field artillery materiel was the philosophy of its use. As the war progressed, an entirely new factor changed completely the old artillery-infantry relationship. The Minie rifle became the universal weapon of the infantry. It would kill at a thousand yards although the target had to be at least as large as a battery of guns to be hit at all frequently. A battery which stayed in the open below this distance soon sacrificed itself. The infantry fired on could retaliate effectively. The old smoothbore musket had only a maximum effective range of 200 yards, but the increase in the range of infantry shoulder weapons was of tremendous importance since smoothbore field pieces were relatively ineffective beyond 1,200 yards. Rifled field pieces were accurate and had plenty of sustained velocity even at two miles but they could not produce enough casualties. The old balance was upset. If the guns were close enough to be effective, the new infantry rifles could silence them quickly. This was especially true as the citizen soldiers became veterans. They were familiar with the sight and sound of artillery and knew its limitations. Experience taught the infantry that when the enemy's guns were too far away to be fired at successfully with their rifles, the guns were not really dangerous. But at Cold Harbor smoothbore pieces were used as monster shotguns right in with the infantry. Grant's costly repulse was caused in part by smoothbore pieces firing canister from *prepared* positions (*not* in the open.) The use of this really effective ammunition at the ranges at which it was deadly was made possible by sheltering the crews of the pieces behind breastworks and giving them the security of the surrounding infantry.

NAVAL ORDNANCE

Meanwhile, the Federal Navy was using the following types of heavy ordnance:[7] (For additional information, see Chapter 17.)

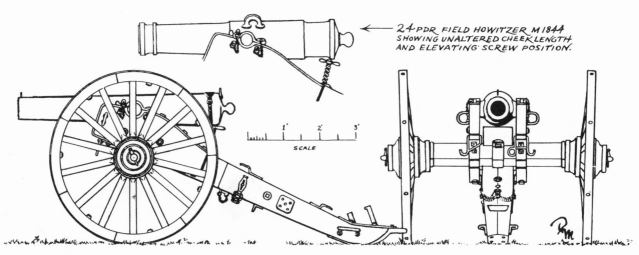

24 PDR FIELD HOWITZER M 1844 SHOWING UNALTERED CHEEK LENGTH AND ELEVATING SCREW POSITION.

12 PDR "NAPOLEON" GUN-HOWITZER M.1857 AS MOUNTED ON MODIFIED 24 PDR FIELD HOWITZER CARRIAGE

STANDARD FIELD PIECE, THE NAPOLEON

Robert L. Miller

Caliber	Weight		Charge Weight	Weight Shot	Weight of Shell
15-inch	42,000		35-50	400-440	330-352
11-inch	15,700		15-20	166	127-135.5
10-inch	12,000 to 16,000		12.5-40	124	95-101.5
9-inch	9,000		10-13	90	68.50-73.50
8-inch	5,500 to 10,000		7-20	65	50-52.75

Caliber	Gun Weight	Diam. of Bore	Charge Weight	Shot Weight	Shell Weight
64-pdr.	10,600		8-16		
32-pdr.	2,700		4.9	32.5	25-26.5
Bronze Howitzer		12-pdr. 24-pdr.	Smooth or rifled		
Rifled Guns (Parrott)					
150-pdr.	16,500	8.00	16	135-154	135
100-pdr.	9,700	6.40	10	70-100	80-100
60-pdr.	4,900	5.30	6	60	50
30-pdr.	3,550	4.20	3¼	30	29
20-pdr.	1,750	3.67	2	20	18
Rifled Guns (Dahlgren)					
20-pdr.	1,340	4.00	2	20	18
12-pdr.	880	3.40	1	12	11

For all these guns, the weights of "bursting charges" were less than the "weights of charges" as given in the above table.

The following data is extracted from *Ordnance Instructions for the United States Navy* (1864), *passim*.

Navy armament

On shore—muskets and carbines
On ship—revolvers, cutlasses, boarding pikes[8]

MACHINE GUNS

The United States Patent Office on July 8, 1856 issued patent number 15,315 to C. E. Barnes of Lowell, Massachusetts, for a crank-operated machine cannon. This weapon had many original improvements, and was the forerunner of a series of crank-operated weapons. The rate of fire depended solely on the speed with which the crank could be turned. This weapon was far ahead of its time, and its development would have placed a reliable machine gun in the hands of the U. S. Army several years prior to the Civil War.

Ezra Ripley of Troy, New York, took advantage of the paper cartridge to patent a machine gun which provided sustained volley fire by a compact firing assembly that allowed the gunner to fire one shot or the whole volley, by a quick turn of the handle. The weapon consisted of a series of barrels, grouped together around a common axis, that were open at both ends for breech loading. The barrels remained stationary during firing. Many features of this weapon, patented in 1861, greatly influenced machine gun design for years to come.

Due to the failure of the Colt revolving rifle, the development of new weapons was turned over entirely to civilians. The military authorities refused to be interested in anything beyond some means of producing volley fire, similar in arrangement to the early organ gun. Perhaps the weapon most in keeping with the acceptable idea of producing volley fire was the Requa battery. This caliber .58 gun was built late in 1861 by the Billinghurst Company of Rochester, New York. It was publicly demonstrated in front of the Stock Exchange Building in New York City in the hope of interesting private capital in manufacturing it for the Federal Army. This gun had 25 barrels, mounted flat on a light metal platform. The sliding breech mechanism was operated by a lever. Charging was accomplished by means of cartridges held in special clips. This early weapon, though crude, had a few unusual features that warrant mention. The clip loading, and the quick means of locking and unlocking, allowed a fair rate of fire. This gun became known as the "covered bridge" gun. During the Civil War, many of the important crossings over streams were in the form of a wooden bridge with roof and sidewalls to protect the floor and under-structures from the weather. As these covered bridges were usually long and narrow, one of these weapons in the hands of an alert crew could break up a quick charge by the enemy, either on horse or afoot. The 25 barrels could be adjusted to the necessary height and width. With a crew of 3 men, the weapon could be fired at the rate of 7 volleys or 175 shots per minute. The effective range was 1,300 yards. In the field the Requa battery had its limitations. Dampness in the unprotected powder train would render it useless. Consequently, it was unfit for offensive service, but very effective in defense of restricted fields of fire.

The next machine gun to be used by the Federal forces was the Ager, better known as the "coffee mill" gun. The nickname was derived from its being crank-operated with a hopper feed located on top so that it closely resembled the contemporary kitchen coffee grinder. The caliber was .58. The Ager weapon was purposely made not to exceed a speed of 120 shots per minute, since it used only a single barrel. The heat from rapid firing was considered a serious drawback. Subsequently, the inventor arranged a very ingenious cooling device for the gun. The barrel was rifled, and the maximum effective range, using the caliber .58 Minie-type bullet and a 750-grain powder charge, was 1,000 yards. The Ager gun was a very advanced weapon for the Civil War era. But there was no military demand for a machine gun. Contemporary authorities condemned it as requiring too much ammunition ever to be practical, although the gun was used in battle in a few isolated instances. President Lincoln was interested in the possible use of the gun by the Army. On December 12, 1861, a letter he wrote to a representative of the makers of the gun shows his position:

"My Dear Sir:

"I do not intend to order any more of the 'Coffee Mill' guns unless upon General McClellan's distinctly indicating in writing that he wishes it done, in which case, I will very cheerfully do it. This is very plain: He knows whether the guns will be serviceable; I do not. It avails nothing for him to intimate that he has no *objection* to my purchasing them."

Eventually there was talk about the Government buying 50 of these guns, but extreme caution is evident in all the correspondence about the weapon.

The North was deprived of a great Ordnance officer when Major General Gorgas joined the Confederacy, but this loss likely was more than offset when Richard Jordan Gatling moved to the North in 1844, hoping to manufacture and market several of his mechanical inventions. Gatling's weapon was the logical outgrowth of the trends portrayed in the Ager and Ripley guns. The Gatling gun is the prototype of one of the most remarkable firing mechanisms of all ordnance history and its inventor is credited generally with being the father of the machine gun. The 1862 Gatling gun was fundamentally the Ager principle, improved by the multi-barrel arrangement of the Ripley gun. As early as 1862 a model of the gun was exhibited before thousands of people in Indianapolis. One of the most interested spectators was the Honorable O. P. Morton, Governor of Indiana, who wrote to the Assistant Secretary of War telling him of the weapon's unusual performance. He suggested that Dr. Gatling's gun be permitted officially to prove its worth. Meanwhile, Gatling continued to improve his gun, including the use of copper-cased rim-fire ammunition. On one of his numerous trips to Washington to interest the Army, Gatling called on Brigadier General J. W. Ripley, Chief of Ordnance, and asked that the weapon be given tests with a view of adopting it. General Ripley refused point-blank to take the gun under consideration. A few days later, one of Gatling's representatives met General Benjamin F. Butler in Baltimore, and asked permission to demonstrate the weapon. At the same time he neglected to mention General Ripley's refusal to become interested. Butler was enthusiastic over the resulting exhibition. He immediately purchased 12 guns, paying $12,000 for the weapons, or carriages, complete with 12,000 rounds of ammunition, and personally directed their use in battle during the siege of Petersburg. Believed by some to be a Southern sympathizer, Gatling had little success in interesting the Army in his weapon prior to 1865. The gun was officially adopted by the United States Army on August 24, 1866, but, of course, the war was over. The Navy adopted the Gatling in 1862. It was used successfully on a small scale in the Franco-Prussian War, while the much publicized rapid-firing weapons of European origin were being proved utter failures. For more than 40 years thereafter, the Gatling was used by practically every major power and influenced world events in no small manner.[9]

MUZZLE-LOADING MUSKETS AND RIFLES

U. S. FLINTLOCK MUSKET, MODEL 1822, CALIBER .69

This is the most familiar of all flintlocks. Made in great quantities until 1840 with slight changes. Made by contract and at Springfield and Harper's Ferry. Complete weight 10 pounds with bayonet 16 inches long. In the 1850's many of these were altered to percussion locks. At the outbreak of the war, as there were not enough of later models available to equip all the troops, many regiments were issued these .69 caliber altered weapons. In several cases the soldiers refused to accept them. The last model flintlock is dated 1840 and was very similar to the 1822 type. The manufacture of flintlocks ceased in 1844.

U. S. PERCUSSION MUSKET, MODEL 1841, CALIBER .69

First issued at the front during the Mexican War and it is claimed the soldiers preferred the old flintlocks. Made at Government armories and by contract. About 1852 many of these muskets were rifled after a plan by Colonel Minie of France, thus becoming the U. S. Minie rifle, caliber .69. A long range rear sight was added. The bayonets for these muskets were the first to have a clasp for better attachment to the barrel. Many were used in the early part of the Civil War.

U. S. RIFLE, MODEL 1841, CALIBER .54

Known as the Mississippi or Yager rifle. Made at Harper's Ferry and Springfield Armories and by contract until 1855. When first made, these rifles were not provided with bayonets but later (1855) a long saber bayonet was added. Many of these weapons were converted to breechloaders in the Civil War, some to the Merrill system and others to the Lindner. As the troops from Mississippi during the Mexican War were the first to be equipped with this weapon they were called "Mississippi Rifles."

U. S. RIFLE-MUSKET, MODEL 1855 (MAYNARD PRIMER), CALIBER .58

This rifle used a priming magazine, the invention of Dr. Edward Maynard of Washington. The Maynard primer was a waterproof tape enveloping patches of fulminate placed at intervals throughout its length. This tape was coiled and placed in a round cavity in the lock plate, a hinged gate covering it. An arm from the hammer pushed the tape along, step by step, causing a patch of fulminate to project over the nipple. The end of the hammer had a sharp edge which came down close to the mouth of the primer cavity and cut off the tape beyond. Ordinary caps could also be used on the gun. Great difficulty was experienced in keeping the tapes dry, they becoming useless if allowed to become damp. Many used from 1861-1865.

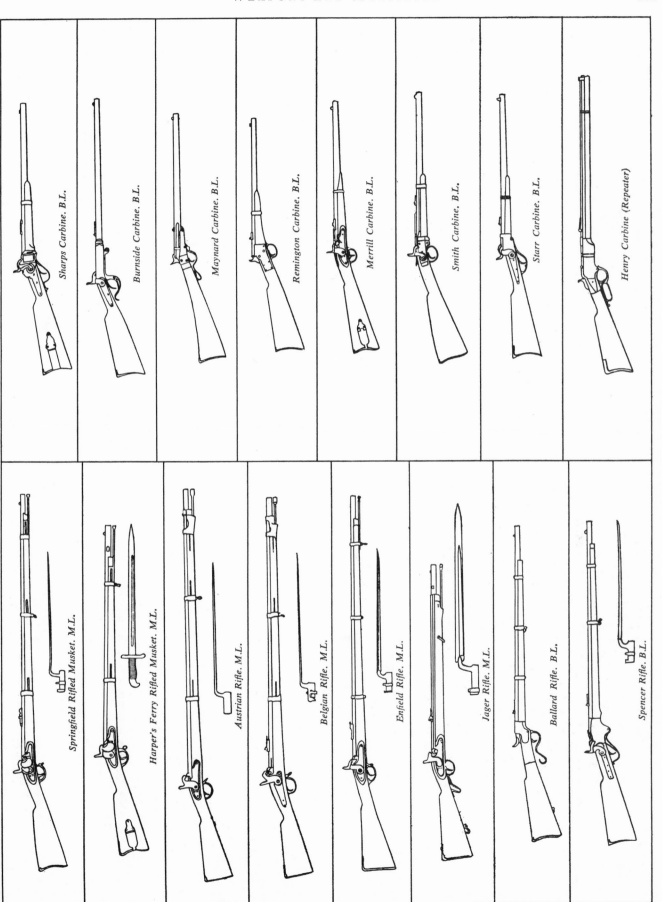

Sharps Carbine. B.L.

Burnside Carbine. B.L.

Maynard Carbine. B.L.

Remington Carbine. B.L.

Merrill Carbine. B.L.

Smith Carbine. B.L.

Starr Carbine. B.L.

Henry Carbine (Repeater)

Springfield Rifled Musket. M.L.

Harper's Ferry Rifled Musket. M.L.

Austrian Rifle. M.L.

Belgian Rifle. M.L.

Enfield Rifle. M.L.

Jager Rifle. M.L.

Ballard Rifle. B.L.

Spencer Rifle. B.L.

RIFLES AND MUSKETS

U. S. RIFLE, MODEL 1855 (MAYNARD PRIMER)

Same lock as the musket but shorter barrel and fitted for a long saber bayonet. Weight with bayonet, 13 pounds.

U. S. RIFLE-MUSKET, MODEL 1861, CALIBER .58

This was the principal weapon of the Civil War. The lock plate and hammer are identical with the Model 1855, but the Maynard primer magazine was eliminated. The U. S. fabricated 801,997 and purchased 670,617 of these during the years 1861-1865. Many firms accepted contracts for these and had to build factories in which to make the muskets. It was late in 1862 before deliveries from contractors began in satisfactory quantities. Some were made in Germany, and one made by Manton, the famous English gunmaker is in the author's possession. The following list shows the Civil War makers of contract muskets and the number of weapons made by each:

Contracts delivered from 1861 to 1865 for Springfield Model Rifled Muskets are shown in the table.

This table is compiled from Senate Executive Document No. 16, 45th Congress, 3rd Session, p. 75.

ENGLISH ENFIELD MUSKET, MODEL 1853, CALIBER .557

Extensively used by both sides in the war. The U. S. purchased 428,000 in the early months of the war and the South received 400,000 during 1861-1862. A short pattern Enfield (Model 1858) with sword bayonet was also used.

U. S. RIFLE-MUSKET, MODEL 1863, CALIBER .58

This weapon shows some changes from the Model of 1861. The hammer, nipple lug, bands, and ramrod

Contract Date	Contractor's Name	Price	Number Delivered
December 26, 1861	Sarson & Roberts	$20.00	5,140
December 26, 1861	A. M. Burt	20.00	11,495
December 26, 1861	J. T. Hodge	20.00	10,500
December 26, 1861	Eagle Manufacturing Co.	20.00	20,000
April 1, 1864	Norwick Arms Co.	18.00	10,000
October 18, 1864	Norwich Arms Co.	19.00	15,000
December 24, 1861	C. B. Hoard	20.00	1,500
December 1, 1863	C. B. Hoard	19.00	11,300
July 13, 1861	Alfred Jenks & Son	20.00	25,000
October 7, 1861	Alfred Jenks & Son	25.00	19,000
December 15, 1863	Alfred Jenks & Son	20.00	48,000
February 1, 1865	Alfred Jenks & Son	19.00	6,000
January 7, 1862	James Mulholland	20.00	5,502
January 7, 1862	William Mason	20.00	30,000
July 13, 1861	Providence Tool Co.	20.00 ⎫	38,000
November 26, 1861	Providence Tool Co.	20.00 ⎬	
May 1, 1864	Providence Tool Co.	19.00	32,000
July 11, 1861 ⎫	Lamson, Goodnow & Yale	20.00	50,000
October 7, 1861 ⎭			
January 7, 1862	Amoskeag Manufacturing Co.	20.00	10,001
November 5, 1863	Amoskeag Manufacturing Co.	19.00	15,000
January 6, 1865	Amoskeag Manufacturing Co.	19.00	2,000
September 28, 1863	Parker, Snow & Co.	19.00	15,000
October 11, 1861 ⎫	C. D. Schubarth	20.00	9,500
November 26, 1861 ⎭			
December 7, 1861	Wm. Muir & Co.	20.00	30,000
December 26, 1861	J. D. Mowry	20.00	10,000
November 27, 1863	J. D. Mowry	20.00	2,000
April 6, 1864	J. D. Mowry	18.00	10,000
October 17, 1863	Eli Whitney	19.00	15,001
September 9, 1862	Savage Arms Co.	18.00	13,500
February 25, 1864	Savage Arms Co.	18.00	12,000
November 6, 1861	W. W. Welch	20.00	16,000
January 12, 1864	W. W. Welch	18.00	1,000
December 14, 1863	E. Remington & Son	18.00	40,000
June 10, 1863	Edward Robinson	20.00	12,000
December 29, 1863	Edward Robinson	18.00	4,000
February 23, 1864	Edward Robinson	18.00	8,000
October 4, 1864	Edward Robinson	18.00	6,000
July 5, 1861	Colt's Patent Fire Arms Company	20.00	25,000
June 5, 1863	Colt's Patent Fire Arms Company	20.00	12,500
March 19, 1864	Colt's Patent Fire Arms Company	20.00	37,500
	TOTAL		643,439

were improved in design. In 1864 another model was brought out very much like the 1863. About the only change was the revival of the band springs and a slight change in the design of the bands. During 1864 Springfield Armory produced 276,200 arms. This was the greatest year's work there. The muskets averaged $10.69 each in cost. This is the last muzzle-loader made by the Government.

U. S. Navy Rifle (Whitneyville), Caliber .69

Known as the "Plymouth" rifle. Made by the Whitney Armory near New Haven, Connecticut. Ten thousand of these were delivered to the Navy in 1863. They were intended to use the famous Dahlgren knife bayonet. This weapon had a 12-inch blade and weighed 2½ pounds. It is worthy of note that this arm was .69 caliber instead of the regulation (since 1855) .58 caliber.

U. S. Rifle (Zouave), Model 1863, Caliber .58

Made by Remington at Ilion, New York. The bayonet was modeled after the 1855 saber bayonet, but was straighter, 2 inches shorter, and ½-pound lighter. This admirably made and exceptionally good military rifle was apparently not used during the war.[10]

Sniper's Rifle

Federal sharpshooters such as Berdan's regiment, used target rifles of various types in the early months of service. Some of these weapons, weighing from 15 to 30 pounds, were equipped with telescopic sights. This type of rifle was of little use in skirmishing because of its weight, but was excellent for use against enemy officers and gun crews. The rifles were specially made target rifles which were obtained by Government agents making a house-to-house canvass for the privately owned match rifles, ideally suited for long range work. One model of these sniper rifles, including the telescopic sight, was made by W. G. Langdon, a Boston watch and clock maker and expert rifleman, who in 1862 contracted to make a score of these rifles for the Federal Government at $150.00 each, telescope included. Langdon claimed to be the inventor of the means of making the seamless drawn steel tube used in the telescopes for these rifles.[11]

Breechloaders

The open-sighted Sharps rifle, using linen or "skin" cartridges, .52 caliber conical ball, was the best single-shot breechloading gun at that time made, a perfectly safe and reliable arm, combining accuracy with rapidity, just what a skirmish line needed for effective work. To their good judgment in choosing this rifle may be attributed their future success in the field, attaining as they did a reputation that eventually made the name of "Berdan Sharpshooters" renowned in foreign lands as well as in the United States. The muzzle-loading target rifles—telescope and globe sights—while of great value before fortifications and for special work, would have been useless in skirmishing. The percussion Sharps declined in popularity as the Spencer, Henry, and other metallic cartridge and repeating arms became more numerous but continued to be used with great success until the end of the war.[12]

Between January 1, 1861, and June 30, 1866, the Government bought the following arms and ammunition from the Sharps Rifle Manufacturing Company:

80,512 Carbines	$2,213,192.00
9,141 Rifles	330,629.97
16,306,508 Rounds of Ammunition	347,410.57

Only one breechloading arm was ordered in greater quantity—the Spencer—but too late for it to be widely used until the last year of the war. It appears that the majority of the Sharps arms possessed by the Federal Army were used by troops in the East.[13]

The Sharps Rifles, Model 1859, was made in both Army and Navy models. These weapons leaked fire between the breechblock and barrel; otherwise, they were excellent capping breechloaders. Their rapidity of fire and their accuracy enabled a soldier marksman to hit his enemy first, and the renown of Civil War units armed with Sharps rifles may have given rise to the laudatory term, "Sharpshooters." The Government bought 9,141 during the war at an average cost of $36.15 each.

Greene Rifle, Model 1857, Caliber .535

This weapon, the invention of J. D. Greene, an Army officer, was the first bolt action gun used by the U. S. The bolt handle was in the rear, same being released by pressing down a spring catch on the tang. It was a percussion arm and had the nipple underneath with a ring-shaped hammer. The cartridge had the bullet in the rear so that there were always two in the gun when loaded. The rear one was intended to act as a gas-check. A few were used in the war; in fact, bullets of this rifle are reported to have been found on the battlefield of Antietam.

Ballard Rifle, Model 1861, Calibers .44 to .54

Made both in rim and center fire. The extractor had to be manipulated by hand, being pushed to the rear to eject the empty shell. The Ballard was made in both rifles and carbines. The rifle took an ordinary triangular bayonet. As there were over three and one-half million cartridges purchased for Ballard arms during the Civil War, they undoubtedly saw service.

Merrill Rifle, Model 1858, Caliber .54

This weapon was equipped with a saber bayonet. To load, the percussion hammer was cocked and the arm was operated by a lever latched under the rear sight base. Back pressure on two flat, knurled sides released, unlatched the lever, and permitted it to be raised backward, withdrawing the hinged, sliding, copper-faced breech bolt and exposing the breech for the insertion of a niter treated paper cartridge. The copper fact on the bolt acted as a gas check. The lever was then lowered forward and latched under the rear sight, closing the breech, and a percussion cap could be fired by the hammer and cone. It is believed that these rifles were made for Merrill by Remington. Seven hundred and seventy Merrill rifles were purchased by the Government during the war between April 1862, and November 1863.[14]

COLT REVOLVING RIFLE, MODEL 1855

The early civilian method of fastening a shoulder stock on the heavy barrel revolvers and making a serviceable repeating shoulder arm led the Colt Company to apply the same idea to a full-fledged rifle. Consequently, the 1855 model revolving rifle was produced. It became the first repeating rifle adopted by the armed service of the United States. This caliber .58 weapon had a full length rifle barrel. But one major weakness prevented widespread use of this weapon. During firing the heavy rifle barrel had to be supported by hand. This had not been necessary in the revolver equipped with the shoulder stock. Sometimes loose powder from a faulty cap or gas leak would cause other chambers to be ignited. When this happened, the soldier using the piece lost his hand or the portion of his arm that happened to be in front of the exploding cylinder. One such accident in a regiment destroyed not only confidence in the weapon, but the morale of soldiers and officers alike. The total failure of the Army's first official attempt to introduce a repeating shoulder weapon into the service gave the conservative element a chance to point out the inevitable disaster that always follows any such departure from what has proved successful over the years. Finally, a board of officers met. After hearing all the evidence, they ordered that the Colt's use be discontinued and the pieces sold for whatever price could be obtained. The highest bid was 42¢ a rifle.[15]

SPENCER RIFLE, MODEL 1860

The Spencer rifle was considered by general officers of both line and staff to be the best rifle in use during the war. This is especially significant in view of the fact that from 1861 to 1865 just about every variety of both breech and muzzle loading weapon was given the exhaustive test of hard use. The Spencer was a seven-shot rifle, loaded through a trap in the butt plate. The loading was a bit slow, with one cartridge at a time, until the appearance of Blakeslee's patent cartridge box containing ten tin tubes, each holding seven cartridges, each tube loadable as a unit. This method was in use during the last two years of the war, although the box was not patented until 1865.

Official U. S. Government records, although incomplete, show that the War Department bought at least 94,196 Spencer cavalry carbines, 12,471 Spencer rifles and 58,238,000 Spencer cartridges. Unrecorded War Department purchases, plus those made direct to the manufacturer from soldiers in the field, and from State and civil organizations brought the sales of the Spencer Repeating Rifle Company up to the 200,000 mark during the war, exclusive of over 30,000 seven shooters made for the Government by the Burnside Rifle Company.

"In spite of initial resistance to their use by Ordnance," wrote Lieutenant Colonel Berkeley R. Lewis, Office Chief of Ordnance, Department of the Army in 1953, "Spencer repeating breechloading carbines were purchased by many units, as these were obviously far superior to any other weapons then available. When the war ended, more Spencer carbines had been purchased by the U. S. Government than any other type of breechloader. These arms were capable of 15 shots per minute, which is good even today. The Spencer design was sound and the arm was very well made. The ball penetrated 13 inches of pine at 50 yards; its maximum range was about 2,000 yards."[16]

HENRY RIFLE, MODEL 1860

In 1860 the New Haven Arms Company concentrated on production of Henry rifles, which used rim fire copper cartridges. The ammunition was a novelty at that time. This company from 1860 to 1866 made only one model of Henry rifle, although it ran the gamut from the plainest grade to the most elaborately ornamented and expensive; the weight was about 10 pounds, the barrel was 24 inches long; and the caliber was .44. The cartridge held 25 grains of powder and a conical bullet of about half an ounce weight—216 grains. The Henry barrel was bored caliber .42, rifled with 6 grooves each about .005 deep, making the actual caliber .43, to use a bullet of caliber .44. The grooves had an increasing, called a "gain," twist, beginning at the breech with one turn in 16 feet and ending at the muzzle with one turn in 2.75 feet.

The Henry rifle was in considerable use during the war; a sporting rifle privately purchased to the extent of about 10,000 by entire companies and regiments of State troops in Federal service. Although, even in sporting model by far the best military rifle in the world, the Federal Government would not buy it. Lack of large funds and Government patronage held the company from expanding to fill its orders, which exceeded by about 20 times the possibilities of manufacture. During and after the war, valuable testimonials of Henry service were written by the commanders of troops that possessed the Henry and thus were enabled to defeat the enemy troops who outnumbered the Federals, often by a large number. The Henry, a 15-shot repeating rifle of excellent accuracy, was considered by many to be the best rifle (carbine) of the war.[17]

CAVALRY WEAPONS

During the Civil War the U. S. Cavalry was generally armed with rifles or carbines, sabers, and revolvers. The rifles carried at the commencement of the war were changed for carbines, and the single loading carbines were, in the latter part of the war, changed for repeating ones. Only one lancer regiment went out, the 6th Pennsylvania, and it changed the lance for the saber in April 1863.[18]

CARBINES (BREECH-LOADING SINGLE SHOT)[19]

Name	Patent date	Caliber	No. sold to U.S.
Jenks	1838	.54	......
Gibbs	1856	.52	1,052
Schroeder	1856	.53	......
Greene	1854	.53	700
Joslyn	1855	.54	......
Cosmopolitan	1862	.50	9,342
Starr	1858	.54	25,603
Smith	1856	.52	30,062
Warner	1864	.50	4,001
Maynard	1851	.50	20,000
Palmer	1863	.50	1,000
Gallager	1860	.54	(many used but no figures given)
Wesson	1859	.44	150
Burnside	1856	.54	56,000
Merrill	1861	.54	14,695
Sharps	1856	.52	80,512
Sharps and Hawkins ..	1859	.56	......

REVOLVERS

The advent of the revolver increased the value of cavalry. In addition to possible shock action, the value of cavalry in combat was to be found in its mobility and ability to displace its firepower quickly from one locality to another. Therefore, its most effective employment was under conditions which not only permitted the fullest use of its mobility, but also the use of maximum firepower. The issue of revolvers to the cavalry increased its firepower as compared to the infantry, which was still armed with muzzle-loaders. The advantage of increased firepower added to its mobility, enhanced the value of the mounted service until recent years, when the issue of repeating arms to the infantry and subsequent motorization caused a decline in the importance of cavalry as a combat branch. But this came after 1865.

The invention of percussion ignition permitted a design that did away with the danger of simultaneous discharge of several chambers, and to Samuel Colt belongs the credit for perfecting the first practicable and working firearm equipped with a mechanically operated cylinder, and its subsequent improvement and development. In addition to the mechanical revolution of the breech, his patents covered a number of other vital points, such as placing the percussion cap cones on the back of the loading chambers, the separation of the cones by metal walls to prevent the ignition of chambers other than the one to fire, and a mechanical method of locking the cylinder at the moment of firing to insure the alignment of the chamber with the barrel. In fact, his patents covered the important and basic principles of revolver construction so thoroughly that it was not until the expiration of the Colt patents in 1856 that practical revolvers could be manufactured by others without infringing the Colt patents.

According to the Colt Fire Arms Company, during the Civil War the Colt Armory furnished the Government with 386,417 revolvers, about 7,000 revolving rifles and carbines and 113,980 muzzle-loading rifle muskets. Colonel Colt died January 10, 1862, his end probably hastened by his labors in connection with supplying the Government with arms in war emergency.[20]

The principal hand gun of the Civil War was the Colt Army model of 1860, six-shot revolver. It was also made in .36 caliber for Navy use at a cost of $27.00 each, to the Government. Some Colts were equipped with shoulder stocks. The Remington revolver was probably as popular as the Colt.

From 1861 to 1865 there were purchased 373,971 revolvers of about 20 different makes, at a cost of six million dollars. In the early days of the war the domestic purchases were supplemented by foreign arms, such as Adams, Lefaucheaux, Perrin, and others, but these were discarded for American arms as soon as the industry was able to supply the needs of the Army and Navy. Of these, the Colt and Remington were the most used. Some of the more commonly used types were: [21]

Name	Date of Patent	Caliber	No. Sold to U.S. Govt.	Cost
Prescott Navy	1860	.36	......	......
Remington Army	1858	.44	125,314	$12.50
Remington Navy	1858	.36	5,000	12.50
Rogers & Spencer ...	1862	.44	5,000	12.00
Pettingill Army	1856	.44 .36	5,000	......
Whitney Navy		.36	11,214	12.00
Savage Navy	1856	.36	11,284	19.00
LeFauchaux (French & Belgian)		.41	12,000	13.00
Wesson & Leavitt ...	1837	.40 .31	......	......
Joslyn Army	1858	.44	1,100	22.50
Adams Army	1853 (England)	.44 .36	......	......
Raphael ....(France)		.41	978	16.50
Perrin ....(France)		.45	200	20.00
Allen & Wheelock ...	1857	.44	500	......
Beal	1858	.44	2,814	......
Starr	1856	.44 .36	47,952	......

MAIN TYPES OF WEAPONS

A definite indication of the main types of weapons in most general use during the war by Federal troops is shown by Circular No. 13, 1865, Ordnance Office, War Department.[22]

Number and Description of Arms Retained by Enlisted Men Under General Order No. 101:

Muskets

Springfield, rifled	96,238
Enfield, rifled	19,882
Austrian	270
Prussian	26
Harpers Ferry	89

Rifles

Spencer	2,844
Henry	808
Sharps	3,454
Ballard	13
Colt	305
Whitney	146
French	406
English, artillery	35
Smith and Wesson	4
Windsor	11
Joslyn	171
United States	15

Swords

NCO's	869
Musicians	105

Sabers

Cavalry	13,437
Artillery	208

Carbines

Spencer	8,289
Sharps	2,549
Burnside	392
Maynard	871
Smith	695
Starr	266
Joslyn	177
Merrill	25
Gallagher	165
French	8
Warner	36
Union	8

Revolvers

Colt	9,047
Remington	9,875
Beal	43
LeFaucheaux	23
Savage	17
Pettingill	93
Starr	831
Whitney	115
Adams	2

AMMUNITION AND PROJECTILES

The reports on the early engagements of the war allude frequently to the great diversity of missiles, showing that every available weapon had been seized upon to arm the troops hastily thrown into the field. These reports have been fully corroborated by the great variety of bullets and projectiles recovered from battlefields in recent years, especially with the aid of mine detectors. In addition to the various U. S. Models, large numbers of foreign weapons, especially

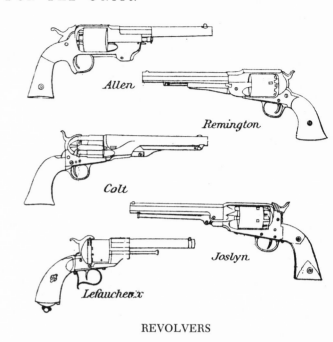

Allen

Remington

Colt

Joslyn

Lefaucheux

REVOLVERS

English, Belgian, Austrian, Prussian, and French were used. And the great variety of breechloading and magazine arms added to the long list of small-arms ammunition utilized in combat.

By far the larger number of shot injuries were inflicted by missiles from small arms. The nature of the missile involved in 141,961 wounded cases has been recorded. Of this number, 127,929 or 90.1 percent, were caused by missiles from small arms. The missiles used with small arms were: spherical balls, usually discharged from smooth-bore muskets; and those of an elongated form, adapted to rifled arms; the latter were either conical, cylindro-conical, or ovoid, varying in size, weight, and volume. The materials composing the missiles were usually lead or lead hardened by an alloy of tin or antimony. The superiority of the elongated missile thrown from the rifled barrel over the spherical ball rests upon the fact that elongated bullets usually have an expansive base, either plain or hollowed, which by the explosion of the charge is intended to fill the grooves of the rifle and give the projectile, as it is driven forward, rotation on its long axis, thus increasing its range and precision.

The records of the Ordnance Office, U. S. Army, show that 33,350 Gardner's "explosive bullets" or "musket shells" were issued to the troops in the early part of the war and that 10,000 of these were abandoned on the field for want of transportation. The Gardner "explosive bullet" was a cylindro-conoidal projectile of lead, made in two sizes; the larger of caliber .58, weighing 451 grains, the smaller of caliber .54, weighing 363 grains. Within the interior was placed an accurately fitting acorn-shaped chamber filled with fulminate, and communicating with a one- and one-quarter time-fuze, which was exposed to the charge at the rear of the missile; the fuze was ignited by the discharge of the piece. The bursting charge was sufficient to rend the bullet and transform it into a jagged, dangerous missile. It is claimed that other forms of projectiles of this nature were provided with a percussion cap which would explode upon contact with even soft tissues.

CANNON PROJECTILES

The large projectiles used with heavy ordnance may be classified under the headings spherical and elongated, the former being generally used with smooth-bore, the latter with rifled guns. Round shot were solid spheres of cast-iron varying in size and weight. A grape-shot was composed of a number of cast-iron balls, generally nine, arranged in layers of three each and kept in position by a series of tables or plates held together by a vertical rod secured by nuts on each end; these missiles varied in caliber to fit guns of various sizes; at the discharge the several parts became separated and each part acted as a distinct projectile. They were superseded by canister for field use after the second year of the war.

A canister shot was a projectile made by enclosing a large number of iron or leaden balls of less size than grape in a cylinder of tin, which was torn asunder at the discharge of the cannon; the contents were scattered, assuming in their forward course something of the nature of a cone dispersion. When used against masses of troops and at short range the canister shot was very destructive.

Shrapnel shells were spherical or elongated, according to the type of cannon in which they were used, and when adapted to smooth bores they were designated as "sperical case shot." They were shells of considerable thickness, filled with musket balls consolidated into matrix of sulphur and resin, and were exploded by a charge of powder filled into their interior, which was ignited by either a time or percussion fuze, as might be desired. They had a long effective range and were calculated to inflict serious injury by the great number of fragments set loose at their explosion.

The projectiles used in rifled guns combined the properties and character of the projectiles described above with the characteristics of guns constructed on the rifled principle. These guns delivered projectiles varying *greatly* in size and weight; the velocity varied with the caliber from 1,090 to 1,550 feet per second; and the range of some exceeded five miles. Whereas case shot broke into many fragments on explosion, some rifled projectiles were cast solid, and were used for breaching or battering purposes. Shells thrown from mortars differed little if any from ordinary spherical shells except in size and in the manner of projection. Their use was generally restricted to sieges. Under the same circumstances hot solid shot were used during the war, but with the intention of destroying property rather than personnel.[23]

ARTILLERY PROJECTILES

Left to right: Grapeshot with metal sabot; spherical case; solid shot with wooden sabot; canister; and grapeshot with wooden sabot. Grapeshot was used by the Navy and coast artillery.

SMALL ARMS CARTRIDGES

Cartridges most commonly used are listed in *Ordnance Memorandum No. 1* for 1865 (pp. 141-142) as follows:

Muskets—Smoothbore	Diameter of ball
buck and ball	.69
elongated, Mefford's	.69
round ball	.73

Muskets—rifled	
elongated ball	.54
elongated ball (.577 and .58)	.574
elongated ball (for pistol carbine)	.574
elongated ball (Johnston & Dow's)	.574
elongated ball (Sharler's patent)	.574
elongated ball (Williams' patent)	.574
elongated ball (French)	.61
elongated ball (or musketoon)	.69
elongated ball	.70
elongated ball	.71
elongated ball	.73

Rifles and Carbines Type	Diameter of Ball
Ballard's carbine, copper	.44
Ballard's rifle, copper	.45
Ball's and Palmer's carbine, copper	.44
Burnside's carbine, metallic	.56
Burnside's carbine, metallic (Poultney's patent)	.56
Cosmopolitan carbine, linen	.52
Colt's rifle, paper	.58
Colt's rifle, sporting size, paper	.44
Gallagher's carbine, metallic	.53
Gallagher's carbine, metallic (Jackson's patent)	.53
Gibbs' carbine, linen	.54
Gibbs' carbine, paper	.54
Greene's carbine or rifle, paper	.546
Hall's carbine, paper	.675
Hall's rifle, paper	.52
Henry's carbine, copper	.46
Henry's rifle, copper	.44
Johnson's carbine, copper	.45
Joslyn's carbine, copper	.54
Lindner's carbine, paper	.574
Maynard's carbine, metallic	.52
Maynard's carbine, metallic (Poultney's patent)	.52
Merrill's carbine and rifle, paper	.56

Rifles and Carbines Type	Diameter of Ball
Remington carbine, copper	.43
Sharps' carbine and rifle, linen	.54
Sharps' carbine and rifle, paper	.54
Sharps' & Hankins carbine, copper	.54
Sharps' & Hankins rifle	.55
Spencer's carbine and rifle, copper (can also be used in Starr's new model carbine)	.55
Starr's carbine, copper	.54
Starr's carbine, linen	.56
Warner's carbine, copper	.515

Pistols	Diameter of Ball
Colt's Navy, linen	.386
Colt's Army, linen	.46

Rifles and Carbines Type	Diameter of Ball
Adams', Allen's, Colt's, Hoard's, Joslyn's, Pettingil's, Starr's, Savage, Remington, Whitney, Navy, paper	.38
Army, paper	.46
Navy, skin	.38
Army, skin	.46
Adams', Allen's, Colt's, Hoard's, Joslyn's, Pettingill, Starr's, Savage, Remington's, and Whitney's *Navy*, Johnston and Dow's water-proof and combustible Army	.38 and .46
LeFaucheaux, copper	.30
LeFaucheaux, copper	.36
LeFaucheaux, copper	.44
Round ball, for smooth-bore pistols	.54

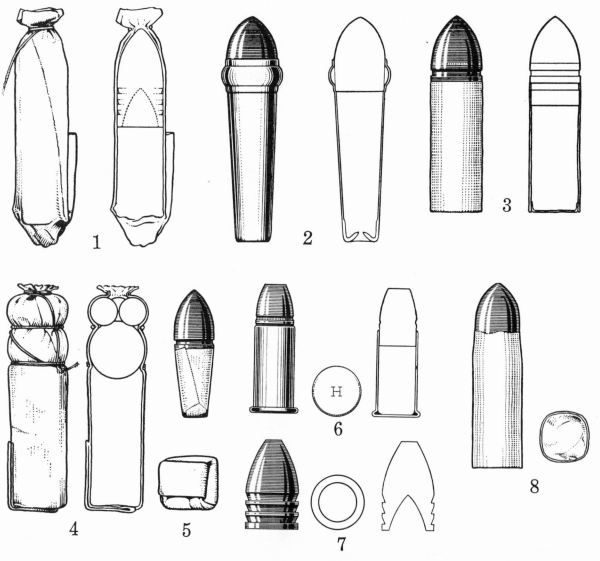

SMALL ARMS AMMUNITION

1. Caliber .58 paper cartridge. 2. Caliber .54 Burnside cartridge with brass case. 3. Caliber .52 Sharps linen case with nitrated paper base. 4. Caliber .69 buck and ball paper cartridge. 5. Caliber .44 Colt pistol paper cartridge. 6. Caliber .44 Henry flat ball with copper case. 7. Caliber .58 Minié ball. 8. Caliber .54 Starr linen cartridge.

EDGED WEAPONS

SWORDS, ARMY OFFICERS'

Commissioned officers of the Federal Army wore swords of almost limitless variety and quality. In addition to militia officers' swords, there were the following main regulation types:

(1) Staff and Field Officer's Sword. On April 9, 1850, the Army adopted a standard sword for all staff officers and for the field officers of infantry, artillery, and riflemen. Like the foot officers' sword adopted the same day, it was based upon a French pattern and was a sturdy and serviceable weapon. Its use was mandatory until 1860 when the frail staff and field officers' sword of that date became optional. Officers who desired a real weapon, however, continued to use it until 1872, when the frail 1860 pattern became regulation.

(2) Medical Staff Swords. The small sword, adopted in 1840, was worn by Army medical officers until 1902. It underwent only minor variations during the 62 years that it remained regulation for Army medical officers. Early specimens have heavy blades, usually elliptical in cross section while post Civil War examples usually had light and frail blades diamond-shaped in cross section.

(3) Pay Department Swords. Throughout most of its history, the Pay Department of the United States Army required its officers to wear swords similar to those carried by the Medical Staff. In fact, the Pay Department sword of 1840 was exactly the same as that described for the Medical Staff, except that the "M. S." (Medical Staff) was replaced by "P. D." (Pay Department).

(4) Corps of Engineers Swords. When the standard foot and field officers' swords of 1850 were adopted, the special sword (pattern of 1840) of the Corps of Engineers disappeared. As with other branches of the service, the 1850 models were worn until 1872 when the frail 1860 staff and field officers'

sword became regulation. However, the Topographical Engineers wore their own model (1839 pattern) until their corps was abolished in 1863. The sword was marked with "T. E." (Topographical Engineers) and corresponded exactly to the 1833 dragoon saber.

SWORDS, NAVY OFFICERS

In 1852, the Navy Department adopted a sword which with only very minor variations was to be worn as long as swords continued to be a part of the uniform of the United States Navy. The only noticeable difference in the appearance of the sword, aside from the etching styles on the blades, that can be noticed in this span of years comprise the variable blade length of a few inches depending upon the wearer's height and a noticeably lighter blade in the later specimens. Also used in the Civil War was a non-regulation sword of English design. An "Officers' Cutlass," similar to the weapon issued to seamen aboard ship, was worn by officers (perhaps by chief petty officers as well), although this weapon was not prescribed by regulations to either officers or chief petty officers.

SWORDS, MARINE CORPS

Marine Corps officers' swords are now very scarce for the Civil War period. Prior to 1859, officers of the Corps wore the characteristic Marine Corps sword with the grips shaped in the Mameluke pattern. In 1859 the Marine Corps Officers were ordered to abandon their distinctive swords in favor of the model 1850 foot officers' sword then worn by the Infantry.

CUTLASSES

Just before or just after the beginning of the Civil War a new model Naval cutlass was adopted by the Navy Department. The traditional date of 1860 has been tentatively accepted as the year this new pattern of cutlass was adopted. This new weapon was patterned after a model that had long been in

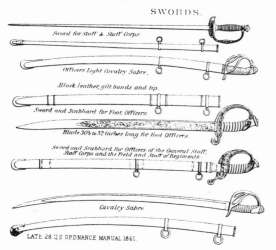

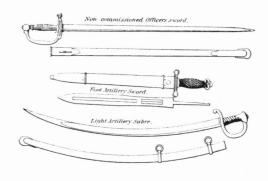

EDGED WEAPONS

use in the French navy, and it remained standard for American sailors for over 75 years. Even though a new model was adopted in 1917, these cutlasses were still to be found in the arms racks of some American naval vessels at the beginning of World War II.

SABERS, CAVALRY

In 1840 the War Department adopted a new model saber for the Army's three regiments of dragoons. This weapon, which followed closely the French light cavalry model of 1822, set the pattern for American cavalry sabers for the next 75 years, and won the name of "Old Wristbreaker" from the men who used it.

About 1860 a light saber was introduced for cavalry. In this new model, which did not immediately supplant the heavy saber, the blade was reduced in width, and the entire weapon was lightened. The exact date of this change is not known, but the light saber is mentioned in the *Ordnance Manual* of 1862, and most of the sabers of the Civil War period and later were made of this pattern. In addition to American-made sabers, the Federal Government during the early days of the Civil War, purchased swords from many sources, both domestic and foreign. Most of the domestic products followed the current official models exactly.

SABERS, ARTILLERY

In 1840 the War Department adopted a special saber based upon a French pattern for the light artillery companies of the regular artillery regiments. A handsome and essentially serviceable weapon, it remained regulation for approximately 50 years.

NONCOMMISSIONED OFFICERS' SWORD

The noncommissioned officers' sword adopted by the War Department in 1840 was based principally upon a type used in the French Army, but was reminiscent also of some models used in Great Britain. It was a handsome and graceful appearing weapon but somewhat heavy in the hilt and ill balanced. Nevertheless, it was worn by American sergeants for over 70 years which included such great conflicts as the Mexican War, the Civil War, and the Spanish American War.

MUSICIANS' SWORD

There is often a tendency on the part of students and collectors to think of the musicians' sword as purely a decoration, but that was not the case. It is true that bandsmen were not normally expected to use their swords in offensive action; but they did accompany the combat troops upon the field of battle and thus there was always the possibility that they might be called upon to defend themselves from a sudden onslaught of the enemy. In such an eventuality, their swords were their only means of defense, and for this reason the musicians in the American Army always carried serviceable weapons. The musicians' sword adopted by the War Department in 1840 was essentially the same as the noncommissioned officers' sword adopted at the same time. The only differences between the two were that the musician's sword did not have the double counterguard and its blade was 4 inches shorter.[24]

KNIVES, ARMY

The Civil War made the bowie knife as popular on the East Coast as it had been west of the Appalachians. Almost every volunteer on both sides wore one. The town of Ashby, Massachusetts, for instance, presented every one of its residents with a bowie knife when he enlisted, as did Shelburne Falls and many other Massachusetts towns. Veterans recalled, however, that the knives were soon abandoned, especially by Federal soldiers who found that their issued weapons were sufficient and that they had enough to carry without them. Confederate soldiers were not so well armed, and, therefore, the big knives remained more popular with them.

Northern soldiers generally carried English-made knives while Confederates relied more on homemade products. However, by the time of the Civil War, the period of knife manufacture in the United States was in full swing. Mounted men particularly favored pocket knives with stone hooks to help care for their horses' hooves on the march; and corkscrews were always useful to a foraging soldier. One type which was sold widely at the beginning of the war was a combination knife, fork, and spoon. Three major types of Civil War knife-fork-spoon combinations are recognized by collectors today, and a few have actually been recovered from battlefield sites.

KNIVES, NAVY

Most sailors carried clasp knives. They were strictly functional, being used to cut and splice ropes and for various other odd jobs requiring a cutting blade. Whittling or carving was one of the sailor's principal amusements during long months at sea. And if a man became tangled in a running line, a good knife with which to free himself often meant the difference between life and death. In the Navy these essential clasp knives were issued to seamen at least as early as the Civil War.

The Navy was the first service in the United States to adopt a knife bayonet. Credit for this innovation belongs to Admiral John A. Dahlgren who in 1856 pointed out the need for a bowie knife type of bayonet for hand-to-hand fighting, and a heavy tool for cutting away damaged naval tackle. Dahlgren devised a heavy bayonet which was adopted as official and used with the so-called Plymouth rifle, another weapon also manufactured according to Dahlgren's specifications. These new bowie bayonets were made under contract by the Ames Manufacturing Company at Chicopee Falls, Massachusetts, and were unique in the history of American naval small arms.[25]

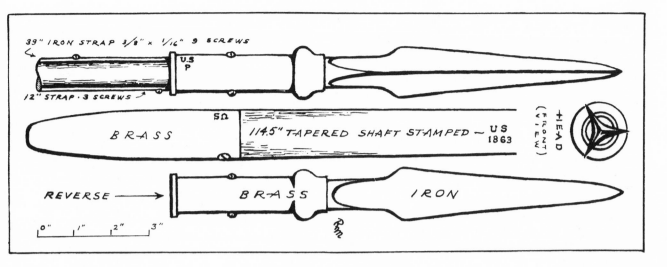

UNITED STATES LANCE

LANCES

The 6th Pennsylvania Cavalry, famed as Rush's Lancers, was armed with lances and served with these weapons in the Army of the Potomac. The Ordnance Department had the lances made under contract. They were an adapatation of the Austrian pattern, about 9 feet long with an 11-inch, three-edged blade. The staff was of Norway fir, about 1¼ inches in diameter with ferrule and counterpoise at the heel—the whole weighing 4 pounds 13 ounces. The people of Philadelphia contributed funds and purchased 1,000 scarlet swallow-tailed pennons for the lances. Although popular with spectators and officers, the men hated the clumsy lance in which they had no confidence. In 1863 the 6th Pennsylvania exchanged the lance for the saber and carbine.

MISCELLANEOUS WEAPONS AND MILITARY TECHNIQUES

General B. F. Butler was a nonprofessional soldier with an extremely bold originality in military technology. Few, if any, new devices appeared during the war of which Butler was not either the first or a very early champion. In the summer of 1861 he became the first American general to employ aerial reconnaissance. "It is greatly to his credit," says the leading historian of Civil War balloon activities, "that he encouraged a branch of military science then in its infancy in this Country, where his administrative superiors failed or refused to recognize its possibilities." Butler heartily endorsed the use of wire entanglements in the trench warfare along the Bermuda Hundred front in 1864. At the same time he devised a kite which was sent over the Confederate lines with a bundle of Lincoln's amnesty proclamations to be released by a string and lowered upon the enemy troops. A submarine was built for him, and what appears to have been a steam-driven helicopter had been nearly completed, with encouraging results,

when construction was halted by his final departure from the Army.[26]

Lincoln also was interested in submarines, including a rocket-driven submarine torpedo. At a demonstration, one of these torpedoes veered from

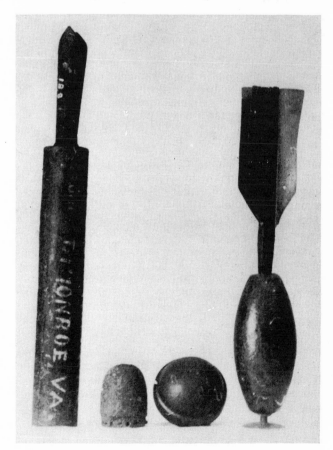

ROCKETS AND GRENADES

Left to right: rocket; rocket projectile found near Petersburg; *Excelsior* hand grenade marked "W. W. Hanes, Pat. Aug. 26, 1862"; and the Ketchum hand grenade marked "Patented August 20, 1861."

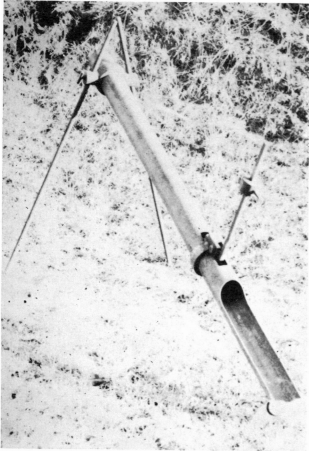

ROCKET LAUNCHER

The Hale rocket launcher. Length 5', range 500-2200 yds., depending on the elevation and on the weight of the rocket. Note similarity to more modern rocket launchers or "trench" mortars.

its course and struck the schooner *Diana*, blowing up her bow and sinking her. So far as is known, this was the first time a ship was sunk by a self-propelled torpedo. (Cushing used a spar-torpedo when he sank the *Albemarle*.)

HAND GRENADES

The most common hand grenade was Ketchum's, patent of August 20, 1861. It is listed in *Ordnance Memorandum* No. 1, 1865, as being of four different weights: 1, 2, 3, and 5-pounds. Also listed were 6 and 12-pound hand grenades. In his *Military Dictionary* (1864) Scott says that a hand grenade 2½ inches in diameter could be thrown about 26 yards. Ketchum's hand grenade was a small oblong percussion shell which exploded on striking a slightly resisting object. To prevent accidents, the plunger or piece of metal which communicated the shock to the percussion cap was not inserted in its place until the moment before the grenade was thrown.

Another type of hand grenade was completely different. This type, known as the "Excelsior," was patented by W. W. Hanes, August 26, 1862. It was

a cast-iron sphere with an inner and outer shell. The inner shell was 2½ inches in diameter and contained the powder. On the outside of this inner shell were screwed 14 nipples which took the regular musket percussion caps. The outer shell was in two halves, in which was inserted the inner shell, the two halves screwing together. Before firing, percussion caps were placed on the nipples; when the grenade struck an object, at least one of the 14 percussion caps was sure to receive the impact and thus explode the shell. Since the outer shell was in two parts, these parts would break up into many destructive fragments. This projectile was so dangerous to handle that only a few were made.

ROCKETS

Ordnance Memorandum No. 1 (1865) lists "War Rockets," Hale's patent, consisting of 2-inch and 3-inch types. (These measurements refer to the interior diameter measurements of the case.) Scott's *Military Dictionary* (1864) defined a "war rocket" as a "projectile set in motion by a force within itself." The Civil War rocket was composed of a strong case of paper or wrought iron, inclosing a composition of niter, charcoal, and sulphur, so proportioned as to burn slower than gunpowder. The head was either a solid shot, shell, or spherical-case shot, with the base perforated by one or more vents. The rockets used by the United States in the war were Hale's, in which steadiness in flight was given to the flight of the rocket by rotation, as in the case of the rifle bullet, around the long axis of the rocket. This rotation was produced by three small vents placed at the base of the head of the rocket. Hale's rocket was improved during the war by placing three tangential vents in a plane passing through the center of gravity of the rocket, and at right angles to the axis. This was accomplished by dividing the case into two distinct parts, or rockets, by a perforated partition. The composition in the front part furnished the gas for rotation, and that in the rear the gas for propulsion. The two sizes of Hale's rockets in use were:

2¼ inch (diameter of case)—weight 6 pounds.
3¼ inch (diameter of case)—weight 16 pounds.

Under an angle of from 4-5 degrees the range of these rockets was from 500 to 600 yards; and under an angle of 77 degrees the range of the smaller rocket was 1,760 yards, and the larger was 2,200 yards. War rockets are usually fired from tubes or troughs, mounted on portable stands or on light carriages.

Hale's rockets saw some combat use. When the war broke out, Hale's offer to come over from England and make rockets for the Union was refused; but his rockets were used.[27]

In addition to rockets, signal flares of different colors were used. The pistols for shooting these flares were of brass and were made in different sizes for the Army and Navy. The flares used were stationary like flares used on railroads today, and did not fire into the air.

GREEK FIRE

Greek Fire for incendiary purposes was employed, probably by both sides in a few instances. The Federals used it at the siege of Charleston in 1863, but its employment led to such representations respecting its barbarity that the use of it was but little resorted to, if at all, during the remainder of the war. Lincoln watched a demonstration in which two 13-inch shells charged with Greek Fire were exploded, each tossing fire 40-50 feet in the air and carpeting the ground over a 50-foot radius with a blaze that lasted ten minutes. But General Ripley refused to approve an order for 2,000 of the shells; however, General Butler took 100 of them on his New Orleans expedition.[28]

INCENDIARY SHELLS AND FLAME-THROWERS

Incendiary shells were invented by an Alfred Berney, whose demonstration before Lincoln of the shells' effectiveness resulted in an order for 1,000 of them. Lincoln and Stanton witnessed the demonstration on May 9, 1863. While they looked on, the inventor sent a woodpile flying into the air in a burst of smoke and flame, detonated two shells in the middle of the wood to suggest their effect on an enemy position and squirted fire from his hand pump. Lastly, he played a stream of fire on three hundred gallons of the fluid, representing the amount thrown in a minute from the nozzle of a steam pump. "The black pool blazed up, and fire billowed into the . . . twilight."[29]

CHEMICAL WARFARE

In May 1862 a letter was written to Lincoln by a New York school teacher named John W. Doughty who knew the properties of chlorine. He proposed the use of heavy shells filled with liquid chlorine. This, he explained to the President, would immediately expand into a choking gas of many times its original volume, which, being denser than air, would sink irresistibly into trenches and bomb-proofs. But there is no evidence that Lincoln actually read Doughty's letter. Someone, probably a White House secretary, referred it to the War Department; thence it went to General Ripley, who ignored it. Doughty wrote Ripley and was told that the Ordnance Department was too busy to test the idea. But the Germans, using a cruder version, were not too busy in 1915 to use the idea with astonishing effect at Ypres.

BREECHLOADING CANNON

Several models of breechloading cannon were offered for trial but the Chief of Ordnance, General Ripley, was not interested in them. One of these weapons was a breechloading iron field piece, about 4½ feet long, with a 2-inch bore. Five ounces of powder could send the gun's 4-pound ball as far as 2½ miles. Moreover, the gun was phenomenally rapid in operation. One had been fired a hundred times in six minutes without overheating.[30]

NOTES CHAPTER 10

1. Bruce, Robert V., *Lincoln and the Tools of War*, pp. 81-82, 264.
2. *Ibid.*, pp. 99-100.
3. *Ibid.*, pp. 284-285.
4. Manucy, Albert, *Artillery Through the Ages*, pp. 17-20.
5. *Ibid.*, pp. 14-20, 61.
6. Weller, Jac, "The Field Artillery of the Civil War," *Military Collector and Historian*, Vol. V, No. 2, 3, 4, June-December 1953.
7. Brandt, J. D., *Gunnery Catechism, Naval Artillery*, pp. 193-196.
8. *Ordnance Instruction for the United States Navy* (1864), *passim*.
9. Chinn, George M., *The Machine Gun*, Vol. 1, pp. 24-57.
10. Catalog, Francis Bannerman Sons, 501 Broadway, N. Y. (1955), pp. 258-259.
11. Stevens, page 6.
12. Stevens, C. A., *Berdan's United States Sharpshooters in the Army of the Potomac*, p. 7.
13. Some were sent to Kansas just before the war.
14. Gluckman, p. 265.
15. Chinn, Vol. 1, pp. 30-31.
16. Buckeridge, J. O., *Lincoln's Choice*, pp. 25-26.
17. Gluckman, p. 318.
18. See the regimental history.
19. Catalog, Bannerman, pp. 260-265.
20. Gluckman, Arcadi, *United States Martial Pistols and Revolvers*, pp. 153-160.
21. Catalog, Bannerman, pp. 266-268.
22. Senate *Report* No. 183, 42nd Congress, 2nd Session, pp. 167-172.
23. *Medical and Surgical History*, Part 3, Vol. 2 (*Surgical History*), pp. 696-704.
24. Peterson, Harold L., *The American Sword 1775-1945*, pp. 13, 32-35, 43-47, 54, 130-148, 161-164, 170.
25. Peterson, Harold L., *American Knives*, pp. 49, 102, 106-107, 137-140.
26. Bruce, p. 73.
27. *Ibid.*, pp. 218-219.
28. *Ibid.*, pp. 179-182.
29. *Ibid.*, pp. 237-238.
30. *Ibid.*, pp. 129-130, 247-248.

CHAPTER 11

Flags, Uniforms, Insignia

THE CIVIL WAR was the last major conflict of the United States in which bright banners and colorful uniforms were present on the battlefield. The rapidly deteriorating battle flags in our State capital show-rooms give but a faint idea of the appearance of thousands of "boys in blue," advancing on the enemy, with colors flying.

These colors were carried in battle and were an especial object of enemy fire, casualties among the standard-bearers being unusually heavy. Most conspicuous of all for heroism were those soldiers, sailors, and marines charged with bearing and guard-in the colors. In numerous instances the color-bearers continued defiantly to wave their cherished emblem in front of the enemy after the cloth had been shot into shreds by hostile fire; and official reports cite repeated instances of mortally wounded standard-bearers trying desperately to hold the colors aloft and refusing to give them up except to another member of the guard or until death relaxed their stubborn hold. An example of this spirit was shown by the color-bearers of the 42nd New York Infantry at Gettysburg:

The color-bearer, Sergeant Michael Cuddy, who established his great and superior courage in the Fredericksburg battle on this occasion displayed the most heroic bravery. When he fell, mortally wounded, he rose by a convulsive effort and triumphantly waved in the face of the rebels, not 10 yards distant, that flag he loved so dearly of which he was so proud and for which his valuable life, without a murmur, was freely given up. (Official Records, Vol. 27, Pt. 1, pp. 451-452.)

THE ARMY

In addition to the national and regimental flags the military forces of the Republic had distinctive flags for armies, corps, divisions, and brigades. For the flags of army corps, the central theme was the insignia of the corps itself. Divisions were indicated by colors: 1st Division, red; 2nd Division, white; 3rd Division, blue; and 4th Division, green. Brigades were indicated by a numerical designation.

FLAGS, COLORS, STANDARDS, GUIDONS

Early in the war militia units and some volunteer regiments carried distinctive flags or guidons, but after a few months' service all units adhered to the Army Regulations in their flags and colors. Flags, colors, standards, and guidons were prescribed in *Revised Regulations for the Army of the United States* (1861) as follows:

ARTICLE L. Sections 1464-1469

Garrison Flag

The garrison flag is the national flag. It is made of bunting, thirty-six feet fly, and twenty feet hoist, in thirteen horizontal stripes of equal breadth, alternately red and white, beginning with the red. In the upper quarter, next the staff, is the Union, composed of a number of white stars, equal to the number of States, on a blue field, one-third the length of the flag, extending to the lower edge of the fourth red stripe from the top. The storm flag is twenty feet by ten feet; the recruiting flag, nine feet nine inches by four feet four inches.

Colors of Artillery Regiments

Each regiment of Artillery shall have two silken colors. The first, or the national color, of stars and stripes, as described for the garrison flag. The number and name of the regiment to be embroidered with gold on the centre stripe. The second, or regimental color, to be yellow, of the same dimensions as the first, bearing in the centre two cannon crossing, with the letters U. S. above, and the number of the regiment below; fringe, yellow. Each color to be six feet six inches fly, and six feet deep on the pike. The pike, including the spear and ferrule, to be nine feet ten inches in length. Cords and tassels, red and yellow silk intermixed.

Colors of Infantry Regiments

Each regiment of Infantry shall have two silken colors. The first, or the national color, of stars and stripes, as described for the garrison flag; the number and name of the regiment to be embroidered with silver on the centre stripe. The second, or regimental color to be blue, with the arms of the United States embroidered in silk on the centre. The name of the regiment in a scroll, underneath the eagle. The size of each color to be six feet six inches fly, and six feet deep on the pike. The length of the pike, including the spear and ferrule, to be nine feet ten inches. The fringe yellow; cords and tassels, blue and white silk intermixed.

Camp Colors

The camp colors are of bunting, eighteen inches square, white for Infantry, and red for Artillery, with the number of the regiment on them. The pole eight feet long.

Standards and Guidons of Mounted Regiments

Each regiment will have a silken standard, and each company a silken guidon. The standard to bear the arms of the United States, embroidered in silk, on a blue ground, with the number and name of the regiment, in a scroll underneath the eagle. The flag of the standard to be two feet five inches wide, and two feet three inches on the lance, and to be edged with yellow silk fringe.

The flag of the guidon is swallow-tailed, three feet five inches from the lance to the end of the swallow-tail; fifteen inches to the fork of the swallow-tail, and two feet three inches on the lance. To be half red and half white, dividing at the fork, the red above. On the red, the letters U. S. in white; and on the white, the letter of the company in red. The lance of the standards of guidons to be nine feet long, including spear and ferrule.

Army, corps, division and brigade flags are illustrated in the following:

(a) *Flags of the Army of the United States carried during the War of the Rebellion 1861-1865; to designate the Headquarters of the different Armies, Army Corps, Divisions and Brigades.* Compiled by the Quartermaster General, U. S. Army.

(b) *The Battle Flags of the Army of the Potomac at Gettysburg, Penna. July 1st, 2nd, and 3rd 1863.* Compiled by James Beale.

On Washington's birthday 1862, the War Department ordered that units would inscribe on their colors the names of battles in which they should participate. The order which contributed much to morale and the building of esprit de corps among the combat units read as follows:

It is ordered that there shall be inscribed upon the colors or guidons of all regiments and batteries in the service of the United States the names of the battles in which they have borne a meritorious part. These names will also be placed on the Army Register at the head of the list of the officers of each regiment.

It is expected that troops so distinguished will regard their colors as representing the honor of their corps—to be lost only with their lives; and that those not yet entitled to such a distinction will not rest satisfied until they have won it by their discipline and courage.

The General Commanding the Army will, under the instructions of the Department, take the necessary steps to carry out this order.

L. Thomas
Adjutant General

UNIFORMS

In 1861 the militia which responded to Lincoln's call for 75,000 volunteers wore their own distinctive uniforms. The variety was almost endless, and especially noticeable in Washington just before First Bull Run. Among the New Yorkers were Highlanders in plaid "trews" (their kilts and bonnets very properly left at home), the blue jackets of the 71st, the gray jackets of the 8th, and Varian's artillery. There were half-fledged Zouaves, like the 14th New York (Brooklyn), and full-rigged Zouaves wearing gray pants and red shirts—the First Fire Zouaves of New York, under Ellsworth. From Rhode Island came Burnside's men

in pleated blue blouses; from Wisconsin came men in fast-fading gray—Blenker's Germans were there—a reserve division in gray from head to foot. The 2nd New York Fire Zouaves had a color-guard, nearly all seven-footers, all in the scarlet fez and breeches of the favorite troops of France. The Garibaldi Guard —mainly Italians—wore a uniform copied from that of Bersaglieri. A French regiment wore the Algerian campaign uniform. (*Photographic History*, Vol. 8, pp 78-80).

A few Zouave regiments, and special units like the regiments of Sharp-shooters kept their distinctive uniforms throughout their service. But the remaining units soon wore out or discarded their fanciful outfits and wore the uniform as had been prescribed in General Orders on March 13, 1861.

The following "Regulations for the Uniform and Dress of the Army of the United States" is reproduced verbatim, as being the best method of furnishing complete and authoritative information on that subject.

General Orders
No. 6

War Department
Adjutant General
Washington, March 13, 61

The Uniform, Dress and Horse Equipments of the Army having been changed in many respects since the "General Regulations" of 1857, the following description of them is published for the information of all concerned:

COAT

FOR COMMISSIONED OFFICERS

1. All officers shall wear a frock coat of dark blue cloth, the skirt to extend from two-thirds to three-fourths of the distance from the top of the hip to the bend of the knee; single-breasted for Captains and Lieutenants; double-breasted for all other grades.

2. *For a Major General*—two rows of buttons on the breast, nine in each row, placed by threes; the distance between each row, five and one-half inches at top, and three and one-half inches at bottom; standing-up collar, to rise no higher than to permit the chin to turn freely over it, to hook up in front at the bottom, and to slope thence up and backward at an angle of thirty degrees on each side; cuffs two and one half inches deep to go around the sleeves parallel with the lower edge, and to button with three small buttons at the under seam; pockets in the folds of the skirts, with one button at the hip, and one at the end of each pocket, making four buttons on the back and skirt of the coat, the hip button to range with the lowest buttons on the breast; collar and cuffs to be of dark blue velvet; lining of the coat black.

3. *For a Brigadier General*—the same as for a Major General, except that there will be only eight buttons in each row on the breast placed in pairs.

4. *For a Colonel*—the same as for a Major General, except that there will be only seven buttons in each row on the breast, placed in equal distances; collar and cuffs of the same color and material as the coat.

5. *For a Lieutenant Colonel*—the same as for a Colonel.

6. *For a Major*—the same as for a Colonel.

7. *For a Captain*—the same as for a Colonel, except that there will be only one row of nine buttons on the breast, placed at equal distances.

8. *For a First Lieutenant*—the same as for a Captain.

9. *For a Second Lieutenant*—the same as for a Captain.

10. *For a Brevet Second Lieutenant*—the same as for a Captain.

11. A round jacket, according to pattern, of dark blue cloth, trimmed with scarlet, with the Russian shoulder-knot, the prescribed insignia of rank to be worked in silver in the centre of the knot, may be worn on undress duty by officers of Light Artillery.

FOR ENLISTED MEN

12. The uniform coat for all enlisted FOOT men, shall be a single-breasted frock of dark blue cloth, made without plaits, with a skirt extending one-half the distance from the top of the hip to the bend of the knee; one row of nine buttons on the breast placed at equal distances; stand-up collar to rise no higher than to permit the chin to turn freely over it, to hook in front at the bottom and then to slope up and backward at an angle of thirty degrees on each side; cuffs pointed according to pattern and to button with two small buttons at the under seam; collar and cuffs edged with a cord or welt of cloth as follows, to wit; Scarlet for *Artillery;* sky blue for *Infantry;* yellow for *Engineers;* crimson for *Ordnance Sergeants* and *Hospital Stewards.* On each shoulder a metallic scale according to pattern; narrow lining for skirt of the

INFANTRY SERGEANT

The Jeff Davis hat with its ostrich plume, the frock coat, shoulder scales, and noncom's sword indicate that this photo was taken about 1861-62. After that period such dress uniforms were generally worn only by garrison troops.

CAVALRY MUSICIAN

Note the Jeff Davis hat and the shoulder scales. Such finery was not in general use after 1862. Many cavalry bugles were shorter than the one shown here.

coat of the same color and material as the coat; pockets in the folds of the skirts with one button at each hip to range with the lowest buttons on the breast; no buttons at the ends of pockets.

13. *All Enlisted Men of the Dragoons, Cavalry, Mounted Riflemen, and Light Artillery* shall wear a uniform jacket of dark blue cloth, with one row of twelve small buttons on the breast placed at equal distances; stand-up collar to rise no higher than to permit the chin to turn freely over it; to hook in front at the bottom, and to slope the same as the coat collar; on the collar, on each side, two blind button holes of lace, three-eighths of an inch wide, and one small button at the button hole, lower button hole extending back four inches, upper button hole three and a half inches; top button and front

ends of collar bound with lace three-eighths of an inch wide, and a strip of the same extending down the front and around the whole lower edge of the jacket; the back seam laced with the same; and on the cuff a point of the same shape as that on the coat, but formed of the lace; jacket to extend to the waist, and to be lined with white flannel; two small buttons at the under seam of the cuff, as on the coat cuff; one hook and eye at the bottom of the collar; color of lace (worsted), orange for *Dragoons*, yellow for *Cavalry*, green for *Riflemen*, and scarlet for *Light Artillery*.

14. *For all Musicians*—the same as for other enlisted men of their respective corps, with the addition of a facing of lace three-eighths of an inch wide on the front of the coat or jacket, made in the following manner: bars

CORPORAL, LIGHT ARTILLERY
Photographed in 1862. The fancy headgear saw little field service.

CAVALRY SERGEANT
Completely equipped for combat. About 1862.

of three-eighths of an inch worsted lace placed on a line with each button six and one-half inches wide, with the bottom, and thence gradually expanding upwards to the last button, counting from the waist up and contracting from thence to the bottom of the collar, where it will be six and one-half inches wide, with a strip of the same lace facing to correspond with the color of the trimming of the corps.

15. *For Fatigue Purposes*—a sack coat of dark blue flannel extending half way down the thigh, and made loose, without sleeve or body lining, falling collar, inside pocket on the left side, four coat buttons down the front.

16. *For Recruits*—the sack coat will be made with sleeve and body lining, the latter of flannel.

17. On all occasions of duty, except fatigue and when out of quarters the coat or jacket shall be buttoned and hooked to the collar.

BUTTONS

18. *For General Officers and Officers of the General Staff*—gilt, convex with spread eagle and stars, and plain borders; large size, seven-eighths of an inch in exterior diameter; small size one-half inch.

19. *For Officers of the Corps of Engineering*—gilt, nine-tenths of an inch in exterior diameter, slightly convex, a raised bright rim, one-thirteenth of an inch wide; device an eagle holding in his beak a scroll, with the word *"Essayons"* a bastion with embrasures in the distance surrounded by water, with a rising sun—the figures to be of dead gold upon a bright field. Small buttons of the same form and device, and fifty-five hundredths of an inch in exterior diameter.

20. *For Officers of the Corps of Topographical Engineers*—gilt, seven-eighths of an inch exterior diameter, convex and solid; device, the shield of the United States, occupying one-half the diameter, and the letters T. E. in old English characters the other half; small buttons, one-half inch diameter, device and form the same.

21. *For Officers of the Ordnance Department*—gilt, convex, plain bordered, cross cannon and bombshell, with a circular scroll over and across the cannon, containing the words "Ordnance Corps" large size, seven-eighths of an inch in exterior diameter; small size, one-half inch.

22. *For Officers of Artillery, Infantry, Riflemen, Cavalry,* and *Dragoons*—gilt, convex; device, a spread eagle with the letter A, for Artillery—I for Infantry—R for Riflemen—C for Cavalry—D for Dragoon,—on the shield; large size, seven-eighths of an inch in exterior diameter, small size one-half inch.

23. *Aides-de-camp*—may wear the button of the General Staff, or of their regiment or corps, at their option.

24. *For all Enlisted Men*—yellow, the same as is used by the Artillery, &c, omitting the latter in the shield.

TROUSERS

25. *For General Officers and Officers of the Ordnance Department*—of dark blue cloth, plain, without stripe welt, or cord down the outer seam.

26. *For Officers of the General Staff and Staff Corps*—except the Ordnance—dark blue cloth, with a gold cord, one-eighth of an inch diameter along the outer seam.

27. *For all Regimental Officers*—dark blue cloth, with a welt let into the outer seam, one-eighth of an inch in diameter, of colors corresponding to the facings of the respective regiments, viz: *Dragoons,* orange; *Cavalry,* yellow; *Riflemen,* emerald green; *Artillery,* scarlet; *Infantry,* sky-blue.

28. *For Enlisted Men*—except companies of Light Artillery—dark blue cloth; *sergeants* with a stripe one and one-half inch wide; *corporals* with a stripe one-half inch wide, of worsted lace, down and over the outer seam, of the color of the facings of the respective corps.

29. *Ordnance Sergeants and Hospital Stewards*—stripe of crimson lace one-and one-half inch wide.

30. *Privates*—plain, without stripe or welt.

31. *For Companies of Artillery equipped as Light Artillery*—sky-blue cloth.

All trousers to be made loose, without plaits, and to spread well over the boot; to be reenforced for all enlisted men.

HATS

32. *For Officers*—of the best black felt. The dimensions of medium size to be as follows:
Width of brim, 3¼ inches
Heighth of crown, 6¼ inches
Oval of tip, ½ inch
Taper of crown, ¾ inch
Curve of head, ⅜ inch
the binding to be ½ inch deep, of best black ribbed silk.

33. *For Enlisted Men*—of black felt, same shape and size as for officers, with double row of stitching, instead of binding, around the edge. To agree in quality with the pattern deposited in the clothing arsenal.

Trimmings

34. *For General Officers*—Gold cord, with acorn-shaped ends. The brim of the hat looped up on the right side and fastened with an eagle attached to the side of the hat; three ostrich feathers on the left side; a gold embroidered wreath in front, on black velvet ground, encircling the letters U. S. in silver, old English characters.

35. *For Officers of the Adjutant General's, Inspector General's Quartermaster's, Subsistence, Medical, and Pay Departments, and the Judge Advocate, above the rank of Captain:* The same as for General Officers—except the cord which will be of black silk and gold.

36. *For the same Departments, below the rank of Field Officers*—The same as for Field Officers, except that there will be but two feathers.

37. *For Officers of the Corps of Engineers*—The same as for the General Staff, except for the ornament in front, which will be a gold embroidered wreath of laurel and palm, encircling a silver turreted castle on black velvet ground.

38. *For Officers of the Topographical Engineers*—The same as for the General Staff, except for the ornament in front, which will be a gold embroidered wreath of oak leaves, encircling a gold embroidered shield, on black velvet ground.

39. *For Officers of the Ordnance Department*—The same as for the General Staff, except the ornament in front, which will be a gold embroidered shell and flame, on a black velvet ground.

40. *For Officers of the Dragoons*—The same as for the General Staff, except the ornament in front, which will be two gold embroidered sabres crossed, edges upward, on black velvet ground, with the number of the regiment in silver in the upper angle.

41. *For Officers of Cavalry*—The same as for Dragoons, except that the number of the regiment will be in the lower angle.

42. *For Officers of the Mounted Riflemen*—The same as for the General Staff, except the ornament in front, which will be a gold embroidered trumpet, perpendicular, on the black velvet ground.

43. *For Officers of Artillery*—The same as for General Staff, except the ornament in front, which will be gold embroidered cross-cannon, on black velvet ground, with the number of the regiment in silver within the bend.

44. *For Enlisted Men*—except companies of Light Artillery: The same as for Officers of the respective corps, except that there will be but one feather, the cord will be of worsted, of the same color as that of the facing of the corps, three-sixteenths of an inch in diameter, running three times through a slide of the same material, and terminating with two tassels, not less than two inches long, on the side of the hat opposite the feather. For *Hospital Stewards* the cord will be of buff and green mixed. The insignia of the corps, in brass, in front of the hat, corresponding with those prescribed for officers, with the number of regiment five-eighths of an inch long, in brass, and letter of company, one-inch arranged over the insignia. Brim to be looped up to side of hat with a brass eagle, having a hook attached to the bottom to secure the brim—on the right side for mounted men and left side for foot men. The feather to be worn on the side opposite the loop.

45. *For Officers of Infantry*—The same as for Artillery, except the ornament in front, which will be a gold embroidered bugle on black velvet ground, with the number of the regiment in silver within the bend.

46. All trimmings of the hat are to be made so that they may be detached; but the eagle, badge of corps, and letter of company are to be always worn.

47. For companies of Artillery equipped as Light Artillery, the old pattern uniform cap, with red horsehair plume, cord and tassel.

48. Officers of the General Staff, and Staff Corps, may wear, at their option, a light french chapeau, either stiff crown or flat, according to the pattern deposited in the Adjutant General's Office. Officers below the rank of Field Officers to wear but two feathers.

FORAGE CAPS

49. For fatigue purposes, forage caps, of pattern in the Quartermaster General's Office: Dark blue cloth, with a welt of the same around the crown, and yellow metal letters in front to designate companies.

50. Commissioned Officers may wear forage caps of the same pattern, with the distinctive ornament of the corps and regiment in front.

CRAVAT OR STOCK

51. *For all Officers*—black; when a cravat is worn, the tie not to be visible at the opening of the collar.

52. *For all Enlisted Men*—black leather, according to pattern.

BOOTS

53. *For all Officers*—ankle or Jefferson.

54. *For Enlisted Men of Riflemen, Dragoons, Cavalry, and Light Artillery*—ankle and Jefferson, rights and lefts, according to pattern.

55. *For Enlisted Men of Artillery, Infantry, Engineers, and Ordnance*—Jefferson, rights and lefts, according to pattern.

SPURS

56. *For all Mounted Officers*—yellow metal, or gilt.

57. *For all Enlisted Mounted Men*—yellow metal, according to pattern.

GLOVES

58. *For General Officers and Officers of the General Staff and Staff Corps*—buff or white.

59. *For Officers of Artillery, Infantry, Cavalry, Dragoons, and Riflemen*—white.

SASH

60. *For General Officers*—buff, silk net, with silk bullion fringe ends; sash to go twice around the waist,

and to tie behind left hip, pendent part not to extend more than eighteen inches below the tie.

61. *For officers of the Adjutant General's, Inspector General's, Quartermaster's, and Subsistence Departments, Corps of Engineers, Topographical Engineers, Ordnance, Artillery, Infantry, Cavalry, Riflemen, and Dragoons, and the Judge Advocate of the Army*—crimson silk net; *for Officers of the Medical Department*—medium or emerald green silk net, with silk bullion fringe ends; to go around the waist and tie as for General Officers.

62. *For all Sergeant Majors, Quartermaster Sergeants, Ordnancy Sergeants, First Sergeants, Principal or Chief Musicians and Chief Buglers*—red worsted sash, with worsted bullion fringe ends; to go twice around the waist, and to tie behind the left hip, pendent part not to extend more than eighteen inches below the tie.

63. The sash will be worn (over the coat) on all occasions of duty of every description, except stable and fatigue.

64. The sash will be worn by "Officers of the Day" across the body, scarf fashion, from the right shoulder to the left side, instead of around the waist, tying behind the left hip as prescribed.

SWORD BELT

65. *For all Officers*—waist belt not less than one and one-half inch, nor more than two inches wide; to be worn over the sash; the sword to be suspended from it by slings of the same material as the belt, with a hook attached to the belt upon which the sword may be hung.

66. *For General Officers*—Russian leather, with three stripes of gold embroidery; the slings embroidered on both sides.

67. *For all other Officers*—black leather, plain.

68. *For all Non-commissioned Officers*—black leather, plain.

SWORD-BELT PLATE

69. *For all Officers and Enlisted Men*—gilt, rectangular, two inches wide, with a raised bright rim; a silver wreath of laurel encircling the "Arms of the United States;" eagle, shield, scroll, edge of cloud and rays bright. The motto, "E PLURIBUS UNUM," in silver

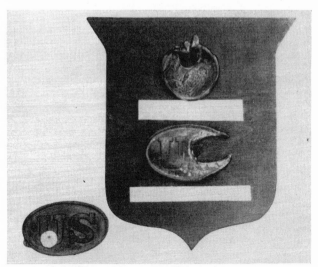

BELT BUCKLE AND BREASTPLATE

The "Eagle Plate" (top) is from the Chancellorsville battlefield, the belt buckle from the Wilderness. Both were penetrated by enemy bullets which killed the wearer. The belt buckle on the lower left still holds a bullet which went partially through it.

letters, upon the scroll; stars also of silver; according to pattern.

SWORD AND SCABBARD

70. *For General Officers*—straight sword, gilt hilt, silver grip, brass or steel scabbard.

71. *For Officers of the Adjutant General's, Inspector General's Quartermaster's, and Subsistence Departments, Corps of Engineers, Topographical Engineers, Ordnance, the Judge Advocate of the Army, Aides-de-Camp, Field Officers of Artillery, Infantry, and Foot Riflemen, and for the Light Artillery*—the sword of the pattern adopted by the War Department, April 9, 1850; or the one described in G. O. No. 21, of August 28, 1860, for officers therein designated.

72. *For the Medical and Pay Departments*—Small sword and scabbard, according to pattern in the Surgeon General's office.

73. *For Officers of Dragoons, Cavalry, and Mounted Riflemen*—sabre and scabbard now in use, according to pattern in the Ordnance Department.

74. *For the Artillery, Infantry, and Foot Riflemen, except the field officers*—the sword of the pattern adopted by the War Department, April 9, 1850.

75. The sword and sword belt will be worn upon all occasions of duty, without exception.

76. When on foot, the sabre will be suspended from the hook attached to the belt.

77. When not on military duty, officers may wear swords of honor, or the prescribed sword, with a scabbard, gilt, or of leather with gilt mountings.

SWORD-KNOT

78. *For General Officers*—gold cord with acorn end.

79. *For all other officers*—gold lace strap with gold bullion tassel.

BADGES TO DISTINGUISH RANK
Epaulettes

80. *For the Major General Commanding the Army*—gold, with solid crescent; device, three silver-embroidered stars, one, one and a half inches in diameter, one, one and one-fourth inches in diameter, and one, one and one-eighth inches in diameter, placed on the strap in a row, longitudinally, and equidistant, the largest star in the centre of the crescent, the smallest at the top; dead and bright gold bullion, one-half inch in diameter and three and one-half inches long.

81. *For all other Major Generals*—the same as for the Major General Commanding the Army, except that there will be two stars on the strap instead of three, omitting the smallest.

82. *For a Brigadier General*—the same as for a Major General, except that, instead of two, there shall be one star (omitting the smallest), placed upon the strap, and not within the crescent.

83. *For a Colonel*—the same as for a Brigadier General, substituting a silver-embroidered spread eagle for the star upon the strap; and within the crescent for the *Medical Department*—a laurel wreath embroidered in gold, and the letters M. S., in old English characters in silver, within the wreath; *Pay Department*—same as the Medical Department, with the letters P.D. in old English characters; *Corps of Topographical Engineers*—a shield embroidered in gold, and below it the letters T.E., in old English characters, in silver; *Corps of Engineers*—a turreted castle of silver; *Ordnance* Department—shell and flame in silver embroidery; *Regimental* Officers—the number of the regiment embroidered in gold, within a circlet of embroidered silver, one and three-fourths inches in diameter, upon cloth of the following

colors: *for Artillery*—scarlet; *Infantry*—light or sky blue; *Riflemen*—medium or emerald green; *Dragoons*—orange; *Cavalry*—yellow.

84. *For a Lieutenant Colonel*—the same as for a colonel, according to corps, but substituting for the eagle a silver-embroidered leaf.

85. *For a Major*—the same as for a Colonel, according to corps, omitting the eagle.

86. *For a Captain*—the same as for a Colonel, according to corps, except that the bullion will be only one-fourth of an inch in diameter, and two and one-half inches long, and substituting for the eagle two silver-embroidered bars.

87. *For a First Lieutenant*—the same as for a Colonel, according to corps, except that the bullion will be only one-eighth of an inch in diameter, and two and one-half inches long, and substituting for the eagle one silver-embroidered bar.

88. *For a Second Lieutenant*—the same as for a First Lieutenant, omitting the bar.

89. *For a Brevet Second Lieutenant*—the same as for a Second Lieutenant.

90. All officers having military rank will wear an epaulette on each shoulder.

91. The epaulette may be dispensed with when not on duty, and on certain duties off parade, to wit: at drills, at inspections of barracks and hospitals, on Courts of Inquiry and Boards, at inspections of articles and necessaries, on working parties and fatigue duties, and upon the march, except when, in war, there is immediate expectation of meeting the enemy, and also when the overcoat is worn.

SHOULDER STRAPS

92. *For the Major General Commanding the Army*—dark blue cloth, one and three-eighths inches wide by four inches long; bordered with an embroidery of gold one-fourth of an inch wide; three silver embroidered stars of five rays, one star on the centre of the strap, and one on each side equidistant between the centre and the outer edge of the strap; the centre star to be the largest.

93. *For all other Major Generals*—the same as for the Major General Commanding the Army, except that there will be two stars instead of three; the centre of each star to be one inch from the outer edge of the gold embroidery on the ends of the strap; both stars of the same size.

94. *For a Brigadier General*—the same as for a Major General, except that there will be one star instead of two; the centre of the star to be equidistant from the outer edge of the embroidery on the ends of the strap.

95. *For a Colonel*—the same size as for a Major General, and bordered in like manner with an embroidery of gold; a silver-embroidered spread eagle on the centre of the strap, two inches between the tips of the wings, having in the right talon an olive branch, and in the left a bundle of arrows; an escutcheon on the breast, as represented in the arms of the United States; cloth of the strap as follows: for the *General Staff and Staff Corps*—dark blue; *Artillery*—scarlet; *Infantry*—light or sky-blue; *Riflemen*—medium or emerald green; *Dragoons*—orange; *Cavalry*—yellow.

96. *For a Lieutenant Colonel*—the same as for a Colonel, according to corps, omitting the eagle, and introducing a silver-embroidered leaf at each end, each leaf extending seven-eighths of a inch from the end border of the strap.

97. *For a Major*—the same as for a colonel, according to corps, omitting the eagle, and introducing a gold-em-

broidered leaf at each end, each leaf extending seven-eighths of an inch from the end border of the strap.

98. *For a Captain*—the same as for a Colonel, according to corps, omitting the eagle, and introducing at each end two gold-embroidered bars of the same width as the border, placed parallel to the ends of the strap; the distance between them and from the border equal to the width of the border.

99. *For a First Lieutenant*—the same as for a Colonel, according to corps, omitting the eagle, and introducing at each end one gold-embroidered bar of the same width as the border, placed parallel to the ends of the strap, at a distance from the border equal to its width.

100. *For a Second Lieutenant*—the same as for a Colonel, according to corps, omitting the eagle.

101. *For a Brevet Second Lieutenant*—the same as for a Second Lieutenant.

102. The shoulder strap will be worn whenever the epaulette is not.

103. The rank of non-commissioned officers will be marked by chevrons upon both sleeves of the uniform coat and overcoat, above the elbow, of silk or worsted binding one half an inch wide, same color as the edging on the coat, points down, as follows:

104. *For a Sergeant Major*—three bars and an arc, in silk.

105. *For a Quartermaster Sergeant*—three bars and a tie, in silk.

106. *For an Ordnance Sergeant*—three bars and a star, in silk.

107. *For a Hospital Steward*—a caduceus two inches long, embroidered with yellow silk on each arm above the elbow, in the place indicated for a chevron, the head toward the outer seam of the sleeve.

108. *For a First Sergeant*—three bars and a lozenge, in worsted.

109. *For a Sergeant*—three bars, in worsted.

110. *For a Corporal*—two bars, in worsted.

111. *For a Pioneer*—two crossed hatchets of cloth, same color and material as the edging of the collar, to be sewed on each arm above the elbow in the place indicated for a chevron, (those of a corporal to be just above and resting on the chevron,) the head of the hatchet upward, its edge outward, of the following dimensions, viz: *Handle*—four and one half inches long, one-fourth to one-third of an inch wide. *Hatchet*—two inches long, one inch wide at the edge.

112. *To indicate service*—all non-commissioned officers, musicians, and privates, who have served faithfully for the term of five years, will wear, as a mark of distinction, upon both sleeves of the uniform coat, below the elbow, a diagonal half chevron, one-half an inch wide, extending from seam to seam, the front end nearest the cuff, and one-half an inch above the point of the cuff, to be of the same color as the edging on the coat. In like manner, an additional half chevron, above and parallel to the first, for every subsequent five years of faithful service; distance between each chevron one-fourth of an inch. Service in war will be indicated by a light or sky-blue stripe on each side of the chevron for Artillery, and a red stripe for all other corps, the stripe to be one-eighth of an inch wide.

OVERCOAT

For Commissioned Officers

113. A *"cloak coat"* of dark blue cloth, closing by means of four frog buttons of black silk and loops of black silk cord down the breast, and at the throat by a long loop *a echelle*, without tassel or plate, on the left side, and a black silk frog button on the right; cord for the loops fifteen-hundredths of an inch in diameter; back, a single piece, split up from the bottom, from fifteen to seventeen inches, according to the height of the wearer, and closing at will, by buttons, and button-holes cut in a concealed flap; collar of the same color and material as the coat, rounded at the edges, and to stand or fall; when standing, to be about five inches high; sleeves loose, of a single piece, and round at the bottom, without cuff or slit; lining, woolen; around the front and lower border, the edges of the pockets, the edges of the sleeves, collar, and slit in the back, a flat braid of black silk one-half an inch wide; and around each frog button on the breast, a knot two and one-quarter inches in diameter of black cord, seven-hundredths of an inch in diameter, arranged according to

ARMY OVERCOAT

This light artilleryman is wearing the sky-blue greatcoat which was used extensively. Note the artillery saber. Photographed in 1862.

drawing; cape of the same color and material as the coat, removable at the pleasure of the wearer, and reaching to the cuff of the coat-sleeve when the arm is extended; coat to extend down the leg from six to eight inches below the knee, according to height. *To indicate rank,* there will be on both sleeves, near the lower edge, a knot of flat black silk braid not exceeding one-eighth of an inch in width, arranged according to drawing, and composed as follows:

114. *For a General*—of five braids, double knot.

115. *For a Colonel*—of five braids, single knot.

116. *For a Lieutenant Colonel*—of four braids, single knot.

117. *For a Major*—of three braids, single knot.

118. *For a Captain*—of two braids, single knot.

119. *For a First Lieutenant*—of one braid, single knot.

120. *For a Second Lieutenant and Brevet Second Lieutenant*—a plain sleeve, without knot or ornament.

For Enlisted Men

121. *Of all Mounted Corps*—of sky-blue cloth; stand and fall collar; double breasted; cape to reach down to the cuff of the coat when the arm is extended, and to button all the way up; buttons (24.)

122. *All other enlisted men*—of sky-blue cloth; stand-up collar; single-breasted; cape to reach down to the elbows when the arm is extended, and to button all the way up; buttons (24.)

123. *For Dragoons, Cavalry, and Mounted Riflemen* —a gutta percha talma, or cloak extending to the knee, with long sleeves.

OTHER ARTICLES OF CLOTHING AND EQUIPMENT

124. *Flannel shirt, drawers, stockings, and stable frock* —the same as now furnished.

125. *Blanket*—woolen, gray, with letters U. S. in black, four inches long, in the centre; to be seven feet long, and five and a half feet wide, and to weigh five pounds.

126. *Canvas overalls for Engineer soldiers*—of white cotton; one garment to cover the whole of the body below the waist, the breast, the shoulders, and the arms; sleeves loose, to allow a free play of the arms, with narrow wristband buttoning with one button; overalls to fasten at the neck behind with two buttons, and at the waist behind with buckle and tongue.

127. *Belts of all Enlisted Men*—black leather.

128. *Cartridge box*—according to pattern in the Ordnance Department.

129. *Drum sling*—white webbing; to be provided with a brass drum stick carriage, according to pattern.

130. *Knapsack*—of painted canvas, according to pattern now issued by the Quartermaster's Department; the great coat, when carried, to be neatly folded, not rolled, and covered by the outer flap of the knapsack.

131. *Haversack*—of painted canvas, with an inside sack unpainted, according to the pattern now issued by the Quartermaster's Department.

132. *Canteen*—of tin, covered with woolen cloth, of the pattern now issued by the Quartermaster's Department.

TENTS

133. *For all Commissioned Officers*—wall tent, with a fly, pattern now issued by the Quartermaster's Department.

134. *For Hospital purposes*—pattern described in General Orders No. 1, of January 19, 1860.

135. *For all Enlisted Men*—Sibley's patent, according to the pattern now issued by the Quartermaster's Department, at the rate of one tent to 17 mounted or 20 foot men. Sheet-iron stoves will be issued with the tents in cold climates, or when specially ordered.

136. *For Officers' Servants and Laundresses*—small common tent, old pattern.

HORSE FURNITURE
For General Officers and the General Staff

137. *Housing for General Officers*—to be worn over the saddle; of dark blue cloth, trimmed with two rows of gold lace, the outer row one inch and five-eighths wide, the inner row two inches and one-fourth; to be made full, so as to cover the horse's haunches and forehands, and to bear on each flank corner the following ornaments, distinctive of rank, to wit: for the *Major General Commanding the Army*—a gold embroidered spread eagle and three stars; for other *Major Generals*— a gold embroidered spread eagle and two stars; for a *Brigadier General*—a gold embroidered spread eagle and one star.

138. *Saddle-cloth for General Staff Officers*—dark blue cloth, of sufficient length to cover the saddle and holsters, and one foot ten inches in depth, with an edging of gold lace one inch wide.

139. *Surcingle*—blue web.

140. *Bridle*—black leather; bent branch bit, with gilt bosses; the front and roses yellow.

141. *Collar*—yellow.

142. *Holsters*—black leather, with gilt mountings.

143. *Stirrups*—gilt or yellow metal.

For Officers of the Corps of Engineers and Topographical Engineers

144. The same as for General Staff Officers.

145. In time of actual field service, General Officers and Officers of the General Staff and Staff Corps are permitted to use the horse equipments described for mounted service.

MISCELLANEOUS

182. General Officers, and Colonels having the brevet rank of General Officers, may, on occasions of ceremony, and when not serving with troops, wear the "dress" and "undress" prescribed by existing regulations.

183. Officers below the grade of Colonel having brevet rank, will wear the epaulettes and shoulder straps distinctive of their army rank. In all other respects, their uniform and dress will be that of their respective regiments, corps, or departments, and according to their commissions in the same. Officers above the grade of Lieutenant Colonel by ordinary commission, having brevet rank, may wear the uniform of their respective regiments or corps, or that of General Officers, according to their brevet rank.

184. Officers are permitted to wear a plain dark blue body coat, with the button designating their respective corps, regiments, or departments, without any other mark or ornament on it. Such a coat, however, is not to be considered as a dress for any military purpose.

185. In like manner, officers are permitted to wear a buff, white, or blue vest, with the small button of their corps, regiment, or department.

186. Officers serving with mounted troops are allowed to wear, for stable duty, a plain dark blue cloth jacket, with one or two rows of buttons down the front, according to rank; stand-up collar, sloped in front as that of the uniform coat; shoulder straps according to rank, but no other ornament.

187. The hair to be short; the beard to be worn at the pleasure of the individual; but when worn, to be kept short and neatly trimmed.

188. *A band* will wear the uniform of the regiment or

corps to which it belongs. The commanding officer may, at the expense of the corps, sanctioned by the Council of Administration, make such *additions* in ornaments as he may judge proper.

BY ORDER OF THE SECRETARY OF WAR:

L. THOMAS,
Adjutant General.

OFFICIAL:
Assistant Adjutant General.

CHANGES IN UNIFORM REGULATIONS

The uniform regulations were changed on a few minor points during the War. These changes were as follows:

Signal Officer:

By General Order No. 32, June 15, 1861, it was provided that the uniform and dress of the Signal Officer would be that of a major of the General Staff.

Chaplains:

By General Order No. 102, November 25, 1861, the uniform for chaplains of the Army was to be a plain black frock coat with standing collar, and one row of nine black buttons; plain black pantaloons; black felt hat, or army forage cap, without ornament. On occasions of ceremony, a plain chapeau de bras could be worn.

This order was amended by General Order No. 247, August 25, 1864, as follows: The coat was to have "herring bone" of black braid around the buttons and button holes; a hat or cap insignia was to be worn, consisting of a gold embroidered wreath, on black velvet ground, encircling the letters U. S. in silver, old English characters.

However, there seems to have been considerable confusion as to the rank, uniform, and duties of chaplains during the war. Accordingly, there was great variety in these particulars. Many new chaplains adopted the ordinary uniform of a captain of Cavalry, with the shoulder straps, sash, and sword included. (H. Clay Trumbull, *War Memories of an Army Chaplain*, p. 2.)

Chaplain Horatio S. Howell, 90th Pennsylvania Infantry was killed by a Confederate soldier during the retreat through the town of Gettysburg. The chaplain was wearing a sword and was shot because he appeared to be a line officer and not a noncombatant. The sword of Chaplain Benjamin R. Miller, 119th Pennsylvania Infantry is a line officer's weapon; it is in the author's collection. Other noncombatants who wore swords were medical officers and even hospital stewards! The author has examples of both. The hospital steward's weapon is a medical officer's sword, inscribed to "Hospital Steward James Kemble, 28th Pennsylvania Infantry."

ARMY—REGULARS AND VOLUNTEERS

By General Order No. 8, December 16, 1861, the following change was ordered for the uniform trousers of regimental officers and enlisted men: cloth to be sky-blue mixture; the welt for officers, and stripes for noncommissioned officers of Infantry to be of dark blue.

INVALID CORPS

General Order No. 124, May 15, 1863, prescribed the following uniform for the Invalid Corps: Jacket —of sky-blue kersey, with dark-blue trimmings, cut like the jacket for United States Cavalry, to come well down on the loins and abdomen. Trousers— Present regulation, sky-blue.

FORAGE CAP—PRESENT REGULATION

The same month (May 29, 1863), General Order No. 158 prescribed the following uniform for officers of the Invalid Corps: *Frock coat*—of sky-blue cloth, with dark-blue velvet collar and cuffs—in all other respects, according to the present pattern for officers of Infantry.

SHOULDER STRAPS

According to present regulations, but worked on dark-blue velvet. Pantaloons—Of sky-blue cloth, with double stripe of dark-blue cloth down the outer seam, each stripe one-half inch wide, with space between of three-eighths of an inch. Insignia (The insignia for branches of service and for indicating rank of officers and men are found in General Order No. 6).

CORPS BADGES

The adoption of a device to designate the organization to which a soldier belonged originated in General Philip Kearny's order, announced in May, 1862, that the officers and men of his division should wear a piece of red cloth on the front of the cap, to indicate that they belonged to his command, and this device was called the "Kearny Patch."

The continuance of its use after General Kearny was killed at Chantilly, Virginia, was authorized by General Orders, No. 49, Headquarters of the 1st Division, Third Army Corps, Sept. 4, 1862, issued as the announcement of General Kearny's death, "to still further show our regard for him, and to distinguish his officers as he wished, each officer will continue to wear on his cap a piece of scarlet cloth, or have the top or crown-piece of cap made of scarlet cloth." —By order of General D. B. Birney, commanding.

The story is current that, to comply with General Kearny's original order, the pieces of cloth were cut from scarlet blankets brought by the general from France.

General Joseph Hooker, commanding the Army of the Potomac, issued, March 21, 1863, a circular concerning the adoption of original corps badges "for the purpose of ready recognition of corps and divisions of this army, and to prevent injustice by reports of straggling and misconduct through mistake as to their organizations."

The corps were usually divided into three divisions, and the color of the badge was determined by the

CORPS BADGES

number of the division:—1st division, red; 2nd, white; and the 3rd, blue—the colors of our flag. When more than three divisions, green was used for the 4th, and orange for the 5th.

The badges were placed upon brigade, division, and corps flags, and also on the wagons, artillery, ambulances, and all other public property belonging to the corps.

General Hooker's circular prescribed for the First Army Corps a sphere; for the Second, a trefoil; for the Third, a lozenge; and for the Fourth, a equilateral triangle. (This corps was disbanded before the actual adoption of the badge.) For the Fifth Army Corps, a Maltese Cross, and for the Sixth, a Greek Cross were prescribed.

The Seventh Corps, Department of Virginia, was discontinued before any order was issued concerning a badge. Major-General J. J. Reynolds, commanding the Seventh Corps, Department of Arkansas, issued a circular, June 1, 1865, giving cuts of the badge adopted, as a crescent partially surrounding a five-pointed star, and might be worn by all enlisted men of the corps.

The Eighth Corps, or Middle Department, used as its badge a star with six rays, but no order was ever issued.

The Ninth Corps was the travelling corps, doing duty in the South, East, and West. General Orders, No. 6, dated April 10, 1864, is the first official announcement concerning its badge and describes it as a shield with a figure nine (9) in the center, crossed with a fouled anchor and cannon. The order states that those who desired might wear a medal of the same design. General Orders, No. 49, dated Dec. 23, 1864, required all officers and men of the command to wear the badge on the cap or hat. The design for this badge was suggested in the Seal of the State of Rhode Island—General Burnside's State.

The Tenth Corps was for a considerable time on duty on the seaboard, and used its strength largely in the building or destruction of fortifications. In General Orders, No. 18, dated July 25, 1864, the trace of a four-bastioned fort was announced as the badge; an appropriate selection.

General Hooker's circular of March 21, 1863, prescribed for the Eleventh Corps a crescent, and for the Twelfth, a five-pointed star. When the Army of the Potomac was reorganized in March 1864, General Orders, No. 10, announced that the troops transferred should preserve their badges and distinctive marks. The combination of the First and Fifth Corps used as a badge for the new Fifth Corps a circle surrounding a Maltese Cross; the Sixth retained the Greek cross as its badge.

No badge for the Thirteenth Corps, Army of the Tennessee, was ever announced in General Orders during the war; but at a meeting of the society of this corps, during the Twenty-first National Encampment of the Grand Army of the Republic at St. Louis, Missouri, September 28-30, 1887, an ellipse, surrounding a canteen, having on one side a picture of General Grant, and on the reverse side the letters U. S., was adopted.

The first official mention of designating the flags in the Department of the Cumberland (original Fourteenth Army Corps) was in General Orders, No. 41, dated December 19, 1862, defining the flags for the different divisions of the department; each flag to be attached to a portable staff. General Orders, No. 91, dated April 25, 1863, announced the substitution of flags to be more plainly marked than those in use. General Orders, No. 62, dated April 26, 1864, rescinded the order of April 25, 1863, and announced the badges of the different corps serving in the department,—the Fourth, Fourteenth, and Twentieth. Paragraph 2, of the order, reads, "For the purpose of ready recognition of the corps and divisions of this army, and to prevent injustice by reports of straggling and misconduct through mistakes as to organizations, the following described badges will be worn by the officers and men of all the regiments of the corps mentioned." For the Fourth Corps (formed by the consolidation of the Twentieth and Twenty-first Corps), an equilateral triangle (the same as announced for the Fourth Corps, Army of the Potomac, but never used).

For the Fourteenth Corps, an acorn. This device, it is said, was suggested by the experience of this command during the fall of 1863. The roads were bad, and supplies could not be brought up. Near their camp was an oak grove, the trees loaded with acorns; here was a substitute for the delayed rations. The acorns were roasted or boiled, ground between stones, and made into a kind of bread; the men pinned the acorns on their breasts, cut them from coins and cloth, wore them as badges, and named themselves the "Acorn Boys."

Before communications were established, these gifts of nature had become an important part of the ration, and, when the order came to select a corps badge, the acorn was chosen by acclamation.

For the Twentieth Corps (formed by the consolidation of the Eleventh and Twelfth Corps), a five-pointed star, the old badge of the Twelfth. For some time men of the Eleventh Corps clung to the crescent, and used it in combination with the star—their new device being a crescent joining the two upper points of the star.

General Orders, No. 10, dated Head-quarters, Fifteenth Army Corps, February 14, 1865, reads, "The following is announced as the badge of this corps: A miniature cartridge-box, black, set transversely on a field of cloth or metal; above the cartridge-box plate will be stamped or marked in a curve, the motto, 'Forty Rounds.'"

An amusing incident is said to have suggested the

badge. The story is that when the Eleventh and Twelfth Corps joined the Army at Chattanooga, Tennessee, naturally a spirit of rivalry sprang up between the boys of the East and the West. The latter spoke of the new arrivals as the men with "paper collars, crescents, and stars." Near the camp of the Eastern men was a division of the Fifteenth Corps lately arrived from Memphis. One of its members, a ready witted Irishman, seeing a group of the Twelfth Corps, said, "Are all you fellers brigadier-ginerals?" "No," was the answer. "Why do you ask" "Shure, you all wear the star." Of course this raised a laugh, and called out the answer that the star was the Twelfth Corps Badge. Then the men wearing the star said, "What is your corps?" Straightening himself up with pride, the Irishman replied, "I belong to the Fifteenth Corps." "Well, where is your badge?" "Badge, is it?" Clapping his hand to his cartridge-box, he said, "This is the badge of the Fifteenth Corps,—Forty Rounds." General Logan, hearing of this, and appreciating the wit and significance of the Irishman's corps badge, declared that this should be the badge of the Fifteenth Corps.

No order was ever issued concerning a badge for the Sixteenth Army Corps. When it was decided by the members to adopt a badge, several designs were made, thrown into a hat, and by common consent the first drawn out was to be accepted. The drawing of this, as first issued, and shown on the old Grand Army Badge, was a circle crossed by two bars at acute angles. The device was a circle, with four minie-balls attached to the circumference at equal intervals, the points towards the center, the spaces between the balls forming a figure resembling a Maltese Cross with curved lines. This was the device adopted, and was called the "A. J. Smith Cross," in honor of the first commander of the reorganized corps.

The badge of the Seventeenth Corps was announced in General Orders, No. 1, dated March 25, 1865, as an arrow. In the order General F. P. Blair, its commander, said, "In its swiftness, in its surety of striking where wanted, and in its destructive powers when so intended, the arrow is probably as emblematical of this corps as any design that could be adopted."

The badge of the Eighteenth Corps was announced in a circular, dated June 7, and in General Orders, No. 108, dated August 25, 1864, Headquarters of the Eighteenth Army Corps. This badge is described as a cross with foliated leaves.

For the Nineteenth Corps, the design for a badge was announced in General Orders, No. 17, dated Headquarters, Department of the Gulf, February 17, 1863, as a four-pointed star, resting on the appropriately colored flags, to denote divisions, and to be habitually displayed in front of the headquarters they

designate. This badge was never worn on the uniform.

The design now known as the badge of the Nineteenth Corps was announced in General Orders, No. 11, dated November 17, 1864, as follows: A fan-leaved cross with an octagonal centre, or the St. Andrew's Cross. Brevet Brigadier-General D. S. Walker said, "We never fired a hostile shot under the Saint Andrew's Cross. The battles of the Nineteenth Corps were fought under the flags with the four-pointed star."

No orders were ever issued concerning a badge for the Twenty-first Corps.

No official order was issued concerning a badge for the Twenty-second Corps. This corps served continuously in the defenses of the National Capital, and adopted as a badge a pentagon, the edge cut into five equal sections, and a circle described in the centre. This design, seems to indicate a space inside of entrenched lines or defensive works.

For the Twenty-third Corps a shield was used as a badge. It was adopted in the spring of 1864, but no order was issued. This corps was originally organized to form with the Ninth the Army of the Ohio, and these commands were intimately associated under General A. E. Burnside. This may have suggested the selection of a badge resembling that of the Ninth Corps. An official order concerning it is found in Special Orders, No. 21, Headquarters, First Division, Twenty-third Army Corps, dated April 15, 1865, which directs that the "badges which have just been issued to this command will be worn on top of the cap and left side of hat."

The Twenty-fourth Corps was composed largely of veterans from the white troops of the Tenth and Eighteenth Corps. The adoption of a heart as the badge was announced in General Orders, No. 32, Headquarters, Twenty-fourth Army Corps, dated March 18, 1865. "The symbol selected is one which testifies our affectionate regard for all our brave comrades—alike the living and the dead—who have braved the perils of this mighty conflict, and our devotion to the sacred cause—a cause which entitled us to the sympathy of every brave and true heart and the support of every strong and determined hand."

The Twenty-fifth Corps was composed of the colored soldiers of the Tenth and Eighteenth Corps. The adoption of the device of a square with a small square set diagonally upon it, was announced in General Orders, Headquarters Twenty-fifth Army Corps, dated Feb. 20, 1865. General Weitzel, in this order, said, "In view of the circumstances under which this corps was raised and filled, the peculiar claims of its individual members upon the justice and fair dealing of the prejudiced and the regularity of the conduct of the troops which deserve those equal rights that have hitherto been denied the majority, the commanding general has been induced to adopted the square as the distinctive badge of the Twenty-fifth Corps. Wherever danger has been found and glory to be won, the heroes who have fought for immortality have been distinguished by some emblem to which every victory added a new lustre. They looked upon their badge with pride, for to it they had given its fame. Soldiers! to you is given a chance, in this spring campaign, of making this badge immortal. Let history record that on the banks of the James thirty thousand freemen not only gained their own liberty, but shattered the prejudice of the world, and gave to the land of their birth peace, union, and glory."

No order was issued concerning a badge for Hancock's First Corps, Veteran Volunteers. The badge used is thus described: "A circle is surrounded by a double wreath of laurel. A wide red band passes vertically through the centre of the circle. Outside the laurel wreath, rays form a figure with seven sides of concave curves. Seven hands, springing from the circumference of the laurel wreath, grasp spears, the heads of which form the seven points of the external radiated figure."

No order was issued concerning a badge for General Philip Sheridan's Cavalry Corps. Early in its service steps were taken to provide an appropriate device, but these were not ready for use until the summer of 1864. "This badge is described as gold-crossed sabres, on a blue field, surrounded by a glory in silver."

No order was issued concerning the badge of General J. E. Wilson's Cavalry Corps. A badge was adopted, used, and is thus described: "A red swallow-tail cavalry guidon, with crossed sabres in the field, suspended from a rifle or carbine."

No order was issued concerning a badge for General Judson Kilpatrick's Cavalry Command. By tacit consent the device of a red swallowtail flag with a small flag in the field, and on one of its streamers the word "Alice," on the other "Kilpatrick's Cavalry;" across the top three gilt stars, surmounted by an eagle.

The Signal Corps used the device of two flags crossed over the handle of a blazing torch, the flags being used for signalling during the day and the torch at night.

Section 1227, Revised Statutes, gives legal recognition to corps badges as follows: "All persons who have served as officers, noncommissioned officers, privates, or other enlisted men, in the Regular Army, volunteer or militia forces of the United States, during the war of the rebellion and have been honorably discharged from the service, or still remain in the same, shall be entitled to wear, on occasions of ceremony, the distinctive army badge ordered for or adopted by the army corps and division respectively in which they served."

NAVY

FLAGS

Flags of the Navy differed according to the rank of the fleet or unit commander. The flag of a rear admiral was rectangular, plain, and blue and was to be "worn at the mizzen." If two or more rear admirals in command afloat should meet, or be in the presence of each other, the senior only was to wear the flag of blue, the next in seniority to wear it of red, and the other or others to wear it of white. Rear admirals, and especially lesser officers, wore broad pendants.

A divisional mark and the mark of a senior officer present were both to be triangular in shape, with a middle part of a different color from the rest, in the form of a wedge, the base occupying one-third the whole hoist or head, and the point extending to the extremity of the fly. For a first division—blue, white, blue; second division—red, white, red; third division —white, blue, white; and for a senior officer present —white, red, white. (*Regulations for the Government of the United States Navy*, 1865)

UNIFORMS

The following regulations for officers' uniforms were issued by the Navy Department, July 31, 1862.

GENERAL ORDERS
UNIFORM FOR OFFICERS OF THE U. S. NAVY

Full dress—Frock coat, epaulettes, cocked hat, sword and knot, plain pantaloons, without lace or cord.

Undress—Same as full dress, without cocked hat, and with or without epaulettes or sword.

Service Dress—Same as undress, but without epaulettes.

In full dress, the coat to be always worn fully buttoned. All officers are required to conform strictly to the uniform prescribed. Officers are to wear their uniform, either full or undress, whenever they make official visits to the President of the United States, the Secretary of the Navy, or to foreign authorities and vessels of war; when acting as members of courts-martial, courts of inquiry, boards of examination, or of special boards, or when attending such boards as witnesses, or in any other capacity. The officer ordering such courts or boards may direct which description of dress to be worn.

Uniform is to be worn by all officers when attached to any vessel of the Navy, to any navy yard, station, recruiting service, hospital, or other naval service for duty, unless absent on leave.

Officers on furlough will not wear their uniform, except on special occasions of public ceremony; and officers, while suspended from duty by sentence of a court-martial, are strictly prohibited from wearing any part of their uniform.

On all occasions of ceremony, abroad or in the United States, when a Commanding Officer may deem it necessary to order the attendance of the officers under his command, he shall be careful in such order to prescribe the particular dress to be worn.

COAT

For an Admiral—Shall be a frock coat of navy-blue cloth, faced with the same, and lined with black silk serge; double breasted, with two rows of large Navy buttons on the breast, nine in each row, placed four inches and a half apart from eye to eye at top, and two inches and a half at bottom.

Rolling Collar; skirts to be full, commencing at the hip-bone and descending four-fifths thence towards the knee, with one button behind on each hip, and one near the bottom of each fold.

Cuffs to be plain, closed, and two and a half inches deep, with one strip of Navy gold lace, three-quarters of an inch wide, below the seam, but joining it, and two other similar strips on the sleeve above the cuff, (separated from each other by the space of three-quarters of an inch) together with three additional strips, each one-quarter of an inch wide, two of them in the spaces thus left, and the third one-quarter of an inch above the upper strip of the three-quarter inch lace (as per pattern.)

For a Commodore—Same in all respects as for an Admiral, except the upper (third) strip of narrow (one-quarter inch) lace on the sleeves above the cuffs.

For a Captain—Same as for a Commodore, except that the cuffs shall have but three strips of gold lace around them, each three-quarters of an inch wide, and placed one-half inch apart.

For a Commander—Same as for a Captain, except that the cuffs shall have two strips of gold lace around them, each three-quarters of an inch wide, separated by the space of three-quarters of an inch, and one strip of lace one-quarter of an inch wide in the space between.

For a Lieutenant Commander—Same as for a Commander, except that the cuffs shall have but two strips of lace around them, each three-quarters of an inch wide, separated by the space of half an inch.

For a Lieutenant—Same as for a Lieutenant Commander, except that the cuffs shall have one strip of gold lace three-quarters of an inch wide, and one strip one-quarter of an inch wide around them, separated by one-quarter of an inch.

For a Master—Same as for a Lieutenant, except that the cuffs shall have but one strip of gold lace three-quarters of an inch wide around the upper edge.

For an Ensign—Same as for a Master, except that the strip of lace around the upper edge of the cuff shall be but one-quarter of an inch wide.

For a Midshipman—The same as for an Ensign, except that medium size buttons shall be substituted for the large buttons; and without lace on the cuffs.

For a Master's Mate—To be a frock coat, of navy-blue cloth or flannel, rolling collar, single breasted, with nine navy buttons on the breast, one button behind on each hip, and one near the bottom on each fold, and none on the cuffs.

Shipped or Rated Master's Mates—Will wear a blue cloth or flannel jacket, rolling collar, double breasted, with two rows of medium size navy buttons on the breast, six in each row; open fly sleeve, with three small buttons in the opening.

Officers appointed on "temporary service" are not required to supply themselves with full dress uniforms, but are required to obtain undress uniforms and side arms.

Coats for all other officers to be the same as those now prescribed for *undress* of their respective grades, except that all cuffs will be closed and without small buttons, and with the same arrangement of lace as that worn by the "line officers" of same relative rank.

Jackets may be worn, as "service dress," by all officers, except at general muster or upon special occasions of ceremony, when a different dress is prescribed by the commanding officer; to be of navy-blue cloth, faced with the same, and lined with black silk serge; double or single breasted, as in the coat; rolling collar, with the same number of small sized buttons on the breast as for the coat, and with the same arrangement of lace on the cuffs, and the same shoulder straps.

PANTALOONS

For all Officers—To be of navy-blue cloth, or white drill, and are to be worn as prescribed by present regulations.

VESTS

For all Officers—Same as now worn.

COCKED HAT

For all Officers—Same as now worn.

CAP

For all Officers—To be of the same shape and dimensions as that now worn, and with the same description of gold lace around it as that prescribed by present regulations; and to have the following devices embroidered on the front above the band, viz:

For an Admiral, a gold wreath of oak and olive branches enclosing a silver five-pointed star one inch in diameter, as per pattern.

For a Commodore, Captain, Commander, and Lieutenant Commander, a gold wreath of oak and olive branches, enclosing a silver eagle and anchor, similar to that now prescribed for Captains, as per pattern.

For a Lieutenant, Master, and Ensign, a gold wreath of oak and olive branches enclosing a silver foul anchor one and a half inches in length, as per pattern.

For a Midshipman, the same as for an Ensign, except that the device on the front shall be a gold wreath of oak and olive branches enclosing a *plain* silver anchor one inch in length, placed vertically, as per pattern.

For a Master's Mate, to have a plain silver anchor in front without a wreath.

Shipped or Rated Master's Mates, to have the same cap as other Master's Mates, without the anchor in front.

EPAULETTES

For an Admiral—To be of the same form and dimensions as now prescribed for a *Captain,* and with the same device (of a silver eagle and anchor on the frog, with two stars above on the strap) as now prescribed for the *Senior Captain.*

For a Commodore—To be of the same form and dimensions as that now prescribed for a *Commander,* with the same device as for an Admiral, except that there shall be but one star on the strap.

For a Captain—To be the same as for a Commodore, without the star on the strap.

For a Commander—The same as for a Captain, except the device on the frog, which is to be a silver foul anchor two inches long, placed horizontally, with a silver leaf on each side, as per pattern.

For a Lieutenant Commander—To be the same as for a Commander, except that the leaves will be embroidered in gold.

For a Lieutenant—To be of the same form and dimensions as now prescribed; the device on the frog to be a silver foul anchor two (2) inches long placed vertically, with two silver bars, each three-quarters (¾) of an inch long and three-sixteenths (3/16) of an inch wide, on each side of the flukes of the anchor, as per pattern.

For a Master—Same in all respects as for a Lieutenant, except that there shall be but one bar on each side of the anchor.

For an Ensign—Same as for a Master, except that there shall be no bars with the anchor.

For all other Officers entitled to wear them, the epaulettes will be the same as now prescribed.

Sword, Sword Knot, and Belt

For all Officers—Same as now prescribed for Commissioned Officers.

Shoulder Straps

For an Admiral—To be of navy-blue cloth, four inches long and one inch and three-eighths wide, bordered with an embroidery of gold one-quarter of an inch in width, with a silver foul anchor one inch and three-quarters in length, placed in the middle, with a silver star five-eighths of an inch in diameter at each end, as per pattern.

For a Commodore—Same as for an Admiral, except that there shall be but one star with the anchor, placed as per pattern. (The crown of the anchor and point of the star each seven-sixteenths (7/16) of an inch from the inner edge of the border of the strap.)

For a Captain—Same as for a Commodore, except that the device shall be a silver eagle and anchor, two inches long, as per pattern.

For a Commander—Same as for a Captain, except that the device shall be a silver anchor one inch and three-quarters in length, placed in the middle, with a silver embroidered leaf nine-sixteenths of an inch at each end, as per pattern.

For a Lieutenant Commander—Same in all respects as for a Commander, except that the leaves shall be embroidered in gold.

For a Lieutenant—Same as for a Lieutenant Commander, except that there shall be, instead of the leaves, two gold embroidered bars on each side of the anchor, each one half inch long and one-eighth of an inch wide, as per pattern.

For a Master—Same as for a Lieutenant, except that there shall be but one bar on each side of the anchor.

For an Ensign—Same as for a Master, but without the bars. Shoulder straps to be always worn as distinctive marks when the epaulettes are not worn.

Buttons

To be the same as now prescribed.

Straw Hats

In summer, or in tropical climates, officers may wear white straw hats, under the same restrictions as in the case of jackets; the body of the hat to be not more than four inches and a half in height, nor the rim more than three and a half inches in width, with a band of plain black ribbon.

Overcoats, for all officers, shall be of navy-blue pilot cloth, double-breasted; rolling collar; skirts to descend to the knee, with the same number of large-sized navy buttons and similarly arranged as for undress, and with the same shoulder straps, and same arrangement of lace on the cuffs. Blue cloth cloaks may be worn in boats, or over the full dress, when rendered necessary by cold or wet weather.

No other changes than those herein specified are to be made in the uniform at present prescribed.

> GIDEON WELLES
> Secretary of the Navy.

Navy Department,
July 31, 1862.

Marine Corps

In 1852 the Navy Department published regulations governing the uniform of the Marine Corps. The Navy Department had earlier (1839) secured the approval of the President of the United States to the same regulations which were in effect a short time, when, in partial imitation of Army uniform modifications, these regulations were again revised. However, these regulations were not strictly adhered to during the Civil War. The Corps continued to supply most of its own equipment, which differed in many respects from that worn by Army units. For instance, a black cowskin knapsack was specified in the 1859 Marine Corps dress regulations. Although white cross belts were not specified in the regulations of 1859, Civil War photographs show them still being worn. The device on all caps was a bugle with an "M" inside its ring; Officers had theirs sewn on a red cloth patch. This was not changed to the familiar globe-and-anchor device until after the war (1868). Although the 1859 regulations ordered Marine NCO's to wear swords the "same as U. S. Infantry"—which meant the straight NCO sword of the model of 1840 with a cast brass hilt—the contemporary illustrations show first sergeants and others carrying the sword authorized for officers. Contemporary photographs bear out this usage.

On January 24, 1859 the dress of the Marine Corps was altered from that worn since 1840 to a more modern style with tunic and cap—a change which the Army had made eight years earlier. The new uniform is illustrated and described in great detail in *Regulations for the Uniform and Dress of the Marine Corps of the United States, October 1859* (Published by Charles Desilver of Philadelphia). The dress uniform prescribed in these regulations was worn by the Corps, with only a few changes, throughout the Civil War and until 1875. Company officers wore the same stiff cap as enlisted men, with gold pommon for full dress. Field officers in full dress wore the chapeau with red feather plume. On top of the officers undress cap appeared for the first time the 4-lobed knot, often referred to as the "clover leaf" or "French love knot" which is today one of the most distinctive features of the Marine officer's uniform. The 1859 regulations provided that Marine Corps officers would wear the regular naval officer's sword with black leather scabbard. Musicians continued to wear red coats. Chevrons were worn with points up at a time when the Army wore them with points down. (See H. Charles McBarron, Jr., "U. S. Marine Corps, 1859-1875" Journal of the Company of Military Collectors and Historians, Vol. I, No. 4, December 1949; and "U. S. Marine Corps, Field Service, 1859-1868," *Ibid.*, Vol. V, No. 2, June 1953.)

CHAPTER 12

Officers and Leadership

IN JANUARY, 1861, there were five officers of general rank in the United States Army. These were: Lieutenant General Winfield Scott, commissioned June 25, 1841; Brigadier General John E. Wool, June 25, 1841; Brigadier General David E. Twiggs, commissioned June 30, 1846; Brigadier General William S. Harney, commissioned June 14, 1858; and Brigadier General Joseph E. Johnston, commissioned June 28, 1860. Scott was retired on November 1, 1861, in place of the younger McClellan; Wool was assigned to the command of a Military Department June 1, 1862; Twiggs was dismissed from the service March 1, 1861; Harney retired August 1, 1863;[1] and Johnston resigned to join the Confederate Army. With the exception of Johnston, these senior officers of the Regular Army were too old for field service in April, 1861, and accordingly the President's first call for troops provided for five major generals and seventeen brigadier generals from the States.[2]

The Government had great difficulty in finding able commanders for the Federal forces in the early years of the war. The higher offices in the Army were for the most part entrusted to graduates of the Military Academy of whom 556 served in the Federal Army. Of these there were: 51 major generals; 91 brigadier generals; 106 colonels; 56 lieutenant colonels; 69 majors; 157 captains; and 32 lieutenants. The captains were mostly artillery officers.[3] The proportion of West Pointers among the officers of the Federal armies was from one and a half to twice as great as among the officers of the Confederate armies. In the Army of the Potomac and in the Army of Northern Virginia, the commanding general, the chief of artillery, chief of cavalry, chief quartermaster, chief commissary, and chief engineer officer were West Pointers.[4] Of the total number of West Point graduates who participated in the Civil War, 73 percent served in the Federal and 27 percent in the Confederate armies.[5] The scramble for high rank among some of the Regular Army officers was too great for President Lincoln to handle himself and the entire business was dropped in the lap of the appointment branch of the Adjutant General's Department. In at least one case the persistence of the wife of a Regular Army major resulted in his receiving a commission as brigadier general.[6]

PROFESSIONAL JEALOUSY AMONG OFFICERS

Although some commanders like Rosecrans kept inefficient generals in command because of an utter lack of firmness and an incapacity to hurt any man's feelings,[7] a more common phenomenon was a situation where professional jealousy prevented wholehearted co-operation between generals, even Regulars. When McDowell failed to advance during the Second Battle of Bull Run, he was denounced as a traitor by men of his own corps. Hooker's habit of criticizing his superiors was well known and he was not admired by the higher officers, who had grown up in the service with him.[8] In this same campaign another general (Fitz John Porter), at a time when he should have been marching his men to the front, took time to write a long letter to a friend in which he openly sneered at his commander. He exhibited himself plainly as "a disaffected subordinate writing professional libels on his superior while he neglected and delayed obedience in so systematic a way as to demonstrate that his commander was likely to fail in any combination which depended on his promptness or efficiency."[9] Even the cooperative spirit of McClellan in this campaign has been questioned. Schurz met some generals on the retreat "who expressed their pleasure at Pope's discomfiture without the slightest concealment, and spoke of our government in Washington with an affection of supercilious contempt."[10]

Although there is no laughter in a bickering between officers of high rank when that bickering can lead to loss of life through unwillingness to cooperate in battle, there is an occasional light moment. Certainly the exchange between Generals Naglee and Keyes provoked many a smile among those who knew the parties concerned. On June 15, 1863, Brigadier General Henry M. Naglee wrote Major General E. D. Keyes as follows:[11]

General:

I am most happy to advise you that I have been transferred with my brigade into the Department of North Carolina.

GENERAL JOSEPH HOOKER AND STAFF

1. Capt. Hall; 2. Gen. Geary (div. comdr.); 3. Gen. Butterfield (chief of staff); 4. Gen. Hooker; 5. Gen. LeDuc; 6. Capt. Kibler. Taken in Lookout Valley, winter of 1863-64.

It may be equally agreeable and satisfactory to you, as it certainly is to myself, to be assured that the separation will be a permanent one.

H. M. Naglee

On June 25, 1863, the following answer came back:
General:

Your letter of the 15th instant has been received. The happiness you express in your announcement of a permanent separation from me, is, I assure you, most cordially reciprocated. I will add, with the risk of being thought to exaggerate, that I do not believe any one of your previous commanding officers was made more happy at parting with you than I was.

Very respectfully, etc.
E. D. Keyes

Some volunteer officers who attained high rank but had not attended West Point believed that they were outside the pale. General Logan complained that the Regular Army officers regarded no man as a competent soldier who did not pass the "sacred portals of West Point; an *ex-cathedra* ban is pronounced by the institution against the volunteer officer, who is then registered as an empyric in the profession of arms." [12] However, Carl Schurz, who attained the rank of major general of volunteers, believed that although there were several volunteer officers of great merit developed during the war, the most efficient officers came from the Academy. [13]

In general it would appear that discipline was stronger in the East than in the West; this is explained partially at least by the fact that in the Eastern armies the number of West Pointers was much larger and their *esprit de corps* more pronounced and exclusive. The volunteers respected the superior training of the Regular officers but some, at least, resented their aristocratic exclusiveness. One writer expressed his dissatisfaction with the fact that there were numerous young men scattered through the Army, whose only point of superiority was that they had graduated at West Point. "This . . . [was] enough to excuse their blunders, their insults, and their unendurable superciliousness." [14] On the whole, however, no commander was more respected than the Regular Army officer who combined his training with courageous and intelligent leadership. He possessed the great advantage over his colleagues in the volunteer forces in that he had the training which they lacked. All else being equal, he was certain to make the best officer. Although McDowell, McClellan, Pope, Burnside, and Hooker failed, it must not be forgotten that Grant, Sherman, Sheridan, and Thomas definitely did not. As the war progressed, the common soldier adopted a "wait and see" attitude with respect to newly assigned generals. By 1864 the Federal soldier was not impressed with bombastic speeches or Napoleonic poses. When Sheridan joined the Army of the Potomac "he simply reviewed each [cavalry] division in turn, and without issuing any high-sounding general orders. The cavalry regarded him perhaps with more curiosity than any other feeling, and waited quietly to see what he would do. It did not take long to find out, for the campaign opened, and it is safe to say that General Sheridan proved all that had been expected of him by General Grant." [15]

POLITICAL APPOINTEES

A second source for general officers was found among well-known supporters of the administration and, in a few cases, equally well-known members of the opposition party. Lawyers who had entered the field of politics and thereby had become nationally known figures were offered commissions. Among the better known generals of this type were Banks, Butler, Baker, Logan, and Blair, several of whom left seats in Congress to serve in the Army. Butler was a general of Massachusetts militia, while Banks had served as governor of Massachusetts and Speaker of the House. Both were made major generals of volunteers, but Frémont, who had unsuccessfully contended with Buchanan for the Presidency in 1856 was made a major general in the Regular Army. It would seem that there was no need of giving to any untried civilian a rank so high that of itself it constituted a constant temptation to entrust him with an important command.[16]

It is difficult at this late day to realize how closely intertwined were politics and military commissions. "The ties of relationship, of friendship, of party consideration, considerations of speculation even, cause to be named for very important positions men totally incapable of filling them."[17] When an influential man raised a regiment, the President often had to accept it, even though there might be good reasons for doubting the man's leadership capabilities. One man would be commissioned a major because he helped to "carry" Pennsylvania; another, because he was a relative of the Secretary of State.[18] The Postmaster General felt no hesitation in personally requesting the President to commission one of his wife's relatives a brigadier general.[19] In fact the whole organization of the volunteer force may be said to have been political though one hears more of "political generals" than of political captains or lieutenants. Cox relates the case of a lieutenant being forced by his captain (a splendid soldier) to resign on account of his general inefficiency. A few months later that same lieutenant took the field again as a lieutenant colonel of a new regiment while the captain still stood at the head of his fraction of a company in the line.[20] As late as 1864 a man was commissioned a quartermaster by one of the governor's council to whom he owed money, and who conceived this as a plan for getting him the ways and means for payment. The quartermaster made and sold pies in partnership with an enlisted man to hasten the liquidation of his debt![21]

The State governors not only issued the commissions to their regiments while still under State control but retained that privilege after those regiments had been mustered into the United States service. General Sherman questioned this right but was informed by the War Department that "vacancies occurring among the commissioned officers in volunteer regiments will be filled by the governors of the respective states by which the regiments are furnished".[22] As the war went on and the ranks of the armies began to thin, instead of filling up the old and tried regiments experienced in field service, the ex-

pedient was adopted of forming new regiments of raw men, from the colonel down; when these came into the field it was not an unusual thing to see new colonels, who had never heard a shot fired and could not give a command correctly, placed over the heads of lieutenant colonels and majors who had been through a dozen battles. Sometimes, to remedy the disadvantages of a poor colonel, the Washington authorities would make him a brigadier general; that is, if he had sufficient political influence to bring to bear. Since the law prescribed the maximum number of major and brigadier generals, political and military pressure combined to keep the list always full. On one occasion Grant wanted to have Brigadier General W. F. Smith, an excellent officer, promoted but there was no vacancy.[23] Sherman spoke out very bluntly when his choices were ignored in favor of two political favorites "who left us in the midst of bullets, to go to the rear in search of personal advancement."[24] On one occasion an inefficient colonel, who had a habit of missing battles, went to Washington on sick leave, but returned later with the stars of a brigadier general.[25] It appears that there was little use for commanders to send worthless officers to the rear. They either came back, sometimes with increased rank won in Washington, or they rested content in some soft place where they could draw their pay in perfect security.

Efficient officers in the field were often discriminated against because their politics were those of the opposition party. Gibbon believed that the war was unnecessarily prolonged because of the fact that generals commanding armies in the field were judged "*not* by their military capacity but by their opinions upon the slavery question or any other political issue."[26] It would appear, however, that the retaining of McClellan in command, despite his insubordinate antagonism to the administration, would indicate a sincere desire on the part of Lincoln to prosecute the war irrespective of political differences. It is a well-known fact that Hancock, although a Democrat, was entrusted with important command. Many of the governors, however, lacked Lincoln's breadth of vision and oneness of purpose; they were influenced by political considerations when, in many cases, they did their country and individuals injustice by the refusal to subordinate party or local interests for the nation's good. The efficient leadership of Colonel Cross in the field did not compensate for his criticism of certain Republican measures, but one of his officers believed that if McClellan and Hooker had at all times been actuated by Cross' firm belief in victory "the army would not have come to look upon a retreat as the natural sequence of a day when we did not succeed."[27] Condemnation of the governors' policy must not be made without reservation. Officers and men in the Federal service were often too prone to carry their politics with them into the

Army. Sharp scrutiny of officers was necessary in many cases; one can appreciate the concern of the secretary of the Republican State Central Committee of Michigan when he discovered that the colonel of a regiment was, as he believed, a "miserable copperhead." In writing to the Governor he advised caution or they might have "another Col. proposing to raise a white flag and march a whole Reg. over to the rebel lines because he didn't like the Emancipation Proclamation."[28]

OFFICERS OF FOREIGN ORIGIN

The support of the important foreign groups was encouraged by the granting of commissions to certain of their influential members. The most prominent of these were: French, Brigadier General Philip Regis de Trobriand; Irish, Brigadier Generals Michael Corcoran and Thomas Meagher; German, Major Generals Carls Schurz, Julius H. Stahel, Franz Sigel, and Brigadier General Alexander Schimmelfennig. Of these de Trobriand and Schurz appear to have been capable officers. Sigel was "entirely unfit" for high command because of deficiency in tactics, logistics, and discipline.[29] Schimmelfennig was chosen because something had to be done that would be "unquestionably in the interest of the Dutch."[30] The Prussian and Austrian armies furnished a large contingent of "shipwrecked officers who mostly had to run away before their creditors, or who escaped the consequences of some duel, breach of discipline, if not some less pardonable sins."[31]

The war gave these officers a new lease on life. In December, 1861, Secretary of War Cameron sent a circular letter to eighteen State governors requesting that they appoint foreign officers of military education to regimental positions believing that such appointments would tend to increase the efficiency of the volunteer forces by giving to inexperienced officers competent instructors and to regiments able and skillful commanders.[32] Despite this official encouragement, the foreign officers who secured positions in the Federal Army did not, as a rule, prove very successful. One of them managed to ruin the 39th New York Infantry before he was cashiered for some irregularities in his pay accounts. The regiment was composed of Germans, Hungarians, Italians, Spaniards, and Swiss. It lost 15 officers through resignation and as many more by dismissal.[33]

UNFIT OFFICERS

There were other ways to ruin regiments too. The colonel of the 1st Massachusetts Cavalry was an admirable disciplinarian and organizer but, according to Charles Francis Adams, "he was all-outside. There was no real stuff in him . . . As an officer, in presence of the enemy on under the stress of campaign . . . [the colonel] was an utter failure and so recognized." Yet this colonel was a West Point graduate and had been a cavalry instructor at the Academy.[34] Another regiment, the 93rd Pennsylvania Infantry, had as its colonel one who "don't look for his rights. He is afraid to speak to a Gen'l. It would be a blessing if they would send him home for he is not fit to be here."[35] When the colonel had difficulty in getting his men camped in a swamp and complained to General Hancock that the whole trouble was the bad state of the ground, the general accurately gauged the difficulty in his statement: "Bad Hell! it's bad luck of the regiment."[36] Many of the early commissioned officers were political hacks who had paid off by State governors for political debts, "Of the art of war proper—of commanding troops—of discipline—of even the subsistence of soldiers, these gentlemen too frequently know little or nothing. The real patriotism of the State [of Iowa] . . . was oftenest in the ranks of the common soldier. The privates had volunteered out of more patriotism, not to get commissions and glory. Mistakes as to military appointments were made by the Governor constantly . . ." Usually the field officers in Iowa had no claim to their commissions but that they wanted the office very badly. Many of these officers by bitter experience learned their business; a few were promoted as the war went on, despite demonstrated unfitness; gradually some were dismissed the service; and very many were compelled to resign the commissions they had only disgraced."[37] Of the first 38 colonels from New York, those officers elected to their positions were not examined as to competency or conditioned in any respect; they were commissioned without question. The result was that about two-thirds of these officers failed to serve their full term of two years, having been discharged or having resigned, in the meantime; at least one-third of them resigned within the first six months.[38]

Regimental commanders were usually selected by the governors of the States in which the regiments were raised. Often indifferent men, with a little skill in drilling soldiers and with no other known qualifications, were sought out and commissioned as colonels or field officers. The Governor of Iowa seemed much less interested in military knowledge than in sobriety. He required a certificate as to the sober habits of all officers elected—but, in spite of this, drunkenness was not less common among officers than was incompetency. Still, as a rule, drunken officers also left the service long before the war ended. "The list of Iowa officers suspended, dismissed, resigned, or forced to go home, is discreditable."[39] A volunteer regiment was considered fortunate if it had among its field officers a lieutenant from the Regular Army or even a person from civil life who had gained some little military knowledge elsewhere.

By a general order the War Department directed that all vacancies among the company officers be filled by elections held in the companies concerned, and all vacancies among the field officers be filled by election among the commissioned officers of the regiment.[40] Some of the selections were very poor; the 115th Illinois Infantry lost 17 officers in three months by resignation and dismissal.[41] One colonel, the son-in-law of a lieutenant governor and a good lawyer, was utterly ignorant of his duties, but nevertheless was given the command of a prisoner of war camp.[42] In one case, the long pursuit of an enemy force ended ignominiously because the colonel in charge of the pickets believed that his general wanted the enemy to clear out and also because the colonel deemed it unwise to disturb his superior after a hard day's work![43] On another occasion, the 3rd Ohio Infantry was aroused at midnight by its colonel, who prepared his men for battle with the following encouraging words:[44]

Soldiers of the Third: The assault on the enemy's works will be made in the early morning. The Third will lead the column. The secessionists have ten thousand men and forty rifled cannon. They are strongly fortified. They have more men and more cannon than we have. They will cut us to pieces. Marching to attack such an enemy, so entrenched and so armed, is marching to a butcher shop rather than to a battle. There is bloody work ahead. Many of you boys will go out who will never come back again.

These cases were not isolated ones, nor were all the incompetents to be found among the colonels. The election of company officers seemed best at the beginning of the war but election of field officers ought not to have been permitted. The evils came of a bad system in which men were commissioned whose only prominence was in local politics—and also the system was bad in that it permitted companies and line officers to elect their favorites to command just as they elected men at home to the Legislature or Congress, regardless of special fitness. The system was very democratic, but pernicious and unheard of in military selections.[45] The young Regulars should have been encouraged to enter the volunteer service. However, the Army would not have been as closely identified with the people if it had come too completely under Regular officers.

OFFICERS' AGES

In the appointment of officers for the volunteer regiments some of the governors discriminated against very young men. Nelson A. Miles was refused a captain's commission in 1861 one the score of youthfulness. He began as a lieutenant at 22 and was a major general 4 years later.[46] Early in the war Cameron believed that no colonel should be over 45 years of age, no lieutenant colonel over 40, no major over 35; no captain should be under 30 and no lieutenant over 22.[47] The ages of officers when commissioned averaged probably about five years higher than the enlisted men.[48] With a few exceptions the great

commanders of the war, on both sides, were considerably above this average. Grant was 39 when the war began; Sherman, 40; Sheridan, 30; Meade and Hooker, 46; Thomas, 45; Rosecrans, 42; Buell, 43; Burnside, 37; and McClellan, 35. Most of the regiments, East and West, went to the front headed by men over 40 years of age. There were several noteworthy exceptions, however, in which youthful officers commanded large units before the war was over; but in all cases they started above the grade of private to their original muster. Custer was the youngest of a quartet of dashing cavalry leaders which included James H. Wilson, 23 years of age, and Judson Kilpatrick and Wesley Merritt, both 25. These four men were all graduates of the Military Academy and served as generals in the field. Henry W. Lawton of Indiana entered the service as a first sergeant and commanded his regiment as a lieutenant colonel when barely 20. Another westerner, Arthur MacArthur of Wisconsin, was denied the chance of going to West Point but at the age of 17 was appointed adjutant of the 24th Wisconsin Infantry. He was promoted to major and lieutenant colonel while still 18 and commanded his regiment at Resaca and Franklin. At Missionary Ridge he won a Medal of Honor for carrying his regiment's flag ahead of the charging line. Of the 2,778,304 Federal soldiers, over 2,000,000 were not 22 years of age at enlistment and 1,151,438 were not even 19.[49]

ELECTED OFFICERS

The company officer at the beginning of the war was more often than not a thrifty middle-aged farmer or a county or town magistrate. Absolutely ignorant of tactics he would find that his habits of mind and body were too fixed for him to learn the new business into which he had plunged. It was a very rare thing for a man of middle age to make a good company officer. A great many who tried at the beginning had to be eliminated. On May 4, 1861, the War Department ordered that two-thirds of the company officers be appointed at the commencement of a regiment's organization; and the remaining one-third should be appointed when the regiment had its full complement of men from among the sergeants, on the recommendation of the colonel of the regiment, approved by the brigade commander. Corporals would then be chosen from among the privates, sergeants from among the corporals, and the first sergeant would be selected by the captain.[50] This order was not applied in the subsequent calls for men, and the general practice in all States was for the men to elect their own company officers. Experience proved that it was unwise to interfere with the results of company officers duly elected. Occasionally a colonel would not recognize the company's choice but friction usually followed such interference. A considerable portion of the officers elected were incompetent to command. Many were elected because of brief terms of service in the Black Hawk or Mexican Wars. Personal courage was not wanting in these men, but they lacked physical strength and stamina. Some were indolent, some had acquired intemperate habits, and the majority of them possessed little military aptitude. Such a man was the captain of Co. "D," 61st Illinois Infantry, whose service in the Black Hawk War gave him "immense prestige" but who never could learn to drill, except the most simple company movements. At drill he would order "Swing around, boys, just like a gate."[51] Even the efficient captains did not necessarily make good field officers or colonels.

TYPES OF OFFICERS

It would appear that there were three general types of officers elected by their companies. The first type, consisting of able, honorable, accomplished men, was animated by the highest motives and governed by a genuine solicitude for the welfare of their men. The second sort was made up of equally brilliant men, but selfish, unscrupulous, and tyrannical. The lower the rank of this type of officer, the more he desired to show his power. Men of this type often secured their elections by bribery. This bribery was possible because of the election system. On Monday a whole company enlisted as privates. On Tuesday three out of the hundred men, not the best or worthiest often, withdrew from the common barracks to a seclusion, a privilege, and a power, which meant a distinction and an advantage that can best be appreciated by an intelligent man who has served as an enlisted man himself. The transition was so sudden, the distinction so absolute, the gulf so broad, that the officer sometimes forgot to be a man; and the private, bewildered, forgot to be a soldier. In one company, ten men were promised sergeancies and twenty-one corporal's warrants by the man who was eventually elected captain. Those who voted against him paid a bitter price for their opposition. The day after the election one of the captain's opponents in the voting, a student at Dartmouth College, failed to hear a command whereupon the captain hit him sharply across the face with his sword. Such officers incited men to desertion or perhaps ultimate revenge. The incident above was related to the author by Color Sergeant Francis H. Buffum, 14th New Hampshire Infantry. The captain decided not to return with the regiment at the end of the war but settled in Georgia where four of his old company looked him up and killed him. A third class of officers may be somewhat loosely characterized as good natured imbeciles. These men avoided ever giving commands of any sort but tried to curry favor with their men. All of this sash-girted rubbish soon floated homeward on the happy currents of eagerly accepted resignations, and better men from the ranks stepped into positions they should have originally occupied.

LOSS OF OFFICERS

Officer ranks were depleted by several causes but whether it was by death, retirement, resignation, or dismissal, the officers who remained on duty had a double burden until new men were commissioned. After a severe campaign it was not unusual to find several companies with no officers at all. The following letter illustrates the problem of filling officer vacancies, a problem which confronted many combat regiments.[52]

INFANTRY LIEUTENANT

This photo of Lieut. C. F. Allen was probably taken during the shaking-down period which occurred when a new unit arrived at the front. He will soon discard his sash and leggings. The blouse is typical of those worn by officers in the field.

Camp of 104 N. Y. Vol.
Thoroughfare Gap, Va.
Oct. 21, 1863

Capt. Wyley

Dear Sir:

As there is but little prospect of receiving any more drafted men at present and as there is no sign by which we can conclude that any of the officers at Richmond will be with us very soon, and as we need more officers I would most respectfully ask that if it is possible and you are able to do duty, you report to the regiment. You have no idea how the few officers we have here have to work. Besides it makes me as much again trouble and work, not having an officer to each Company. Muster day is near at hand and we should have at least one officer to a Company, and how to get along farther without more officers I know not. We have had a pretty hard campaign since we left the Rapidan in Marching and night duty. We made a quick march from there to Centerville. March from Raccoon Ford to near Culpepper, C. H. thence to Kelly's ford in one day. Camped there one day thence to Bristow in one day. Thence to Centerville by noon the next day. That afternoon the division was sent to the stone bridge over Bull Run and was ordered to post a picket line of five hundred (500) men from the bridge down to Cub Run and up to form a junction with the pickets of the 6th Corps on our right. Got through after daylight and then was recalled across Cub Run. Remained there until midnight when I was ordered to take command of four regiments and go to Bull Run bridge to support the cavalry there without an aide or any help except one orderly. Stayed there fortifying on each side of the bridge four days when we moved with the Corps to Haymarket. The next day I was put on duty as division officer and was ordered to withdraw the pickets about 8 o'clock. And we marched through the gap where we are now in camp.

I hope you will oblige me by coming as soon as you possibly can to help us. Lt. Rose is here awaiting the sentence of a Court martial for disobedience of orders. Will be dismissed, I think, at least. Lt. Stark is discharged, thank the Lord, he wishes me to recommend him for the Invalid Corps as 1st Lt. which I think I will not do in a way that will help him much. Hoping to see you soon and with regards to all with you, I am Sir,

Yours

Gilbert G. Prey

At no time during the war was the hardship anything at all equal to the summer of 1864. While the work was most severe and unremitting, there were fewer officers to perform it. The pay amounted to very little. Several sergeants in the 1st Massachusetts Cavalry, (and other regiments), declined a promotion, which brought with it excessive responsibility and totally inadequate pay, in some cases indebtedness instead of pay. During this period not a single squadron in the 1st Massachusetts was commanded by an officer of higher rank than second lieutenant. Only two captains were present on duty, and each commanded a battalion. Several companies had no officers, and were assigned to officers commanding other companies.[53] Some enlisted men even had little desire to take on the responsibilities of the higher noncommissioned grades. One ex-officer considered the first sergeantcy of a company to be the most difficult position he ever had in the Army.

If any one thinks that the life of an orderly [first] sergeant in active service is an amiable one let him try it. When the men are not growling about you the Captain is growling at you, and you are constantly between two fires. About one-third of the men in Company 'A' had been members of the "Old Battalion," and the town meeting tactics that prevailed in the militia had not quite died out. I was a recruit, and my promotion was not hailed with joy by the old men. They drew up a petition, asking for a change, and some twenty men signed and, through a committee, presented it to the Captain. "What is this?" said the Captain. "A petition for a change in first sergeant," was the reply. "Petition! This is mutiny. Go to your quarters, and if I hear more of this I will have every man court-martialed and sent to Dry Tortugas." There was no more trouble.[54]

In killed and mortally wounded the ratio of officers to men was 1 to 18, but the organizational ratio at muster in was 1 to 25. Only one officer died for every ninety men who died of disease.[55] The reasons for the disproportionate losses of the enlisted men by disease are several. In the first place, the officers received better shelter and food. They had superior advantages for maintaining personal cleanliness and not being crowded together as much as their men were therefore less subject to contagious diseases. As prisoners of war they were generally treated more leniently than were their men. By no means the least potential cause was the superior morale, the hopefulness and elasticity of spirit, which is given to a man by investing him with a commission and its accompanying authority, responsibility, and chances of advancement.

RETIREMENT AND RESIGNATION

Commissioned officers who had completed forty consecutive years in the Regular Army were permitted to retire by making personal application to the President. All commissioned officers of the Regular Army who became incapable of performing the duties of their office were likewise placed on the retired list and withdrawn from active service and command.[56] Any Regular Army officer was permitted to resign by making application through his commanding officer to the Adjutant General of the Army. Officers of the volunteer service could tender their resignation by applying through their immediate commanders to the commander of the Department or army corps in which they served. The commander was authorized to grant the discharge; he then notified the Adjutant General who communicated the information to the governor of the State concerned.[57] Cases of resignation by volunteer officers became so numerous after Bull Run that the War Department ordered increased vigilance on the part of regimental, brigade, and Department commanders to prevent abuse, and directed them to insist on the observance of regular channels in the forwarding of applications. In each case a clear statement was required as to the cause which led to the resignation.[58]

EXAMINING BOARDS

A system of examing boards was established to examine the capacity, qualification, propriety of conduct, and efficiency of any commissioned officer of volunteers. The boards were to consist of from three to five officers appointed by generals commanding departments or detached armies. If the board's report was adverse, the commission of the officer should be vacated on approval of the President. It was provided that no officer should sit on the board whose rank or promotion would be affected and at least two officers should be of equal rank to the accused.[59] These boards improved discipline and raised the dignity of the officer class in the estimation of the men by purging the personnel of the list of officers. By far the most numerous type of officers brought before these boards were incompetents whose riddance was necessary for the good of the service.

The examiners always favored those who were known to be disposed to learn their profession but those convicted of downright ignorance had no mercy shown to them. One Regular officer thought it hard for prominent citizens recently commissioned who had generously spent their time and money to raise regiments not to be permitted to reap some benefit for their labor and sacrifice. "It did seem a little cruel to examine them in Army regulations and tactics!"[60] The inefficient field officers of one regiment were examined and informed that they either resign or charges would be preferred against them. It was a bitter disappointment to them all; they were happy and contented in their positions; one of them wondered why they had not been left alone, remarking that "we were all making a good living."[61] A good examining board was able to form a just estimate of a man's fitness for command. One observer believed that there should be a board with every army or corps headquarters.[62] Regimental commanders had a strong role in recommending who should ap-

pear before these boards and at times their selections were probably influenced by personal reasons.[63]

The examining boards for candidates for commissions as colonels of regiments were very rigid in their standards. The applicants were required to show, first of all, a thorough knowledge of Casey's *Tactics*. Since General Casey himself was in charge of the examinations, the questions on his system of tactics were detailed and extensive. In addition, the aplicant had to have a good knowledge of history, geography, arithmetic, algebra, and geometry. Then came the "Army Regulations," "Articles of War," and muster and pay rolls. In fact, the applicant had to be fully as well posted for a second lieutenant's commission as many colonels of volunteers were in these subjects. During the two-weeks stay of one applicant, two lieutenant colonels and many line officers were rejected as unfit for second lieutenants. In addition to the tests outlined above, the applicants were subjected to a searching physical examination and no matter how well an applicant may have done in the other tests, if he was not passed by the medical authorities he was rejected.[64]

DISMISSAL

In the summer of 1862, at Stanton's wish, Congress passed a law authorizing the summary dismissal of officers at the discretion of the President.[65] "Move or be removed" was the rule. Stanton used this law to rid the service of officers who were continually absent from their commands for one purpose or another. Often an officer who had been dismissed would proceed to Washington and demand a revision of his case and reinstatement into his former position.[66] Some officers, like the lieutenant who had been dismissed for drunkenness on duty, would appeal to the governor of their State, often asking for a new commission in another regiment.[67] Usually these appeals were of little avail and by 1864 there were comparatively few incompetents left in the Federal Army. With Grant came stricter discipline; many generals were sent to Washington and the soldiers saw no more of them.[68]

NOTES, CHAPTER 12

1. United States War Department, Adjutant General's Department, *Official Army Register for 1861*, pp. 3-4. "General Order No. 94," November 1, 1861, *General Orders for 1861*. "General Order No. 58," June 4, 1862, *General Orders for 1862*, Wool was retired August 1, 1863. "General Order No. 5," March 1, 1861, *General Orders for 1861*. Adjutant General's Department, *Official Army Register for 1864*, p. 60.

2. *Official Records*, Third Series, Vol. 1, p. 69, There was a total of 3,549 commissioned officers included in the April 15, 1861 call for 75,000 men.

3. Upton, p. 237.

4. This was also true in other armies.

5. Close to relative white populations of the North and South.

6. Fry, James B., *Military Miscellanies*, pp. 280-281.

7. *Official Records*, First Series, Vol. 30, Part 1, p. 220.

8. *Official Records*, First Series, Vol. 32, Part 2, pp. 467-469.

9. Cox, J. D., *The Second Battle of Bull Run as Connected with the Fitz-John Porter Case*, p. 13.

10. Schurz, Carl, *Reminiscences*, Vol. 2, p. 382.

11. Keyes, E. D., pp. 478-479.

12. Logan, John, *The Volunteer Soldier in America*, p. 582.

13. Schurz, Vol. 2, pp. 348-349.

14. Hepworth, G. H., *The Whip, Hoe, and Sword*, pp. 239-240.

15. Crowninshield, p. 202.

16. Ropes, J. C., *The Story of the Civil War*, Vol. 1, pp. 112-113.

17. Lecomte, Ferdinand. *The War in the United States,* pp. 93-94.

18. *The Spectator,* Vol. 34 (July 27, 1861), p. 806.

19. Croffut, p. 65.

20. Cox, Vol. 1, p. 439, Cox states that this was not a singular instance but one that occurred "literally by the thousand . . ." *Ibid.*

21. Livermore, *Days and Events,* p. 461.

22. Colonel Dwight A. Woodbury, 4th Michigan Infantry to Governor Blair (Michigan), August 29, 1861. Manuscript letter in Burton Historical Collection.

23. *Official Records,* First Series, Vol. 31, Part 3, pp. 122, 277, 458, 571; Vol. 32, Part 2, pp. 79-80.

24. *Ibid.,* Vol. 38, Part 5, p. 247.

25. Testimony of General Gibbon before the Committee on the Conduct of the War, Committee's Report, Second Series (1865), Vol. 1, p. 447.

26. Gibbon, p. 242.

27. Livermore, *Days and Events,* p. 257.

28. Secretary W. S. Wood, Republican State Central Committee, Detroit, September 15, 1864, to Governor Blair. Manuscript in Burton Historical Collection.

29. *Official Records,* First Series, Vol. 3, p. 95; Vol. 36, Part 2, p. 840.

30. Lincoln to Stanton, Fry, *Military Miscellanies,* p. 281.

31. Salm-Salm, pp. 24-25. See also Agassiz, p. 262.

32. Upton, pp. 242-243.

33. Perhaps the mixture of nationalities was to blame.

34. Adams, Charles Francis, *An Autobiography,* p. 138.

35. Waltz, Henry J. Lieutenant, 93rd Penn. Infantry, Entry for July 7, 1864. Petersburg, Va. Diary in author's possession.

36. Westbrook, R. S., *History of the 49th Pennsylvania Volunteers,* p. 102.

37. Byers, S. H. M., *Iowa in War Times,* pp. 72-73.

38. Burt, Silas W., p. 31.

39. Byers, pp. 72-73.

40. United States War Department, "General Order No. 49," August 3, 1861, *General Orders for 1861.*

41. Royse, p. 64.

42. *Official Records,* Second Series, Vol. IV, pp. 195-208.

43. Croushore, p. 91.

44. Ford, ed., *Memoirs of a Volunteer* (John Beatty, 3rd Ohio Infantry), pp. 25-26.

45. Byers, pp. 72-73.

46. Miles, *passim.*

47. *Official Records,* Third Series, Vol. 1, pp. 227-228.

48. Later men were commissioned from the ranks.

49. *Photographic History,* Vol. 8, pp. 194-196.

50. United States War Department, "General Order No. 15," May 4, 1861, *General Orders for 1861.*

51. Stillwell, L. *The Story of a Common Soldier of Army Life in the Civil War 1861-1865,* p. 12.

52. Letter of Gilbert G. Prey, 104th New York Infantry, October 21, 1863, Manuscript in author's possession.

53. Crowinshield, p. 233.

54. Adams, (19th Massachusetts Infantry), pp. 21-22.

55. Killed and mortally wounded during the War totalled 5,221 officers and 90,886 enlisted men, *House Executive Documents,* 39 Cong., 1 Sess., Documents 1, Part 1, p. 73.

56. United States War Department, "General Order No. 54, August 10, 1861, *General Orders for 1861.*

57. *Ibid., Revised Regulations for the Army of the United States 1861,* Article 5, Section 25; Article 52, Section 1647, p. 497.

58. *Ibid.,* "General Order No. 51," August 3, 1861. *General Orders for 1861.*

59. *Ibid.,* "General Order No. 49," August 3, 1861, *General Orders for 1861.*

60. Howard, Vol. 1, p. 168. The officer was Colonel Henry W. Slocum.

61. Ward, George W., *History of the Second Pennsylvania Veteran Heavy Artillery,* p. 18.

62. *Army and Navy Journal* Vol. 1 (May 7, 1864), p. 614.

63. Such appeared to be the case in the 5th New Hampshire Infantry.

64. Norton, p. 184.

65. United States War Department, "General Order No. 91," July 29, 1862, *General Orders for 1862.*

66. *Army and Navy Journal,* Vol. 1 (April 16, 1864), p. 564.

67. Lieutenant Frederick Haxford, 19th Michigan Infantry, to Governor Blair, August 7, 1862, Manuscript in Burton Historical Collection.

68. Wilkeson, p. 38.

CHAPTER 13

Discipline

A S SOON AS a Federal unit completed its organization the officers commenced the process of instilling discipline into the command. Many observers considered the man in the ranks to be of excellent quality but the deficiency too often was in the quality of the officers.[1] Until the weeding-out process was completed the officers did not stand towards the men in the relations that officers should occupy towards those whom they were to put into battle and hold up to their work. There was probably considerable truth in the statement of the veteran who believed the awful death-roll of the Federal armies was lengthened at least on-fourth, probably one-third, by the want of wholesome though irksome discipline during the first months in service.[2] In many cases this lack of discipline continued throughout the entire term. Those regiments subjected to the strictest discipline invariably made excellent records in combat and usually lost the fewest men from disease. Laxity of discipline was not so much indicated by outward mutiny as by a mild but dangerous defiance of, or contempt for, those necessary rules which long experience had found to be necessary for an efficient organization. Many Federal soldiers agreed with the enlisted man who held that "that soldier is best whose good sense tells him when to be merely a part of a machine and when not."[3] Lack of discipline often prevented the exploitation of Federal successes. At Gettysburg, for example, very few Confederates were captured following Picket's repulse. This was due in part, to the men not waiting for orders from their colonels. They started to leave their lines to collect souvenirs and otherwise trifle instead of staying together, ready to make a counter-attack.[4] The idea appeared to be fairly generally held that the Federal volunteer forces could get along without discipline. Nevertheless, some volunteer regiments were very well disciplined.

Poor Officers the Cause of Poor Discipline

Much of the whole problem of poor discipline can be attributed to the kind of officers selected, for "there was no such thing in the late war as a regiment of cowards. Inefficient or timid officers may have given their commands a bad name, and caused them to lose confidence in success, and hence to become unsteady or panicky. The average American is not deficient in true courage. Careful drill and discipline make good soldiers."[5] A volunteer officer believed that there was no regiment in the army so good that it could not be utterly spoiled in three months by a poor commander, nor so poor that it could not be altogether transformed in six by a good one. The difference in material he believed, was nothing— "white or black, German or Irish; so potent is military machinery that an officer who knows his business can make good soldiers out of almost everything, give him but a fair chance."[6] This ability to make or unmake an organization is well illustrated by Mott's division which was Hooker's old fighting division on the Peninsula and later, but in the Wilderness Campaign had served under two commanders of such little merit or force of character as to render it practically worthless.[7] One officer of high rank, previously eminent in civil life, could only vindicate himself before a court-martial from the ruinous charge of false muster by summoning a staff officer to prove that it was his custom to sign all military papers without looking at them.[8] An officer riding through a regimental camp "whose utterly filthy condition seemed enough to send malaria through a whole military department," was asked by the colonel, almost with tears in his eyes, to explain to him why his men were dying at the rate of one a day.[9] Yet this regiment had been in service nearly a year and its colonel had had almost two years of service with the Army of the Potomac.

Discipline In Regular Army

Discipline in the Regular Army had been rigid before the war when its enlisted men were mainly drawn from the immigrant class. Some splendid achievement was required to enable the noncommissioned officer to take a seat among his former chiefs; it was only in 1861 that a commission was appointed for the examination and regular admission of a certain number of noncommissioned officers to the rank of officers.[10] Throughout the war the exacting discipline of the Regular Army tended to discourage volunteer enlistments in its ranks. With the volunteers some of the lack of discipline was really a lack of soldierly etiquette. In many regiments the men failed to salute officers. They performed guard duty with languid indifference. New regiments would often ridicule other volunteer organizations that were properly dressed and equipped and well disciplined.[11] Regular Army officers had difficulty in dealing with raw volunteers who were totally different in attitude from the enlisted men whom they had commanded before the war. On one occasion a general fell afoul of a gawky lieutenant who a few weeks previously had been a carpenter. The lieutenant, dressed in trousers and a red shirt, and barefoot, was seated on the head of a barrel, eating an apple and gossiping with a sentry. On the appearance of the general this volunteer officer saluted but did not rise or cease munching his apple, whereupon the general endeavored to explain to him military courtesy and finally "with an expression of disgusted despair . . . stalked away to blow up a sentry whom he found sitting down on post."[12]

VOLUNTEERS INTOLERANT OF ARMY DISCIPLINE

Much of the formality of military practice appeared as a useless waste of time to volunteers. Men who had been working all their lives for a purpose could see little use in pacing up and down doing nothing.[13] It took some time to instill into the volunteer soldier, accustomed to the democracy of civil life, the realization that a system of "caste" existed in the army and that one of the first essentials of military life was conformity to that system. One officer believed the army to be an aristocracy on a three-years' lease and that the undemocratic character, so often lamented in West Point and Annapolis, was in reality their strong point.[14]

The criticism was often made that in the Federal Army many soldiers were relatively superior to their officers.[15] Early in the war McClellan reported the dissatisfaction of the men with their immediate commanders.[16] Indeed one observer believed that most of the evils in the army were directly attributable to the officers. Holding that the men were as good as could be desired the observer believed that they could be brought to as high a state of discipline and drill as in the Regular Army "if only the officers . . . [could] be taught to at least imitate gentlemen, and gain the respect and confidence rather than the good will and votes of their men."[17] The lack of respect engendered by poor leadership resulted too often in the men obeying only those commands that recommended themselves to their common sense. In nine cases out of ten the soldier utterly detested being commanded while the officer, in his turn, equally shrank from commanding. War to both was an episode in life, not a profession, and military subordination, which needs for its efficiency to be fixed and absolute was by common consent reduced to a minimum.[18] An efficient organization necessitated the erection and maintenance of the intangible wall separating officers and men, but the entire process was complicated by the fact that often the men were from the same community with brothers, fathers, and sons serving in the same company, the son, perhaps, being senior to his father!

The community in which the company was raised usually possessed what a foreign writer labeled "a very peculiar and repulsive form of aristocracy, an aristocracy of local political notabilities . . ."[19] Many of the political leaders were commissioned by the State governors as officers in the volunteer regiments but actual field service tended to eliminate the incompetent ones if they had not resigned or been dismissed before reaching the front. As the war progressed, there was a noticeable improvement in the quality of leadership. Colonel Theodore Lyman who had just returned from Europe to serve on Meade's staff in 1863 observed the firm, quiet bearing of both the high and low officers. He was able to pick out those who had seen combat "by their subdued and steady look."[20] The discipline was not always what would have been considered discipline in continental armies but the men had bravery, enthusiasm, and intelligence.

SOLDIERS VALUED GOOD COMMANDERS

A Regular Army officer noted the intuitive judgement of the volunteers which they formed in regard to their officers, more especially the commanders of armies irrespective of the personal popularity of the officers themselves. In many cases the utmost confidence was placed in officers who never seemed to excite any especial enthusiasm among the men. This judgement was sometimes hasty but seldom very far wrong, and when unjust was speedily corrected. Up to the Battle of Chancelorsville, for example, few commanders had enjoyed greater personal popularity among the troops than had "Fighting Joe" Hooker. He had an attractive, winning way and was always well received by the men. After the battle this feeling entirely changed and there was something in the air of the men which said as plainly as words: "We have no further use for you; you are a failure." Of Chancellorsville, Hooker himself admitted that he was not hurt by a shell in that battle and, added the general, "I was not drunk. For once I lost confidence in Hooker, and that is all there is to it."[21] Success was usually the criterion by which the men evaluated their leaders. "Grumble as much as they might at hard work, long marches, and short rations, the results, when they became apparent, atoned for everything."[22] A soldier in front of Vicksburg noted in his diary July 3, 1863 that "the boys are beginning to think Grant is Napoleon. He has completely wiped out his Shiloh Affair."[23] The lack of aggressiveness of Buell was compared to the similar trait in McClellan by men who found it exasperating to feel that all the hard campaigning had been so utterly fruitless.[24] After Antietam, McClellan's men could not understand why the battle was not renewed since they were convinced that there were ample forces and ammunition to continue the fight. In at least one brigade the men had lost all confidence in their leaders; they felt they were being out-generaled and believed that Lee's army and not Richmond should be the objective point since the rebellion could never be put down until that army was annihilated.[25]

Soldiers resented the loss of thousands of their comrades in such futile enterprises as the assault on Lee's lines at Fredericksburg and noted with concern the lack of unison between their corps commanders. The men respected true leadership and regretted the fact that Burnside lacked "the mental force to wield and bind these discordant, disintegrating elements into one solid, compact, adhesive mass, subject to his will and guided by his judgment . . ."[26] A successful general like Sherman, on the other hand, earned the unbounded confidence of his men because they knew that no man was more unwilling to waste their lives in futile frontal assaults when flanking would achieve the same results.[27]

MARTINETS DISLIKED

The average soldier fully realized that battle casualties were a necessary concomitant of warfare but he entertained little respect for the martinet. One of this type incurred the enmity of his entire command as a result of his insisting on frequent roll calls, drills, inspections, and reviews in the midst of an arduous campaign. One such "whipper-snapper little general," (J. W. Davidson) insisted on these reviews and drills during an expedition in which it either rained or snowed 43 days out of 110.[28] Officers who insisted on such formalities beyond a necessary degree usually found themselves relieved from command duty in a short time. On the other hand, some officers were martinets but their physical courage in combat and their ability to fight the enemy well tended to counteract strict adherence to regulations. Such a commander was Winfield Scott Hancock who was probably the best corps commander on the Federal side, but a man who insisted on following regulations at all times. For example, when Sheridan left the Valley to join Grant he was succeeded by Hancock who at once made himself immensely unpopular by issuing an order forbidding all men in the ranks to wear boots. "It was an unnecessary and contemptible order, and caused much suffering in the midst of the prevailing snow, ice and mud.[29] Late in 1862, when some men of Hancock's corps deliberately left the ranks to go after some sheep, these men were fired upon with live ammunition, i. e. ball cartridges. Hancock was so enraged at this foraging that he instructed each division commander to assemble a court-martial for the trial of these offenders. Consequently, every evening after going into camp, these courts were in session. Sharp and summary were the punishments. Some of such infractions of discipline became themes for humorous discussions among the soldiers for months after they recovered. On one occasion, for example, the head of the column was continuously feeling its way forward. Due to expected contact with the enemy, Hancock ordered skirmishers to deploy. Soon these men were seen running to and fro along a fence; then they appeared to be running to the rear. Their actions amazed and perplexed the general, who turned to the colonel in command saying: "Colonel, what is the meaning of this; your men are running to the rear; have they struck the enemy? Your skirmishers are being driven in by the rebs." The colonel retorted that his men never ran from the enemy. But taking a close look with his field glasses, the colonel saw his men running this way and that, and muttered, "Enemy! The rebs be d—d! It is a d—d flock of sheep they are after." There was a well-attended court-martial that evening.[30]

The average soldier instinctively recognized genuine solicitude and interest when displayed by their officers. They felt little respect for Howard who, a very religious man, nevertheless never actually helped his men solve their personal problems.[31]

LITTLE RESPECT FOR RANK

Respect for rank was more often than not conspicuous by its complete absence.[32] The war correspondent Russell noted that General McDowell was not saluted by the many soldiers whom he encountered, although his rank was clearly visible to them.[33] Even army commanders late in the war were not always referred to in the most dignified terms. On one occasion a surgeon complained to General Meade that the men were calling him "old pills" and requested that the general have it stopped. Meade just at that moment was apparently not in the best possible frame of mind. He seized hold of his eye glasses, conspicuously large in size, clapped them on his nose, glared through them at the medical officer and exclaimed: "Well, what of that? How can I prevent it? Why, I hear that, when I rode out the other day, some of the men called me a 'd—d old goggled-eyed snapping-turtle,' and I can't even stop that!" The medic was forced to be satisfied with this explosive expression of a sympathetic fellow being and to take his chances as to obnoxious epithets in the future.[34]

Although Meade was thereafter called "Old Snapping Turtle" by his staff,[35] he was by no means the only general with a nickname. Many generals had "old" in front of the nickname because they appeared old to the young soldiers who were in their late teens while many generals were in their forties. General French, who was constantly blinking, was "Old Blinky," Grant was "Old Seven Jaw," while Howard, who prayed regularly and publicly, was "Old Prayer Book." Others were: "Pop" Thomas, "Uncle Billy" Sherman, and "Black Jack" Logan. Nicknames were even more common among the men. One soldier was called "Little Mother" because he had a needle book with thread and when a comrade lost a button he would go and get "Mother" to fix it.[36] In the 13th New Hampshire Infantry, a very strong man was nicknamed "Old Bones," a weak man "Grunty," a story-teller was called "Old Yarn," while one soldier who always smelled of everything before he would eat it, was called "Smellee."[37] Units had nicknames, as for example the Ninth Army Corps was called "Burnside's Geography Class" because it had fought in so many States.[38] Some batteries named their guns; for example, "Baby Waker," "Whistling Dick" and "Brick Driver" were guns of the 3rd Rhode Island Heavy Artillery which pounded Fort Sumter so heavily in 1863.[39]

MEN ADMIRED BRAVE OFFICERS

The nature of the war was such that officers led their men in combat, and personal courage was an essential quality for the officer who wished to earn and retain the respect of his men. Cowardly officers were sometimes unceremoniously sent to the rear by men who refused to serve under them.[40] The officers and men of one regiment caused a resolution be introduced in their States House of Representatives that their colonel be requested to resign because of cowardice at Bull Run.[41] Probably no Federal commander was more unfavorably criticized by his men for non-appearance at the front than was General McClellan. He was not on the field at Malvern Hill. Heintzelman, late in the afternoon, signalled to him that his absence was noticed and "was the subject of unfavorable comment among the officers and men." It appears that during most of the battle McClellan maintained his headquarters on a gunboat.[42] Although McClellan was personally brave he disliked the sights of the battlefield and did not exploit to the fullest at the front his personal appeal which was very strong at the opening of the Peninsula Campaign. At Antietam in one sector he sent infantry forward to cope with the infantry and artillery because he had failed to acquaint himself with the nature of the opposition in that area. In the assault that followed, the men noticed the general hiding behind a haystack while in sharp contrast they watched their divisional commander advancing with his front line, almost alone, afoot, and with his bare sword in his hand. This was General Richardson, the divisional commander, who was killed in this action.[43]

Many Federal assaults failed because commanders were absent at critical moments to direct the men. In the costly assault on Port Hudson, June 14, 1863, there was a strange lack of commanders at the vital points. "Not a single general, and not a single Regular officer that I know of, went near the ramparts during the whole day. The entire storming business was left to the management of volunteer colonels and lieutenant colonels, many of them belonging to nine-months' regiments, and none of them acquainted with the mysteries of fortifications.[44]" Later on, the survivors of the assault were marched to the rear where they were addressed by their commander, General Banks, but although called on for three cheers for their general, the men looked on in sullen silence. Of 6,000 men engaged in the assault, 203 were killed, 1,401 wounded, and 188 were missing[45]

Late in the war the attempt to effect a breakthrough on the Petersburg front collapsed because, according to Grant, the troops were not properly commanded, the divisional commanders did not go forward with their men but allowed them to go forward alone.[46] One of these divisional commanders remained in his bomb-proof and, while his men were being slaughtered in the Crater, told a staff officer who came for instructions that the brigade commanders should get their men out and press forward.[47]

There were 2,537 officers of general rank in the Federal army or about one for every regiment.[48] The casualties in killed among them were 1 army commander; 3 corps commanders; 14 division commanders; 33 brigade commanders. In addition 37 brigade commanders with the rank of colonel were killed in action; and 35 general officers died of disease during the war.[49] A volunteer officer noted with approval that his corps commander, General Humphreys, rode from one end of his line to the other ceaselessly, until his earth-works was completed—"a practice of this admirable officer which . . . [the volunteer] never knew to be pursued by any other corps commander . . ."[50] From the available evidence it would appear that the soldiers held in highest respect those officers who *led* them into action, officers who were brave and who displayed a genuine interest in the welfare of their men. The personality of the general was also important; there is probably considerable truth in the soldiers' belief that the best generals were those who had the common touch.[51]

MUTINY

Mutiny in the Federal Army was rare after 1861. Disaffected officers solved their problems by obtaining positions in new regiments or by resignation, while enlisted men either made the best of the situation or deserted. Many soldiers recorded in their diaries sentiments similar to the following: "It sometimes seems as though some of the officers think privates nothing but animals and treat them as such, but we have our rights and can maintain them if we only will get up the energy to do it."[52] Usually the soldier's resentment confined itself to his secret communion with his diary; his "energy" to do something about it availed him nothing, and his only alternative was desertion. Most of the men were sensible enough to refrain from so flagrant an act as mutiny and left "the entire monopoly of insubordination to a few regiments, mostly composed of European adventurers.[53]

In the West the news of the removal of Fremont created a great sensation among the German troops who declared that if he were superseded they would not fight,[54] but no open mutiny appears to have taken place. Three of Sherman's seven regiments mutinied after Bull Run over the question of their length of service. These regiments had enlisted for "three years or the War," understanding that the war would be over in a few weeks and that the "three years" phrase was merely a precautionary measure on the part of the government. The men felt tricked when the other Bull Run veterans went home after their three-month service was completed.[55] These three regiments were the 13th, 21st, and 79th New York Infantry.[56] Most of the trouble, however, took place in the 79th New York Infantry, which was largely composed of men of Scotch descent. The regiment participated in the Battle of Bull Run and acquitted itself well, losing heavily in officers and men. Soon after the battle the regiment had lost by death or resignation its colonel, major, nine of its ten captains, and many lieutenants. As a result, this organization was left in a condition peculiarly unfavorable for discipline. One of its members began to repent bitterly of having cast in his lot with a foreign regiment composed of men who lacked the feelings of Americans and who could not, when a reverse came, "be inspired to renewed efforts for the cause."[57] The mutiny was crushed by the appearance in front of the camp of some Regular Army infantry, cavalry, and artillery forces under a Regular officer who had orders to mow the mutineers down if they did not submit. The regiment had its colors taken away; much publicity was given to the affair, and so quickly and efficiently was the matter handled that the entire outcome was most salutary. The army commander believed the trouble arose rather from poor officers than from the men.[58] In fact, the Provost Marshal of Washington knew of only two cases where regiments refused to go to the front. In one of these the men of a new regiment refused to embark at all because they believed their colonel and lieutenant colonel to be entirely worthless. The sequel, in which the lieutenant colonel afterwards landed in the Old Capital Prison for horse stealing shows they were not entirely wrong.[59]

ABSENTEEISM

Although the problem of mutiny was solved by swift and summary action, absenteeism and desertion remained to blight the Northern war effort until the very end. Absenteeism ofter resulted from the abuse of leaves of absence granted to troops who visited the large centers of population for pleasure or on visits to their families. One foreign observer [60] believed it not uncommon for a force to have one-third of its members absent because of abuse of leave or

without leave at all. Many officers and soldiers were put on the sick list as a matter of favoritism in order to visit their homes. Halleck had medical boards reexamine men in the hospitals at St. Louis, with the result that about three-fourths of the patients were reported fit for duty.[61] The great number of officers absent from their regiments in the summer of 1862 prompted the War Department to call attention to Army Regulations which permitted leaves of absence to be granted only by the Secretary of War in time of war except when a certificate of medical officer should show beyond doubt that a change of location was necessary to save life or prevent permanent disability. All officers of Regulars and Volunteers, except those on parole, were to be considered "absent without leave" unless they were found at their posts within 15 days of the issuance of the order.[62] State governors were requested to give publicity to the order which was followed by a similar one a few days later applying to enlisted men.[63] Since April 7, 1862, the military commanders had been ordered to submit reports tri-monthly to the Adjutant General in which they were to list the names, organizations, and residences of all soldiers furloughed or discharged by them. Their responsibility also included the collection and forwarding of stragglers to their units.[64]

The problem of absenteeism in the Army of the Potomac became acute in the summer of 1862 due to the failure of the Peninsula Campaign. It a letter of July 15, 1862, McClellan informed the President that 40,000 men were absent from the army, half of whom were fit for duty. The general believed that many of the absentees were actually sick or wounded but many also were malingerers. He requested a press attack on the absentees and the employment of deputy marshals to round them up. The summary dismissal of officers and the publication of their names was also suggested. Many of the malingerers escaped by accompanying the wounded on the hospital boats where there was no opporunity to examine permits.[65] As a result of this letter, the President ordered that all leaves of absence and furloughs would be revoked on August 11th and all officers and men were to join their commands forthwith under the penalty of dismissal from the service or such penalty as a court-martial might direct.[66] The only excuses that would be accepted were: an order or leave from the War Department; disability from wounds received in service; and disability from disease that rendered the party unfit for military duty. Any officer or private whose health permitted him to visit "watering places or places of amusement, or to make social visits, or walk about the town, city, or neighborhood in which he may be," can considered fit for military duty and to be evading duty by absence from his unit. The order further provided that on August 18th at 10 a.m. each regiment and corps should be mustered and absentees marked. Those fit for duty were to be regarded as absent without cause, their pay was to be stopped, and the men dismissed from the service or treated as deserters. No officer was to be restored to his rank until he had established before a court of inquiry, appointed by the President, that his absence was with good cause. United States marshals, mayors, chiefs of police, sheriffs, postmasters, and justices of the peace were authorized to act as special provost marshals to arrest any officer or private fit for duty who was absent from his command without just cause. Such agents were to receive five dollars and "reasonable expenses" for each absentee conveyed to the nearest military post.[67]

A temporary improvement was soon apparent. The stragglers were promptly gathered in and hotels and bar-rooms were swept of officers of all grades absent without leave. Many officers and men had somehow become separated from their regiments, often through no fault of their own, or "with less than the frequent scoldings in general orders would have one believe." A camp was set up near Alexandria, Virginia under Colonel J. S. Belknap of the 85th New York Infantry to collect these strays. In the last three weeks of September and in October, there were sent to the Army of the Potomac 65,000 men of whom 16,000 were convalescents and stragglers.[68] The situation in September, when McClellan reported [69] that in one of his corps there were 13,000 men present and 15,000 men absent, was improved by the employment of deputy provost marshals ordered by the War Department.[70]

The problem of absenteeism was little better in the West, where General Buell reported 14,000 from his army on June 24th.[71]

After the disastrous Battle of Fredericksburg, absenteeism increased again and in January, 1863, there were 8,987 officers and 282,073 men absent from duty.[72] Only a part of these were really sick or disabled; the remainder were mostly deserters, stragglers, malingerers. On his assumption of the command of the Army of the Potomac in January, Hooker found the number of absentees from that army to be 2,922 officers and 81,964 men.[73] scattered all over the country and the majority absent from causes unknown. The officers' abuse of their leave privilege had so bad an effect on their men that Halleck instructed courts-martial in all parts of the country that they had the power to sentence officers absent without leave to be reduced to the ranks and to serve three years or during the war as privates.[74] In June, the War Department directed that all brigadier generals who had been absent more than thirty days from duty on account of sickness other than those wounded in battle should report their state of health; those unfit for duty were to be honorably discharged.[75] Examining boards were established in

Annapolis and Cincinnati before one of which officers who had left their commands in consequence of ill health were ordered to appear as soon as they were able to travel. They underwent an examination by the board and were recommended, according to their condition, for light duty, further leave of absence, or medical treatment in a general hospital of the city where the board was in session. If found fit for duty they were ordered forthwith to their regiments.[76] Before these boards were established there had been from one to two hundred officers monthly reported absent without leave. By March 1, 1865, this number had decreased to 30 for an eleven-month period. Sick and wounded officers were generally employed, as soon as convalescent, in recruiting service and when recovered were sent to the front to replace others who required relief.[77]

In the last two years of the war there was much stronger enforcement of the furlough and leave regulations. When Colonel Russel A. Alger, 5th Michigan Cavalry, failed to join his command after having previously abused the leave privilege, he was recommended by his superiors, Generals Sheridan, Torbert, Merritt, and Custer for dismissal. Colonel Alger resigned September 16, 1864, and his resignation was accepted.[78]

DESERTION

Unlike the absentee who merely overstayed his leave or somehow got temporarily "lost," the deserter left the ranks with the intent of abandonment of the service. Although volunteers in 1861 possessed abundant patriotism, they had no knowledge of military law and obligation. They had no conception of discipline. Many of them became what the Provost Marshal General termed "technical deserters" or men who actually did desert their original commands but subsequently joined other branches of the service without the inducements of bounty, and proved to be good and faithful soldiers.[79] Many men in a Pennsylvania regiment stationed in Washington took "French leave" during Lee's invasion of their native State, returned to their homes, and joining the Army of the Potomac at and around Gettysburg, were engaged in defending their homes and firesides. Many such were killed or captured and are recorded as deserters to this day. When a man failed to answer to his name at roll call he was reported a deserter unless accounted for later. If he turned up again, well and good; if he did not, the charge remained against his name without further inquiry on the next muster roll. Many Federal soldiers simply disappeared; the lack of "dog tags" often rendered identification of their bodies impossible; others were killed by guerrillas, evacuated to hospitals of other units and died alone and their remains hidden; while not a few were their identity unknown by the hospital staff.

During the war there were 201,397 desertions of which 92,095 occurred prior to April 1, 1863. From that date to the end of the war the Provost Marshal General's Bureau returned 75,909 to their regiments. In addition there were 161,286 desertions for failure to appear when drafted.[81] Desertion in the Regular Army was much greater than in the Volunteers due to the foreigners in the former who possessed neither national nor local pride. The ratio of desertions in the Regular Army was 244.25 per thousand; in the Volunteers it was but 62.51 per thousand. The volunteer army contained in its every company the seeds of envy, discontent, and insubordination resulting largely from the exertions of the petty political leaders of districts where the companies were raised. When the men elected their officers the majority vote decided the election and issues not connected with the military service often governed them. A dissatisfied and often highly intelligent minority was frequently the result, and desertion, both before and after sufficient trial to prove the fitness or unfitness of the officers, occurred, and was regarded by the parties resorting to it more as a refusal on their part to ratify a contract than as the commission of a grave crime.

The large bounties paid to men enlisting in the Federal Army was a great inducement to desertion and led to the infamous class of "bounty jumpers" which became especially prominent in the latter part of the war. The most extreme case was the man who confessed to have jumped the bounty 32 times! He finally landed in the Albany penitentiary.[82] Lack of adequate means for the arrest of deserters and adequate punishment encouraged desertion in the early part of the war. The absence of men from the ranks meant a heavier burden on those who remained with the colors. Exaggerated talk by the deserters concerning the harsh treatment inflicted by the officers tended to discourage volunteering. The lack of vigor in dealing with the evil in the early stages of the war was in reality harsh cruelty to those who remained true to their flag. Lives were lost, battles were lost, the war itself was prolonged as a consequence of the depletion of the ranks of the armies by desertion.

The lack of effective measures to deal with the problem of desertion was particularly observable in 1861 and 1862. Prior to the commencement of the war, the Army Regulations authorized a reward of thirty dollars for the arrest and delivery of a deserter to an officer of the Army.[83] Although it was up to officers to arrest deserters, the police of the cities did most of the arresting themselves for the reward. However, but few arrests were made.[84] On September 7, 1861, the reward was reduced to five dollars.[85] The following April the duty of collecting stragglers and deserters was assigned to the military commanders of cities.[86] In September of that year a Provost Marshal General of the War Department was assigned to duty in Washington to handle the desertion problem but the man selected for the position accomplished little. The first really effective machinery to combat the evil of desertion was set up in March, 1863, with the establishment of the Provost Marshal General's Department. The new Provost Marshal General, Colonel Fry, maintained his headquarters in Washington and from there sent out helpful information on deserters to the provost marshals to seek out, arrest, and return the deserters. In July, 1863, the reward for apprehending a deserter was increased to ten dollars:[87] a few months later it was further increased to thirty dollars;[88] but all rewards were stopped in March, 1965. The same month an act was approved which provided that all deserters who did not return within sixty days would lose their right to become citizens and would be disqualified from holding office under the United States.[89]

The course of desertion in the Federal Army fluctuated as the army won victories or incurred defeats. It is entirely possible that desertion in the East more than doubled desertion in the West.[90] It must be confessed that the records bear this out. The main reasons would seem to be the consistent records of defeat suffered by the Army of the Potomac up to July, 1863, and the quality of replacements received by that army from that date to the end of the war. The absenteeism and desertion under McClellan has already been noted. They increased appreciably under Burnside in whom the men had no confidence after his leadership at Fredericksburg. The month of that battle there were over 100,000 men absent from their commands.[91] The Emancipation Proclamation on January 1, 1863, aroused the opposition of a considerable number of troops, "some of whom went so far as to say that they would not have entered the service if this action of the government had been anticipated.[92] Disease in the form of diarrhea, typhoid, and scurvy appeared in the Army of the Potomac. The army had not been paid for six months and letters from destitute families increased the soldiers' dissatisfaction. Friends and relatives sent civilian clothing to aid the soldiers in desertion.[93] Confederate agents established rail and water routes whereby Federal deserters were returned North. Many deserters escaped in this way until two privates under the direction of the Provost Marshal of Washington "deserted" and returned later to give the necessary information that resulted in the stoppage of these routes.[94]

One of the most potent causes for desertion in the the Army of the Potomac was the scarcity of furloughs and leaves of absence during this period. When Hooker succeeded Burnside, he did much to ameliorate this condition by granting furloughs and leaves as generously as possible. On March 10, 1863, the President issued a proclamation declaring that all soldiers absent from their regiments without leave who should report themselves to certain designated rendezvous on or before the first day of April (1863) would be restored to their regiments without punishment. Those who did not so return would be treated as deserters. The President called on all "patriotic and faithful citizens" to resist "evil-disposed and disloyal persons" who were enticing and procuring soldiers to desert and absent themselves.[95] The same month as the President's proclamation the War Department ordered that: commanders of regiments, independent companies, batteries, detachments; surgeons in charge of hospitals or detachments; and commanding officers of men on detached service, should report monthly the names and descriptions of all deserters from their repective commands to the Provost Marshal General.[96] The result of this increased attention paid to suppressing desertion was that a definite improvement was noted in 1863 over the preceding year. Stricter discipline plus an awakening public consciousness as to the odious nature of desertion did much to combat desertion in the volunteer regiments. The rate of desertion in 1864 was higher because of the nature of recruits sent to replace the casualties among the volunteers of 1861 and 1862. An inferior class of men enlisted in the Army through the medium of bounty and substitute brokers.

Desertion was especially characteristic of troops from large cities. Fry believed that desertion was a crime of foreign rather than native birth and that but a small proportion of the men who foresook their colors were Americans. "It is a notorious circumstance that the great mass of the professional bounty jumpers were Europeans." The manufacturing States led in desertion and the towns and cities in these States were crowded with foreigners. The ratio per thousand of desertion was as follows:[97]

All loyal States	62.51
New York	89.06
New Jersey	107.00
Connecticut	117.23
Maine	43.90
New England	74.24
West	45.51
White	62.51
Colored	67.00

The Confederate General Breckinridge spoke of the men, "chiefly foreigners" who came over into his lines.[98] However, the numbers of Germans and Irish in the Northern army has been overstated by Southern writers.[99] Colonel Lyman of Meade's staff believed the Germans were handicapped by not knowing the language but added bitterly: "By the Lord! I wish these gentlemen who would overwhelm us with Germans, Negroes, and the offscourings of great cities, could only see—only *see*—a Rebel

regiment, in all their rags and squalor. If the had eyes they would know that these men are lik wolf-hounds, and not to be beaten by turnspits. Lyman believed that the trouble was the lack of machinery to work up the poor material and the lac of adequate punishment for the scoundrels, vaga bonds, and aliens who would not fight and coul not be made to fight.[100] Desertions were greatly in creased by a proclamation from General Lee offerin to send Federal deserters North to their home Thousands probably availed themselves of this op portunity; a few enlisted in the Rebel service. Th majority of deserters re-enlisted in the Federal serv ice. Several thousand did take refuge in Britis provinces although some, desiring to return, wer pardoned by the President. [101]

The majority of deserters in 1864 and 1865 appea to have been enlisted men who had been regularl enrolled but who had never reached the regiment to which they were assigned. Grant believed tha out of every five men enlisted in 1864 he receivec but one.[102] Lincoln is reported to have said in thi connection: "We get a large body of reenforcement together, and start them to the front; but after de ducting the sick, the deserters, the stragglers anc the discharged, the numbers seriously diminish b the time they reached their destination. It is lik trying to shovel fleas across a barnyard; you don get 'em all there."[103] The need for replacements dur ing the latter part of 1863 and 1864 continued to be acute and more drastic measures were employec against deserters than formerly. Sometimes bounty jumpers attempting to desert were shot, with n attempt made to arrest them.[104] Although the figur of 121 has been given as the number shot durin the war, this is probably an understatement.[105] Th execution of a deserter was a public spectacle anc was viewed by units as large as divisions. The natur al repugnance of men to serve on the firing squad was lessened somewhat by allowing one rifle tc be loaded with a blank cartridge, hence each mem ber of the squad could comfort himself with the thought that he may have been given that particula rifle. Sometimes a deserter was captured by his orig inal unit and when this happened, short shift wa made with him. When a company of the 71st In diana Infantry captured one of their own number they all begged for permission to shoot him. "The number detailed was fifteen, and fifteen bullets were found in his body.[106]

INITIAL PUNISHMENTS

Punishment for cowardice and desertion tended to be comparatively mild in the early part of the war, but grew progressively more severe as the conflict wore on. Every regiment had a number of men who ran away during a battle or left their units with no intention of ever coming back. At first such offenders were given rather light sentences. On October 10,

1863, an artillery brigade was called out to witness a "somewhat sad and novel scene," the branding and drumming out of service of deserters from the batteries. The brigade was formed into a hollow square facing inward, with a battery forge in the center, the blacksmith blowing the bellows. The deserters were brought into the square under an infantry guard and took position near the forge. The deserters were then partially stripped of their clothing, irons were heated, and the letter "D" was burned upon their left hip. Their heads were then shaved after which they were marched about the square under guard, led by a corps of fife and drummers playing the "Rogue's March." It was a painful and humiliating sight but undoubtedly left its salutary impression, as was designed, upon all who witnessed it.[107] A man in the 63rd Pennsylvania Infantry was branded for deserting although he was only a deserter technically, since he did not go over to the enemy nor did he go home. But he left his command and went on a huckstering tour, buying goods from the settlers and peddling them through the different camps making money at the business. Of course, being absent from the ranks and unaccounted for, he was marked on the rolls as a deserter. He was arrested, returned to his unit, regularly tried and found guilty. His sentence was that he should have the buttons cut off his uniform, have his head shaved, be branded on the hips, and then drummed out of camp. The sentence was carried out. A lid of a cracker box was then hung on his back with the word *Deserter* painted on it in large black letters. Eight men then formed behind him with bayonets fixed, the band preceded him, playing the "Rogue's March," and, accompanied by hundreds of spectators, he was escorted from camp. As he left the men gave him the "parting salute," which consisted of throwing after him old shoes, tin pans, and other articles. He was turned loose to go where he saw fit, dishonored and disgraced forever. Feeling deeply his disgrace, he never returned to his home and his comrades and friends never heard of him again.[108] When substitutes and bounty-jumpers purposely shot off the index fingers of their right hands, thus disabling them for firing the musket, the men were warned that in any future cases, no ether or chloroform would be used in dressing the fingers thus mutilated. In a few days, a man purposely blew the end off his index finger. The finger was dressed without the use of any anaesthetic; the man, a big fellow with a strong voice, howled loud and long. The job hurt of course, but without doing to him any special injury. "No more index fingers were blown off in the Thirteenth after that noisy case."[109]

EXECUTIONS

But as the draft got into full gear and the regiments began to receive trash as replacements, de-

DRUMMING OUT OF CAMP

THE PENALTY FOR DESERTION

sertion and cowardice began to be severely punished. The death penalty, which Lincoln had often set aside in previous cases of desertion, began to be used more often, and executions were carried out rapidly, inexorably, and publicly. The executions, witnessed by whole brigades, divisions, and corps, apparently made a deep impression on the spectators. Many diarists and letter writers described them for the folks back home and posterity. On June 19, 1863, a soldier of Co. "G" 5th Ohio Infantry wrote in his diary a description of one of these executions. Because his description is a contemporary one and the execution is fairly typical of others described in regimental histories, it is given here in the soldier's own words:

At 11 o'clock the troops were formed in line and a order read to them, informing them that between the hours of 12 noon and 4 p.m. 3 Deserters would be shot to death by Musketry by order of a Courtmartial with the approval of Gen. Hooker. By 12 noon all the troops composing the 12th Corps were in line to witness the execution of the Sentence. At 1 p.m. the party approached. First came a army wagon containing the Coffins of the three condemned men. Next a ambulance carrying the condemned men themselves, with their hands pinioned behind them. Then followed the shooting party from the 46th Regt. P. V. numbering about 30 men, arrived at the place of execution. The coffins were taken out of the wagon and one placed before each grave which had been dug previously. Then the guard stepped up to the ambulance, tied a handkerchief around the eyes of one of the prisoners and escorted him to the coffin whereupon he was seated and his feet tyed to the coffin. The same was done with the other two men and then the shooting party took their positions. The Provost martial now stepped forward and read in a loud and clear voice the sentence of the Court. Next the Minister

came forward asking the Almighty to have mercy on the souls of the prisoners. After he stepped back the shooting party came to a ready and in a few more moments a Volley of Musketry insured that the law had been apeased and the souls of the Victims winged their flight to the throne of the Almighty. May God have mercy upon their souls.[110]

After the Gettysburg campaign there was a marked increase in desertions. The sympathy with criminals in 1861 and 1862 had made those of 1863 bold and audacious. "The execution of a score of bad men in 1862 would have saved the lives of many good men in 1863 and 1864[111] When the 1864 campaign opened up, a new, tough attitude was clear to all. Old charges of desertion were kept on file; if the man concerned should desert again, he would incur the death penalty. Such was the case of a private of Co. "K" 19th Massachusetts Infantry who was warned that his next offence would be his last. "While he had promised that [he would serve faithfully], he did not intend to, and was only kept in battle at the Wilderness by fear of death from the officers. On the 18th [May, 1864] he deserted while under fire, was captured the 19th, tried by drum-head court-martial the 20th, and ordered to be shot at 7 a.m. on the 21st." The man was executed, and while some "may think the killing unjust and cruel, it was not. At that time there were in the ranks of every regiment, men who had no interest in the cause. They had enlisted for the bounty and did not intend to render any service. They not only shirked duty, but their acts and conversation were demoralizing good men. The shooting changed all this. Men who had straggled and kept out of battle now were in the ranks, and the result to our Corps alone was as good as if we had been reenforced by a full regiment."[112]

But in other corps, at least, the desertions continued. Late in the fall of 1864 there were many executions of men caught in attempting to desert to the enemy, so many as to season the nerves of the unwilling witnesses. There were so many deserters, in fact, that shooting gave way to more ignominious hanging, and even this soon ceased to affect the sensibilities of the men. There was a current joke in the 11th Maine Infantry that the company cooks would hover around a gallows tree until its victim was lowered, when they would scramble for the scaffolding to cut up the wood for their cookfires. The 11th Maine, having lost no man by execution for desertion, was relieved by special order from attending military executions, as its members were considered to need no warning.[113] As for the condemned deserters, they apparently were not contrite about their activities, but rather seemed to the onlookers to be indifferent or, in some cases, aware that they were in the spotlight. However, a deserter from the 5th New Hampshire realized and regretted his acts. Before he died he made a moving speech to the spectators urging them to "be true to the oath which you have taken, and you will feel better in your own heart. It is only since I received my sentence that I have realized the full enormity of my errors; you should do so whilst you have yet time." Before he was executed this unfortunate man, who had deserted several times, shook hands with the firing squad, and sincerely asked God to have mercy on him.[114]

MILITARY LAW AND COURTS-MARTIAL

Much of the problem of maintaining discipline lay in the fact that too much of the operation or imposition of discipline itself was transferred from the military service where obedience, above everything else, should have reigned. The average Federal officer or soldier prided himself on his individual privileges and his right to be free. The result was a multiplicity of courts of inquiry and courts-martial, diverting, at every turn, a good number of soldiers from active service without aiming, most frequently, at any results. Veritable lawsuits bristling with incidents of every kind, were always pending by the dozen in each division, in which the question in the greater part of the European armies, would have been one of the simple competence of superior or general officers. The officers had too little the habit of using their disciplinary power and made too many concessions to the whims of the soldiers.[115]

By law, courts-martial could pronounce upon the slightest breaches of discipline but a thousand ways were found to evade sentence. An officer who neglected his duty would be placed under arrest as if in preparation for trial. At the end of eight days[116] he would be released and told that the matter would not be pursued further, a decision in which he naturally hastened to acquiesce.[117] In more serious cases he would be confined to his tent in arrest for three or four weeks and warned if he made any complaint against such illegal proceeding the President would be requested to relieve him. General Order 91 required that a copy of the charges should be furnished the accused officer within 8 days of his arrest and that he should be brought to trial within 10 days thereafter.[118] The General-in-Chief believed the machinery of courts-martial to be too cumbrous for the trial of military offences in time of actual war. He complained that to organize such courts it was often necessary to detach a large number of officers from active duty in the field and then a single case would sometimes occupy a court for many months. The general believed that enforcement of discipline in the field involved prompt trial and punishment.[119] The court-martial had a double function, depending on the gravity of the charges brought before it. Acting as a simple court it could recommend the President to suspend or dismiss the party accused. As a military tribunal it was invested by the Constitution itself with judiciary power to try

THE GUARD HOUSE
At David's Island, New York Harbor.

special cases and could impose pecuniary fines and corporal penalties extending even to death.[120]

Officers had to be tried by court-martial and they could not be punished without a formal sentence. As mentioned above, this brought in many cases, practical immunity to officers accused of insubordination towards their superiors, owing to the length of time it took to bring them to trial. More often than not they escaped entirely. However, there were exceptions. On June 11, 1863, a lieutenant of the 21st New Jersey Infantry had his sword broken over his head, his shoulder straps and buttons cut off, his pistol broken, and was otherwise publicly disgraced in front of his brigade. This officer had been tried by a court-martial and convicted of cowardice at Chancellorsville. The sentence and manner of its execution were ordered to be published in the newspapers of the county where the regiment was raised. As one spectator expressed it: "When I saw the look of shame and humiliation on the face of that young soldier, I felt that I would rather have died many times over, facing the enemy on the field of battle, than to have undergone that terrible ordeal.[121] Attitudes had changed so much that a year later, when a lieutenant in a Pennsylvania regiment was drummed out of camp for cowardice, he was followed by men with fixed bayonets who prodded him along, while a fifer and drummer played the "Rogue's March.[122]

General Schofield believed that incompetent brigade and division commanders should have been court-martialed for sacrificing their men. In the Atlanta campaign he sent to the rear, in permanent disgrace, a divisional commander who, contrary to Sherman's instructions, had sacrificed his men in a hopeless assault upon a fortified position. But he never heard of another similar case of even approximate justice to an officer of high rank.[123] In the case of a lieutenant who had lent money at very high usury to his men, the regimental commander preferred charges with the result that the officer had to stand disarmed in the center of a hollow square where he was reprimanded in general orders in the most cutting terms. The officer was returned to duty but the narrator declares that had he been subjected to such disgrace, he would have tried to leave his bones on the next battlefield.[124]

Whereas, the most that officers received as punishment was usually dismissal, the soldiers were punished in a variety of ways. Their legal punishments by sentence of court-martial according to the offense and jurisdiction of the court were: death, confinement; hard labor; ball and chain; confinement on bread and water diet; solitary confinement; forfeiture of pay and allowances; discharges from service; and reprimands; and, when noncommissioned officers, reduction to the ranks. Solitary confinement, or confinement on bread and water, was not to exceed 14 days at a time and not to exceed 84 days in any one

year. The power to pardon or mitigate the punishment ordered by a court-martial was vested in the authority confirming the proceedings and in the President of the United States. Also, a military commander superior to the officer confirming the proceedings could suspend the execution of the sentence when, in his judgment, it was void upon the face of the proceedings, or when he saw a fit case for executive clemency. [125]

CRUEL PUNISHMENTS

In the fall of 1861, the inhabitants of Washington observed with astonishment soldiers who had been guilty of some violation of discipline, usually insolence or drunkeness, tied to the carriage of a gun, or half suspended by their thumbs, while others were gagged.[126] Punishments as severe as these, and in some cases much worse, continued to be inflicted throughout the war although contrary to Army Regulations and the Articles of War. Much depended on the president of a court-martial as to the nature of the punishment meted out. One court, which had as its president a West Pointer, sentenced a soldier who had been absent without leave for five days, to hard labor on fortifications for three years and loss of all pay and allowances except enough to cover his washing bill.[127] On the other hand, another West Point graduate only resorted to arbitrary punishment once in his command; he sentenced an unmilitary sentinel to stand on the head of a barrel for several hours and the soldiers' ridicule of the man was sufficient to make further punishment in that command unnecessary.[128] A similar punishment was given a "bibulously inclined" soldier who rather foolishly rode off with a general's horse.[129]

The most common punishment seems to have been confinement in the guardhouse and the most brutal was probably tying on the rack. In between these extremes were varied forms of camp drudgery, such as digging holes and filling them up again, or carrying a log of wood on the shoulder while walking post. Many organizations had a Black List as it was called, on which the names of all offenders against the ordinary rules of camp were kept for frequent reference, and when there was any particularly disagreeable task about camp to be done, The Black List furnished a quota for the work. This was in addition to the regular policing up required of everyone. Among the tasks that were considered interesting and profitable for the black-listed to engage in were digging and fitting up new company sinks (or latrines as they are known today) and filling up abandoned sinks. A favorite treat meted out to the unfortunates in the cavalry and artillery units was the burying of dead horses or cleaning up around the picket lines where the animals were tied.[130] A common form of punishment was to have the offenders sit for hours at a time on a horizontal bar a dozen feet above the ground.[131] In the Ninth Army

Corps cowards were forced to stand on barrels placed on top of the breastworks with placards of "coward" suspended from their necks, a pretty severe punishment if they had any shame left.[132] As mentioned previously, some deserters were executed. Others were sent to the Dry Tortugas, Florida for imprisonment during the war.[133] "Tying on the spare wheel" was used in some commands, especially in the artillery units. Extending upward and rearward from the center of every caisson was a fifth axle to which was attached a spare wheel. A soldier to be punished was placed on this wheel so that his legs spanned three spokes and his arms stretched until there were three or four spokes between his hands. A moderate punishment involved the offender remaining on the wheel for five or six hours. If a more severe punishment was desired, the wheel was given a quarter turn so that the offender's position was not upright but was now horizontal. He had to exert all his strength to keep his weight from pulling heavily and cuttingly on the cords with which he was tied. If one cried out he was gagged. "Tying on the spare wheel was the usual punishment in the artillery service for rather serious offenses; no man wanted to be tied up but once. Another less frequently employed punishment was "tying on the rack." This could very easily cripple a man for life. In the rear of every battery wagon was a heavy, strong rack on which forage was carried. The rack extended about two feet behind the wheels and its edge was about one inch thick. The offender was led to the rack, his hands dragged forward as far as possible without lifting his feet from the ground, and then bound to the felloes of the wheel. One foot was then bound to the felloe of one wheel and the other foot bound to the felloe of the other wheel. The whole weight of the soldier was thus thrown on his chest which bore heavily against the sharp edge of the rack. He was always gagged since no man could endure the supreme pain inflicted by this torture without screaming. Strong and determined men would faint in less than ten minutes to be cut down and never again serve in the Army. In some cases men would beg to be killed rather than be tied on the rack.[134]

ARMY PUNISHMENT

In the infantry a form of punishment known as "bucking and gagging" was employed. The soldier would be forced into a sitting position, a musket placed under his legs, and his hands placed under the musket and tied. Then a bayonet would be put across his mouth and held in position by rope tied behind the soldier's head. If kept in this position for any considerable length of time the soldier on being released would be unable to walk a step.[135] Tying up by the thumbs was a fairly common form of punishment. The man's thumbs would be tied to the branch of a tree at such height that he would be forced to stand on tiptoe during the length of his punishment.[136] Drumming out of camp was a form of punishment administered for cowardice. The coward, stripped of his uniform and equipment, was marched through the camp with guards urging him on with their bayonets. Often a fife and drum corps brought up the rear, droning out the "Rogue's March." The coward was hissed and jeered at throughout the whole march. There were no restraints put upon the language of his recent associates as they reviled him until he had crossed the camp boundaries and disappeared.[137]

NOTES, CHAPTER 13

1. Testimony of General Irvin McDowell, December 26, 1861, Joint Committee on the Conduct of the War. Committee's *Report*, First Series (1863), Vol. 1, p. 132; General Silas Casey in *Army and Navy Journal*, Vol. 1 (October 10, 1863), p. 99; "What We Have Neglected. A Reserve Corp—Incompetent Officers, *Ibid.*, Vol. 1 (August 29, 1863), p. 11.

2. Buffum, p. 141.

3. *Battles and Leaders*, Vol. 2, p. 557.

4. Testimony of General John Gibbon, April 1, 1864, Joint Committee on the Conduct of the War. Committee's *Report* (1865), Second Series, Vol. 1, p. 443.

5. Keifer, Vol. 1, p. 181.

6. *The Atlantic Monthly*, Vol. 14 (September 1864), p. 355.

7. Agassiz, p. 93, One general said to Meade; "General, I don't *want* Mott's men on my left; they are not a support; I would rather have no troops there, *Ibid.*, p. 110.

8. *The Atlantic Monthly*, Vol. 14, (September 1864), p. 354.

9. *Ibid.*, p. 355.

10. Comte de Paris, Vol. 1, p. 22.

11. How quickly they forget their own inexperience!

12. Croushore, p. 23.

13. The men took great pleasure in ridiculing unnecessary drill.

14. *The Atlantic Monthly*, Vol. 14 (September 1864), p. 349.

15. *Ibid*. See also Meade, Vol. 1, p. 231.

16. *Official Records*, First Series, Vol. 2, p. 752.

17. *Army and Navy Journal*, Vol. 1 (Aprl 7, 1864), p. 547.

18. *The Atlantic Monthly*, Vol. 14, (September 1864), p. 350.

19. "The American Aristocracy," *The Spectator*, Vol. 34 (July 27, 1861), p. 806.

20. Agassiz, pp. 11-12.

21. Bradford, Gamaliel, *Union Portraits*, p. 64.

22. Gibbon, pp. 424-425.

23. Wells, *The Diary of Seth J. Wells*, p. 87. Wells served with the 17th Illinois Infantry.

24. Hinman, p. 302.

25. Entry for October 28, 1862, Lane, *A Soldier's Diary*, p. 21.

26. Entry for December 28, 1862, *Ibid.*, p. 23.

27. Some men contrasted him with Grant.

28. Elliott, pp. 31-32.

29. Buffum, p. 317.

30. Rhodes, p. 133.

31. Alexander Hays, for example.

32. But not in Regular Army units.

33. Russell, Vol. 2, p. 138.

34. Porter, *Campaigning with Grant*, pp. 247-248.

35. Not to his face. But the enlisted men were less tactful.

36. He was one of the few who still kept his housewife.

37. Thompson, p. 542.

38. Fenner, Earl, *The History of Battery "H", 1st Rhode Island Light Artillery*, p. 33.

39. Denison, Frederic, *Shot and Shell: The Third Rhode Island Heavy Artillery Regiment in the Rebellion*, p. 175.

40. Jackman, Lyman, *History of the Sixth New Hampshire Regiment in the War for the Union*, pp. 99, 109.

41. Benedict, Vol. 1, pp. 88-89. The regiment was the 2nd Vermont Infantry.

42. Beach, Witt., *The First New York (Lincoln) Cavalry*, pp. 149-150.

43. Livermore, *Days and Events*, pp. 133, 137-138, 143-144.

44. Croushore, p. 143, 145.

45. Livermore, Numbers and Losses, p. 101.

46. Testimony of General Grant before the Joint Committee on the Conduct of the War, December 20, 1864. Committee's *Report*, Second Series (1865), Vol. 1, p. 110.

47. *Battles and Leaders*, Vol. 4, pp. 555-556.

48. Phisterer, pp. 247-316. This includes officers holding the rank of General by brevet.

49. Fox, pp. 40-43.

50. Livermore, *Days and Events*, p. 421.

51. Kearny was a good example.

52. Entry for November 1, 1863, diary of David H. Haines, 4th Michigan Cavalry. Manuscript in Burton Historical Collections.

53. Comte de Paris, Vol. 1, p. 270.

54. Letter of First Lieutenant Benjamin F. Fish, First Div. "Union Home Guard," St. Louis, October 5, 1861. Manuscript in Burton Historical Collection.

55. Letter of General Sherman, August 19, 1861. Thorndike, p. 126. See also McClellan, pp. 99-100.

56. About 100 mutineers were placed in irons on a prison ship.

57. Lusk, William C. (editor), *War Letters of William Thompson Lusk*, p. 73, Lusk was a member of the 79th New York Infantry.

58. McClellan, pp. 99-100.

59. Doster, William E., *Lincoln and Episodes of the Civil War*, pp. 148-149.

60. Lecomte, p. 98.

61. *Official Records*, First Series, Vol. 8, 647.

62. United States War Department, "General Order No. 61," June 7, 1862. *General Orders for 1862*.

63. *Ibid.*, "General Order No. 65," June 12, 1862, *General Orders for 1862*, men not reporting were to be classed as deserters.

64. *Ibid.*, "General Order No. 36," April 7, 1862.

65. Joint Committee on the Conduct of the War, *Report*, First Series (1863), Vol. 1, pp. 343-344.

66. United States War Department, "General Order No. 92," July 31, 1862, *General Orders for 1862*.

67. *Ibid.*, This order was repeated in "General Orders, No. 101" and 102, War Department, August 11, 1862, which ordered the Courts of inquiry and revoked the leaves of absence and furloughs mentioned in "General Order No. 92." *General Orders for 1862*.

68. *Battles and Leaders*, Vol. 2, pp. 543-544.

69. McClellan to the Adjutant General, September 28, 1862, Joint Committee on the Conduct of the War, *Report*, First Series (1863), Vol. 1, p. 506.

70. United States War Department," "General Order No. 140," September 24, 1862. *General Orders for 1862*.

71. *Annual Cyclopedia* (1862), p. 21.

72. Annual Report of the General-in-Chief, November 15, 1863, House *Executive Documents*, 38 Cong., 1 Sess., Document 1, p. 44.

73. Testimony of General Hooker before the Joint Committee on the Conduct of the War, March 11, 1865, *Report*, Second Series, Vol. 1, p. 112.

74. *Annual Cyclopedia* (1863), p. 25.

75. United States War Department, "General Order No. 196," June 29, 1863, *General Orders for 1863*.

76. Report of Secretary of War, December 5, 1863, *House Executive Documents*, 38 Cong., 1 Sess., Document 1, p. 9.

77. Report of Secretary of War, March 1, 1865, *House Executive Documents*, 38 Cong., 2 Sess., Document 83, p. 4.

78. Transcript of Alger papers in William L. Clements Library.

79. *House Executive Documents*, 39 Cong., 1 Sess., Document 1, Part 1, pp. 89-90.

80. Ward, (2nd Pennsylvania Heavy Artillery), p. 30.

81. *Official Records*, Third Series, Vol. 5, p. 109, 670, 677-678.

82. *Ibid.*, p. 725.

83. United States War Department, *Regulations for the Army of the United States, 1857*, Article 18, Section 152, p. 21.

84. *Official Records*, Third Series, Vol. 5, pp. 676-677.

85. United States War Department, "General Order No. 73," September 7, 1861, *General Orders for 1861*.

86. *Ibid.*, "General Order No. 36," April 7, 1862, *General Order for 1862*.

87. *Ibid.*, "General Order No. 222," July 16, 1863. *General Orders for 1863*.

88. *Ibid.*, "General Order No. 325." September 28, 1863.

89. *Official Records*, Third Series, Vol. 5, p. 677.

90. Immigration was heavier in the East.

91. *Official Record*, Third Series, Vol. 2, p. 939.

92. Banes, Charles H., *History of the Philadelphia Brigade*, p. 148.

93. Soldiers' mail contained many urgings to come home.

94. Doster, pp. 99-101.

95. United States War Department, "General Order No. 58," March 10, 1863, *General Orders for 1863*, lists the rendezvous and officers.

96. *Ibid.*, "General Order No. 72," March 24, 1863.

97. *House Executive Documents*, 39 Cong. 1 Sess., Document 1, Part 1, pp. 75-76.

98. *Official Records*, Fourth Series, Vol. 3, p. 863.

99. The actual number of foreigners has been ignored.

100. Agassiz, pp. 208-209.

101. *Annual Cyclopedia* (1864), p. 37.

102. *Official Records*, First Series, Vol. 42, Part 2, p. 783.

103. Porter, pp. 192-193.

104. Wilkeson, pp. 12-13.

105. See *Annual Cyclopedia* (1864), p. 37, which asserts that the death penalty was "unsparingly used."

106. Bardeen, pp. 287-288.

107. Rhodes (Battery "B" 1st Rhode Island Light Artillery), p. 241.

108. Hays, *Under the Red Patch*, No. 41-42.

109. Thompson, (13th New Hampshire Infantry), p. 227.

110. Diary of August G. Werthmiller, Co. "G" 5th Ohio Infantry. Manuscript in author's possession.

111. Rhodes, (Battery "B" 1st Rhode Island Light Artillery), pp. 233-234.

112. Adams (19th Massachusetts Infantry), p. 94.

113. *The Story of One Regiment: the Eleventh Maine Infantry Volunteers in the War of the Rebellion*, pp. 234-235.

114. Child, William, *A History of the Fifth Regiment, New Hampshire Volunteers*, pp. 242-245.

115. Lecomte, pp. 97-98.

116. United States War Department, "General Order No. 91," July 29, 1862, *General Orders for 1862*.

117. Comte de Paris, Vol. 1, p. 268.

118. United States War Department, "General Order No. 91," July 29, 1862, *General Orders for 1862*. See also Comte de Paris, Vol. 1, p. 268.

119. Halleck's annual report, November 15, 1863, *House Executive Documents*, 38 Cong., 1 Sess., Document 1, p. 44.

120. Comte de Paris, Vol. 1, p. 268.

121. Bidwell, Frederick David, *History of the Forty-Ninth New York Volunteers*, pp. 149-150. See also, Stevens, *Three Years in the Sixth Corps*, p. 221.

122. Thompson, (13th New Hampshire Infantry), pp. 328, 408.

123. Schofield, p. 182.

124. Livermore, *Days and Events*, p. 64.

125. United States War Department, *Revised Regulations for the Army of the United States 1861*, Article 38, Sections 895, 899.

126. Comte de Paris, Vol. 1, pp. 22-23.

127. Croushore, p. 45.

128. Gibbon, pp. 36-37.

129. Roe, A. S., *The Tenth Regiment Massachusetts Volunteer Infantry 1861-1864*, p. 41.

130. Billings, *Hardtack and Coffee*, p. 145.

131. Wilkeson, pp. 5-6.

132. This was on the Petersburg front.

133. Soldiers convicted of insubordination were also confined on this island prison. Buffum, p. 153. For a description of this prison by an officer who served with the guard detail, see Prentice, "On the Dry Tortugas," *McClure's Magazine*, Vol. 18 (April 1902), pp. 564-570.

134. Wilkeson, p. 33.

135. Usually reserved for extreme cases of insubordination.

136. Wilkeson, p. 35.

137. Billings, *Hardtack and Coffee*, pp. 155-156.

CHAPTER 14

Morale

THE MORALE of the Federal volunteer fluctuated at various periods throughout the war. While it is impossible to measure exactly the morale of an army, a regiment, or even a man, one does observe certain factors that result in either a raising or lowering of the general morale of a large body of troops. This is true, to a certain extent at least, in the Federal Army. Although the men of the North believed in an early victory, their subsequent disappointments did not deter them from prosecuting the war to the successful finish. The loyal men of the Army refused to be disheartened by the terrible lists of casualties, the hardship endured, and the battles lost through incompetent leadership.[1]

SOLDIERS' CONFIDENCE IN THEIR OFFICERS

Morale in a unit was directly affected by the soldier's confidence in their officers, especially in their regimental commanders. There was also a direct relationship between good discipline and high morale; that discipline had be to strong and gained through mutual respect, not through fear of punishment. The Northern volunteer did not take easily to discipline of any kind. Although brave, individualism of the volunteers rendered discipline difficult to achieve and maintain; their obedience resembled the obedience which children render to one of their number whom they have selected to be their captain. The attitude of the men towards their officers varied according to the conduct of the officers themselves. A sentinel who killed his colonel was acquitted in spite of strong evidence of his guilt. The officer was unpopular although a splendid disciplinarian.[2] The volunteers respected most those officers who were personally brave in action and they liked to see their commanders enduring the same hardships that they were forced to undergo. Fortunate was the regiment which began its service under an officer like Colonel Edward E. Cross of the 5th New Hampshire Infantry who so impressed those under him with his spirit that the regiment as little contemplated retreating as he himself did. Cross embodied what the Federal soldiers admired most in their officers; "he was a very brave man, and clearheaded in a fight; he took the most excellent care of

his men in a sanitary way, and was a good disciplinarian.[3] His men submitted to the discipline because they came to learn that it was an intelligent discipline enforced for their own good.

GRUMBLING NOT A MEASURE OF MORALE

The initial reaction of the men to their first hardships was usually the crucial test of their morale. As the men met the discomforts of camp, new diet, inclement weather and inadequate housing, so they endured to the end of their military service. Those who sputtered and growled the worst, together with those who were carefree, taking the mud, storms, and vicissitudes of Army life as good jokes—these were good for every strain and hardship as a general rule. But the quietly despondent ones, the homesick boys, and there were many, were enrolled inevitably for early death or speedy discharge from the service. The volunteer who wrote home that he had "forgotten how to take cold or get sick"[4] was fairly sure of lasting the war out, barring wounds or death. A soldier in the 83rd Pennsylvania Infantry pointed out in a letter home that "there are a few who are constitutional grumblers. They never are satisfied with any treatment or any regulation. They find fault with everything. In fact, if they ever get to Heaven, they'll be finding fault with the music!"[5] Some of the grumbling was justified. Histories and reminiscences are replete with criticism of such installations as the convalescent camp at Alexandria, Virginia. One soldier recorded in his dairy that although he had been in this camp only a week, the time already was much too long. Although he disapproved of grumbling, he did not believe that the camp was as well supplied with food and comfortable quarters as its proximity to Washington would have warranted." The *quantity* is not so much to be complained of as the *quality*. Spero meliora."[6] At other times the grumbling was directly caused by laziness. One soldier, who probably hesitated to complain openly, let off steam to his home folks in the following words:[7]

"The Sholder straps wants to put on stile and they hav us out choping the stumps out and they set back and drink. When I want to work, I work, and when I dont feel all rite I dont work. Then I get right up

214

GENERAL GRANT EMERGING FROM THE WILDERNESS
The soldiers of the Army of the Potomac, who too often had been ordered to retreat after a battle, were given a great lift in morale when Grant headed *toward* Richmond after the Battle of the Wilderness.

and walk off. You can take a horse to water but you cant mak him drink."

The grumblers were always good for laughs, then and now. One man in the 13th New Hampshire Infantry surprised his comrades by suddenly giving up the use of profane language. His explanation was that "no hard words can possibly do the weather and mud here any degree of justice, and he (was) tired of trying." [8] There was constant complaint about the food. An Illinois soldier claimed the beef his regiment received was so worthless "that one can throw a piece up against a tree and it will just stick there and quiver and twitch for all the world like one of those blue-bellied lizards at home will do when you knock them off a fence rail with a stick." Hardtack was so often infested by worms that soldiers nicknamed it the "worm castle." A sergeant described his beloved as follows: "My girl is none of your one-horse girls. She is a regular stub and twister. She is well-educated and refined, all wildcat and fur, and union from the muzzle to the crupper." Private George Hunter of Pennsylvania wrote: "I am well convinced in my own mind that had it not been for officers this war would have ended long ago." Another soldier said he "wished to God one half of our officers were knocked in the head by slinging them against the other half!" [9] The officers, too, showed flashes of humor. When an engineer lieutenant was told to itemize what he would need to mount a cannon in the deep swamp facing Fort Sumter, he sent in a regular requisition for materials and also called for "one hundred men, eighteen feet high, to wade through mud sixteen feet deep." [10]

SOLDIERS NOT IMPRESSED BY HOKUM

The average volunteer possessed a surprising ability to gauge the results of the operations in which he participated. Roseate bulletins describing victories

when he knew his army was whipped, and general orders of congratulations for successful movements which he knew covered up inglorious retreats, did not deceive him in the least. Talk from speakers' platforms of "eyes gazing with rapturous delight on the Old Flag" or "it is dying in an ecstasy of sacrifice that makes the glory of the world," was to him pure hokum. Some soldiers thought that to die under any circumstances was not an act that brought thrills of "voluptuous sweetness" to anyone, unless he was a lunatic. Each soldier believed himself to be immune; to him it was always the man in the next rank who was to be the victim. [14]

FIGHTING MEN HELD OTHERS IN CONTEMPT

The fighting element of the army held in cool contempt the "population (of the camps) constitutionally opposed to warfare, such as cooks, ambulance nurses, stretcher bearers, shirks, and sometimes surgeons . . . no matter whether necessity or inclination . . . (kept) them to the rear . . ." [12] The three-year volunteers had little respect for the nine-month men, especially those who had seen no action. When a veteran regiment heard a short-term regiment complaining of delay in their muster out, the veterans invited them to fight, pointing out that the short-termers would not have anything to tell of the war unless something were done for them in that way. [13] In some cases there was jealousy of three-year regiments who, in consideration of a furlough and another bounty, had re-enlisted just before the expiration of their term of service. Troops stationed in Washington or otherwise permanently located in or near some city or military station were variously called "Bandbox heroes," "Parlor Cadets," and "Lincoln's Pets." This was especially true of the heavy artillery regiments that performed garrison duty in the defenses of Washington until 1864. Many believed that these artillerymen had enlisted to serve out the war in a safe place, but the evidence is that some of these regiments were originally enrolled as infantry units and believed that they would be sent to the front. Until Grant ordered them to the front in the spring of 1864 these men were scoffed at by the other services. In the 1st Maine Heavy Artillery the men had chafed and fretted, sulked and swore all those months, and when at last they did receive the order, they left their camp with cheers, being glad to go and see service.[14] There appears to have been a well-nigh universal contempt for the draft dodgers and perhaps this attitude was fairly well expressed by the soldier who wrote his civilian brother that he would like to see the young men show their patriotism and if they would not serve voluntarily, they should be forced to do so.[15] Even then, these draft dodgers often proved of no value when they did get into combat. For example, at the Battle of Winchester, September 19, 1864, "two *things* in Union uniform were observed playing a queer trick. One of them laid himself on the ground, while the other carefully shot him through the calf of the leg. They then exchanged places, and marksman No. 1 got a Minie ball put through his calf. There was no danger in the operation; and it was a good passport for several months in hospital, no duty, and an easy life. The turmoil of the fight prevented their exposure."[16]

SOLDIERS RESENTED PACIFIST POLITICOS

Soldiers in the field also resented the activities of Democrats in the North who were pro-Southern and who opposed the war aims of Lincoln and the Republicans. Most soldiers realized that many of their comrades were Democrats; they respected these men even though they did not agree with them politically. As an Ohio soldier said:

"There are two parties that call themselves democrats. One is them that are in for the Union and to whip the rebles. Them are demercrats. Then these that are in for peace and are going to rebell agance the draft and agance the prosecution of the war. They are peace men and butternuts and them kind of men. The demercrats are down on them as much as republicians is. It is the opinioned of all the soldiers, with few exceptions, that the peace men of the north is what is carion on the war. If the soldiers do what they say they will of both partys, the peace men in the north will not get as much sympathy as the rebles in the south."[17]

Eventually many of these young men were conscripted but, with some exceptions, they were not of the same caliber as the original volunteers who held them in little respect.

TROOPS EMBITTERED BY GRAFT AND IRREGULAR PAY

Soldiers in the Army of the Mississippi possessed in 1863 an almost universal feeling of intense bitter-ness, from the conviction that they were being used principally for the benefit of cotton speculators, officers, and outsiders.[18] The failure to pay the troops regularly contributed to low morale. There was very low morale among Missouri troops in 1864 because of this reason, resulting in depredations by the men who had lost all hope of receiving their pay. Their commander feared that the troops would abandon all organization and go home. The officers had received no pay for twenty months.[19] In the Army of the Potomac, soldiers resented the publication of reports by newspapers that they were living in comfort with nothing to be desired.

FEAR OF CONFEDERATE PRISONS

Newspaper reports were not necessary to encourage the Federal soldier to resist capture if at all possible. Many Federal soldiers risked everything rather than be taken prisoner. When the 10th Massachusetts Battery was attacked by Confederate Infantry its supporting troops gave way, but the battery continued to fire until overpowered. The few survivors who were not killed or wounded decided instantly to attempt to run the guantlet of fire because "against the horrors of Rebel prisons on the one hand we (had) only to balance the chances of being shot while retreating."[20] Despite the evidence of recent scholarship to show that the Confederate prisons did not deliberately starve Federal prisoners, and that much of the atrocity flavor to the newspaper accounts was but a reflection of war psychosis in the North,[21] Federal soldiers *knew* that a great many of their comrades who were taken captive never returned and that those who did return were often in poor physical condition.

COLLECTIVE COURAGE SUBSTANDARD

Because the North was the invader, her armies were more often than not the assaulting troops and conducted most of the sieges. The Federal soldier displayed from the very first a great deal of personal bravery. But "collective courage," a distinctive trait of well-trained armies, was lacking. Federal troops had been accustomed to complete freedom of action before their enlistment, and long habits of training were necessary before they could function smoothly as a unit. They went into battle in a spirit of obedience which the Count of Paris thought rather rational than passive; they were actuated more by a sense of duty as citizens than by the habitude of the disciplined soldier who forgets his own volition to follow that of his chief.[22] Because of the independence of the Federal volunteer, more than one general saw a certain victory turned into defeat, while on the other hand, the most disastrous defeats could almost always be remedied. If the soldiers believed further effort useless they retreated despite all efforts of their officers to stop them. The retreat seldom degenerated into a rout because the men refused to believe themselves beaten. They were only intent on reaching better positions which, in their minds, gave better promise of being defended than those they were evacuating. Federal volunteers were usually capable of being rallied.[23] Too often, however, they retired in regular order and suffered heavily in so doing, while their opponents employed an open-order style of fighting and in retreating went rapidly in irregular formation, thus presenting a poor mark for musketry.[24] The "fugitives" were a much misrepresented class. Actually, when defeated, the soldiers did not fly at full speed for any considerable distance. They soon dropped into a walk even though the bullets were still whizzing around them. Although cool, however, they usually wanted to find their own company, or at least their regiment before continuing the fight. Officers, too, appeared bewildered, and often instead of rallying the men in their immediate vicinity would go off in search of their units; but if a superior officer would order such lost officers to take command of squads of soldiers they would do so. Apparently their morale was restored by the authority and responsibility thrust upon them.

LOW MORALE FROM ASSAULTING FIELDWORKS

As their enemy came to learn the wisdom of digging entrenchments and protecting those entrenchments with obstructions in front, the Federal infantry was forced to assault them with a certainty of losing heavily in the process. Beyond a reasonable proportion of perhaps four to one, numbers amounted to nothing in making such assaults. Often a single division was just as good for an assault as two corps. It was not physically possible for numbers to succeed in certain assaults even if the immediate commander was willing to sacrifice the men, and if the men were willing to be sacrificed. As the officers and men came to see what was involved in frontal assaults on entrenched positions, there came to be a general unwillingness among commanders and men to sacrifice or to be sacrificed beyond what seemed to them a reasonable expenditure of life for the object to be gained. By the latter part of 1864 assaults of this nature could only be successful if made when the positions to be carried had been but recently occupied and the fortifications were very slight. After several days' occupation the positions became im-

SUNKEN ROAD AND STONE WALL NEAR FREDERICKSBURG
Burnside gravely damaged the morale of his troops by hurling them against this strong Confederate position in December, 1862.

pregnable. The idea became increasingly prevalent that there was no necessity of fighting the enemy on unequal terms. This was not due to cowardice but good sense. The veteran Federal soldier fought very much as he had been accustomed to work his farm or run his sawmill; he wanted to see a fair prospect that it was going to pay. As General Schofield said: "To mass troops against the fire of a covered line is simply to devote them to destruction. The greater the mass, the greater the loss—that is all."[25]

The hurling of masses of men on entrenched positions resulted not only in heavy casualties but also in an appreciable drop in morale among the survivors. After the failure of his June 14, 1863 assault on Port Hudson, General Banks offered "various glories" to volunteers for what was to be known as the "forlorn hope," but those regiments that had suffered most severely in the first assault sent very few volunteers for the second. For instance, the 8th New Hampshire, which had already lost more than two-thirds of its numbers in the unsuccessful assaults, did not furnish a single officer or soldier.[26] The Federal soldiers were grimly appreciative of the few opportunities they had of repelling enemy assaults on *their* entrenched positions; and they made the enemy pay heavily for such attempts. During the siege of Knoxville, Federal troops repulsed a Confederate infantry attack with a loss to themselves of 13 killed and wounded. The enemy lost from 1300 to 1500 men, a very large proportion of whom were killed.[27]

Cavalry Morale Improved

The cavalry fared better than the infantry, especially in the first two years of the war when they were used mainly for scouting and escort duty. Greatly inferior to the Confederate cavalry from 1861 to the spring of 1863, they did not really "find themselves" until completely re-organized under Hooker. On the Peninsula and even at Antietam, the Federal cavalry had done little beyond rounding up stragglers. In the spring of 1863 the Federal horsemen were collected into large units and sent out to fight the enemy horse. At Brandy Station, June 9, 1863, they acquitted themselves very well. This battle really made the Federal Cavalry.[28] Up to that time they had been confessedly inferior to the Southern horsemen, but they gained on that day the confidence in themselves and in their commanders which enabled them to contest so fiercely the subsequent battlefields of June, July, and October. By 1864, Federal cavalry was not only well trained but possessed a firm belief in its ability to defeat Confederate cavalry whenever encountered. In the Shenandoah Valley, Sheridan's cavalry repeatedly charged Confederate infantry protected by stone walls, riding right up to and in some cases over the walls before retreating in fairly good order, and, although under a furious fire, "with apparently no more of panic than if they had been fighting a sham battle."[29]

Artillery Had High Morale

The artillery branch of the Federal Army possessed high morale from the very beginning of the war and never lost it. One writer believed it to be the steadiest of the three arms because "the piece is subject to neither fear nor panic, it does not move easily, and the cannoneers are nothing without it."[30] At all events, its fighting won the admiration of the enemy and foreign observers alike. From Bull Run to Appomatox, Federal artillery, supported or unsupported, took a heavy toll from the excellent Confederate infantry troops who learned in the course of the war the wisdom of "opening out" as they approached the well-served Federal batteries.[31] At Gaines' Mill the artillery did their whole duty; in the words of a war correspondent "they peopled Hades."[32] Those who lost their guns stood by them until half the battery's men and horses were struck down and the ammunition completely expended. In several instances the men dragged their guns off by hand. Artillerymen were bayoneted at their guns for having cut the throats of uninjured horses to prevent them falling into the hands of the enemy. An English observer reported that although many guns fell into the hands of the Confederates the "heaps of blue-jackets round them told that they had been heroically defended.[33] Had the guns not been sold as dearly as they were, had they been brought off when it was still "safe," the main body of the Federal infantry must have surrendered. Such defense was typical throughout the war. At Malvern Hill Federal artillery mowed down desperate infantry assaults by a hitherto victorious enemy and prevented a major breakthrough which could have resulted in disaster to McClellan's army. At Cold Harbor during the 1864 campaign, a Confederate noticed with admiration an unsupported Federal battery which increased the rapidity of its fire as its difficulties mounted, showing no signs of becoming wild or hurried. Every shot went straight to the object against which it was directed; every fuse was accurately timed, and every shell burst where it was intended to burst. Several of the guns were dismounted, and dead horses were strewn in rear. The loss among the men was appalling, but the battery commander fought on as coolly as before, and with their glasses the enemy could see him calmly sitting on his large gray horse directing the work of his gunners.[34] Federal artillery in the West was equally good. The 11th Ohio Battery at Iuka although surrounded on three sides repulsed five enemy charges, losing 77 out of 80 horses and half its men in killed and wounded. After killing and wounding about 800 enemy infantrymen the "survivors were finally choked from the guns they would not abandon." A Confederate prisoner said later: "Those battery boys had so much spunk that we took pity on a few who were left."[35] There were exceptions, but in the main, Federal gunners served their pieces with efficiency and devotion. Regular artillery units were well trained and rendered efficient service; they were soon matched by volunteer batteries equally good.

REGULAR ARMY

Except in the artillery service and in the higher echelons of leadership, the contribution of the Regular Army to the winning of the war was negligible. Whereas the volunteers lost 353,730 by death, the Regular Army lost but 5,798. Of every thousand men killed in battle and died of wounds, 21 were Regulars, 948 (nearly) were volunteers, and 31 were colored; of the same thousand, 123 (nearly) were cavalry, 32 were artillery, and 845 (nearly) were infantry. The volunteers lost 107,787 killed and mortally wounded and 221,494 by disease while the Regular Army lost 2,283 killed and mortally wounded and 3,092 by disease.[36] The ratios per thousand of men furnished by the three services were:

Regulars	25.29
Colored	70.58
Volunteers	904.13

Of every thousand men killed in battle or died of wounds, the volunteers contributed 43 more than their proportionate number, the Regulars 4 less, and the colored troops 39 less.[37]

FOREIGNERS

The white volunteers included large numbers of foreigners, especially Germans and Irish. As soldiers in the field, some of the German troops were nearly useless because they spoke no English. Under good officers some did tolerably well in simple line formations, but others were only interested in plunder and not in fighting.[38] Hancock's troops behaved badly at Ream's Station, August 25, 1864, especially three New York regiments that were officered by men who could not speak English. In this engagement only 99 officers and men were killed and 501 wounded and 1752 missing. Many of the foreigners were substitutes.[39] The German troops apparently surrendered readily; at New Market, Virginia, nearly all the prisoners were Germans. Two cadets from the Virginia Military Institute captured 23 of them.[40] The Irish appear to have fought well, especially the famous Irish Brigade in the Army of the Potomac. One foreign observer believed it to be but "simple justice to allow that the native soldiers have borne themselves, as a rule, better than the aliens. The Irish Brigade . . . has performed good service . . . but the Germans have not been distinguished either for discipline or daring."[41] However, this appraisal of the Germans in the Federal Army is not in accord with a more recent analysis[42] which characterizes them as "somewhat slow in response but . . . stable and solid in battle; they learned, in fact, to do some skillful fighting." Much of the attitude toward the Germans which was rather generally held during the war was due to the rout of the 11th corps at Chancellorsville and its subsequent defeat on the first day at Gettysburg. In both battles, native Americans were also routed and no objective analysis of the 11th Corps' defeats can ignore the important factors of faulty tactical disposition and inept leadership.

NEGRO TROOPS

The employment of colored troops by the Federal government met with considerable opposition, not only from civilians but also from many Regular officers and volunteers who believed it to be a white man's war. When the order arming the Negroes was read to an Irish regiment the men hissed.[43] While there were many soldiers who favored the emancipation of the Negro, others believed a system of servitude preferable to immediate emancipation because the Negro would become a worthless vagabond if free.[44] It was often asserted that freed slaves would not make good soldiers and could not be subjected to military discipline.[45] Sherman believed that the Negroes were not the equal of white men and should be used mainly as pioneers and servants, and later on as garrison troops.[46] The general would not use them for skirmishing and picket duty because soldiers must do many things without orders, using their common sense, as for example, men on picket duty. "Negroes are not equal to this."[47] An aide to General Meade in a letter of May 7, 1864, wrote that they did not dare trust them in the line of battle. The aide said in part: "Ah, you may make speeches at home, but here, where it is life or death, we dare not risk it. They have been put to guard the trains and have repulsed one or two little cavalry attacks in a creditable manner; but God help them if the grey-backed infantry attack them."[48]

Negro troops went into action for the first time July 16, 1863, at James Island, South Carolina. Some of them were taken prisoner and the enemy proclaimed that such prisoners would be turned over to State authorities to be tried under the local laws relating to servile insurrection, and that white men commanding them would be dealt with as outlaws although there is no evidence that this was ever done.[49] It is unquestionably true, however, that officers and men of Negro units who were captured received unnecessarily rough treatment. The excessively large number of colored troops killed in the capture of Fort Pillow, April 12, 1864, caused intense indignation in the North. The Confederate commander, General Bedford Forrest, justified the act by holding that Negroes were property and not prisoners of war.[50] A more reasonable explanation was offered by the Confederate general, S. D. Lee, who held that it was "a servile race armed against their masters, and in a country which had been desolated by almost unprecedented outrages."[51] Federal colored units saw little action in the war but the consensus of opinion seems to be that they fought fairly well.[52] The fact that they were very likely to be killed after capture[53] made their employment as assault troops a delicate one. They were used with reluctance by the Federal commander in the assault on the Petersburg Crater but the entire operation was badly executed and many of the colored troops were captured by an enraged enemy and promptly dispatched.[54] The Negro recruit was amenable to discipline and learned drill quickly. He was more docile and obedient; he worked better, but his officers deemed him "more timorous" than the white.[55] All observers agreed that the colored troops recruited from free States were superior to those recruited from slave States. The Negroes' superstitious nature was sometimes a handicap to their reliability on outpost duty. One officer recorded in his journal how the coming of darkness filled the colored troops at his fort with fear. When any unusual sound was heard such as a bird stirring in the bushes or the song of a whippoorwill, some Negro was sure to interpret it as an omen of coming evil, and thus "an alarm . . . (was) given by firing which . . . (was) generally followed by a stampede *not to the front.*"[56] Surgeons of enrollment boards said, in general, that the Negroes were about the same as whites in physical aptitude for military service.[57]

The problem of accepting colored volunteers arose soon after the fall of Sumter. In May, 1861, General Butler at Newport News, Virginia, was asking General Scott what to do with "this species of property" that was being utilized by the enemy in the construction of batteries.[58] Some use had already been made of fugitive Negroes in the Quartermaster Department.[59] On May 6, 1862, the United States agent in charge of "contrabands" in South Carolina was apprised of the intention to organize at least one regiment of colored troops, giving them pay, food, clothing, and training "in the same manner with other troops.[60] A regiment raised by General Hunter was disbanded, however, on August 10, 1862, due to lack of support from the War Department. Hunter was a firm believer in the potentialities of the Negro soldier.[61] In the summer of 1862 the President was authorized to receive into the service of the United States "for the purpose of constructing intrenchments, or performing camp service, or any other labor or any military or naval service for which they may be found competent, persons of African descent.[62] The first troops mustered in under this act were the "First Louisiana Native Guards," subsequently designed the "73rd Regiment, United States Colored Troops."[63] The Enrollment Act of March 3, 1863, included among those liable to draft all male citizens of the prescribed ages; this was interpreted to include free Negroes but met with such bitter opposition in the border States that in those sections its enforcement was hampered.[64] Negroes could only be accepted as substitutes for their own race due to disparities in pay and bounties with the whites.[65]

Several colored regiments had already been raised when the Bureau was a part of the Adjutant General's Office[66] and provided field officers to supervise the organization of the colored troops as well as boards to examine applicants for commissions in new Negro regiments.[67] Recruiting of the colored troops soon became a system. The Adjutant General, Lorenzo Thomas, was ordered to the Mississippi Valley to superintend the formation of the colored units. The noncommissioned officers were generally appointed from white regiments, but as intelligent blacks were found they were made corporals and sergeants.[68] Almost without exception all the commissioned were white.[69] The best material for the line officers in the colored regiments was found to exist among the noncommissioned officers and privates of the volunteer regiments. They were, as a rule, "vastly superior" to the commissioned officers who applied for field appointments.[70] The number of applicants for commissions amounted to 9,019, of which 3,790 were examined. Of this number 1,472 were rejected and 2,318 received appointments.[71] Some of the early appointments were made by General Butler in New Orleans; many of these were unfit and were later dismissed from the service.[72] The total number of colored troops (including their white officers) enlisted in the war was 186,017.[73] The number of colored soldiers was 178,975 but the largest number in service at any one time was 123,156, the number on the rolls July 15, 1865.[74]

Although one historian[75] maintains that "there can be no question as to the value of the Negro soldier in the War" the fact remains that they saw little active service. Colored troops were not severely exposed to field service proper; their battle mortality was but 16.11 per thousand as compared to the white volunteers' 35.10. The rate of mortality by disease among the colored troops was 141.39 per thousand while the white mortality was 59.22. It may be assumed that where one man died of disease, at least five others were seriously sick, a large proportion of the colored troops must have been constantly upon the sick-list.[76] The Provost Marshal believed the reason to be one of morale and not physical. The colored men had "lack of heart, hope, mental activity" which could be improved by a higher moral and intellectual culture. The colored regiments were well led; their officers lost in killed and mortally wounded 1 in 42 while the men lost 1 in 66; in disease the officers lost 1 in 77 but their men lost 1 in 7. Desertion for white and black volunteer regiments was approximately the same.[77]

MILITARY REVERSES AFFECTED MORALE

Morale in this heterogeneous Federal Army fluctuated according to the vicissitudes of war but throughout the protracted struggle there were enough faithful soldiers, possessed of their President's grim determination to fight the war to a finish, to insure final victory. The North expected an easy victory in 1861; the early volunteers had no doubt as to their ability to defeat their adversaries with speed and ease. Far sighted men like Sherman were openly derided because they expressed the conviction the war might well be long and bitter. The soldiers themselves were optimistic; in one company the estimated number of "rebels" that one Yankee could comfortably handle ranged from five to twelve.[78] Before Bull Run the Federal troops received minor setbacks at Big Bethel, Vienna, and Blackburn's Ford where there was much talk of ambuscades and "masked batteries." These reverses probably had little effect on the morale of the early Federal volunteers whom Davis believed inferior to the Confederates in self-reliance and the habitual use of fire arms.[79] As the troops crossed Bull Run they laughed at precautions being taken to cover their retreat. The defeat itself was not due to lack of courage on their part [80] nor was the retreat a complete rout.[81] Many units preserved their organization throughout the entire retrograde movement.

Most of the troops who fought at Bull Run returned home and three-year regiments poured into Washington. Morale was high among these new units; they "did not despair of the Union, and only prayed that they might be ably led against the enemy, that their services and sacrifice might contribute decisively to success."[82] The fall of 1861 was utilized by the young commander, McClellan, in organizing and training the Federal Army. The weather and roads were ideal for a movement during October and November; the army was in excellent spirits, but no aggressive attempt of any sort was made to reduce the enemy batteries on the Potomac River.[83]

But McClellan waited too long. Due to poor roads, fighting in the Civil War was generally seasonal. During the latter part of November there set in a long spell of stormy and miserable weather. The ground became a mass of mortar; the tents were flooded; the weather became dismal and gloomy and stayed that way. The men were unable to leave their quarters, except when they were compelled to stand guard. Sometimes they were almost to their knees in mud with the cold rain falling on them and chilling them to the bone. All began to grow restless and impatient. Letters from home informed the men in the field that a great change had taken place; all manufacturing concerns had started up with a boom and wages were higher than ever before. Those who had remained at home were making money, while many of the wives and children of the soldiers were beginning to feel the cold grip of want and were suffering from sickness, cold, and hunger. "Those big-hearted Union-savers who said, 'go boys, go and save our beloved country, and we will take care of your families and see that they do not suffer', had

forgotten their promises." Soldiers' wives and children soon had nothing to depend upon but the scanty $13.00 a month which was paid them at irregular intervals. To make it worse, all the necessities of life began to go up in price, and the mother of a large family began to be heavily pressed for the bread for herself and her hungry brood. She told her soldier husband of these troubles in her letters; consequently, many of the men began to feel the corroding of the fetters which bound them to a military life from which there was no escape. Their friends and neighbors at home were reaping a golden harvest, while their loved ones were experiencing increasing difficulty in getting a mere subsistence. All this angered the soldiers; "their faces became gloomy and their hearts grew sad; and in many cases the results soon became apparent." Some became homesick, which is "the worst sickness that can befall a man, a sickness that mocks at medicine and the doctor's skill." These men were sent to the hospital where many sank, despite the doctors' care, and passed away from life.[84]

The unfortunate affairs at Ball's Bluff affected generally only those regiments who participated in the battle. For the others, although there was an increasing desire on the part of many to see their homes, if only for a brief period, most of the men were impatient for something to do to end the war.[85] The men, generally, were possessed a high resolve, fervid enthusiasm, and intense susceptibility to patriotic appeals. The glad and joyous confidence in the speedy success of the Union cause, which animated officers and men, sought some embodied object, and as a result, created that ideal of their first leader (McClellan) which defeat and disgrace could not shatter.[86] The Army of the Potomac was now a well-disciplined and drilled organization of more than a hundred thousand men, and in better heart to do fighting than it ever was in later years. During its first engagements all were anxious to get into the fighting, even officers' servants and other detailed men, taking their guns and their places in the ranks of their own free will.[87]

This army under General McClellan was made up largely of the flower of the manhood of the Northern and Eastern States; the officers were men and soldiers of a very high type.[88] The army's confidence in its leaders was disturbed by the month's delay in taking Yorktown, but the men remained cheerful despite rain and often insufficient rations. At Gaines' Mill the Federal right was crushed while the center and left, under McClellan's own eye, were held passive in front of a skeleton line. Nevertheless the men believed Richmond would be taken; they still trusted their commander and cheered him at every opportunity. During the Seven Days their morale remained unaffected; they had become accustomed to military life and even after defeat they were always ready to resume the offensive.[89] The enemy was decisively repulsed at Malvern Hill and the men, believing that their retreating was finally over, were amazed when McClellan lead them to Harrison's Landing and then back to Washington.[90] Although McClellan was in advance of his army during the retreat, seeking defensive positions, he boasted to the President on July 2, 1862, that he had only lost one gun and one wagon.[91] A week later he reported to Stanton that the enemy was in full retreat![92] It can scarcely cause surprise that the Administration was bewildered by such a man who expressed fear one moment and bravado the next. McClellan was forced to transfer many of his units to Pope, who was given command of a new army. The transferred units were torn by loyalty to the old commander and antagonism toward the new. Brigade and divisional commanders showed by every word and act their disapproval of the change, while during the battle (Second Bull Run) which Pope conducted, one corps commander (Porter) held his men in the rear although in "plain hearing at less than 3 miles distance, of a furious battle, which raged all day."[93] The men who were engaged "made a splendid fight," at one time even breaking the enemy line but there was too much attacking piecemeal.[94] Pope and his army retired to the defenses of Washington defeated, humiliated, and discouraged. The attitude of the troops was one of mortification and rage, tempered slightly with disgust.[95] It appeared to some that the army was sullenly waiting to be slaughtered.[96]

Thousands of stragglers hurried to the defenses of Washington the command of which, including all the troops for the defense of the capital, was soon given to McClellan again.[97] The army welcomed him back because they believed in the main that he had shown great ability; they accepted his estimate of the enemy's numbers and were inclined, therefore, to hold the Administration responsible for sacrificing them by demanding the impossible.[98] Later disasters only served to strengthen this delusion. At Antietam, McClellan, who "would have been an excellent chief of staff but was unfit for the command of any army."[99] sent in his troops a corps at a time. It was the bloodiest single day's battle of the war; between sunrise and four o'clock in the afternoon the Federal forces lost 2108 killed, 9549 wounded and but 753 missing out of 53,000 engaged. McClellan had 75,000 on the field. Lee used all of his 51,000 men, losing 2,700 killed, 9,024 wounded, and about 2,000 missing.[100] One of McClellan's corps commanders, impatient at having been compelled by the remissness of his commander to waste the precious hours of the early morning, attacked in column of brigades with no skirmish line. The brigades were so close[101] behind each other that there was insufficient space to admit their changing front. The men, full of confidence, advanced until they met at close

range a terrible and sustained fire, which was impossible for them to return, nor could the leading brigades change front. In a very few minutes one division alone lost over 2,200 officers and men out of a strength of 5,500.[102] Despite such sacrifice the enemy was allowed to escape. After the battle, morale throughout the Federal forces elsewhere was raised by reports of McClellan's "great victory."[103] The administration was not similarly impressed, however, and the "Little Napoleon" was removed, an act which "greatly depressed" many in the Army of the Potomac.[104]

MEN DEPRESSED BY McCLELLAN'S REMOVAL

So depressed were many of the men at this time, that their letters reflected their general state of morale. The following is an example of this:[105]

Ever since the war broke out I have been desirous of entering into the service, but while my wife was living I did not think it was my duty to do so. Being troubled with rheumatism I failed in my first attempts to enter the army, but finally enlisted and I was accepted on the 15th day of August last. We were in camp at Worchester two weeks and then took passage in the steamer Merrimack in Boston for the city of Washington. After a very unpleasant voyage of four days (owing to the crowded state of the boat) we landed in that city. Since then we have been almost constantly on the march from place to place. Some of our marches made in the hot weather were very severe. We were near by but not in the battles in the state of Maryland. An error in an order alone prevented our regiment from being in the battle of Antietam. We arrived on the field of battle soon after its occurence and witnessed the effects of that terrible slaughter of human life. We marched from there to various points in Maryland and crossed the Potomac on the 26th instant in a severe rain storm and suffered much in consequence. We have since then closely pressed the Rebs in their retreat south. Our artillery and cavalry have had almost daily skirmishes with them. Of how the war goes on, or the Union cause goes on, we know but very little except what comes under our immediate observation. We get no daily papers, or at least, not until they are 8 or 10 days old. The weather since we have been in this state has been cold and very uncomfortable. Most of the time we have had sufficient to eat by patronizing the suttlers and with what the government furnishes. But at present we are very scantily supplied. The government furnishes no vegetables of any kind, nothing but hard bread and meat with coffee and a very little sugar. While we were in Maryland our hard bread was very poor, the most of it being wormy and all of it was moldy or musty. But now what we have is of good quality. There is much dissatisfaction among the soldiers in this wing of the army (because of their treatment with regards food and pay). Much more than is supposed to be the case at the North. In fact, I think ⅘ of them are getting to regard the cause for which they left their homes and families with indifference, and care but little how the war ends so that it ends soon. They are willing to fight if that will aid in hastening their return to their homes. The impression is pretty general among us that the war has been and will be unnecessarily prolonged from political and selfish motives. We, that is the Mass. 35th, were promised that if we would enlist that we should not have to guard rebel property, that the time of such foolishness had passed

BATTLE OF ANTIETAM
Thousands of Federal soldiers were sacrificed near Dunker Church by these massed attacks.

away. But in this matter we were deceived and sadly disappointed. Everything belonging to the Rebs here is protected and guarded even to a straw stack except fences which we *will* have for fuel, but that I suppose the government will pay well for. Now when we are hungry, to be forbidden to take even a chicken from our enemies under penalty of being sent to Harper's Ferry to work on the public works is very trying to our remaining patriotism. Nevertheless the "boys" do forage a little now and then. Three of our company were caught in the act the other night and narrowly escaped sent to the public works. If they had been so sent I most think it would have created mutiny in the regiment. The President's proclamation freeing the slaves after the 1st of January is laughed at for the reason that his previous one is not enforced. Although we are suffering for food, close by is a large mill owned by rebels who won't even sell us a meal for our currency and their mill and property is guarded by our troops. This with hundreds of similar things convinced me that it is not the wish of our generals to hasten the war to a close. The most painful thing to me about the business is to witness the effect upon the soldiers of being away from the restraints of society. Many of them seem to lose all respect for themselves or others and give loose rein to every evil fashion that they have an opportunity to gratify. Profanity and vulgarity of the most horrid and low description is shamefully indulged in even by officers. In our company, for instance, every officer, commissioned and non-commissioned, uses profane language more

or less. A sick man here receives but little attention, scarcely as much as a sick horse or mule. It is wonderful how in different we become to scenes of suffering and death. A man dies in the morning and is buried without coffin or shroud before night and no more attention is paid to it than if he were a brute. But when I think that each soldier that dies here leaves a circle of friends to mourn their loss my heart aches, and I am glad that they do not and cannot see how he has been treated.

DEFEAT AT FREDERICKSBURG RUINED MORALE

The new commander, General Burnside, appears to have been well liked by the army and it was hoped by the men that he would push things with more vigor than had his predecessor.[106] Burnside did not live up to expectations; possessing "astounding ignorance" of the terrain in front of him, he refused to credit information as to terrain features which made his ill-fated attack hopeless from the start.[107] "As the observer stood on the range of hills which impend over Fredericksburg on the south, and glanced his eye down upon the town, he might have challenged the most deeply read student of military history to produce any precedent in which battle has ever been delivered under circumstances more unfavorable to the assailing party, or upon ground from which any great master of the art of war would more naturally have recoiled, had the initative remained within his own option."[108] The men themselves knew the hopelessness of their commander's attack. Their enemy had entrenched the hills and planted cannon upon them, "tier after tier as thick as they could work them, their light artillery upon the first hills, and heavy artillery upon higher hills."[109] In front of these batteries the enemy had a line of infantry posted in rifle pits, while sharpshooters were concealed in great numbers all over the undulating plain which had to be crossed by the Federal infantry. Behind a stone wall on the main hill itself (Marye's Heights) the enemy had posted his men six ranks deep.[110] thus insuring an uninterrupted rate of fire. Under such circumstances the men could expect but one result and although they charged up the sloping hill again and again they only rushed upon their own destruction. "The rebels fired their artillery so rapidly that it seemed one continual roar and we could not distinguish the discharge of a single cannon . . . the rebel infantry sent perfect showers of bullets to meet us, yet we kept steadily on until we had drove the rebel infantry back to their entrenchments."[111] After this disaster the morale of the Army of the Potomac just about collapsed completely. As one soldier expressed it: "I should not care for this (the loss of his leg) if we had been put in where we had the least chance. It's gone for nothing."[112] There now existed a total want of confidence in those who managed the operations of the Army of the Potomac; survivors resented repeated mistakes in strategy and grossest blunders in movement and began to consider further effort unreasonable and criminal. In one regiment on the first roll-call after the battle only 70 men responded where one year before 1,000 men had answered to their names.[113] Prisoners told the enemy of their disgust with the repeated failures of the Federal forces.[114] Straggling soldiers returned to camp, "muddy, wet, ugly, sour, and insubordinate."[115]

The men felt that their lives were being made the playthings of high officers in command; they felt that they were sacrificed and imperiled at Antietam, through the blunderings of incompetents, and thrown against the impregnable entrenchments of Marye's Heights by obstinate stupidity. Those indeed were dark days. "The men moved about the duties of the camp with sad hearts and dejected mien. At every turn they missed many of the familiar faces of officers and comrades." There was considerable sickness, the hospital accommodations were inadequate and meager, the wounded did not receive proper care and doubtless many lives were lost on this account. "I do not believe I have ever seen greater misery from sickness than exists now in our Army of the Potomac."[116] For the army, the Falmouth camp after Fredericksburg and until April 1863, was the Valley Forge of the War. The bands were forbidden to play pathetic or plaintive tunes, such as "Home, Sweet Home," "Annie Laurie," and "Auld Lang Syne" lest they serve to depress and unnerve the suffering men.[117] Some regiments, not in the Army of the Potomac, were in similar shape. In order to keep *their* morale up, they were told at retreat parade that the Federal forces had won a great victory.[118] Posterity agrees with an evaluation of the Federal soldiers' fighting spirit at Fredricksburg which has been so well set forth in our time: "Whatever credit may be gleaned from the Northern hopes on the Rappahannock during the winter of 1862-1863 belongs to the fighting men of the Union Army, who went into action under a terrific handicap of inept leadership at the army and ground division levels . . . the troops who shattered themselves against the stone wall (in six massive but unsupported attacks) before Fredericksburg were as sound and courageous as any who ever wore the uniform of the American soldier."[119]

MORALE GOOD AFTER CHANCELLORSVILLE

A successor to Burnside was difficult to find. So infatuated were some sources with McClellan that one paper believed it should be he, maintaining that the army and the people would unanimously approve the choice.[120] "Fighting Joe" Hooker was finally selected and soon the morale of the men rose again; the new commander not only reorganized them but visited various units, infusing a good deal of his own confident spirit into his officers and men.[121] An Ohio soldier recorded in his diary[122] the morale in the Army of the Potomac just prior and during the Battle of Chancellorsville. The following excerpts from this heretofore unpublished diary are fairly typical of the experiences of the other soldiers, and reveal an unusual ability to depict the mood of the men as they marched to battle.

April 21, (1863)
The air was clear and a new moon was riding brightly in the heavens. It was a glorious scene—the large camp last night. The forest was lighted with innumerable campfires. Groups of men were sitting around, conversing or singing Union and love songs. Late we received notification that a mail would leave at 6 o'clock in the morning and soon a number of boys were engaged writing to the loved ones at home. I had none to write to.

April 29:
Arose at daylight. Was very sore; all the limbs of my body ached. We crossed the Rappahannock at about 7 a.m. on pontoons. The 5th Corps is in our rear. The 11th Corps commenced crossing at 9 p.m. last night and troops have crossed ever since. We met with no resistance of any kind. We marched till quite late and then halted. Our cavalry captured about 65 Rebs who were building a bridge across the Rapidan. They were a good looking set of men. It was an entire surprise. In the evening the 11th Corps passed us and also the 5th. The men were in fine spirits and were singing martial airs as they marched

along. About 9 p.m. we again took up the line of march and crossed the Rapidan. The Rebs had erected piers and on each pier was a log fire burning, illuminating the scene. The river is deep and very swift. A beautiful scene—those masses of men crossing over on thick plank, the water boiling, rushing mildly along, the steady tramp of the crossing men—all lighted up by the blazing fire of pine boards and knots; it was one of the most impressive scenes I ever witnessed.

May 1:

A very pleasant morning. The sun is shining warm and the birds are warbling their morning songs of thanksgiving to the all-kind Creator of all that is good. The Brass Band of the 27th Regt. O.V.I. is playing and the forest is full of sweet echoes, recalling bygone and lovely, peaceful scenes of former years. The boys are cleaning their arms. The clicking of a lock or the ring of the steel ramrod as it rebounds from the polished breech may be instantly heard. Cartridges were given out a few minutes ago and everything indicates work, bloody and hot, to be close at hand.

(Later)

We are laying in the woods waiting for further orders. About 12½ we were ordered to fall in. We then marched out on the plank road about 1 mile when we turned to our right and went into the woods where we formed a line of battle and loaded our pieces. After about for ½ hour laying around we marched forward through woods and creeks and lay'd in a small open field. A shell came and struck near on our left, exploding and wounding 2 of the 29th Regt. O.V.I. After a little while we fell back again the same way we came. Musketry increased on our left and grew heavier every moment. About 5 p.m. the Rebs attempted to storm our battery but were received in an ambush and received a terrible fire from our massed infantry. They were repulsed and then our artillery opened on them a terrible fire of grape, cannister, shell and solid shot. They came twice and both times were repulsed. During the fight we were laying down on our arms. The fight was about 200 yd. on our left. About dusk the Rebs commenced skirmishing on our right but after some heavy cannonading were repulsed. We laid down on our arms during the night. The men all done splendidly, being cool and determined everything work as it ought to and everything would come out all right.

May 2:

Day clear and warm. Laid around camp, lounging around doing nothing. At 4 p.m. we received suddenly orders to fall in in light marching order. skirmishing commenced in the front and grew heavier every minute. Troops came from the right wing on a double quick to reinforce the center of our line. Artillery opened and for a while a continuous roar of musketry and artillery could be heard on the right, increased with the yell of the charging regiments and groans of the wounded. (the Rebels) succeeded in turning our right flank and totally surprising the 11th Corps. Stragglers came running from the field but we compelled them to go back to their respective regiments.

May 3:

We had lain about 15 minutes when a shell came skreeching through the air from the Battery opposite our centre cutting the knapsack of Ransom's back, striking about 1 foot in front of me, covering my face with dirt and little stones, which hurt me severely. It then rebounded, passed through the left shoulder of Thomas Mundy, then tearing off Geo. Morris right arm near the shoulder and then exploded, killing a commissioned offi-

cer of the 147 PA and 1 private. Geo. Morris arm was found laying about 12 feet from him. Morris and Mundy were conveyed to the hospital, Morris using the last accommodation there, then walked to United States ford, a distance of about 4 miles.

At Chancellorsville the Federal troops fought well, confident in their leader and hopeful of winning a complete and decisive victory, and were puzzled as to the cause of their leaving the field. They were in no sense demoralized [123] but knew that they had fought well and were eager for the time when they could again meet the enemy, "could it only be under a general who equalled the ability on the other side." [124] General Hooker, rather than the Army of the Potomac, was defeated at Chancellorsville. The army as a whole was never given the chance to win. [125]

MORALE HIGH AT GETTYSBURG

Meade, the successor of Hooker, probably did not possess the ability his men would have hoped for, but at Gettysburg the Federal forces were defending their own soil and their morale was high. It had to be to defeat an enemy whose officers talked of going on to Philadelphia and New York while the Confederate soldiers had the air of men who were used to conquer, believing in those who led them, and not doubting that when they saw the Yankees they would drive them again. [126] At Gettysburg the Federals fought very stubbornly but Meade did not follow up his victory. As the Ohio diarist put it: "The boys are disappointed that Lee succeeded in duping our Gen." [127]

THE COMING OF U. S. GRANT

The Army of the Potomac did little until the following spring when Grant was appointed to command all the Federal armies. His task was no easy one; Richmond, the ultimate objective, was so strongly entrenched that one man inside was more than equal to five outside besieging or assaulting. [128] Realizing this fact, Grant gathered for active duty at the front those men who, for one reason or another, had been spending the war in garrison or on detail far from the clash of arms. The ranks of the veteran regiments in the field were augmented by the return of detailed men and the arrival of brand new recruits. Many men were ordered to the ranks who had not carried a musket since the day of enlistment.

The transportation being reduced to one wagon to a brigade, some of the men who were ordered back to live duty were drivers of mule teams. Among these was a private in the 19th Massachusetts Infantry whose unit one day was passing the wagon train when a mule set up one of those unearthly snorts. The ex-mule driver looked at the mule and said: "You need not laugh at me; you may be in the ranks yourself before Grant gets through with the army." [129]

The Army of the Potomac had yet to win a complete victory but it contained a nucleus of veterans.

When Grant took command, the army accepted his reputation as of little worth because he had not yet met Bobby Lee.[130] He was soon to show them that the old habit of fighting a battle and then retreating for several weeks' rest was a thing of the past.[131] On May 5, 1864, Grant entered the Wilderness where the musketry and cannon continued from daybreak until night. Although the enemy was behind breastworks the Federals charged into them, fighting with the greatest determination and continued to do so.[131] It was a harder campaign than any of the men had ever endured before[132] but Grant's refusal to turn back was the turning point in the fortunes of the Army of the Potomac, which had at last found its hero.[133] As the casualty lists mounted there were increasing signs of demoralization because of what some termed "useless butchery."[134]

Morale was probably at its lowest after Cold Harbor where the Federals in a frontal assault lost about 12,000 killed and wounded in half an hour.[135] The night before Cold Harbor the old soldiers discussed McClellan's campaign in 1862. Some of the men were sad, some indifferent; some so tired of the strain on their nerves that they wished they were dead and their troubles over. The infantry knew that they were being called upon to assault perfect earthworks, and though they had resolved to do their best, there was no eagerness for the battle. The impression among the intelligent soldiers was that the task cut out for them was more than men could accomplish.

One reason for low morale was that the men did not see their generals at the front. One soldier has said that he saw Grant and Meade under fire on only one occasion during the entire campaign, and then they were only within range of rifled cannon.[136] One Confederate believed the repulse at Cold Harbor was inflicted with a loss to the defenders of about 100 men.[137] Despite repeated orders to renew the attack the men refused.[138] It became a saying in the army that when the veterans got as far forward as they thought they ought to go "they sat down and made coffee."[139] Much fault was found with the fact that generals launched good troops against entrenched works which the generals had not inspected. Men commented on the fact that army and corps commanders remained away from the front.[140] Some of the severest losses after Cold Harbor occurred among the new troops who joined the army during the campaign and had not had previous experience in attacking breastworks. Many of the veterans units were decimated. Gibbon's division which had a strength of 6,799 officers and men at the opening of the campaign, lost 47 per cent, mostly killed and wounded, in three weeks. In June the percentage leaped to 72. By the end of July he had lost 9 out of 17 brigade commanders and 40 regimental commanders were killed or wounded.[141] The effect of such slaughter was not in numbers alone but in the quality of men lost. The very best officers and bravest men were those who fell. It was soon apparent that the effect of these losses and the general wear and tear of the campaign had begun to work upon the efficiency of the army.[142]

The failure of the Petersburg Crater operation added to the low morale of the army, especially in the 9th Army Corps which had suffered heavily in the fiasco.

MORALE GOES UP

Victories in the Shenandoah Valley, Mobile Bay, and in the West raised the spirits of the men in the Army of the Potomac who had no intention of permitting a negotiated peace and expressed their approval of the further prosecution of the war in the presidential election. The end of the year found the soldiers confident of a speedy end to the war. This general optimism was shared by all and the 1865 campaign was waged by officers and men who knew that the war would soon be over.

APPOMATTOX

Many soldiers knew the end was in sight during the early part of April 1865, but were surprised when it did come at Appomattox. A drummer boy, writing from Farmville, Virginia the day before Lee surrendered recorded in his diary:[143]

We commenced our march about half past 10 a.m. and continued marching till half past 8 p.m. when we reached this place. The Army were in fine spirits last night and the bands were playing through the streets. We threw our pontoons across the Appomatix River. Our army are still pursuing the Rebs and have taken a great many prisoners. This town is fairly situated and contains a population of 1,400 inhabitants. There is quite a number of tobacco manufactures here. Our men have been through a great many stores. Tobacco is laying all over the streets. There was fourteen factorys here before the war. The Rebs retreated across the Bridge last night and burnt it.

April 9th:
We started away about 8 o'clock a.m. and continued our march until half past 3 p.m. Reports say that Gen. Lee has surrendered unconditionally and is waiting until tomorrow to give up his sword. Firing this morning in our front. Cloudy most all day.

The men of the Army of the Potomac received news of Lee's surrender with a joy only they could completely appreciate and understand; behind these veterans lay four years of some of the toughest and certainly the most frustrating fighting American soldiers have ever endured. As Charles Cox wrote to a friend on the greatest event of his life, so did his comrades write or think in those days after Appomattox:[144]

Camp near Nottoway Court House, Va.
April 23, 1865
Dear Friend:

I received your ever welcome letter by last evening's mail and now seat myself to try and compose an answer.

Lee surrendered at Appomattox Court House. We were in the front line of battle. The fight had just commenced when a flag of truce appeared on the Rebel skirmish line and we were halted. An aide of our Division rode along and told us Lee was going to surrender. We had marched very hard and a long distance and were tired, half starved, dirty and ragged but I would not have missed being in line that morning for a fortune. When the news was told us that Lee was going to give up the men got perfectly wild with joy and shouted until they were hoarse, for my part I almost cried with joy. I could not shout, the sad news of the President's death has cast a gloom over the whole army and for once all party differences were forgotten. I think any death too good for his murderer . . . I don't think we will ever have to fire a shot at Johnnie again. The war is over for certain and I hope I will be home by 4th of July. All that remains of the Rebel army is Johnston's and Kirby Smith's forces and they will soon be obliged to give up. I have got an easy time of it now, no picket or guard duty to do, but I guess I will soon be in the Company again. As there is but little going on here at present except drilling and other camp duties I will close.

I remain yours truly, Give my love to all.

Charles R. Cox

MORALE HIGHER IN WEST

The Western armies had, as a rule, been more successful throughout the war and their morale tended to be consistently higher than that of their comrades in the East. Although outnumbered at Wilson's Creek by about two to one, they had inflicted greater damage than they received.[145] They captured Forts Henry and Donelson and fought the enemy to a draw at Shiloh, finally winning the field. Shiloh, which was fought at a time when the Army of the Potomac was marking time in front of Yorktown, was a soldier's fight. There was little strategy but as Sherman said later: "We fought, and held our ground, and therefore counted ourselves victorious. From that time forward we had with us the prestige. That battle was worth millions and millions to us, by reason of the fact of the courage displayed by the brave soldiers on that occasion; and from that time to this, I never heard of the first want of courage on the part of our Northern soldiers."[146]

The battle may well have had the effect of lowering the morale of Confederate troops in the West; at least, some claim that "the South never smiled after Shiloh."[147] At Stone's River Federals fought an approximately equal enemy force, inflicted as many casualties as they received,[148] and kept the field. Brilliantly led by Grant they triumphed at Jackson and Champion's Hill, and then besieged and captured Vicksburg, which "in celerity of movement, and in the vigor and decision of its steps . . . was the most remarkable of the war."[149] The fall of Vicksburg and Port Hudson, plus the defeat of Lee at Gettysburg, led some to hope for an early termination of the war if the leaders would push things.

Many of the Western troops were constantly disappointed at the failure of Eastern forces from whom they expected much. One soldier, writing in April 1862, told his father that he and his comrades were waiting anxiously to hear that the Army of the Potomac had done something of which "200,000 well armed and well drilled men may not be ashamed, something more than merely taking an evacuated village (Centerville) armed with quaker guns." This soldier, on hearing that McClellan was being serenaded, believed the music of the brass bands at Washington to be more pleasing to the general's ear than the booming of cannon or rattle of musketry.[150] Some believed that they were fortunate in being so far removed from Washington and its interference. When Eastern troops arrived in the West in 1863 they were sneeringly saluted by calls of "Bull Run" and "Fredericksburg."[151] The Easterners, on the other hand, observed in the Western troops "an air of independence hardly consistent with the nicest discipline" although they admired the Westerners' cool reliance in battle.[152] Apparently the Westerners were better marchers and more democratic than the better-disciplined Easterners with whom they had little comradeship. One observer believed the Eastern armies to be composed of "citizens, the West of pioneers."[153] The larger size of the Westerners was commented on at the final review in May 1865. The main reason that Eastern armies were better disciplined than the Western armies (apart from the pioneer-type of soldier in Western units), was the fact that the Eastern armies had a higher proportion of West Point graduates than did Western units. This was true, not only in higher echelons of command but down to regimental and battery level.

RELATIVE COMBAT WORTH

Any comparison between the relative fighting ability of the sections is impossible to make because the situations were not the same. It would certainly appear that the best Confederate leaders were in the army opposing the Army of the Potomac. The difference between Bragg's army in the West and the Army of Northern Virginia was "very striking" to Colonel Blackford, who compared the demoralization of Bragg's men with the morale of Lee's men who always believed they were doing the proper thing, whether it was advancing or retreating.[154] In commenting on the Federal army in the West, Meade called them "an armed rabble" while Grant repeatedly said that the fighting in the Wilderness threw in the shade anything he ever saw, and that he had not expected such resistance.[155] Other officers who had fought with both armies said that the Eastern troops were "fifty per cent" better than the Western, and that the good enemy soldiers had always been kept near Richmond except when Longstreet went temporarily to the West.[156]

Longstreet's corps fought with the Western enemy forces at Chickamauga, but according to some participants, the fighting of the Federals at Chickamauga greatly surprised Longstreet's men who "never saw such a fool lot of Yankees . . . (who did not) know when to run."[157] In this battle the Federals were driven back through no fault of the men themselves but "smarting under the mortification of a disaster for which they knew they were not responsible and which was not caused by any lack of bravery or discipline on their part, they were resolved to be driven no further and facing the advancing foe, they savagely stood at bay."[158] One Confederate general reported that he had never known Federal troops to fight so well.[159] The Confederates, outnumbering the Federals, defeated them but lost more heavily than their opponents in so doing.[160]

MORALE IN WEST RAISED BY VICTORIES

After Chickamauga, Federal operations were uniformly successful. The men's morale remained high until the end of the war, while that of the enemy steadily deteriorated after the removal of Johnston. At Franklin, November 30, 1864, a Confederate force of 26,897 launched a frontal assault on 27,939 Federals protected by entrenchments and lost 5,550 killed and wounded to their opponents 1,222.[161] The enemy loss included 12 generals killed and wounded and 1 taken prisoner; the loss in morale to the enemy was serious.[162]

Like their comrades in the Eastern armies the Western troops were heartily in favor of the draft from the moment of its inception, one soldier terming the last call for 500,000 men, the boldest act of Lincoln's administration which, although costing the President many votes among civilians, would be more than made up in the Army.[163] Soldiers at the front were eager to see the draft enforced, and were even willing to guard their "wide mouth and fire in the rear neighbors" far enough to the front so that they would "become most intamately (sic) acquainted with their Rebel brethren."[164] On the other hand, the worthless riff-raff that filled some of the regiments were just as worthless as those in the Eastern armies. Sherman believed that some of the older regiments in September 1864 were discouraged because of failure to replace their losses which in certain units ranged as high as 70 percent.[165] This did not prevent the successful completion of the march through Georgia. After arriving at Savannah, Georgia, a soldier in the 14th Army Corps wrote a friend:[166]

We hav maid a larg march since I wrote the last leter to you and we hav got throo Georgia. We would bee clean throo iff the River was not high. We started from Atlanta on the 10th of last month and we got in Savannah day before last and the city is all right. They did not disturb any thing. Every thing looks lovly hear. We hav got plenty of every thing and that is all we can ask for. The Rebs went flying high. They crost the river right in front of the town. They laid a pontoon bridg a crost the river and laid straw on the bridge so our men could not hear them crost the bridge and they did not get thier hevy guns a crost the river. They left all thier

guns except thier small arms and men. They left thier railroad cars on the track in good running order and you never saw sutch a pile of rice in your life. They is houses full of it and the flower mills was full of flower. I suppose they will kneed that before long. But old Pop Sherman was to clos on to them. They thought it was getting unhelthy in Savannah. So they got up and lit out for Som Whair els, I dont know whare. The cuntry that we cam throo is plaid out. You could harley feed a cat. Martin, I can show you how to skin a chicken when I get home. I have just lernt the rinckle how to pull the chicken legs.

The Federal victories in the fall and winter of 1864 raised the hopes of the depleted regiments for a speedy termination of the war, hopes that were realized in the spring of the following year. But even at the end, the men of Sherman's army were not sure but that the fighting might drag on well into the summer. Only a week before Lee surrendered and eight weeks before Johnston also gave up, the Western troops had every reason to expect months of fighting ahead. After arrival in North Carolina, they took stock of the situation. The Ohio soldier who described the march through Georgia in such succinct (and ungrammatical!) terms wrote from Goldsboro, North Carolina on the 1st of April:[167]

Your welcom leter came to hand and I was every so glad to hear from you wonce more that you was still a live and injoying good helth. Your leter was the first news that I had from home for nearly two month and so i sat right down and red it over three or four times. it was the best news that (I) herd . . . (we are) hoping this war will soon com to a close. But it is very hard to tell when this will be settled. But we can liv in hopes that it wont bee long. I hope not.

Well Martin we have maid a very large march since I last rote to you. We had a hard time to get so long but we got throo all right at last. We have very bad roads to travell over and we had so mutch rain and we could not hardley get the wagons along. We had to fil the roads for nearly one hundred miles and som times we would start be fore sun up and work all day and all night and som was getting sick all the time and some times the rivers was so hie that it would brak bridges and that would make us stop for som time. But we had lots of fun in all the rest. We lived at the top of the pot all the time and the worst was the boys shoes ware out before we got throo and I was one of them lucky ones. My feet hurts the ground for about fifty miles and I did not like to do that, you know.

The surrender of Johnston to Sherman on April 26, 1865, virtually ended all military operations of any real significance.

AWARDS—BADGES AND MEDALS

Expedients to spur morale during the war were slow in coming. Even as late as March, 1863, Lecomte, the Swiss observer, commented on the lack of stimulation to the "military zeal" of the Federal army. In addition to lack of honorable distinctions, decorations, good music, bright uniforms, he noticed no distribution of brandy and a severe prohibition against making booty.[168] Although Lecomte was partly in error in these observations there was some truth in what he said. As late as December 1864, the service journal was commenting on the fact that very few except the wounded had anything to show that they had offered themselves for their country's defense.[169] Hooker probably did more than any other Federal commander to correct this evil when he instituted army and corps flags, corps badges, and inscriptions of battles on regimental colors.[170] Special medals were struck for Gillmore's campaign against Fort Sumter in 1863 and Butler's campaign before Richmond in 1864. The latter was specially designated for colored troops.[171] Early in the war, medals had been awarded to the commands which had defended Forts Sumter and Pickens. Also medals were awarded to the 17th Army Corps. Sumter was again involved when Major General Quincy A. Gillmore had 400 "medals of honor" struck off for gallantry during the operations before Charleston, South Carolina, July to September, 1863. Butler's medals were issued to 200 members of the colored troops of the 25th Army Corps. The Gillmore medals were made by Ball, Black, and Company of New York. On one side was a representation in relief of Sumter in ruins; and on the other, a facsimile of the general's autograph. Neatly engraved on each medal was the name, rank, and regiment of the recipient. A certificate was awarded with each medal. Although all regiments participating in the siege of Sumter were invited by General Gillmore to send in the names of deserving soldiers, a few regiments declined on the grounds that every man of the unit had been "gallant and meritorious."[172] On May 27, 1863, troops of Kearny's old division were paraded to witness the presentation of another decoration, the "Kearny medal". These badges of honor were of bronze in the form of a Maltese cross, suspended from a bar, and were presented by a number of patriotic Philadelphians at the suggestion of General Birney to such enlisted men as had particularly distinguished themselves in action by gallant conduct and conspicuous bravery. The recipients of the medals were noncommissioned officers and privates recommended by their superior officers for this distinction. Speeches appropriate to the occasion were made by General Birney and the brigade and regimental commanders of his division. Among the numbers of the 63rd Pennsylvania Infantry there was a diversity of sentiment as to the value of the decoration; some who had been promoted from the ranks and whose commissions were awaiting their acceptance, begged the commanding officer to withhold their promotion and permit them to accept the medal for which they had been recommended, preferring it to a lieutenant's shoulder straps. Others regarded it as a meaningless bauble and signified their willingness to "trade it off" for a square drink of whiskey.[173] A special medal to Grant was approved by Congress December 17,

1863, which body also expressed joint resolutions on sixteen other occasions to commanders for gallantry and good conduct. Only one of these military commanders was below the rank of general.[174] The European officers who approached Adjutant General Townsend in 1861 for positions in the Federal Army were often men who had earned decorations in other campaigns. These medals or orders were the "objects of envy" to many young aspirants for military glory. Many persons who had been in foreign armies came to offer their services to the Government of the United States, and there were many men in the U.S. volunteers who had served abroad. Both types of men were in the habit of wearing these foreign decorations on their uniforms.[175]

In 1861 Townsend urged upon Scott and the Senate Military Committee the advisability of awarding medals in the Federal service but they objected on the grounds that wearing of decorations would be unpopular because it was contrary to the spirit of American institutions.[176] The next year, however, Congress authorized the President to cause two thousand "medals of honor" to be struck which should be presented in the name of Congress to such noncommissioned officers and privates as should most distinguish themselves by their gallantry in action, and other soldier-like qualities.[177] During Lee's invasion of Pennsylvania in June-July 1863, an "appropriate Medal of Honor" was authorized for the "emergency troops" who volunteered for temporary service.[178] As a result of this second authorization, many of the Medals of Honor were awarded for service at Gettysburg. The 27th Maine Infantry got the majority of these, being thus rewarded for "volunteering to remain in service and participate in the battle of Gettysburg after their term of service had expired."[179] Most of the remainder were given men who captured enemy battle flags; a few were given to the first sergeants who escorted Lincoln's remains to Springfield, Illinois. In all, a total of about one thousand Medals of Honor were awarded military personnel for Civil War service. This compares with 95 given to soldiers for World War I service, and about 300 to all branches of the armed forces in World War II. In his annual report of 1864, General Townsend recommended the award of a gold or silver medal to officers who, although entitled to a Medal of Honor,[180] did not receive it because of the idea that the appropriate way to reward them for distinguished bravery would be in the conferring of brevet promotions at a later date.

The first occasion of the presentation of Medals of Honor to enlisted men in the Army of the Potomac, occurred September 15, 1864, when medals were presented to a sergeant in the 3rd Delaware Infantry, a private in the 18th Massachusetts Infantry, and a private in the 11th Pennsylvania Infantry.[181] In at least one instance, a regimental commander awarded decorations to men in his regiment. When the 2nd Connecticut Infantry was mustered out, its colonel presented gold medals, for bravery on the field, to Color Sergeant Austin P. Kirkham and Sergeant Robert Leggett.[182] A very unusual event was the presentation of a beautiful gold medal to Captain Henry L. Cranford, a man who had repeatedly distinguished himself by gallantry. The medal in the shape of recipient's corps badge, is beautifully inscribed with the officer's name, the battles he had fought in, and the inscription, "from the Brigade Commd'r and Staff, June 1, 1863."[183]

PROMOTIONS

Promotions and furloughs were the most common means of rewarding bravery and soldierly conduct. Promotion from the ranks was the usual thing and men thus advanced often proved to be among the best officers. In fact, the original idea was that this would be done. On May 4, 1861, the War Department ordered that two-thirds of the company officers of the infantry and cavalry regiments should be appointed in the same manner as the officers of like rank in the existing Army; and the remaining one-third, when a regiment reached its full complement of enlisted men, *would be appointed from the ranks*. These men were to be taken from among the sergeants, on the recommendation of the colonel of the regiment, approved by the general commanding the brigade.

After the completion of the organization of a regiment of cavalry or infantry, one-half of all the vacancies which might occur in the lowest grade of commissioned officers, by promotion on otherwise were to be appointed as above, from the ranks.

Corporals were to be taken from the privates; Sergeants from corporals. The First Sergeant was to be selected by the captain from among the sergeants of the company.

The regimental noncommissioned staff were to be appointed from the sergeants of the regiment by the colonel.[184]

Many competent volunteer officers failed to receive promotion. The best principle was that of promoting only competent men. Unfortunately this principle was too often violated by State governors who had no opportunity to observe the candidates but nevertheless refused to defer to the judgment of regimental commanders.[185] In the high echelons, officers were kept on the roster after it was proven that they were incompetent and when no army commander would willingly receive them as his subordinates. Nominal commands at the rear were multiplied where many incompetents passed no small part of the war "waiting orders."[186] Since the total number of general officers was limited by law, it followed that promotion had to be withheld from many who had won it in the field. Brevets were given to conciliate those who should have received actual promotions. Promotions in the Regular Army were pushed by Halleck; in

the volunteers by political friends.[187] The question of assignments and promotions was always an embarrassing one for commanders in the field. Grant was forced to wait for months before he secured the promotion of an officer who he believed possessed "one of the clearest military heads in the army," and to be as well qualified as any man in the service for the largest commands.[188] The wish of Sherman that no promotions be made of officers who went home on sick leave or by "cause other than wounds in battle" was disregarded, much to his disgust.[189]

Promotion of company officers in the Regular Army was according to a fixed plan, which provided that one-half of all vacancies occurring in the lowest grade of commissioned officers in regiments after completion of organization should be filled by promotion from the ranks. Also one-third of the original company officers were appointed from the ranks.[190] Automatic promotion for the vacancies in the noncommissioned officers was established. All vacancies in the established regiments and services of the Regular Army was by seniority up to the rank of colonel, except in cases of disability or incompetency. Many civilians were commissioned in all grades except general directly in the Regular Army during the war, often without examination.[191]

Initially, the volunteers had a promotion system similar to that of the Regular Army.[192] This system, however, does not appear to have been strictly adhered to and each State followed its own method of filling vacancies. Some States like Illinois based their promotion system on seniority[193] but many believed that such a system should have been superseded for one whereby commanders could make battlefield promotions.[194] One regimental commander urged his superiors to promote worthy, battle-tested sergeants; he also filled all his noncommissioned vacancies, writing on the warrants, "For especial gallantry at Antietam" which had "a very happy effect."[195] In general, promotion to the noncommissioned ranks appears to have been fairly rapid and impartial. Favoritism did not play the role it played in the officer ranks.

BREVET RANK

By a general order March 24, 1863, the President was authorized to confer, with Senate approval, brevet rank upon such commissioned officers of the volunteers or other forces as had been or should thereafter be distinguished by gallant actions or meritorious conduct.[196] Although such brevet rank did not entitle the officers to any increase of pay or emoluments according to this order, later interpretation allowed Regular officers to draw the pay of their brevet rank when on detached service, court-martial duty, or assigned to duty by the President. However, a brevet in the volunteers could under no circumstances bring additional pay. The brevet rank enabled the President to confer, in the way of rewards, titles which were wholly independent of the rules of seniority. Lyman reports the arrival of 253 brevets at headquarters of the Army of the Potomac in December 1864. These brevets ranged from first lieutenant to major general; the only disappointed officer appears to have been a general whose brevet promotion would have made him rank the Adjutant General of the Army, and therefore was not made.[197] After the war there were wholesale promotions by brevet. Many regimental commanders were made generals by brevet in this way. These and many other brevet promotions were dated March 13, 1865, and it at once became a standing joke in the Army to refer to "that bloody day, the 13th of March." Heading the list and generally with the highest rank were those officers whose service during the war had been in Washington and other cities, many of whom had not heard a hostile shot fired during the whole war.[198] The honor of receiving a brevet for gallantry on the battlefield was diminished by the promiscuous issuance of these promotions; an officer who had not been in the field at all would be breveted to the highest rank for "faithful, meritorious and distinguished services" in a staff department, while far below him would appear the name of another officer who had repeatedly distinguished himself in combat and who perhaps had been wounded several times.

LEAVES AND FURLOUGHS

Aiding materially in the maintenance of morale was the general pay raise in 1864 which affected all enlisted men, white and colored. Nostalgia, that great enemy of a soldier's morale, was to some extent offset by the granting of leaves of absence to officers and furloughs to the men. Army regulations provided that no leave of absence would be granted an officer during the season of active operations except on urgent necessity nor should any company be left without at least one commissioned officer.[199] Leaves were not to exceed 7 days, except on "extraordinary occasions" until an officer had served with his unit at least two years; leaves of absence on account of sickness had to be accompanied by a medical officer's certificate. Furloughs to enlisted men were granted only by the commanding officer of the post or regiment. Soldiers on furlough were not permitted to take their arms and accouterments with them.[200] Apparently it was easier for officers to obtain leave than for enlisted men. Occasionally, in cases of peculiar family affliction, the latter were granted furloughs but such exceptional amenities only intensified the tedium of those who could not go. Officers and men were quite often the center of attraction while home from the front. A wounded officer, who had returned to his regiment after a furlough at home, received the following letter from his lady friend:[201]

You must have enjoyed youself very much while at home last summer. Of course you received lots of atten-

tion from all the pretty girls (wounded officers always do). I have heard them wish that they might get slightly wounded, just enough to make it interesting and then come home for a while. I had a friend who was wounded in his thumb—he expected he would lose it, but was fortunate enough not to. He came home on a furlough and as his wound did not prevent his receiving or making calls, his time was pretty well occupied. One thing I am sure of, our soldiers do not get any more attention than they deserve.

All sorts of reasons were given by the men in order to get home. Because the education of some of the men had been limited, especially in the case of men from rural areas, their written requests for leave were often brief and ungrammatical. Morale was helped when the general who received the following letter[202] proved to be an understanding family man!

General Sir I request a furlow of .. days to visit my home in the State of New Hampshire to arrange some unseteled business also to make some important famley arangments of GRATE importance to myself and famley.

Respectfully yours

This soldier had six children, the youngest a year old, and "General Sir" granted him a "furlow" immediately.

The large amount of absenteeism during the Peninsular Campaign caused the War Department to call attention to the regulations which prohibited commanding officers from granting leaves of absence in time of war, such authority resting only with the Secretary of War. All volunteer and Regular officers absent on leave were ordered to return to their regiments, while those invalid and wounded officers able to travel were ordered to report either to Annapolis in the East or Camp Chase, Ohio in the West for examination.[203] A few days later the War Department expressly prohibited the granting of furloughs by company or regimental commanders. Military commanders were allowed to issue written furloughs to men at home not to exceed 30 days in cases of serious disability from wounds or sickness on presentation of a reputable physician's certificate.[204] The practice of granting furloughs to enlisted men was discontinued July 14, 1862,[205] and a little later this order was repeated with the added inclusion of leave for officers.[206] At the same time, the extension of sick leaves was revoked.[207]

Such prohibition of leaves and furloughs did not check absenteeism and desertion in the least, on the contrary the men just "went home" anyway. Realizing this, General Hooker finally received Halleck's permission to grant leaves and furloughs to a certain percentage of his command. Leaves were not to exceed 10 days except to men from the more remote States; these men received at the rate of two for every hundred men. Married men received preference. In an army general order, Hooker listed those units which his inspectors had found to be below standard in appearance and soldierly conduct; personnel of these units were deprived of all leaves and furloughs until further notice. The names of the "good" regiments and batteries were published along with an order that the original quota of two per hundred enlisted men and two officers per regiment would be raised to three in each case.[208]

When the army went into winter quarters there was always a regular epidemic of applications for leave or furlough. The officers discovered patriotic services to back up their applications. They all had been in service since the First Bull Run, had been wounded six times, and had never been absent a single day; their wives were very sick; their mothers were not expected to live; and they could easily bring back fifty volunteers with them to fill up their regiment![209] An order of December 1863 granted to enlisted men in the general hospitals furloughs up to 30 days depending on the distance to their homes and their "good conduct." Only five percent could be absent from any one hospital at a time.[210] It was also provided the same month that soldiers returning to their regiments from furlough and who were unable to provide their own transportation, were to be furnished transportation, subject to later deduction of the cost from their pay.[211] During the winter, leaves and furloughs were granted more freely than at any other time, but with the coming of spring the officers and men were ordered to return for the spring offensives.[212]

Welfare Activities

Those who could not go home on leave or furlough were partially compensated by the receipt of letters and boxes from home. Of great assistance also were the Sanitary and Christian Commissions who played an important part in maintaining morale. Although most of the men objected to the over-emphasis these agencies placed on religious salvation, the contributions of reading material especially was most welcome. Regiments in the field and in camp were often visited by agents sent by their State; sometimes, indeed, their governor himself would show up in camp with speeches and occasionally more concrete testimony of his patriotic support in the form of food, medicines, and other useful items. The President became a familiar figure to the men encamped around Washington, visiting their camps after Bull Run and at various other times throughout the war. He was always received with great enthusiasm because of his informality and, more especially, the greatness of his character which was instinctively sensed by his men. He visited the Army of the Potomac after Antietam and shortly before Chancellorsville. Grant and the army were honored by the President's presence at City Point and later in Richmond itself. In later years veterans were proud to be able to tell their listeners that they had "seen the President."

Propaganda

Standing in the first rank among the leaders of the nation's morale were the members of the clergy. Those who did not serve as chaplains at the front remained behind as inspirers in the pulpit or comforters in the homes of bereavement. The Northern clergy supported a powerful drive for peace before the war, but slowly and surely came to regard the war as a wicked rebellion. It was a clergyman who wrote one of the best sellers of the war period, *The Man Without a Country*, which greatly strengthened the morale of the Union case.[213] Such men as the eminent divine, Henry Ward Beecher, told their audiences that the enemy was "hot, narrow, and boastful" and had to be whipped.

Another source of propaganda, the press, had its correspondents on all fronts. Affected by their news were not only the civilians at home but the soldiers as well. Newspaper agents sold their papers in the camps and at the front; in some areas these agencies were given to disabled veterans.[214] Correspondents became practically staff members of some of the higher ranking officers; when one general refused to take two of them into his mess, they proceeded to write letters to their papers describing the general as incompetent and his command as demoralized, drunken, and undisciplined.[215] A steady flow of atrocity stories emanated from the pen of such men as "Carleton" of the Boston *Journal* whose writing was a mixture of nauseous religious drivel and name calling.[216] Some of the men believed that although many chaplains and Christian Commission men were useless, the war correspondents were worse because they wrote up spectacular lies to "sell" their papers.[217] Certain it is that the reputations of many commanders and units were made or unmade by these war correspondents. Illustrated papers like *Harper's Weekly* and *Frank Leslie's Illustrated Newspaper* had wide circulation. Many of their patriotic cartoons resembled in purpose and motif those that appeared so commonly on the envelopes and letter heads of the period.

In addition to Carleton's books there were others that had wide circulation and must have had considerable morale effect. An "impressed New Yorker" described his personal experiences in *Thirteen Months in the Rebel Army* which purported to exhibit the "power, purposes, earnestness, military despotism, and demoralization of the South."[218] The ex-editor of the Knoxville *Whig*, William G. Brownlow, published his fiery denunciation of Rebeldom in 1862. Driven out of the State of Tennessee, Brownlow delineated the barbarities of the enemy in that State and, in asserting his desire to see the State restored to the Union, he expressed the hope he could point out to the triumphant Federal army such men as deserved to hang, suitable limbs from which to hang them, and the privilege of placing the rope around their infernal necks![219] A similar propaganda book of the same region came from the pen of Junius Henri Browne, Special War Correspondent of the New York *Tribune*. In one place in his book Browne relates the crucifixion of a deserter from the Confederate Army.[220] Similar barbarities were reported from the beginning to the end of the war. According to a New York *Herald* correspondent, the enemy fired on nurses and set fire to hospitals with red hot shot, along with other "diabolical deeds which have, as yet, only been equalled by the East India Sepoys and the Tartars of old." The Boston *Post* told of bleeding soldiers being tied to trees and bayoneted.[221] Early the next year a chaplain reported the finding of two Massachuetts soldiers in the woods horribly mutilated—"the work of Rebels."[222] Stories of attempted poisoning of Federal soldiers were not infrequent.[223]

Among the best sources for propaganda were the experiences of escaped or released Federal prisoners of war. During the postwar years scores of books and articles were published giving the experiences of Federal soldiers in Confederate prisons.[224] One of the very earliest of these books, written by an officer captured at Ball's Bluff, described the shooting of Federal prisoners for inadvertently leaning from the prison windows.[225] A prisoner in the West asserted that some of the Federal wounded captured at Shiloh were allowed to lie two weeks without attention, "their wounds . . . tainted with putrid flesh and alive

with crawling maggots!"[226] Towards the end of the war the Joint Committee on the Conduct of the War published its report on "Returned Prisoners" which, with the aid of photographs, attempted to "prove" the horrible conditions in the Confederate prison pens.[227]. At the same time the Committee published its findings on the Fort Pillow Massacre which "revealed" an indiscriminate slaughter of Federal Troops carried out by the enemy "with a furious and vindictive savageness . . . never equalled by the most merciless of Indian tribes."[228] The famous *Report 67* was followed up by the evidence taken by United States Sanitary Commission on conditions in enemy prisons.[229] All such propaganda devices undoubtedly had some effect on the soldiers, although possibly the civilians were the more affected. There is no way of knowing how important such propaganda was in getting men to the recruiting stations. There can be no doubt, however, that propaganda was unnecessary to prevent the Federal soldier from believing prison life to be an easy existence. He knew that in them mortality was extremely high, just as well as he knew that his enemy fought with admirable skill an determination. Occasionally a soldier believed that "the rebs" drank a whiskey and gunpowder mixture before going into combat[230] but most evidence indicates that Federal soldiers held the courage and fighting ability of their adversary in very high respect.

NOTES, CHAPTER 14

1. Especially true of the Army of the Potomac.
2. Byers, S. H. M., *With Fire and Sword*, 26-27.
3. Livermore, *Days and Events*, pp. 255-256.
4. Letter of Lieutenant Charles A. Phillips, 5th Massachusetts Battery, February 14, 1862. Cowles, p. 132.
5. Norton, p. 75. Letter written May 1, 1862, on the Peninsula.
6. Buffum, diary. Entry for February 1, 1865. "Camp Distribution," Alexandria, Virginia.
7. Letter of Daniel Stine, Co. "H" 11th Ohio Infantry. Manuscript in author's possession.
8. Thompson, p. 25. Quoted from a diary entry dated November 24, 1862.
9. Address of Bell Irvin Wiley to the Civil War Round Table, Washington, D. C., March 1956.
10. *The Story of One Regiment* (11th Maine Infantry), p. 138.
11. Some men believed they would be killed.
12. Dwight, "How We Fight at Atlanta," *Harper's New Monthly Magazine*, Vol. 29 (October 1864), p. 666.
13. Entry for July 22, 1863, Journal of Major Harrison Soule, 6th Michigan Heavy Artillery. Manuscript in Michigan Historical Collections.
14. Buell, Augustus, *The Cannoneer*, pp. 169-170.
15. Letter of Hospital Steward James Vernor, 4th Michigan Cavalry, March 26, 1863. Manuscript in Burton Historical Collections.
16. Buffum, p. 220.
17. Letter of Jacob C. Houser, 110th Ohio Infantry, Washington, D. C. December 30, 1863. Manuscript in author's possession.
18. *Official Records*, First Series, Vol. 22, Part 2, p. 106.
19. *Ibid.*, Vol. 34, Part 2, p. 439.
20. Billings, (10th Massachusetts Battery), p. 321.
21. Federal veterans would have disagreed!
22. Comte de Paris, Vol. 1, pp. 190-191. ". . . il attatque resolument, mais froidement," Chanal, p. 242.
23. *Army and Navy Journal*, Vol. 2, (March 18, 1865), p. 467.
24. Hence their losses were lower.
25. Schofield, p. 146.
26. Inept leadership gave this unit low morale.
27. *Official Records*, First Series, Vol. 31, Part 1, pp. 277-278. See *Ibid.*, pp. 461, 487, 490, 519-520 for Confederate accounts.
28. Baylor, George (Co. "B" 12th Virginia Cavalry, C. S. A.) *Bull Run to Bull Run*, p. 146.
29. Gordon, John B. (Lieutenant General, C. S. A.) *Reminiscences of the Civil War*, p. 44.
30. *Army and Navy Journal*, Vol. 2, March 25, 1865, p. 483.
31. Buell, *The Cannoneer*, p. 288.
32. Letter from White Oak Swamp, June 29, 1862, Gilmore, p. 13.
33. "An English Combatant," *Battlefields of the South, From Bull Run to Fredericksburg*, p. 342.
34. Eggleston, G. C., (Sergeant-Major, Lamkin's Virginia Battery, C. S. A.), in *Battles and Leaders*, Vol. 4, p. 232.

35. Neil, *A Battery at Close Quarters*, pp. 11-13. Ohio Commandery, Loyal Legion of the United States.

36. *Official Records*, Third Series, Vol. 5, pp. 664-665, 671.

37. *Ibid.*

38. Letter of August 8, 1864, Agassiz, p. 208. Lyman's experience was that they had "no native courage to compare with Americans." See also letter of May 28, 1864. *Ibid.*, p. 131. Of course such a judgment is only subjective; the German soldier is not deficient in courage. Obviously the lack of knowledge of English and the fact that many were substitutes contributed a great deal to the alleged lack of courage.

39. Hancock's report quoted by Billings, 10th Massachusetts Battery, pp. 332-333.

40. Wise, John S., *The End of an Era*, pp. 301, 304.

41. Lawrence, p. 249.

42. Lonn, *Foreigners in the Union Army and Navy*, p. 649.

43. *The Atlantic Monthly*, Vol. 14, September 1864, p. 355; Kansas Commandery, Military Order of the Loyal Legion of the United States, Publication 14, p. 11.

44. Entry for December 25, 1862, diary of Colonel Oliver L. Spaulding, 23rd Michigan Infantry, Manuscript in Michigan Historical Collections.

45. Report of Secretary of War, December 5, 1863, *House Executive Documents*, 38 Cong., 1 Sess., Document 1, p. 7.

46. Sherman to John A. Spooner, recruiting agent for the Commonwealth of Massachusetts, July 30, 1864, *Army and Navy Journal*, Vol. 2, August 27, 1864, p. 7.

47. Sherman to Halleck, September 4, 1864, *Official Records*, First Series, Vol. 38, Part 5, p. 793. Sherman asserted that the men of his army shared in this opinion. *Ibid.*

48. Agassiz, p. 102.

49. Negro prisoners were often abused by civilians.

50. Williams, George W., *A History of the Negro Troops in the War of the Rebellion, 1861-1865*, p. 266.

51. *Battles and Leaders*, Vol. 4, p. 418.

52. Cox, Vol. 2, p. 408; *Civil War Papers*, Vol. 1, p. 159; *Army and Navy Journal*, Vol. 1 (July 2, 1864), p. 741; July 9, 1864, p. 758.

53. This was true of the Crater and at Fort Pillow.

54. *Battles and Leaders*, Vol. 4, pp. 563-564; *Southern Historical Society Papers*, Vol. 18 (1890), pp. 1-38; Vol. 25 (1897), pp. 79-86; Vol. 33 (1905), p. 364.

55. Wilson, Joseph T., *The Black Phalanx*, pp. 280-285.

56. Entry for November 12, 1863, Journal of Major Harrison Soule, 6th Michigan Heavy Artillery, Manuscript in Michigan Historical Collections.

57. *House Executive Documents*, 39 Cong., 1 Sess., Document 1, p. 251.

58. Butler to Scott, May 27, 1861, *Official Records*, First Series, Vol. 2, p. 53.

59. Butler to Scott, May 24, 1861, *Ibid.*, p. 649.

60. *Ibid.*, Third Series, Vol. 3, pp. 29-30.

61. *Ibid.*, Second Series, Vol. 1, p. 822; Third Series, Vol. 2, pp. 198, 290, Lincoln shared in this belief. See Randall, James G., *The Civil War and Reconstruction*, pp. 504-505.

62. United States War Department, "General Order No. 91," July 29, 1862, *General Orders for 1862*.

63. September 27, 1862. *House Executive Documents*, 39 Cong., 1 Sess., Document 1, p. 67.

64. *Official Records*, Third Series, Vol. 3, pp. 416-420, 1192.

65. "Circular 54," Provost Marshal General's Office, July 20, 1863, *House Executive Document*, 39 Cong., 1 Sess., Document 1, Part 2, pp. 111-112.

66. United States War Department "General Order No. 143," May 22, 1863, *General Orders for 1863*.

67. *Ibid.*, "General Order No. 144," May 22, 1864, *General Orders for 1864*; *Official Records*, Third Series, Vol. 3, pp. 215-216.

68. Annual Report of Secretary. of War, March 1, 1865, *House Executive Documents*, 38 Cong., 2 Sess., Document 83, p. 29.

69. The only exception I can find is an officer mentioned by Schouler in *A History of Massachusetts in the Civil War*, Vol. 2, pp. 583-584. The officer was First Lieutenant Stephen A. Swailes, 54th Massachusetts Infantry.

70. *Army and Navy Journal*, Vol. 1, January 30, 1864, p. 363.

71. Report of Secretary of War, November 22, 1865, *House Executive Documents*, 39 Cong., 1 Sess., Document 1, Part 1, p. 29.

72. Holbrook, Wm. C., *A Narrative of the Services of the Officers and Enlisted Men of the 7th Regiment of Vermont Volunteers*, p. 57.

73. *Official Records*, Third Series, Vol. 5, p. 661.

74. Report of Secretary of War, November 22, 1865, *House Executive Documents*, 39 Cong., 1 Sess., Document 1, Part 1, p. 29.

75. Shannon maintains that what the colored troops lacked in initiative they made up by the superior training they received from their better selected officers.

76. Report of Provost Marshal General, March 17, 1866, *House Executive Documents*, 39 Cong., 1 Sess., Document 1, Part 1, p. 76.

77. *Ibid.*, White desertion was 62.51 per thousand; colored desertion was 67.00. *Ibid.*

78. Andrews, E. Benjamin, *A Private's Reminiscences of the First Year of the War*, p. 7.

79. Davis, Jefferson, *The Rise and Fall of the Confederate Government*, Vol. 1, pp. 341-342.

80. Johnston, Joseph E., *Narrative of Military Operations Directed During the Late War Between the States*, p. 50.

81. Entry for July 21, 1861, diary of Private George Vanderpool, 3rd Michigan Infantry. Manuscript in Burton Historical Collection.

82. Webb, A. S., *The Peninsula*, p. 9.

83. Ropes, Vol. 1, pp. 220-224.

84. Hays, *Under the Red Patch*, pp. 44-45.

85. Banes, Charles H., *History of the Philadelphia Brigade*, pp. 34-35; "Carleton," *Following the Flag*, p. 46.

86. Walker, Francis A., *History of the Second Army Corps*, p. 12.

87. Hyde, T. W., *Following the Greek Cross*, p. 35.

88. No series of defeats had yet occurred.

89. Ropes, Vol. 2, p. 183.

90. Banes, pp. 88-89.

91. *Official Records*, First Series, Vol. 2, part 3, p. 287.

92. *Ibid.*, pp. 308-309.

93. Pope to Halleck, September 1, 1862, quoted by French, *The Army of the Potomac from 1861 to 1863*, pp. 152-154.

94. Longstreet, James, *From Manassas to Appomatox*, pp. 182, 187, 200; Stiles, Robert, *Four Years Under Marse Robert*, p. 123.

95. General McClellan's removal was resented.

96. *Glimpses of the Nation's Struggle*, First Series, p. 303; Meade, Vol. 1, p. 309. Letter of September 12, 1862.

97. *Official Records*, First Series, Vol. 12, Part 3, pp. 798, 807. McClellan was given the command September 2, 1862.

98. Cox, Vol. 1, pp. 352-353.

99. Alexander, E. P., *Military Memoirs of a Confederate*, p. 224.

100. Livermore, *Numbers and Losses*, pp. 74, 92-93.

101. From 50 feet to 30 paces. Palfrey, F. W., *The Antietam and Fredericksburg*, pp. 83-84.

102. 2nd Division of the 2nd Corps (Sumner). *Official Records*, First Series, Vol. 19, part 1, p. 193; Ropes, Vol. 2, p. 364.

103. McClellan was inaccurate.

104. Meade, Vol. 1, p. 325, Letter of November 8, 1862.

105. Letter of William A. Plaisted, Co. "C," 36th Massachusetts Infantry, November 12, 1862. Manuscript in author's possession.

106. Letter of Lieutenant Charles H. Salter, Co. "B," 16th Michigan Infantry, November 27, 1862. Manuscript in Burton Historical Collection.

107. *Personal Recollections of the War of the Rebellion,* Vol. 2, pp. 304-305.

108. London *Times* narrative, Headquarters of General Lee near Fredericksburg, December 12, 1862, quoted in Moore, *Rebellion Record,* Vol. 6, p. 108.

109. Letter of Lieutenant Charles H. Salter, Co. "B," 16th Michigan Infantry, December 21, 1862. Manuscript in Burton Historical Collection.

110. Alexander, pp. 305, 308.

111. Letter of Lieutenant Charles H. Salter, Co. "B," 16th Michigan Infantry, December 21, 1862. Manuscript in Burton Historical Collection.

112. Hopkins, W. P., *The Seventh Regiment Rhode Island Volunteers in the Civil War, 1862-1865,* p. 49.

113. Child, William, *A History of the Fifth Regiment New Hampshire Volunteers in the American Civil War 1861-1865,* pp. 166-167.

114. All men realized that their capture was in a hopeless attempt.

115. Thompson, p. 103.

116. Page (14th Connecticut Infantry), pp. 104-106.

117. Thompson, p. 104.

118. Related to the author by Color Sergeant Francis H. Buffum, 14th New Hampshire Volunteers, July 1927.

119. Stackpole, Edward J., *Drama on the Rappahannock: The Fredericksburg Campaign,* p. 270.

120. "The General Mismanagement of the War," New York *Herald,* No. 9614, January 10, 1863, p. 4.

121. Gates, Theodore, *The Ulster Guard and the War of the Rebellion,* p. 358.

122. Diary of August G. Werthmiller, Co. "G," 5th Ohio Infantry. Manuscript in author's possession. George Morris was discharged October 16, 1863; Thomas Mundy died on the field.

123. Letter of Surgeon David P. Chamberlin, 4th Michigan Infantry, May 12, 1863. Manuscript in Burton Historical Collection.

124. Hyde, pp. 135-136.

125. Stackpole, Edward J., *Chancellorsville: Lee's Greatest Battle,* p. 367.

126. They believed this battle would end the war.

127. Entry of July 13, 1863, Werthmiller's diary.

128. Grant, U. S., "Preparing for the Campaigns of '64," *Battles and Leaders,* Vol. 4, p. 110.

129. Adams (19th Massachusetts Infantry), p. 86.

130. Grant had difficulty in overcoming this feeling of inferiority on the part of some of his officers.

131. *Battles and Leaders,* IV, 163.

132. Letter of Lieutenant Charles H. Salter, Co. "B," 16th Michigan Infantry, May 15, 1864, Manuscript in Burton Historical Collection.

133. Dana, Charles, *The Life of Ulysses S. Grant,* pp. 200-201. See also Porter, p. 79.

134. *Battles and Leaders,* Vol. 4, pp. 143-144.

135. Livermore, *Numbers and Losses,* p. 114.

136. Wilkeson, pp. 93, 127.

137. Blackford, Charles M. (ed.) *Letters from Lee's Army,* pp. 250-251. Fox does not give the Confederate loss, but it was small although probably greater than Blackford estimated.

138. *Battles and Leaders,* Vol. 4, pp. 218, 227.

139. Gibbon, pp. 229-230.

140. Wilkeson, pp. 93, 121-122.

141. Gibbon, p. 228; Humphreys, p. 249, letter of September 6, 1864; Croushore, p. 165, letter of August 8, 1864;

testimony of General Meade before the Joint Committee on the Conduct of the War, Committee's *Report,* Second Series, Vol. 1, p. 36.

142. *Ibid.*

143. Entry for April 8, 1865. Diary of Fred Stearns, Co. "L," 1st New York Engineers. Manuscript in author's possession.

144. Letter of Charles R. Cox, Co. "F," 1st Maryland Infantry, April 23, 1865. Manuscript in author's possession.

145. August 10, 1861. Livermore, *Numbers and Losses,* p. 78.

146. Speech at St. Louis, July 19, 1865, quoted by Remlap, *The Life of General U. S. Grant,* p. 63.

147. Probably said originally by George W. Cable.

148. Livermore, *Numbers and Losses,* p. 97.

149. Pollard, Edward, *Third Year of the War,* pp. 43-44. Pollard's comment is of special interest because he was a Southerner.

150. Letter of Lieutenant William C. Stevens, 3rd Michigan Cavalry, April 5, 1862. Manuscript in Burton Historical Collections.

151. There were several fights between Eastern and Western units.

152. *Battles and Leaders,* Vol. 4, p. 671.

153. True to a certain extent.

154. Letter of October 25, 1863, Blackford. *Letters from Lee's Army,* p. 224.

155. Agassiz, p. 126. But Meade never served in the West.

156. *Ibid.* The Confederate general, D. H. Hill, apparently believed the Northwest reared some of the best Federal soldiers. *Battles and Leaders,* Vol. 2, p. 575.

157. Clark (ed.) *Histories of the Several Regiments and Battalions from North Carolina in the Great War 1861-65,* Vol. 2, p. 703.

158. Howe, David, *Civil War Times,* p. 190.

159. Report of Major General T. C. Hindman, C. S. A., *Official Records,* Vol. 30, Part 2, p. 305.

160. Livermore, *Numbers and Losses,* pp. 105-106.

161. *Ibid.,* pp. 131-132. In addition the Confederates probably had several hundred more slightly wounded. *Ibid.,* p. 139 (note).

162. Report of Lieutenant General S. D. Lee, C. S. A., Hood, *Advance and Retreat,* pp. 340-342.

163. Letter of Major William C. Stevens, 9th Michigan Cavalry, near Atlanta, Georgia, August 26, 1864. Manuscript in Michigan Historical Collections.

164. Entry for November 14, 1863, Journal of Major Harrison Soule, 6th Michigan Heavy Artillery. Manuscript in Michigan Historical Collections.

165. Sherman to Halleck, September 4, 1864, *Official Records,* First Series, Vol. 38, Part 5, p. 793.

166. Letter of Daniel Stine, 11th Ohio Infantry, December 24, 1864. Manuscript in author's possession.

167. *Ibid.,* letter of April 1, 1865, Goldsboro, North Carolina.

168. Lecomte, p. 96.

169. "Medals for Soldiers," *Army and Navy Journal,* Vol. 2, December 17, 1864, p. 262.

170. "General Order No. 19," February 22, 1862, Headquarters of the Army, Adjutant General's office, *General Orders for 1862.*

171. See Williams, *A History of Negro Troops in the War of the Rebellion, 1861-1865,* Frontispiece.

172. Eldredge (3rd New Hampshire Infantry), pp. 1013-1014.

173. Hays (*Under the Red Patch*), page 187.

174. Lieutenant Colonel Joseph Bailey, 4th Wisconsin Infantry, who rescued a gunboat flotilla under Rear-Admiral David D. Porter, Phisturer, pp. 64-66.

175. *Uncle Sam's Medal of Honor,* page 409.

176. Rodenbough, *The Bravest Five Hundred of '61*, page 481.

177. United States War Department, "General Order No. 91," July 29, 1862. *General Orders for 1862*. The metal was bronze.

178. *Ibid.*, "General Order No. 195," June 29, 1863, *General Orders for 1863*.

179. Adjutant General's Department, *Medals for Honor awarded for Distinguished Service during the War of the Rebellion, passim*.

180. Report of Secretary of War, March 1, 1865, *House Executive Documents*, 38 Cong., 2 Sess., Document 83, page 18.

181. Kings, W. C. and Derby, W. P., *Camp-Fire Sketches and Battlefield Echoes*, page 285. The men were: Sergeant John Shilling, 3rd Delaware; Private T. C. Anderson; 18th Massachusetts; George H. Reed, 11th Pennsylvania.

182. Croffut, W. A. and Morris, John M. *The Military and Civil History of Connecticut during the War of 1861-65*, pp. 99-100.

183. The medal is in the possession of the recipient's grandson, Colonel F. L. Cranford, a veteran of World War II.

184. United States War Department, "General Order No. 15," May 4, 1861, *General Orders for 1861*.

185. Testimony of Brigadier General John Gibbon before the Joint Committee on the Conduct of the War, April 1, 1864, Committee's *Report*, Second Series, Vol. 1, pp. 445-446.

186. Cox, Vol. 1, page 172.

187. *Ibid.*, Vol. 2, page 134.

188. General W. F. Smith, *Official Records*, First Series, Vol. 31, Part 3, pp. 122, 277, 458, 571; Vol. 32, Part 2, pp. 79-80.

189. *Ibid.*, Vol. 38, Part 4, pp. 433, 439, 443; Part 5, pp. 241, 260, 271.

190. United States War Department, "General Orders No. 16," May 4, 1861, *General Orders for 1861*.

191. *Army and Navy Journal*, Vol. 1 (October 10, 1863), page 99.

192. United States War Department, "General Order No. 15," May 4, 1861, *General Orders for 1861*; "General Order No. 16," May 4, 1861, *Ibid.*

193. Elliot, page 10; Royse, page 24.

194. *Army and Navy Journal*, Vol. 1 (September 12, 1863), page 35.

195. Hyde, page 109.

196. United States War Department, "General Order No. 73," March 24, 1863, *General Orders for 1863*.

197. Letter of December 6, 1864, Agassiz, page 289; Gibbon page 373. At the close of the war, in one regular regiment alone, 21 of its 45 officers had received brevets. Comte de Paris, Vol. 1, page 22.

198. Gibbon, pp. 371-372. See also Phisterer, pp. 248-251, 257, 267, 290-316.

199. United States War Department, *Revised Regulations for the Army of the United States 1861*, Article 21, Paragraph 175.

200. *Ibid.*, Article 22, Paragraphs 182, 185, 190-191.

201. Letter to Major Henry A. Wiley, 104th New York Infantry, July 17, 1864 from an unidentified female admirer. Manuscript in author's possession.

202. Thompson (13th New Hampshire Infantry), page 219.

203. United States War Department, "General Order No. 61," June 7, 1862, *General Orders for 1862*.

204. *Ibid.*, "General Order No. 65," June 12, 1862.

205. *Ibid.*, "General Order No. 78," July 14, 1862.

206. *Ibid.*, "General Order No. 102," August 11, 1862.

207. *Ibid.*, "General Order No. 100," August 11, 1862.

208. Bigelow, pp. 490-491, 494-495.

209. Letter of December 10, 1863, Agassiz, pp. 59-60.

210. United States War Department, "General Order No. 391," December 9, 1863. *General Orders for 1863*.

211. *Ibid.*, Circular of December 24, 1863.

212. *Battles and Leaders*, Vol. 4, page 103.

213. Dr. Edward Everett Hale.

214. "The Circulation of Newspapers and Periodicals Among the Troops, etc." New York *Herald*, No. 9760 (June 5, 1863), page 1.

215. Cox, Col. 1, pp. 76-77.

216. Charles Carleton Coffin. See his *Following the Flag* and *My Days and Nights on the Battlefield*.

217. The men resented any reflection on their units.

218. Stevenson, *Thirteen Months in the Rebel Army*.

219. Brownlow, *Sketches of the Rise, Progress, and Decline of Secession, with a Narrative of Personal Adventures Among the Rebels*, p. 438.

220. Browne, *Four Years in Secession*, pp. 154-155.

221. Victor, *Incidents and Anecdotes of the War*, page 186. This book appeared in 1862.

222. "A Piece of Barbarism," New York *Times*, February 23, 1862, quoted in Moore, *Rebellion Record*, Vol. 4, page 45.

223. The Louisville *Democrat* and Albany *Journal*, quoted in Moore, *Rebellion Record*, Vol. 3, page 46.

224. These works vary greatly in style and quality.

225. Harris, *Prison-Life in the Tobacco Warehouse at Richmond* (1862), page 33.

226. Geer, *Beyond the Lines: or a Yankee Loose in Dixie* (1863), page 65.

227. *House Reports*, 38 Cong., 1 Sess., Report 67 (May 9, 1864).

228. *House Reports*, 38 Cong., 1 Sess., Report 65 (May 9, 1864), pp. 100-101.

229. United States Sanitary Commission, *Narrative of Privations and Sufferings of United States Offices and Soldiers While Prisoners of War in the Hands of the Rebel Authorities*. This book appeared in September, 1864.

230. Keeler, page 54.

CHAPTER 15

Life in Camp, Prison, and Hospital

SOLDIER life in the Federal Army varied greatly with units and localities but, in general, it was the life of youthful volunteers who were determined to have as good a time as their ingenuity and Army discipline would permit. Before departure for the seat of war they were usually allowed free rein until their officers had learned how to enforce discipline. Many soldiers continued their ordinary duties of home life until drilling commenced. In some regiments many men spent most of their time out of camp altogether.[1] Those whose homes were too remote for frequent visits were honored by receptions and dinners at which they occupied the post of honor while listening to the fervent orations of local dignitaries. Friends, relatives, and peddlers flocked to the camps to watch the fledglings as they were exercised in sharp dashes at the double-quick and the elementary drill maneuvers. Occasionally the men were taken on what was then termed long marches. Policing of camp and drill were varied by visits to town, visits that were often marked by turbulent convivialities. After all the members of the regiment had arrived, the men were often granted a week's furlough to visit their homes; shortly after their return the unit would receive traveling orders and proceed to the front, usually by rail.

FIELD CAMPS—WINTER QUARTERS

Most of the active campaigning in the war was seasonal. When in the field the men went into bivouac if in the presence of the enemy and constructed whatever shelter was possible. Regulations prescribed the lay-out of infantry, cavalry, and artillery camps, and fairly uniform adherence to these rules was observed by most units. When in towns the troops occupied available buildings.[2] On the approach of winter the men built comfortable log huts, often with fireplaces when stoves were not available.[3] Some huts were floored with boards from packing boxes,[4] and in general the comfort of each hut was only limited by available materials and the owners' ingenuity.

In some camps the men had names for each street. Often these names would be inscribed on a piece of board nailed to a tree or corner of a hut. Several of the worst sort of huts would be labelled "Home, Sweet Home." In the camp of the 13th New Hampshire Infantry there were: Lincoln Street, Burnside Avenue, Starvation Alley, and Mud Lane; and for

WINTER QUARTERS
A card game in camp. Notice the youth of the drummer boy; also the various types of shelters used for the winter quarters. The barrel on the roof is an improvised chimney.

living quarters, such names as Astor House, Swine Hotel, Dew Drop Inn, and We're Out. An especially muddy place near the chaplain's tent was called Holy Park.[5] Many of the huts had crude chimneys made out of sticks and mud. These chimneys often caught fire in the cold nights when too strong a fire was kept up, and it was a common sight to see the inmates of a tent suddenly sally forth and kick over the chimney in order to save their tent or hut. These chimneys often figured in practical jokes which were perpetrated by the mischievous soldiers on their comrades. One trick was to quietly slip up and place a board over the top of the chimney which would soon smoke out the inmates. Another trick which caused much profanity, was that of sneaking up when the tent was closely tied shut, and throwing several blank cartridges down the chimney. These would fall into the fire and explode and scatter the fire and ashes all over the sleeping soldiers inside. This would cause a sudden rush from the tent, but the perpetrators by this time would have made themselves scarce; and well for them that they had, or they would have been severely injured.[6] The following letter describes life in camp fairly accurately and is also indicative of how the veteran soldier lived in the "off season" of fighting.[7]

Camp near Weldon Road, Va.
November 25, 1864

Dear Friend:

Your ever welcome letter has been received and I now proceed to answer it. I am glad to hear of you and the family being blessed with health. I am well and hearty and hope this scratch will find you the same. Everything is as usual. The ground which freezes hard during the night thaws during the day and is very muddy. We were out on battalion drill this morning but the mud will prevent drilling for a time. I wish you could see some of the log houses here. They are put up as well as those at home and some of them a great deal neater. The camps look like villages and of a night a person almost thinks they are in town, but all the citizens wear the same colored clothes and there is no ladies about, so it is a dull city. You may well say there is but little fancy work in battle. There is plenty of music from bullets, solid shot, canister and shells but I can't say I fancy the sound of it, and I don't think there is many who do. If you ever see a man bragging, you can set him down as being out of shelling distance at the time of a fight. Some of those fancy officers who run around Washington—just get them out here and you would see the difference soon. It is no use to put on airs here. Those fancy officers are splendid marks for the Johnnies' sharpshooters. Among the rebs you can't tell an officer from a private, only in a few cases . . . Our orderly sergeant died at White Hall Hospital on the 18th inst. He was thought a great deal of in the Company and it seems like I have lost some of my own folks, when I think of his death. He was wounded on the 18th of August on the Weldon Road. Give my love to all of the family and keep a share for yourself.

I remain yours truly
Charles R. Cox.

P. S. You must excuse this poor letter.

CAMP VERMIN

In camp the men were occupied with policing up, cooking, cleaning of weapons and accouterments, and washing their clothes.[8] Much of the laundry consisted of boiling the clothes to rid them of lice or "graybacks," as they were termed by the men. The extermination of this ever-present pest "interested the soldiers far more than those other questions of state sovereignty, confiscation, finance, and the Negro-which put the statesmen at Washington to their best trumps. Indeed, the minds of the soldiers were exercised with far greater activity in planning campaigns against the *pediculus,* than in thinkng about those which were directed against Lee, and Bragg, and Hood, and Joe Johnston."[9] Apparently these pests were no respecters of rank, for a "robust brigadier-general . . . afterward President of the United States," was observed by a soldier of the Sherman brigade busily engaged in chasing lice along the seams of his nether garments, while discreetly sheltered behind the largest tree in the area.[10] The lice problem was at its worst during a campaign when men lacked a change of clothing or the opportunity to wash. On arrival in camp the soldiers had time to boil their clothes, clean themselves and equipments, and if necessary, draw new clothing.

ARTICLES OF WAR READ PERIODICALLY

Once every three months the men listened to the reading of the Articles of War by their regimental or battery commander.[11] Early in the war, some regimental and battalion commanders had the Articles of War read to their men every Sunday. The 19th Massachusetts Infantry was marched out on Sundays by companies, were then seated in the shade (if available!), and listened to the reading of the Articles of War by their officers. As one veteran recalled them: "Whatever you did, you were to be shot, or such other punishment as may be inflicted by courts-martial."[12]

MUSTERS

Regulations called for a muster of all troops at time of paying the men off. These musters were to take place when troops were paid, i.e., the last day of every other month, beginning with February. Musters were made by an Inspector-General, if present, otherwise by an officer specially designated by the commander of the army, division, or department; and in absence of either an Inspector-General or officer specially designated, the muster was made by the post commander.

All stated musters of the troops were supposed to be preceded by a minute and careful inspection in the prescribed mode; and if the command was more than a company, by a review, before inspection. The mustering officer inspected the companies in succession, beginning on the right. He then went back to the first company and mustered it in the following manner: The company being at *Order Arms,* with open ranks, as when inspected, the captain ordered the company to *Support-Arms*. The mustering officer then called the roll—each man answering distinctly *Here*, and then bringing his piece down to the *Order*.

After mustering the companies, the mustering officer, attended by the company commanders, would visit the guard and hospital to verify the presence of the men reported there. Muster and pay rolls were then made out on the printed forms furnished from the Adjutant-General's Office. One copy of each muster roll was transmitted by the mustering officer to the Adjutant General's Office in the War Department within 3 days after muster. These were for the purpose of having a permanent record of every man on file for future use and reference.[13]

ENTERTAINMENT

Occasionally an itinerant photographer would arrive in camp and take group pictures of the regiment, often by squads and companies. Individual photographs and daguerreotypes were usually taken at permanent establishments in the towns and cities. At Arlington Heights, Virginia, the wife of a photographer wrote (September 24, 1862), that she had finished 73 pictures of soldiers in one day. At such a rate, she said, it certainly makes a very busy day; in a few days it may be quiet, as most of them are under marching orders.[14] Life in camp was by no means an endless monotony of work and drill. When neighboring regiments from the same State were encamped close to each other, there followed mutual visits of friends and relatives. On New Year's Day 1864, Battery "H" 1st Rhode Island Light Artillery had a turkey supper and invited as guests the 3rd New Jersey and 2nd Maine Batteries. After the supper, in the absence of the fair sex, the men arranged what was known among the soldiers as a "stag dance" with the ladies left out. The men who impersonated the ladies were distinguished from their partners by white handkerchiefs tied on their right arms. And then the fun began. First a Grand March—"then came the ball consisting of Quadrille, Lancers, Cotillion, Spanish Quadrille, Portland Fancy, followed by an old fashioned Irish Break Down (with no broken heads, however)." The dance lasted until two o'clock the next morning and was thoroughly enjoyed by all.[15]

MAIL AND PERIODICALS

The arrival of the mail played a great part in camp life. Along with the mail came enormous packages of newspapers which were quickly distributed to the most remote corners of the camp. In every tent the latest news brought by the leading newspapers was read in the evening and eagerly discussed, while the soldier on duty, if he thought himself unobserved, walked up and down with his musket in one hand and his newspaper in the other.[16] Because many

ARRIVAL OF NEWSPAPERS

regiments had newspaper men in their ranks, such units often published their own newspapers. These were usually small affairs and generally ran only a few issues. One such paper was published by the 50th Illinois Infantry. Its first title was *The Fiftieth* but was soon changed to *The Camp Prentiss Register* in order to insure a wider interest and circulation. "It was an extremely loyal as well as an ably conducted paper, and served to relieve the camp of much of the tedium incident to army life."[17]

The arrival of boxes from home was always a great event for the recipients who generally shared the contents with their less fortunate tent mates. Books and periodicals sent from home were supplemented by reading matter furnished by civilian agencies, especially the Christian Commission. One soldier observed that the novels of Thackeray and Charles Lever were widely read in his regiment, while *The Atlantic Monthly* and *Harper's Weekly* were by far the most popular periodicals.[18] While the Army of the Potomac was encamped around Washington in the winter of 1861, its men organized lyceums, debating societies, and schools in Latin and German. Some of the men who had been denied the opportunity of attending school earlier in life were instructed in the three R's.[19] Many of the older men had never learned to read or write, and often letters were written for these soldiers who could not write for themselves. Generally the party for whom the letter was being written desired that it be written "just as I would write it, you know." Some of the requests were very amusing. They generally followed a certain sequence. First of all came very affectionate words to the wife; then the children were attended to; then items of business; then connections of the family. Next would come a joke or two for old Jake or Sally, then a little final gush, couched more or less in special terms and which must be written word for word, because those words were agreed upon when the soldier left home. These words would be fully understood at home but were worse than Greek to the writer.[20]

SPORTS

As one would expect with such a preponderance of boys in their teens, the Federal volunteers entered into games and sports with all the enthusiasm of a college undergraduate. Sham battles with other regiments were staged whenever possible. Companies and even regiments participated in snowball fights. One of these took place between the 2nd and 12th New Hampshire Infantry Regiments, in which "tents were wrecked, bones broken, eyes blacked, and teeth knocked out—all in *fun*." [21]

PETS, MASCOTS, AND SOUVENIRS

Characteristically enough, individuals and units made pets of almost every species of fowl and animal; Reference has already been made to the eagle "Old Abe," in the 8th Wisconsin Infantry. This veteran survived all the battles of his regiment; in action he was carried on a standard by one of the tallest men in the regiment.[22] The 12th Wisconsin Infantry went to the war with a bear, while the 35th Ohio Infantry had a dog which went through all the battles of the regiment without a scratch.

Some soldiers collected souvenirs, often with fatal results, since unexploded shells seemed to have had a special fascination for recruits. In fact, it is not too much of an exaggeration to say that almost every regiment lost some man through carelessness with weapons or souvenirs. For example, a lieutenant emptied a shell of its powder (as he thought) with the idea of using the shell as an andiron in the fireplace of his hut. About ten o'clock at night the shell exploded, demolishing the hut, lifting the roof, knocking the chimney and fireplace to pieces, and seriously injuring the lieutenant. The explosion was taken to be a signal gun, announcing an attack by the enemy, and resulted in arousing the whole force in that camp area. In the same regiment, another man picked up a safer souvenir—a New Testament which belonged to Sergeant J. H. Prickett, 25th South Carolina Infantry. The Federal soldier took the souvenir home with him and twenty years after the war was able to return it to the father of the Confederate sergeant who died in a Northern prison camp. This Testament was the only item the bereaved father had to remind him of his son.[23]

SUTLERS

Pay day was usually followed by visits to the sutlers. Even at the front an occasional enterprising sutler would show up. On June 9, 1864, two sutlers in an open buggy drove towards the front through the lines, peddling tobacco. They had gone through three or four lines of entrenchments, winding in and out in a zig-zag fashion through the openings covered by curtains when enemy bullets wounded the horse and killed one of the men. The other man turned to drive back, with his dead companion still in the buggy, when the horse, frantic with pain, started on the run, utterly unmanageable, and crashed over into a trench with the horse, both men, and buggy ending up in a heap. The soldiers near the scene made a rush and scramble for the tobacco and, after getting that, they lifted out the occupants of the buggy. "The horse had to be killed, the buggy was ruined, and the pedler came back across the field alone, carrying the harness on his arm, a poorer and a less careless man."[24] Sutler's rates were usually very high.

OFFICER'S EXPENSES

Officers felt the pinch more than the enlisted men. They were compelled to have civilians for servants, if they could find any. These servants, frequently Negroes, would usually be able to beg, borrow, buy, or steal something for the officer's dinner during the

A Warm Breakfast — Winter

The Chief Cook.

An Evening Meal — Summer Camp

OFFICERS' COOKS AND SERVANTS

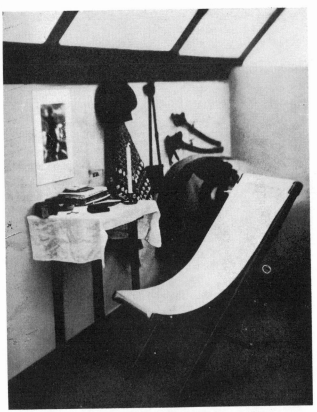

A PICTURE FOR THE HOME FOLKS

The occupant of this tent probably had this picture taken
to show his wife how comfortable his quarters were. The
shawl, hanging conspicuously by the bed, was probably made
by the wife and sent to him while his regiment was in winter
quarters—that was before the day of knitted sweaters. Notice
the haversack or dispatch case hanging near the swords. This
is a rare photograph.

day's march. They came to be called "strikers" and
there was great rivalry among them in getting food
and little articles of luxury. Commonly, three or four
officers would mess together; sometimes the officers
of a company or battery would unite into a common
mess. In this manner, the smartest strikers would pool
their foraging talents. But by the middle of 1864,
the pay of the officers did not go very far. In one
regiment the officers calculated that in favorable
times an officer would owe the Government about
$25.00 a month, instead of coming out ahead. Officers
had to pay 25¢ a pound for beef, 51¢ for coffee, etc.
Beef had formerly cost 7¢ and coffee 15¢ a pound.
In addition to charges for servants, officers also were
charged 40¢ a day for riding a Government horse.
All these expenses applied only to officers who also
had to furnish their own uniforms and weapons.[25]

BASEBALL

Besides the popular game of quoits,[26] checkers
and chess, cards, boxing, and football, there was
baseball.[27] Although baseball existed before the war
it became generally known throughout the Army
by the return of men from furlough in 1862 who

told their regiments of the marvelous new game
which was spreading through the Northern States.
Some of the games were free-scoring affairs; for example, the final score between two officer teams in
the 11th New Jersey Infantry was 40 to 15! The
game took place in April 1863. Baseball appears
to have been more popular in the East than in the
West.[28] According to legend, Abner Doubleday developed the game of baseball in 1839 when he was
in school at Cooperstown, New York. Doubleday,
who rose to the rank of major general during the
war, was particularly conspicuous at Gettysburg.
While the Army of the Potomac was in camp at
Falmouth the baseball fever broke out. One could
see thousands of men, representing almost every company in the 9th Army Corps engaged in playing baseball. Two hundred games would be going on at the
same time on some days; at other times probably
double that number would be underway on the
level plain.[29] It was the old-fashioned game, where
a man running the bases must be hit by the ball to
be declared out. This baseball craze began with the
men, then the officers began to play. Finally, one
regiment would challenge another. For example,
the 19th Massachusetts Infantry challenged the 7th
Michigan Infantry to play for $60.00 a side. The game
was witnessed by nearly the entire division. The
Massachusetts regiment won and the $120.00 was
spent on a supper with both clubs being present as
guests. "It was a grand time, and all agreed that it
was nicer to play *base* than *Minie ball.*"[30]

OTHER SPORTS

The men often hired local Negroes to sing and
dance, an entertainment which was a source of un-
ending amusement. Cockfights were popular, as were
such sports as boxing, wrestling, and tossing some
unsuspecting victim in a blanket. Life in camp varied from day to day and the following letter[31] is
probably typical of thousands of others in its description of the everyday life of the soldier:

Halls Hill, December 3, 1861
4 p.m.
Dear Sister

I just received your letter that was written Sunday
and I hasten to answer for you do not mention having
received any money by *Express.* Why you have not I
can't imagine for I sent twenty dollars by Adams Express
and have the receipt for it.

I have been having the toothache some but have got
along first rate and if it troubles me much more I shall
have it pulled. The hospital steward is an excellent hand
for that it is said.

In rainy weather we take lots of *comfort.* Have no
playing to do except it may be a little practice, so we
lay around the tent, read, write, play checkers, *once in
a while* a game of Euchre and enjoy ourselves as well as
possible. But for all this laziness I feel just as if I could
go to work tomorrow and if I was at home and work as
long and as hard as ever . . .

We got our swords Sunday, we only have twelve for

the band. I was one of the unlucky ones to get one. I say *unlucky* ones because it is so much more *brass* to take care of and I hardly think I shall ever have occasion to use it. If you send me another box put in a couple of papers of tripoli or some such thing for cleaning brass for I believe the Sutlers do not keep it. They (the Sutlers) keep every thing almost that can be imagined that a soldier would be likely to ask for and made good profits. The most I buy of them is butter and molasses. Butter is worth 28¢ per lb. and molasses 80¢ per gallon but the molasses we get of the Maine Sutler is the best I ever ate in my life, about as nice as honey. Two of us "go in together" and take turns buying butter and molasses. It does not amount to a great deal. The Sutlers are making a good thing now, selling boots and gloves. The "*Army*" does not find anything for the feet but shoes and those are not the thing for mud. I have a good pair of bootees that I bought in Washington and a pair of government shoes. Besides boots bring a dollar or a dollar and a half more than they do at home, but I should rather pay the difference then send home for a pair on account of getting a fit.

Ronald
18th Mass.

SOLDIER LANGUAGE

Although most of the contemporary literature was discreetly silent on the subject, it is evident from letters, diaries, and journals of the men themselves that soldiers' "vices" were by no means nonexistent. The profanity of the day would excite the admiration of a first sergeant of 1917 or 1941; it was forceful, picturesque, and frequent. The choice of personal expletives has been preserved in the statement of charges and specifications in the records of courts-martial. Examples may be found in United States War Department, "General Orders 188, 199, 225," 1863, *General Orders for 1863*.

TOBACCO AND WHISKEY

The use of tobacco was very general; Federal pickets exchanged their coffee and newspapers for tobacco with the enemy, while cases were known of men leaving the line of battle to ransack a tobacco storehouse.[32] At the Battle of Opequon a group of officers smoked with great pleasure some tobacco furnished by a comrade during a lull in the fighting.[33] When the 5th Massachusetts Battery found a barn with five thousand dollars worth of cured tobacco in it, they were told by their officers to help themselves. If tobacco was not available the men smoked oak leaves and other substitutes but with little pleasure.[34]

Foreign observers believed drunkenness was a much too common vice among the Federal soldiers, necessitating in some cases the prohibition of its use even in moderation.[35] A study of the court-martial cases would tend to bear this out. Certain prominent generals, reported as "unwell" by the papers, were actually drunk while leading their troops in action.[36] In one engagement, the corps, division, and brigade commanders were "incapacitated" but their emphatic orders to the troops cost the lives of several men who had no choice but to obey.[37] On the other hand, although some believed the use of whiskey should be abolished in the Army, others counseled its continued use in moderation.[38] The whiskey ration was certainly appreciated by the men after a severe battle which had strained their mental and physical faculties to the breaking point. After Shiloh the Sherman brigade was issued rations of whiskey or "commissary" as it was called, about two or three times a day. All enjoyed it and nobody became

RELAXING IN CAMP
The soldiers in the middle are probably playing poker. One of them is wearing his cartridge belt, an indication that he is a member of the interior guard.

intoxicated except a few who managed to get an extra supply.[39] Intoxication itself was not a military offense and was therefore not punishable. When men had been in idleness for months, often desperate with malaria, and restless under the irksome restrictions of military life, they were often ready to try or do anything. Many officers and men turned to whiskey, which was easy to get.[40]

CAMP FOLLOWERS AND PROSTITUTES

In the early part of the war many units were supplied with other diversions by camp followers who as late as the Antietam campaign hovered around the army. Then, as now, the larger town and cities had their "establishments" for the entertainment of the soldier. Because of their higher rate of pay, officers were especially welcome, but unfortunately for morale and discipline, they appear to have been the least circumspect in their actions. In such cities as Washington the counterfeiters and confidence men assembled from all sections of the country. Petty thieves and pickpockets were common. To entertain the soldiers there were dancers and singers, comedians, prize fighters and gamblers, vendors of obscene literature and proprietors of "rum-jog shops." On many streets were brothels, and the prostitutes were followed by doctors promising cures.[41] A young Michigan soldier stationed in Nashville reassuringly wrote his mother:[42]

There is another institution that I will speak of just to show what kind of a city the south praise and call the "flower of Tenessee." (I pray God to keep all such flowers out of my garden, and out of my hands) it is the institution sanctioned by law, and licensed by military authority, there is one street running the whole length of Nashville, where evry house is kept by courtesans . . . this st is called "Smoky-row" and there are . . . "Patrolls" [to keep order]; there is a hospital kept by Uncle Sam where these courtesans are brought evry ten days, and examined by the Surgeon if found to be sound they are given a license for ten days. for which they pay one dollar, if not they are kept there and doctored untill they are. there are between 1400 and 1500 licenses given evry ten days . . . there are a great many kept by officers who do not get licenses . . .

It is unneccessary to add that most diaries and letters failed to record such diversions as might have proved to be a source of embarrassment in later years.

GAMES AND GAMBLING

The almost universal time killer in camp was cards. Some commanding officers forbade gambling in their commands. On December 10, 1861, the colonel of the 63rd Pennsylvania Infantry issued a regiment order which stated:[43]

"All gambling and card playing is positive prohibited in this camp. Persons disobeying this order will be severely punished."

But gambling could not be stopped. It was the pastime of many soldiers, especially the bounty jumpers who carried it on very extensively. Thousands of dollars would change hands in one day's playing, and there were many ugly fights, caused by these bounty jumpers cheating each other at cards.[44] Some of the decks of cards had replaced the symbols of card suits—clubs, diamonds, hearts,

RECREATIONAL ITEMS
Tobacco, dice, cards, and liquor —what the soldier most desired during his off-duty hours. What important item is missing? The bottle (Hooker's?) was found on the Chancellorsville Battlefield, the cards and pipe at Cedar Mountain, and the dice at Antietam.

spades—with such patriotic symbols of the American flag, a shield, a star, and an eagle. Other decks used pictures of officers as the symbols. The games varied, but were practically always for stakes. In one regiment where poker was the favorite, games could be found in almost every company street, "officers as well as men taking a twist at the tiger."[45] These card games often led to quarrels, but they helped pass the time away, especially when books and other reading materials were scarce. It was observed that many soldiers would throw away their packs of cards before going into combat.[46]

A dice game called "Chuck-or-Luck" seems to have been one of the most popular gambling games. This game kept more men on their knees than did the chaplains; the officers had a similar game called "Sweat-Board," in which the stakes were much higher.[47] At payday the Chuck-or-Luck banks were set up at convenient places, such as at the springs where the men obtained their water. At each bank there would be ten to twenty soldiers down on their knees laying their money on certain figures laid out on a board while a "banker" threw the dice. After each throw the banker picked up the largest number of dollars. Some of the men would lose an entire month's pay in a few days.[48]

The men would bet in many ingenious ways, based on different schemes and devices. On one occasion, the attention of an officer was drawn to a group of soldiers assembled in a big circle on the parade ground. Coming up to the men he saw a circle on a board, with the circle about a foot in diameter. A very novel type of gambling was going on. Each one participating placed a "gray-back" (or louse), at the center, and the one reaching the edge first, won the stakes.[49] In some regiments, the officers, particularly in the quartermaster or commissary department, owned horses kept for racing. Some the these were thoroughbreds; and while in winter quarters, running races, usually quarter races, was an element of amusement. One such occasion occurred while the cavalry was together just before coming to the Wilderness, in 1864, and considerable money was dropped in the 1st Massachusetts, by betting on Tom Taylor, against an unknown, which turned out to be a pure-bred racing horse.[50]

CLUBS, ASSOCIATIONS, LODGES

More serious officers and men founded clubs or continued their association with organized groups of which they had been members before enlistment in the Army. A group of the 100th Indiana Infantry organized a Masonic lodge under a special charter[51] while at Fort Monroe the 10th New York Infantry organized a working lodge of Master Masons in a casemate where thirty-four members entered, passed, and were raised. "Frequently gray-clad soldiers of the Southern Army—prisoners within the lines—found their way to the spot and sat in lodge with their more fortunate brethren."[52] The community of interest between members of such fraternal organizations as the Masons was remarkable in that it overrode the animosities of the battlefield. There were many examples of this throughout the war. On one occasion a wounded captain of the 146th New York Infantry gave the Masonic sign of distress. His signal was seen by a Confederate surgeon who chanced to be riding past. This officer at once dismounted, examined the captain, and by skillful amputation of an arm managed to save his life. The surgeon was Doctor Todd, a brother of Mrs. Lincoln.[53]

THEATRICALS

When in winter quarters the troops broadened their entertainment to include concerts and the theater. General Sedgwick's brigade built a theater which accommodated several hundred men, was lighted with gas, and equipped with a dress circle and an orchestra pit.[54] One of the few cases of planned entertainment occurred in the 9th New York Infantry while in garrison on Roanoke Island. Lacking sufficient drill to keep them busy, and with wounded men returning from furlough elaborating on the royal reception received while at home, it was decided that some radical departure had to be made to lift the men out of their low spirits and cause them to forget their loneliness. A reading room, post office, and debating club were organized. Gymnastic equipment was sent down from the North; and, in addition, baseball, boxing, and wrestling events were scheduled regularly. In the evenings the "Zouave Minstrel and Dramatic Club," a regimental organization, presented burlesques on Shakesperian plays in addition to the ever-popular minstrel shows. Regular admission was charged and the proceeds sent to widows of men who had died while serving with the regiment.[55] In Suffolk, Virginia, a regiment presented a Christmas parade which was fully as colorful as a modern circus procession. Eight magnificent horses, "gayly trimmed" with laurel, holly, and ribbons, pulled a wagon filled with members of the regimental band. Much in evidence on the wagon was a large American flag. Behind the wagon marched twenty or thirty of the regiment in masquerade costume, some with masks and others with painted faces, but all curiously dressed in women's clothes, bear skins, or ill-fitting men's attire. This motley crowd, mounted on kicking mules and condemned horses, represented the Southern Confederacy returing to its allegiance.[56] A brigade in the 1st Army Corps constructed an "opera house" during the winter of 1864; the house itself was built of logs, with a roof made from shelter tents and wagon covers. The dress circle and parquette were furnished with log seats for two hundred men although more than double that number crowded into the building "to listen to the charming melodies, not indeed, of Verdi and Donizetti, but of Foster and his imitators.[57]

VISITORS

In the mud at Brandy Station that same winter, officers of the Army of the Potomac met their wives with ambulances at the railroad station. These women had taken advantage of the lull in active operations of the army to visit their husbands. Soon groups of these reunited couples could be seen riding about the countryside. Others listened to band music while partaking of meals which sometimes included such items as soup, fish, roast beef, turkey, and pie.[58] Many of the women preferred to live in nearby towns because of the lack of comfort they found in the military quarters. Livermore believed the presence of these wives in camp was injurious to the "martial spirit" of their mates and interferred in some cases with discipline,[59] while Lyman noted the "sound of revelry and champagne corks" within the tents.[60]

Senators and governors arrived and were honored by impressive reviews. Some of these dignitaries and several distinguished generals on the night of Washington's Birthday repaired to a large hall constructed of pine boards where the 2nd Army Corps' commissioned personnel presented a supper and dance. Regimental flags and stacked arms lent a martial air to the occasion which was graced by Vice-President Hamlin and his daughter. We are assured that the "toilets of the ladies were magificent, and the officers of the corps proved they were as successful upon a ball-room floor as upon the field of battle." [61] A year later Lyman visited a large building, constructed by the 50th New York Engineers, which was used both as a church and a theater. The structure holding one-half a regiment at a time, was illuminated by a rustic chandelier, while the stage was lighted by the rays of Army lanterns and candles reflected from tin mess plates.[62]

BREAKING CAMP

With winter gone, the armies prepared to move. An extensive weeding-out process now took place, eliminating the non-fit. With the exception of some of the replacements of the latter half of the war, the men in the service, and more especially those at the front, were the hardiest and best of the original enlistees. One observer estimated that about one-fifth of the men who enlisted were not tough enough nor brave enough to be soldiers.[63] A regiment on arrival at its station would number a thousand strong but in six months it could muster only six or seven hundred men for fighting duty. The rest vanished in different ways; some had deserted, some had died of hardship or disease, or nostalgia; as many more has been discharged for physical disability; others were absent sick, or had received furloughs by shamming sickness; others were on special duty as

bakers, hospital nurses, wagoners, quartermaster's drudges, while a few were working out sentences of courts-martial. A division of 15,000 men soon dropped to 10,000 and even 8,000. Companies soon lost one if not two of their three officers. Strikingly illustrative of this is the Secretary of War's report [64] on the strength of the Army as of May 1, 1864. On that date the military forces totalled 970,710 officers and men, distributed as follows:

In field hospitals or unfit for duty	41,266
In general hospitals, or home on sick leave	75,978
Absent on furlough or prisoners of war	66,290
Absent without leave	15,483
On detached service in the Military Departments	190,348
Available force "present for duty"	662,345

Shortly before leaving for the front the sick and disabled were turned over to general or semi-permanent hospitals, thus leaving only those fit for duty to make the trip which was by rail or water as far as possible.

The breaking up of a large camp was a sad occasion for many of the men for whom their huts and surroundings had been home for several months. The men had become acquainted with many soldiers in neighboring regiments and had come to know the local citizens, often on a friendly basis. As the men prepared to leave their camp they had to dispose of articles of furniture and various household conveniences. All must be destroyed, left, or given away; scarcely anything could be sold. Friendly citizens would be freely remembered in the forced distribution. Usually confusion would reign when camp was being broken. "Hundreds of contrabands, all ages, are begging and pilfering, and carrying off all they can hold in their arms, or cram into their capacious bags and pockets; little teams, gathered here from the farmers in the vicinity and from . . . [neighboring towns] are all about camp, driven by white natives, and all being loaded with plunder gotten by stealing or begging; many of the soldiers were drunk; bonfires are fed with numerous contrivances and conveniences the men have made for themselves; wives are parting from husbands . . . There are sweethearts here too . . . Some of the houses, huts and tents are burning, and amid the bustle, smoke and hot hurrying, the lines are formed, company by company; we shoulder arms, turn our backs upon . . . [the] Camp, give three rousing, but not altogether spontaneous cheers . . . and at 9 a.m. are away." [66]

Too often, however, troops would burn all their huts before leaving camp with the result that there was no shelter at all for other units which might use the same camp area again. There are many descriptions of troops breaking camp but one of the best is that of one of McDowell's regiments just before First Bull Run. The large amount of baggage carried could only have occurred early in the war. According to the narrator, about 30 four-mule wagons were used for the transportation of tents and camp equipment. With a Washington citizen as guide, the march was to be accomplished before daybreak.

"The night was cloudy, with occasional showers. To give light for the necessary work of moving, the men set fire to the dried cedars, which had served as shades and ornaments. The effect was splendid. There was little noise, for silence has been enjoined; and the figures of the men tugging away at bundles, packing and repacking, hurrying hither and thither, and leading over obstructions, with the images of the long-eared mules reflected on the white-covered wagons, which were alternately brilliant in the glare, or darkened in the shadow, as the flames flashed up in wreathing spires, or the smoke rolled in clouds of pitchy blackness, made altogether a scene of wildness fit for the pencil of Salvator Rosa." How many times was this goblin picture, with every conceivable variation, repeated during the war! [66]

CONFEDERATE PRISONS

Captured Federals, whether wounded or unwounded, were hastened as rapidly as possible to the rear to prevent their recapture. Long marches and railroad trips eventually brought them to their destination, usually one of the larger prison camps such as Libby or Andersonville. Generally speaking, the treatment of captured Federal soldiers was good when their captors were combat troops. However, the local militia units, often composed of older

men or youngsters, who were not eligible for combat duty, seemed anxious at times to prove their military prowess or to impress the Southern civilians. In such cases the Federal prisoners' treatment was not always what it should have been. Despite attempts by later writers to show deliberate exaggeration by ex-Federal prisoners of war, the conditions in those prison pens must have been horrible. [67] Officers were segregated in separate prisons and, as a rule, their living conditions were superior. Of 48 "good, healthy robust young men" from one company of the 85th New York Infantry, 30 died there; all the officers of the regiment (they were captured at the same time as their men) returned home. Everyone knew what Andersonville meant; there were no illusions as to the conditions and high rate of mortality there.[68] Not only did the press contain accounts of prison conditions, but many Federal soldiers saw their comrades after their return from prison camps. An officer of the 19th Massachusetts Infantry described what he saw as follows; [69]

We went from Charlotte to Goldsboro where we saw the worst sight that the eyes of mortal ever gazed upon. Two long trains of platform cars, loaded with our men, came in. Not one in fifty was able to stand. Many were left dead on the cars, the guards rolling them off as they would logs of wood; most of them were nearly naked, and their feet and hands were frozen; they had lost their reason; could not tell the State they came from, their regiment or company. We threw them what rations we had, and they would fight for them like dogs, rolling over each other in their eagerness to get the least morsel. I took a little fellow in my arms and carried him across the street; he could not have been over sixteen years old, and did not weigh more than fifty pounds; he died just as I laid him down.

Another account, in a letter [70] written during the

PERSONAL TREASURES
Daguerrotypes; inkwell from camp at Falmouth; diary of Lieut. Fred Frank, 11th Indiana Infantry; writing portfolio of Pvt. Chas. Cox, whose letters are quoted in this book; and a watch presented to Capt. G. H. Amidon by Co. E, 4th Vt. Vols.

ANDERSONVILLE PRISON IN 1864

A remarkable photograph which plainly shows the crowded and unsanitary conditions which caused such an appalling death rate at this prisoner-of-war concentration camp in Georgia. Note the proximity to the camp of the large open latrine in the foreground. This undoubtedly was the cause of much fatal dysentery.

war, describes the condition of paroled prisoners as they arrived at the exchange point, Cox's landing on the James River.

"We arrived at the landing a few minutes before the rebel flag-of-truce boat [which] had the Confederate flag flying at the stern, and was towing a barge filled with our sick soldiers, the boat itself being a dirty affair. In a few moments more, six hundred of our men, half of them commissioned officers, including two brigadier generals, were on the shore; and those of them who could walk immediately started for Aiken's landing, at some distance below, where our flag-of-truce boat lay. The rest filled a long line of ambulances, and fully two hours were consumed before they were all transferred to our own boat. Such a looking set of men I never saw before, and hope never to see again. Hatless, shirtless, shoe-less, wrapped up in old bed-quilts of as many hues as Joseph's coat their feet wound with rags, and many of them barefoot (and the wintry, ice-cold mud six inches deep) their clothing in tatters, their hair long and matted, dirty and unshaven, and all looking as pale and thin as though wasted with consumption or fever. Many were carried on board our boat on stretchers, too weak and sick to stand. Just before our boat moved off a band struck up the Star Spangled Banner and the poor emaciated fellows tried to cheer. They were too weak to give a very loud one, but I never heard a more impressive cheer in my life."

Because of the controversial nature of the entire problem of treatment of prisoners the following statistics are given: [71]

	FEDERAL soldiers	CONFEDERATE soldiers
Died in Prison	26,249	26,774
Exchanged and paroled ..	154,059	350,367
Released on oath		71,889
Escaped	2,696	2,098
Joined Confederate army .	3,170	
Joined Federal Army		5,452

But the really significant fact is that athough the Confederacy held less than half as many prisoners as the Union, almost exactly the same number died in prison, or to put it otherwise, prison life in the South was twice as noxious as in the North. This was not because the Union men were in prison longer, either; some of the biggest Union hauls came very early in the war, at Fort Donelson and in the operations at New Orleans and along the Carolina coast. The Union prisons were no rose gardens, as the figures demonstrate, but they were nothing like the places that killed off one man out of every seven confined.[72]

On arrival within the prison proper the newly captured Federals were invariably called "Fresh Fish" by the older inmates until a new group arrived.[73] In every prison there were pickpockets, thieves, and even murderers among the prisoners themselves. This was especially true after large quantities of the Eastern cities' riffraff had been captured in Grant's 1864 offensive. The prisoners themselves executed a few of these hoodlums in self-protection.

Life in the enlisted men's prisons could not have

been aught but monotonous and disheartening. Poor diet, inadequate shelter, and poor medical service kept their physical powers so low that a slight scratch often meant gangrene and death. The poor sanitary facilities were not improved by volunteers who were often too lacking in discipline to observe even the simplest rules of good health. Prisoners varied their carving of chess men and pipes with attempts to tunnel out to freedom. A few of these attempts were successful but more were discovered by alert guards or "tipped off" by Confederates disguised as Federal prisoners. The constant rumors of exchange led to the disease facetiously termed "exchange on the brain."[74]

Life in the officer prisons was better. Putnam relates that when his group arrived at Danville in the fall of 1864, the men turned in early due to sufficient heat and blankets. Sleep was difficult for men who had had their overcoats and a large number of their shoes confiscated and were left with but scraps of blankets for the group.[75] For entertainment these officers sang such songs as "Marching Through Georgia," but as the winter wore on and hope for an early exchange faded, the more frequent selections were "Mother, Will You Miss Me?" and "Tenting On The Old Camp Ground." The difficulty of finding occupation during the long hours of the day was partially overcome by water and wood parties, always, of course, under guard. Chess tournaments eventually stopped because playing demanded too much concentration of men weakened by lack of sufficient food. Some of the officers developed hitherto unknown

ANDERSONVILLE RELICS

These articles are representative of the crude implements used by Federal prisoners in the notorious Andersonville compound. Also it is one of the first collections of Civil War relics, and was displayed at the Metropolitan Fair of the U. S. Sanitary Commission in New York City in 1864.

talents as raconteurs while others conducted classes in Spanish and German.[76] The all-absorbing topic of conversation for officers as well as men was the possibility of exchange.

The principal place of confinement for Federal soldiers was at Andersonville, Georgia. Out of 45,613 prisoners confined there, 12,912 died, or, 28 per cent. The greatest number present at any time was 33,114 —on August 8, 1864. The greatest number of deaths in any one day was 127—on August 23, 1864. The daily average of deaths was 29.75.[77] In any discussion of prisoners of war, it should be pointed out that efforts were made to exchange the most disabled soldiers and they are the ones who were in the most weakened state when exchanged. Grant did not favor exchange of prisoners because of the poor condition of the Federal soldiers he would get in return. Sherman refused to accept a proposition which would release to him the prisoners at Andersonville in exchange for soldiers taken from Hood in the Georgia campaign.[78]

HOSPITAL LIFE

Life in the hospitals was naturally much better than in prison pens; the wounded and sick Federals were either removed to large hospitals near their homes or they were often visited by friends and relatives in the large government hospitals around such cities at St. Louis and Washington. In the hospitals themselves the nurses, male and female, were aided by women volunteer workers who received and registered donations, issued clothing, and prepared special drinks and delicacies for the men.[79] These volunteers helped the men to pass the tedious period of convalescence by playing games with them or writing their letters home. The situation on the hospital transports, however, was marked by lack of system and supplies in 1862 coupled with great overcrowding,[80] a situation which still existed as late as May 1864.[81]

Hospitals varied greatly in their facilities and to a large extent were as good as the available supply of medical personnel and supplies would permit. Often the soldiers received meager care through no fault of the doctors; there simply were no adequate facilities available. This was especially true in the early period of the war. The following letter[82] was written by a company commander who was killed in action at Cold Harbor. The letter illustrates the genuine interest that an excellent officer had in his men, and also points up the inadequate hospital facilities that too often characterized the Federal Army in 1861 and 1862.

Mr. James M. Crafts
    Dear Sir
    Your letter of 2d inst. reached me this morning and I reply immediately in order to relieve your mind from

FIELD HOSPITAL

ts uncertainty in regard to your son Irving. I am most happy my dear sir to write you that Irving is yet alive and, what is better, fast improving in health. He has indeed been very sick, so sick that for a while we did despair of his life. His long illness has, of course, very much reduced him, but he is gaining, his appetite is good and as soon as the sore on his back is healed, he will be about as strong again. Irving has had during his sickness all the attention it was possible to give him, situated as we have been with our regiment scattered over one hundred miles and our hospital stores divided but everything the Surgeon advised for his good I have obtained if possible, paying for it as in other cases out of the Company fund . . .

We have had a great deal of sickness among the men since occupying Washington and I have had the sad duty of laying six of my boys beneath the sod.

W. A. Walker,
Capt. Co. C, Mass. 27th.

Hardship Furloughs

One of the best applications for furlough was written by a man in the 16th Maine Infantry; he must have been very well versed in the Holy Scripture. By the end of December 1863, applications for furloughs had been so frequent that Sergeant-Major Maxfield believed his only chance to get a furlough would be to base it on Biblical text. Accordingly he sent in his application, basing his request on Deuteronomy, Chapter 20, Verse 7: "And what man is there, that have betrothed a wife, and hath not taken her? Let him go and return unto his house, lest he die in battle and another man take her." The Sergeant-Major told his comrades that if the application were approved, he would ask for an extension, referring again to Deuteronomy, this time to Chapter 24, Verse 5, which says: "When a man hath taken a new wife, he shall not go out to war, neither shall he be charged with any business; but he shall be free at home one year, and shall cheer up his wife which he hath taken." Much to the Sergeant-Major's surprise (apparently he underestimated the religious training of his superiors!), he obtained his furlough, while the applications of two officers, who applied at the same time, were disallowed.[83]

Furloughs were granted to sick and wounded soldiers just as sick leaves of absence were granted officers. Except for some unusual family affliction at home it was very difficult for an enlisted man to receive a furlough during the war.

Furloughs to Vote

The only exceptions to this were the furloughs to re-enlisted veterans and the furloughs granted both officers and men to permit them to participate in political campaigns in their States. It is difficult to ascertain just how widespread the furloughing of individuals was but we do know that during February 1864, while the armies were in winter quarters, certain new Hampshire regiments were sent home in a body to vote in what was well known would be a critical election for the administration. That election was, perhaps, the most important ever held in that State; it was the first prophetic voice of the people in the presidential campaign. Before the 14th New Hampshire Infantry was sent home a quiet canvass of the unit was taken to ascertain its corporate attitude[84] while in the 2nd New Hampshire Infantry "it was not a mere accidental coincidence that all the men who went were legal voters, and that their furloughs brought them home at the date of the annual State election."[85] This regiment had 450 men furloughed for a period of 20 days for this purpose. The 14th Regiment's furlough was for 12 days, and the same time was granted the 13th Regiment. Free transportation was furnished the soldiers for the entire round-trip. In the 13th Regiment all men were required to wear side-arms, and to be on special duty and under military orders. Officers wore their swords, men their bayonets—all these weapons had to be worn wherever the men went, and when they voted. This was considered advisable because threats had been made in New Hampshire that the soldiers would not be allowed to go home and vote, even though only those men voted who were actually legal voters in the town where they went to vote. At some of the polls there were civilians who would have prevented the soldiers from voting had it been possible.[86] Party feeling in the State was high. Angry discussions and numberless personal collisions marked "town-meeting day" for while "the boys did not exactly carry to the polls a chip on each shoulder, they were not in a mood to be jostled to any great extent: and the Copperhead had a hard time of it where the soldiers were numerous enough to start a little political 'camp-fire' in the midst of the assembled voters."[87] A few persisted in voting according to old predilections but they were in no way proscribed afterward. The soldiers' vote in this spring election helped to insure the State remaining Republican but in the fall presidential election the soldiers' votes, except in Maryland, were of little consequence in the final result.[88]

The voting by the soldiers in the fall of 1864, however, is significant in that it indicates the general attitude of the Federal soldier toward the administration and the prosecution of the war. The War Department prescribed regulations in respect to the distribution of election tickets and proxies in the Army in a general order, October 1, 1864. This order provided for the designation of an agent for each army corps by the State executive or the State committee of each political party who should take the tickets and proxies to corps headquarters for distribution. Each political party was allowed one civilian inspector per brigade to be present at the elections. Political speeches, harrangues, or canvassing among the troops were forbidden while commanding officers were enjoined to take all necessary steps to secure freedom and fairness in the election.

Summary dismissal was ordered for any officer or private who should wantonly destroy tickets or who should prevent their proper distribution among the troops. This penalty was also ordered for any officer or man who made a false return or interfered with the election.[89] These elections in the field were subjected to no undue influence.[90] Regimental commanders designated officers to serve as "Inspectors" and "Clerks of Elections."[91] Lyman thought the vote was 5 to 1 for Lincoln which he correctly believed showed that the men identified the administration with the support of the war.[92] Actually the percentage of the soldiers' vote cast and counted in all the States was 75% for the Union ticket and 25% for the Democratic. The voting, of course, varied greatly in different regiments. The 6th Wisconsin Battery cast its entire 75 votes for Lincoln[93] while in the 7th New Hampshire Infantry there were only 14 for Lincoln and 2 for McClellan, many not caring to exercise the privilege.[94] Some of the State elections in which soldiers participated are of interest in that the candidates were at the same time officers in the field. In 1863 a divisional commander ran as Democratic candidate for the governorship of Iowa

ABSENTEE VOTING

Absentee voting authorization for Coal Heaver Charles E. Lewis, USS *Nyack*, in the Presidential election of 1864. Shortly after the election the *Nyack* participated in the attack on Fort Fisher, North Carolina.

against an Iowa colonel on the Republican ticket. The colonel won even without the soldiers' vote.[95]

RELIGION

The religious phase of the soldiers' life was entrusted to the chaplains. Each volunteer regiment was allowed one chaplain who initially received his appointment by the regimental commander on the vote of the field officers and company commanders on duty with the regiment at the time the appointment was made. The chaplain so appointed had to be a regularly ordained minister of some Christian denomination and received the pay and allowances of a captain of cavalry.[96] Similar regulations provided for the appointment of chaplains in the Regular Army.[97] In May 1862, each permanent hospital was allowed a chaplain to be appointed by the President.[98] In July, the Federal authorities ordered that all captive Confederate chaplains be immediately and unconditionally discharged, asserting that the principle that chaplains should not be held as prisoners of war was then recognized.[99] This principle was reiterated two years later.[100] About this time, also, the rank of chaplain was recognized as being a noncommand rank in the Regular and volunteer service of the United States; chaplains were included among those entitled to pension rights. The chaplains' duties were definitely prescribed: they were to render monthly reports to the Adjutant General of the Army as to the "moral condition and general history of the regiments, hospitals, or posts to which they . . . [were] attached"; they were to hold "appropriate religious services" at the burial of soldiers who died in their commands to which they had been assigned to duty; and they were to conduct public religious services at least once each Sabbath, when practicable.[101]

Despite the advantage that their education gave them in publicizing their contributions to the welfare of their charges, the evidence would indicate that far too many of the chaplains were ill-fitted for their positions. Many men became chaplains merely by submitting an application without sufficient credentials from responsible people who actually knew the training and experience to be as claimed. To restrict the number of incompetents or charlatans as much as possible, the Government emphasized that chaplains had to meet the requirements of Section 8 of the Act of July 17, 1862, as follows:[102]

"No person shall be appointed a chaplain in the United States Army who is not a regularly ordained minister of some religious denomination, and who does not present testimonials of his present good standing as such minister, with a recommendation for his appointment as an Army chaplain from some authorized ecclesiastical body, or not less than five accredited ministers belonging to said religious denomination."

Many chaplains were ministers who had mistaken their profession or who could not find or keep churches. In expressing the hope for a government investigation to weed out the incompetent pretenders, the service journal quoted a general who said that the chaplains in his department were "a set of time-serving rascals—fonder of luxurious ease, more grasping, not only of less use, but far more injurious to good order and good morals than any men in his command."[103] One colonel could not see "how a chaplain could benefit a regiment" but admitted that the Government must have known what it was doing in assigning a chaplain to his regiment and therefore *his* chaplain had to earn his keep. The colonel ordered the chaplain to preach twice on Sunday, and to hold prayer meetings in the companies during the week. Also, the chaplain had to visit the hospital and guard house and be present and deliver a parting benediction to all detachments about to depart on expeditions![104] In one brigade the commander had his chaplains pull down fences that they might do something to earn their salaries. While some lacked adaptability, others lacked the stamina necessary for active campaigning and soon resigned. Although eleven chaplains were killed in action,[105] some were arrant cowards and were laughed at by men who faced danger bravely.[106] The following incident[107] occurred during the Chancellorsville campaign and illustrates the soldiers amusement at the failure of some chaplains to practice what they preached:

In easy range of the rebel guns, we were mustered for pay. At four o'clock p.m. it was proposed by a congress of chaplains to hold divine service in the brigade, preparatory to the general slaughter anticipated during the next forty-eight hours. Everything was quiet over the river, and not a sign betrayed to the innocent twelve hundred dollar shepherds, the gathering storm, as they collected in the center of a hollow square, and fervently pleaded the cause of the Lord and the country. They were eloquent in their appeals to our patriotism, and pictured in glowing colors the halo of glory that would enfold the martyred dead . . . counseling all to stand firm, to shrink not from the terrible ordeal through which we were called to pass, to be brave and heroic, and God being our shield we would have nothing to fear—when came a slight puff of smoke, followed by another, and yet another, in quick succession, just across the river, and then a rushing sound like trains of cars and terrific explosions all around us of (whole blacksmith shops). The explosion of shells, the neighing of horses, and the sharp commands were almost drowned by the shouts and laughter of the men, as the brave chaplains, hatless and bookless, with coat-tails streaming in the wind, went madly to the rear over stone-walls, through hedges and ditches, followed by "Come back and earn your twelve hundred dollars," "Stand firm! Be brave and heroic and put your trust in the Lord!"

In addition to the noble Christian men, the Army was cursed with a lot of scalawags, who fitted themselves for chaplains how, when, or where, nobody knows.

The Secretary of War reported on June 19, 1862,

that although the rolls of 676 regiments were then on file in his office, there appeared to be only 395 chaplains on duty, of which number 29 were absent on leave or detached service and 13 were absent without leave. Recognizing the need of adequate measure "to purify and invigorate this branch," the Secretary stated in this report that he could but reiterate what the Adjutant General had previously reported, that is, that the main flaw was in the mode of appointment of chaplains. It was recommended that no person be eligible to an appoinment as chaplain who, in addition to being a regularly ordained minister of some religious denomination, should not also be able to procure credentials of his good standing, piety, intelligence, and devotion to duty from the presiding authorities of his church. The Secretary called attention to General Orders 15 and 16, May 4, 1861, pointing out that the appointing power was not used conscientiously by the officers. The preferences of the men were not consulted: "The men are not thought of; mere *social* influences carry the day, and the consequence is that persons are appointed chaplains who take but little interest in the men, and are, in turn, but little thought of by the latter. Such chaplains can effect no good, and their office thus degenerates into mere sinecure." [108]

The religious life of the soldiers was probably a personal one. Many soldiers carried their own New Testaments and religious objects. Pocket Bibles were printed in several languages and for different faiths. If the chaplain was a sincere, hard-working, religious man, he was respected as such. But most soldiers disliked long sermons or preaching.[109] It is difficult to assess the effect of chaplains on the religious life of the men because much of the material is only available in regimental histories, and ex-chaplains or clergymen wrote many of those histories. This difficulty is illustrated by the conflicting accounts about enforced religious services and prayer meetings. In one regiment, where apparently the religious services were voluntary, the ex-chaplain in the regimental history said: [110] "We had delightful prayer meetings in the open air nightly, and much tenderness in religious matters was manifested by some of the younger men. . . . A regimental church was organized, composed of the professing Christians. The Communion of the Lord's Supper was administered to them at intervals of three months while we continued in the service."

In another regiment the chaplain held prayer meetings every night in which he urged his listeners to be ready to die, pointing out that even if death did not come they would be in better shape to live. Apparently the officers considered their rank entitled them to admittance into Heaven, since few attended these meetings although strongly encouraging the men to do so.[111] Soon after Antietam there was a religious revival in many units, and this gave hope

to many homes in the North that Christianity was gaining many converts among the soldiers.[112]

The propensity of the soldier to find humor in every facet of his army life was often manifested even in religious matters.[113]

On one occasion the 1st Vermont Heavy Artillery while garrisoning a fort, had on guard a private who knew the Bible thoroughly. The guardhouse was located just inside the Fort entrance, and a bridge spanned the moat to the entrance. The officer of the day came to inspect the guard after midnight. It was a dark, rainy night. The private, on hearing the approach of the officer of the day called out "Who comes there?" Just at that moment the officer stumbled and fell headlong into the moat, but as he fell, he exclaimed in a loud voice "J . . . s C . . . t!" The private faced about and promptly called out "Turn out the Apostles, J . . . s, C . . . t." Then, with commendable foresight, he helped the officer out of the moat.[114]

The Catholic regiments, naturally, had chaplains of their own faith; there appears to have been little friction between them and the Protestant chaplains.[115]

Typical of the better type of chaplain was Dr. James J. Marks, of the 63rd Pennsylvania Infantry. Survivors always spoke enthusiastically of his active work, especially in cheering up the men during the long, cold, and stormy winter of 1861-1862. Chaplain Marks understood the men's problems and "he began at once to devise plans to divert their thoughts as much as possible from brooding over their home troubles." He started various projects of an interesting character; gave lectures every week on pleasant subjects, and as he had traveled extensively in the Holy Land, his lectures on Palestine were highly appreciated. He organized a night school, a debating society, and various other devices to amuse the men. He had a large hospital tent which was used for worship and for entertainments. Scarcely an evening passed that it was not well filled. "The good work done by this aged minister during the gloomy winter will never be fully appreciated." [116]

Catholic chaplains were generally excellent men who were conspicuous for their front line service. Probably the best known of these Catholic chaplains was Father William Corby of Notre Dame, who gave general absolution while standing on a boulder during the second day's fighting at Gettysburg. Catholics were concerned that men of their faith in non-Catholic regiments were unable to receive the sacraments when they had most need of them.

Early in 1862 there were 472 army chaplains. Among these were 22 Catholic priests and 450 Protestant chaplains. The proportion of Catholic to Protestant chaplains was therefore, about 1 to 20, but Catholics believed the ration of their faith to Protestants in the Army to be at least 1 to 6. Where the regiment was entirely Catholic, there was a Catholic chaplain. But there were regiments where one-third were Catholic, and yet no Catholic chaplain in the brigade, or in the whole division.[117] This problem was not solved during the war. In battle, Catholic chaplains sought out all of their faith whenever possible in order that all could receive absolution.

MUSIC

Occasionally the chaplain was a good singer and organized a regimental glee club.[118] Those were "singing days" and the troops sang on the march and around the evening campfire.[119] In addition to the routine bugle calls, many regiments had fife and drum corps and, until the fall of 1862, large brass bands. At formal guard mount and dress parades these bands provided music which did much to inspire the soldiers. Some hospitals had their own bands; at burials the men marched with reversed arms to the death march, "Pleyel's Hymn." This was the most commonly played music for burials; the "taps" of today was a later adaptation of the "Tattoo" of 1861-1865.

Up to July 1862, the infantry call for "Taps" was that set down in Casey's *Tactics*. Soon after the Seven Days battles on the Peninsula, General Daniel Butterfield wrote out "Taps" (as we know it today) and directed a bugler of his brigade to sound the new version thereafter in place of the regulation call as provided for in Casey's manual. It was soon adopted by other commands of the Army of the Potomac and was carried to the West by the Eleventh and Twelfth Corps when they went to Chattanooga in the fall of 1863.

Late in the war, Frank Moore published a collection of soldiers' songs under the title "Songs of the Soldier." This was one of many such collections. One of the most popular of the war songs was Julia Ward Howe's "Battle Hymn of the Republic," which she wrote while in Washington in November 1861. This hymn was usually sung on lofty occasions; its very grandeur precluded its general use. The song was more often sung to the words of "John Brown's Body" or "We'll Hang Jeff Davis on a sour-apple tree." Also popular was "When Johnny Comes Marching Home" which in 1863 was parodied into a short ballad ridiculing the incompetent leaders of the Army of the Potomac from McDowell to Hooker.[120]

The Confederate war songs "Dixie" and "Maryland, My Maryland" were quite familiar in the Federal camps. During its successful campaign in the Shenandoah Valley in 1864, the entire 19th Army Corps joined one evening in singing "Yes, We'll Rally 'Round the Flag, Boys."[121] As the long war dragged on, such songs as "Tenting Tonight" and "In the Prison Cell I Sit" became more and more frequent. A song which Sherman detested, "Marching Through Georgia," was very popular in the last few months of the war.

A comprehensive treatment of the music of the Civil War would fill a large and entertaining volume. The bugle-call at reveille, on the skirmish line, or guiding the evolutions of squadron or battery, continued to echo in veterans' ears long after the war.

In camp and on the march the different "calls" formed an important and perpetual element. Doubtless the disgruntled or worn-out soldier questioned the rapturous melody of the drum sounding the call for another detail to appear in front of the adjutant's quarters. But in spite of all unpleasant suggestions,

FIFE AND DRUM CORPS

Regimental field music. When a unit reached the front the musicians generally ceased to function as such. They acted as litter bearers, in evacuating the wounded. At other times their music helped keep up the morale of the men in ranks.

it was true that much of the genuine romance of camp life was associated with the routine calls. There was no finer inspiration than the first burst, crash, and roll of reveille when a crack drum-corps with melodious shrill fife rallied upon the color line and roused an entire regiment as by an electrical shock. The effect was intensified when, in a great army stretching out for miles, a single bugle-note gave the signal, and then, as by magic, from every direction broke out the accelerating roll of drums, the screech of fifes, and the blare of artillery and cavalry bugles.

Then came breakfast call and, often at 8:30, sick-call, with the faithful soldier who had fought off disease mingling with the chronic "dead-beats" who deliberately cheated the Government and who shifted every burden of duty on to their overworked comrades.

The calls and marches accompanying guard-mounting at 9 a.m. gave the drummer the fullest opportunity for displaying his skill while playing the detail to the guard house, when the band ceased its escort, the review before the officer of the day being passed, and the parade dismissed.

Every call, march, and air of drum-corps and band entered into the very life of a regiment, and was valued beyond the power of a civilian to appreciate. The evening calls of "supper," "tattoo," and "lights out" were full of music and meaning, and each breathed forth its own suggestions. A military camp at the hour of tattoo was a study; games, letter-writing, reading, mending, lounging on bunks, story-telling, pondering on objects far away but near to the soldiers heart—these were intruded upon by the ra-a-a-at tat-tat-tat of the drum-major, in his preliminary flourish, as he initiated the stereotyped measures of the bed-time concert.

"Lights out" were hopelessly incongruous. They were always either too late or too early. If the sergeant of the guard, who walked every company street immediately after the call, commanding "Lights out!" could have gathered up the comments which were occasionally hurled after him, he could have given the public a most remarkable and startling collection of strong language. It often occurred that said executor of taps-law was not more than three tents away before candles were lighted again, and penny-ante progressed, necessitating another tour by the irate sergeant. And something else sometimes happened, for the audacious gamester wound up his fun with a night in the guard-house.

The acme of musical demonstration was reached in the dress-parade, and it was never determined whether a crack drum corps or a fine band appeared to best advantage on those occasions. For martial music, purely, a drum corps stood by itself, but a band had obvious advantages which constantly helped morale.

Up to the time of the Civil War it was a popular notion that armies marched to battle inspired by the patriotic strains of bands, and the martial airs of fife and drum. So far as modern warfare is concerned, this is no longer so—and in the Civil War, musicians were present either as buglers (and they were few), but mainly occupied in carrying stretchers to remove the wounded. But men in the hospital were invigorated by the airs they had come to love from their boyhood.

The music of the Union had many parts and moods and renderings. In addition to instrumental performances, vocal music in the Army was well-nigh universal, and in quality it ranged from the veriest crudities of expression up to the productions of skill and taste. In nearly every regiment the musical side of Army life furnished a curious and interesting study. In many cases a regimental glee club was organized. Due to the lack of many types of entertainment now available to the American soldier, music played a very important role in the morale of the Federal soldier.

BURIALS

An important part of the soldiers' life in camp was the burial of their comrades who were killed in battle or died of disease. Some regiments refused to permit strangers to bury their men, hoping for similar treatment if their turn should come. Soldiers killed in battle were buried in their blankets unless comrades saw fit to get old boards and make coffins, which was seldom done. The government sent no coffins to the front but at large assembly points and at the general hospitals coffins were furnished. Metallic caskets, "air tight," indestructible, and free from encroachments of vermin or water" were advertised by commercial firms who indignantly disclaimed any connection with rival companies using sheet iron and similar materials.[122] Embalmers did a thriving business during the war and their "ghastly advertisements" met the eye of visitors in Washington[123] and other large centers as well as at the front. A visitor to the Army of the James noted the roadside dotted with the "neat prospectus of the Embalmer-General to the Army, whose suggestive notices had greeted the eyes of each soldier as he marched to the front." When a staff member pointed out their demoralizing influence, General Butler ordered the embalmer to desist from this method of advertising.[124] At times rival embalmers would send their teams along the front handing out handbills with the heading "The Honored Dead" and containing "an incongruous mixture of the claims of sentiment and the cash cost of caring for a dead comrade."[125] One firm attempted to get a bill through Congress which would have given the firm exclusive right to embalm bodies; this firm also attempted to have Congress authorize a corps of embalmers for each division. The firm charged $50.00 for an officer and $25.00 for an enlisted man. A correspondent had to admit that the bodies looked as lifelike as if they were asleep.[126] Later these prices were raised to $80 and $30 respectively. The embalmed bodies were placed in long boxes, lined with zinc, on the lid of which was written the full name of the deceased and the address of his parents. In the box, beside the body, were placed the papers and other personal effects. Many of these boxes were to be seen on all trains and transport ships.[127]

By General Order 169, October 27, 1862, commanding officers of regiments and batteries were required to transmit after every battle or skirmish a correct return of the killed, wounded, and missing in their commands.[128] In addition, quarterly returns of deceased soldiers had to be rendered to regimental headquarters and the Adjutant General's Office which included in the case of each soldier: name, rank, unit circumstances of death, money due the soldier, money due the government, and such miscellaneous debts as sutler and laundry accounts.[129] In April 1862, each commanding general was directed to reserve plots of ground near every battlefield and to inter therein the remains of the dead. Each grave was to be marked with head boards bearing numbers which should correspond with a register to be kept of the burial ground.[130]

In July, the President was empowered to purchase cemetery grounds to be used as national cemeteries for Federal troops who should die in service.[131] Many soldiers, however, were buried where they fell, by comrades who marked their graves with boards on which was inscribed the soldier's name, regiment, and state. These boards were respected by everybody; they made it easy for the parents to find the bodies of their sons and, after shipping their remains home, to give them a formal burial. One observer commented on the great number of fathers she saw on such an errand.[132] Whenever possible, the surviving members of the regiment would go over the battlefield, checking to see if they could identify the bodies of their unit who had not been properly buried and also to see if the head boards were properly marked. A week after the Battle of Cedar Creek,

a lieutenant went over the field and located the graves of many of his unit. At one of these graves he found a veteran soldier, sitting all by himself, crying over a brother "whose remains laid in the cold ground."[133] Many of the graves were marked by the Sanitary Commission, which, in addition, sent a record to the Hospital Directory of the Commission at Washington along with the effects of the deceased. From Washington the effects and a letter of particulars and sympathy were dispatched to the family concerned.[134] Occasionally while on transports, the men would witness a burial at sea. On the second day out in sailing to Louisiana, men on the transport *Daniel Webster* witnessed such a burial. The band played a dirge on the quarter-deck, and the shrouded body was laid on a plank in an open port hole. "The splash, the plunge, the unmarked entombment, completed a burial most beautiful and fitting."[135]

Officially, the Quartermaster's Department was assigned the duty of burying the Federal dead. The records of the Department showed the internment in cemeteries of 116,148 persons, of whom 98,827 were loyal, 12,596 disloyal, and of whom 95,803 were whites and 20,345 colored persons.[136] This was exclusive of those who fell in battle and were buried immediately on the field by their comrades. Sherman states that about half the Federal graves in the national cemeteries were marked "unknown."[137] The Department marked the graves of 12,912 soldiers at Andersonville, 451 of which were labelled "Unknown U. S. Soldier."[138]

TOTALS OF WAR CASUALTIES

During the war there were 304,369 total deaths in the Federal armies of which 26,168 are known to have died in Confederate prisons. The discharges for disability amounted to 285,245. A total of 280,040 Federal soldiers were wounded and 184,791 were captured or missing. One out of every seven died in captivity, one out of about every nine died in the service, while one out of about every thirteen men died of disease and unknown causes. About ten percent of the Federal forces were wounded in action.[139]

NOTES, CHAPTER 15

1. Billings, *Hardtack and Coffee*, p. 212.

2. United States War Department, *Revised Regulations for the Army of the United States 1861*, Article 36, paragraphs 515-553.

3. *Photographic History*, Vol. 8, pp. 224-225, 231.

4. Letter of Captain Charles A. Phillips, January 4, 1863, Cowles, p. 523.

5. Thompson, pp. 106-107.

6. Hays, *Under the Red Patch*, p. 41.

7. Letter of Charles R. Cox, 1st Maryland Infantry, Camp near the Weldon Road, Virginia, November 25, 1864. Manuscript in author's collection.

8. See photographs in *Photographic History*, Vol. 8, pp. 187, 201-202.

9. Hinman, pp. 193-194; Billings, *Hardtack and Coffee*, pp. 79-83.

10. Hinman, p. 195.

11. Cowles, pp. 143-144.

12. Adams, p. 10.

13. United States War Department, *Revised Regulations for the Army of the United States 1861*, Article 31, Sections 327-334.

14. Letter of Mrs. H. E. Pearce, a photographer's assistant, September 24, 1862. Manuscript in author's collection.

15. Fenner, Earl, *The Story of Battery "H," First Regiment Rhode Island Light Artillery in the War to Preserve the Union 1861-1865*, pp. 30-31.

16. Comte de Paris, Vol. 1, p. 285.

17. Hubert, Charles F., *History of the Fiftieth Regiment Illinois Volunteer Infantry*, p. 41.

18. Brainard, p. 154.

19. "Carleton," *Following the Flag*, p. 46.

20. Thompson (13th New Hampshire Infantry), p. 163.

21. March 24, 1864. Haynes, p. 212.

22. Williams, John M., *The Eagle Regiment*, p. 91.

23. Thompson (13th New Hampshire Infantry), pp. 217, 274-275.

24. *Ibid.*, p. 370.

25. Crowninshield, pp. 234-235, 298.

26. Howe, *Civil War Times*, pp. 66-77. Howe was in Co. "I," 79th Indiana Infantry.

27. Photographs of men playing these games appear in *Photographic History*, Vol. 8, pp. 241, 243.

28. Marbaker, Thomas D., *History of the Eleventh New Jersey Volunteers*, pp. 49-50.

29. Thompson, p. 113.

30. Adams, pp. 60-61.

31. Letter of Roland Breland, member of the band, 18th Massachusetts Infantry. December 3, 1861. Manuscript in the author's possession.

32. *Army and Navy Journal*, Vol. 1 (January 9, 1864), p. 314.

33. Croushore, p. 184.

34. Cowles, pp. 292, 511.

35. Lecomte, pp. 74-75; Russell, Vol. 2, p. 270.

36. Gilmore, pp. 219, 221, 223.

37. Page (14th Connecticut Infantry), p. 225.

38. *Army and Navy Journal*, Vol. 2 (February 11, 1865), p. 391; (March 25, 1865), p. 486; (April 15, 1865), p. 534.

39. Hinman, p. 159.

40. See Deforest's description of conditions in Camp Parapet, Louisiana in 1862. Crushore, p. 41.

41. The VD rate was highest in units near large cities.

42. Letter of Franklin H. Bailey, 4th Michigan Cavalry, November 17, 1863. Manuscript in Michigan Historical Collection.

43. Hays, *Under the Red Patch*, p. 49.

44. Blanding, S. F., *In the Defences of Washington*, p. 8.

45. Page, 14th Connecticut Infantry, p. 65.

46. According to many veterans.

47. Curtis, O. B., *History of the Twenty-fourth Michigan of the Iron Brigade*, pp. 138-139.

48. Entry for November 23, 1863, Clark, pp. 153-154.

49. Hubert, C. F., *History of the Fiftieth Regiment Illinois Infantry in the War for the Union*, p. 201.

50. Crowninshield, p. 290.

51. Masons were active while in the service.

52. Fox, p. 478.

53. Brainard, pp. 76-77.

54. Letter of Lieutenant Charles H. Hutchins, 5th Michigan Infantry, February 24, 1862. Manuscript in Burton Historical Collection.

55. Graham, pp. 193-200.

56. New York *Herald*, No. 9609, January 5, 1863, p. 2.

57. *Frank Leslie's Illustrated Newspaper*, Vol. 18, March 26, 1864, p. 7.

58. Agassiz, pp. 64-67, 72.

59. Livermore, *Days and Events*, pp. 322, 324.

60. Letter of January 29, 1864, Agassiz, p. 65.

61. *Army and Navy Journal*, Vol. 1, March 12, 1864, p. 484.

62. Agassiz, pp. 311-312, 317; *Photographic History*, Vol. 8, p. 257.

63. Croushore, pp. 35-36.

64. Report of Secretary of War, November 22, 1865, *House Executive Documents*, 39 Cong., 1 Sess., Document 1, Part 1, p. 5.

65. Thompson, p. 250.

66. Lord, Jesse H., quoted by Croffut and Morris, p. 88.

67. See photographs of Libby and Andersonville in *Photographic History*, Vol. 8, pp. 57, 75, 129. The comparison with the Federal prison at Elmira is striking. *Ibid.*, p. 81.

68. Langworthy, Daniel, *Reminiscences of a Prisoner of War and His Escape*, pp. 16-17.

69. Adams, pp. 177-178.

70. Letter of February 25, 1865. Thompson (13th New Hampshire Infantry), pp. 535-536.

71. Pratt, Fletcher, *Stanton: Lincoln's Secretary of War*, p. 486.

72. *Ibid.*, pp. 486-487.

73. Sturgis, Thomas, *Prisoners of War 1861-1865*, p. 289.

74. Abbott, A. O., *Prison Life in the South*, pp. 169-170.

75. Men went to bed early to keep warm.

76. Classes in foreign languages were held.

77. Fox, p. 51.

78. Cruel but realistic!

79. Letter of August 1862 (anonymous), *Notes on Hospital Life*, p. 23.

80. United States Sanitary Commission, *Hospital Transports* (1863), pp. 32-33, 40, 61, 73-74, 100.

81. Reed, W. H., *Hospital Life in the Army of the Potomac*, pp. 11-12.

82. Letter of Captain W. A. Walker, Co. "C," 27th Massachusetts Infantry, Washington, North Carolina, November 17, 1862. Manuscript in author's possession.

83. Small, A. R., *The Sixteenth Maine Regiment in the War of the Rebellion*, p. 159.

84. Buffum, pp. 149-151.

85. Haynes, pp. 211-212.

86. Thompson, pp. 237-238.

87. Buffum, pp. 149-151.

88. Benton, J. H., *Voting in the Field: A Forgotten Chapter of the Civil War*, p. 26.

89. United States War Department, General Order No. 265. October 1, 1864, *General Orders for 1864*.

90. Benton, p. 320; Entry for November 8, 1864, Clark, ed., *Downing's Civil War Diary*, p. 227.

91. Curtis, O. B., *History of the Twenty-fourth Michigan of the Iron Brigade*, p. 280.

92. Letter of October 14, 1864, Agassiz, p. 245; Benton, pp. 319-320.

93. Entry for November 8, 1864, Jones, J. L., *An Artilleryman's Diary*, pp. 267-268.

94. Little, p. 334. The "Iron Brigade" cast 543 votes for Lincoln and 116 for McClellan, Curtis, (24th Michigan, "Iron Brigade") p. 280, while in the 11th Iowa Infantry the vote was: Lincoln 314, McClellan 42. Clark, ed., *Downing's Civil War Diary*, p. 227.

95. Entry for October 13, 1863, Clark (ed.) *Downing's Civil War Diary*, p. 147.

96. United States War Department, General Order No. 15, May 4, 1861, *General Orders for 1861*.

97. *Ibid.*, General Order No. 16, May 4, 1861.

98. *Ibid.*, General Order No. 55, May 24, 1862, *General Orders for 1862*.

99. *Ibid.*, General Order No. 90, July 26, 1862.

100. *Ibid.*, General Order No. 190, May 3, 1864. *General Orders for 1864*.

101. *Ibid.*, General Order No. 158, April 13, 1864.

102. *Ibid.*, General Order No. 126, September 6, 1862, *General Orders for 1862*.

103. *Army and Navy Journal*, Vol. 1, December 19, 1863, p. 261. Another general, however, differed greatly from this view.

104. Soldiers of other generations have made similar comments.

105. Fox, p. 43.

106. Trumbull, *War Memories of an Army Chaplain*, pp. 8-9.

107. Small, (16th Maine Infantry), pp. 101-102.

108. Letter of Secretary of War, June 19, 1862, *House Executive* Documents, 37 Cong. 2 Sess., Document 136, p. 1.

109. Trumbull, p. 66.

110. Haines, (15th New Jersey Infantry), pp. 15-16.

111. Van Alstyne, p. 31.

112. Similar revivals were held in the West.

113. Specially true under poor chaplains.

114. Anson, Charles H., "Reminiscences of an Enlisted Man," *War Papers,* Vol. 1, p. 288.

115. Trumbull, p. 23.

116. Hays, *Under the Red Patch,* pp. 44-46.

117. Blied, Benjamin J., The Reverend, *Catholics and the Civil War,* pp. 112-113.

118. Much of the singing was impromptu.

119. Robinson, "My Experiences in the Civil War," *Michigan History Magazine,* Vol. 24, Winter Number 1940, p. 34.

120. Billings, *Hardtack and Coffee,* p. 71. For "Taps" see Butterfield, p. 47.

121. Buffum, p. 312.

122. Advertisement in *Army and Navy Journal,* Vol. 2, September 24, 1864, p. 79.

123. Howe, *Reminiscences,* p. 270.

124. "A Visit to General Butler and the Army of the James," *Fraser's Magazine for Town and Country,* Vol. 71, April 1865, p. 438.

125. Trumbull, pp. 224-225.

126. "Miscellaneous" (Contributions by a Washington correspondent), *Frank Leslie's Illustrated Newspaper,* Vol. 14, May 3, 1862, p. 30.

127. Salm-Salm, p. 42.

128. United States War Department, General Order No. 169, October 27, 1862, *General Orders for 1862.*

129. Kautz, August V., *The Company Clerk,* pp. 75, 76.

130. United States War Department, General Order No. 33, April 3, 1862, *General Orders for 1862.*

131. *Ibid.,* General Order No. 91, July 29, 1862.

132. Salm-Salm, p. 73.

133. Entry for October 26, 1864. Diary of Lieutenant Fred Frank, 11th Indiana Infantry. Manuscript in author's possession.

134. Letter from City Point, Virginia, July 23, 1864. Gilmore, pp. 181-182.

135. Buffum, p. 161.

136. Report of the Secretary of War, November 22, 1865, *House Executive Documents,* 39 Cong., 1 Sess., Document 1, Part 1, p. 39.

137. Sherman, Vol. 2, p. 394.

138. Report of the Secretary of War, November 22, 1865, *House Executive Documents,* 39 Cong., 1 Sess., Document 1, Part 1, p. 39.

139. Phisterer, pp. 70-71, 74-75.

CHAPTER 16

Life at the Front

ACTIVE campaigning generally began in the spring once the roads were in any kind of condition which permitted military movements. These movements involved a tremendous area of conflict and long rail and water movements before the troops went into action. The general reader fails to realize that most of the Federal soldiers who were in combat did their fighting in engagements which are not famous and in places which most people have never heard of. Gettysburg's place in the history of American arms is well established, but it was only one of 892 major and more than 5,000 minor batles or engagements that occurred during the period 1861-1865.[1]

MOVEMENT TO THE FRONT

The early stages of moving to the front was usually by rail or transport. If the trip was by rail there were often many of the men who had never seen a railroad locomotive or car before in their lives. Occasionally a man would fall asleep or miss his footing and would fall under the wheels and be killed. If the trip by rail was in a loyal State the civilians along the rail line would often organize for the purpose of supplying the soldiers with food and refreshment. But if the move was on the water, especially the open sea, the men were probably in for a rough trip. One veteran insisted that "in no place is the life of a soldier so hard as on a transport. Crowded between decks like cattle, unable to cook or even make coffee, they must subsist on what rations are issued and drink water from the casks. The crews are always liberally supplied with miserable whisky, which they sell at a high price to those who will buy, and a few men are always found in every regiment who will get drunk if they have a chance. On shore the guard house can be resorted to, but on board ship there is no relief from the unbearable nuisance."[2] When a transport ran into a storm, a soldier believed he had never observed more ludicrous wretchedness in a small area than he did on that voyage. The utter disgust with life itself was comically pitiful. About one-third of the narrator's regiment were helplessly sick, while not more than one-fourth entirely escaped. As many of the men as possibile remained on deck, and the rails were constantly fringed with sufferers heaving—not the lead. The condition of things below was indescribable.[3]

MARCHES

The last stages of going up to the front were made by marching. In the beginning of the war the Federal soldier was a poor marcher. The raw recruits invariably burdened themselves with useless knick-knacks, absurd comforts, and impossible luxuries. In one overloaded regiment the men were exhausted in a very short march and those "lagging, fagged-out green volunteers, panting over a two-mile march, must have been objects of ridicule to a veteran of the Army of the Potomac."[4] Many of the infantrymen did not know how to husband their strength for a long march. They had no idea of how to buckle on their knapsacks; they even carried very light weights on their shoulders in a clumsy fashion. On the march the usual formation was column of fours.[5] In some units it was seldom that men were permitted to file into the woods, or even rest in the shade, no matter how hot the day.[6] The value of regular halts was recognized, however, in some quarters. In an article entitled "The March of the Brigade," the service journal advocated a halt of ten minutes during the first half hour of the march, a halt of ten minutes at the end of each hour, and a halt of seventy minutes near the middle of the day's march. This article also commended what was in general practice at the time, that is, the employment of advance, rear, and flanking guards while marching.[7] It was customary to have the marching column followed by ambulances under a medical officer to pick up the sick stragglers while a field officer took the malingerers into custody. Roll call was taken immediately after halting from the march. Following close on the heels of each large unit was the provost guard which was assigned the duty of preventing straggling during the march and in battle. The Provost Marshal of the Army of the Potomac, General M. R. Patrick, was so efficient that he was kept on in that capacity under the various successive commanders from McClellan to Grant although very eager for a field command. He was given very extensive powers and was only beholden to the commander himself.[8]

The music of a band had the power to make the men forget their weariness but most Federal bands were abolished in 1862. Illustrative of the morale value of martial music was the reaction of the 11th Ohio Battery after the Battle of Corinth. This and other Federal units were pressing closely on a retreating enemy but on the second night's march the men could only stumble along, almost dead with fatigue. Suddenly a band struck up the familiar song "John Brown's Body," other bands joined in, and soon the men were awake and swinging along without a thought of their weariness.[9]

Since much of the movement of Federal troops was in hostile territory, it was often necessary to employ local guides. In June 1864, the 93rd Pennsylvania Infantry was guided on its march by a man who got the regiment on the wrong road. However, "some said that the General was drunk. Perhaps he was, for we lost the road 3 different times, and when we did move we went like a bullgine. We went about 4 miles and when we stopped we had about 50 men in our regt, all plaid out and grate many was sun struck. A grate many horses and mules gave out. As soon as a horse or a mule give out, then they shoot him. i tell you the smell is enough to kill men."[10] And only five months earlier this same regiment participated in a march in which five men froze to death, while the rest of the men were so cold that they "almost maid the woods shake with [their] shiveren."[11] One of the Confederates' most powerful allies was the mud. It seemed in constant league with them, an efficient and defensive adversary which

took the military valor all out of a man. The soldiers declared that although Virginia was once in the Union, she was now in the mud. "One would think, from reading the Northern newspapers, that we had macadamized roads over which to charge the enemy." The following well-known expression was proverbial among the stay-at-homes: "Why doesn't the army move?" "It would have been most pleasing to have seen those, who supported us at so safe a distance in the rear, at the cry of 'On to Richmond,' plod over a five-mile course in the Virginia mud, loaded with a twenty-or forty-pound knapsack, and a haversack filled with three or four days' rations. Without exaggeration, Virginia mud has never received full credit for the inconvenience it afforded the rebels during the war. It has never been fully comprehended, and, in order to do so, one must march in it, sleep in it, and be encompassed round-about by it. Great is mud!—Virginia mud."[12]

A regiment prepared to march in this manner: About sunset the regimental drummer beat an officers' call; commanders of companies gathered around at the Colonel's headquarters; and an order was read: "The Thirteenth will march at six o'clock tomorrow morning, in light marching order, with three days' cooked rations and sixty rounds of ball cartridge per man." Captains informed their men, examined arms and equipments, saw that every man had his blankets, his shelter tent, and a complete uniform. Lieutenants and sergeants attended to rations and other matters. Raw rations of beef and pork were drawn by the Commissary, brought to the several company cooks' tents, and at once put over the fires. A few pieces of raw pork were cut

MOVEMENT BY RAIL

MARCH AND BIVOUAC

Normally the artillery, messengers, and wagon trains marched in the road, while the infantry columns moved in the fields to either side.

up and distributed among the men, for some of them preferred to receive it raw, and to broil it on a stick, or spider, over some little bivouac fire, or at a halt in the march. Boxes of hard tack arrived, and a fixed number of the crackers was counted out to each man. Some men needed more, some less, and the "divvy-ing" and "evening-up" was accomplished among themselves. Boxes of ammunition arrived. Each box, containing 1,000 cartridges and weighing from 60 to 80 pounds, was lugged by two men. The captain, if he was wise, attended to the distribution of the am-munition himself, and saw that every man took his 60 rounds. If possible the camp-guard was changed, weak men and those capable of performing only light duties relieved the strong and able men, so that all who were able to march could have a good night's rest before starting. The whole affair of getting ready to march occupied an hour only of the evening, and the men turned in at the usual hour. No one knew what might come on the morrow, and all pre-pared for the worst.

Next morning the Regiment is called at 4 a.m. The roll is called. At the Surgeon's call or previously it is determined what men are able to march, and what men not, and who may be depended upon to guard the camp in the absence of the command. The command is at once made up, a trusty rearguard selected, breakfast eaten, the cooked rations distributed, an informal inspection made of every man and his belongings, blankets are rolled, each man's blankets in a long roll, the ends of the roll brought together and tied, forming a sort of "horse-collar," all is made ready and the muskets are stacked along the several company streets.

Due notice is given, the drums beat a quick assembly, the men fall into line along their musket stacks, the roll is again called. The colors are brought out, markers are placed to designate the line, companies take their arms, march to the regimental street—"front street"—and the

line is formed. In a veteran regiment an assembly of this kind is made strictly according to regulations, but to the casual observer appears absolutely informal. If the men are to move in heavy marching order they take knapsacks and all, the teams carrying the officers' baggage.

When all is ready the Colonel takes command, gives the order to march, places himself with staff at the head of the column, and at the quick step of a lively march played on fife and drum, or by the band, the command moves out of camp in column of fours, by the right flank, guns on the shoulder, each man with his roll of blankets thrown diagonally across his shoulders, every haversack, canteen, and cartridgebox is full, and the dusty blue column moves away; soon the music ceases, the route-step is taken, the files spread apart until the road is well filled, and the jaunty, joking, merry, laughing host passes out of sight—to fell or to fall.[13]

The march was a vast migration, with long ammu-nition and supply trains disposed for safety along the inner roads, guarded by infantry, the artillery being next in order. The cavalry functioned as feelers of the army and protected its front, rear, and flanks; while behind, trailing along every road for miles, were the rabble or stragglers—laggards through sick-ness or exhaustion, squads of recruits, convalescent from the hospitals, and special duty men going to rejoin their companies. Each command had its route laid down for it every day, the time of starting set by the watch, and its place of bivouac or camp as-signed, together with the time for its arrival.

If two roads came together, the command that reached the junction first kept moving on, while the next to arrive would halt by the wayside or file into the fields, stack arms, build fires, and make their coffee. An observer standing by the roadside while the troops were filing past would see the men in "route step," is it was called—that is, not keeping time —and only four abreast, since a country road seldom permitted any more to march side by side, and still allow space for the aides, and orderlies to gallop in either direction along the column. If the march had just begun, one would hear the sound of voices everywhere, with roars of laughter in spots, marking the place of the company's humorist. Later on, when the weight of knapsack and musket began to tell, these sounds died out, a sense of weariness pervaded the dusty masses streaming by, varied only by the shuffle of a multiple of feet, the rubbing and straining of innumerable straps, and the flap of full "canteens and haversacks, 'three days' cooked rations and forty rounds' stored therein. So uniformly would the mass move on that it suggested a great machine, requiring only its directing mind." [14]

Advice to the volunteers as to the best way to survive long marches varied from good common sense to the ridiculous. The importance of care of the feet, clean clothing, correctly packed knapsacks, and encouragement on the part of officers was stressed in the service journal. [15] Some of the counsel, however, was not entirely divorced from mercenary motive. An advertisement in *Leslie's*, for instance, called the attention of the volunteer to "Galvano Electro Magnetic insoles" and "voltaic belts." Supporting the claims of these indispensables was a testimonial from a major of the 2d Fire Zouaves (Excelsior Brigade) whose feet had been "badly abused" but in one week were cured by these patent metallic soles. [16] One of the most potent causes for straggling was blistered feet. Marching on feet in such a condition was "an incessant bastinado applied by one's own self, from morning to night"; heat, hunger, thirst, and even fatigue were nothing compared with that torment. All soldiers agreed that soaping the inside of their stockings was helpful, but while some believed in washing the feet before starting out in the morning [17] others took exactly the opposite view, holding that the *only* time to wash one's feet was in the evening. [18]

In the early months of the war, several books and pamphlets on health care which were rather extensively purchased by men entering the service for the first time. Most of these publications were of little value and soon disappeared from the camps. One of these, entitled the *Soldier's Health Companion* contained such advice as the following: [19]

Wash the scalp thoroughly every morning. Let the whole beard grow. This protects the lungs against dust and the throat against winds and cold in winter. In the summer, it induces a greater perspiration of the skin—hence greater coolness of the parts outside, while the throat is less feverish and dry.

The author sincerely believes, that by keeping the mouth and teeth shut, a person can sleep in any malarious region, or mingle in any out-door infection with impunity. Even the animals—Nature's own followers—always keep the mouth closed.

When bathing, never remain in the water over five minutes; three minutes is generally sufficient.

Sentinels, to stay awake, should take spirits of hartshorn, or Scotch sneezing snuff. Also wash the eyes with a little brandy.

When on the march, if feet blister, draw a piece of yarn through the blister with a needle; cut the yarn off, leaving two short ends projecting; this allows the water to discharge and in the morning the feet will be found perfectly well.

Wounds can be healed by washing them a number of of times a day with warm soap suds and half as many times with cider brandy, and drop upon the wounds some warm, soft tallow. This will prevent maggots.

Western troops were probably the best marchers; they marched with a long swinging stride several inches longer than that of troops from the Eastern States. [20] Nevertheless, the Easterners developed into good marching troops and on occasion turned in very creditable marching performances. The 12th Connecticut Infantry marched 34 miles in one day while serving with Banks in Louisiana. [21] Sheridan's army in the Shenandoah Valley marched well during a season which saw 46 days pass with no rain; [22] while some divisions at Gettysburg marched 36 miles in one day, and then fought for two days after that, with scarcely anything to eat or drink. When accompanying infantry on the march, the artillery and wagon trains used the roads while the foot soldier marched on the open land on both sides, but more often the infantry preceded the trains which were kept to the rear for safety's sake.

Once in the enemy country the troops, whether green or veteran, had to be constantly on the alert. Not only a vigilant enemy army but also an embittered citizenry had to be contended with and often one little mistake meant death or capture. As would be expected, new troops were often either too careless or too cautious. When the 14th New Hampshire Infantry approached enemy held territory the men saw Confederates behind every bush. As the regiment advanced the report came in that the enemy was throwing up entrenchments on the opposite side of a river. As they later described it:

It was evident that the main body of the Johnnies were in hiding, as only one or two scouts were in sight. The troops were hurried up, every officer who had a glass anxiously surveyed the situation, and a general plan of attack was discussed. The position was approached with great caution, and the men wondered how many would be likely to get hit in crossing to the assault. After a long delay, it was decided to send a reconnoitering party over to investigate. The forlorn hope was generally commiserated and little hope was expressed of seeing them again alive. Yet they did return unharmed and reported that the dangerous spade had been doing its work on the Rebel side of the Potomac; but the fact was, that two colored individuals had come down to the shore with the dead body of a friend, and the excavations so much dreaded were strictly confined to legitimate grave-digging. The first shell of the bombardment had scattered the formidable party of two, they unceremoniously dumping the corpse on the ground in their flight. [23]

Except for such amusing interludes, however, it was all serious business. As a lieutenant expressed it in his diary, written at the front:

"We had no sleep for 3 nights. We had very hard work to keep awake with all the firing but we dare not sleep; we must keep our eyes open to watch rebs, for they need watching. *They take the advantage whenever they can get it.*[24] Some who needed 'watching' were the garrillia [who] bother our rear very much [including] this Mosby [who] is the biggest pest to our Army. He is here and there and everywhere. He is after our trains always."[25]

Some of Mosby's aggressiveness was explained by another diarist who wrote that "Mosby and his guerrillas bother the camps. They are getting quite bold.

Who wonders when citizens are shot in cold blood. Done by 3 Pa Cav."[26] No one was safe from such enemy harrassment as partisan leaders like Mosby could offer. These irregular troops had a special fondness for supply trains both wagon and rail. When a soldier, writing from Parole Camp, Annapolis, sent his girl a valentine, he also added: "I am sure you will get it if the Rebs don't get it first, for they are nastey boys and they fired into the train ahead of the one I came down from the Ferry [Harper's] in. I was badly scared, you better believe, and I thought of corn meal and Georgia about that time, but I came through all safe and sound and I am here in this confounded camp and it is cold enough to freeze an Esquemaux."[27]

INFANTRYMAN
ON PICKET

A TRUCE

Federal and Confederate pickets trading coffee and sugar for tobacco. They also swapped newspapers, jackknives, buttons, canteens, and gossip.

PICKETS

On approaching the enemy, each unit supplied pickets to prevent surprise. If cavalry troops were present they were used as mounted patrols while closer in to the main infantry body a line of sentinels (more commonly called pickets) was established. These pickets were supported by a line of supports and a body of reserves. Each unit was responsible for maintaining contact with the units on its right and left.[28] The pickets of each unit were under the orders of an officer of the day. The picket line in the presence of the enemy was generally posted in three lines: First, the line of sentries; second, the picket supports, about thirty yards in rear of the sentries; and third, the guard reserves, about three hundred yards farther in the rear, depending upon the topography of the country. Each body constituted one-third of the entire force, i.e. one-third was constantly on duty as sentinels, one-third as picket supports, and one-third as guard reserves. The changes were made every two hours, usually, so that each sentry served two hours on post and four hours off. The latter four hours were spent half on guard reserve and half as picket supports. The supports were divided into companies, and posted in concealed positions, near enough to the sentry line to be able to give immediate support in case of attack, while the guard reserves, likewise concealed, were held in readiness to come to the assistance of any part of the line. Ordinarily this part of the picket force was able to sleep during its two hours of reserve service. The support, however, while resting, had to remain alert and vigilant. It was the duty of the picket line to prevent a surprise, it had to repel any sort of attack with all its power. In the first instance the sentinel had to promptly challenge any party approaching.

The usual formula was: "Halt! Who comes there?" If the approaching party failed to obey the command to halt, it was the sentinel's duty to fire at once, even though he be outnumbered a hundred to one, and if it cost him his life. Many a faithful sentinel lost his life in his fidelity to duty under such circumstances. For although the picket was there to prevent a surprise, the attacking party was equally bent on getting the advantage of a surprise, if possible, and many were the ruses adopted to capture sentinels before they could fire their guns. The sentry was expected to fire his gun, even though he be captured or run through with a bayonet the next instant. This delay gave the alarm, and the other sentries and picket supports opened fire at once, and the reserves immediately joined them, if necessary, to hold or impede the progress of the enemy. The picket force had to fight so that time might be gained to sound the "long roll" and to assemble the army. Many of the picket fights were so saucy and stubborn that the attacks were nipped in the bud, the enemy believing the army was there opposing them. In the meantime, mounted orderlies would be despatched to army headquarters with such information of the attack as the officer of the day was able to give.[29] The regiments comprising a brigade were sent out in turn on picket service alternately. They remained out three days, and the men were well pleased with it when the weather was pleasant, since they were exempt from all drills and camp duties. It always gave them an opportunity to do some foraging on the sly, and many a chicken's life went out and many a potato patch yielded its quota to furnish a supper around a camp fire in the dark woods. The picket posts were about 100 yards apart, but this was arranged to suit the lay of the land, and sometimes they were much closer. At these posts six men were stationed, and they generally constructed a bush shelter where they slept while off duty. The advance line was usually placed along a road or path and stood about twenty paces apart. A signal and countersign were given each one, and when anyone approached the picket, he had to give the signal; he then advanced and gave the countersign which, if correctly given, permitted that person to pass. However, after dark it was extremely dangerous to approach a picket. Often, when in the proximity of the enemy, the pickets were ordered not to challenge anyone coming from the direction of the enemy, but to fire at once.[30]

Although intercourse with the enemy was strictly forbidden, the men were on the most friendly terms, amicably conversing and exchanging such commodities as coffee, sugar, tobacco, corn meal, and newspapers. It was a singular sight to see the soldiers of two great hostile armies walking about unconcernedly within a few yards of each other, with their bayonets sticking in the ground, bantering and joking together, exchanging the compliments of the day and even saluting officers of the opposing forces with as much ceremony, decorum, and respect, as they did their own. The keenest sense of honor existed among the enlisted men of each side. It was no uncommon sight, when visiting the picket posts, to see an equal number of "gray-backs" and "blue-bellies" as they facetiously termed each other, enjoying a social game of Euchre or Seven-up and sometimes the great national game of draw poker, with army rations and sutler's delicacies as the stakes.[31]

Picket duty was often a good place to catch up on letter writing. The following letter,[32] published here for the first time, is indicative of the nature of picket duty and what the men often described in letters when they had plenty of time to write:

From Albert Anderson   Army of the Shenandoah
Co. "H", 1 D. C. Vols.   Sloughs Brigade, Siegels
                              Division, June 20, 1862

Dear Aunt—

Being on pickett duty to day I take an opportunity to write to you again whilst I am lying under the shade of a tree and have nothing else to do in particular. I have no news to tell you of much account excepting that all the boys are well again except Murphy. He is sic yet and is talking of coming home which I expect he will do. Fremont is sending all his sic and wounded to Winchester and Harpers Ferry. The road is all the time full of ambulances and other convances carring sic and wounded. We all are looking for old Jackson every day. We are rebuilding the bridge over the Shenandoah. The first brigade has gone ahead and I expect we will go too in a day or two. The weather is different here to what it is down in the district. It is almost cold enough for frost here of nights and the sun shines hot in the daytime. There is not one young man in a days travel about here or in any part of Virginia in which we have been yet. They have all enlisted or been pressed in service, both young and old, that was able to carry a gun. We have arrested a good many secess soldiers since we have been out here. We bring in one or two every day. The mountains out here are full of them and we have to be very careful how we go about here I can tell you. I am sic and tired of these old hard crackers and old salt beef. There is but few beeves around in this neighbourhood but plenty of sheep, but I can't bear sheep meat and all the chicken is disapeared entirely. I don't believe there is one chicken, duck, or goose or turkey to be found in 5 miles of this place. We got them all when first got here though we sent out a forageing party today for beef. There is plenty hogs about here but there is so many old dead horses about here that ain't fit to [eat]. You must know I won't anyhow. Buter is cheap

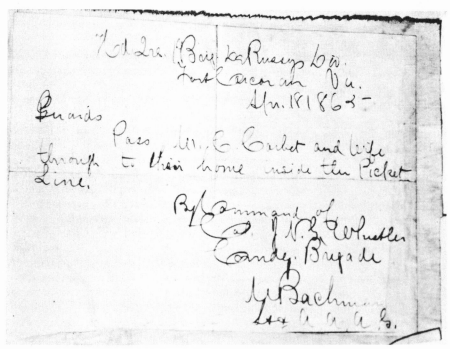

A CIVILIAN PASS

This pass was issued to a couple whose house lay within the picket line protecting the approaches to Fort Corcoran, a part of the defenses of Washington.

ON THE BATTLE LINE

Grover's 2d Division, 19th Corps, during the battle of Opequon, September 19, 1864. Note the excellent targets which the mounted officers make, even though they are in rear of the line.

here, only 25-30 cents a pound, eggs 12½-15 cents a dozen, bread is high—15 and 20 cents for a small loaf and without one bit salt in it. I aim very well satisfied out here and so is Billy Cox and Anderson though I would like very much to see you all once more, I shan't be able to see you untill the war is over as I expect we will, if successful, push on down towards Richmond unless I should get wounded. Then I might see you but I stop scribling now. Excuse this penciling, I [have] no ink.

All the two Billys and Fred sends love to you all. Jo is well and on pickett with me. I remain your afectionate Nephew—   Albert Anderson

P. S. Direct your letters to Winchester, Va. in care of Capt. Coleman, Co. H 1 D.C.Vols.

ON THE BATTLE POSITION

Whether acting offensively or defensively the main line was protected by skirmishers and often sharpshooters. A line of active skirmishers was a serious hinderance to a close column of an attacking enemy. Experience taught the wisdom of letting volunteer troops, and indeed all soldiers, understand what was to be attempted. Instant obedience to all commands, but especially "Halt" and "Cease Firing" was essential. Before going into action efficient officers checked the weapons of their men to be sure they were loaded and in good order. When possible men were fed before combat. With new troops it was found advisable to commence firing as soon as possible in order to occupy their attention.[33] A small regimental guard of six to twelve men under a good officer was of value in checking disorder and retreat, but such a provision does not seem to have been widely employed. In its stead was the provost guard which was usually too far to the rear to check incipient panics.

EFFECTIVENESS OF FIRE

Excessive quantities of ammunition expended by a regiment was considered a disgrace in the latter part of the war; other circumstances being the same, those troops were best and bravest who brought out

of action the greatest number of cartridges in their boxes.[34] Although men were weighted down with too much ammunition in the early stages of the war, this was a trifling evil compared with the encouragement given to the prevalent idea that he who fired the greatest number of rounds in battle was the best soldier. One observer was struck with the remark made by a Confederate prisoner to his captors: "We never carry more than forty rounds into action, and usually expend about ten."[35] However, under certain circumstances an excessive use of ammunition appears to have been justified. When the enemy charged in mass formation, seeking to smash through by sheer weight of numbers, the men wanted to get as much lead out as possible. Due to the close proximity of the enemy's jumping off position, it was necessary to repel an attack by opening fire immediately and to throw out so heavy a fire that few enemy survivors would reach the defended position.

Often a heavy fire would be opened in anticipation of a heavy attack by the enemy. In the trenches before Petersburg an attack was expected on the morning of August 21, 1864. Accordingly, "About 11 a.m., all along the lines here in our immediate vicinity, our troops in the front trenches—some 3,000 men— commences firing as rapidly as possible. The enemy replies, and soon the discharges of musketry blend in a continuous roar. Pretty soon also the artillery on both sides joins in the fray, and the noise becomes tremendous, continuing for an hour or two in all. During this affair 80 men of the 13th [New Hampshire] have fired over 4,000 rounds of ball cartridge— about 50 rounds per man. At the same average the 3,000 men must have fired above 150,000 bullets at the enemy's lines. It is wonderful how very few men are struck amidst the shower of flying lead and iron. This demonstration appears to be made by the Union troops here for the purpose of covering sundry movements on the Union left."[36]

Ordnance reports would certainly indicate that most of the Federal missiles never found their mark. Almost 90½ million pounds of lead, 26½ million pounds of powder, and nearly 13 million pounds of artillery projectiles were used to kill an indeterminate number of Confederates by Federal forces which lost slightly over 110,000 killed in the process.[37] At Gettysburg the Federal artillery fired thousands of rounds; at battles like Chickamauga the Federal infantry fired millions of rounds.[38] Fox estimates that the Confederate armies lost in the aggregate nearly 10 percent in killed and mortally wounded while the Federals lost but 5 percent.[39] This disparity is partially explained by the fact that the Federals had many regiments that never saw action at all and as many more who were under fire but a few times. Two Federal corps at Chancellorsville did not fire a shot; at Gettysburg the entire Sixth Army Corps was in reserve; while at Antietam, McClellan chose to keep large forces inactive although the enemy's line was so attenuated that "there appeared to be hardly one man to a rod of ground."[40] The Confederate commanders displayed a great ability in always confronting their enemy with an equal force at the point of contact.

NUMBER OF MEN USED IN BATTLE

In comparing the actual performance in the field of the troops on the two sides, a mere statement of the numbers enrolled and the terms of service are not all that should be considered. The irregular organizations on the enemy's side were probably of little value in active operations in the field, except in attacks against small bodies of men, and supply installations. The same is true for the "emergency men" and some of the other short-term troops in the Federal Army. Also, 60,000 men of the Veteran Reserve Corps were not available for service in the field; and the enlistment of 300,000 men was so near the close of the war that many did not see active service, and the records show that over 250 regiments never went into action. The number of men in the Federal Army, serving three years was 1,556,-678 and they opposed 1,082,119 Confederates. The objective reader studying the figures of men involved on both sides will come to realize that the fighting ability of both sides must command our admiration. There were 48 battles in the war in which each side had at least 1,000 killed and wounded. In these 48 battles the total number of men involved on the Federal side was 1,575,033; of this total there were 176,550 killed and wounded. In these 48 battles a total of 1,243,528 opposed the Federals, and of this number, 187,124 were killed and wounded. In other words, the Federals had 112.09 hit per 1,000 men; the Confederates had 150.47 hit per 1,000 men.[41]

Due to the misunderstanding about the relative numbers of men involved in particular battles, it should be pointed out that Federal regiments did not go into battle with full ranks. Instead of the 1,000 men originally enlisted in each Federal regiment, the average regimental strength "present for duty" in the following battles was:[42]

Shiloh	560
Fair Oaks	650
Chancellorsville	530
Gettysburg	375
Chickamauga	440
Wilderness	440
Sherman's Army, May 1864	305

The attrition was due to losses in action, desertions, and discharges for various causes, especially physical disability. Moreover, in the Federal Army a regiment of infantry 1050 strong regularly had about 70 noncombatants and, too often, men employed as company clerks and officers' servants were kept out of battle. These 70 men included:

10—Staff
20—Musicians
40—Wagoners, men detailed at headquarters and in Medical Departments and in Quartermaster.

The Federal commanders too often neglected to exclude the noncombatants in their reports of units "present for duty equipped," while the enemy counted only those men *actually present* with sword or musket.[43]

SKULKERS

Another element which sapped the fighting strength of the Federal Army was the inclusion in its ranks, from late 1863, to the end of the war, of the bounty-jumpers and many of the substitutes. Some of these men deserted at the first opportunity; some even misbehaved so as to be arrested and thus avoid duty. In some regiments, they were marched into the fight, occasionally without muskets or equipments, with the veterans under orders to shoot them immediately if they shirked their duty or tried to run. Usually it was understood that such orders would not be carried out "but the Subs, as was intended, took the order to be one made in dead earnest. A more thoroughly scared gang of cowards than these fellows were, when the bullets began to fly, no man ever looked upon. They had to face the music for once." These men seized the first musket and set of equipment they came across and they were cured thereafter of getting up mock riots for the purpose of avoiding duty.[44] To prevent cowards from escaping front line duty, both infantry and cavalry units were used to assist the provost guard. At Cedar Creek (October 19, 1864), men leaving the front were stopped by Custer's cavalrymen who were deployed across the open fields to turn back all skulkers. When wounded men showed their wounds the saber barrier was raised.[45] At the Wilderness, sentries paced to and fro in the woods on each side f the main roads, or stood leaning against trees ooking in the direction of the battle line, which was ar ahead of them in the woods. When one of these entries was asked what he was doing he said he was sending stragglers back to the front" and no enlisted nan could get past him unless he could show blood. Wilkeson observed one of these sentries as he halted a private, who came hastening down the road. The soldier, who was going to the rear, paid no attention o the command to halt. Instantly the sentinel's rifle was cocked, and it rose to the shoulder. He coolly covered the soldier and sternly demanded that he show blood. The man had none to show. The coward-y soldier was ordered to return to his regiment, and greatly disappointed, he turned back. Wounded nen passed the guard without being halted. These guards seemed to be posted in the rear of the battle-ines for the express purpose of intercepting the flight f cowards.

"At the time," said Wilkeson, "it struck me as a quaint idea to picket the rear of an army which was ighting a desperate battle." [46]

ATTACK FORMATIONS

Many Federal commanders in the earlier part of the war were too prone to charge in European fash-on. New troops at Antietam were sent to the assault our lines deep. Cheered on by a band in rear and ed by their commander on horseback, "this magnifi-cent array moved to the charge, every step keeping ime to the tap of the deep-sounding drum." The re-ult was inevitable. Waiting until these troops were almost close enough to see the eagles on their but-ons, the enemy fired with such appalling effect that the entire front line, with few exceptions, went down in the consuming blast." [47]

In Sumner's charge at Antietam there was very ittle distance between the lines—no more than thirty paces. Not a regiment was in column—there was ab-solutely no preparation for facing to the right or left n case either of their exposed flanks should be at-acked. The total disregard of all ordinary military precaution in their swift and solitary advance was so nanifest that it was observed and criticized as the devoted band moved on. A single regiment in column on both flanks of the rear brigade might have indeed changed the results of the battle. Sumner had marched this division into an ambush. There were some ten Confederate brigades on his front and flank and working rapidly round the rear of his three bri-gades. The result was never in doubt. His fine divi-sion was at the mercy of the enemy. The fire came upon them front and flank and presently from the rear. Change of front was impossible. The only fire delivered by the 20th Massachusetts Infantry of the second line was delivered when the men faced to the rear. Nearly 2,000 men were disabled in but a moment and their severe losses were entirely uncompensated. There is no reason for believing that they had in-flicted any appreciable damage on the enemy. What General Sumner may have expected or even hoped to accomplish by his stupid manner of advance is diffi-cult to conjecture. His old-fashioned training may possibly have planted in his mind some notions as the effect of a mass attack or he may have had some vague idea that he could use infantry the way he believed cavalry could be used, i.e. he could cut his way out if surrounded. This excellent division went into action with 3,000 men; it lost 355 killed, 1,579 wounded, and 321 missing, a ghastly total of 2,255 or just about 50 percent. [48]

Troops in other, more intelligently-led units found the fighting completely unlike anything they had heard about or read in books. Some of the action took place in "an old chopping all grown up with bushes so thick that . . . [the men] couldn't hardly get through—but . . . [they] were so excited that the 'old scratch' himself couldent have stopt . . . [them] —[they] *rushed* on to them every man for himself— all loading and firing as fast as he could see a rebel to shoot at." [49]

FIGHTING IN THE WOODS

Much of the terrain in the south resembled that of the Wilderness which, with its second-growth of thicket, thorny underbrush, and twisted vines, was an almost impossible labyrinth. In general, the fighting took place in wooded country and although the men were "deployed," actually in close order according to tactical teachings of the day, they usually were preceded by strong skirmish lines, which took ad-vantage of cover. The Federals were generally the assailants, so that in a wooded and broken country the enemy had a positive advantage, for "they were always ready, had cover, and always knew the ground to their immediate front."

Victories were difficult to exploit because habitu-ally the woods served as a screen, and the Federals often did not realize the fact that their enemy had retreated till he was already miles away and was again entrenched, having left a mere skirmish line to cover the movement, in turn to fall back to the new position. [50]

FIGHTING SPIRIT

Many observers have noted the difference in the combat spirit of the Federals and Confederates. Many believed the Confederates to be superior in combat which lasted a comparatively short time, while the Federals seemed to excel at prolonged battles and sieges. Even the cheers in battle were different. None of the old soldiers who ever heard the Rebel yell could ever forget it. "Instead of the deep-chested manly cheer of the Union men, the rebel yell was a falsetto yelp which, when heard at a distance, reminded one of a lot of school boys at play. It was a peculiar affair for a battle yell, but though we made fun of it at first, we grew to respect it before the War was over. The yell might sound effeminate but those who uttered it were not effeminate by any means. When the Union men charged, it was with heads erect, shoulders squared and thrown back, and with a firm stride, but when the Johnnies charged, it was with a jog trot in a half-bent position, and though they might be met with heavy and blighting volleys, they came on with the pertinacity of bull-dogs, filling up the gaps and trotting on with their never-ceasing 'Ki-Yi' until we found them face to face." [51]

EXAMPLE OF INFANTRY COMBAT

By 1864 both armies were professionals at combat. At the Battle of the Wilderness the Federals could not use artillery; it was an infantry battle and a soldiers' battle too. There was little evidence of generalship on the Federal side and, in fact, the higher command was seen but little in that battle. One of the best descriptions of infantry combat in the war has been given us by an artilleryman whose unit was not in action but who went in person to the front line to see what war was like. Here is his account:[52]

By noon I was quite wild with curiosity, and confident that the artillery would remain in park, I decided to go to the battle-line and see what was going on. I walked out of camp and up the road. The wounded men were becoming more and more numerous. I saw men, faint from loss of blood, sitting in the shade cast by trees. Other men were lying down. All were pale, and their faces expressed great suffering. As I walked I saw a dead man lying under a tree which stood by the roadside. He had been shot through the chest and had struggled to the rear; then, becoming exhausted or choked with blood, he had lain down on a carpet of leaves and died. His pockets were turned inside out.

A little farther on I met a sentinel standing by the roadside—Sends stragglers back to the front. Moved on—came on a second line of battle. I heard the hum of bullets as they passed over the low trees. Then I noticed that small limbs of trees were falling in a feeble shower in advance of me. It was as though an army of squirrels were at work cutting off nut and pine cone-laden branches preparatory to laying in their winter's store of food. Then, partially obscured by a cloud of power smoke, I saw a straggling line of men clad in blue. They were not standing as if on parade, but they were taking advantage of the cover offered by trees, and they were firing rapidly. Their line officers were standing behind them or in line with them. The smoke drifted to and fro, and there were many rifts in it. I saw scores of wounded men. I saw many dead soldiers lying on the ground and I saw men constantly falling on the battle-line. I could not see the Confederates. I pushed on, picking my way from protective tree to protective tree, until I was about forty yards from the battle-line. The uproar was deafening; the bullets flew through the air thickly. Now our line would move forward a few yards, now fall back.

I stood behind a large oak tree, and peeped around its trunk. I heard bullets "spat" into this tree and I suddenly realized that I was in danger. My heart thumped wildly for a minute; then my throat and mouth felt dry and queer. A dead sergeant lay at my feet, with a hole in his forehead just above his left eye. Out of the wound bits of brain oozed, and slid on a bloody trail into his eye, and thence over his cheek to the

ground. I leaned over the body to feel of it. It was still warm. He could not have been dead for over five minutes. I unbuckled the dead man's cartridge belt, and strapped it around me, and then I picked up his rifle. I loaded it, and before I fairly understood what had taken place, I was in the rear rank of the battle-line, which had surged back on the crest of a battle billow, bare-headed, and greatly excited, and blazing away at an in-distinct, smoke-and-tree obscured line of men clad in gray and slouch-hatted. The fire was rather hot, and the men were falling pretty fast. Still, it was not anywhere near as bloody as I had expected a battle to be. As a grand, inspiring spectacle, it was highly unsatisfactory, owing to the powder smoke obscuring the vision. At times we could not see the Confederate line, but that made no difference; we kept on firing just as though they were in full view. We gained ground at times and then dead Confederates lay on the ground as thickly as dead Union soldiers did behind us. Then we would fall back, fighting stubbornly, but steadily giving ground, until the dead were all clad in blue.

ENTRENCHMENTS AND SIEGE WARFARE

Entrenchments were used extensively by both sides during the latter part of the war. Sherman and Grant believed in "digging in" wherever opportunity afforded. At the beginning of the war both sides were adverse to entrenchments, believing that manual labor detracted from the dignity of a soldier and that their differences should be settled by a "fair, stand-up fight in the open."[53] But by spring of 1864 the Federals were very aware of what was involved in charging enemy positions. Confederate fortifications were elaborately constructed of heavy timber banked with earth to the heighth of about four feet, above which was placed what was known as a "head log," raised just high enough to enable the muskets to be inserted between it and the lower work. Pointed logs formed an abattis, in front of which there would be a deep ditch.[54] In the siege of Petersburg one soldier commented in his diary: "Talk about MacClellan digging—Grant has done more of that in this campaign than has been done before in the whole war."[55]

Heavy firing continued for weeks at a time in siege operations of this type and losses were only kept comparatively low by extensive trench systems. Regiments would serve four days in the front rifle-trenches and two out, alternately; always going in after dark. The majority of men hit were shot through the head. Along the line of one division, the casualties averaged 15-20 a day.

The mortars on both sides made great havoc and were a terror to the men. Men were torn completely to pieces when hit by one of their projectiles. At Petersburg the Federals used a 100-pound Parrott, called the "Petersburg Express" which sent a shell into Petersburg every 15 minutes. The gun fired directly over the rifle trenches. In the field at Petersburg it was found impossible to have any hospitals at or near the front rifle-trenches. When a man was sick or wounded, he had to be carried to a field hospital in the rear, a distance usually of at least a mile. From the field hospital he would be evacuated to a base hospital at City Point. Surgeon's call was held once a day in the trenches, with a surgeon and hospital steward present with each regiment. It was sure death for a man to show his head above the works, which were pierced with numerous small holes to watch and shoot through.[56]

There was some humor amid the death and monotony of a long siege. During the Petersburg siege, Finnegan's brigade of Mahone's division, composed principally of Florida troops, deserted in such numbers to the Federals, that soon they were coming over every night. This was a considerable annoyance to the staff officers at headquarters, who were awakened at all hours of the night to receive these Confederate deserters. One of the staff officers, in a spirit of fun, sent a polite note one evening to General Finnegan, requesting him to come over and take command of his brigade.[57]

TRUCES

The high command on both sides arranged formal truces for burying the dead, while the common soldiers arranged their own informal truces just to chat and swap with each other. The writer has yet to find a single example where the soldiers of either side violated these unofficial truces, and they were held many times during the course of the war. On one occasion a field of corn was situated between Federal and Confederate positions. This field was bisected by a deep ditch which, by tacit agreement, constituted the dividing line of the belligerents in their ownership of the coveted roasting ears. It was agreed that the soldiers of the two armies would take only what was on their own side of the ditch. A Federal soldier found a number of a Florida regiment on the Federal side of the ditch with his arms full of fine roasting ears, and the Johnnie would not turn the corn back to the "rightful owners." A fist fight ensued with a ring formed by soldiers of both sides to see fair play. The Federal soldier won the fight and Johnnie Reb left the corn and retired to his own lines amid the cheers of the spectators. Not an angry word was spoken on either side, and the combatants shook hands when the victory was won. Similar contests were not infrequent during this most peculiar fratricidal war that was ever maintained between soldiers of the same nationality.[58]

On another occasion a small body of Federals penetrated deep into the Dismal Swamp and lost their way. While stumbling about in the thick undergrowth, vainly looking for a trail, they were accosted by a similar body of Confederate scouts who were in a similar predicament. The Confederates asked the Federals where they were going and were told that they were trying to find the way out of this damn swamp. The Confederates at once announced that "if you'uns will show we'uns out, we'uns will show

SOUVENIRS
Confederate canteen marked "A. J. B. 45 Ala. Inf." and "W. Zimmerman, Co. H, 50 Ind. Volunteers." A. J. Bethune, the original owner, was captured at Ackworth, Ga., June 11, 1864. The metal object is a home-made iron knuckle taken from a Confederate at Gettysburg.

you'uns out." The result was a very friendly meeting, an exchange of souvenirs, and a mutual escape from the swamp to their respective commands.[59] Incidents of this nature occurred by the thousands. Almost every regimental history contains at least one example. Diaries and letters home contain many more. On November 11, 1864, a private in the 1st Maryland Infantry wrote a lady friend as follows: [60]

"Dear Friend Annie—I hope you will excuse me for not writing to you before. This leaves me in possession of excellent health and I hope will find you enjoying the same blessing. Everything has been very quiet here for several days and our pickets and the Johnnies are on very friendly terms, exchanging papers, tobacco, etc. The last time I was out I exchanged a copy of the Baltimore American for a Richmond Enquirer with one of the 6th Virginia. He was a tolerable good looking fellow and it did not seem as if we were enemies. We met between the lines and after talking a while we shook hands and went back to our different rifle pits. Although everything was quiet the next moment we might be firing at each other. I have seen pickets fight all the morning and in the evening be exchanging papers and on good terms. . . . We have been reduced down to nine men for duty [in our company] but now we have fourteen, I believe. The 2nd Sergeant has been in command ever since the battle of August 18th. Since then we have been in many battles and skirmishes but Thank God I am still unhurt."

Charles R. Cox
Co. "F" 1st Md. Vet. Infy.
2nd Brig. 2nd Div. 5th Corps
Army of the Potomac
Camp near Weldon Railroad, Va.
November 11, 1864

LOSSES AT COLD HARBOR

By 1864, men in the Army of the Potomac had learned the value of hasty entrenchments in a campaign which amazed its participants by its magnitude and a succession of events unparalleled for rapidity. Men received no rest for days and nights at a time; the booming of cannon and the rattling of musketry echoed unceasingly through the Wilderness, around the hillocks of Spottsylvania, along the banks of the North Anna, and among the groves of Bethesda Church and Cold Harbor.[61] Realizing that one man behind entrenchments was equal to five in the attack,[62] Grant endeavored to outmaneuver his opponent but at Cold Harbor he attempted a frontal assault and was repulsed with very heavy loss. He endeavored to break through by sheer weight of numbers; the units, massed in column, were forbidden to deploy. The charge was made with uncapped guns, the orders being to take the works with the bayonet. Confederates firing through slits in their entrenchments were never in danger; during the truce that followed the slaughter, one Confederate officer remarked that "it seemed almost like murder to fire upon you."[63] The battle was kept up all day and the wounded came in very fast. "We have a grate many wounded here, more then we had at any other battle, yet the battle was kep up untill after dark and the wounded are coming in all night." Thus wrote a man who had served in a regiment which had participated in every battle of the Army of the Potomac since early 1862. "Our losses are heavy, but we have the best of the enemy. We drive them at every point and take their works whenever we charge on them *but we lose many men by these charges.*"[64]

Grant's tactics at Cold Harbor have been severely censured and he himself later admitted his error but he was undoubtedly influenced by Upton's successful assault a month earlier at Spottsylvania. Covered by an artillery preparation, Upton's assaulting column of four lines had ben led quietly to within 200 yards of the enemy entrenchments without being observed. The charge was well planned and excellently led; after a few seconds of hand-to-hand fighting the column poured over the first line of works capturing a large number of prisoners. It pressed forward and extending to the right and left captured the second line of trenches. As Upton correctly stated later, the enemy's line was completely broken and a major breakthrough was achieved. This breakthrough, however, was not exploited due to the nonarrival of supports. Enemy reinforcements arrived and, attacking Upton in front and on the flanks, compelled him to retire. Enemy casualties in the initial assault were about 1,000 in killed, wounded and prisoners; while his loss was even heavier in the attempts to oust Upton from the entrenchments.[65]

SHERMAN DUG IN

Sherman's army in the West had completely adopted the principle of digging in immediately after the halt. Each man was his own engineer. After the officers had selected the general defensive line each company and regiment fortified its own ground. A hasty barricade was constructed in case the enemy attacked at once; the front rank taking all the guns and protecting the rear rank which hastened off at a double quick to collect rails, logs, rocks, anything that would stop a bullet. In five minutes the men could prepare for an assault, and although outnumbered, could repulse such assault with but slight loss if they were veteran troops.[66]

VARIOUS DEFENSE WORKS

General Butler used telegraph wire as wire entanglements in front of his entrenchments at Drury's Bluff in 1864. The enemy were repulsed in charging these positions; "in falling over the telegraph wire [they] were slaughtered like partridges."[67] In siege operations at Charlestown the Federals used Greek fire and calcium lights;[68] while gabions, rolling saps, abatis, and chevaux-de-frise were extensively employed by both sides in the latter part of the war.[69] The enemy used mine fields at Fort Fisher.[70] The Confederates had buried several large "torpedoes" (as they were called) in the sand over which an attacking force would have to pass. Wires had been attached to each "torpedo" and, in turn, connected to a magnetic battery inside the fort. Had not a shell exploded and ruined the connecting wire, many lives would have been lost during the assault on Fort Fisher.[71]

BOOBY TRAPS

More common, however, than buried shells or torpedoes which used a battery for detonation, were booby traps which were also buried but exploded on contact. The Confederates used these at Yorktown.[72] Chaplain Marks of the 63rd Pennsylvania Infantry saw one of these booby traps go off, thus demonstrating the "devilish ingenuity of the wretches." A soldier of a New York regiment, while getting water at a spring, saw a pocket knife lying on the ground. Picking it up, the soldier found a cord tied to it. Without any suspicion he gave it a pull and the next instant was torn into fragments, since the cord had been fastened to the machinery of a concealed torpedo, and the slight pull had exploded it. These "torpedoes" were actually shells, buried in such a way that only the capped nipple was at the surface of the ground; when stepped on they would explode. General McClellan was so angry over the use of such "infernal machines" that he had a "number of Rebel prisoners go over the ground and completely remove the buried torpedoes. Of course they ran great risks, but none were injured, as they well knew where they were hidden. Rebel papers roasted McClellan, calling such handling of prisoners of war as cruel, barbarous, and not warranted by the usages of war. They had not a word to say against the savage barbarity of those who planted these deadly engines in the pathway of the army."[73] The Federals also used booby traps, but not to the extent that their enemy did. This was natural since the Confederates were on the defensive and therefore employed more defensive devices than the attacking Federals. Booby traps were used by Federal troops during the Atlanta campaign. On August 13, 1864, a soldier in the 100th Indiana Infantry, serving under Sherman, described the Federal use of booby traps and also has left behind a good description of rail line destruction as performed during the March to the Sea.[74] "We have been tearing up Rail Road. The way this is done is to string the troops out along the track, two men to a tie. The men stick their guns with their bayonets on into the ground close behind them so as to have them handy in case of an attack, and then at a Yo Heave! every man grabs a tie and lifts. Up comes the whole track and slowly tips over. Then with sledge hammers, hand spikes, or any thing else handy, the ties are knocked loose from the rails, the fish plates unbolted, the pine ties made into piles, set on fire, and the rails laid on top. When they get red hot in the center about 20 men get hold of the ends and wind them edgewise around a telegraph pole or small tree. That fixes them. The deep cuts we fill with brush and tree tops and put shells in them that will explode if the Johnnys try to clean them out."

UNUSUAL WEAPONS

Explosive bullets were used by both sides. If a soldier was not instantly killed when hit by an explosive bullet, he generally died later from the copper which remained in the wound and poisoned the victim's blood. The device used was a conical copper bullet, containing a charge of high explosive. Some Federal soldiers believed that the enemy got their explosive bullets from the British via the blockade.[75]

Both sides used hand grenades, mortars, signal pistols, and observation balloons. The war, in certain of its phases, strongly presaged the trench warfare of 1917-1918. With the troops the poetry of war soon lost its pomp and show.

VETERANS

Practical utility replaced gay dress or "nodding plumes." Dusty, ragged, and unshaven, the appearance of the men became in accordance with their surroundings. Death was always imminent and in a few months boys matured into men.[76] If a man was wounded so as to be unfit for any more service at the front, he either received a discharge for disability or was transferred to the Veterans Reserve Corps (Invalid Corps). Many men wished either to be returned to their regiments or be discharged from the service. The following letter[77] expresses this attitude which was very generally true for most of the veteran regiments:

Elmira General Hospital
Ward No. 1
December 11, 1863
My Ever Dear Friend Captain:
My wound is no better. Captain, I do not think I will be fit for the field again. Will you send a final statement and recommend my discharge. I do not want to be attached to the accursed Invalid Corps, if I am not fit for the field I am not fit to do duty in the Invalid Corps.
To my much esteemed friend from

Clet Barnes.

LOOTING AND FORAGING

American soldiers are notorious souvenir hunters and the Federal troops were no exception. In especial demand were enemy canteens and currency. In addition to such souvenirs as the soldiers got by swapping during a truce, some Federal soldiers had little compunction at taking just about anything they saw in civilian homes. Looting and destruction of property were forbidden[78] but some regimental commanders "looked the other way."

There were very few cases of criminal assault.[79] An English observer reported seeing little looting on the Peninsula,[80] but in Fredericksburg there was considerable pillaging. Stores and homes were looted.[81] The control of looting depended to a considerable extent on the attitude of the commander.[82]

Sherman ordered his army to forage liberally on the country and ordered each brigade commander to organize a "good and sufficient" foraging party under a "discreet" officer to carry this into effect. Sherman's order[83] on foraging provided that:

The army will forage liberally on the country during the march. To this end, each brigade commander will organize a good and sufficient foraging party, under the command of one or more discreet officers, who will gather, near the route traveled, corn or forage of any kind, meat of any kind, vegetables, corn meal, or whatever is needed by the command, aiming at all times to keep in the wagons at least ten days' provisions for the command, and three days' forage. Soldiers must not enter the dwellings of the inhabitants or commit any trespass, but during a halt or a camp, they may be permitted to gather turnips, potatoes and other vegetables, and to drive in stock in sight of their camp. To regular foraging parties must be entrusted the gathering of provisions and forage at any distance from the road traveled.

To army corps commanders alone is entrusted the power to destroy mills, houses, cotton gins, etc.; and for them this general principle is laid down: In districts and neighborhoods where the army is unmolested, no destruction of such property should be permitted; but should guerrillas or bushwhackers molest our march, or should the inhabitants burn bridges, obstruct roads, or otherwise manifest local hostility, then army commanders should order and enforce a devastation more or less relentless, according to the measure of such hostility.

As for horses, mules, wagons, etc. belonging to the inhabitants, the cavalry and artillery may appropriate freely and without limits; discriminating, however, between the rich, who are usually hostile, and the poor or industrious, usually neutral or friendly. Foraging parties may also take mules or horses to replace the jaded animals of their trains, or to serve as pack mules for the regiments or brigades. In all foraging of whatever kind, the parties engaged will refrain from abusive or threatening language, and may, where the officer in command thinks proper, give written certificates of the facts, but no receipts; and they will endeavor to leave with each family a reasonable portion for their maintenance.

Negroes who are able-bodied and can be of service to the several columns, may be taken along; but each army commander will bear in mind that the question of supplies is a very important one, and that his first duty is to see to them who bear arms.

Some of Sherman's foragers were summarily executed on capture.

Sheridan, while a guest of Bismarck during the Franco-Prussian War, declared against humanity in warfare, contending that the correct policy was to treat a hostile population with the utmost rigor, leaving them, as he expressed it, "nothing but their eyes to weep with over the War."[84] In the Shenandoah Valley, Sheridan ordered his cavalry to burn everything that could be of any use to the enemy and this was thoroughly done. After one of his favorite aides, Captain Meigs, son of the Quartermaster General of the Army, had been murdered by guerrillas, Sheridan ordered that in retaliation all houses and barns for a circuit of several miles be burned down. One diarist recorded that "the sky after sundown was deeply colored by the blaze of burning buildings" and later he noticed as many as ten and twelve fires burning at the same time.[85]

Some of this retaliation was justified. Sick and wounded soldiers, left behind during a retreat, were often never heard of again, and to this day are carried as "Missing" on the regimental rolls. Many reenlisted veterans who fell behind during a march were killed for the large amounts of money they were known to have on their persons. Captured colored troops and their white officers were often given especially rough treatment. But bushwhackers spared no one. Their ranks were recruited from criminals and deserters from both armies; booty was their sole interest, and they did not take prisoners. On December 10, 1864, on the Weldon Railroad raid, "the bodies of several Federal soldiers were found, who had been bushwhacked and murdered. In retaliation, all the houses were burned as the command marched in."[86] This succinct account was published in the history of the 1st Massachusetts Cavalry. Recently a letter came to light which was written five days after the event, and which corroborates the historian of the 1st Massachusetts. The letter was not written for publication and its authenticity can not be questioned.[87]

Camp 1st Md. Inf.
Near Fort Davidson, Va.
December 15, 1864
Dear Friend Annie:

Your welcome letter received in due time but you must excuse my seeming neglect for not answering it before. This is the first chance I have had to do so. I am not very well but in good spirits, I am suffering from a severe cold, my throat and breast is very sore. Well, it turned out just as I predicted in a former letter. We had to leave our good quarters at daybreak on the 7th instant. The 5th Corps, 2nd Div. 2nd Corps and two brigades of Gregg's Cavalry started down the Jerusalem Plank Road. That night we crossed the Nottaway River, rested about 2 hours and went on our way again. On the evening of the 8th we got in sight of the Weldon Road. You are probably aware that the Johnnies had built a branch road some distance in our rear connecting that road with the South Side Road and were using it to carry supplies to Petersburg and Richmond. That night we commenced tearing up the road, burning the ties and bending the rails. We laid down to rest near day. It was very cold and next morning when we awoke the ground was frozen hard around us. We went on next day still working on the railroad. That night we tore it up past the Black Water River (I think that is the name of it). It rained very hard and it froze as it fell. You can judge how much we slept. Next morning we started back on the road near Sussex Court House. We found three of Company A of our regiment who had straggled, murdered and stripped of their clothing. Numbers of our soldiers were found all along the road murdered. It was done by citizens. As we went down safeguards were put on their property and that is the way we were repaid. As soon as the men were found orders were issued to burn everything for five miles on each side of the road. It was done with a vengeance. It was a track of fire day and night and was a sublime but awful sight. In one cellar three of the 2nd Corps were found murdered and buried. The owner of the house was hung without judge or jury. There was no fighting of consequence, what was done was done by the Cavalry. We destroyed over 20 miles of the road besides thousands of dollars worth of property. The whole country was left a barren waste. It was an awful sight to see those who the guerillas had killed. I have walked over battlefields where the dead and wounded lay in piles but I never saw anything that harrowed my feelings so before. But enough of it. I would like to forget it if I could. None but devils could do such deeds. We marched very fast and many of the men laid down exhausted is the cause of so many meeting such an inhuman death. The cavalry burnt the houses in our rear while we marched along. You must excuse this dismal letter but it is true, it would take me a day to tell all that happened on the march I have been in all the fights on our flag except Front Royal and the Wilderness. I have been very lucky. So you think you will be an old maid. It is a good tale to tell Marines but it is no use to tell Vets that. Somebody will be around after while and you will forget all about the old maid. Give my love to all and keep a share.

Yours truly,

C. R. Cox

P.S. Get Frank Leslie's as I expect there will be an account of the move in it, as the "Special Artist" was along with us.

BATTLE MORTALITY

Battle mortality tended to range highest in the northern tier of States, whether Eastern or Western. The proportion per thousand for some of the areas for deaths in action and from wounds was as follows:

New England	44.76
Iowa	45.44
Michigan	44.82
Wisconsin	42.01
Border States	25.32

The explanation given of this higher battle mortality of the extreme Northern section of the country was that this region was far removed from the seat of war and hence it was not necessary for any portion of the troops raised in it to remain at home on garrison duty. These troops were, therefore, kept almost constantly at the front. A remarkable exception to the above was the case of Kansas, a frontier State, which nevertheless showed the highest battle mortality of all (61.09). The Provost Marshal ascribed this fact to the "peculiarly pugnacious" population of Kansas which induced over half the able-bodied men of the State to enter the Army without bounty and to increase their exposure to the casualties of battle after they were in the service.[88]

A study[89] made after the first year of the war showed that mortality of the armies recruited in the West (and which as a rule operated in the West) was almost precisely three times (3.01) that of the troops recruited in the Middle and New England States (which as a rule served in the East). The Western rate of death from wounds received in action was 4.9 times that of the Eastern armies, while the rate of death from disease and accident was 2.8 times that of the Eastern forces.

SICK RATES

A similar contrast was observable in the rates of sickness in the troops of the two sections. The rate of sickness among Western armies (161 per 1,000 men) was more than twice that of the Eastern armies (76 per 1,000); while the average constant sickness rate for the entire Federal military forces, from all available returns, was 104.4 per thousand. The constant sickness rate for commissioned officers was only about 65% of that of the enlisted men; the rate for officers was 68.8 per 1,000 men, and the rate for enlisted men was 105.9 per 1,000 men.

As with the rates of mortality, the rates of constant sickness appear to have been greater in the fall than in the summer, and greater in the winter than in the fall; these rates per thousand were:

Summer	70.2
Fall	92.2
Winter	117.9

Qualified observers believed that the excess of sickness and mortality rates of the Western armies at this period of the war was due not only to the greater activity of Western forces in the field but also to badly chosen camp sites, very probably a result of looser discipline. The diet also in many Western regiments lacked desiccated vegetables, nor was the food prepared as well as in the Eastern regiments. But probably the longest single factor was "the greater disposition on the part of the soldiers to neglect appliances for personal comfort; and to the greater neglect of, or a lack of means for enforcing cleanliness of person and camp."

MISSING IN ACTION

In every battle, East or West, there was a surprisingly large number of men who failed to answer roll call after the fighting had ceased. These men were carried as "Missing in Action" and, although some were later identified as killed or prisoners of war, many were never heard from again. In 48 battles, including 21 minor engagements the "captured and missing" totalled 41,786, as contrasted with 34,532 killed and 168,777 wounded. In other words, there were more captured and missing than there were killed in these battles. Among the missing there must have been many wounded men, and many who were killed. The nature or history of any particular battle will generally throw some light on the fate of the missing. From Fredericksburg and Cold Harbor but few of the missing ones ever returned; they fell close to the enemy's works, and in the repulse, or swift retreat, were left to be buried by the enemy. But in actions like Ream's station or Poplar Spring Church, the history of the fight tells of flanking movements with large captures of prisoners from certain divisions, and it can be justly inferred that the missing were captured men, as an examination of the muster-out rolls will show.[90]

LACK OF IDENTIFICATION

If there had been a regular issue of identification tags to all military personnel, the number of men permanently listed as "missing" would have been appreciably less.

But it is only in recent years that American soldiers have been provided with dog tags or similar means of identification. Before World War I soldiers went into combat with no assurance that in case of death their bodies could be positively identified or their ultimate fate revealed to next of kin. This was especially true of the Federal troops of 1861-1865. It is a matter of record that 184,791 men of the Federal Army were captured or missing during the war. Included in the missing were thousands who, buried on the many battlefields of the war, are to this day "unknown." Often strangers to the burial parties assigned to the last hurried rites, these men are "those who never came back." Many men who died under the surgeon's knife at field hospitals in rear areas were only "bodies" to hospital attendants. The graves of thousands more who died in Confederate prisons are marked by the one word "unknown." As the statistician Phisterer has put it:[91]

"All who served during the war know that at times men disappeared or failed to turn up, who, it was morally certain, had not deserted; still they could not be accounted for, never were heard of again, and undoubtedly lost their lives in some way and owing to the war."

When one examines regimental histories or reports of adjutant generals of the States, he is struck by the frequency of such entries as "Never heard from" or "Missing at the battle of ——." Is it any wonder that for decades after the war, many applications for widows pensions were extremely difficult to process?

Much of the heartache caused by uncertainty of a son's fate would have been spared the mother if the Government had issued some means of identification to the soldiers. On several occasions men going into combat improvised means of identification which their Government had neglected to provide. For instance, at Cold Harbor a member of Grant's staff noticed the men, in preparation for what was obviously to be a desperate assault, calmly writing their names and home addresses on slips of paper, and pinning them on the backs of their coats, so that their dead bodies might be identified upon the field.[92] History records that many of those slips of paper were useful before the day was over.

However, some soldiers on their own initiative made reasonably sure of their identification in case they became casualties. Often such items of equipment as haversacks and knapsacks were stenciled with the owner's name and regiment. Occasionally a soldier would scratch his name and unit in the soft lead which formed the back of the brass U. S. buckle of his waist belt. Several of these buckles can be seen in such museums as the one at Gettysburg. Notebooks, diaries, and letters from home were invaluable in identifying a man killed in battle.

The more farsighted (or pessimistic) soldiers provided themselves with items sold by private concerns before leaving their home state or purchased them from enterprising sutlers on arrival at the theater of war. These items were of two general types. The first type was the more expensive and more widely advertised. These were of gold or silver and quite ornate. Generally they consisted of the soldier's name and unit engraved on the metal shaped in the form of the badge of the corps to which the wearer belonged. One should not confuse these privately purchased badges with the officially authorized corps badges worn on the cap or hat. Incidentally, corps badges and identification insignia of any kind were much more in evidence in the Eastern armies than in the Western armies.

The second type of identification medium was very similar to the dog tags used by American troops in World War I but were brass or lead instead of aluminum. They had a hole for attaching the tag by string around the neck. Many of these tags are in private collections today. One collector has over a hundred of them; his collection has four brass and three lead variations of this second type. Brass ones have on one side an eagle or shield and such phrases as: "War of 1861," "War of 1861, 2, and 3," "War for the Union," or "Liberty, Union and Equality." The other side is blank except for the soldier's name, unit, and sometimes a list of battles in which he had par-

ticipated. The author's collection contains one which was carried by Frederick Gridman, Co. C, 1st New York Mounted Rifles. Before purchasing this dog tag, Gridman had already fought at First Bull Run, as shown on the tag. All lettering was machine stamped. On one occasion, at least, nearly an entire regiment went into an active campaign with this type of disc. In July, 1864, the 14th New Hampshire Infantry while passing through Charlestown, West Virginia, on its way to the campaign in the Shenandoah Valley, purchased many of these brass discs from a sutler who had set up his tent by the roadside. He stamped each disc purchased with name, company, and regiment.[93]

The lead type of circular identification disc included on one side such legends as "Gen. Geo. B. McClellan, U.S.A." and "First in the hearts of his soldiers," or the New York State coat of arms with "Union and Constitution" and "N.Y.S. Vols." with the dates "1776" and "1861." These lead types were blank on the other side except for the soldier's name and regiment.

All the badges and circular discs mentioned here, and other types as well, were used by Federal soldiers and certainly reduced to some extent, at least, the frequency of that terse but indefinite word "missing." Careful investigation into official records and museums has disclosed no reference to an official issuance of identification media of any kind to Federal troops in the Civil War.

COMMENTS ON LOSSES

Battles and wars are considered great in proportion to the loss of life resulting from them. Bloodless battles excite no interest and a campaign of maneuvers is accorded but a small place in history. There have been battles at least as decisive as Waterloo and Gettysburg but they cost few lives and never became historic.

It is difficult to comprehend fully what is implied by the figures which represent the loss of life in a great battle or war. It is only when the losses are considered in detail—by regiments for instance—that they can be definitely understood. As the regiment was the unit of organization in the Federal Army, it was to the Army what a family is to the city. It had a known limit of size and its losses were intelligible, just as loss in a family can be understood, while the greater figures of the city's mortuary statistics leave no impression on the mind.

There were over 2,000 regiments in the Federal Army. On some of these the brunt of battle fell much heavier than on others. Some never saw any combat at all; others were continually at the front. It is from this latter group that the so-called "fighting regiments" came. Some of the fighting regiments were led by excellent officers and their losses were not in vain, but some regiments incurred frightful loss through faulty orders or incompetent leadership, and the survivors did not have the satisfaction of knowing that the sacrifice had been justified. For example, the 1st Maine Heavy Artillery lost all its men in battle within the period of ten months. During that short period, this regiment was several times called on for suicidal frontal assaults. At Petersburg it charged with about 900 men in line and lost 632 in killed and wounded. Only a month earlier at Spottsylvania, it had lost 82 killed and 394 wounded in another hopeless undertaking. On the other hand, the 5th New Hampshire Infantry, which sustained the greatest loss in battle of any Federal infantry regiment, incurred its losses entirely in aggressive, hard, stand-up fighting; none of it happened in routs or through blunders.[94]

ENGINEERING FEATS

Many Federal successes were gained with no loss of life or an insignificant number. During the Red River campaign, the Army saved Admiral Porter's fleet by a brilliant piece of engineering which prevented the loss of a fleet worth two million dollars. Porter's fleet had advanced above the falls at Alexandria, was ordered back, but found that the river was so low as to imprison 12 vessels. Lieutenant Colonel Joseph Bailey, Acting Engineer, 19th Army Corps, obtained permission to build a dam in order to raise the level of the water and permit the ships to move again. The dam was begun April 30, 1864, and the work was finished on May 8, "almost entirely by the soldiers, working incessantly day and night, often up to their necks in water and under the broiling sun. Bailey succeeded in turning the whole current into one channel and Porter's squadron passed below to safety." [95]

A similar exploit, comparatively bloodless but very valuable to the Federal cause, was the installation of the "Swamp Angel" during the Siege of Charleston. This project was commenced August 4, 1863, and was finished August 19th. In these two weeks, Federal troops placed in a swamp a 16,500-pound cannon, in position, ready to fire. The gun position was located at a point approachable only at high water and at a distance of 8,800 yards from Charleston—a little short of 5 miles. The mud of the swamp

at the gun position was 16 feet deep. A lieutenant of engineers said: "The thing is impossible," but the colonel of the 1st New York Engineers told the lieutenant: "There is no such word as impossible; the battery must be built at the point indicated." The engineers used an immense platform of large logs in double layers, crossed and interlocked and firmly fastened. This platform was towed out to the gun site; when in the right place, it was covered with thousands of bags of sand until it was firmly imbedded in the swamp. The bags were then covered with two layers of heavy plank. Side walls were built 12-15 feet thick, using bags of sand, as the best protection against enemy shelling. Piles were driven at points where the gun would rest. The "Swamp Angel" was then rafted to the platform site, put into position, and opened fire on the enemy.

These 200-pound Parrotts, such as the "Swamp Angel," carried as far as 9,760 yards by actual measurement.[96]

SOLDIERS RETAINED WEAPONS

With the end of the war, the vast armies of the Republic were quickly disbanded and then men, about a million of them, quietly returned to their homes. On June 15, 1865, the War Department announced that all soldiers who wished to retain their arms and accouterments could do so by paying therefor their value. Soldiers who wished to take advantage of the offer, originally made on May 30, 1865, had to signify their intention before leaving the field, so that the prices could be entered and charged on the muster-out rolls. The prices fixed by the Ordnance Department were as follows: [97]

$ 6.00—Muskets, all kinds, with or without accouterments.

$10.00—Spencer carbines, with or without accouterments.

$ 8.00—All other carbines and revolvers, with or without accouterments.

$ 3.00—Sabers and swords, with or without belts.

On June 15, 1865, soldiers who were honorably discharged were permitted to retain, without charge, their knapsacks, haversacks, and canteens.[98]

NOTES CHAPTER 16

1. Stackpole, Edward J., *They Met at Gettysburg*, p. xxi.
2. Adams, 19th Massachusetts Infantry, p. 25.
3. Buffum, p. 158.
4. *Ibid.*, p. 66.
5. A photograph of the 22nd New York Infantry in this formation appears in Vol. 8, p. 203 of *Photographic History*.
6. Usually due to overzealous and green officers.
7. *Army and Navy Journal*, Vol. 1 (April 23, 1864), p. 582.
8. Cox, Vol. 1, p. 265-266.
9. Neil, Henry M., *A Battery at Close Quarters*, pp. 20-21.
10. Entry for June 1, 1864, diary of Lieutenant Henry J. Waltz, 93rd Pennsylvania Infantry. Manuscript in author's possession.
11. *Ibid.*, entry for January 1, 1864.

12. Rhodes (Battery "B" 1st Rhode Island Light Artillery), p. 83.
13. Thompson (13th New Hampshire Infantry), pp. 539-540.
14. Rhodes, (Battery "B" 1st Rhode Island Light Artillery), p. 95.
15. "Simple Hints on Marches of Infantry," *Army and Navy Journal*, Vol. 1 (September 5, 1863), p. 26.
16. *Frank Leslie's Illustrated Newspaper*, Vol. 15 (October 18, 1862), p. 63.
17. Croushore, pp. 92, 94.
18. Buffum, pp. 199-200.
19. *The Soldier's Health Companion*, pp. 30-34, 40-41, 52.
20. *Photographic History*, Vol. 8, p. 205.

21. Croushore, p. 102.

22. Buffum to author.

23. Buffum, p. 78.

24. Entry for June 17, 1864, diary of Lieutenant Henry J. Waltz, 93rd Pennsylvania Infantry. Manuscript in author's possession. (Italics are author's.)

25. Ibid., Entry for August 20, 1864.

26. Entry for January 19, 1864, diary of Hospital Steward Emery T. Getchell, 1st Maine Cavalry. Manuscript in author's possession.

27. Letter of F. M. Byrne, 4th Battalion (V.R.C. ?), Parole Camp, Annapolis, Maryland, February 12, 1865. Manuscript in author's possession.

28. General Order No. 69, February 25, 1862, Headquarters, Army of the Potomac.

29. Hitchcock, F. L., War from the Inside (132nd Pennsylvania Infantry), pp. 168-170.

30. Hays (Under the Red Patch), pp. 47-48.

31. Ibid., pp. 270-271.

32. Letter of Albert Anderson, Co. "H" 1st District of Columbia Infantry, June 20, 1862. Manuscript in author's collection.

33. Army and Navy Journal, Vol. 2, February 25, 1865, p. 420.

34. Ibid., Vol. 2, March 4, 1865, pp. 435-436.

35. Ibid., Vol. 1, August 29, 1863, pp. 11-12.

36. Thompson, pp. 445-446.

37. Official Records, Third Series, Vol. 5, pp. 664-665, 1042-1043.

38. Fuller, J. F. C., The Generalship of U. S. Grant, p. 60.

39. Fox, p. 555. The Federal wounded amounted to about 10 percent. Phisterer, p. 71.

40. McClellan, H. B., The Life and Campaigns of Major-General J. E. B. Stuart, p. 132.

41. Livermore, Numbers and Losses, pp. 62-63, 65.

42. Ibid., p. 68.

43. Ibid., pp. 67-68.

44. Thompson, 13th New Hampshire Infantry, p. 261.

45. Buffum, Francis H., "A Wounded Man," Stories of the Soldiers, Vol. 2, p. 187.

46. Wilkeson, pp. 58-59.

47. Gordon, John B., Reminiscences of the Civil War, pp. 84-87. See the photograph of the battle haze at Antietam in Photographic History, Vol. 1, p. 65.

48. Palfrey, Francis W., The Antietam and Fredericksburg, pp. 83-90.

49. Letter of William H. Brearley, Co. "E" 17th Michigan Infantry. Camp on the Antietam River, September 26, 1862. Manuscript in Burton Historical Collection.

50. Sherman, Vol. 2, p. 394.

51. Hays, (Under the Red Patch), pp. 240-241.

52. Wilkeson, pp. 58-63.

53. "Entrenchments and Fortifications," Photographic History, Vol. 5, p. 194.

54. Rhodes, Battery "B" 1st Rhode Island Light Artillery, p. 283.

55. Entry for September 8, 1864, diary of Corporal William Boston, Co. "H", 20th Michigan Infantry. Manuscript in Michigan Historical Collections.

56. Thompson, (13th New Hampshire Infantry), p. 437.

57. Hays, (Under the Red Patch), p. 271.

58. Ibid., pp. 269-270.

59. Thompson, (13th New Hampshire Infantry), pp. 154-157.

60. Letter of Charles R. Cox. Co. "F" 1st Maryland Infantry camp near Weldon Railroad, Virginia, November 11, 1864, Manuscript in author's possession.

61. "Carleton," "The May Campaign in Virginia," The Atlantic Monthly, Vol. 14, July 1864, p. 124.

62. Grant, U. S., "Preparing for the Campaigns of '64.", Battles and Leaders, Vol. 4, p. 110.

63. Bartlett, A. W., History of the Twelfth Regiment New Hampshire Volunteers in the War of Rebellion, p. 205.

64. Entry for June 2, 1864, diary of Lieutenant Henry J. Waltz, 93rd Pennsylvania Infantry. Manuscript in author's possession. Italics are author's.

65. Walker, pp. 460-461.

66. Harper's New Monthly Magazine, Vol. 29 (October 1864), p. 664. The ratio of 1 to 3 is given as the estimate of the number of the enemy that Federal troops could thus repulse. See pictures of entrenchments around Atlanta in Photographic History, Vol. 5, pp. 197, 199, 201.

67. Battles and Leaders, Vol. 4, p. 212; Bartlett, pp. 190-192.

68. Official Records, First Series, Vol. 28, Part 2, p. 37.

69. See Photographic History, Vol. 5, pp. 197-209, 215.

70. Lamb, (Colonel, C. S. A.), "The Defense of Fort Fisher," Battles and Leaders, Vol. 4, p. 643.

71. Sands, Francis P. B., "The Last of the Blockade and the Fall of Fort Fisher," War Papers No. 40, D. C. Commandery, Loyal Legion of the United States, p. 27.

72. Entry for May 4, 1862, diary of Private George Vanderpool, 3rd Michigan Infantry. Manuscript in Burton Historical Collection. See also Medical and Surgical History of the War of the Rebellion, Part 3, Surgical Vol., p. 699; and Cowles, pp. 244-245, 248.

73. Hays, Under the Red Patch, p. 83.

74. But due to Federal shell fire the connecting wire was cut.

75. Hays, Under the Red Patch, p. 470.

76. An interesting contrast in demeanor and appearance can be made by comparing photos of soldiers taken early in their service and at the time of discharge.

77. Letter of Clet Barnes, Elmira General Hospital, December 11, 1863. Manuscript in author's possession.

78. Billings, Hardtack and Coffee, p. 237.

79. Official Records, First Series, Vol. 38, Part 4, pp. 273, 297-298.

80. Chesney, Charles C., A Military View of Recent Campaigns in Virginia and Maryland, p. 36.

81. Thompson (13th N. H. Inf.), p. 41.

82. Cox, Vol. 2, p. 306.

83. Special Field Orders No. 120, November 9, 1864, Headquarters Military Division of the Mississippi, In the Field, Kingston, Georgia.

84. Adams, Charles Francis, Studies Military and Diplomatic 1775-1865, pp. 266-267.

85. Entries for September 29, October 4, October 7, 1864, diary of Lieutenant Frederick Frank, Co. "K," 11th Indiana Infantry. Manuscript in author's possession.

86. Crowninshield, p. 247.

87. Letter of Charles R. Cox, 1st Maryland Infantry, December 15, 1864. Manuscript in author's possession.

88. Report of the Provost Marshal General, March 17, 1866, House Executive Documents, 39 Cong., 1 Sess., Document 1, p. 74.

89. Elliott, E. B., "Mortality and Sickness of the U. S. Volunteer Forces," (May 18, 1862), Bulletin No. 46, United States Sanitary Commission.

90. Fox, pp. 23, 424.

91. Phisterer, p. 71.

92. Porter, p. 174.

93. Related to the author in 1927 by Color Sergeant Francis H. Buffum, 14th New Hampshire Infantry.

94. Fox, pp. 1-2, 125.

95. Photographic History, Vol. 6, pp. 230-231.

96. Burlingame, John K., History of the Fifth Regiment of Rhode Island Heavy Artillery, pp. 179, 300.

97. United States War Department, General Order No. 101, May 30, 1865, Circular No. 24, June 10, 1865, Ibid.

98. Ibid., General Order No. 114, June 15, 1865.

CHAPTER 17

The Navy and Marine Corps

A UNION VICTORY without the naval contribution was probably an impossibility. Without the blockade, the river operations, the control of the Mississippi, and the international effect of Northern supremacy on the seas, it is very doubtful if the North could have won the war. The blockade was the controlling condition of Union success. This success was made possible by the undisputed naval and maritime supremacy of the national government. Cut off from the outer world and all exterior sources of supply, reduced to a state of economic helplessness by the inexorable blockade, the Confederacy was pounded to death. In other words in the game of warfare, maritime supremacy on the part of the North—what Admiral Mahan developed historically as the Influence of the Sea Power—even more than compensated for the military advantage of the defensive, and its interior strategic lines, enjoyed by the South. This being so, the greater command of men, supplies, munitions, and transportation by the North worked its natural result.

The work of the United States Navy was an affair of long patience unrelieved by many prospects of brilliant exploits and lacking the exhilaration of frequent combat. It therefore required discipline and morale all the more. But the reward was great because the blockade was one of the effective agencies in deciding the issue of the war. The Navy entered into the struggle as the essential pivot on which turned many of the most important of the land movements such as Grant's operations in Virginia. The capture of Hatteras Inlet (August 26, 1861) and of Port Royal (November 7, 1861) were strategically of the utmost importance since they distinctly foreshadowed the process of devitalization as a result of which the Confederacy ultimately collapsed. The taking of New Orleans, from every point of view, must be considered as one of the most important events of the war; it was a knife-thrust in the very vitals of the Confederacy. The sinking of the *Alabama* by the *Kearsarge* was of no moment in terminating the war but its psychological effect in Europe at a critical period was very significant.

The South, before the war, did not consider the matter of a blockade, as an element of a war with the North, to merit consideration at all. For instance, James H. Hammond, then in the Senate from South Carolina, in a speech delivered in 1858, thus summarily dismissed the idea of a blockade as an absurdity: "We have three thousand miles of continental seashore line so indented with bays and crowded with islands that when their shore lines are added, we have twelve thousand miles . . . Can you hem in such a territory as that? You talk of putting up a wall of fire around eight hundred and fifty thousand square miles so situated! How absurd!"

The Confederacy was admittedly inferior in its navy but this was not due alone to the newness of the Southern nation; Southerners had never been notable as a seafaring or ship-minded people. The South lacked the industrial means of shipbuilding and the technique of ship operation. Therefore, to acquire new warships the Confederate government looked to England and Europe and at the same time attempted to exploit the Northern blockade in the diplomatic field.

The Civil War was waged in an era of transition in naval architecture and fighting methods. Yet, in spite of the number of ships built and equipped during the war, many of them being new types to naval warfare, the total cost of the Navy during the war was just over $314,000,000, or only 9.3% of the total cost of the war. Much of the credit for this remarkable increase in numbers and new models of ships must go to Secretary Gideon Welles. When "the old man of the sea" took over in March 1861, his Navy Department was top-heavy with a superabundance of old officers and a radical deficiency in the junior grades. The Navy, moreover, had been hampered by traditions and a spirit of routine difficult to eradicate in a short time. Above all, the supineness of the Navy Department during the closing months of the Buchanan administration, bred of a deliberate policy of inaction and a determination to abstain from any step which might be construed as coercion, had served to seriously cripple the Navy when the crisis suddenly developed. If there was not actual treachery on the part of Toucey (Welles' predecessor) and many of his subordinates in the Navy Department, the effect was nearly the same, so that the Government in April 1861 found itself in an almost complete state of naval unpreparedness.

THE NAVY

The Navy Department

When the Lincoln administration came to power in 1861, the Secretary of the Navy under the Buchanan administration, Isaac Toucey of Hartford, Connecticut, was succeeded by his fellow townsman, Gideon Welles, whose experience as chief of the Bureau of Provisions and Clothing in the Navy Department, 1846-1849, had familiarized him with the details of department work. Under Welles, as Assistant Secretary, was appointed Gustavus V. Fox, a brilliant naval officer, whose 18 years in the service had well fitted him for the work he was to take up, and whose talents and foresight later provided valuable aid to the Secretary.[1]

Welles *Diary* is a source of great value, not only for naval matters but also for political observations.[2]

The vast operations of the Navy Department during the war were naturally divided into two main branches: one relating to affairs belonging particularly to the Navy, and perhaps more specially to professional matters; and the other embracing civil transactions and the whole business machinery and operations of the Department. At the head of the first named of these branches was placed the Assistant Secretary, who, himself having been an officer of the Navy of long experience, was supposed to be a competent judge of whatever belonged to ships, their outfit and armament, and of such plans as might be proposed for increasing the efficiency of the Navy. The head of the other branch was called simply the Chief Clerk, a name which does not adequately describe the importance of the officer, for upon him was laid not merely the superintendence of the clerical force, but the direct management of the business operations of the Department. He was really a confidential secretary placed over one branch of the affairs of the Department, while the Assistant Secretary supervised that which belonged specifically to the ships, their materiel, and operations. Of course the plans and suggestions of both these officers were submitted to and decided upon by Welles himself.[3]

Fox was named Assistant Secretary of the Navy on August 1, 1861. Without any doubt this was one of the most important appointments made during the war.[4] The post was created for Fox because up to that time there had been no Assistant Secretary. From then on, Welles had by his side a trained seaman.[5] In William Faxon, the Chief Clerk of the Navy Department, Welles found an extremely capable assistant, whose business ability and mastery of detail were rewarded in the last months of the war by his being appointed Assistant Secretary while Mr. Fox was abroad.

BUREAUS

The Navy Department was broken down into functional bureaus as follows:[6]

Yards and Docks
    Rear-Admiral Joseph Smith (May 25, 1864 to April 30, 1869)
Ordnance and Hydrography (in 1862 "Hydrography" was transferred to the Bureau of Navigation)
    Captain A. A. Harwood (April 24, 1861 to July 22, 1862)
    Rear-Admiral John A. Dahlgren (July 22, 1862 to June 24, 1863)
    Commander Henry A. Wise (June 25, 1863 to June 1, 1868)
Navigation ("Office of Detail" attached April 28, 1865)
    Rear-Admiral C. H. Davis (July 17, 1862 to April 27, 1865)
Equipment and Recruiting
    Rear-Admiral Andrew H. Foote (July 17, 1862 to June 3, 1863)
    Commander Albert N. Smith (June 4, 1863 to September 8, 1866)
Construction, Equipment, and Repair (Afterwards changed to Construction and Repair. For "Equipment," see Bureau of Equipment and Recruiting)
    Chief Naval Constructor John Lenthall (November 17, 1853 to January 22, 1871)
Provision and Clothing
    Pay Director Horatio Bridge (October 1, 1854 to July 11, 1869)
Medicine and Surgery
    Surgeon William Whelan (October 1, 1853 to June 11, 1865)
Steam Engineering
    Engineer-in-Chief B. F. Isherwood (March 26, 1861 to March 15, 1869)

NAVY YARDS

Servicing the vessels of the Navy, whether on the blockade or engaged in other duties were the Navy yards. These were located at:

Portsmouth, New Hampshire; Boston, Massachusetts; New York, New York; Philadelphia, Pennsylvania; Washington, D. C.; Mare Island, California; Sackett's Harbor, Maine; Norfolk, Virginia; and Pensacola, Florida.

The Navy with which the North ended the war belonged to a different era from that with which it started, the men to a different class. Very early in 1862, the number of artisans and laborers employed by the Government Navy yards was increased from less than 4,000 to nearly 17,000, and these were constantly employed in the construction and equipment of new ships, embracing all the improvements that could be effectively used, as soon as they were shown to be practical. In addition to these 17,000 men, there were fully as many more engaged by private contractors, building and equipping other vessels for the service. Also, as early as 1862, the Navy maintained hospitals at Boston (Chelsea), New York, Philadelphia, Norfolk, Mound City, and Mare Island. It had magazines at Portsmouth and Boston, and the Naval Observatory at Washington, D. C.

ORDNANCE DEPARTMENT

Despite the timely improvements in armaments by John A. Dahlgren, few excellent guns of large caliber had been produced by the opening of the war. The paucity of efficient cannon in the possession of the Northern government in April 1861, is surprising: on hand were 2,468 heavy guns (1,872 of which were 32-pounders of an obsolete pattern) and 557 light guns, also of an old pattern. There were only 305 9-inch Dahlgrens and 32 11-inch guns of the same type. Unfortunately, many of the Dahlgren pieces were at Norfolk and hence were seized by the enemy, while others were aboard ships at sea. The Navy Department actually had at its disposal about 50 efficient guns. Therefore, the Government had not only to create ships but also to provide armaments for those ships.

It was fortunate for the North that it had Dahlgren in its Navy Department; his great service to the war was not in winning battles but in designing, casting, and improving armament. He developed the famous system of heavy ordnance. It is not too much to claim that Dahlgren during the decade preceding hostilities was laying the foundations for Union victory in the Civil War. By his inventive genius in the construction of ordnance and by his plan for arming steam vessels of war, he did more for the Navy possibly than any other single person. He increased the destructive power of cannon fourfold. For sixteen years, while in charge of ordnance matters at the Washington Navy Yard, he introduced and improved a workshop which became the foundation for an effective ordnance establishment. He developed a "boat howitzer," a type of gun suited to both field and naval service; he developed several large guns of his own design, which were of solid cast iron, thick at the breech; and introduced innovations which completely revolutionized the armament of the Navy.

In the War, the Federal Navy broke away from the old tradition that the effectiveness of a fighting vessel is in proportion to the number of guns she carries. The distinct tendency became not to divide the weight she could safely bear among numerous guns of small caliber, but rather to have fewer guns of higher efficiency. Many of the Federal gunboats carried 100-pounder rifles. The Federal practice was to increase the weight of the shot, at the expense of the velocity if necessary, and to use, in any event, for breaking walls and smashing armor plate, a heavy projectile, and then, by rifling or otherwise improving the gun, to increase velocity and range. Such naval powers as England acted on the opposite theory; the English had no smooth-bore cannon other than the 8-inch 68-pounder, while the Federal Navy had in actual service on their vessels, 9-inch, 10-inch, 11-inch, and 15-inch smooth-bore guns, and even

NAVAL GUN AND CREW
This crew on a Federal gunboat is armed with cutlasses and revolvers for close combat.

cast a 20-inch gun; and 200-pounder rifles were even found on gunboats as well as 100-pounders. Some Army batteries before Charleston were equipped with 300-pounder Parrott rifles. The armor of the *Atlanta,* said to be equal to 5 inches of solid iron, was pierced by a shot from a 15-inch gun and the ship captured. The heavy Parrott rifles pierced armor plate of 4-5 inches thickness with ease.

Shells for the Dahlgren guns were provided with fuses that could be set to explode just about where and when the gunner wished to have them do so. But whether the damage to be done by a 15-inch round shot smashing its way through a ship's side would be greater or less than that of a rifle projectile boring its way through was a question that had not been decided. It was granted that the rifle had the longer range. With a reasonable elevation a rifle would carry 3 to 4 miles, and do some damage when the projectile arrived, while the effective range of the smooth-bore was 1500-1600 yards, though gunners made efforts, when the right time came, to run in to a range of 600 yards or less instead. But, on the whole, it was the belief among American naval officers before the Civil War that the big Dahlgren smooth-bore was the best gun afloat. So it came to pass that the newest and best ships of the Navy were armed with the Dahlgren gun.

Rifled guns were gradually introduced during the war. These were chiefly Parrott guns, 20-30, and 100-pounders. The Parrott gun of the smaller calibers was serviceable, but as a heavy gun it was dangerous, and occasionally burst. In the Western flotilla, when it was transferred to the Navy, there were several Army rifled 42-pounders, which were so dangerous as to be nearly useless.

In addition to the improvements in heavy ordnance, a corresponding advance was made in the construction of carriages for mounting and maneuvering them in broadsides and in pivot. This problem was a vital one, and not easily solved, especially in connection with maneuvering during the violent rolling and pitching motion of a ship at sea; even when the batteries were used in ordinary weather, the problem was a serious one. A series of well-conducted experiments at the Washington Navy Yard and on board the ordnance practice ship *Plymouth,* under the command of Dahlgren, resulted in the complete solution of the difficulties so far as the 9 and 11-inch guns were concerned: that is to say, a broadside carriage for the 9-inch, and a pivot carriage for the 11-inch, both of *wood,* were designed and constructed for the frigates of the *Merrimac* class, and were found to be as perfect in their operation as could be expected. The difficulty, however, of obtaining seasoned timber during the war led the attention of the Chief of Naval Ordnance to the possibility of substituting iron for wood in the construction of these carriages, and the first trial of iron was made in the carriages

of the *New Ironsides.* These were found to be better than those made of wood, and the days of wooden carriages were numbered. Iron was a necessity in the carriages of the Monitors, and the genius of Ericsson soon overcame all mechanical difficulties in the methods of movement and compression. He designed and successfully tested a carriage upon which the 15-inch guns could be mounted and worked in broadside without difficulty or danger—the momentum of these heavy guns being easily controlled by means of a rotary compressor.

Additional information on Naval Ordnance is given in Chapter 10.

GROWTH OF THE (NAVY SHIPS)

At the time of Lincoln's inauguration, March 4, 1861, the Navy Department was organized on a peace establishment. Such vessels as were in condition for service were chiefly on distant stations, and those which constituted the home squadron were, for the main part, in the Gulf of Mexico. Congress had adjourned without making provision for any extraordinary emergency, and the appropriations for naval purposes indicated that only ordinary current expenses were anticipated. Events of the next few weeks called for extraordinary action on the part of the Government, including a large augmentation of the naval force, and the recall of almost the whole of the foreign squadrons for service on the coasts of the United States. The total number of vessels in the Navy, of all classes, on March 4, 1861, was 90, carrying, or designed to carry, about 2,415 guns. These vessels had a complement, exclusive of officers and Marines, of about 7,600 men, and nearly all of them were on foreign stations. The home squadron consisted of 12 vessels, carrying 187 guns and about 2,000 men. Of this squadron, only 4 small vessels, carrying 25 guns and about 280 men, were in Northern ports. Morale was low; demoralization prevailed among the officers, many of whom left the service soon after Sumter. But the crews were true and reliable and maintained, through every trial and under all circumstances, their devotion to the Union. Unfortunately, however, comparatively few of these men were within call of the Department. They, as well as their ships, were abroad.

Immediate action was imperative, but no legislative provision had been made for increasing the Navy. Only a feeble force of men and vessels, scarcely sufficient for ordinary police operations, was available on the Atlantic coast. Without waiting the arrival of vessels from the foreign squadrons, the Department directed such ships as were dismantled and lying in the various navy yards to be repaired and put in commission. The Department also began to purchase vessels of many types and to construct new vessels. By December 1861, the total number of vessels, including those newly-purchased and vessels under construction, was 264, with 2,557 guns. The aggregate number of seamen had increased from 7,600 on March 1, to 22,000 by December 2, 1861.

The proclamation of April 1861, placing the entire coast from the mouth of the Chesapeake to the Rio Grande under blockade, found the North with a naval force inadequate to the task, even if every vessel had been on blockade duty. By December 1862 the blockade began to be made more effective, chiefly through the expansion of the Navy to 427 ships. Welles could well be proud of this tremendous effort which his Department had made since the beginning of the war. It was unquestionably no exaggeration when the Secretary claimed that "the annals of the world do not show so great an increase in so brief a period to the naval power of any country."

The increase in naval strength was truly a remarkable achievement and must be considered as one of the decisive contributions to the Northern victory. The following tabulation indicates the strength in ships, exclusive of losses, from the time of Lincoln's inauguration to December 1864:

Date	No. of Vessels	No. of Guns	Tonnage
March 4, 1861	69	1,346	
Dec. 1861	264	2,557	218,016
Dec. 1862	427	3,268	340,036
Dec. 1863	588	4,443	467,967
Dec. 1864	671	4,610	510,396

In all, during the period March 4, 1861-December 4, 1865, the Federal Navy was increased by the construction of 208 vessels, and the purchase of an additional 418.[7]

COMMISSIONED PERSONNEL OF THE FEDERAL NAVY

No less than 322 officers resigned from the United States Navy and entered the Confederate Navy, 243 of them being officers of the line. Thus nearly a fourth of the officers of the Navy at the beginning of 1861 espoused the cause of the South. About 350 Southern-born naval officers remained loyal to the Union. Of 38 Southern captains, 16 resigned; of 64 commanders, 34 resigned; of 151 lieutenants, 76 resigned; of 128 acting midshipmen, 106 resigned. In other words, over one-fifth of all the officers forsook their allegiance for political reasons. Admiral Ammen wrote:

For half a century, perhaps, there had existed a kind of culture of fealty to a State, instead of the government which they served; it was paraded as a dogma and was in a degree acknowledged by some officers from the South in the military service of the government, more than half of whom, prior to the Civil War, either came from the slave States or had married within them. Able and educated men, acknowledging this doctrine, thought they had only to resign to hopelessly embarrass the Government.

Demoralization prevailed among the officers, many of whom, occupying the most responsible positions, were merely marking time until they saw how their individual States were going to react to the secession of the lower South.[8]

Although founded only a decade before the war, the Naval Academy supplied the service with some of the excellently-trained officer personnel required for active service. The Academy and public property attracted the attention of the disloyal elements in the Annapolis area. Demonstrations were made towards seizing the property, and also the frigate *Constitution*, which had been placed at Annapolis for the benefit of the young men who were being educated at the Academy. Prompt measures rescued the frigate and Government property. The corps of midshipmen, under the Commandant of the Academy, contributed, in no small degree, to this result. As it was impossible, in the then existing condition of affairs in Annapolis

GUNBOAT CONVERTED FROM FERRY

This ship, the *Commodore Perry*, was used for patrolling the Pamunkey River.

and in Maryland, to continue the school at that place, and as valuable public property was in jeopardy, the Academy was moved to Newport, Rhode Island. The War Department offered Fort Adams for the temporary occupation of the students, which was at once accepted, and the school, with the frigate and other public property were removed to the fort. Although the numbers at the Academy were reduced by the resignation of nearly every student from the Southern States, and by a call of the upper classes to active duty, the junior classes remained to form a nucleus to re-establish and give vitality to the institution. The number of midshipmen authorized by law was 515 but as late as December 1862, there were only 376 at the Academy. By November 12, 1863, this number had risen to 463. On May 21, 1864, with the danger of enemy interference removed, Congress directed that the Naval Academy be returned to Annapolis before the commencement of the opening of the 1865-1866 academic year. This was accomplished by September 1, 1865. Commodore George S. Blake, who was superintendent in 1861, continued at the head of the Academy for the entire period of the war.[9]

However, the Naval Academy could not begin to supply all the officers needed. In consequence of the wholesale resignations at the outbreak of the war, whereby about 20 percent of the officers left the Naval service of the United States, resort was made at once to Volunteers, chiefly from the merchant marine, of whom some 7,500 were appointed altogether. The regular officers continued to form about one-seventh of the whole service and of course filled the most important positions. A large proportion of the volunteers rendered excellent service, although it is true that previous military training would have contributed considerably to their efficiency. The Navy Department deemed itself fortunate when it could secure volunteers with nautical experience, let alone previous military training.

One of the most serious difficulties of the personnel situation arose from the long continued and vicious system of seniority promotion in the Navy, combined with the absence of any provision for retirement. The inevitable result was to repress individual initiative—to make routine men. As promotion was sure there was little incentive to effort. The senior grades were filled with men most of whom had passed their sixtieth birthday, while many able officers were stagnating in the lower grades. Some lieutenants had been 34 years in the service yet never had risen to the responsibilities of command. Many of the 78 captains at the head of the list were gallant veterans who had rendered noteworthy service in the "old Navy," but had already grown too old for active service at sea. Of the 114 commanders, those at the head of the list were between 58 and 60 years of age; of the 321 lieutenants, those at the head of

the list were between 48 and 50. Only a few of the junior officers were graduates of the Naval Academy, some dozen or more of the younger lieutenants and less than 100 masters and midshipmen being at the foot of the list.

Such was the pressing need for trained officers in the subordinate grades that the three upper classes at the Academy were ordered into active service. Some of these lads became lieutenants at the age of 19. A remedy for the accumulation of dead wood at the top among naval officers was found in December 1861, when Congress passed a law retiring all officers at the age of 62, or after they had been in the service for a period of 45 years.

Though thousands answered the call for naval volunteers, more men were at all times needed than could be supplied. An exceedingly valuable contribution to the volunteer force were the merchant captains and mates from the Northern seaports and the Great Lakes.[10] Many of the volunteer officers possessed great ability and some of them, at the end of the war, were taken into the Regular service, where they rose to high rank, filling with credit some of the most important posts.

Meanwhile, Congress passed an act "to establish and equalize" the grades of line officers of the Navy.[11] The active list of line officers was divided into 9 grades, taking rank according to the date of commission in each grade, as follows: Rear-Admiral, commodore, captain, commander, lieutenant commander, lieutenant, master, ensign, and midshipman.

It was further enacted that the relative rank between officers of the Navy and the Army should be as follows, lineal rank only being considered:

Rear-Admiral—Major General
Commodore—Brigadier General
Captain—Colonel
Commander—Lieutenant Colonel
Lieutenant Commander—Major
Lieutenant—Captain
Master—First Lieutenant
Ensign—Second Lieutenant

At the same time, Congress passed legislation which would correct many of the abuses in the promotion system in the Navy. Hereafter, "no line officer of the Navy upon the active list, below the grade of commodore, nor any other naval officer, would be promoted to a higher grade until his mental, moral, and professional fitness to perform all his duties at sea should be established to the satisfaction of a board of examining officers, appointed by the President of the United States." Such an examination board was to consist of not less than 3 officers, senior in rank to the officers to be examined. Any of the officers in the naval service, by consent of the Senate, could be advanced, not exceeding 30 numbers, in his own grade, for distinguished conduct in battle, or extraordinary heroism.[12] A "volunteer Lieutenant"

GROUP OF NAVAL OFFICERS
Between decks on a Federal warship. Straw hats were popular with naval officers on duty in Southern waters.

was theoretically outranked by a regular "Lieutenant" and in turn outranked an "Acting Volunteer Lieutenant," but in practice it was a question of who was in charge of what job, the additions to the titles being mere verbal decoration.

A "master" would rank about with a first-class warrant today; he took a salute but had no commission, and when in charge of a ship carried the courtesy title of "Captain." The rank of "Ensign" began to appear in the Federal Navy in 1863, usually with "Acting" attached; he was below a "Master." [13]

Enlisted Personnel of the Federal Navy

Of the 51,000 men in the Federal Navy during the war, not a third could have been called sailors. A great majority rated as "landsmen," were so in fact as well as name, and at least 12,000 to 15,000 of the men serving in the fleets along the coast and on the rivers had never set foot on a ship before enlisting. [14]

The question of finding seamen to man the ships was just as grave a problem as securing the vessels themselves, a fact which becomes apparent with the simple statement that the number available at all the Union naval stations in April 1861 totaled only 200. However, the expansion was rapid, and by July 1863 the number of seamen in service, including those on the Mississippi flotilla, was about 34,000. This expansion may perhaps be best grasped by noting the sharp contrast between 7,600 sailors at the opening of hostilities and 51,500 officers and sailors at the close of the war. Still, the demand for *trained* and *experienced* seamen was greatly in excess of the supply. The men enlisted were for the most part landsmen with little or no knowledge of seafaring life, steamboat hands, or even soldiers transferred

from the Army. The chief cause for the deficiency of Navy personnel was the high Federal bounties paid for enlistment in the Army, which tempted into the Army many sailors whose service would have been much more valuable on the sea. Congress took steps to meet this situation by authorizing bounties for sailors and by providing for the transfer to the naval service of sailors who had enlisted in the Army. As a result, the receiving ships were soon filled to overflowing. [15]

The liberal bounties offered by the States and local communities for Army volunteers, and the absence of any provision for transfers between the two services, also made it more difficult to secure naval enlistments. After the establishment of the draft, mariners were equally subject to its provisions. The States were not credited on their quotas with men furnished the Navy until 1864, and as a result many trained seamen were forced into the Army. Eventually extraordinary inducements were held out to secure naval volunteers and sometimes $1,000 was paid to secure a single seaman. The Navy and Marine Corps, both below strength, were supposed to receive conscripts from the draft of March 14, 1864.

In 1864 the following regulations of the War Department, adopted by the Navy Department, were published for use by the Navy. The regulations provided that no person under the age of eighteen should be mustered into the United States service, and the oath of enlistment taken by the recruit would be taken as conclusive as to his age. The regulations also provided for penalties for officers who would enlist minors. The Navy Regulations of 1864 provided for the enlistment of boys, 13 years of age or over. These boys had to be at least 4 feet, 8 inches tall, unless they were apprentices. No person was to be entered as landsman who was over the age of 33 unless he possessed some mechanical trade, nor could he be enlisted if he were over 38 years of age, without special permission of the Navy Department.[16]

Crews on Federal men-of-war were a mixture of races and nationalities. From one-third to one-half of the crews, to strike a fair average, on the war vessels of the United States Navy had been born abroad.[17] As early as September 25, 1861 the Navy Department officially sanctioned the enlistment of Negroes in the Navy. While the Congress and Army procrastinated, the Navy had from the very first received, protected, and employed for wages able-bodied colored men. The Navy really inaugurated the policy of emancipation.[18]

Among the Confederate prisoners at Point Lookout many became "galvanized Yanks" and enlisted in the Federal Navy.[19] And, at times, some Army units got rid of men they did not want for one reason or another in the following manner as described by a soldier of the 4th Illinois Cavalry, January 31, 1862:

"Our Captain did some weeding out today. There is a fleet of gunboats just completed here. Men were wanted to man them, and not wanting to wait to enlist them, there was a call for volunteers . . . from regiments here to be transferred to the gun-boats. But the Captain took it upon himself to detail such men that he would rather spare and told them they had to go, and they went. They were mostly Norwegians and Germans that could hardly speak English. Some of the other companies furnished some men for the gun-boats also, and some companies did not furnish any. Charley Walsh who was under arrest for drunkeness and attempting to kill Lieutenant Hapeman, was given the privilege to take service on a gun-boat or stand a court-martial. He chose the former."[20]

Disputes about enlistment date and enlistment terms were similar to those which arose in the other services. For instance, the men who shipped at Chicago during the latter part of 1861, claimed their discharge on the grounds of "expiration of term of enlistment." These men maintained that at the time of their enlistment "no one thought the war would last but a few months."

Many of the enlistment papers contained no mention of "term of enlistment" and no signature by any recruiting officer. Strange as it may seem, this was fairly typical of the way recruiting records were kept, early in the war, at most of the recruiting stations for the flotilla in the West.[21] The situation was somewhat better in other places, however.

NUMBERS AND CASUALTIES

Figures on naval enlistments vary with various sources. Much of the confusion arises from the fact that many men re-enlisted. Fox gives the total number of men in the Navy during the war as 132,554. Of this number, 7,600 were already in service at the outbreak of hostilities.[22] However, the number of men credited to the several States as having been furnished to the Navy and Marine Corps was 105,963, including re-enlistments. The actual number in naval service was 84,417 men, of whom 4,588 died. An estimated 4,649 deserted.[23] A total of 1,804 were killed and mortally wounded, including 342 scalded to death and 308 drowned in action. The number of wounded was 2,226.[24] Although the exact number of prisoners is not available it could not have been large. It is interesting to note that while Grant refused to exchange prisoners of war with Lee, naval prisoners were exchanged by negotiations between the Secretaries of the Navy on the two sides.

UNIFORMS

The naval officer's uniform was based upon the dress regulations of March 8, 1852 and July 31, 1862. The following is a composite description based on the 1852 and 1862 regulations. While the officers uniform was precisely described in the dress regulations of March 8, 1852 and July 31, 1862, the dress of petty officers and crew was only described in very general terms in the regulations, and exhibited great differences. The only rank insignia authorized was the eagle-anchor-star device, worn on the right sleeve by boatswain's mates and higher ratings, and on the left sleeve by other petty officers. In photographs this device varies in design as does the top of the cap and the cap ribbon.

For service at sea the men wore blue woollen or white duck frocks and trousers, and blue or white cloth caps, in various mixtures as each commander might direct, "having proper regard for the comfort of the crew." There were at least three different methods of cutting the yoke of the blouse.[25]

For additional information on Navy and Marine Corps flags and uniforms, see Chapter 11.

PAY

The pay of the officers and men in the Navy, unlike that of the volunteers enlisted in the Army, was regulated by the length of term of service and by the duty the officer was called upon to perform. The captain's rank, which was the highest position held in the Federal Navy at the opening of the war, was the only one in which the length of service did not bring an increase of pay. The pay scale tapered down through the various grades of seamen, until the "boys," which included all the youngsters engaged in the positions of "powder-monkeys," "water-boys," and various other duties, received eight or nine dollars a month and their rations.

The Register of the Navy of the United States, January 1, 1863, listed the yearly pay as follows, except for retired personnel, and men on leave or awaiting orders:

Rank	At sea	On shore
Rear-Admiral	$5,000.00	$4,000.00
Commodore	4,000.00	3,200.00
Captain	3,500.00	2,800.00
Commander	2,800.00	2,240.00

Lieutenant Commander . .	$2,343.00	$1,875.00
Lieutenant	1,875.00	1,500.00
Master	1,500.00	1,200.00
Ensign	1,200.00	960.00
Midshipman	500.00	
Fleet Surgeon	3,300.00	
Surgeon	3,000.00	1,600.00
Assistant Surgeon	1,500.00	1,050.00
Paymaster	3,100.00	1,400.00
Assistant Paymaster	1,500.00	1,000.00
Chaplains	1,875.00	1,500.00
Boatswain, Gunner, Carpenter, Sailmaker . .	1,450.00	800.00
Engineer	2,600.00	1,800.00
Assistant Engineer	1,250.00	750.00
Engineer-in-chief	3,000.00	
Naval Constructor	2,600.00	
Clerk	1,500.00	400.00

Enlisted men—per month

Rank	Pay
Yeoman	$24.00
Armorer	20.00
Mate	20.00
Master-at-arms	25.00
Ship's corporal	20.00
Coxswain	24.00
Quartermaster	24.00
Quarter Gunner	20.00
Captain of forecastle	24.00
tops	20.00
afterguard	20.00
hold	20.00
Cooper	20.00
Painter	20.00
Steward	20.00
Nurse	14.00
Cook	20.00
Master of the band	20.00
Musician 1st class	15.00
2nd class	12.00
Seaman	18.00
Ordinary seaman	14.00
Landsman	12.00
Boy	8.00
Fireman, 1st class	30.00
2nd class	25.00
Coal heaver	18.00

Food

By Public Law No. 81, "An act to establish and regulate the Navy Ration," approved August 29, 1842, the Navy ration consisted of the following daily allowance of food for each person:

One pound of salted pork with half a pint of peas or beans; or one pound of salted beef, with half a pound of flour, and a quarter of a pound of raisins, dried apples, or other dried fruit; or one pound of salt beef, with half a pound of rice, two ounces of butter, and two ounces of cheese, together with fourteen ounces of biscuit and one quarter of an ounce of tea; and a weekly allowance of half a pound of pickles or cranberries, half a pint of molasses, and half a pint of vinegar.

Fresh meat could be substituted for salt beef or pork and vegetables or sauerkraut for the other articles usually issued with the salted meats. It was per-

mitted to substitute one pound of soft bread, or one pound of flour, or half a pound of rice for fourteen ounces of biscuit; half a pint of wine for a gill of spirits; half a pound of rice for a pint of beans or peas; half a pint of beans or peas for half a pound of rice.

No commissioned officer or midshipman, or any person under 21 years of age was permitted to draw the spirit part of the daily ration, but would be paid the value of the same in money.

Welles early realized that such a ration as that prescribed in the 1842 law would not meet the needs of the service. Accordingly, in his report of July 4, 1861, he recommended a modification of the law, and his suggestion was followed. Since nearly the entire naval strength of the United States was employed on blockade duty, extending along the entire Atlantic coast, it was obviously essential that the blockading vessels remain on duty at their stations as long as possible, to guard the coast and prevent illegal commerce. To perform this mission satisfactorily it was essential that the crews have frequent supplies of fresh provisions to maintain health. Welles pointed out that his Department had already begun to send to these blockading ships the necessary fresh supplies, and he proposed that the Navy be permitted to continue to supply the crews in this manner until the war was over. Communication with each of the principal stations would be established by despatch boats, which would not only carry fresh provisions, but would also "carry to and receive from the squadrons letters, would take recruits to their ships, and would evacuate sick and wounded, while at the same time performing their main function of maintaining an effective coastal blockade."

Discipline

The *Regulations for the Navy of the United States* (1864) is a book of 278 pages, which served the Navy in similar fashion as the book on Army Regulations served the land forces. These naval regulations were the boiled down version of a long series of laws passed by various Congressional Acts for the Government of the Navy. Many of these laws dated back to the period of the War of 1812 and had to be revised to meet the many changes which had taken place in the Navy over the period of half a century. Among the changes was a gradual reduction in the severity of punishments meted out to naval personnel. Courts-martial procedure was stream-lined and made more precise. The most frequently used naval court was the summary court-martial. This was established for the trial of lesser offenses which the commanders of vessels deemed deserving of greater punishment than they were legally authorized to inflict upon petty officers and men under their command, but not sufficiently serious to require trial by a general court-martial.

A commander of a vessel of the Navy could inflict

the following on petty officers, seamen, or Marines, without sentence of a general or summary court-martial:

1. Reduction of any rating established by himself.

2. Confinement, with or without irons, single or double, for not more than ten days.

3. Solitary confinement on bread and water not exceeding five days.

4. Solitary confinement not exceeding seven days.

5. Deprivation of liberty on shore.

6. Extra duties.

Summary courts-martial could inflict the following punishments:

1. Discharge from the service, with bad conduct discharge.

2. Solitary confinement in irons, single or double, on bread and water, or diminished rations for no more than 30 days.

3. Solitary confinement in irons, single or double, for no more than 30 days.

4. Solitary confinement for no more than 30 days.

5. Confinement not exceeding 2 months.

6. Reduction to next inferior rating.

7. Deprivation of liberty on shore on foreign station.

8. Extra police duties, and loss of pay, not to exceed 3 months, could be added to any of the above-mentioned punishments.[26]

There must have been many occasions for punishing minor infractions of naval regulations and ships' routine while at sea. This was especially true in the case of ships on blockading duty. Also, when any ship was in port, Marine sentries were lined up along the ship's side to prevent the men going ashore without permission. These sentries were stationed at each gangway on a platform arranged on the ship's side, and on the forecastle. When at sea these above-mentioned Marine sentries were dispensed with. But there were other parts of the ship where Marine sentries were on duty constantly, day and night. They were posted outside the cabin door, captain's orderly, spirit room, orlop deck abaft, and the "brig" where prisoners were confined. If at any time a sentry was needed for other parts of the ship, the Marines were used for this duty.[27]

General courts-martial were convened for the following types of serious offenses: mutiny; disobedience of orders, or assaulting a superior officer; intercourse with the enemy; desertion; sleeping on watch; willful stranding of a vessel or malicious injury to a vessel; striking the flag without proper authority; cowardice; neglecting to prepare for battle; spying; murder; cruelty to subordinates; profane swearing, drunkenness, gambling, theft; dueling; and many others. Punishment involved death, or as the court-martial directed, except that flogging was not permitted.

Courts of Inquiry could be ordered by the President of the United States, the Secretary of the Navy, or the commander of a fleet or squadron, provided such a court did not consist of more than 3 members, all commissioned officers, including a judge advocate. But such a court could only state facts, and was not to render an opinion unless expressly required to do so in the order for convening, and the party whose conduct was the subject of inquiry, or his attorney, was permitted to cross-examine all the witnesses.[28]

INNOVATIONS

The Civil War was not only the first war in which naval operations on a vast scale were conducted after the introduction of steam, but it was also the first war in which use was made of certain modern appliances which revolutionized the art of naval warfare. Extensive use was made for the first time of ironclads, rifled ordnance, rams, and torpedoes. For the first time was witnessed the maintenance of a steam blockade, as well as the employment by the enemy of swift steam cruisers, which proved a serious threat to the commerce of the nation. It saw a blockade instituted which was effective and conducted on so vast a scale as to make it without parallel to anything previous in history.

Regardless of ridicule, and the almost invincible prejudice against monitors of some of the older and most distinguished officers of the Navy, such as Du Pont, the Navy Department persevered in building ironclads and monitors, faster and more powerful each year. The result was that toward the end of the war the United States, which at the beginning of the conflict had only a skeleton navy of a type soon to be outmoded, possessed a fleet which could bid defiance to England and France, which "in consequence, let us alone to work out our destiny." There can be little doubt that the monitors and other ironclads produced by Welles and the Navy Department had more effect in restraining England and France from intervening in the struggle and from continuing to give hospitality to Confederate commerce destroyers than all the expostulations of the State Department delivered through our ambassadors, Adams and Dayton.[29] The following description of the various classes of monitors was written during the war and is of especial interest in the comparisons it contains between the Federal Navy and its potential enemies in Europe.[30]

One of the features of the Federal Navy was the "tin-clad" fleet, especially constructed to guard the rivers and shallow waters of the West and South. The principal requirement of these "tin-clads" was that they be of very light draft, to enable them to navigate across the shoals in the Mississippi and other rivers on which they operated. The lighter class of these vessels drew less than two feet of water, and it was a common saying that they could "go anywhere where the ground was a little damp." They were small side- or stern-wheel boats, and were armored with iron plating less than an inch in thickness, from which they derived the name of "tinclads." Though insufficient protection to resist a heavy shell, this light plating was a good bulletproof, which would withstand the fire of a light field piece, unless the shell chanced to find a vulnerable spot, such as an open port hole. These boats were armed with howitzers, and their work against field batteries or sharpshooters on shore was particularly effective. The heavier class of boats that were used in the river offensive and defensive work was armed with more guns of larger caliber, and their armor plating was somewhat heavier than that of the little vessels designed to get close to the shores. The little boats, however, took their full share in the heavy fighting; and on the Red River, with Admiral Porter standing at her helm after the pilot had fallen, the *Cricket*, one of the smallest of these light-armored boats, fought one of the most valiant small naval contests of the war. Others of these boats won distinction in their actions against shore forces and heavier vessels.[31]

SQUADRONS OF THE FEDERAL NAVY

To enforce the blockade it became necessary from the very beginning of the war to concentrate almost all the naval forces of the United States along the Atlantic Coast from the Chesapeake Bay to and in the Gulf of Mexico. This extensive line of seaboard, embracing an extent of nearly 3,000 miles, with its numerous harbors and inlets, was deemed too extensive for a single command. Accordingly the naval force, by July 4, 1861, was organized in two squadrons. The command of the first of them, the Atlantic Squadron, was entrusted to Flag-Officer Silas H. Stringham, and the second, or Gulf Squadron, was given to Flag-Officer William Mervine.

It was early found necessary to place a flotilla on the lower Potomac. This force, known as the "Potomac Flotilla" succeeded in keeping the Potomac River open until the enemy had erected batteries on the Virginia shore, thereby making all passage on the river exceedingly dangerous. Before the end of 1861 it was found necessary to divide the blockading squadrons, since the duties imposed on the two squadron commands were too extensive for each of them to handle. Accordingly both the Atlantic and Gulf Squadrons were divided. The task of blockading the coast was unattractive and devoid of adventure, since the enemy had no large navy to combat.

By December 1, 1862 the naval force was distributed as follows:

North Atlantic Squadron—Guarded the Virginia and North Carolina coasts. On January 1, 1865, the squadron, commanded by Rear-Admiral David D. Porter, consisted of the following ships: First rate—6, second rate—9, third rate—34, fourth rate—63. The squadron also had an ordnance ship, tug, launch, and various installations, including the naval station at Beaufort. By December 1863, this squadron had closed its coast line fairly effectively with

A SHIP THAT MADE HISTORY

Deck of the *Monitor* after her historic battle with the *Merrimac*. Note the dents in the turret, made by cannon balls.

the single exception of the port of Wilmington. Some of the fastest steamers from overseas had, under cover of darkness, succeeded in eluding capture, but most of these fast steamers had been caught or driven ashore by the end of 1863. The number of vessels and personnel employed in this squadron was greater than that of any other squadron, and its importance was at least as great as any other in the service. In January 1865, the squadron assisted in the capture of Fort Fisher; an incessant fire was poured into the fort by 44 naval vessels.

South Atlantic Squadron—This squadron was charged with patrolling the coast from the line which separates the two Carolinas and extended to Cape Florida. On January 1, 1865, this squadron, commanded by Rear-Admiral J. A. Dahlgren, consisted of the following ships: First rate—0, second rate—2, third rate—17, fourth rate—61.

It also had a store ship and a naval battery under its jurisdiction. During a good part of the war, the squadron was hammering away at Fort Sumter and the immediate enemy fortifications around this fort. Although not successful in taking the fort, the squadron was justly proud of the fact that "not a single blockade runner has succeeded in reaching the city for months, and the traffic which had earlier been carried on with large profits was stopped. The coast entrusted to this squadron was about 300 miles in extent, a considerable portion of it being a network of inlets and sounds. Within the limits of this command were two of the chief sea ports of the enemy— Charleston and Savannah. They were not taken until near the end of the war.

East Gulf Squadron—The Gulf Squadron was divided into the East and West Gulf Squadrons on February 21, 1862. The East Gulf Squadron comprised the southern and western portions of the Florida peninsula, commencing at Cape Canaveral on the eastern coast and extending to Pensacola. There were few important military operations in this area, and the squadron contented itself with keeping a close watch of the coast and of the adjacent waters. This vigilance resulted in the capture of many prizes and the almost entire annihilation of all illicit traffic by the end of 1863. During 1864, the limits of the squadron were extended so as to include the waters of the Bahamas and the vicinity of Cuba.

West Gulf Squadron—This squadron guarded a coast which commenced at (and included) Pensacola and extended westward to the Rio Grande, and was, from a variety of reasons, one of the most important and responsible commands ever entrusted to a naval officer. From the harbors and rivers subject to that blockade there had been exported before the war vast amounts of cotton, sugar, and other products. Within those limits were the ocean outlets of the great central valley of the Union. The Navy selected D. G. Farragut as commander of this squadron, "in the confident belief that his courage and energy were equal to the exigency." Farragut had already shown considerable courage and energy in the capture of New Orleans and the opening up of navigation of the Mississippi. Elements of the squadron were active in the Vicksburg and Port Hudson campaign. The ships bombarded enemy positions for long periods of time from the water, and even landed naval ordnance which was used as land artillery, entirely manned with naval personnel. The squadron established an effective blockade of the Red River and thus intercepted the supplies from Texas destined for the Confederate armies. The enemy felt this to be one of the most serious and fatal blows inflicted on them during 1863, and from the effects of it they never fully recovered. The Rio Grande, being the boundary between the United States and Mexico, was open to navigation of both countries, and could not be blockaded. The enemy devised several schemes to exploit this situation, and under the guise of neutral trade, Matamoras suddenly became a great commercial center. However, the occupation of such localities as Brownsville ended Matamoras' commerce and by the end of 1863, the town of Matamoras was becoming "as insignificant as it was before the rebellion." Elements of the Squadron participated in the Battle of Mobile Bay, August 5, 1864. On January 1, 1865, the West Gulf Squadron, commanded by Commodore James S. Palmer, consisted of the following ships: First rate—0, second rate—5, third rate —11, fourth rate—61. By 1865, the squadron had a naval rendezvous at New Orleans and its own naval hospital and was responsible for Mobile Bay, the coast of Texas, Southwest Pass, and the Mississippi River. The appointment of Palmer to the command of the squadron was but temporary, since Farragut had been placed in command of the Fort Fisher expedition.

Mississippi Squadron—This large organization was charged with overcoming the enemy and restoring the National control of the great central valley of the Union. In slightly more than two years, the squadron grew from nothing to an organization of 100 vessels, carrying 462 guns, with crews amounting to about 5,500. The capture of Arkansas Post in January 1863, and the captures of Vicksburg and Port Hudson in July 1863, were among the successes in which this squadron took a prominent part. In the absence of naval installations along the Mississippi River, it was necessary to have supplies sent out from the central and secure position at Cairo. The squadron was composed mainly of boats that had been employed in the carrying trade; and were purchased, strengthened, and fitted for war purposes. They were necessarily inferior to naval-built vessels in strength, since they were lightly armed and armored, and consequently much more vulnerable. However, their cost was much less than that of iron-clads or ocean-going vessels. The Mississippi Squadron was gradually reduced after April 1865, and on August 14, 1865 ceased to exist.

Pacific Squadron—The vigilance of this squadron, and the cooperation of the custom-house and revenue authorities on the West Coast, resulted in suppression of all attempts by the enemy to fit out "piratical cruisers" on the Pacific. In July 1863, the American steamer *Pembroke* was fired upon by Japanese vessels in Japanese waters. The *Wyoming* proceeded to the scene of the attack and engaged Japanese land batteries and small naval force. After an hour's fighting the *Wyoming* withdrew, having sunk two Japanese craft, damaged the shore batteries, and vindicated the honor of the American flag. During 1864 no hostile craft made its appearance in the Pacific and commerce was carried on without interruption, other than that caused by the measures of foreign powers in an attitude of hostility towards each other. The blockade of Mexico's Pacific ports by the French fleet necessitated close surveillance by the U. S. naval elements. Whereas most of the squadrons were discontinued after the end of the war, the Pacific Squadron was expanded and strengthened.

West India Squadron—This squadron was discontinued October 3, 1864 because the principal objectives for which it had been created no longer were important. The chief duties of the West India Squadron were turned over to the East Gulf Squadron. In 1864, there were no special occurrences in the squadron's convoying of the California steamers.[32]

FLOTILLAS

In addition to the squadrons, the Federal Navy had flotillas both in the East and West. In the east, the "Potomac Flotilla" performed service which was probably among the most fatiguing and discouraging of the war. The crews of the vessels spent a great portion of their nights in rowing up and down the river on picket duty, watching for mail-carriers, smugglers, and spies of all kinds; and in the daytime the ships were often aground on the bars and shoals, in spite of all precautions. They were in hourly danger of being fired upon by masked batteries, which could be constructed unseen in the thick undergrowth of the shores; quarters in the little steamers were exceedingly uncomfortable; the prizes were rowboats and small, worthless river craft. For their reward, these hard-working, much-enduring men received too often only the complaints of the Country that nothing was done, and sneers at the inefficiency of the Navy Department, and especially of the Potomac Flotilla.[33]

In the West a "Western Flotilla," also known as the "Mississippi Flotilla," under A. H. Foote was very prominent at Fort Henry and Fort Donelson. Ap-

parently this flotilla was enlarged and became the nucleus of the "Mississippi Squadron" in 1862.

THE BLOCKADE

The blockade which the United States proclaimed, and at last succeeded in enforcing, against the ports of the Southern Confederacy, was of twofold character; it was both military and commercial, was recognized by the Supreme Court of the United States as being valid, and sanctioned by both municipal and international law. By the amended proclamation of President Lincoln April 27, 1861, the whole seacoast of the South Atlantic and the Gulf of Mexico was interdicted from commercial relations with any foreign shore. To supplement this proclamation the Secretary of the Treasury on March 31, 1863, published regulations governing internal and coastal commercial intercourse. The following sections were especially significant:

Section I. No goods, wares, or merchandise, whatever may be the ostensible destination thereof, shall be transported to any place now under the control of insurgents, nor to any place on the south side of the Potomac River; nor to any place on the north side of the Potomac, and south of the Washington and Annapolis railroad; nor to any place on the eastern shore of the Chesapeake; nor to any place on the south side of the Ohio River below Wheeling, except Louisville; nor to any place on the west side of the Mississippi River below the mouth of the Des Moines, except St. Louis, without a permit of a duly authorized officer of the Treasury Department.

Section III. No clearance or permit whatsoever will be granted for any shipment to any port or place affected by the existing blockade, except for military purposes, and upon the certificate and request of the Department of War or the Department of the Navy.

Section XV. No vessel, boat, or other vehicle used for transportation from any place in the loyal states, shall carry goods, wares, or merchandise, into any place, section, or State, restricted as aforesaid, without the permit of a duly authorized officer of the Treasury Department, application for which permit may be made to such authorized officer near the point of destination as may suit the convenience of the shipper.

The blockade of a coastline of 3,549 miles in length, greater in extent than the whole coast of Europe from Cape Trafalgar to Cape North, was an undertaking without precedent in history. During the War of 1812, when England had 800 naval vessels in commission, not a single port of the United States was thoroughly closed. Immediately after closing the ports of the States in rebellion, and giving that act the character of a blockade, the efforts of the Navy Department were directed towards securing several harbors at comparatively equidistant points, as bases for operations for the squadrons, where Federal naval units could receive their supplies and maintain themselves at their stations and on their cruising ground, without returning to Northern ports for repairs and re-equipment. To have pulled blockading ships off their stations for long periods of time would not only have endangered the efficiency, but in some instances might have involved an abandonment of the blockade. With these considerations in mind, the Department sent out various coast expeditions which resulted in taking possession of or closing all the ports except Wilmington by the end of 1864. For various reasons, Cape Fear River was more difficult to blockade than any port on the coast of the United States. The two main entrances were 40 miles apart, and these two were subdivided into several others, each of which afforded an entrance to vessels. The water shoals gradually and regularly to the shore line, and numerous isolated batteries were erected along the coast, so that a blockade runner of light draught was not forced to make directly for the entrance, but could run close under the land protected by the batteries, and pass in over the bar at leisure. When coming out, a steamer could select its own time and place; it could pass either up and down the coast before making a break for it, or it could proceed straight out to sea, trusting for escape to the night and favoring darkness and mists, and the fact that it was under full speed, while the blockading vessels had to remain at low steam. Almost every vessel employed in violating the blockade was constructed in England with great skill, regardless of cost, and with the sole purpose of engaging in trade, the profits of which were almost as remunerative as those connected with the slave trade.[34]

The great contribution of the Federal Navy to winning the war was in the blockading service on the Atlantic and Gulf coasts. So successful was this blockade that although in the early months of 1864 about two of every three blockade-runners evaded capture, the noose grew steadily tighter before the year was over. By December of the year, 40 out of 66 were captured while they were trying to enter a given port. During the war 1,149 prizes were taken, in addition to which 355 vessels were burned, sunk, driven on shore, or otherwise destroyed, and a few were wrecked. The total loss has been computed at 1504 vessels of all classes. The gross value of the cargo condemned in prize courts before November 1, 1865, totaled nearly $22,000,000, a sum subsequently enlarged by fresh condemnations. The value of the vessels captured and destroyed amounted to about 7 million dollars, so that the ultimate total loss to owners of the ships and cargoes mounted to at least thirty-one million dollars, a low estimate.[35] By the end of 1861, the blockade had become so effective that in 1861-1862 the total cotton exported from the South was only 13,000 bales as against the 2,000,000 of the corresponding season before the war. During the quarter beginning September 1, 1861, less than 1,000 bales of cotton left Charleston Harbor, as against 110,000 for a like period in 1860. Some of this decrease was due to the fact that the new Confederacy was not producing the same amount of

cotton nor endeavoring to export as much as had the ante-bellum South.[36] The total length of the Atlantic blockade was over 3,500 miles. In addition the Navy had to patrol some 4,000 miles of inland waterways. This totals nearly 10,000 miles—a colossal undertaking, and it was accomplished.[37]

SOUTHERN PRIVATEERS

The Federal Navy was also confronted with privateering activity on the part of the enemy but most of this activity was confined to 1861. After that year, not only were Confederate ports closed to Southern privateers by Federal blockading squadrons, but such was the menace of the blockade in shutting off foreign markets that Southern ships could perform both a more gainful and a more patriotic service by running the blockade as cargo carriers than by acting as privateers. The South employed some famous cruisers to prey on Northern shipping and these cruisers gave the American merchant marine a setback from which it did not recover until World War I. The earliest of these Confederate cruisers was the *Sumter*, a screw steamer of 500 tons which was the first ship of war to fly the new Confederate flag on the high seas. The *Sumter* captured 18 ships before it entered the blockade running business. More famous still was the *Alabama* which captured 62 merchant ships, but more than met its match in the *Kearsage*, in one of the famous battles of naval history. It is interesting to note that the crew of the *Alabama* was made up chiefly of Englishmen, not Southerners. Other Confederate cruisers, such as the *Shenandoah, Florida, Tallahassee,* and *Georgia*, contributed their share in destroying the merchant marine of the United States. But the bulk of the Federal fleet was kept on blockading duty rather than sent out to bring these cruisers to bay. The cruisers were too slippery and fast to catch; moreover, the blockade was gradually choking the Confederacy to death.

LIFE ON BOARD SHIP

The life of enlisted men on the blockading vessels was monotonous in the extreme. Only a few on the smaller or the faster ships saw very much of excitement, and except for the bombardment of the forts, very little fighting. From the time a man enlisted on the receiving ship until his term of service was up, very few of the sailors ever set foot ashore. In consequence, there was much grumbling in many of the forecastles.[38] The lack of exercise and nutritious food was felt by officers and men. Scurvy, the dreaded pest of ship life in the old Navy, was only avoided by the occasional relief which came to them from the steamers bringing supplies of fresh meats and vegetables in amounts about enough for two or three days. The diet for the rest of the month was composed mainly of salted meats, cheese, hard bread, bad butter, inferior coffee, and positively bad tea.

It is surprising that the morale and efficiency of the personnel was not ruined under such conditions.[39]

The crews of the ships despatched on foreign service and in search of the Confederate cruisers were picked men, although many of them came from the volunteers. Because of the rapid enlargement of the Navy, there was very little attempt made to do more than work new men into useful shape at first. The adage of the old service was, "It takes three years to make a sailor," and sailors, in the proper sense of the term, most of them never became. But on the regular ships of the Navy all the old order was maintained, chiefly by the warrant officers, chief petty officers, quartermasters, boatswains, mates, and gunner's mates.

The crew proper was divided primarily into two watches, starboard and port watch; and secondarily into subdivisions. The ship's guns were divided into divisions, each generally under command of a lieutenant, assisted by a midshipman. To each gun was assigned a crew that, in the muzzle-loading days of the war, was made up of 1 captain, 1 second captain, 2 loaders, 2 rammers and spongers, 4 side-tacklemen, 5 train-tacklemen, and 1 powder boy—sixteen in all. Their titles indicate clearly their positions at the gun in action.[40] On the gunboats in the Mississippi and the converted merchantmen, there was very little chance for enforcing the strict rules that governed life on the regular vessels. The men in some cases had greater comforts, and in others much less. It was a question of give and take and make the best of it between officers and crew. With the introduction of the monitors there came into sea life an entirely new existence. At sea, if the weather was rough the men were corked up like flies in a bottle. Under a hot sun the sleeping quarters below became almost unbearable, and the iron decks so hot that they almost scorched the feet.

For those sailors in combat either with enemy fighting ships or with enemy land-based artillery, the price paid in suffering was certainly as great as that paid by the soldiers. To the perils of wounds from

RELAXATION ABOARD

Federal Tars off duty. Several games of checkers are being played, clothes repaired, and some music offered. Notice the Negro sailors, and the youth of many of the crew.

ammunition and suffering from cold and lack of food, there were the added dangers of drowning after the ship was blown up, of being pinned down and burning with the ship, and of being scalded to death by escaping steam if a shell struck the engine.

ACCOMPLISHMENTS

The success of the Federal Navy must be measured by how it solved its strategic and operational role in the overall Northern blueprint for victory. On December 1, 1861, Secretary of the Navy Welles outlined three different types of naval operations, which the situation confronting the Country demanded on an extensive scale. These were:

1. The closing of all the enemy ports along a coast line of 3,000 miles, by means of an international blockade, including the naval occupation and defence of the Potomac River from its mouth to the Federal capital, as the boundary line between Maryland and Virginia, and also the main commercial avenue to the principal base of Federal military operations.

2. The organization of combined naval and military expeditions to operate in force against various points of the enemy coast, rendering efficient naval cooperation with the position and movements of such expeditions when landed, and including also all necessary naval aid to the Army in cutting off intercommunication with the enemy and in its operations on the Mississippi and tributaries.

3. The active pursuit of enemy cruisers which might escape the vigilance of the blockading units and put to sea from enemy ports.

GALLANTRY IN THE NAVY

The Federal Navy still awaits a comprehensive treatment of its many tactical successes; only the over-all naval strategy of the war is comparatively well known and appreciated. The great victories at New Orleans in April, 1862; the naval victories of Farragut, Porter, Worden, and Cushing have been receiving greater attention in recent years. What is not so well appreciated, however, is the gallantry displayed in battle by the men of the Federal Navy, even when the odds at times were hopeless. One such occasion occurred March 8, 1862, when the Confederate ironplated giant frigate *Virginia* (the old *Merrimac)* rammed and shelled the wooden ship *Cumberland,* whose crew stuck heroically to the sinking vessel and went down with flags flying. A survivor thus describes the action [pages 294-98]; [41]

* * *

FIGHT BETWEEN THE CUMBERLAND AND THE MERRIMAC

Saturday the eighth of March was a beautiful spring day, mild bright, and clear. The *Cumberland* was lying at single anchor with her sails loosed to dry, when at twelve thirty p.m., the writer as Officer-of-the-Deck, reported that the *Merrimac* had just hove

in sight, a long distance off in the direction of Norfolk. Owing to the mirage, her movements were much obscured, and her progress was so slow that at first it seemed doubtful if she was really coming out. But surmises were dispelled as the large, low hull came in view abreast of Craney Island, heading for the mouth of the Elizabeth River.

Our Captain (William Radford) was temporarily absent on court martial duty at Hampton Roads. The Executive Officer, Lieutenant George U. Morris, ordered all hands called. The sails were promptly furled, and then the quick beat to "quarters" aroused everyone and warned that the long-expected occasion had finally come. More than an hour of doubt followed while the *Merrimac* was hidden by a high bluff at the mouth of the James River. We could not see whether, after leaving the Elizabeth River, she was proceeding towards the squadron in Hampton Roads, or heading for the anchorage of the *Cumberland* and *Congress* off Newport News.

Meantime the *Cumberland* presented an inspiring sight; a splendid type of an old-time frigate; towering masts, long yards, neat and trim man-of-war appearance, with her crew standing at their guns for the last time; cool, grim, silent and determined Yankee seaman, the embodiment of power, grit, and confidence. I firmly believe that the sheer force of their confident determination to conquer would have prevailed over the armor and ram of the *Merrimac,* but for the handicap of sail motive power.

At 2:30 our doubts as to the objective chosen by the *Merrimac* were set at rest by her reappearance from behind the bluff, heading in our direction. As she passed the *Congress,* anchored below us, the latter opened with her whole broadside; but it merely rattled from the sloping armor like hail upon a roof, This effect caused us neither surprise nor shaken confidence in our own powers, since the *Congress* armament could fire nothing to compare with the solid shot of 80 pounds which we could deliver.

Disdaining to reply to her weaker antagonist, the *Merrimac* steamed slowly across the bow of the *Cumberland* and maneuvered for a ramming position. We had much difficulty in bringing any guns to bear. The springs which had been run long before, to provide against this very contingency of having to swing the ship to meet maneuvers of a mobile enemy, now proved useless from the fact of the turn of the tide having swung the *Cumberland* athwart the channel; thus bringing the springs in line with her keel. Three times the gun deck divisions were sent from one battery to the other without gaining any opening, while the head rigging prevented the 10-inch forecastle pivot gun from firing. At last the *Merrimac's* bearing changed sufficiently to starboard to permit our opening fire with a few forward 9-inch guns and the bow pivot gun. The enemy at once replied with her 7-inch rifle and broadside guns, sometimes aiming

RAMMING THE CHARGE
Note the powder monkey, whose duty was to carry charges from the magazine to the crew.

the latter at the small fort on shore, whose fire could have no material effect upon the action.

The *Merrimac's* first shot passed through the starboard hammock netting, killing and wounding nine marines, and knocking down, but not injuring, their commander, Lieutenant Heywood. These men, the first to fall, were promptly carried below, and their groans were something new to us and served as an introduction to a scene of carnage unparalleled in the war. The *Merrimac* continued to lay about 300 yards sharp on the starboard bow, raking the *Cumberland* with every shot from her broadsides, while we could reply only by extreme train with the few guns already mentioned. It was a situation to shake the highest courage and the best disciplined, but our splendid crew never faltered.

Of even the few guns that could bear, No. 1 on the gun deck was fired but once. The second shell from the murderous 7-inch rifle burst among the crew as they were running the gun out, after loading for a second shot, literally destroyed the whole crew except the powder boy, and disabled the gun for the remainder of the action. The captain of this gun, a splendid seaman named Kirker, rated commodore's coxswain, had both arms taken off at the shoulder as he was holding his handspike and guiding the gun. He passed me while being carried below, but not a groan escaped from him.

At this time the spring from the starboard quarter was manned on the spar deck, with the object of bringing the broadside to bear, but for the reasons previously explained the attempt proved futile. Events followed too fast to remember them in detail, during fifteen minutes of the most gruelling punishment. The dead were thrown to the disengaged side of the deck; the wounded carried below. No one flinched, but everyone went on rapidly loading and firing;

the places of the killed and wounded being taken promptly by others, in accordance with previous drill and training. The carnage was frightful. Great splinters torn from the ship's side and decks caused more casualties than the enemy's shell. Every first and second captain of the guns of the first division was killed or wounded, and with a box of cannon primers in my pocket, I went from gun to gun firing them as fast as the decimated crews could load.

The *Merrimac* was not satisfied even with the great advantage of gunfire incident to her raking position. The resistance from the *Cumberland* promised such delay, damage, and expenditure of ammunition as would handicap further operations against the Federal fleet, and Captain Buchanan decided to ram. The *Merrimac* struck the *Cumberland* upon the starboard bow, the ram penetrating the side under the berth deck, and for a few minutes holding the two ships together. As the *Cumberland* commenced to sink, the *Merrimac* was also carried down until her forward deck was under water. This situation presented an opportunity which unfortunately our officers on deck failed to seize. If our anchor had been let go it would have fallen on the *Merrimac's* deck and probably have held the two ships together; thus sinking the *Merrimac* with the *Cumberland*.

But no such action was taken. The ram was broken off in the *Cumberland's* side by the combined strain of the *Cumberland's* sinking and the swinging of the *Merrimac* under the influence of the tide. The current brought her up broadside to us, and whether from demoralization over the narrow escape, engines caught on center, or from some other reason, there she lay for some moments without moving; finally giving the *Cumberland* her first fair opportunity to fight back. That it was quickly and fully exploited regardless of our sinking condition, and notwith-

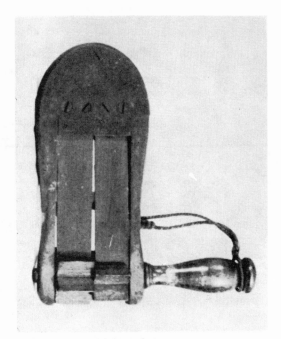

NAVAL ALARM DEVICE
This rattle was used to call men to their battle stations.

standing the carnage that surrounded us, is sufficient justification for the emphasis which I have placed upon the qualities of that peerless crew.

Three solid broadsides in quick succession were poured into the *Merrimac* at a distance of not more than one hundred yards. Confederate officers have told me that it made her fairly reel. Cheer upon cheer went up from the *Cumberland*, unfortunately only to be followed by exclamations of rage and despair as the enemy slowly moved away. But in spite of her armor she was not unscathed. Noting the small effect of our fire upon her sides, the gun captains had been instructed to aim only at the gun ports, with the result that the muzzles of two of her broadside 9-inch guns had been shot away.

The water was rising rapidly, the *Cumberland* going down by the bows. The forward magazine was flooded, but the powder tanks had been whipped out and carried aft, whence the supply of powder to the forward guns had been subsequently maintained. As the water gained the berth deck, which by this time was filled with the badly wounded, heart-rending cries above the din of combat could be heard from the poor fellows as they realized their helplessness to escape slow death from drowning.

Having reached a position free from our fire the *Merrimac* hailed the *Cumberland* and asked if she would surrender. The reply went back from Lieutenant Morris, "Never! We will sink with our colors flying"; whereupon the enemy resumed her old raking position on our starboard bow and again opened upon the doomed ship. The first cutter was sent with a hawser from the port quarter to a nearby

schooner, and another effort made to bring our broadside to bear, but by that time the *Cumberland* was too waterlogged to be moved.

While the foregoing was in progress the writer gathered together the remnants of the first division, some thirty men, and took them forward, with the object of transporting No. 1 gun to the bridle port, in a position where it would bear upon the *Merrimac*. The tackles had been scarcely hooked, when a shell, passing through the starboard bow, burst among them, killing and maiming the greater number. At about this time Master's Mate Harrington had his head shot off, and fell a corpse at my feet, in the act of receiving an order to slip the cable. There were few men left in the first division, which I had commanded for so long. Not a gun's crew could be mustered from the six crews of brave fellows who had gone into action so confident in their ship only three quarters of an hour before. No men ever stood at their guns better than that first gun deck division of the *Cumberland*.

The appearance of the gun deck forward at this time can never be forgotten. It was covered with the dead and wounded and slippery with blood. Some guns were left run in from their last shot; rammers and sponges, broken and powder-blackened, lay in every direction; the large galley was demolished and its scattered contents added to the general bood-spattered confusion.

Meanwhile the water had been rapidly gaining in spite of the efforts of the after division which had been sent to the pumps. The *Merrimac* must have noted our rapid sinking, but for some reason which I have never understood, unless to give a final *coup de grace*, she rammed the *Cumberland* a second time, striking her abaft the fore channels but doing no special damage.

By this time, even if there had been a sufficient number of men left, there was no longer any powder to serve the guns of the first division. The writer started aft, and on the way the ship gave a lurch forward, and water commenced pouring in through the bridle ports. Manifestly she was sinking so rapidly that no time could be lost. The order was passed for "every man to look out for himself;" an order never given until the last extremity.

The survivors rushed aft, some up the ladders from the berth and gun decks, others along the spar deck. Fortunately, all the boats had been lowered before the action commenced, and two of the largest were uninjured. Some of the survivors jumped into these boats moored astern, some climbed the rigging, and still others saved themselves on gratings and wooden material from the deck.

In this moment of dire confusion, with the water closing over the doomed ship, the last gun was fired, sounding her death knell. It was generally believed that this act of heroism was performed by Coxswain

Mathew C. Tierney, who had been mortally wounded and who perished in the ship.

I was one of the last to leave the main deck, the water then being up to the main hatch. Turning to the wardroom hatch ladder, almost perpendicular from the ship having a heavy list to port, I found it blocked by our fat drummer, Joselyn, struggling up with his drum. The peril was imminent, and, throwing off coat and sword, I squeezed through a gun port. In doing so, however, the heel of my boot became jammed against the port sill by the gun, which, from a position partially inboard had been slid outboard by the listing of the ship. For a few precious moments it seemed as though I must be carried down with the rapidly sinking ship; but with much difficulty, from a bent position I finally succeeded in wrenching off the boot-heel and thus freeing my foot. Then jumping into the icy water, encumbered by boots and clothing, I swam to the launch astern and was picked up exhausted. Later the drummer was also rescued while using his drum as a life buoy.

Almost immediately the *Cumberland* took one final plunge, bow first and stern high in the air, and settled beneath the waters. With difficulty the boat was shoved clear of the sinking vessel, whose flag, though almost within our reach, was left to wave over the glorious dead who had defended its honor with their lives.

Thus perished the *Cumberland*. No vessel ever fought more splendidly against odds so great that but one result was possible. She fought to the bitter end until the waters closed over her last gun.

Few battles of the war, ashore or afloat, resulted in so large a proportion of casualties on either side.

On the day of this desperate fight the crew of the *Cumberland* numbered 299 bluejackets and 33 marines; of whom 80 were killed or drowned, and about 30 wounded saved. Thus the total casualties were more than 33% of those engaged. The brunt of the fight fell upon my division, which lost more than half of its 85 men.

It is not easy to estimate all the damage done to the *Merrimac*. Two of her crew were killed, and numbers wounded, among the latter being Captain Buchanan; an able officer who was a great loss to the Confederacy. The flagstaff and the muzzles of two guns were shot away. Many of the plates on the casemates were loosened. The smokestack was so perforated with shot holes, as to fill the gun deck with smoke and seriously interfere with the working of her battery, and to greatly decrease the draft of the boilers, and hence to lower her speed. Finally the ram was wrenched off in the *Cumberland's* side causing the *Merrimac* to spring a leak.

But for the assistance rendered by the *Minnesota* in getting the *Monitor* ready for action, the latter could not have put up such a good fight as she did on the morning following her arrival. If on this occasion, the *Merrimac's* smokestacks had been intact, the handicap which she suffered of not being able to maneuver as handily as the *Monitor*, would have been much reduced; and when the opportunity to ram presented itself she is likely to have struck the *Monitor* squarely instead of a glancing blow. Moreover if the *Merrimac's* ram had been in place, it is my belief, formed after an inspection of the *Monitor* only a few days later, that even the glancing blow would have sunk the *Monitor*. Therefore I am firmly convinced that the great sacrifice made for the honor

SOUVENIRS OF THE FIGHT
Leather powder bucket from the *Cumberland;* a brass signal pistol; and a brass signal lantern.

of the flag by the crew of the *Cumberland*, though it failed to save their ship, resulted in the much greater achievement of saving the fleet, if not the Union.

History gives no example of braver resistance in the face of utter hopelessness, no precedent of a sterner feeling of "never surrender," than was shown by the *Cumberland* on the 8th of March, 1862. With the steadying influence of but few officers, exposed to a terrible shell fire for the first time in their lives, with little opportunity to fight back, seeing great numbers of their comrades mangled and killed before them, with the rising water pouring over the decks, and the ship trembling in her last throes; the manner in which those decimated guns' crews stood unflinchingly at their quarters until the word was passed from their officers, "Every man look out for himself;" was truly sublime and ought to embalm the name of *Cumberland* in the heart of every American; regardless of the military results accomplished. Without hope of assistance, against fearful odds, those splendid fellows fought to the bitter end, and the ship was their tomb. Let their memory be kept green in the hearts of their countrymen, and if their example stimulates the youth of coming generations to be true to their country and their flag, it cannot be said they died in vain.

* * *

CUSHING'S HEROISM

Soon after the end of the war, Admiral Farragut told the Secretary of the Navy that "while no navy had better or braver officers than ours, young Cushing was the hero of the war." Yet this young man, because of a harmless prank, was forced to leave the Naval Academy where a report on him in February 1861 said: "General conduct, bad; aptitude for the naval service not good; not recommended for continuance at the Academy." (!) Yet Cushing was shortly, on five different occasions to receive commendation and thanks from the Secretary of the Navy, and for his most daring and successful exploit the thanks of Congress. This exploit has been described as follows: [42]

* * *

The Navy unsuccessfully attempted to destroy the *Albemarle*, a powerful ram, by sowing mines in the river. The presence of the ram enabled enemy blockade runners to slip into Albemarle Sound. The Navy Department learned that the *Albemarle* was lying at the wharf at Plymouth some eight miles from the mouth of the river. In October 1864, a steam launch, equipped with spar torpedoes, under Cushing, arrived at the mouth of the river. At midnight October 27th the launch, with its engines muffled by tarpaulins to shut off the light and sound, approached the *Albemarle*. The launch traveled at low speed so as to reduce the noise of the engines. The night was dark and stormy with now and then a heavy fall of rain. Running cautiously under the trees on the right bank, the launch proceeded on its way up the heavily-guarded enemy river. Cushing hoped to land unobserved, board the ram from the wharf, and bring her down the river. To carry this out the attack would have to be a surprise. But this plan had to be discarded, because as the launch approached the wharf area, a dog barked, and a sentry, aroused, discovered the boat and hailed her. Receiving no reply he hailed again and fired. The time for surprise was past; Cushing drove his launch straight at the ram, about 200 yards away. The *Albemarle's* crew opened with rifle fire which Cushing answered with canister from the howitzer on the launch. Continuing straight on, the launch struck the boom of logs protecting the ram, and passing over them, the torpedo-span was lowered. Going ahead slowly now, until the torpedo was well under the *Albemarle's* bottom, Cushing detached it with a vigorous pull. Wating until he could feel the torpedo touching the vessel, he pulled the trigger-line and exploded it. Cushing ordered the crew to save themselves. Most of them, however, were captured or drowned. Cushing escaped by swimming. The *Albemarle* keeled over and sank at her moorings.

* * *

The war ended with the Stars and Bars still floating over the great southwest port of Galveston. The surrender of this port on June 2, 1865, may be regarded as the final act in the naval war.

THE MARINE CORPS

The war brought no great fame to the Marine Corps. It was increased only to a maximum of 3,900 officers and men, and most of these were required aboard ship. Marines formed part of several land operations but their greatest combat service was rendered as gun crews in battle aboard naval vessels and in the other assignments they had to perform while at sea.[43]

Fundamentally, the Marine Corps was subject to the laws and regulations established for the government of the Navy, except when detached for service with the Army by order of the President of the United States. The Corps was subject to either the laws governing the Navy or the Commandant of the Marine Corps.[44]

When Marines were received on board a vessel they were entered separately on the vessel's books as part of the complement, or as supernumeraries, as the situation required, on the same footing as the seamen with respect to "provisions and short allowances." Marines were not to be diverted from their appropriate duties, or called upon to coal ship or work as mechanics, except in case of emergency. When a detachment of Marines joined a vessel-of-war for sea duty, it was always to be accompanied by the officers attached to the detachment. Since occasions arose when it was necessary to use Marines at the "great guns" of the men-of-war, they were instructed as full gun crews by their own officers, Marines or the Army, according to the particular service with which the Corps was associated.

During the war the Marine Corps actually served two masters. The regulations for the recruiting service of the Army applied to the recruiting service of the Corps so far as was practicable. Exercises and formation of Marines at parades, reviews, inspections, escorts, guard mountings, funerals, challenges of persons, police and regulations for camp and garrison duties, and salutes, were the same as those established for the Army. However, any Marine detachment serving within a Navy Yard was subject to the orders of the Commandant of the Yard; and no part of the detachment could be relieved or withdrawn from the Yard, except on order of the Commandant of the Marine Corps, approved by the Secretary of the Navy. Marines also could be assigned as members of regular gun crews under naval officers. This was done by the ship's commander but only in cases of emergency. When Marines were not on guard, or on duty as sentinels, Marines were subject to the naval officers exactly as the seaman were.[45]

PERSONNEL

In 1861, the United States Marine Corps had a total of 63 officers as follows: [46]
Commandant: Colonel John Harris
General Staff:

Adjutant and inspector, Major H. B. Tyler
Paymaster, Major W. W. Russell
Quartermaster, Major William B. Slack
Assistant Quartermaster, Captain W. A. T. Maddox
1 lieutenant colonel
4 majors
13 captains
20 first lieutenants
20 second lieutenants

Colonel Harris died in 1864 and was succeeded as Commandant by Colonel Jacob Zeilin. During the war the Corps was enlarged and on January 1, 1865, consisted of the following officers: [47]

Colonel Commandant	1
Generals staff	5
Colonel	1
Lieutenant Colonel	2
Majors	4
Captains	19
First Lieutenants	30
Second Lieutenants	22
	——
	84

Meanwhile the enlisted force of the Corps was being increased. By July 4, 1861, the Corps as a result of two increases in personnel, numbered 2,500 enlisted men. The new men, who were "able-bodied and of a superior class" were very readily obtained. But the increased demand for guards on men-of-war necessitated a further increase in the Corps so that by October 1861, the report of the Commandant showed the actual strength of the Corps, ashore and afloat, to be 2,964. A year later the Commandant, in his annual report, stressed the need for an increase of 500 men with a proportionate number of officers.

UNCERTAIN STATUS

Nevertheless, the Corps remained small in size and more or less ignored by the press and public. One of the main reasons certainly, was the uncertain status of the Corps with relation to the Army and Navy. As Secretary Welles said in his December 1862 report:

There has always been a divided opinion among naval officers in regard to maintaining a distinct organization of marines for service on ships-of-war, even before the great change which the service has undergone by the introduction of steamers, with their corps of engineers, firemen, and attendants. An incongruity attaches to the system, for the marines are partly under the Army laws and regulations, and partly under the Naval code. On shore they are paid by a Marine paymaster, on shipboard by a Navy paymaster. They are subsisted on the Army ration on shore, while on shipboard they have the Navy ration. Consequently the condition of the Marines varies from shore to ship, or ship to shore, as they may be employed.

The Commandant thought that it would be better if the Corps were to be permanently attached to either the Navy or Army, instead of occupying an equivocal attitude as regards both. He requested that the Commandant be made a brigadier general and thereby have rank corresponding with like commands but the rank of the Corps Commandant was only colonel throughout the entire war.

In his December 1863 report, Welles reported difficulty in keeping up a full complement of the Corps because of the high bounties paid for Army recruits. Many Marines, whose time had expired, though preferring to remain with their old Corps were induced by extraordinary bounties to enter the Army. It was not the policy of the Navy Department to resort to the system of bounties for either the Marine Corps or the Navy, but Welles cautioned that circumstances might make it necessary. The Commandant recommended that the Corps be increased from its authorized strength of 3,000 men to a total of 3,500. This number would be sufficient for the Corps to meet its current requirements since a large portion of the vessels in commission did not require a Marine guard. On a few important occasions a battalion of Marines was detailed for Army duty, but the lack of equipment and other causes rendered their employment in a service to which they are not drilled, and to which they do not belong, a question of doubtful expediency. And, again, the Secretary suggested the advisability of attaching the Corps *permanently* to either the Navy or Army. Welles also urged once more that the Commandant be brigadier general.

In 1864 the Secretary made little mention of the Corps except to point out that it was unable to comply with all the requisitions for guards on ships at sea. However, when in action, the reports from the several squadrons and vessels of the service showed that, in the gallant deeds of the Navy, the Marines bore an honorable part. A year later, with the war over, Welles reported that the strength of the Corps had not changed materially and that the greater part of the Corps had been actively engaged with the squadrons in the naval operations of the last year of the war.[48]

UNIFORMS

Just as today, the Marine Corps wore its own distinctive uniform. On January 24, 1859 the dress of the Corps was altered from that worn since 1840 to a more modern style with tunic and cap—a change which the Army had made eight years earlier. The new uniform is illustrated and described in great detail in *Regulations for the Uniform and Dress of The Marine Corps of the United States, October 1859.* One of the few photographs of Marines during the Civil War is found on page 68, Volume 6, of *Photographic History of the Civil War* which shows the dress uniform of the Corps. Company officers wore the same stiff cap as enlisted men, with gold pompom for full dress. Field officers in full dress wore the chapeau with a red feather plume. On top of the officer's undress cap appeared for the first time the 4-lobed knot, often referred to as the "clover leaf" or "French love knot," which is today one of the most distinctive features of the Marine officer's uniform. Officers wore the regular naval officers sword with black leather scabbard. The Marine Band, justly famous then as it is today, also wore a distinctive uniform.[49]

PAY AND ALLOWANCES

Annual pay and emoluments for officers of the Corps were as follows:

Colonel Commandant	$3,186.00
Colonel	2,529.00
Lieutenant Colonel	2,239.00
Staff Major	2,154.00
Major	2,010.00
Staff Captain	1,752.00
Captain	1,428.00
First Lieutenant	1,308.00
Second Lieutenant	1,248.00

All commissioned officers below the rank of major received $10.00 a month for "responsibility of" clothing, arms, and accouterments, when commanding guards of vessels in active service, with guard complements of at least 40 men, and at the shore naval stations. All commissioned officers were also entitled to one additional ration for every 5 years' service.[50]

EMPLOYMENT

The role of the Marine Corps during the war was similar to that of more recent campaigns. Marines were used on ships, at sea, in landing operations, and as infantry battalions with the Army in land operations. In addition to serving as gun crews on men-of-war, Marines on ship were organized as a unit under their own officers and would be placed on parts of the spar or upper deck as the ship's captain would direct. If an attempt by the enemy to board seemed imminent, the Marines would be located behind the Navy pikemen "or at any other place from which their fire on an assailing enemy may be most effective, and least dangerous to our own men." On such occasions the Marines were formed with loaded muskets and fixed bayonets.[51]

The following excerpts from letters show that such service was of real value, and also indicates that some people in authority were considering seriously a transfer of the Corps to the Army. On November 25, 1863, the Corps Commandant informed Rear Admiral Porter that the Corps could not increase the Marine complement at the Cairo station. He pointed out to Porter that the call for Marines to supply guards for vessels was so frequent that it kept their numbers very much reduced at all the different stations. He assured the Admiral that he would do his best to send out more Marines and added: "It is a pleasure to send Marines to an officer that appreciates them as I know you do."[52] Porter had earlier been apprehensive that the Navy would lose the Marine Corps altogether. On January 11, 1863, he had written to a Marine officer:[53] ". . . I would consider it a great calamity if the Marine Corps should be abolished and turned over to the Army. In its organization it should be naval altogether. A ship without Marines is no ship of war at all. The past efficiency of our Marine Corps fills one of the brightest pages in the history of our Country, and the man who proposes such a measure cannot know much about the service, or is demented. When they take away the Marines from the Navy they had better lay up all large vessels. I wish anyone could see the difference between the Marines out here and the people they call soldiers; they would not talk of abolishing the Corps. I can only say, God forbid that it should come to pass."

Although a small force numerically, the Marines were well armed and disciplined and saw action from the very beginning of hostilities. They were used in the abortive attempt to reinforce Fort Sumter in January 1861, and were participants in the successful reinforcing of Fort Pickens in April. On the night of the 20th of the same month, a body of Marines assisted in destroying the Gosport, Virginia, Navy Yard, to prevent it falling intact in the hands of the enemy.

In July 1861, a battalion of Marines under Major

John G. Reynolds was assigned to McDowell's army in the Bull Run campaign. This battalion numbered 12 officers and 336 men. In the battle of July 21st, the battalion broke line several times but reformed again until a general rout took place in which the Marines participated. Major Reynolds said in his report that the conduct of the Marines was such as to elicit the highest commendation. The battalion was composed entirely of recruits, who had been in the service only three weeks and had hardly learned their facings when committed to battle. The officers were in about the same position. Only 5 officers, 9 noncommissioned officers, and 2 musicians were experienced from length of service. The battalion lost: killed, 1 lieutenant and 9 privates; wounded, 1 brevet major, 1 lieutenant, 1 corporal, and 16 privates; missing, 16 privates; total casualties, 44.

Throughout the war the Marines participated in both sea and land operations, and even in the July 1863 draft riots in New York City. Attached to the various naval squadrons, Marines were active in the naval battles including Mobile Bay, where they conducted themselves with "the usual distinguished gallantry of their Corps."

The last major land action in which the Marines participated was at Fort Fisher in January 1865. 1400 Marines and sailors participated in the direct assault. It was a frontal attack against an enemy protected by the walls of the fort. The assault failed but at other positions the fighting was maintained by the Army. The ships assisted the assaulting troops, constantly hurling their shells into the traverses not occupied by Federal troops, but filled by the enemy; sometimes, however, failing to hit enemy troops and killing the Federal soldiers. Eventually the fort was taken after what Admiral Porter termed the most terrific struggle he ever saw. In the assault on the fort by the Marines and seamen, the assaulting party was divided into four lines, the first line being composed of Marines. There was no time for the Marines to organize their attacking unit due to the fact that they were thrown together in small detachments from the various ships without previous drill together. Despite this disadvantage, the attack of the Marines and seamen diverted the enemy's attention from the attack of the land forces. In the triumph for the Union forces, with which the fight ended, glory and honor were won equally by the Marines and seamen, who, in the face of a terrible fire, and against extremely heavy odds, bravely aided to make victory possible, and by the soldiers who succeeded in entering and seizing the enemy stronghold.[54]

The Marine Corps displayed exceptional gallantry in the war. The failure to permit it to be a truly significant force in terms of numbers was an error which the Corps regretted as much as anyone. Its small size and the "neither fish nor fowl" status it held with respect to the Navy and Army, certainly hampered the Corps' opportunities in the war. However, when opportunities on land and sea were present, the Corps seized on them eagerly and the members displayed combat spirit of a high order.

NOTES CHAPTER 17

1. *Photographic History*, Vol. 6, pp. 50-52.
2. See Naval Bibliography.
3. Boynton, Charles B., *The History of the Navy during the Rebellion*, Vol. 1, p. 20.
4. This worked very well.
5. The two made an ideal combination.
6. Hamersly, Thomas H. S., *General Register of the United States Navy and Marine Corps*, pp. 4-5.
7. *Reports* of Secretary of the Navy, July 4, 1861 to December 4, 1865, *Passim*.
8. Ammen, Daniel, *The Atlantic Coast*, 5-6.
9. *Reports* of Secretary of Navy, 1861-1865, *passim*.
10. *The Union Army*, Vol. 7 (*The Navy*), pp. 23-24.
11. United States War Department, "General Order No. 91," July 29, 1862, *General Orders for 1862*.
12. Public Act No. 50, July 16, 1862.
13. Pratt, Fletcher, *Civil War on Western Waters*, p. 10.
14. *Photographic History*, Vol. 6, p. 286.
15. Lonn, *Foreigners in the Union Army and Navy*, pp. 618-620.
16. *Regulations for the Navy of the United States* (1864), Article 23.
17. Lonn, *Foreigners in the Union Army and Navy*, p. 642.
18. Boynton, Vol. 1, pp. 28-29.
19. Haynes (2nd New Hampshire Infantry), p. 205.
20. Avery (4th Illinois Cavalry), pp. 51-52.
21. *Official Records*, Series 1, Vol. 24, pp. 167-168.
22. Fox, p. 537.
23. War Department, *Memorandum Relative to Probable Number and Ages of Federal Veterans*, pp. 3-4.
24. Fox, p. 537.
25. McBarron, Jr., H. Charles, "U. S. Navy, Service Dress 1862-1863," *Journal* of Society of Military Collectors and Historians, Vol. 5, No. 2, June 1953.
26. Harwood, A. A., *The Practice of Naval Summary Courts-Martial*.
27. Marine sentries were subject to orders which passed through the officer in command.
28. *Laws of the United States Navy* (1865), Articles 1-23.
29. It soon became more than a mere "paper" blockade.
30. Boynton, C. B., *The Navies of England, France, America, and Russia*, pp. 33-40.
31. *Photographic History*, Vol. 6, pp. 62, 64.
32. The material on the squadrons is from the *Reports* of the Secretary of the Navy, 1861-1865, *passim*.
33. *Photographic History*, Vol. 6, p. 94.
34. *Report* of Secretary of the Navy, December 2, 1864.
35. Lonn, *Foreigners in the Union Army and Navy*, p. 641.
36. *Photographic History*, Vol. 6, pp. 26-28.
37. See reports of Secretary of Navy.
38. *Photographic History*, Vol. 6, p. 282.

39. Apparently the Sanitary Commission didn't serve the Navy.

40. *Photographic History*, Vol. 6, pp. 283-284.

41. Selfridge, Jr., Thomas O., *Memoirs*, pp. 44-56.

42. Soley, J. R., *The Blockade and the Cruisers*, pp. 101-105.

43. McBarron, Jr., H. Charles, "U. S. Marine Corps 1859-1875," *Military Collector and Historian*, Vol. 1, No. 4, December 1949.

44. DeHart, William C., *Observations on Military Law and the Constitution and Practice of Courts Martial*, p. 8.

45. *Regulations for the Navy of the United States* (1865) Paragraphs 977-978, 980, 983, 985-986, 996-997, 1008.

46. *Register of the Commissioned and Warrant Officers of the Navy of the United States including Officers of the Marine Corps 1861*, pp. 76-79.

47. *Ibid.*, 1865, pp. 106-109.

48. Reports of the Secretary of the Navy for 1861-1865.

49. McBarron, *op. cit.*

50. *Register of the . . . Navy . . . Including Officers of the Marine Corps*, 1863.

51. *U. S. Navy Ordnance Instructions*, 1860, paragraph 71.

52. *Official Records* (Navy), Series 1, Vol. 25, p. 590.

53. *Ibid.*, Series 1, Vol. 24, p. 150.

54. Aldrich, M. Almy, *History of the United States Marine Corps*, pp. 129-192.

CHAPTER 18

The Home Front

ABRAHAM LINCOLN was at the head of a Nation torn asunder by armed rebellion, with dissension in his own Party and opposition from the Democrats. Foreign nations were neutral officially, but several of the more powerful were, if not actively hostile to the United States, at least sympathetic to the South. The population of the North was non-homogenous, many native-born were lukewarm or apathetic to the war aims, and in the field the Army of the Potomac was unsuccessful in nearly every major engagement up to that at Gettysburg. All of Lincoln's political acumen and skill, and great determination, were required to hold the leaky ship together and maintain it steadily on its course.

FOREIGNERS IN THE NORTH

In 1860 the foregn-born element in the population of the United States was very large in proportion to the native-born population. This situation was partly due to the extensive immigration from Ireland after the potato famines and from Europe, especially Germany, after the 1848 revolutions. By far the greater part of these foreigners had located in the Northern States. In 1860 there were only 233,650 foreign-born persons in those States which later made up the Confederacy, while there were 3,903,672 foreign-born in the strictly Northern States. Excluding the border States, this means that for every white immigrant in the slave States there were eight in the free States. These foreigners tended to congregate in certain sections of a city or to acquire neighboring farms in a rural locality to which the name "German settlement," "Swedish settlement," or "Swiss colony" became attached. Here the tongues of Europe were used almost exclusively, and newspapers in these languages also entered the homes.[1]

The loyalty of these foreign-born Americans who had settled in the North was to the Union. Although retaining a natural interest in the countries of their origin, they believed in democracy; they had left the Old World to seek a new lfe in America; and they were among the first to volunteer to fight for their newly-adopted country. International relations interested them at least as much as they did native-born Americans, but, with the exception of the Finian movement, the foreign-born kept no significant link with the past. The war itself absorbed their attention as it did most other Americans.

FOREIGN RELATIONS

No discussion of the North in wartime would be at all adequate without some comment on the relations of the United States with foreign powers. The most important of these powers was England, whose upper classes tended to favor the South but whose lower classes were largely in sympathy with the North. During the war the so-called Palmerston-Russell ministry was in power in England, and remained in firm control of the government until October 1865, following the collapse of the Confederacy. The three leading men in this ministry were: Lord Palmerston, Premier; Lord John Russell, Secretary for Foreign Affairs; and William Gladstone, Chancellor of the Exchequer. From the very beginning of the war, Palmerston was sympathetic to the Confederacy; his instincts as a member and representative of the British privileged classes were hostile to the more democratic North. After the defeat of the Federal forces at Second Bull Run, Lord Palmerston wrote to Russell suggesting whether the time had not come "for us to consider whether, in such a state of things, England and France might not address the contending parties and recommend an arrangement upon the basis of separation." This was received favorably by the Foreign Secretary (Russell) who replied that he was decidedly of the same mind as the Premier: "I agree with you that the time is come for offering mediation to the United States government, with a view to the recognition of the independence of the Confederates. I agree further that, in case of failure, we ought ourselves to recognize the Southern States as an independent State. For the purpose of taking so important a step, I think we must have a meeting of the Cabinet."

Palmerston acquiesced in this and told Russell that the plan was excellent and as to timing of the recognition, he suggested that . . . "if France and Russia agree—and France, we know, is quite ready and only waiting for our concurrence—events may be taking place which might render it desirable that the offer

303

should be made before the middle of October [1862]."

Meanwhile events were moving rapidly forward on the war front which tended to strengthen European belief in the inevitability of a Southern victory and the ultimate establishment of an independent Southern nation. Throughout the months of July and August 1862, the cause of the Union has sustained an almost unbroken series of reverses. The Confederacy had not only made good its right to be recognized as a belligerent, but it was so far, a victorious one. The Mexican expedition of the French Emperor having overrun that country, Napoleon III was urging the British Cabinet to take a aggressive attitude towards the United States which would inevitably have proved the first step toward an armed intervention, and the consequent breaking of the blockade. The great Lancashire cotton famine, necessarily incident to the blockade and confidently relied on throughout the Confederacy to compel intervention in its behalf, was at its height. If gold in New York stood at a premium of 50, cotton stood at 200 in Liverpool. The looms were idle, and a long and sustained wail of famine and pitiable agony went up from the most crowded districts of Great Britain. The crisis was at hand. For some strange reason the meeting of October 23rd was not held. Earlier in the same month (October 7) Gladstone delivered his famous Newcastle speech in which he declared that Jefferson Davis had made a nation and that the independence of the Confederacy and dissolution of the American Union was certain.[2]

It must be stressed that most enlightened and educated foreigners believed, until July 1863, that the Confederacy could not be defeated. Most of the aristocracy wanted to see the United States go to pieces. Through all the diplomatic maneuvers there ran the central question of recognition of the Confederacy and the related questions of mediation, intervention, and the demand for an armistice. Had the South won on any of these points, victory would have been well-nigh assured. However, Lee's repulse at Antietam and Lincoln's emancipation proclamation caused several responsible British leaders to urge that England continue to maintain strict neutrality. Although England did maintain neutralty for the entire war, some of her actions caused great irritation in the North, and aroused ill-will and hostility which prevented understanding between the involved parties for many years.

One of the first British actions to cause wide-spread resentment on the part of the North was the Queen's proclamation of neutrality, May 13, 1861. Despite the anger of the North, the recognition was proper under international law and was imitated in other countries. It did involve a recognition of Confederate belligerency. Lincoln realized full well the importance of the North's relations with England and sent there one of his best men to handle the various and delicate problems that were sure to arise. The character and ability of that Ambassador, Charles Francis Adams, were as valuable as Federal military victories in contributing to ultimate success in the war. This is especially noteworthy when we recall that Adams faced an extremely difficult task in London. Southerners were jubilant at the attitude of the English towards the United States. "America can expect no sympathy or assistance in Europe from any Government. They all hate us and fear us, even the most liberal."[3]

Although space does not permit an extensive discussion of the North's international relations with foreign countries, it should be pointed out that the ruling classes of England and France were little less than hostile to the Federal cause. But Russia was friendly. although not out of any sympathy for the Union. Russia's handling of the perennial Polish question had occasioned a joint remonstrance against Russia (April 1863) by England, France, and Austria. Anticipating the possibility of war, Russian statesmen did not want their ships in home waters where they might be trapped by the British Navy. A visit to some friendly neutral country was indicated. American ports, in addition to other advantages, offered a point of departure for operations against enemy commerce in case war should break out, as well was for possible attacks upon enemy colonies. Accordingly, Russian fleets visited our East and West coast in 1863 and returned to Russia in April 1864.

Relations with England and France were not so friendly. The French adopted a policy of "wait and see" and looked to see which way England would jump. Emperor Napoleon III was in sympathy with the South but there was a strong anti-slavery sentiment in France during the war. Though encouraging the South by glowing promises, France gave less aid and comfort to the Confederacy than did England. France did send troops to Mexico. It now appears that Confederate diplomats were ready to make an actual alliance with France. French troops eventually pulled out of Mexico after Napoleon saw the handwriting on the wall, especially after the arrival of substantial United States forces on the Rio Grande in 1865.

Although there were several crises in the relations between the North and Great Britain, bringing the two countries close to war on a few occasions, cooler heads on both sides prevailed and a war, which could only have been disastrous to the North, was averted. Public opinion was aroused both in England and in the North when the Federal warship San Jacinto stopped the British merchant ship Trent and took off two Confederate diplomats, Mason and Slidell. In England the people were "frantic with rage." War preparations were carried to the point of sending 8,000 troops and war material to Canada and Henry Adams wrote from England that war was imminent. Eventually the United States retreated from its strong stand and a friendly letter to Lord Lyons ended the matter. Much more serious than "The *Trent* affair" was the damage done by such English-built warships as the *Alabama,* not only to American merchant marine but also to British-American relations. The North was fearful that the Laird rams, built in England for the Confederacy, would "lay under contribution any of the loyal cities on the coast or could break the blockade at any point." But Union victories at Gettysburg and Vicksburg stalled a British parliamentary motion for recognition of the South. Adams finally succeeded in dissuading the British government from turning over the powerful rams to the Confederacy and the last real crisis was over. From the autumn of 1863 until the end of the war there was a notable relaxation of tension between the United States and England, and in foreign affairs generally. A great factor underlying this change was due, of course, to the improved military position of the North after July 1863. Closely tied in with the refusal of European countries to recognize the Confederacy was the issue of slavery. Lincoln's Emancipation Proclamation was a master stroke and its effect, as well as Gettysburg and Vicksburg, was very evident in the North's international relations from 1863 to 1865.[4]

POLITICS IN THE NORTH

On March 4, 1861, the first successful presidential candidate of the new Republican Party assumed office. Few Presidents have been less known on entering office than was the strange, new man from Illinois, whose homely appearance was ridiculed by his critics, who quickly spoke of him as the "baboon" or "gorilla." Lincoln, a minority President, was distrusted by the South and, quite generally, by the "first families" in the North. Many of the more experienced public leaders in the North believed that Seward would be the directing force in the new administration and that Lincoln would be President in name only.

Lincoln's real leadership began on that March 4, 1861, when he delivered the first of those incomparable state papers of his, which have become classics. For his cabinet, Lincoln chose rivals within his own party, nor did he exclude Republicans who had formerly been Democrats. The Democratic Party was a real force in Northern politics. It is essential to remember that the Democratic Party was so strong in the North in 1862, that it could have seized the Federal Congress had the South been restored in that year to the Union. However, as the war progressed this party of compromise lost its hold on the political machinery. Meanwhile, a limited group within the Republican Party, the Radical Republicans, seized the reins. This transformation of the Republican Party and its attainment of dominating power was one of the major political developments of American history. The most bitter and fateful wartime disputes were not between Republicans and Democrats, but rather the differences within the Republican Party, as a result of which Lincoln's moderating influence was defeated.[5]

One of the pernicious byproducts of the Radical Republican element was the Committee on the Conduct of the War. This Committee was made up of Radical Republicans, mainly lawyers, with practically no military experience of any kind. The most prominent and powerful member of the Committee was Ben Wade, who exercised a controlling influence. This committee conducted investigations of military affairs, mostly of those in the Eastern theater. The most systematic of these investigations related to the Army of the Potomac. With the exception of Grant, an inquiry was made into the administration of all the generals in command of that Army.[6] The son and biographer of Meade says: The Army of the Potomac unfortunately furnished, through its proximity to the Capital, a fine opportunuity to the committee for the exercise of its peculiar theories as to the proper mode of conducting a great war, and at the Committee's door can justly be laid the incentives to most of the intrigues, rivalries, and dissensions that marred the otherwise brilliant record of that army.[7]

The tangible evidences of the Committee's work are the eight large volumes of testimony, papers, and reports. Less tangible, but none the less significant, is the sorry record made by these radicals and other partisan Republicans who held back the promotion of Democrats in the Army whose brilliant combat records were ignored simply because of partisan politics. The most outstanding Democrats were Generals McClellan, Hancock, and Logan, but some lesser officers like General Gibbon and Colonel Cross of the 5th New Hampshire Infantry suffered to some extent as a result of political discrimination which had a definite effect on their military careers.

In 1862, the opposition to the Lincoln administration became intense. Military failure increased the impression of incompetence at Washington. The defeats on the Peninsula, at Second Bull Run, the inactivity after Antietam, the calls for immense numbers of additional volunteers, and the general lack of coordination in the direction of military operations —all these developments had their political repercussions as the months of failure and frustration passed on. In addition to the military reverses must be added the traitorous activities of many "Copperheads" in the North. For example, the Council Bluffs (Iowa) Copperheads gave General Dodge and his family trouble throughout the war. The so-called Peace Men in Iowa in 1862 were determined to have the soldiers back home by the end of the year. But the boys in the trenches before Vicksburg in 1863, at

Corinth and on other battlefields wrote home a series of resolutions, a paragraph of which was decidedly to the point:

"We regard the teachings of the so-called Peace Men of Iowa as not tending to stop the war, but only to prolong it; and that we will hold them responsible for the lives of all loyal soldiers sacrificed by reason of such disloyal conduct." [8]

Against a background of dissension and disloyalty Lincoln startled the Country with his "proclamations," the Proclamation of Emancipation, September 22, 1862, and that of September 24, 1862, by which a general suspension of the habeas corpus privilege was authorized and the military trials in suppressing disloyalty announced. By these measures the President severely offended the conservatives, both within his own party and among the Democrats. It would indeed be difficult to name *any* faction which in the fall of 1862, was pleased with Lincoln. The harrassed President, without winning the hearty support of the abolitionists, had alienated moderate Republicans and War Democrats. As for the opposition Democrats, Lincoln had put excellent ammunition into their hands. As a result, it was only by the slenderest margin that Lincoln's party retained control of Congress in the Congressional election of 1862. Five important states which Lincoln had carried in 1860 now sent Democratic delegations to the House of Representatives, while a sixth sent an evenly balanced delegation.

As 1863 dragged along, conditions became no better for the Republicans. The military reverses of Fredericksburg, December 13, 1862, and Chancellorsville, May 1-3, 1863, coupled with the March (1863) conscription law, increased the dissatisfaction of the public with the Administration. July brought good news from Gettysburg and Vicksburg, but it also brought the draft riot in New York City. The North felt a sense of frustration when Meade failed to follow up his victory at Gettysburg. And when, at the end of the year Lincoln launched his amnesty policy and his plan for easy restoration of the Southern States, he stirred up such bitter opposition in his own party that his enlightened program proved impossible of fulfillment.

Events of May and early June 1864, an important period because of the approach of Presidential nominations, were not such as to increase the prestige of the Administration. The terrific losses of the Wilderness and Cold Harbor had brought Grant no closer to Richmond than McClellan was in 1862. Despite some opposition, Lincoln received his party's nomination in the Republican convention in June. But as the weeks dragged on during the summer of 1864, with the frightful loss of life in Virginia, and the sense of discouragement culminating in the Early raid and the narrowly averted capture of Washington, the clouds of depression, defeatism, and political opposition thickened and darkened. The Democrats played a waiting game, postponing their convention to the end of August. Meanwhile, various forms of peace agitation and efforts toward negotiation were taking shape. Vallandigham, having escaped from the South and returned via Canada to Ohio, was attacking Lincoln and urging peace. This peace movement actually was the inevitable expression of a war-weary and heart-sick nation. Various peace missions to the South failed, however, because of Southern insistence on independence and there was no opportunity to consider such points as amnesty, State restoration, and compensation to slave owners, on which Lincoln stood ready to offer generous pledges.

In the midst of the uncertainty at home and the campaigning, seemingly without results, at the front, a movement within the Republican Party was under way to force Lincoln to withdraw in favor of a "more vigorous" candidate. To many, this seemed the only solution to the Party's and the Country's woes. Grant seemed to be accomplishing nothing and apparently Lee was as invincible as ever. Three years of war and hundreds of thousands of casualties had gone for naught; Sherman was apparently getting nowhere, and Early had almost captured Washington. There was talk of naming Grant, Butler, or Sherman for President, and Farragut as Vice President.

Meanwhile, the Democrats met in Chicago on August 29th. Their convention represented a union of War Democrats and Peace Democrats; and to please the War Democrats, McClellan was nominated for the Presidency, with his running mate being Pendleton of Ohio. The Peace Democrats were permitted to draft the party platform. With Vallandigham as their outstanding leader, they demanded in the platform a cessation of hostilities so that, at the earliest possible moment, peace could be restored on the basis of Federal Union of the States. This was not a peace-at-any-price declaration; it proclaimed reunion as the condition of peace. The objectives were good but the weakness lay in assuming that the South would give up the main purpose for which it was fighting and would agree to an abdication by the Southern Government.

McClellan, embarrassed by the peace plank, campaigned as a war leader, insisting on the preservation of the Union as the object of the war. On September 2nd important newspaper editors were seeking to promote the movement to oust Lincoln in favor of some other candidate. But suddenly all this changed. Atlanta fell, Sheridan was victorious in the Shenandoah Valley, while Farragut had earlier won a brilliant victory at Mobile Bay (August 5, 1864). The Republicans decided to stick with Lincoln. Lincoln won the election in what aproached a landslide although there were significant Democrat minorities in New York, Pennsylvania, Ohio, Indiana, and Illinois. The Democrats failed because they took up the cry of peace, denounced all others as abolitionists, organized secret societies, and wrote a platform to conciliate a minor group which had assumed leadership. Had McClellan been elected he probably would have held true to his known war record and his campaign declarations, and would, therefore have refused peace on terms involving a Union surrender.[9]

DISLOYALTY AND THE FIFTH COLUMN

Most Democrats in the North were loyal to the United States, although opposing the administration policies on partisan grounds. But from the very beginning of the war, the North was flooded with Southern correspondents, runners, smugglers, incendiaries, mail-carriers, and spies—both amateur and professional. Washington, itself a hotbed of treason, was set in an area of disloyalty that reached from lower Maryland to southern Delaware. Even after the blockade was established there was plenty of contraband trade by water, but before that it was carried on wholesale; and traffic by land routes was increasing. Conspiracies, such as a plan to seize the navy yard and arsenal at Philadelphia, flourished on every hand. The Confederate States had been preparing for war months before hostilities opened. The newly appointed superintendent of West Point, P. G. T. Beauregard of Louisiana, had resigned to become a Confederate general. Many experienced officers of the higher grades in both Army and Navy had gone South. Their resignations were accepted without question; some who remained at their posts were known to be unfaithful.

There was much treason in Washington, and even more suspicion of disloyalty. High-ranking officers as well as Senators, representatives, and other government officials went South to join the forces of their native states.

Baltimore, another center of disloyalty, showed its strong Southern sentiment as early as April 19, 1861, when mobs of its citizens attacked the 6th Massachusetts Infantry on its way to the defense of the Capital. These troops had to fight their way through a mob which hurled stones and fired guns at the Northern militiamen, who lost 4 killed and 31 wounded.[10]

Much of the disloyalty throughout the North during the Civil War was inextricably entangled with partisan politics. Democrats were strong in Ohio, Indiana, and Illinois; substantial elements of their populations were friendly to the South and bitterly regretted the war, which they blamed upon Republican politicians. In Indiana Lincoln's opponents obtained control of the legislature. Such things as aiding desertion, discouraging enlistment, resisting arrests, de-

THE BALTIMORE RIOTS

stroying enrollment lists, and circulating disloyal literature were among the charges against anti-administration elements. Even more serious accusations referred to such matters as recruiting for the enemy, distributing arms and ammunition so that "rebel" raids in the North might be assisted from the rear, plotting the release of Confederate prisoners, and planning the detachment of a "Northwest Confederacy" which by dividing the North was to promote Confederate success. Though some of the bolder schemes of the Knights (see below) slanted toward treason, the main agitation of such leaders as Vallandigham was carried on in mass meetings urging a negotiated peace. In addition to these Confederate sympathizers there were Confederate agents in the North who attempted to find unofficial means of obtaining funds. In Illinois the "Copperheads," to use the contemporary term of reproach for those Democrats who were outspoken in their opposition to the Lincoln Administration, controlled the legislature of 1863, and agitated for an armistice.

These anti-Republican groups formed secret organizations with the usual concomitants of mystery and rumor. Some Democrates in Ohio, Indiana, and Illinois established an organization known as the "Knights of the Golden Circle," then as the "Order of American Knights," and later as "Sons of Liberty." The secret societies were reported to comprise hundreds of thousands of members, in communication with the enemy. In their efforts to promote a Union defeat, they perpetrated outrages upon Unionists, stole military supplies, destroyed bridges, bushwacked, mapped fortifications, carried treasonable correspondence, and intimidated voters. On September 24, 1862, Lincoln issued a general proclamation providing that during the existing "insurrection" all persons discouraging enlistment, resisting the draft, or guilty of any disloyal practice, were subject to martial law and liable to trial by courts-martial or military commissions. Touching such persons, the suspension of the habeas corpus privilege was authorized. The number of arrests ran into the thousands. After a series of litigations on cases arising from arbitrary arrests, the Supreme Court was asked to review the sentence passed on Vallandigham by a military commission. On May 1, 1863, Vallandigham in a political speech in Mount Vernon, Ohio, had asserted that the war was not for the Union, but for the liberation of the blacks and the enslavement of the whites. He was placed under military arrest, tried by a military commission, and found guilty of declaring disloyal opinions with the object of weakening the Government. The Commission sentenced Vallandigham to close confinement during the war. Lincoln, however, banished him to the Confederacy, since he realized full well that there were thousands more like Vallandigham and that severe treatment would only help their cause. Val-

landigham escaped in 1864 and was active in the 1864 Presidential campaign but was not interfered with despite his vicious partisan activities.[11]

During the war the East experienced some violent incidents. Massachusetts, Connecticut, New York, New Jersey, and Pennsylvania were all reputed to have chapters of the Knights of the Golden Circle. A sore spot of opposition to the draft was Cass Township in Schuylkill County, Pennsylvania. In October 1862, more than 500 coal miners, mostly Irish-born members of the Molly Maguire organization, forcibly prevented a trainload of draftees from leaving Tremont and Pottsville. That area, plus certain parts of Philadelphia, Pittsburgh, and Berks and Cambria counties, remained troublesome throughout the war, and many draft evaders took refuge in the sparsely settled northwestern portion of the State. On July 13, 1863, the great New York draft riot began, provoking reverberations in Troy and other cities of that State, uneasiness in New Haven and Hartford, and a brief flare-up in the north end of Boston which the prompt and vigorous action of Governor Andrew, contrasting with the temporizing course of New York's Seymour, quickly put down. Confederate agents also gave the section some attention. On October 19, 1864, Confederates in civilian clothing, under Lieutenant Bennett H. Young, slipped over the Canadian border to St. Albans, Vermont, looted three banks of more than $200,000, killed one citizen, and then rushed back to Canada, where the courts found reasons to avoid acting against them. Somewhat later the Confederate guerrilla John Yates Beall, who had been unsuccessful in an attempt to surprise the U. S. revenue cutter *Michigan* on Lake Erie in order to use it as a means of setting free the Confederate prisoners at Johnson's Island, was apprehended in a train-wrecking venture near Niagra Falls and executed. And on November 25th a bizarre effort was made to set on fire a number of hotels in New York City, including the Astor, St. Nicholas, Metropolitan, and Fifth Avenue, plus, of all things, Barnum's Museum. One participant, Robert Kennedy, was captured and hanged after confessing his part in the scheme.

The Peace Democrats in the East never succeeded in capturing the party machinery as they did in the Middle West. Men like Governors Seymour of New York and Joel Parker of New Jersey bitterly denounced arbitrary arrests and suppression of disloyal newspapers without being willing to admit the circumstances that provoked them or attempting to cooperate with the Federal authorities in working out a more discriminating system. Such men attacked the Emancipation Proclamation as though it represented the primary goal of the Administration rather than recognizing the truth that it had been adopted as an essential weapon for preserving the Union, and they indirectly fostered resistance to conscription by constantly endeavoring to cast doubts on its legality. They did not oppose the war; they merely indulged themselves in a fussy constitutionalism and in irresponsible criticism, with the determined purpose of making political capital. That such actions might contribute to the dissolution of the Union was to them, apparently, a regrettable but unavoidable hazard.[12]

DRAFT RIOTS OF 1863

On July 11, 1863 the draft began in New York City. It had commenced a few days earlier in Rhode Island and Massachusetts. The draft act itself had been approved on March 3, 1863. According to Governor Seymour, the rioting which broke out in New York City on July 13, 1863, was caused by the way the draft was made, that is, the Governor received no notice as to the exact date the draft would commence. However General Fry, Provost Marshal General of the Army, declared that the real cause of the riot was due primarily to the fact that: "In a community where a considerable political element was active in opposition to the war the war was conducted, if not to the war itself, and where there was a strong opinion adverse to the principles of compulsory service, certain lawless men preferred fighting the government at home, when it made the issue of *forcing* them by lot to fight its enemies in the field."[13]

The riot in New York did not occur without previous warning. There were several indications in May and June that the people were dissatisfied with the prospects of a Federal draft. While the enrollment was in progress some of the officers had met with opposition, stubbornness, and bad language. One officer was attacked and nearly killed. The drafting began in the ninth district in New York City on Saturday, July 11, 1863, and no trouble was encountered. About 1300 names were drawn that day. The publication of these names in the Sunday morning papers revealed to the people the great number of laboring men drafted in proportion to the men of more ample means. At once some of the bolder spirits determined to prevent the official notification to the draftees and to stop further drafting. This determination was, during the day, disseminated throughout the Irish wards. On Monday morning isolated groups visited the factories and other places where men were working, and induced the laborers to lay down their tools and join in the fight. Drafting in the district began but after about 75 or 100 names had been drawn, a member of the mob fired a pistol and a shower of brickbats through the windows broke up the proceedings. The officers were routed and the building set on fire. Firemen were prevented from extinguishing the flames and a detachment of the Invalid Corps, which was rushed up, was speedily disarmed and routed. Police were equally ineffectual to deter a rapidly increasing mob, which soon turned its attention to more profitable and enjoyable pursuits.

The riot soon took on the form of wholesale pillage, particularly of saloons, stores stocked with drygoods, jewelry, and other valuables, and hardware stores where guns might be obtained. By the middle of the afternoon a large part of the mob was hilariously drunk. At five o'clock the prejudice against Negroes was combined with desire for plunder, in the sacking of a Negro orphan asylum. Far into the night conflagration and occasional murder of Negroes or suspected abolitionists and police officers continued. Military personnel were treated no better. The riot continued for several days without abatement. Battle-tested regiments from the Army of the Potomac arrived, which restored quiet by Thursday night, July 16th. It was the presence of several regiments in the city in the following month which permitted the draft to be made without further bloodshed. Hundreds of people were killed in the July 1863 riots in New York City, while the fire loss reached $1,500,000.

There were minor riots in Troy, New York, and in Boston, Massachusetts, but the presence of troops kept outrages and demonstrations at a minimum. Boston was better supplied with militia than New York City since she was farther from Lee's army, and was therefore able to call out several units at once. When a crowd of 500 to 1000 people attacked the Cooper Street Armory, the soldiers fired canister into the crowd and followed it up with a bayonet charge. Other attacks by mobs were met so efficiently by police and militia that the rioters lost all courage and dispersed quietly. Although there was resistance to the draft in 1864, this resistance was in scattered areas and was much easier to handle than the New York City riot.[14]

CIVIL LIBERTIES

In time of National emergency certain civil liberties must and do take second place to the paramount issue at stake, that of the Nation's survival. Naturally, this was true for the North when war powers and extra-legal procedures were instituted and maintained. The lines between State and Federal functions; between executive, legislative, and judicial authority; and between civil and military spheres were either blurred or disappeared "for the duration." Probably no President in our history carried the Presidential power, independently of Congress, as far as Abraham Lincoln did. He began his administration by virtually declaring the existence of a state of war all by himself (April 15, 1861), while Congress did nothing but acquiesce in his action months later. By issuing his proclamation Lincoln committed the Government to acknowledgment of the status of the war with the South. The Federal Government, by Lincoln's proclamation, declined to regard the struggle as analogous to a regular war between nations. Space does not permit a detailed discussion of the technicalities involved in this attitude by the Government, but it should be pointed out that such an attitude caused complications involving the North's relations with foreign powers, especially with regard to enforcement of the blockade of the Southern coasts. The United States technically held the Southerners' guilty of rebelling against the Government to which, from the Union standpoint, they owed allegiance. The Lincoln administration spoke of the Southern movement as an "insurrection," a "rebellion," or a "private combination of persons." The Federal Government did not carry this insurrectionary theory so far as to be inhumane; it yielded to the extent that it treated captured enemy personnel as prisoners of war; crews of Confederate privateers were treated as naval prisoners, not as pirates; and Southern citizens supporting the Confederacy were not punished for treason. The Supreme Court went along with this interesting mixture of theory and practice, and the Court's decisions were fitted into a convenient pattern which one historian[15] labels the double-status theory—i.e. that the United States "sustained toward the enemy the double character of a belligerent and a sovereign, and had the rights of both."

In the treatment of "disloyal" practices the Government under Lincoln carried its authority far beyond the normal restraints of civil justice. The North employed the doctrine of "military necessity." Lincoln suspended the habeas corpus privilege and resorted to summary arrest by executive authority which was assumed in disregard of both the judiciary and Congress. On September 24, 1862, despite previous action seeking to prevent arbitrary arrests from getting out of hand, Lincoln issued a general proclamation providing that during the existing "insurrection" all persons discouraging enlistment, resisting the draft, or guilty of any disloyal practice, were subject to martial law and liable to trial by courts-martial or military commissions. The number of these arrests ran into the thousands.[16]

On legal and constitutional points the President's acts were defended in the official opinion of his Attorney General. According to the arguments presented, there was no violation of the Constitution, since that instrument permits suspension of the habeas corpus privilege when the public safety requires it during a rebellion, and does not specify which branch of the Government is to exercise the suspending power.

Despite these reductions in the power and authority of the peacetime governmental apparati—both national and local—Lincoln's practice fell short of dictatorship as the word has come to be understood at the present time. Lincoln did not think of suppressing his legislature and ruling without it; he did not "pack" his Congress, nor eject the opposition. It is true that the arbitrary arrests were made, in many cases, in direct contravention of the rights guaranteed all Americans by the Constitution. On the other hand, Lincoln never considered having a drastic military regime. The harshness of war regulations was often tempered by leniency. Lincoln was generous in releasing political prisoners, whom he refused to treat as war criminals. In the suppression of anti-governmental activity the Government under Lincoln was milder than that of Woodrow Wilson. As for dictatorships, the pattern simply does not fit the Lincoln government.

PROPAGANDA

Any adequate appreciation of the North's use of propaganda in the war can best be acquired by reading the newspapers of the period, the printed version of speeches and sermons delivered, and the surprisingly large number of pamphlets which were printed for propaganda purposes. It is only possible here to sketch briefly some of the main themes which were used to influence national and international opinion. In comparison with the professional propagandists of the last half century, the writers of 1861-1865 appear naive and clumsy in their efforts to mould opinion for their cause. And it should be pointed out, much of the propaganda was by individuals and comparatively small independent groups rather than by Government supported and financed organizations such as functioned in 1914-1918 and 1939-1945. Also, some of the propaganda themes grew out of an actual ignorance of the real situations. For example, a common theme was that the enemy won through superior numbers. A widely read description of the Battle of Bull Run, written the day after the battle, by a correspondent of the New York *Times*, gives the number of Confederates engaged as "at least 60,000" as opposed to 26,000 Federals.[17] The correspondent is approximately correct with respect to the latter figure but has doubled the size of the enemy's forces. Both the press and the pulpit quoted "actual" cases of atrocities committed by the enemy, but the most successful propaganda appears to have been the effect on public opinion engendered by articles and photographs concerning the enemy's treatment of Federal prisoners of war.

Opinion during the war was shaped both by voluntary propagandist groups and by the inevitable product of war psychology. As far as official propaganda in the North is concerned, the only concerted and sustained effort was made for the purpose of influencing foreign sentiment. In 1861 the Federal Government sent a propaganda commission to Europe in the attempt to influence England and France by furnishing to the news agencies and the clerics, and through them the populace, a clear concept of the causes of the Civil War. This mission consisted of Archbishop Hughes of the Roman Catholic Church, Bishop McIlvaine of the Protestant Episcopal Church, and Thurlow Weed. The Archbishop was to win the support of the Papacy, of Napoleon, and of other Catholic rulers; McIlvaine was to make his appeal to the English clergy; and Weed was to labor with journalists and public leaders in order to counteract Confederate journalistic enterprise abroad. Other emissaries followed from time to time during the war, but none except Weed appears to have been very successful.[18]

At home, much of the oral propaganda was expressed in the pulpit, at Union mass meetings, and, of course, at town meetings called for the purpose of raising volunteers. Propaganda clubs sprang into existence, of which the best known was the Union League. The League began in Philadelphia in 1862, and spread to New York and Boston. Soon it appeared in Baltimore, Washington, and San Francisco. Within a year it had spread over 18 Northern States and even among unionists in the South. Primarily the League was a rallying point for citizens' support of the Union cause. It distributed war literature, raised money for soldier relief, helped recruit white and Negro troops, and took the lead in voluntary efforts during some emergencies. The Union League also participated in pro-Administration politics. Propaganda activity in the North appeared also in the work of the Loyal Publication Society of New York and of a similar society in New England. In a way, also, the Sanitary Fairs, bond-selling campaigns, and recruiting drives served as media for propaganda.

In the recruiting drives the call of Country was mingled with various other appeals, such as appeals to race and the advantages of enlisting in a local area which was generous in its bounties for enlistment.

Lincoln's role in promoting morale was not an organized "White House publicity." His manner of speaking to the public was by a well-timed letter to an individual, delegation, or group, which was in reality intended for the Nation's ear. Although his utterings were never bloodthirsty, Lincoln made it very clear that he intended that the United States would win the war and destroy Southern resistance to the Federal Government. Men and women both in the United States and abroad have come to regard Lincoln's inaugural speeches, his address at Gettysburg and his letter to Mrs. Bixby as classics in language and in depth of understanding and vision. The North was very fortunate to have Lincoln as its main spokesman; the South had no spokesman who even approached him in effectiveness or breadth of vision.

THE PRESS

It was important that the people at home receive news of the armies that their enthusiasm might be kept high, and it was equally important that the soldiers should also get the news. The soldiers wanted to know what the people at home thought of them, how the situation of the armies was being described, and what was being written about the battles. The Northern newspapers under the inspiration of professional rivalry kept both the North and South remarkably well informed of everything going on within the Union lines and not infrequently prepared the Confederate generals for the next move of the Federal Army.

It is doubtful whether any war has ever been as fully "covered" as the Civil War. The leading New York dailies spent huge sums on their "war departments"—half a million being spent by the *Herald* alone—and an army of "specials" was placed in the field whose stories form a notable record of adventure and activity. The war for the Union was the heyday of the special reporter. Only occasionally were journalists excluded from military areas; ordinarily they were made welcome and given special privileges. Government passes were extended to them. They had the use of Government horses and wagons; they were given transportation with baggage on Government steamers and military trains. Enjoying the confidence of admirals and generals, they were seldom at a loss to obtain the information they were being well paid to get. They heard an immense deal of officers' talk and could pick up snatches of military intelligence. The censoring function was never carried very far by the Federal Government. For a time this function was exercised by the State Department; then it was transferred to the War Department, but at no time did it amount to more than a rather ineffective effort to prevent leakage of official information which the Government wished to keep secret and the supervision of telegraphic communication which was under Government control.[19]

Freedom of the press was not extinguished under Lincoln. It is true that a few newspapers were suppressed. The Chicago *Times*, an anti-Lincoln paper, was suspended by military order of General Burnside (June 1863) because of "disloyal and incendiary sentiments," but the President promptly revoked the order. Some other papers were suspended or suppressed. However, the Government as a general rule refrained from control of news, whether good or bad. Scores of newspapers throughout the Country, including some that were very prominent, continually published abusive articles during the Lincoln administration without encountering the suppressing hand of government. Lincoln expressed his attitude in a letter to General Schofield as follows: "You will only arrest individuals and suppress assemblies or newspapers when they may be working palpable injury to the military in your charge, and in no other case will you interfere with the expression of opinion in any form or allow it to be interfered with violently by others."[20]

With the exception of the Democratic press, Republican newspapers were of three types so far as their attitude towards Lincoln was concerned: (1) Administration journals which supported the Presi-

THE PRESS
Headquarters of the New York *Herald* in the field.

dent (e.g. the Washington *Chronicle,* Philadelphia *Inquirer);* (2) conservative papers which on the whole, supported the war by the North but did not hesitate to condemn certain acts or methods of the President (e.g. the New York *Times,* the Cincinnati *Commercial);* radical journals which not only censured the President for particular acts but also opposed his general war policy (e.g. the New York *Tribune,* the New York *Evening Post,* the Chicago *Tribune.*)

From the standpoint of the Government and the generals most of the newspapers' activity was highly dangerous to the Country's welfare. Not only was valuable information constantly exposed, but discontent in the Army resulted from an airing of petty complaints, the names of generals and lesser officers were paraded to gratify personal ambition, sensational newswriting was unduly stimulated, and the very elements out of which war is engendered—hatred and misunderstanding—were intensified. Good "copy" for a day's reading being the object, truth and accuracy became altogether secondary considerations. The average reporter, under the pressure of a constant demand for news, would just as soon chat with a disgruntled subordinate officer and print his story as to search for reliable information from a reliable source. Besides, the safe source would not talk. As the "specials" were in nearly ever case civilians without military expertness, they often incorrectly interpreted what they saw, and of course, erred grievously when they presumed to foretell coming movements.

In the case of local papers with limited constituencies there was the necessity of playing up the exploits of favorite sons. Their little heroes became big fools, as Sherman observed, when these accounts were copied in the metropolitan dailies. No sooner was a battle fought than every colonel and captain in it became illustrious. For a month after Shiloh the average newspaper reader in Illinois and Missouri would have supposed that McClernand's and Lew Wallace's achievements on that field were far superior to Sherman's, whereas in reality their parts were indeed quite subordinate. It was the hard-headed and efficient general who was most likely to be played down, while those who "achieved dazzling glory" were almost always of second-rate quality. Because the laconic Grant would not disclose his plans to visitors, the newspapers denounced him as idle, intemperate, and incompetent, such men as Fremont and McClernand being designated as suitable successors. Sherman had only disdain for the "cheap flattery of the press." There was, however, during the war no real suppression of opinion.[21]

One of the main difficulties was that the generals did not quite know how to deal with newspaper men. There was nothing in Scott's *Tactics* or Hardee's *Tactics* or Jomini's *Art of War* about newspaper correspondents. No military authority had yet determined how much, if anything, of an army's plans should be confided to journalists. So the generals were friendly or aloof, according to temperament. Their trust in the newsmen varied. A few told reporters all they knew; most were pleasantly vague.[22] When a general attempted to keep a reporter out of camp the attempt would often backfire. G. W. Smalley of the New York *Tribune* was ordered to leave the Federal lines; he proceeded to get an appointment as volunteer aide on General Sedgwick's staff and was even entitled to wear a sash and side arms.[23] General Jacob D. Cox has left us an illuminating picture of the problems which confronted commanding officers early in the war. Cox relates that:

We were joined at Charleston by two men representing influential Eastern journals—were told that the quartermaster would furnish them with a tent and transportation but that their dispatches should be subject to inspection by one of the staff to protect us from the publication of facts which might aid the enemy. This seemed unsatisfactory . . . they intimated that they expected to be taken into my mess and to be announced as volunteer aides with military rank. They were told that military position or rank could only be given by authority much higher than mine, and that they could be more honestly independent if free from personal obligation and from temptation to repay favors with flattery . . . [they replied to this officer with]: "Very well; General Cox thinks he can get along without us, and we will show him. We will write him down."

They left the camp the same evening, and wrote letters to their papers describing the army as demoralized, drunken and without discipline, in a state of insubordination, and the commander as totally incompetent. The relations of newspaper correspondents to general officers of the Army became one of the crying scandals and notorious causes of intrigue and demoralization.[24]

Since there were no regulations governing newspapermen in the early weeks of the war, their conduct was governed by the military commanders and the discretion of the reporters themselves. As early as July 12, 1861, the interested parties agreed:

That all members of the Press may report by telegraph the progress of all battles occurring and shall be afforded official help for that purpose. That the previous order, requiring every message to be submitted to the inspection of Grant's staff at Army Headquarters is revoked. The newspapermen agreed: That no reports of arrivals, departures, or other movements of troops shall be forwarded by telegraph, nor any statistics of army strengths or munitions; That no mutinies or riots among the soldiery be sent by telegraph. Nor any predictions of movements to ensue. That Mr. Burns of the telegraph office shall be stationed as the censor to maintain observance of the rules.[25]

Shortly thereafter, the rules were tightened and more clearly laid down in War Department *General Order No. 67*, (August 26, 1861) which provided that

By the 57th article of the act of Congress entitled An Act For Establishing Rules and Articles For The Government Of The Armies Of The United States, approved April 10, 1806,

"Holding correspondence with or giving intelligence to the enemy, either directly or indirectly," is made punishable by death, or such other punishment as shall be ordered by the sentence of a court-martial. Public safety requires strict enforcement of this article. It is therefore ordered that all correspondence and communication, verbally or by writing, printing, or telegraphing, respecting operations of the Army or military movements on land or water, or respecting the troops, camps, arsenals, entrenchments, or military affairs, within the several military districts, by which intelligence shall be, directly or indirectly, given to the enemy, without the authority and sanction of the General in command, be and the same are absolutely prohibited, and from and after the date of this order persons violating the same will be proceeded against under the 57th Article of War.

Newspaper men were generally careful in their association with leaders in Lincoln's military family. Most Washington newspapermen had access to Secretary of War Cameron, although the New York *Tribune* enjoyed his special favor. When Stanton took over the position of Secretary of War, his favorite came to be the New York *Herald*. Later, however, Stanton kept reporters out of the War Department and took none into his confidence. If Cameron had been as scrupulously careful, Sherman's dislike for the press might not have been so intense. Sherman, on one occasion, was discussing military matters with Cameron, and indicated that it would be better not to continue the discussions until all strangers had left the room. Cameron claimed that everyone present was his friend, and told Sherman he could speak his mind freely. However, he neglected to tell Sherman that two newspapermen

SUPPORT FROM THE HOME FRONT

Exterior of the New York Metropolitan Fair, which opened April 10, 1864. Similar fairs were held in other large cities, being heavily attended by throngs curious to see the exhibits of war equipment and relics. By means of these fairs the Sanitary Commission raised $2,-738,868 for soldier relief.

were present, representing the New York *Tribune* and the *Philadelphia Press*. Sherman proceeded to give an earnest recitation of the military situation in Kentucky, pointing out that 200,000 men would be needed for an offensive to win the whole central south area for the Union. Cameron threw up his hands and said, "Great God! Where are they to come from?" In a short time newspapers were telling their readers that "the painful intelligence reaches us, in such form that we are not at liberty to disclose it, that General William T. Sherman is insane."[26]

But Sherman was not the only victim of reporters' distortion of the truth. Many of the prominent generals received similar treatment. In 1862, newspapermen became increasingly critical of Halleck, even contrasting "Old Brains" in his slow, mincing campaign (Corinth) with Grant's aggressive moves against the enemy. This was too much for Halleck, who banished all newspaper correspondents from the army. General Meade meted out the same punishment to a reporter who was critical of Meade's suggestion to retreat after the second day's battle in the Wilderness. On this occasion Meade expelled the reporter from the lines, but before leaving the reporter had to wear placards on his chest and back with printing saying "Libeller of the Press." He was then paraded past Meade's old division, drawn up in long lines, while a band played the "Rogue's March." Meade wrote his wife that "the sentence was duly executed, much to the delight of the whole army, for the race of the newspaper correspondents is universally despised by the soldiers."[27] When General Hunter was removed from command during the siege of Charleston he attributed his removal to Horace Greeley. Hunter wrote Greeley a stinging letter mentioning, among other things, the *Tribune's* persistent war cry of "On to Richmond," in which movement, "you shed much ink and other men some blood."[28]

Two other victims of Greeley's paper were *Tribune* correspondents Albert D. Richardson and Junius Henri Browne, who were captured in the Vicksburg campaign and not released for a year and a half, but held in enemy prison camps. These reporters were victims of Confederate spite against Greeley and his newspaper.

There was several hundred newspapermen who covered the war. It is quite probable that William Swinton was the most serious and scholarly. However, it was not the *Times*, but the *Herald* which was the liveliest newspaper and the one which earned more money than any other in America.[29] In January 1863, the *Herald* was being sold at 10¢ each in the Army camps, and later on even followed the soldiers on raids into enemy-held territory. One man thought the *Herald* sold ten to one over any other paper which was sold to the soldiers.[30] A soldier in another unit considered the Philadelphia *Inquirer* to be the soldiers' favorite, though many read the *Tribune, Herald,* while Frank Leslie's and Harper's illustrated weeklies found ready sale among the soldiers if they had money to buy them; and if they did not have money, generally some soldier would steal one, which was passed around until all had seen it.[31] Newspapers were eagerly looked for and quickly distributed through the camp of the 1st Massachusetts Cavalry by boys mounted on horses. The Philadelphia *Inquirer* was the newspaper which brought the latest news, and was most sought after, since it arrived each afternoon of the day of publication.[32]

THE PULPIT

Anti-slavery agitation in the North prior to the war was more of an evangelism rather than a movement backed by any individual sect. Many Northern religious writers even defended slavery. The denominations most active in the abolition movement were the Quakers, Baptists, and Methodists. In 1844 both the Methodists and Baptists split into northern and southern groups over the question of slavery. As a general rule, churches in the South were powerful supporters of slavery; but in the North, such churches as the Presbyterian and Congregational were either divided on the question or lukewarm. Nevertheless, many believed that the pulpit could be "justly held to have done much towards precipitating the Rebellion, as well as aiding it during the whole course of its progress . . . Politicians, secular and religious journals, pamphleteers, men in all classes of society, freely lay the blame of this Rebellion, in a great measure, or wholly, at the door of the Church; charging the ministry, more especially, with having caused it."[33] Contemporary writers made frequent reference to the role of the pulpit in the mass meetings to raise recruits and, of course, quoted at length the obituary sermons delivered when local sons had fallen in battle.

Members of the various sects were very active and helpful while serving with the Sanitary and Christian Commissions, and the Young Men's Christian Association. Some individuals also performed useful service while serving as chaplains in the armed forces. But as indicated earlier in this book, many chaplains were of no use at all, and some were a disgrace to their calling. It is probable that at least half of the chaplains never served out their term of service; regimental histories are replete with examples of chaplains who either served a short period before resigning, or were not with their units for weeks at a time. The total number of chaplains is not available, but possibly the figures for Connecticut would be a fair average for the other States. Of 49 chaplains sent out from Connecticut: 12 were mustered out of the service by expiration of term; 9 were honorably discharged; 27 resigned; 1 died; 2 were wounded; and 1 was captured by the enemy.[34]

The chaplain was not accustomed to life among people the majority of whom were strangers to him, and probably not inclined to his way of life or mode of thinking. The rough camp life and exposure to storms and hunger for which his sheltered life had not prepared him. His delicate constitution, housed so long, fed on the best prepared food regularly, soon broke down. "After the first few months, sick at heart because he could not hold his services regularly, and sick in body because of exposure, he resigned and returned to post up his former flock on the terrible hardships of army life." [35]

However, chaplains are of especial significance to a study of the North in war time. They were often the most literate men in their units and as such wrote letters home for the soldiers and also for publication in local newspapers. In addition, many of them wrote the histories of their respective regiments and some of these histories began to appear even before the war ended.

The Church in the North considered the South to be engaged in a rebellion against lawful Government, gotten up by "disappointed demagogues." The Federal Government, "in the exercise of its constitutional rights, and in the discharge of its God-given duty, sustained by the people, is engaged in putting down this rebellion by Heaven's ordained means, the sword." [36] Northern religious leaders were active for the Union cause both at home and abroad. Henry Ward Beecher spoke to thousands in England; men like Phillips Brooks worked both in his own church and among the troops. In the hospitals able lecturers and the best preachers contributed to the welfare of the men. At Chestnut Hill in Philadelphia, Phillips

Brooks preached in December 1864. "It was hardly a Trinity Church audience, but he spoke to more than a thousand men from about every State in the Union, and every one of them had a rebel shot-mark on him." [37] To a lesser degree, such a scene was repeated in many varied surroundings throughout the North from 1861 to 1865.

NON-MILITARY EVENTS—1861-1865

Because of the military drain upon manpower and the stimulation of industry, a condition of labor shortage appeared which was partially met by immigration. In the early part of the war there was a marked decline in immigration as compared with the 1850's. On July 4, 1864, Congress passed a law providing for the importation of contract-labor. Immigrants entered the country during the war years as follows:

1861	142,000
1862	72,000
1863	132,000
1864	191,000
1865	180,000

It is interesting to note that in the year following the war (i.e. 1866), the figure was 332,000. Many aliens promptly advanced on the road to citizenship or entered the service as aliens. However, those foreigners who had not voted nor declared their intention of becoming citizens were exempt from military duty. Many of these immigrants took advantage of the Homestead Act of May 20, 1862, which gave a quarter section of unoccupied land to homesteaders on payment of nominal fees after five years of actual residence. During the year ending June 1864, 1,261,-

WAR SOUVENIRS
Part of the exhibit at the Metropolitan Fair.

000 acres were taken under the operation of the act. The Union Pacific Railroad Company, a Federal corporation, established by statutes of July 1, 1862, and July 2, 1864, became truly significant in the western settlements after the war, although a little progress was made during the war period.[38] Such projects as the Atlantic cable, begun before the war, had to wait until the fighting was over before they could be completed. The great industrial and technological advances of the 1850's were only slowed down by the war; in fact, after 1862, war prosperity began to make thousands of people richer. Railroad earnings were enormously increased. Money changers and war profiteers were growing wealthy.

Among the wartime measures of permanent importance was the Act of 1862 for the establishment of "agricultural and mechanical colleges" in the States through the aid of Federal land grants. The act embodying this scheme for the advancement of higher education was called the Morrill land grant act, after Justin S. Morrill of Vermont, who fostered the movement in Congress.

War Financing

In financing the war, the Federal Government found itself involved in four major problems: loans, taxes, the paper money problem, and the creation of a national banking system. Speaking broadly, the Government financed itself during the war chiefly by loans and paper money; the sums collected in taxes were relatively small. The Government issued immense amounts of paper money and a considerable volume of short-term loans at high interest. The total amount received from loans, including treasury notes, during the war (i.e. for the four fiscal years 1862-1865 inclusive) was 2,621 million dollars as compared to 667 million received from taxes. When the Government encountered serious difficulty in selling bonds, it made the powerful firm of Jay Cooke and Company the sole subscription agent for the distribution of the bonds of the United States. Cooke thus came to be known as the "financier of the Civil War." Another source of revenue was the income tax law of August 5, 1861. This was the first income tax ever levied by the United States Government. But the most important of the wartime taxes were the various internal revenue duties. The internal revenue law of July 1, 1862, has been described as an attempt to tax everything; spirituous and malt liquors and tobacco were relied upon for a very large share of revenue, but almost everything was included in this taxation.

WEAPONS DISPLAY AT
SANITARY FAIR

In addition to taxes and loans the Government had recourse to large amounts of paper money. The legal tender act of February 25, 1862, authorized the issue of $150,000,000 of non-interest bearing "United States notes," soon to be dubbed "greenbacks." Congress was soon asked for more paper money. Subsequent increases were approved, so that by the close of the war a total of $450,000,000 of legal tender notes had been authorized. At the time of the war, the United States lacked a uniform system of banking and bank-note currency, and one of the important matters of war finance was the creation of such a system. The law of June 3, 1864, is the legislative basis of the national banking system as it emerged from the war.[39]

FREEING THE SLAVES

Certainly one of the most far-reaching events of the Lincoln Administration was the Emancipation Proclamation and the subsequent legislation, including the act of March 3, 1865, which created the Freedmen's Bureau. Although both Lincoln (1861 inaugural speech) and Congress (Crittenden resolution, July 22, 1861) disclaimed fighting to free the slaves, the facts of war soon forced the Federal Government to alter its policy. One of these facts of war was the question of what to do with fugitive slaves who made their way to Federal lines. General B. F. Butler, a lawyer in civilian life, while in command at Fort Monroe, refused to give up Negro slaves, declaring that he needed workmen, that the slaves were being employed in the erection of enemy batteries, and that the fugitive slave act of the United States did not affect a foreign country, which Virginia claimed to be. While military commanders like Fremont and Hunter attempted to free slaves in the districts under their command, Lincoln reserved for himself the emancipation of slaves. It should be emphasized that Lincoln's fundamental and permanent solution of slavery was in terms of "compensated emancipation." Although the District of Columbia adopted the principle of compensated emancipation, Lincoln's scheme of State emancipation with Federal compensation failed. But Lincoln realized that the international aspects of slavery policy were of pressing importance, and that a proclamation of emancipation was absolutely essential for the salvation of the Union. On September 22, 1862, after Lee had been turned back at Antietam, Lincoln issued the preliminary proclamation. On January 1, 1863, the definitive proclamation was issued, its chief provision being that in regions then designated as "in rebellion" (with some exceptions) all slaves were declared free. It is important to note that Lincoln issued the proclamation as commander-in-chief of the Army and Navy and characterized it as an act warranted by the Constitution *upon military necessity.* Reaction in the North varied from approval to doubt and resentment. A natural accompaniment of emancipation was the use of colored men as Federal soldiers. Shortly before the end of the war, a Federal institution known as the Freedmen's Bureau was established to regulate and rehabilitate the Negroes in the Southern States. Most of the activities of the Bureau took place during the reconstruction period, but the Bureau itself was a wartime measure.

CONFEDERATE PRISONS IN THE NORTH

With the exception of the few areas in the North where fighting occurred, as the Antietam and Gettysburg, few Northern civilians ever saw the enemy at all. The exception involved those citizens who lived in the neighborhood of Federal prisons where enemy prisoners of war were kept. Occasionally, too, troop trains with Confederate prisoners would be seen enroute to these prisons. There was a total of 24 military prisons, of which the more important were Point Lookout, Md.; Camp Morton, Indianapolis; Camp Chase and Johnson's Island, Ohio; Camp Alton and Camp Douglass, Illinois; Old Capitol Prison, Washington, D. C.; Rock Island, Illinois; and Elmira, New York.

Johnson's Island was an ideal prison, located in Lake Erie, about three miles from shore. Confederate officers were confined there, but not in large numbers. The location was healthy, and very few deaths occurred, the latter fact being due to two causes: The location was healthy, and the officers were in splendid trim when they went there.

Rock Island Prison, located at Rock Island, Illinois, was 1,250 feet long by 878 feet wide, and contained about 25 acres. It was enclosed by a plank fence, with a "dead line" 20 feet from the fence. The prison, which existed 16 months, saw 9,536 men confined there of whom 1,960 died and 45 escaped.

Camp Chase and Point Lookout were rated as unhealthy prisons. The following table gives official record of number of prisoners, number of deaths, and percentage of deaths.

	No. of prisoners	Deaths	Percentage
Camp Alton	7,117	2,218	31
Camp Chase	14,227	2,166	15
Camp Douglass	22,301	4,039	18
Camp Morton	10,319	1,556	15
Elmira Camp	12,123	2,963	24
Fort Delaware	22,723	2,513	11
Rock Island	9,536	1,960	20
Point Lookout	38,053	3,446	9

It seems rather strange that the ratio of deaths should be so low at Point Lookout, but when the facts are known it only goes to prove that there is more reason for the large percentage of deaths at Elmira. All prisoners received at Point Lookout were direct from the field, as it was the nearest point to the combat zone. After prisoners had been kept there awhile many of them were sent on to Elmira. Had they been held at Point Lookout instead of being un-

ELMIRA PRISONER-OF-WAR CAMP
A total of 12,122 Confederate prisoners were confined at Elmira, New York, of whom 2,917 died and 17 escaped.

loaded on Elmira, the death-rate at Point Lookout would have been vastly higher at Point Lookout and much lighter at Elmira. A great proportion of those forwarded were actually sick or so near it that they became ill soon after reaching Elmira.[40]

The Federal Government also confined Confederate prisoners in so-called permanent prisons at Fort Lafayette, New York Harbor; Fort Warren, Boston Harbor; Fort Delaware, Delaware; and Governor's Island, New York Harbor.[41] The largest military prison in the North was the one located at Elmira. While figures vary somewhat, it is known that about 12,000 prisoners were confined there and that about 3,000 of them died. The greatest mortality occurred in March 1865, in which month 495 died.[42]

Possibly the best known of military prisons was Point Lookout. Through the Governor of New Hampshire the government decided that the garrison at Point Lookout would be the three New Hampshire regiments that had suffered the most in the field. Each of the three regiments selected—the 2nd, 5th, and 12th New Hampshire Infantry Regiments—has left much information in its regimental history; as a result we know much more about conditions at Point Lookout than at most other military prisons. In February 1864 the 4th and 36th United States Colored Troops arrived at Point Lookout to release the white regiments for active field service in Grant's 1864 offensive. But for the white troops that had seen so much of the dark, rough side of a soldier's life and had just been through the Gettysburg campaign, Point Lookout was a military paradise, "where they could find and enjoy in quiet safety, the rest and relaxation that their nerves and muscles so greatly needed, and which the mind did not fail to appreciate." [43]

The men enjoyed to the utmost the good things which went with Point Lookout—the bathing, fishing, and boating, and the oysters and crabs. The river front of the 2nd New Hampshire's camp was soon lined with a fleet of dugouts which had been gathered in from up the river. When off duty the men were given every privilege consistent with military discipline. It was not long, however, before detach-

ments of prisoners began to arrive from New York, Baltimore, and Washington. As a result, it was soon apparent that more guards were required; before long half of the entire force was on duty each day, the men often standing a beat twelve hours out of the twenty-four. The arrangements for the reception and care of the prisoners were as humane as was possible for the control of large bodies of men in enforced confinement. The prisoners had proper and sufficient shelter, both tents and blankets. They had the same rations as their guards, and far better conveniences for cooking them, and there was a plentiful supply of excellent drinking water. The sanitary arrangement of their camp was perfect, the sinks being upon piles out over the waters of Chesapeake Bay.

Applications began to pour in upon the provost marshal to take the oath of allegiance and go north. This was not surprising, considering the manner in which the rebels had filled up their ranks by a merciless conscription, sweeping in many who had but little sympathy with the Confederate cause. There were also many who wished to enlist and fight for the Union. Two full regiments of "Galvanized Yanks" —the First and Second United States Volunteers— were organized from these, and sent to fight Indians in the West, where they did good service without danger of being captured and shot as deserters by their former associates. Many also enlisted in the Navy, and quite a sizeable detachment was received in the 2nd New Hampshire, "where, without exception, they made a record as brave and true soldiers second to none." [44] The regiments of "Galvanized Yanks" were officered by men who were commissioned from the three New Hampshire regiments. Most of the Confederate prisoners who took the oath of allegiance to the United States went North and found work where they could, not daring to return to their homes in the South, even if they had been allowed to do so.[45] When the prison was first opened up, none but relatives were allowed to visit the prisoners, and then only in cases of illness or other urgent reasons.[46] Many prisoners manufactured rings, fans, pipes, chains, charms, etc., which they readily exchanged with their guards for greenbacks or Government scrip.[47] This practice of making such articles as rings, pipes, and other items appears to have been fairly common in other prisoner of war camps as well. For example, among the many unusual items in the Civil War collection of Dr. Hermann W. Williams (Washington, D. C.) is a pipe which was presented to his grandfather. The pipe is inscribed as follows:

To Major S. K. Williams
8th Regt. V.R.C.
1st of January 1865
by F. X. Morel
Prisoner of War
Camp Douglas, Ill.

Although items made by Federal prisoners while in Confederate prison camps are fairly common, similar items made by Confederate prisoners are quite rare. The Williams' pipe shows exquisite workmanship and is indicative of the high esteem in which the recipient was held by the prisoner who gave him the memento.

PAROLE CAMPS

As a result of the Confederate practice of paroling captured Federals immediately after capture, as after Shiloh and the battles on the Peninsula, the Federal Government began a system of handling these paroled troops. At first it was customary to discharge men from the service when they had been returned to Federal lines on parole. But since such men were lost to the service, the War Department, on June 28, 1862 established parole camps at Annapolis, Camp Chase, and Benton Barracks, Missouri. All men on parole were ordered to report to the camp designated for their section of the country. All furloughs were recalled and no more were to be issued.[48] But trouble broke out at once. The prisoners quartered at Benton Barracks had returned to their lines with the expectation that they would receive eight months' back pay and a furlough to their homes until they were exchanged. The majority of the prisoners, who were from Iowa, objected to being sent to a camp outside their own State. Moreover, slight preparations had been made to receive them, and they found themselves without camp equipment, cooking utensils, and other necessities. There were no officers to look after their welfare. And even more seriously, they were ordered under arms to relieve a regiment which had been on guard duty. Such duty was in direct contradiction to their paroles "not to bear arms or to aid the United States directly or indirectly until they were exchanged." After a rather lengthy series of opinions on the question, it was decreed that paroled officers could drill paroled men for purposes of discipline but could not request them to serve as guards, or perform any functions which might release others for service in the field.

Soon a more serious problem developed in the Federal armies. Generals in the field found that the system of paroles established by the cartel on prisoner of war exchange actually acted as an inducement for soldiers to fall into the hands of the enemy in order to be paroled and sent home. Stanton believed that the solution to this was to closely confine such men, drill them diligently every day, and not to give them leaves of absence. Governor Tod of Ohio came up with another solution which was soon adopted. The Indians in Minnesota had gone on the warpath and were causing the Government considerable trouble. As Tod put it—"What could be better than to send the homesick soldiers against this new foe?" However, the men refused to be armed or to do any duty whatsoever, numbers deserted, and all were opposed to the idea of an Indian campaign. The Confederate authorities protested against this contemplated use of paroled prisoners and Adjutant General of the United States Army informed Stanton that the project was illegal. Also, Pope's campaign against the Indians had been successful and there no longer was any necessity for sending the paroled prisoners to fight the Indians.

Even with the passing of the Indian danger, prisoners in the parole camps did not return to obedience. In some camps the officers were as insubordinate as the men. Disorders continued in these camps where the type of men appears to have been low. With the exception of entire regiments (such as the 9th Vermont Infantry) captured through incompetence in high places, many of the men had voluntarily surrendered to take a "little rest from soldiering." The tendency to fall into the hands of the enemy did not cease. It was not even necessary for the men to be captured since a number adopted the practice of forging parole certificates and wandering off to parole camps. William H. Hoffman, Commissary General of Prisoners was finally convinced of the necessity of having the parole camps in the several States, but the need for parole camps was soon to pass.[49] From 1863 on to the end of the war, there was an ever-decreasing tendency of the enemy to parole Federal prisoners. Generally, these prisoners were hurried south to such places as Libby, Tyler, or Andersonville from which the survivors were eventually exchanged or were released after the fighting was over.

FIGHTING ON NORTHERN SOIL

In addition to several small affairs in the border States, in Maryland and Pennsylvania, including such incidents as the St. Albans raid, there were two important campaigns culminating in major engagements on Northern soil—Antietam and Gettysburg. These have been described in detail, as have the 1864 attack on Washington and the burning of Chambersburg, Pennsylvania. It is pertinent to note the reaction of the people of the North to the presence of the enemy on their soil. In general, the people of Maryland were loyal to the Union and often did not attempt to conceal their sympathy for the Federal cause. In Pennsylvania the loyalty was unquestionably as sincere but was occasionally tempered with a local concern for property which irritated Federal soldiers from other States who were fighting to rid the State of the invader.

One of the most patriotic of towns was Frederick, Maryland. The following description applied to the reception accorded many units as they passed through the town during the September 1862 campaign.[50]

"As we entered Frederick we noticed that nearly every house had the American flag displayed from house top, window or porch, and a word of welcome to the troops as they passed by. From balcony and windows fair faces smiled, and handkerchiefs and scarfs waved to greet the Army of the Union, as they passed along the streets from which, only the day before, the Confederates had been driven, after a brisk skirmish."

In Washington and Baltimore the evidences of the existing war were abundant, but in cities like Philadelphia and New York, they had nearly disappeared by mid-1863. The Soldiers' Rest in Philadelphia (also known as the Cooper Union Refreshment Saloon) reminded the soldier on furlough that "sympathy for the defenders of the Union was still warm." Chestnut Street was as gay as in the palmiest days of peace. In New York, Broadway teemed with activity, and its merchants were making princely fortunes. Fashion had never been arrayed more extravagantly, promenades never more brilliant, and places of amusement never more crowded. Except for the old barracks in the park and the few soldiers who found a temporary home at the Rest, there was little to be seen which indicated the existence of a gigantic civil war. The same was true of Providence, Rhode Island. Westminster Street was as lively as before the first gun was fired on Sumter; familiar faces were met at every corner; the cars were, as usual, bringing and carrying their living freight; the ships at the wharves were loading and unloading with unabated activity; smoke was going up from the numerous factories, foundaries and machine shops, and scarcely noticeable was the depletion in population made by the thousands sent to the front. Thus it was throughout the North; with the exception of a recruiting station here and there, nothing looked like war. Soldiers at the front compared their monthly pay (sergeant $17.00; corporal $14.00; private $13.00) with $70.00, which was the approximate amount received by a good mechanic for the same period of time.[51]

The first large scale fighting in the North, Lee's invasion of Maryland in 1862, for the first time brought the war to the North. In "A Woman's Recollections of Antietam"[52] an eye witness has left us a graphic account of the civilians' reaction to the horrors of war as they occurred, literally in their own backyards. It was not long before the wounded came to the town in an endless line of wagons. As the narrator described it:

Our women set bravely to work and washed away the blood or stanched it as well as they could, where the jolting of the long rough ride had disarranged the hasty binding done upon the battlefield. But what did they know of wounds beyond a cut finger or a boil? Yet they bandaged and bathed, with a devotion that went far to make up for their inexperience. Then there was the hunt for bandages. Every housekeeper ransacked her stores and brought forth things new and old. I saw one girl, in despair for a strip of cloth, look about helplessly, and then rip off the hem of her white petticoat. The doctors came up, by and by, or I suppose they did, for some amputating was done—rough surgery, you may be sure. The women helped, holding the instruments and the basins, and trying to soothe or strengthen. They stood to their work nobly; the emergency brought out all their strength to meet it.

It was not long before the whole town was a hospital.

In contrast to the Antietam campaign which was over in a very short time, the Gettysburg campaign lasted long enough for the State authorities to have time to call out the militia units in an attempt to slow down Lee's invading troops. As early as June 20th, an Army officer arrived in Gettysburg and addressed a public meeting in which he advised all ablebodied male citizens to arm themselves and to be ready, at a moment's warning, for the defence of their homes and their State.[53] But an effort to form an infantry company and to arouse the people generally was unsuccessful. This was due to the reluctance of the majority of citizens to desert their homes and families in the hour of danger while they went to defend the less exposed parts of the State. Some were unwilling, from political motives, either to go themselves, or to see their friends go into an organization which might seem to be a support of the Administration, or which might, perhaps, cause their absence from home at the time of the fall election! "Some also, who were brave and patriotic in words, could not make up their minds to expose themselves to the hardships of camp-life, and to the perils of the battle-field." During the battle itself, some of the citizens of Gettysburg left their houses but found to their sorrow when they returned that their houses had been pillaged by the enemy during their absence, while most of those who remained at home during the three-days' battle were able to save their property. During the actual fighting, many of the women and children went into the cellars as places of greatest safety.

A year after Gettysburg, citizens of another town in Pennsylvania saw war at first hand. This time it was Chambersburg, but this invasion was characterized by practically no fighting though a great deal of deliberate destruction. Whereas Lee had enforced rigid and scrupulous protection of property in his 1863 campaign, General McCausland permitted his men to indulge in indiscriminate robbery. "Hats, caps, boots, watches, silverware, and everything of value, were appropriated from individuals on the streets without ceremony; and when a man was met whose appearance indicated a plethoric purse, a pistol would be presented to his head with the order to 'deliver,' with a dexterity that would have done credit to the freebooting accomplishments of an Italian brigand." The commander of the expedition, General McCausland, acted in similar fashion. He gave notice to the citizens of Chambersburg that unless $500,000 in greenbacks or $100,000 in gold were paid in half an hour, the town would be burned. He was promptly told that the town could not and would not pay any ransom. The burning began, even with no time given to remove women, children, the sick, or even the dead.[54] In a few hours, the major portion of Chambersburg, and its chief wealth and business, were destroyed; three million dollars worth of property were sacrificed; and three thousand people made homeless, and "all without so much as a pretence that the citizens of the doomed town or any of them, had violated any accepted rule of civilized warfare."

MORALE ON THE HOME FRONT

Since practically all the fighting took place in Southern States it is but natural to think primarily of the Confederacy when discussing the war in terms of misery and suffering. The North suffered too; its cities, towns, hamlets, and rural communities watched bulletin boards and newspapers which listed native sons who would never come home; its streets were tramped by wrecks of men who had survived battle and prison pen. In some localities hardly a family escaped the loss of father, son, or brother. Many families read of Lee's surrender with the bitter realization that not a single male member would be coming home with their decimated regiments. This was characteristic of the Civil War because the regiments were locally raised units, with towns sending their able-bodied men out in companies. As a result, the town suffered as the company and regiment suffered; if the military unit incurred heavy casualties in battle or losses by disease, the town or county represented suffered in equal proportion.

The Northern people, having a more diverse civilization and being farther removed from the battle fronts, felt the conflict less directly than did the people of the South. Yet their suffering should not be minimized. Illinois with a population of 1,711,000 furnished 259,000 enlistments; Massachusetts with 1,231,000 furnished 146,000; Connecticut with 460,000 furnished 55,000 men; Michigan with 749,000 furnished 87,000; and other States in like proportion. Although these figures include re-enlistments, they indicate the percentage of the North's male population at the front.

As the weary weeks dragged on the struggle and main interest were in Virginia, where the course of the war proved discouraging in the extreme. The gallant but frustrated Army of the Potomac suffered a maddening series of defeats. Even Antietam and Gettysburg were marred by the failure to exploit the defeats inflicted on the enemy. To understand what the Northern people felt as they lived through all this, one must supply the sense of duration, of time suspense, of hope endlessly deferred while increasing sacrifices were demanded. Letters like the following which were written with no thought of publication give us some slight conception of the mental suffering of a father in the North: [55]

Springwater, N. Y.
February 26, 1865

My Dear Son:
Your telegram was duly received. You cannot imagine the pleasure it afforded us to learn that you were out of the hands of the Rebels. I wrote you to Richmond and to Dansville and Robert wrote you at every point where we thought you might be but received no intelligence whatever until about four weeks ago when we received six letters in two days. On the receipt of these letters I started for Washington to get you and G. Snyder on the special list of exchange. I suceeded in so doing through the War Department.
Your ma's health is very poor, so much so that we have serious doubts for her. I suppose you will come home as soon as you can on furlo or some how and see us. Colonel Murdock of the 97 died a few days before I got to Washington at the home of Mrs. Bannaman. He was made Brig. General a few days before his death. His son was with him through all his sickness. His wife came the day after his death. They payed him all the attention at this funeral that any officer could wish. They boar his body on one of the guns that belonged to his brigade, fired a salute in front of the house, shattering the windows very much.
All send love from your affectionate father
John Wiley.

Most parents were less fortunate, being forced to wait until the war was over to welcome their sons back from prisoner of war camps. However, it is completely impossible to measure the grief of parents whose sons never returned at all.

PROFITEERING

In disgusting contrast to the cost in human life and suffering was the fact that thousands fattened on the war and selfishly desired it to continue. When the future builder of the Union Pacific Railroad, G. M. Dodge, went to join his regiment on active duty at the outbreak of the war, a New York money-lender chided him for hurrying west merely to organize a regiment. The man of finance told Dodge: "I am sorry you left New York when you did. If you had remained here a few days longer we could have made something out of the war contracts. Undoubtedly there has been, and will be, good pickings. If this war is to be protracted there will be plenty of good chances, and if it lasts two years it will pay us to spend some time in Washington." [56]

Money changers and war profiteers continued to grow rich. Hartford, Connecticut was waxing fat and people of the money-getting type were interested in

Army operations not from the patriotic motive but for their effect upon the stock market. Railroad earnings were enormously increased. The stock of the Erie Railroad rose from 17 to 126½ in three years.

Despite the hundreds of thousands of men in the armies, crop production was well sustained. Areas open to grain production were increased in the western States; and where men were lacking, women and children did the heavy field work. The shortage of raw materials obtainable from the South was partially made up in the stimulation of wool production as well as flax and hemp as substitutes for cotton, while sugar was imported from Cuba. Crop deficiency in Europe increased the foreign demand for American grain. There was, however, in agriculture no such war boom as in manufacturing and trading. Moreover, much of the profit in agriculture was taken by middlemen and brokers.

LABOR

The stimulation of business and the military drain upon manpower naturally produced a condition of labor shortage. Although labor conditions only improved to a limited degree, wage increases were obtained by pressure tactics. Unionism grew and strikes multiplied. In 1864 there were over one hundred strikes. Race riots occurred in such cities as Brooklyn and Cincinnati when white laborers objected to employment of Negroes. In general it appears that labor was at a great disadvantage during the war as compared with the employing class. Wage increases for the war years amounted to 50 or 60 percent as compared with price increases of 100 percent. Employers used cheap labor where possible and at the end of the war, the laborer suffered a cut in wages so that his condition was undoubtedly worse than in 1860.[57]

INDIFFERENCE

Along with the enhanced prosperity went an indifference on the part of the many people in the North. Immense crowds nightly filled the theaters and places of amusements. Washington was gay with dinners, receptions, and elegant parties. In saloons, winter gardens, skating carnivals, billiard tournaments, burlesque shows, and cock fights, the crowds gathered to be amused and forget the war. Crime was on the increase in the cities though probably not throughout the North as a whole. Crooked politicians protected vice; drunken brawls were common; concert saloons were scenes of debachery; and prostitution was flagrant both in the cities and in the vicinity of army camps.

CORRUPTION

Even worse than the indifference to the war was the corruption. Unbelievable profits were to be had in cotton, which in 1864 could be had in the South at 20¢ or less and would bring $1.90 at Boston, and much of the trading in this commodity was illicit. The brother of General Butler in New Orleans, who was in Louisiana "for the sole purpose of making money," succeeded to the extent of several hundred thousands of dollars. The Government was swindled in its military contracts. Enormous commissions were paid to men who merely obtained contracts for producing firms. Traffic with the enemy offered many scandals. Yet in contrast to the many instances of profiteering and dishonesty, other instances could be presented of men in high place such as M. C. Meigs, Quartermaster General, who made a fine record of supplying the Army with the strictest honesty so far as the activities of his office were concerned. The Lincoln Administration had an honest man for President and honest men at the heads of the Departments (after Cameron resigned). But the system of governmental transactions with private firms permitted "legitimate" profits out of all proportion to service rendered. Lobbying for government business was very active in Washington, being indulged in by public men of high respectability, and downright swindling was an all-too-prevalent evil.

PATRIOTISM

But the North was not all pleasure and corruption. Another, and larger segment of the population was wholeheartedly behind the war and aided in every way possible the humanitarian enterprise and welfare activity. The Federal Government itself devoted far greater attention to the hospitalization and general care of the troops than in former wars. Aiding the Government were the Sanitary and Christian Commission. Contributions to such agencies were voluntary, systematic drives being conducted to obtain funds, chiefly by "Sanitary Fairs" in the cities. At the fair in Chicago in September 1863, the sum of $78,000 was raised; at Brooklyn in October, 1864, the sum of $400,000; at New York in December, 1863, $1,000,-000.[58] The Cooper Shop Volunteer Refreshment Saloon in Philadelphia fed over 600,000 soldiers during the war.[59] The food was good, plentiful, free, and was supplied by patriotic donations of money and time by patriotic citizens of the city. Sometimes the patriotism was colored by a romantic interest in the men at the front with perhaps the hope that the recipient of this interest would react in concrete terms! Often when girls of marriageable age would knit socks or mittens for soldiers whom they did not know, the girls would include a demure note in the box, and would not neglect to add their name and address! At other times, soldiers at the front would advertise in the newspapers for correspondents. Often the advertisements would be answered, couched in the Victorian language of the day. However, the soldier who received the following letter [60] valued it enough to preserve it, but it is not possible to determine to what extent further correspondence and possible conclusions resulted from the reply.

Chelsea, April 22, 1864

Sir:

Feeling a deep interest in those who have so nobly sacrificed all for the defense of our glorious country and seeing your brief advertisement in one of our daily papers, I thought I would avail myself of this good opportunity of helping one brave soldier to while away a few moments of the tedious camp life, for having friends in the Army, I can deeply sympathize with others, and I will say "God prosper them in all of their undertakings" for they, of all others need his aid and blessing while separated from their homes and dearest friends. But I am afraid I am presuming too much in so lengthy a note for this, the first, therefore, after politely requesting a Carte de Visite, also an answer to this note if the correspondence is designed, I will close by bidding you "adieu."

Amy L. H.
Chelsea, Mass.
Box 124

Despite the Victorian tone of the letter it should be noted that Amy wanted a Carte de Visite which meant she would have a photograph of the soldier whose advertisement she was answering. The reader today cannot help but be impressed with the high tone of the letter and also of the unsophisticated eagerness of both parties to find common cause amid the stern realities of the war itself.

NOTES ON CHAPTER 18

1. Lonn, *Foreigners in the Union Army and Navy*, pp. 1-3.
2. Adams, C. F., *Studies Military and Diplomatic*, pp. 387, 408.
3. Adams, C. F., *A Cycle of Adams Letters*, Vol. 1, p. 66.
4. Randall, pp. 462-469, 657-663.
5. *Ibid.*, pp. 594-595.
6. See the Committee reports.
7. Meade, George, *The Life and Letters of General George Gordon Meade*, Vol. 2, pp. 170-171.
8. Copperhead snakes struck without warning.
9. Randall, pp. 594-624.
10. Nicolay, John, *The Outbreak of Rebellion*, p. 87.
11. Randall, pp. 389-402.
12. Gray, Wood, *The Hidden Civil War*, pp. 215-217.
13. Fry, James B., *New York and the Conscription of 1863*, p. 33.
14. *O.R.*, Vol. 27, Pt. 2, 881-90.
15. Randall, p. 384.
16. Randall, pp. 382-404.
17. New York *Times*, July 22, 1861, quoted by Moore, Frank, *Rebellion Record*, Vol. 2, p. 371.
18. Randall, pp. 636-637.
19. *Ibid.*, pp. 641-642.
20. *Ibid.*, p. 403.
21. *Ibid.*
22. However, some of the generals talked too freely.
23. Some became aides.
24. Cox, Jacob D., *Military Reminiscences of the Civil War*, Vol. 1, pp. 76-78.
25. New York *World*, July 13, 1861.
26. Cincinnati *Commercial*, Dec. 11, 1861.
27. Meade, Vol. 2, 202-3.
28. *11th Maine Infantry*, p. 136.
29. Because it had more newsmen in the field.
30. Thompson (13th New Hampshire Infantry), pp. 98, 184.
31. Hays (63rd Pennsylvania Infantry), p. 145.
32. Crowninshield, p. 106.
33. Stanton, R. L. Reverend, *The Church and the Rebellion* (1864), pp. V-VI (preface).
34. Bradford, James H., Chaplain, "The Chaplains in the Volunteer Army," Loyal Legion, Commandery of the District of Columbia, *War Papers*, No. 11, p. 4.
35. *Ibid.*
36. Stanton, p. 549.
37. *Stories of our Soldiers*, Vol. 2, p. 189.
38. Randall, pp. 377-379, 629-630.
39. *Ibid.*, pp. 444-458.
40. Holmes, Clay W., *The Elmira Prison Camp*, pp. 254-255.
41. *Official Records*, Series 2, Vol. 3, pp. 8, 10, 32, 48-49.
42. Fox, p. 51.
43. Bartlett (12th New Hampshire Infantry), p. 145.
44. Haynes (2nd New Hampshire Infantry), pp. 199-205.
45. Bartlett, p. 148.
46. *The War and the Christian Commission*, p. 18.
47. Bartlett, p. 149.
48. United States War Department, General Order No. 72, June 28, 1862. *General Orders for 1862.*
49. Hesseltine, pp. 74-91.
50. Rhodes (Battery "B," 1st Rhode Island Light Artillery), pp. 120-121.
51. *Ibid.*, pp. 161-162, 265.
52. Mitchell, Mary Bedinger, "A Woman's Recollections of Antietam," *Battles and Leaders*, Vol. 2, pp. 686-695.
53. This description of the Pennsylvania campaign is taken from M. Jacobs' *Notes on the Rebel Invasion of Maryland and Pennsylvania*, published in 1864.
54. Schneck, B. Reverend, *The Burning of Chambersburg*, (1864), *passim*.
55. John Wiley to Major H. A. Wiley, 104th New York Infantry, February 26, 1865. Major Wiley had been captured on the Weldon Railroad, August 19, 1864. Manuscript letter in author's possession.
56. Bitterness was often directed against hometown slackers.
57. Randall, p. 631 (quoting Emerson D. Fite, *The Presidential Campaign of 1860*, pp. 184-187.)
58. *Ibid.*, pp. 634-635. Much of the material for this chapter is from this excellent treatment by Randall.
59. Moore, James, *History of the Cooper Shop Volunteer Refreshment Saloon*, p. 207.
60. Manuscript letter in author's collection, dated April 22, 1864.

CHAPTER 19

Veterans, Cemeteries, Monuments

ON APRIL 14, 1865, the United States flag, which just four years before had been lowered on the formal surrender of Fort Sumter, was again raised over that fort by Major-General Robert Anderson, with appropriate ceremonies, national in their character and importance. On the 2nd of April, Jefferson Davis had made a hurried departure from Richmond, stopping at Danville to issue a proclamation to the effect that the events of the last ten days would leave the Confederate armies "free to move from point to point, to strike the enemy in detail far from his base."

END OF HOSTILITIES

However, on April 9th, General Robert E. Lee surrendered the Army of Northern Virginia to General Grant and on the 14th General Joseph E. Johnston opened negotiations for the surrender of his troops to General Sherman, the details being formally consummated on the 26th of that month. Mobile had been surrendered on the 12th to a combined military and naval force, while Federal cavalry divisions were routing and scattering enemy cavalry forces in other sections of the South. Elements of two of these cavalry units, the 1st Wisconsin and 4th Michigan Cavalry Regiments, on May 10th captured the fleeing leader of the Confederacy, Jefferson Davis. Only one significant enemy force remained, that composed of the troops of the Trans-Mississippi Department under General E. Kirby Smith, and these forces surrendered May 25th to General E. R. S. Canby, commanding the Military Division of the Gulf. All significant military operations ceased and for all practical purposes the war was over. A formal and legal date for the end of the war was set as April 2, 1866, by Andrew Johnson, who officially declared that day that the "insurrection is at an end, and is henceforth to be so regarded."

In the meantime the Freedmen's Bureau, created by act of March 3, 1865, was being expanded under the aegis of the five military districts set up in the South. Each of these districts was assigned to high-ranking Federal generals who had at their disposal occupation troops considered sufficient to maintain order and to enforce the laws of the Nation. Schofield was appointed for the district comprising Virginia; Sickles for North and South Carolina; Pope for Georgia, Alabama, and Florida; Ord for Mississippi and Arkansas; Sheridan for Louisiana and Texas. There were numerous changes in these appointments: Stoneman, A. S. Webb, and Canby were the successors of Schofield; Meade followed Pope; and a series of generals succeeded to other commands. Among the less objectionable to Southerners were Hancock and Meade; the more objectionable included Sheridan, Sickles, and Pope.

Earlier, Sheridan had been sent to the Mexican border with a sufficient number of veteran regiments to stall and eventually crush the French plans for permanent occupation of Mexico. Grant was convinced that "the French invasion of Mexico was linked with the rebellion," while Sheridan learned that Texas troops violated their surrender terms and "had marched off in several organized bodies, carrying with them their camp equipage, arms, ammunition, and even some artillery, with the ultimate purpose of going to Mexico." [1]

At the suggestion of Secretary of War Stanton it was decided that the armies of Meade and Sherman should be formally reviewed in the city of Washington before their final discharge from the service of the United States. It is regrettable that elements of the Navy and Marine Corps were not included. The Army of the Potomac, the Army of the Tennessee, and the Army of Georgia therefore marched to the vicinity of Washington to be reviewed on May 23 and 24, 1865, for which the necessary orders were issued by Lieutenant General Grant. The Army of the Ohio remained in North Carolina under command of Major-General John M. Schofield.

The public and private buildings of the National Capital were profusely decorated, triumphal arches and reviewing stands were erected at different points, and vast crowds gathered from all sections to honor the returning veterans. Representatives of various States had erected stands which were filled by their sons and daughters, who, while heartily joining in the honors accorded to all the troops, enthusiastically applauded those who represented their own particular States. The principal reviewing stand was erected near the Executive Mansion, and was occupied by President Johnson and his cabinet, by diplomats and envoys of foreign nations, and by governors of States. Among the latter were some especially esteemed by the soldiers and honored by the nation for their invaluable and patriotic services as "war governors," notably John A. Andrew of Massachusetts, and Andrew G. Curtin of Pennsylvania. On the first day Grant occupied a position near the President with distinguished naval officers and Generals Sherman, Howard, Logan, and others, whose troops were to parade on the next day. Fortunately excellent photographs of the review have been preserved [2] as well as several contemporary accounts by the participants.

This greatest of all American military parades involved some 150,000 men—the Army of the Potomac, 80,000; the Army of the Tennessee, 36,000; and the Army of Georgia, 33,000. Never before or since in the United States has such a pageant been witnessed. Washington was thronged with visitors and along the route of march even the roofs and trees were black with people.

During this parade, Sherman and his Westerners were favorites. They seemed to be taller, leaner—also shaggier—than the Easterners. They gave the appearance of being hardened campaign veterans.

A *New York World* reporter concluded that the Army of the East had been composed of citizens, the West of pioneers. Charles A. Page of the *New York Tribune* declared that the Westerners' "faces were more intelligent, self-reliant and determined."[3] Generals of both Eastern and Western armies made comparisons also.

Although Sherman was critical of Eastern troops, Meade supported his army by stating that it suffered 60 percent of all Union casualties.[4]

COST OF THE WAR: NUMBERS AND LOSSES

The complete cost of the war, apart from loss of human life and limb, includes a variety of factors: billions of treasure (Federal, Confederate, State, local, and unofficial); untold retardation of economic development; ruined homes, roads, buildings, and fields; billions of dollar-value in slaves wiped out; a shattered merchant marine, with a loss of vessels estimated at $20,000,000. At the end of the war the national debt was $2,845,907,626, to which must be added the expenditures of States, counties, and municipalities for such items as bounties and relief for soldiers' families. Far worse than the monetary cost of the war has been the wretched, intangible heritage of hate, extravagance, corruption, truculence, partisan excess (which has lasted for decades), and intolerance.

It has become traditional to strew flowers over these wretched memories and to assume that the vast holocaust was either a necessary sacrifice for the Union or so gallant an adventure for the South as to constitute a justifiable failure. These are sentiments. The proven fact is the failure of statesmen North and South to manage the crisis of 1860-61, when, for instance, the device of a fully representative official national convention, earnestly recommended by moderates, was not tried, while truculent shoutings and strident declarations, having produced the impression that bloodshed was inevitable, made it a reality.[5]

With the possible exception of World War II, the war of 1861-1865 was the hugest of American wars. Participation of the United States in World War I fell short of the Civil War in duration, in the number who served in fighting sectors, and more especi-

COST OF WAR
Dead near Dunker Church, Antietam Battlefield.

ally in casualties and the proportion of soldiers to total population. Because of the lack of reliable and comparable records it is not possible to say, except by more or less reasonable conjecture, actually how many men served in the Federal and Confederate armies. Many Southerners have been inclined to accept the estimate that the Confederate armies numbered 600,000, while those of the Union numbered 2,778,304. This estimate cannot be accepted. The figures cited are extremes in both cases—too low for the Confederate armies and too high for the Federal armies. They were cited in *Southern Historical Society Papers*, Vol. 32, p. 46, by a writer who approached the whole question of comparable forces in a subjective manner and with what can fairly be interpreted as the intention of perpetuating the Southerners' claim that they were only defeated by superior numbers. It is true that the South was outnumbered but not to the extent its apologists have claimed.

In order to make the best showing possible, for their own people as well as for posterity, the Confederate authorities endeavored to show that the South never, from Sumter to Appomattox, had over 600,000 men in arms; and these, first and last, were opposed by, as they assert, some 2,800,000 men on the Federal side. Because the Federal records are much more complete, it is easier to analyze the 2,800,000 figure which is quoted by Southern writers as the size of the Federal Army. It is true that there were 2,898,304 enlistments in the Federal Army during the war. But it must be remembered that there were many more "enlistments" than individual soldiers, since many of the men enlisted several times, and also that an "enlistment" is not a definite unit of comparison because of wide variations in length of service. Some Federal enlistments were for two or three weeks, many were for three months, nine months, twenty-four months; others were for three years. Many were the occasions when whole regiments reenlisted. Desertion and bounty-jumping accounted for many repeaters. Over 300,000 Federal men enlisted just before the close of the war, few of whom, if any, participated in active service. Fox believed that it was doubtful if there were 2,000,000 individuals actually in Federal service during the war.[6] Livermore estimated that on the basis of a three-year enlistment period, the equivalent figure of "2,898,304 *separate enlistments* would be 1,556,678.[7]

Livermore estimated 1,082,119 as the total Confederate levies on a three-year basis.[8] These figures of Livermore have been accepted by some historians. Randall is inclined to take Livermore's work as one of the important exhibits in the testimony rather than as a definitive verdict on the whole case.[9] It certainly has been much more scientifically arrived at than was the figure of 600,000 given by General Early, Alexander H. Stephens, and others who gave

no sources for their figures at all. As Livermore said: "It is a part of human nature which persuades the losers in war to believe that the result must have come from a great disparity in numbers. The sustained conflict and terrible loss of four years of war placed the reputation of Southern valor so high that exaggerated statements of numbers cannot further exalt it in the estimation of the world. To prove that the estimated ratio of four to one between the two armies is not founded in fact does not diminish that reputation."[10]

But let us assume for a moment that the figure of 600,000 for the Southern armies is correct. What does this mean? It means, first of all, that the North had to conquer an extremely formidable defensive force operating in a hostile territory of some 712,000 square miles—a region considerably (30,000 square miles) larger than the combined European areas (prior to 1914) of Austria, Hungary, Germany, France, and Italy, with Belgium, Holland, and Denmark thrown in. This vast space was inhabited by five million people of European descent, with three millions of Africans who could be depended upon to produce food for those of European blood in active service. In the course of the conflict, and before admitting themselves beaten, every white male in the Confederacy between the ages of 17 and 50 capable of bearing arms was called out. Wherever necessary to enforce the rigorous conscription, the Confederate authorities suspended the writ of habeas corpus and appropriated, by the most drastic legislation, labor, property, and lives of the inhabitants. There can be no question that Federal soldiers were reporting the truth when they wrote home that every able-bodied man in their areas was in the Confederate service. The struggle lasted four years and during that period, under any recognized method of computation, the Confederacy, first and last, contained within itself some 1,350,000 men capable of doing military duty. This figure is in accordance with the figures of the census of 1860. During the war the Confederate Army was re-enforced by over 125,000 sympathizers from the sister slave States not included in the Confederacy. (The number is probably much higher.)[11] The upshot of the contention thus is, out of a population of 5,600,000 whites, only 475,000 put in an appearance in response to the often reiterated and *enforced* call to arms in the South—a trifle in excess of one man to each twelve inhabitants. Yet the South Africans, in a defensive struggle with Great Britain operating in a territory of 160,000 square miles—less than a fourth of that included in the Confederacy—put into active service one in four of their population, as against one in twelve in the Confederacy. The preponderance of force opposed to the South Africans was five to one; the preponderance of force in the case of the Confederates, according to their historians, was at most four and a half to one.[12]

Such an estimate, were it based on fact, would be

discreditable to the Confederate cause. As a matter of historical fact the Southerns turned out in force and fought to a finish. Undoubtedly there was, towards the close of the war, a large desertion from the Confederate ranks. The total number of Confederate deserters is given as 104,428, while the number of Federal desertions is 125,000.[13] If one accepts the Confederate figures of 600,000 for the C. S. Army and 2,800,000 for the U. S. Army, this means that one out of every six Confederates deserted while only one out of every twenty-three Federals deserted! But even more significant are the official Confederate figures themselves. For example, the tabular statement of the Confederate Bureau of Conscription gives 566,456 as the number of volunteers and conscripts in January 1864, from only six of the eleven Confederate States, namely, Virginia, the Carolinas, Georgia, Alabama, and Mississippi.[14] Again, if one accepts the figure of 600,000 this means that the above-mentioned six States in a period of more than a year, and the other five States for the *entire period of the war* could only raise 33,544 men!

There is another body of evidence which should not be ignored. The census of 1890 recorded 432,020 Confederates and 1,034,073 Federal veterans then living. To reconcile this evidence with the Southern estimate of 600,000 Confederates to 2,800,000 Federals would imply that over 70 percent of the Confederate soldiers lived until twenty-five years after the war, while only 37 percent of the Federal soldiers survived for that period.[15] It is perhaps fair to give the preponderance of Federal forces to Confederate forces as two and a half to one. With such superiority, the victory of the Federal Army is all the more remarkable. As the aggressor, the North needed the superiority it unquestionably had. What is not so generally realized today is that in 1861 the military experts of Europe believed the South invincible. In that year a census had just been completed, and every fact and figure now open to study was then well known to Europeans and Southerners. From the spring of 1861 to July of 1863 "no unprejudiced observer anywhere believed that the subjugation of the Confederacy and the restoration of the old Union were reasonably probable, or, indeed, humanly speaking, a possibility." Mr. Gladstone, a contemporary observer not unfriendly to the Union side, only expressed the commonly received and apparently justified opinion of all unprejudiced onlookers, when at Newcastle, in October 1862, he publicly declared that "Jefferson Davis and other leaders of the South have made a nation." No community, it was argued, numbering eight millions, as homogeneous, organized, and combative as the South, inhabiting a region of the character of the Confederacy, ever yet had been overcome in a civil war; and there was no sufficient reason for supposing that the present case would prove an exception to a hitherto universal rule.[16]

So far as casualties are concerned, "if writhing and gasping men can be reduced to 'reports' and statistics," the war cost a million casualties. Total deaths in the Federal Army have been figured at 360,222, of which 110,070 were from battle wounds. Wounded Federals have been said to number 275,175. On the Confederate side the number of dead estimated to be 258,000, of whom 94,000 are estimated to have been killed or mortally wounded in battle; and the number of wounded survivors has been estimated at 235,000. This means that the Federal Army had a total number of 385,245 hit as compared with 329,000 on the Confederate side.[17] In addition to the above, the Federal Army lost 249,458 men who died of disease and accidents,[18] 184,791 who were captured and missing,[19] and at least 26,168 men who are known to have died while prisoners of war in the hands of the enemy.[20] Almost half of the total number of deceased prisoners (12,630) died in one year at Andersonville.[21]

A comparison of numbers and losses naturally leads to the question whether one side showed martial capacity and a *Kampfgeist* superior to that of the other; and here it must be recognized that other elements beside mere numbers and losses should be taken into consideration. In physical resources, such as transportation, arms, munitions of war, food, clothing, and hospital supplies, the South was at a great disadvantage. The superiority of the North in these respects counterbalanced many men. To invade and hold a constantly increasing territory required many more troops than would have been needed in the Federal Army for actual fighting, and many Northern soldiers were employed in noncombatants' work, such as was done by Negroes for the Confederate Army. The long and determined struggle by the South against superior numbers and materiel must always command admiration. However, in justice to the Federal soldier, it must be pointed out that the enemy had the advantage of being on the defensive. The Confederate generals, especially at the outset, were superior; they were bolder in taking risks than their opponents. Federal generals were warring to *preserve* a government; Confederate generals were warring to *destroy* a government.

Illustrative of the contrast in opposing leadership was the direction of forces at Antietam. McClellan, with an available force of 75,000 men, allowed only 53,000 of those men to open fire at a Confederate force of 51,844.[22] The brilliance of Confederate leadership (and the frequent lack of it among Federal generals) often led to such a tactical disposition of opposing forces that the Federal "superiority" in numbers was more on paper than on the battle line.

Cemeteries and Battlefield Monuments

Even before the war was over, the North had shown great interest in insuring that its dead be identified where possible, and decently interred in

well-marked graves which would be safe from moles-
tation or destruction. It was the practice of new regiments in the field to send home the first of its members who died. This became too expensive and impractical after the regiment embarked on its first
campaign. Occasionally the more wealthy families
would send for or go in person and recover their
sons' bodies and ship them home at their own expense. But the vast majority of Federal soldiers were
hastily buried and, if time and circumstances permitted, the burial places were marked with crude
headboards. But due to the lack of means of identification and the proclivity of the enemy to remove all
valuables and even clothing from dead Federals, it
was often impossible to identify the dead after a
battle. As a result, almost one half of all Federal
dead are in graves marked "unknown." This unfortunate situation existed despite excellent preparations
made by the War Department in the very first year
of the war.

On September 9, 1861, the Secretary of War
directed that the Quartermaster General of the Army
should cause to be printed and placed in every hospital of the Army, blank books and forms for the
purpose of preserving accurate and permanent records of deceased soldiers and their place of burial,
and that he should also provide proper means for a
registered headboard to be secured at the head of
each soldier's grave. By an act of Congress, approved
July 17, 1862, the President was authorized to purchase cemetery grounds and to have them securely
enclosed that they might be used as national cemeteries for the soldiers who died in the service of the
United States. On April 13, 1866, it was provided by
Public Resolution No. 21 "that the Secretary of War
be authorized to take immediate measures to preserve from desecration the graves of soldiers of the
United States who fell in battle or died of disease
during the War of the Rebellion, and to secure suitable burial-places, and to have these grounds enclosed, so that the resting-places of the honored dead
may be kept sacred forever." On February 28, 1867,
an act to establish and protect national cemeteries
was approved, which provided in detail for the purchase of grounds, and the management and inspection of cemeteries; also for the punishment of any
person who should mutilate monuments or injure the
trees and plants.

In accordance with the foregoing and the orders
issued by the War Department from time to time,
every effort was made to collect the remains of the
dead, to inter them decently, and to record all the
facts known in connection with each grave.

In 1883 there were 79 National Cemeteries with a
total of 318,870 interments. Almost half of these were
unknown soldiers! (Known—171,302; Unknown—147,-
568). Of the whole number of interments indicated
above, 17,700 were of civilians and Confederates,

leaving about 300,000 as the number of Union veterans interred in National Cemeteries two decades
after the war.[23]

The first national cemetery was that of Gettysburg,
which was preserved largely through the efforts of
the State of Pennsylvania. As early as August 1863,
one month after the battle and about three months
before Lincoln made his immortal address at the
battlefield site, several acres where the fighting had
been heaviest were purchased as a Soldiers' National
Cemetery, by authorization of the Governor of the
State of Pennsylvania. Because of the national character of the cemetery the governors of all the States
having soldiers lying in this battlefield became interested in making the cemetery a truly national one.
Accordingly, a landscape gardener laid out the
grounds in State lots, apportioned in size according
to the number of marked graves each State had on
the battlefield.

To preserve the identity of the dead it was necessary to remove the remains as rapidly as possible.
The marks at the graves were only temporary; in
many instances they consisted of a small rough
board on which the name was faintly written with
a lead pencil. Such markings would soon be effaced
by the weather and the boards were also likely to
be thrown down and lost. The graves which were
unmarked were often only level with the surface of
the earth, and the grass and weeds were growing
over them; by fall the leaves of the forests would
cover them so that they might be entirely lost. Accordingly, bids were let for the removal and re-burial
in the National Cemetery of all Union dead on the
field. Thirty-four bids were submitted ranging in
amount from $1.59 to $8.00 per body. The lowest
bidder got the contract and did an excellent job
under great difficulties. He was able to identify the
bodies in many unmarked graves by various means.
Some of the remains were identified by letters, papers,
receipts, certificates, diaries, memorandum books,
photographs, marks on the clothing, belts, cartridge
boxes. Money and other valuables were found, and,
when the residence of relative or friends was known,
were immediately sent to them. Those items not sent
to relatives or friends were carefully packed up and
marked, and every effort made to locate the proper
recipient for the effects.

After purchasing the ground, the State Agent for
Pennsylvania was successful in getting the Quartermaster General of the Army to furnish coffins for
the dead soldiers. On Thursday, November 19, 1863,
the cemetery grounds were "solemnly dedicated to
their present sacred purpose by appropriate and im-
posing ceremonies." On December 17, 1863, commis-
sioners from 12 States assembled in Harrisburg,
Pennsylvania and steps were taken for development
and continuance of the National Cemetery.[24]

Some of the items listed as being found with the

bodies are of pathetic interest. Here are a few:

Charles Sets. Pocket book, and hair of father, mother, sister, and brother.

Unknown. Ornamental article, consisting of cross, figure of the Virgin Mary, Apostles, etc.

Unknown. Ambrotype of young lady, letter.

Sergeant L. H. Lee. Two combs, diary and bullet that killed him.

Solomon Lesser. $30.00 in gold, $6.00 in greenbacks, and certificates of deposit for $300.00 in German Savings Bank, N.Y.

Unknown. Twenty cents.

Unknown. 20th Maine Regiment, Testament, and letter signed Anna Grove.

As the Quartermaster Department completed its task of disinterring and reburial of the Federal dead in a battlefield area, it issued an official report of the number of graves located, including the names of all known dead with their units. These reports appeared as individual General Orders of the Quartermaster General's office. These reports were then assembled, bound in permanent form and designated Roll of Honor. A total of 27 volumes were issued from 1865 to 1871. The titles vary with various issues. Examples are:

"Names of Soldiers who died in Defense of the American Union interred in the National Cemeteries at Washington, D. C. from August 3, 1861 to July 30, 1865." (Washington 1865). "The Martyrs who, for our Country, gave up their lives in the Prison Pens in Andersonville, Ga." (Washington 1866).

Photographs and descriptions of the time give us a good idea of the rugged terrain, often forests, where the dead were buried. The *Photographic History of the Civil War* shows many of the battlefields and the crude graves and headboards of dead Federals. (For examples, see the photographs on page 279 of Volume 9.) The photographs of battlefields can be supplemented by descriptions of the fighting areas written shortly after the war was over. In the summer of 1865 and the following winter, J. T. Trowbridge visited the South, "spending four months in eight of the principal States which had lately been in rebellion." He visited the most famous of the battlefields and followed in the track of the destroying armies. Although Trowbridge was mainly concerned with receiving correct impressions of the country, of its inhabitants, of the great contest of arms just closed, he has left a vivid description of what the battlefields looked like right after the war. In reading such descriptions we get a much better appreciation of the devastation and, incidentally, of the difficulties facing the Federal Government in locating and identifying its dead. Typical of these descriptions is the following of the Wilderness battlefield: [25]

"We passed some old fields, and entered the great Wilderness—a high and dry country, thickly overgrown with dwarfish timber, chiefly scrub oaks, pines, and cedars. Poles lashed to trees for tent supports indicated where our regiments encamped; and soon we came upon abundant evidences of a great battle. Heavy breastworks thrown up on Brock's cross-road, planks from the Plank Road piled up and lashed against trees in the woods, to form a shelter for our pickets, knapsacks, haversacks, pieces of clothing, fragments of harness, tin plates, canteens,

UNBURIED DEAD AT COLD HARBOR

some pierced with balls, fragments of shells, with here and there a round-shot, or a shell unexploded, straps, buckles, cartridge-boxes, socks, old shoes, rotting letters."

Although the United States Government had collected its unburied dead a few weeks earlier, Trowbridge found the unburied remains of several soldiers which had been overlooked by the burial parties. In a cemetery near by there were seventy trenches, each containing the remains of many of the dead, and each marked with a headboard inscribed with the invariable words: "Unknown United States Soldiers, killed May 1864." As if in complaint against the neglect of the unburied remains found in the woods, someone had thrown three human skulls over the paling into the cemetery, where they lay blanching among the graves.[26]

Even a decade after the war, mementoes of the fighting and marks of the contest were yet to be found on many Southern battlefields. A visitor to Cedar Mountain in 1874 noted that nearly every foot of the area within a circumference of several miles had been trodden by both armies. The country was dotted with the remains of old camps. Whole forests had been levelled, leaving stumps to show where oak and pine had flourished. The ground was honeycombed with rifle pits and billowed with earthworks. On visiting his old regiment's campsite, the visitor found that even the corduroy walks in the company streets were still intact. Heaps of worn canteens and rotted portions of haversacks and shoes marked the places where new supplies had been distributed just before the beginning of the final march across the Rapidan. As the veteran looked around at the old camp ground he realized that almost ten years had passed since his unit had occupied the site. Now, with the lonesome and oppressive silence of the place, broken only by the occasional "caw" of a crow or the flapping of a buzzard's wings, "it was easy to re-people this deserted village with the ghosts of its former martial inhabitants."[27]

As the country as a whole, and the veterans in particular, displayed an ever increasing interest in the various combat areas of the war, the Government bought sections of the battlefields from their owners and established those areas as national parks. At the present time the Government, through the National Park Service of the Department of the Interior, has established national parks on the following battlefields:

Fort Sumter
Harpers Ferry
Manassas (Bull Run)
Fort Donelson
Shiloh
Pea Ridge
Fort Pulaski
Antietam
Stone's River
Vicksburg
Gettysburg
Fredericksburg (includes Spottsylvania, Chancellorsville, Wilderness)
Chickamauga-Chattanooga
Kenesaw Mountain
Brice's Cross Roads
Richmond National Battlefield Park (includes several small parks, Beaver Dam, Cold Harbor, Malvern Hill, etc.)
Petersburg
Tupelo
Appomattox

The best marked battlefields are Gettysburg, Vicksburg, and Antietam, where the positions of most of the Federal and many of the Confederate regiments are well marked by permanent monuments and markers. Among the first battlefields to be marked with monuments was Bull Run, right after the end of the war. These monuments are two tall shafts of native brown sandstone which stand, one in the yard of the Henry House, the other in front of the "Deep Cut" on the old railroad grade half a mile northwest of Groveton. Both were erected during the winter of 1864-1865 by General William Gamble's Separate Cavalry Brigade, which was stationed at Fairfax Court House. They were dedicated on the same day —June 10, 1865, with speeches at the Henry House site and military ceremonies at both monuments by Federal troops and artillery which fired salutes.[28] Several photographs of these ceremonies were taken and can be seen in the ninth volume of *Photographic History of the Civil War*. The Deep Cut marker, concealed a half mile from the nearest road by a tangle of woods and poison ivy, is seen by few visitors today, and has been damaged by souvenir hunters. Owing to the spectacular nature of this vestige of the battlefield the Deep Cut is well worth a visit.

It was not until May 10, 1940, that the Bull Run battlefield was designated as a Federal area. The 1,731 acres of Federal land in the park comprise portions of both the First and Second Bull Run battlefields. The best known of all battlefield parks in the United States is Gettysburg. In 1895 this battlefield was made a national military park and the Gettysburg Battlefield Memorial Association transferred its holding of 600 acres of land, 17 miles of avenues, and 320 monuments and markers to the Federal Government. Today the park extends over more than 5 square miles, has 29 miles of paved avenues, and 2,390 monuments and markers. The area of the National Cemetery is 20 acres. At Gettysburg, 18 States were represented in the Federal Army and 12 in the Confederate. Maryland contributed military units to both armies.

For some time after the war most veterans of both the Federal and Confederate armies were too preoccupied with establishing homes, returning to school, or working at their occupations to visit the battlefields. The exception was the individual who needed additional material for a projected history of his regiment. By the 1880's, however, the veterans had gotten married, established their homes and businesses, and were becoming nostalgic about their war service. Many regimental histories were being written and such veterans' organizations as the G.A.R. and Loyal Legion were very active. Towns, counties, and States were preparing histories of their localities in the various battles which were being marked with regimental and other unit monuments. Often the ceremonies at the dedication of such monument were elaborately planned and heavily attended by veterans and high civic officials.

Memorial Day (or Decoration Day) was a gala national occasion, being organized and sponsored in each community by the Grand Army of the Republic. It is now a legal holiday in all the Northern States and in the territories. This practice of commemorating the men who gave their lives for their Country began in 1868 when General John A. Logan, then commander in chief of the G.A.R., designated May 30th as a day for decorating with flowers the graves of men who had fallen in the Civil War. The order was widely observed, the most important ceremony being at the National Cemetery, Arlington, Virginia, where General James A. Garfield was the speaker. Francis H. Buffum, a veteran of the 14th New Hampshire Infantry, who died in 1927, held the unique record of delivering 60 consecutive Memorial Day addresses, more than any other person in the country. Beginning with Rhode Island in 1874, the Northern States one by one adopted May 30th as a legal holiday. Confederate Memorial Day, a legal holiday in most of the Southern states, was established April 26, 1865. On that day, a group of women in Vicksburg, Mississippi, decorated soldiers' graves in their community. Confederate Memorial Day falls on a different date in many areas of the South.

Much attention in the North was attracted to the transfer of Connecticut's battle flags from the State arsenal to the new Capital in Hartford on September 17, 1879. All soldiers and sailors who had served in the war were the guests of the city in order to escort the old colors. These veterans, marching in their old regimental groups, were given an ovation by the local populace and an estimated 100,000 visitors. The entire affair was given wide press publicity and details appeared in book form.[29] Two years later the 71st New York National Guard Regiment visited New Orleans where the regiment fired a volley over the graves of the Confederate dead in Greenwood Cemetery. The local press made much of this tribute by the 71st and pointed out that the act would be productive of great good—"proving to the Southern people that the men of the North are as magnanimous in peace as they found them brave in war."[30]

The same year the 1st Regiment, Connecticut National Guard visited Yorktown, Virginia, in connection with the centennial celebration there of the British surrender of 1781. The 1st Regiment also visited Charleston, South Carolina. The Regiment was composed mainly of younger men who had not served in the war, and there was little fraternization.[31] Two years later (May 23, 1883) at the annual reunion of the 28th New York Infantry at Niagara Falls, New York, the flag of the 28th captured at Cedar Mountain was returned by the Confederate regiment which had captured it in 1862. This regiment, the 5th Virginia Infantry, was represented by 83 men, while a total of 153 Virginians made the trip. A year later, the 28th visited Virginia and made a special trip to Lexington to place flowers on the grave of Lee.[32]

In November 1882, a Federal veteran conceived the plan for an excursion of battlefields in the Shenandoah Valley by veterans of all the Union regiments which had fought in the 1864 Valley campaign. The veteran, a member of the editorial staff of the *Boston Herald* wrote a series of articles on his proposed plan in the *Herald*. The idea of such an excursion was entirely novel, and at once met with widespread approval. The excursion, lasting from September 15 to 24, 1883, was a huge success with many Federal regiments represented. Among the excursionists was General William H. Emory, wartime commander of the Nineteenth Army Corps who told his veterans that by participating in this excursion they had inaugurated a novel episode in the history of war.[33] The excursion attracted national attention, both because of its originality and because of the favorable response from Confederate veterans. In 1885, a similar excursion was made under the same management but this time with the added feature of a rifle competition between picked Blue and Gray teams. The match was won by the Blue team 56 to 46 before a large and intensely interested crowd.[34] Because of the wide-spread interest in the successful excursions of Sheridan's veterans to the Shenandoah Valley, other groups were organized and excursions were made to other sections of the South. On February 26, 1885, veterans of the 9th Connecticut Infantry, in impressive ceremonies in New Orleans, returned the tattered battle flag of the 3rd Mississippi Infantry to survivors of that regiment.[35] Often these excursions were written up in publications of the reunion activities of the regiments involved.

Naturally, the excursions and reunions evoked reminiscing on the part of the veterans. Much of the valuable anecdotal material now available on the war period can be found in these small volumes of reunion proceedings. One of the best of this type of war literature is the *Souvenir of Excursion to Battlefields by the Society of the Fourteenth Connecticut Regiment and Reunion at Antietam, September 1891*.[36]

Veterans Societies

Most Americans are "joiners" and the veterans of 1861-1865 were no exception. While there were several organizations of Federal war veterans after 1865, undoubtedly the most powerful was the Grand Army of the Republic. The soldiers' endorsement was very valuable for political candidates to have, and a man's military record was scanned closely around election time. Illustrative of the importance of Civil War service is the fact that of the eight men occupying the White House from the close of the war to the end of the century, only one had not served in the war. In many States the situation in State and local politics was hardly less striking. This was also true of judges in various courts, and, to a lesser extent perhaps, true also for appointment to United States embassies and legations overseas. Justice Oliver Wendell Holmes, Jr. was perhaps the last of the noted jurists who had fought in the war. The early post-war Congresses must have resembled a veterans' reunion with their many ex-soldiers functioning as either Republican or Democratic legislators.

Although primarily a huge club of ex-soldiers, the G.A.R. was a powerful factor in politics in the North and mid-west, just as in the South the Democrats were powerful. There is no doubt both parties angled for the soldier vote and capitalized on the motives of military patriotism for partisan uses. Outside the South, soldier preference in Federal appointments became a fact, and pension claims were actively pushed. The *National Tribune,* a paper established in 1877 by George E. Lemon, the most powerful pension attorney in Washington, was especially active. The tradition that the Republican Party had

saved the Country, together with the constant emphasis upon the debt which the Country owed its ex-soldiers, and the important fact that it was the Republicans who had favors to grant, caused the G.A.R. to stray from its initial policy of nonpartisanship.[37]

At the start of the Civil War pensions totalled approximately $90,000,000. Under the Arrears Pension Act they increased to 250 million dollars. In the prosperous 1880's many private pension plans developed, which President Cleveland, in one of his vetoes, declared were only raids on the public treasury. In 1890 Civil War veterans (Federal Army, Navy, Marine Corps) incapacitated for manual labor gained a qualified service pension. In 1904, age was made a pensionable disability, Civil War veterans becoming eligible at age 62.

The first G.A.R. post was organized at Decatur, Illinois on April 6, 1866, by Dr. B. F. Stephenson and Rev. W. J. Rutledge, who had been respectively surgeon and chaplain of the 14th Illinois Infantry.[38] The first national encampment was held at Indianapolis on November 20, 1866, with representatives from 10 States and the District of Columbia. Membership was limited to persons who had served during Civil War in the United States Army, Navy, or Marine Corps, or in State regiments in active service under United States general officers. Its official objectives were fraternity, commemoration, and assistance to its members; it was very active in establishing soldiers' homes and memorials, and in caring

REUNION IN 1884
Group of Union and Confederate veterans at stone marking where Jackson fell at Chancellorsville. Do you recognize Rosecrans, Hunt, Robinson, Dickinson, Kniflin?

for and educating soldiers' orphans. The G.A.R. resolved in 1869 that it would not engage in partisan politics; in practice, however, it was a powerful political force for a generation for pension legislation and for objectives which it considered patriotic. An interesting exception to the general practice of the G.A.R. to accept all honorably discharged men who served in the Federal Army, Navy, and Marine Corps, was the exclusion of some Mormon veterans for almost half a century. The national president of the Ladies of the Grand Army of the Republic (an auxiliary organization) had her attention called to a small group of veterans, the Lot Smith Company, Utah Volunteers, who although eligible for G.A.R. membership, had been denied that privilege because of their religion. Through the efforts of this lady, these survivors of the Company were admitted to the G.A.R. in 1910.[39] The first national commander was Gen. S. A. Hurlburt of Illinois; the second was Gen. John A. Logan, also of Illinois, who held the office three years, and was succeeded by Gen. A. E. Burnside. The organization grew slowly, but in 1890 reached a peak membership of 409,489. By the end of 1950 there were only nine surviving members, the youngest, 103 years old, the oldest, 109. At the 1949 meeting the members decided that that would be the final encampment and no new commander was elected to succeed Theodore A. Penland.

The name of James Albert Hard, who died at Rochester, N. Y., on March 12, 1953, at the amazing age of 111 years and 8 months, will go down in American history as that of the last combat soldier of the Federal Army. At the time of his death one other man who wore the blue was still living; Albert Wolson, of Duluth, Minnesota, then 106 years old. But Mr. Wolson enlisted as a musician under the age of 18 in a Minnesota heavy artillery regiment only six months before the close of the war. Mr. Hard, on the other hand, volunteered for service in the Federal Army on April 16, 1861, only four days after the firing on Fort Sumter. This truly representative enlisted man of the Federal Army was born on July 15, 1841. When he died he had not only outdistanced all his Civil War comrades in longevity, but he had established other records. Certainly very few Americans of either sex or any generation had attained such length of years, and by a wide margin he had exceeded the ages at death of the last recorded survivors of any previous American War. Daniel F. Bakeman, last veteran of the Revolution, died in 1869, aged 109 years, 6 months; Hiram Cronk, last survivor of the War of 1812, died in 1905, just past the age of 105; and Owen T. Edgar, last Mexican War soldier, died in 1929, aged 98 years 2½ months.[40]

The original badge of the Grand Army of the Republic was adopted in 1866, but the one finally adopted and which is most familiar to us today, was completely different. In 1870, this new badge was adopted and became the official badge. In several respects it resembles the Medal of Honor authorized by Congress during the Civil War. Description of the Badge:

The badge is bronze, made from cannon captured in different decisive battles during the late rebellion, and in form a five-pointed star, similar in design to the two hundred medals of honor authorized by act of Congress to be given to soldiers and sailors most distinguished for meritorious and gallant conduct during the late war. In the centre of the badge is the figure of the Goddess of Liberty, representing *Loyalty;* on either side a soldier and a sailor clasping hands, representing *Fraternity,* and two children receiving benediction and assurance of protection from the comrades, representing *Charity.* On each side of the group is the National flag and the eagle, representing *Freedom,* and the axe or Bundle of Rods, or Fasces, representing *Union.* In each point of the star is the insignia of the various arms of the service, viz; the *Bugle* for Infantry, *Cross Cannon* for Artillery, *Cross Muskets* for the Marine, *Cross Swords* for Cavalry, and the *Anchor* for Sailors. Over the central group are the words "Grand Army of the Republic," and under, the word and figure, "1861-Veteran-1886," commemorating the commencement and close of the rebellion, and also the date of the organization of the Order. On the reverse side is a Branch of Laurel—the crown and reward of the brave—in each point of the star. The National Shield in the centre, surrounded by the twenty-four recognized Corps' Badges, numerical arranged, each on a keystone, and all linked together, showing they are united, and will guard and protect the Shield of the Nation. Around the centre is a circle of stars, representing the States of the Union and the Departments composing the Grand Army of the Republic. The clasp is composed of the figure of an Eagle, with Cross Cannon and ammunition, representing Defense; the Eagle with drawn sword hovering over and always ready to protect from insult or dishonor the National Flag, which is also the Emblem and Ribbon of the Order."

In 1884 the G.A.R. adopted a button to be worn by the members on the left lapel of the coat. These and the badges were made from Confederate cannon made by English firms; and by Noble Brothers, Rome, Georgia; Quimby and Robinson, Memphis; John Clark, New Orleans; and A.B.R. Brothers, Vicksburg.[41]

There were several patriotic organizations established to cooperate with the G.A.R. The first of these, the Bosworth Relief Corps, was formed in Portland, Maine, in 1869. The first State organization of women was organized at Fitchburg, Massachusetts, April 1879, under the title Woman's Relief Corps. This organization was accepted in 1881 by the G.A.R. and was authorized to add to their title "Auxiliary to the Grand Army of the Republic." In 1883 the G.A.R. invited all existing Ladies' Auxiliaries to form a union of all the various women's auxiliary societies. This was accomplished with the exception of the ladies representing New Jersey, who maintained their own organization, the Ladies Loyal League, which later became the Ladies of the G.A.R.

By 1888, the Woman's Relief Corps had 63,214 members. The difference between the Woman's Relief Corps and the Ladies of the G.A.R. was that whereas the former accepted for membership "all loyal women, whether of kin to the veterans or not," the latter required that a member be "the mother, wife, sister or daughter of an honorably discharged soldier, sailor or marine who served in the late rebellion." In 1878 an organization of Sons of Veterans was formed in Philadelphia. By 1888 this organization had nearly 60,000 members. Applicants for membership had to be at least 18 years of age; their fathers must have been deceased or honorably discharged Union soldiers or sailors. Applicants were also accepted if they were sons of members of the organization.

In addition to the above, there were three other veteran societies of lesser significance. The first of these, the Union Veteran Legion, composed almost exclusively of G.A.R. members, was organized in Pittsburgh in March 1884. Membership was restricted to officers, soldiers, and Marines of the Union Army, Navy, and Marine Corps during the war of the rebellion, who volunteered prior to July 1, 1863, for a term of three years, and were honorably discharged for any cause after a service of two continuous years, or were at any time discharged by reason of wounds received in the line of duty; but no drafted person, nor substitute, nor any one who has at any time borne arms against the United States is eligible.

In 1886 the Union Veterans' Union of the United States was organized in Washington, D. C. The main purpose of this organization was "to recognize the rights of the soldier to positions of public trust, and the preferment of our members over others for employment by the Government or by individuals, other things being equal." At least six months' continuous service (unless discharged on account of wounds) in the Army, Navy, or Marine Corps of the United States, between April 12, 1861, and April 30, 1865, and an honorable discharge therefrom, was required for membership. Part of this service must have been at the front. The third of these organizations, the Veterans' Rights Union, was formed in 1882 to gain preference for veterans in the civil service of the United States.

From the end of the war until 1874, there were numerous efforts made to organize the Federal ex-prisoners of war into associations, all of which failed until April 9, 1874, when such an organization was formed under the title of National Union of Andersonville survivors. Warren Lee Goss of Norwich, Connecticut was elected president. In 1886, John McElroy, editor of the *National Tribune* was elected president, and the next year the national organization of Federal ex-prisoners of war became the Union Ex-Prisoners of War Association. At that time it had about 2,000 members. The object of the organization was "to strengthen the ties of fraternal fellowship and sympathy, formed by companionship in arms during the war for the Union, among the survivors of Rebel Military Prisons."

Entirely different from the societies discussed above were the organizations formed by men who had served in a particular unit and who wished to perpetuate the friendships associated with their wartime unit. The parting of the veterans at their places of final discharge from the service inspired the desire to keep those friendships through life. Only a few regiments failed to arrange for future meetings at times which would commemorate some important event of their past history. The Third Army Corps Union was the first military society organized during the war. The Third Army Corps was formed March 16, 1862. The 1st Division of this corps, after the death of General Kearny at Chantilly, September 1, 1862, was commanded by General D. R. Birney, at whose headquarters a meeting of officers of the corps was held September 2, 1863, to form an association, the main object at that time being to secure funds for embalming and sending home for burial the bodies of officers killed in battle or dying in hospitals at the front. Later this organization actively supported the raising of money to establish a fund for assisting deserving officers who were wounded or disabled in the service, and also to aid the widows and families of deceased members of the corps. The motto of the organization, emblazoned on its beautiful gold badge, was *Dulce et decorum est pro patria mori.* This was the first association formed by Federal veterans; it antedated by many years the Army and Navy Union, Loyal Legion, G.A.R. and the other Civil War veterans' societies.[42] All officers and enlisted men of the Third Army Corps, or who participated in the battles of the corps, were eligible for membership.

Society of the Army of the Tennessee. This was the second society organized during the war. The preliminary meeting for the formation of the society was held in the Senate Chamber at the State Capital, Raleigh, North Carolina, April 14, 1865. Membership in the society was restricted to officers who had served with the "Old Army of the Tennessee." Major-General John A. Rawlins was elected President of the society. He was succeeded by General W. T. Sherman. An interesting amendment to the constitution of the society provided that any member could designate by will the relative to whom membership should descend. In default of such declaration, the eldest son was the one who inherited his father's title to enrollment in the society.

Society of the Army of the Cumberland. This society was organized in Cincinnati, Ohio, February 16, 1868. Membership was open to all officers and enlisted men who served in the Army of the Cumberland. Major-General George H. Thomas was president until his death in 1870; he was succeeded by

General W. S. Rosecrans who served 1870-1871; in 1872 General Philip H. Sheridan was elected President of this society.

Society of the Army of the Ohio. The Society of the Army of the Ohio, Major-General John M. Schofield, President, and the Society of the Army of Georgia, Major-General Henry W. Slocum, President, were organized at Chicago, December 15, 1868, when a reunion of these Western societies was held. General Grant, then President-elect of the United States, so intimately associated by service with them, was present, the central figure of a notable group: Grant, Sherman, and Thomas.

Society of the Army of the James. This society was organized in Boston, September 2, 1868, General Charles Devens, Jr., President. Meetings were held in 1871, 1874, and 1876, and the society then became incorporated with the Society of the Army of the Potomac.

Society of the Army of the Potomac. Surprisingly enough, the veterans who had served with the best-known army of the Federal forces did not organize a society until July 5, 1869, when the society was organized in New York City. All officers and soldiers who served in the Army of the Potomac and in the Tenth and Eighteenth Army Corps, Army of the James, were eligible for membership. An interesting feature of this society was its provision for a president elected at large and a vice-president from each Army Corps, the Artillery Corps, Cavalry Corps, Signal Corps, and General Staff. Presidents included such generals as Sheridan, Meade, Hooker, Burnside, McDowell, and Hancock.

Society of the Army of West Virginia. This society was organized at Moundsville, West Virginia, September 22, 1870. General Rutherford B. Hayes was the first president of this society. Large and interesting reunions were held each year.

Society of the Army and Navy of the Gulf. On July 8, 1869, this society was formed at Long Branch, New Jersey, by officers who served in the Department of the Gulf. Admiral D. G. Farragut was president until his death, when he was succeeded by General Sheridan.

Society of the Burnside Expedition and of the Ninth Corps. This society was organized in New York city, February 8, 1869. The first President was General A. E. Burnside. Probably connected with this society was a veterans' organization known as Roanoke Associates, which included veterans of all branches of service. The Roanoke Associates held reunions on the anniversary of the Battle of Roanoke Island, February 8, 1862.

Pennsylvania Reserve Association. This association was formed by representatives of the 15 Pennsylvania regiments organized in 1861 under the title of "Pennsylvania Reserve Corps." In 1866 a permanent organization was formed "to cherish the memories, per-petuate the friendships, and continue the associations formed in the field." The first president was Governor A. G. Curtin who had organized the Pennsylvania Reserve Corps in 1861.

Cincinnati Society of Ex-Army and Navy Officers. This society was organized in Cincinnati, October 2, 1874, "to preserve a feeling of friendship and cordiality among those who served in our National forces during the struggle for the preservation of the Republic, and also to keep a record of its members." Colonel Stanley Mathews was the first president. Meetings were held quarterly with an annual meeting and banquet.

Signal Corps. The United States Veteran Signal Corps Association was organized at Boston, November 14, 1867, Lieutenant J. Willard Brown, president.

Navy Veterans Organizations. The following associations were composed exclusively of men who had served in the Navy during the war: (1) The Farragut Veteran Association of Philadelphia—Commander, George L. Varnick. (2) Connecticut Naval Veteran Association—President, Charles A. Stillman. (3) The Farragut Veteran Association of the Port of New York—Commander, S. L. B. McCallmount. (4) The Naval Veteran Legion of California—President, Martin Murray. (5) The Essex Association of Naval Veterans, of Essex, Massachusetts—Commander, E. A. Winn. (6) Naval Veteran Association of the Gulf, of New Orleans—President, T. J. Woodward. (7) Commodore Foote Naval Veteran Association, St. Louis, Missouri—Commander, J. C. Parker. (8) The "Kearsage" Association of Naval Veterans, of Boston, Massachusetts—Commodore, P. H. Kendricken. (9) The "Monitor" Association of Naval Veterans, of Camden, New Jersey—Commander, R. A. Pierson.

On January 13, 1887, representatives from a number of these associations met in New York City, and formed the "National Association of Naval Veterans" with Charles W. Adams as Commodore.[43]

MILITARY ORDER OF THE LOYAL LEGION OF THE UNITED STATES

On April 15, 1865, the day after Lincoln's assassination, several officers of the Federal Army met informally, without notice, at the office of Colonel Thomas E. Zell, the head of a well-known publishing house in Philadelphia. At this meeting, as at many other similar impromptu meetings of loyal people that day in all parts of the country, the appalling tragedy which had occurred at Washington was the main topic of discussion. It was determined by those present at this particular assembly to call a mass meeting of citizens for the purpose of expressing public sentiment in regard to the great crime which had been perpetrated, to declare anew allegiance to the Union, and to provide for a proper representation from Philadelphia at the obsequies of the martyred President at the National Capital.

The public meeting called under these circumstances was held April 20th, five days later, and was attended by an immense number of people. Among other proceedings Colonel Zell presented a motion, which was adopted, to the effect that a society should be formed to commemorate the events and principles of the war for the Union then drawing to a close. Subsequent meetings were held and the first public meeting of the Loyal Legion was held May 31, 1865.

The hereditary feature of the Order was adopted after heated dispute and in spite of earnest objections. It was copied from a similar feature in the Society of the Cincinnati, which began with about 100 members but has been perpetuated by direct and collateral descendants of its founders. In 1899 the Loyal Legion had more than 8,000 members of the First Class (original members) on its rosters. It was thought that "from the lineage of this vast membership . . . [the] Order should be perpetuated through many generations or for ages." Samuel Brown Wylie Mitchell is the first name on the lists of the Loyal Legion; his diploma and insignia are No. 1. Mitchell was Major and Surgeon of the 8th Pennsylvania Cavalry and served from August 1, 1861 to August 24, 1865.

The Order of the Loyal Legion is constituted of officers and honorably discharged officers of the Army, Navy, and Marine Corps, Regular or Volunteer, who actually served in the war. These are members of the First Class. Members of the Second Class are the oldest sons or lineal descendants of members of the First Class. On the death of the person whom they represent they may become members of the First Class by inheritance. Members of the Third Class are civilians distinguished by acts of eminent patriotism during the war for the Union.

Each State was organized as a "Commandery." By the turn of the century the following Commanderies had been organized in the following order:

Commandery	Dating from	Number of members August 1, 1899
Pennsylvania	April 15, 1865	1,175
New York	January 17, 1866	1,296
Maine	April 25, 1866	163
Massachusetts	March 4, 1868	929
California	April 12, 1871	714
Wisconsin	May 15, 1874	222
Illinois	May 18, 1879	663
District of Columbia	February 1, 1882	747
Ohio	May 3, 1882	856
Michigan	February 4, 1885	310
Minnesota	May 6, 1885	313
Oregon	May 6, 1885	70
Missouri	October 21, 1885	305
Nebraska	October 21, 1885	117
Kansas	April 22, 1886	216
Iowa	October 20, 1886	255
Colorado	June 1, 1887	237
Indiana	October 17, 1888	308
Washington	January 14, 1891	71
Vermont	October 14, 1891	105

Commanders-in-Chief to 1899 were: General George Cadwallader until 1879; General W. S. Hancock to 1886; General P. H. Sheridan to 1889; General R. B. Hayes to 1892; General Lucius Fairchild to 1895; General John Gibbon—1896; Admiral Bancroft Gherardi to October 18, 1899; General J. M. Schofield.

The insignia of the order is a cross of eight points, gold and enamel, with rays forming a star, pendant from a red, white and blue ribbon. In the center is the inscription *Lex Regit, Arma Tuenter* (Law Rules, Arms Defend). On the other side is "M. O. Loyal Legion U. S. MDCCCLXV." Each member has a diploma which, with the insignia, bears a number corresponding to that of the sequence in which he is registered on the rolls of the order. A rosette or button of red, white, and blue is worn for recognition. There is no uniform, but on occasions of ceremony members may wear the uniform of their rank in the service.

In each State Commandery at its various meetings "papers," as they are called, were read by members appointed for the purpose. The papers were histories of campaigns, of battles, or of isolated events in the war, or they were essays on various military and naval topics. As one member said, if all the papers read in the various commanderies since their organization should be compiled and judiciously edited, they would form a library of war literature unequaled in interest by any similar collection in the world. Some commanderies did preserve the papers in printed form, often bound in convenient volumes of several papers each; these collections are of considerable value now for the personal accounts they contain.[44]

POLITICAL CLUBS

Although the G.A.R. and other veteran societies disclaimed any connection between their organizations and the political parties of their time, political events so motivated and aroused many veterans that they were induced to form hundreds of political clubs, under such titles as "Boys in Blue," "Soldiers and Sailors Leagues," "White Boys in Blue," "Conservative Army and Navy Union," "Colored Soldiers Leagues," and others. Both political parties were represented in National conventions of soldiers and sailors held in September, 1866.

THE MOST IMPORTANT VETERAN ASSOCIATIONS

Although there was obviously a plethora of veterans organizations after the Civil War, the two most important were the Grand Army of the Republic and the Military Order of the Loyal Legion of the United States. The G.A.R. was by far the largest of all veteran societies, perhaps because it accepted enlisted men as well as officers; while the Loyal Legion was necessarily restricted in size because of its limitation of membership for commissioned officers. Whereas the G.A.R. as an organized group contributed practically nothing to Civil War literature, many Loyal Legion organizations in the various States produced some extremely worthwhile material through the medium of the papers delivered at the meetings of the Loyal Legion.

Today's Activities

In recent years the various Civil War Round Tables have carried on this tradition of presenting papers to their members; most of the leading authorities on the war have appeared as guest speakers to these Round Table gatherings. Still another indication of interest felt by many Americans in the war is the constant increase in the number of people who are searching for artifacts and relics on battlefields by using mine detectors.

Since the end of the war, groups of veterans have visited the battlefields at which their units were present, often holding reunions on those fields and Civil War literature is filled with accounts of these reunions. Unquestionably, the largest of all Civil War reunions was held on the battlefield of Gettysburg on the occasion of the 50th anniversary of the battle. In early July 1913, a total of 54,000 veterans, from every section of the Country, witnessed the impressive ceremonies at Gettysburg, culminating in a re-enactment of Pickett's charge which was participated in by survivors from both sides who had been there in person on July 3, 1863. The average age of the veterans who in 1913 made the pilgrimage to Gettysburg was 72 years, but only 9 out of the 54,000 died from the excitement and heat of the week-long visit during the height of the summer. Present as main speaker on July 4, 1913 was President Woodrow Wilson.[45] Again in 1938, on the 75th anniversary, Union and Confederate veterans met at Gettysburg, this time less than 2,000 of them. "America has never seen anything finer and more illustrative of abstract manhood than is the gathering at Gettysburg. One could cheer were it not for a catch in the throat!" [46]

Civil War Centennial

More recently, the Congress of the United States has passed a joint resolution to establish a commission to commemorate the one hundredth anniversary of the Civil War. The Joint Resolution is contained in Public Law 85-305, 85th Congress, H. J. Res. 253, September 7, 1957.[47]

Preliminary plans of the Commission call for the establishment of an historical section to assist States and localities in organizing observances of anniversaries of Civil War events. However such assistance is to be in the nature of advice and guidance only, since it is hoped the States and localities will take the initiative in such commemorations. The Commission also plans to cooperate closely with the Secretary of the Interior and the Director of the National Park Service in support of the program to complete the preservation and development of the 26 Civil War battlefields, memorials, and historic sites in the National Park System so that fitting observances may be held on the appropriate dates.

Under the aegis of the Commission a program of publications, including the revision and re-issuance of important out-of-print works, basic sources, guides, and indices will be encouraged. The Commission promotes the collection, codification, and dissemination of such basic materials as manuscripts, newspapers, and pictures. These and similar steps are being taken by the Commission to promote among the American people the fullest understanding of the heroism and sacrifice displayed by the people on both sides in the war.

NOTES CHAPTER 19

1. Sheridan, P. H., *Personal Memoirs*, Vol 2, pp. 211, 213.
2. *Photographic History*, Vol. 3, p. 349; Vol. 4, p. 257; Vol 7, p. 11; Vol. 8, p. 39; Vol. 9, pp. 109, 233-237, 259; Vol. 10, pp. 162-163, 290.
3. Haynie, pp. 324-34. Page, pp. 397-97.
4. The best comments are by generals who served in both the East and the West. Page, pp. 391.97.
5. Randall, pp. 687-688.
6. Fox, p. 527.
7. Livermore, *Numbers and Losses*, p. 50.
8. *Ibid.*, p. 61.
9. Randall, p. 686.
10. Livermore, *Numbers and Losses*, pp. 2-3.
11. See Adams, C. F., *Studies Military and Diplomatic*, p. 238 note.
12. *Ibid.*, pp. 239-240.
13. Livermore, *Numbers and Losses*, p. 5.
14. *Official Records*, Series 4, Volume 3, p. 102.
15. Randall, pp. 686-687.
16. Adams, C. F., *Studies Military and Diplomatic*, pp. 235-236.
17. Randall, p. 687; Livermore, *Numbers and Losses*, pp. 47-48, 65.
18. Livermore, *Numbers and Losses*, pp. 47-48.
19. Phisterer, pp. 70-71.
20. *Ibid.*
21. *Official Records*, Series 2, Vol. 7, pp. 541-545, 708.
22. Livermore, *Numbers and Losses*, pp. 70-71.
23. Phisterer, pp. 77-79.
24. *Report of the Select Committee Relative to the Soldiers' National Cemetery, March 1864* (Harrisburg, 1864).
25. *Trowbridge, J. T., The South: A Tour of its Battle-Fields and Ruined Cities*, p. 125. (Hartford, 1866).
26. *Ibid.*, p. 126.
27. Cowtan, Charles W., *Services of the Tenth New York Volunteers (National Zouaves) in the War of the Rebellion*, pp. 448-450.
28. Hanson, Joseph Mills, *Bull Run Remembers*, p. 176.
29. *History of Battle-Flag Day September 17, 1879*, Hartford, 1879.
30. Cowan, John F., *A New Invasion of the South*, p. 20.

31. Rathbun, Julius G., *Trip of the First Regiment, C. N. G. to Yorktown, Va., and Charleston, S. C.* Hartford, 1882.

32. *A Brief History of the Twenty-Eighth Regiment New York State Volunteers,* pp. 90-91.

33. Buffum, Francis H., *Sheridan's Veterans,* Vol. 1, September 15-24, 1883, p. 96.

34. *Ibid.,* Vol. 2, September 15-24, 1885, p. 40.

35. Murray, Thomas H., *History of the Ninth Regiment Connecticut Volunteer Infantry, "The Irish Regiment"* . . . *1861-65,* pp. 222, 238.

36. Written by Chaplain H. S. Stevens and published in Washington, 1893.

37. Randall, p. 745.

38. Beath, Robert B., *History of the Grand Army of the Republic,* pp. 33-34.

39. Fisher, Margaret M., *Utah and the Civil War* (1929), pp. 144-145, 147.

40. Hanson, pp. 169-170.

41. Beath, pp. 653-657.

42. Hays (63rd Pennsylvania Infantry), pp. 214-215.

43. Beath, pp. 11-24.

44. Calkins, E. A., "History of the Loyal Legion," *War Papers,* Vol. 3, Loyal Legion of Wisconsin, pp. 343-352.

45. *Fiftieth Anniversary of the Battle of Gettysburg.* Report of the Pennsylvania Commission, Harrisburg, Pa. 1913, pp. 53, 174.

46. *Fort Worth (Texas) Morning Star,* quoted in *Pennsylvania at Gettysburg,* Vol. 4, p. 453. See also p. 135.

47. Public Law 85-305, 85th Congress, House Joint Resolution 253, September 7, 1957.

CHAPTER 20

Battle Losses, Victories, Defeats

GETTYSBURG was the greatest battle of the war. The strategic issues involved were the most important; it was the "High Water Mark" of the Confederacy. In this battle, not only were the contending armies large, but they were at their best in point of discipline and experience; while the loss of life exceeded that of any other battle of the war.

Antietam was the bloodiest battle. More men were killed on that one day than on any other one day of the war. There were greater battles, with greater loss of life, but they were not fought out in one day as at Antietam. At Gettysburg, Chancellorsville, and Spottsylvania, the fighting covered three days or more; at the Wildnerness, Cold Harbor, Shiloh, Stone's River, Chickamauga, and Atlanta the losses were divided between two days of fighting; but at Antietam, the fighting commenced at sunrise, and by five o'clock that afternoon it was over.

BATTLE LOSSES

For the historian, the principal sources for battle losses are to be found in:

Phisterer, *Statistical Record of the Armies of the United States, 1883;* Fox, *Regimental Losses in the American Civil War, 1889;* and Livermore, *Numbers and Losses in the Civil War in America, 1900.* The statistics of these three men vary somewhat, due mainly to the period in which each did his research. As more information became available (this is especially true of the issuance of the *Official Records*) the statistics on battle casualties became more reliable. Since Livermore completed his research more than a decade after both Phisterer and Fox, most historians accept Livermore's figures as being least liable to error. Much of the adjustment made by Livermore was possible by the identification as "killed in action" many men who had been reported during the war as "missing" by unit commanders immediately after an engagement.

As regards the loss in the Federal armies, the greatest battles of the war are listed in the following table. "P" refers to Phisterer; "F" refers to Fox; while "L" refers to Livermore.

Battle	Source	Killed	Wounded	Missing	Total
Gettysburg	P	2,834	13,709	6,643	23,186
	F	3,070	14,497	5,434	23,001
	L	3,155	14,529	5,365	23,049
Spottsylvania	P	(Figures not available)			
	F	2,725	13,416	2,258	18,399
	L	(Figures not available)			
Wilderness	P	(Figures not available)			
	F	2,246	12,037	3,383	17,666
	L	2,246	12,037	3,383	17,666
Antietam	P	2,010	9,416	1,043	12,469
	F	2,108	9,549	753	12,410
	L	2,108	9,549	753	12,410
Chancellorsville ...	P	1,512	9,518	5,000	16,030
	F	1,606	9,762	5,919	17,287
	L	1,575	9,594	5,676	16,845
Chickamauga	P	1,644	9,262	4,945	15,851
	F	1,656	9,749	4,774	16,179
	L	1,657	9,756	4,757	16,170
Cold Harbor	P	1,905	10,570	2,456	14,931
	F	1,844	9,077	1,816	12,737
	L	(Figures not available)			
Fredericksburg ...	P	1,180	9,028	2,145	12,353
	F	1,284	9,600	1,769	12,653
	L	1,284	9,600	1,769	12,653
2nd Bull Run	P	(Figures not available)			
	F	1,747	8,452	4,263	14,462
	L	1,724	8,372	5,958	16,054
Shiloh	P	1,735	7,882	3,956	13,573
	F	1,754	8,408	2,885	13,047
	L	1,754	8,408	2,885	13,047
Stone's River	P	1,533	7,245	2,800	11,578
	F	1,730	7,802	3,717	13,249
	L	1,677	7,543	3,686	12,906
Petersburg (Assault)	P	1,298	7,474	1,814	10,586
	L	(Figures not available)			

It is interesting to note that several major battles are ahead of Gettysburg so far as percentage of loss is concerned. The following table gives a partial list of major battles with the percentage of Union losses in *number of men hit* in the respective engagements:

Battle	Number Engaged	Killed and Wounded	Percentage
Wilderness & Spottsylvania (May 5-12, 1864)	88,892	26,302	29.6
Stone's River	41,400	9,220	22.2

Gettysburg	83,289	17,684	21.2
Chickamauga	58,222	11,413	19.6
Shiloh	62,682	10,162	16.2
Antietam	75,316	11,657	15.4
Second Bull Run & Chantilly	75,696	10,096	13.3
Winchester (Sept. 19, 1864)	37,711	4,680	12.4
Chancellorsville ...	97,382	11,116	11.4

But casualties were also heavy in many of the little-known battles which are rarely mentioned in histories of the war. For example, at Olustee (Florida), on February 20, 1864, a small Federal force was defeated by the enemy. Of the 5,115 Federals engaged, 1,355 were killed or wounded, a percentage of 26.5.

At Groveton, August 28, 1862, Gibbon's "Iron Brigade" (King's Division) of 1,800 men and two regiments of Doubleday's brigade were attacked by the divisions of Ewell and Taliaferro of Jackson's corps under Jackson's direction. The action which lasted only an hour and a half was stopped by darkness. But in that brief space of time the fighting was maintained with great obstinacy and the losses were very severe on both sides. Doubleday lost nearly one-half of those of his troops who were engaged. It was a regular stand up fight, the opponents standing completely in the open, 100 yards apart, and neither side yielded an inch. This battle was the baptism of fire for the Iron Brigade which lost about one third of its 1,800 men in killed and wounded. (At Gettysburg this same brigade entered the battle with 1,883 men. It lost 162 killed, 724 wounded, 267 missing; a total of 1,153 casualties or 61 percent. Most of the missing were killed or wounded.)

VICTORIES

In connection with battle statistics the question naturally arises—which were victories, and which were defeats? It is impossible to give answers which will satisfy proponents of both the Union and Confederate points of view. However, there are certain facts relative to these statistics which the dispassionate reader will concede possess a certain degree of validity. These observations are based on the military axioms—that when an army retains possession of the battlefield and buries the enemy's dead, it certainly cannot be considered as a defeated army; and that when an army abandons the field, either slowly or in rout, and leaves its dead and wounded in the hands of the enemy, it certainly should not claim a victory. In the following battles the Federal armies remained in undisturbed possession of the field, the enemy leaving *many of their wounded and most of their dead on the field:*

Rich Mountain, W. Virginia
Williamsburg, Virginia
Crampton's Gap, Maryland
Mill Springs, Kentucky
Fort Donelson, Tennessee

Shiloh, Tennessee
Pea Ridge, Arkansas
Roanoke Island, North Carolina
New Berne, North Carolina
Carter's Farm, Virginia
Prairie Grove, Arkansas
Nashville, Tennessee
Antietam, Maryland
South Mountain, Maryland
Kernstown, Virginia
Baton Rouge, Louisiana
Iuka, Mississippi
Corinth, Mississippi
Chaplin Hills, Kentucky
Resaca, Georgia
Atlanta, Georgia, July 21-22
Piedmont, Virginia
Bentonville, North Carolina
Gettysburg, Pennsylvania
Magnolia Hills, Mississippi
Raymond, Mississippi
Champion's Hill, Mississippi
Stone's River, Tennessee
Missionary Ridge, Tennessee
Fort Stevens, D. C.
Opequon, Virginia
Cedar Creek, Virginia
Five Forks, Virginia
Sailor's Creek, Virginia

The Federal armies were successful, also, in the following assaults. They were the attacking party, and carried the forts, or entrenched positions, by storm:

Fort Harrison, Virginia
Fort McAllister, Georgia
Fort Fisher, North Carolina
Fort Blakely, Alabama
Marye's Heights, Virginia (1863)
Lookout Mountain, Tennessee
Cloyd's Mountain, West Virginia
Utoy Creek, Georgia
Rappahannock Station, Virginia
Jonesboro, Georgia
Petersburg, Virginia

In the following assaults or sorties, the Confederates were the attacking party, and were repulsed:

Helena, Arkansas
Fort Sanders, Tennessee
Franklin, Tennessee
Wauhatchie, Tennessee
Allatoona Pass, Georgia
Fort Stedman, Virginia
Peach Tree Creek, Georgia
Ezra Chapel, Georgia

DEFEATS

In the following battles the Confederates remained in undisturbed possession of the field, the Federal armies leaving their unburied dead and many of their wounded in enemy hands:

First Bull Run, Virginia
Ball's Bluff, Virginia
Belmont, Missouri
Front Royal, Virginia
Port Republic, Virginia

Wilson's Creek, Missouri
Pocotaligo, South Carolina
Maryland Heights, Maryland
Shepherdstown, Virginia
New Market, Virginia
Seven Days, Virginia
Manassas, Virginia
Cedar Mountain, Virginia
Richmond, Kentucky
Fredericksburg, Virginia
Chancellorsville, Virginia
Winchester, Virginia (1863)
Chickamauga, Georgia
Olustee, Florida
Sabine Cross Roads, Louisiana
Wilderness, Virginia
Spottsylvania, Virginia
Drewry's Bluff, Virginia
Monocacy, Virginia
Brice's Cross Roads, Maryland
Island Ford, Virginia
Deep Bottom, Virginia
Ream's Station, Virginia
Hatcher's Run, Virginia

In the following assaults the Confederates successfully repulsed the attacks of the Federals:

Chickasaw Bluffs, Mississippi
Secessionville, South Carolina
Fort Wagner, South Carolina
Kenesaw Mountain, Georgia
Vicksburg, Mississippi (May 19)
Vicksburg, Mississippi (May 22)
Port Hudson, Louisiana (May 27)
Port Hudson, Louisiana (June 14)
Cold Harbor, Virginia
Petersburg, Virginia (June 17-18)
Petersburg Mine, Virginia

NUMBER OF ENGAGEMENTS

There were 112 battles in the war, in which one side or the other lost over 500 in killed and wounded. Fox states there were 1,882 general engagements, battles, skirmishes, or affairs in which at least one regiment was engaged. Phisterer lists 2,261 battles and engagements in his book, *Statistical Record of the Armies of the United States*. Other authors have compiled similar lists of the battles and engagements of the war. The reader is especially referred to the following:

Dyer, Frederick H., *A Compendium of the War of the Rebellion* (1908).

Fox, William F., *Regimental Losses in the American Civil War* (pp. 426-464, 540-551).

Strait, N. A., *An Alphabetical List of the Battles of the War of the Rebellion* (Washington, D. C. 1882).

Strickler, Theodore D., *When and Where We Met Each Other* (Philadelphia, 1899).

Werner, Edgar A., *Historical Sketch of the War of the Rebellion* (Albany, 1890).

COMPARISONS

Because certain Federal corps saw much more action than others, the regiments associated with those fighting corps suffered heavier battle casualties than regiments in corps which saw little combat in the war.

Many regiments escaped heavy battle losses but suffered severely from disease. The 16th New Hampshire Infantry was in service only nine months, had no killed or wounded at all, but lost 221 men from disease in its short term of service. Some regiments lost heavily by battle and disease, e.g. the 8th New Hampshire Infantry which had 102 men killed in battle and which lost another 258 men by disease. On the other hand, the 5th New York Infantry lost 177 men killed or died of wounds but lost only 34 men by disease during its two years of service. A low rate of losses by disease generally reflected excellent discipline in a regiment.

Comparisons of the Civil War with two world wars of the 20th Century are of interest though obviously they must be made with caution. The following table applies only to the 18 Northern States and omits such States as Colorado and Nevada because their contributions to the Federal Army were negligible. Such border States as Kentucky, Missouri, and Tennessee were also omitted because they contributed substantial forces to both sides. To present as fair a comparison as possible, the figure of 2,213,363 is used as the size of the Federal armed forces but actually the figure is very probably much closer to 1,500,000. Also, it should be noted that the population figures for these comparisons are given only to the closest census year figures, e.g. 1910 for World War I; 1940 for World War II; and 1860 for the Civil War. For convenience, figures for percentages and proportions are rounded off to the nearest tenth. All statistics are from the *World's Almanac* for 1959.

War	Population	Total Mobilized	Percentage Mobilized	Casualty Percentage Among Armed Forces
1917-18	91,972,266	4,734,991	5.1	7
1941-46	131,669,275	16,112,566	12.2	6
1861-65	18,691,421	2,213,363	11.7	29

War	Killed	Died of Disease, etc.	Wounded	Ratio of casualties per military population	Ratio of dead per total pop.
1917-18	53,402	63,114	204,002	$\frac{1}{287}$	$\frac{1}{788}$
1941-46	291,557	113,842	670,846	$\frac{1}{122}$	$\frac{1}{324}$
1861-65	140,414	224,097	281,881	$\frac{1}{29}$	$\frac{1}{51}$

Although these statistics are not precise they are sufficiently accurate to indicate very strongly that the Civil War directly affected a larger segment of the Country's population than either World I or II. If the figures for the Confederacy were included, the comparison would be even more striking. While no attempt is made here to deprecate the Nation's sacrifice in the world wars, it is suggested that the War of 1861-1865 called for greater sacrifice on the part of the average family in the North than was exacted in 1917 and even in 1941. There were comparatively fewer families in the Civil War which did not suffer loss of at least one of its members than was the case in the global struggles of this century so far as the United States was concerned.

Comparisons of battles of the Civil War with those of other American wars are interesting but prove nothing except to illustrate the American soldier's fighting spirit. However, because of the similarity in numbers involved and duration of combat, the following comparison of the Federal Army of the Potomac with the American forces at Iwo Jima presents some interesting statistics. The reinforcements to the Army of the Potomac (Ninth Army Corps and some individual regiments) are offset in this comparison by the fact that the strength of the Japanese force at Iwo Jima was inferior to Lee's army. Fighting in both cases took place in exceedingly rugged terrain.

Battle	Strength U.S. Forces	Dates of Fighting	Duration	Casualties	%
Iwo Jima	111,308	Feb.19-March 16, 1945	26 days	25,992	23.3
Wilderness Spottsylvania	127,471	May 5-June 4 1864	31 days	48,802	38.3

Although the number of Federals officially reported as killed was 6,815, this figure should be increased substantially from the list of missing, which amounted to 7,457. (The total of killed at Iwo Jima is 6,775 which included the missing.) The figures for the Wilderness, Spottsylvania, and Cold Harbor are treated as one continuous battle in this comparison. This is fair, since the Army of the Potomac confronted the same antagonist (Lee's Army of Northern Virginia) during 31 days of almost continuous combat.

CHAPTER 21

Major Units, Commanders, Citations

MANY of the leading figures of the war wrote their memoirs and all of the more important Federal military and naval commanders have their biographers. A selected list of both memoirs and biographies can be found in the chapter on bibliography. For the reader who wishes a short but accurate factual outline of an officer's service, the following books are recommended:

Army:

George W. Cullum, *Biographical Register of the Officers and Graduates of the U. S. Military Academy,* Vol. 1 (1802-1840) Vol. 2, (1841-1867).

Guy V. Henry, *Military Record of Civilian Appointments in the United States Army,* 2 volumes.

Thomas H. S. Hamersly, *Complete Regular Army Register of the United States for One Hundred Years (1779 to 1879).*

William H. Powell, *Records of Living Officers of the United States Army* (1890).

Navy and Marine Corps:

Thomas H. S. Hamersly, *General Register of the United States Navy and Marine Corps . . . For One Hundred Years (1782-1882).*

Lewis Randolph Hamersly, *The Records of Living Officers of the U. S. Navy and Marine Corps* (Seventh Edition, 1902).

GENERALS

There is much more difficulty in selecting "leading" military commanders from the list of Federal Army personnel than from the Navy. This is due to some extent because of the much larger list of Army commanders to choose from, but also because of the fact that there was a total of 1,706 men who were general officers in the war.

BREVETS

The vast majority of these officers were generals by brevet only and some never had a large command during the entire war. For example, Theodore A. Ripley, a company commander who was never promoted at all during his service in the field and was mustered out as a captain, on March 13, 1865 was brevetted a brigadier general.

The list of the commissions by brevet is a document of 178 pages by which brevets seemed to have been conferred very much as one would sow grain, broadcast, without any very definite idea as to where or how the honor was going to fall. On looking over the list a singular anomaly was perceived. At the head and generally with the highest rank were placed officers whose service during the war had been in Washington and other cities, many of whom had not heard a hostile bullet fired during the whole war. Thus the head of a staff department in Washington who had not been in the field at all would rank men who had commanded with distinguished ability, armies in the field! Some who had acted as staff officers to generals would rank generals who had themselves commanded armies and corps. The day selected for the dating of these brevet commissions was March 13, 1865, although no one seemed to know why this particular date was choosen. At all events, "it at once became a standing joke in the army to refer to 'that bloody day' the 13th of March, for services, on which so many Brevets had been conferred." John Gibbon was brevetted four times, Major, Lieutenant Colonel, Colonel, and Brigadier General, all for gallant and meritorious services during the war, and all these brevets date from that "bloody day" the 13th of March, 1865!

THE CHIEF EXECUTIVE

President:
Abraham Lincoln (Illinois)

Vice-President:
Hannibal Hamlin (Maine)
Andrew Johnson (Tennessee)

Secretary of State:
William H. Seward (New York)

Secretary of War:
Simon Cameron (Pennsylvania)
Edwin M. Stanton (Pennsylvania) Jan. 15, 1862

Secretary of the Navy:
Gideon Welles (Connecticut)

Secretary of the Treasury:
Salmon P. Chase (Ohio)
W. P. Fessenden (Maine) July 1, 1864
Hugh McCulloch (Indiana) March 7, 1865

Secretary of the Interior:
Caleb B. Smith (Indiana)
John P. Usher (Indiana) January 8, 1863
Attorney General: Edward Bates (Missouri)
James Speed (Kentucky) December 2, 1864
Postmaster General:
Montgomery Blair (Maryland)
William Dennison (Ohio) September 24, 1864

THE ARMY
WAR DEPARTMENT

Secretary of War:
Joseph Holt—January 18, 1861
Simon Cameron—March 5, 1861
Edwin M. Stanton—January 15, 1862
Assistant Secretaries of War:
Thomas A. Scott—August 3, 1861
Peter H. Watson—January 24, 1862
John Tucker—January 29, 1862
Christopher T. Wolcott—June 15, 1862 to January 23, 1863
Charles A. Dana—August 1863
(Scott was appointed under the act of August 3, 1861, authorizing the appointment of one Assistant Secretary of War. Subsequently three Assistant Secretaries were authorized by law.
Adjutant-General's Department:
Colonel Samuel Cooper—resigned March 7, 1861
Brig. Gen. Lorenzo Thomas—assigned to other duty, March 23, 1863
Col. Edward D. Townsend
Quartermaster Department:
Brig. Gen. J. E. Johnston—resigned April 22, 1861
Brig. Gen. Montgomery C. Meigs
Subsistence Department:
Col. George Gibson—died September 29, 1861
Brig. Gen. Joseph P. Taylor—died January 29, 1864
Brig. Gen. A. E. Eaton
Medical Department:
Col. Thomas Lawson—died May 15, 1861
Col. Clement A. Finley—retired April 14, 1862
Brig. Gen. William A. Hammond
Brig. Gen. Joseph K. Barnes—appointed August 22, 1864
Pay Department:
Col. B. F. Larned—died September 6, 1862
Col. Timothy P. Andrews—retired November 29, 1864
Brig. Gen. Benjamin W. Brice
Corps of Topographical Engineers: (this corps was consolidated with the Corps of Engineers under act of March 3, 1863)
Col. John J. Abert—retired September 9, 1861
Col. Stephen H. Long
Corps of Engineers:
Brig. Gen. Joseph G. Totten—died April 22, 1864
Brig. Gen. Richard Delafield

Ordnance Department:
Col. Henry K. Craig—until April 23, 1861
Brig. Gen. James W. Ripley—retired September 15, 1863
Brig. Gen. George D. Ramsay—retired September 12, 1864
Brig. Gen. Alexander B. Dyer
Bureau of Military Justice:
Major John F. Lee—resigned September 4, 1862
Brig. Gen. Joseph Holt
Provost Marshal General Department:
Brig. Gen. James B. Fry

FIELD ARMIES

Army of the Potomac:
Maj. Gen. George B. McClellan—July 1861
Maj. Gen. A. E. Burnside—November 5, 1862
Maj. Gen. Joseph Hooker—January 25, 1863
Maj. Gen. George G. Meade—June 27, 1863
Army of Virginia:
Maj. Gen. John Pope—June 26, 1862
(Broken up in September 1862)
Army of the Ohio:
Maj. Gen. D. C. Buell, November 9, 1861
Maj. Gen. W. S. Rosecrans—October 30, 1862
Maj. Gen. J. M. Schofield—January 28, 1864
Army of the Cumberland: Originally was the Army of the Ohio—became the Army of the Cumberland October 24, 1862 under Maj. Gen. George H. Thomas, October 1863
Army of the Tennessee:
Maj. Gen. H. W. Halleck—1862
Maj. Gen. U. S. Grant—October 16, 1862
Maj. Gen. W. T. Sherman—October 27, 1863
Maj. Gen. J. B. McPherson—March 12, 1864
Maj. Gen. O. O. Howard—July 30, 1864
Maj. Gen. John A. Logan—May 19, 1865
Other armies were:
Army of the Mississippi
Army of the Gulf
Army of the James
Army of West Virginia
Army of the Middle Military Division

ARMY CORPS

First Army Corps, Army of the Potomac: Created by Order of the President March 8, 1862. Announced March 13, 1862, General Order, No. 101, Army of the Potomac, to consist of Franklin's, McCall's, and King's divisions. Merged into the Department of the Rappahannock, April 4, 1862, by order of the President. Recreated, September 12, 1862, General Order No. 129, Adjutant-General's Office, by changing the designation of the Third Army Corps, Army of Virginia. Transferred to the Fifth Army Corps, by General Order, No. 115, Adjutant-General's Office, March 23, 1864.

Commanders:
  Maj. Gen. Irvin McDowell, March 14, 1862
  Maj. Gen. John F. Reynolds, Sept. 29, 1862
  Brig. Gen. J. S. Wadsworth, January 2, 1863
  Maj. Gen. John F. Reynolds, January 4, 1863
  Brig. Gen. J. S. Wadsworth, February 27, 1863
  Maj. Gen. John Newton, July 2, 1863

First Army Corps, Army of Virginia: Organized by Order of the President, June 26, 1862, from troops in the Mountain Department. Designated the Eleventh Army Corps, Army of the Potomac, by General Order No. 129, Adjutant-General's Office, September 12, 1862.

  Commander: Maj. Gen. F. Sigel, June 29, 1862

First Veteran Army Corps (Hancock's): Created by General Orders, No. 287, Adjutant-General's Office, November 28, 1864, to consist of men who had served not less than two years. Discontinued, July 11, 1866.

  Commander: Maj. Gen. W. S. Hancock, November 28, 1864

Second Army Corps, Army of the Potomac: Created by Order of the President, March 8, 1862. Announced March 13, 1862, General Orders, No. 101, Army of the Potomac, to consist of Richardson's, Blenker's, and Sedgwick's divisions. Discontinued by General Orders No. 35, Army of the Potomac, June 28, 1865.

Commanders:
  Brig. Gen. E. V. Sumner, March 13, 1862
  Maj. Gen. D. N. Couch, October 7, 1862
  Maj. Gen. John Sedgwick, December 26, 1862
  Maj. Gen. O. O. Howard, January 26, 1863
  Maj. Gen. D. N. Couch, February 7, 1863
  Maj. Gen. W. S. Hancock, May 22, 1863
  Brig. Gen. William Hays, July 3, 1863
  Maj. Gen. G. K. Warren, August 16, 1863
  Brig. Gen. J. C. Caldwell, December 16, 1863
  Maj. Gen. W. S. Hancock, December 29, 1863
  Maj. Gen. G. K. Warren, January 9, 1864
  Brig. Gen. J. C. Caldwell, January 27, 1864
  Maj. Gen. G. K. Warren, February 6, 1864
  Maj. Gen. W. S. Hancock, March 24, 1864
  Maj. Gen. A. A. Humphreys, November 26, 1864
  Brevet Maj. Gen. F. C. Barlow, April 22, 1865
  Maj. Gen. A. A. Humphreys, May 5, 1865
  Brevet Maj. Gen. G. Mott, June 9, 1865
  Maj. Gen. A. A. Humphreys, June 20, 1865

Second Army Corps, Army of Virginia: Created by Order of the President, June 26, 1862, to consist of troops in the Department of the Shenandoah. Designated the Twelfth Army Corps, Army of the Potomac, by General Orders, No. 129, Adjutant-General's Office.

Commanders:
  Maj. Gen. N. P. Banks, June 26, 1862
  Brig. Gen. A. S. Williams, September 3, 1862
  Maj. Gen. J. K. F. Mansfield, September 15, 1862
  Brig. Gen. A. S. Williams, September 17, 1862

Third Army Corps, Army of the Potomac: Created by Order of the President, March 8, 1862. Announced March 13, 1862, General Orders, No. 101, Army of the Potomac, to consist of Porter's, Hooker's, and Hamilton's divisions. Discontinued, March 24, 1864, General Orders, No. 115, Adjutant-General's Office, March 23, 1864. First and Second Divisions transferred to the Second Army Corps, and the Third Division to the Sixth Army Corps.

Commanders:
  Brig. Gen. S. P. Heintzelman, March 16, 1862
  Brig. Gen. George Stoneman, October 30, 1862
  Maj. Gen. D. E. Sickles, February 8, 1863
  Maj. Gen. D. B. Birney, May 29, 1863
  Maj. Gen. D. E. Sickles, June —, 1863
  Maj. Gen. William H. French, July 7, 1863
  Maj. Gen. D. B. Birney, January 28, 1864
  Maj. Gen. William H. French, February 17, 1864

Third Army Corps, Army of Virginia: Created by Order of the President, June 26, 1862, to consist of the troops under McDowell, except those within the fortifications and City of Washington. Designation changed to the First Army Corps, Army of the Potomac, by General Orders, No. 129, Adjutant-General's Office.

Commanders:
  Maj. Gen. Irvin McDowell, June 26, 1862
  Maj. Gen. Joseph Hooker, September 7, 1862
  Maj. Gen. George G. Meade, Sept. 17, 1862

Fourth Army Corps, Army of the Potomac, until August 1862: Department of Virginia until August 1, 1863: Created by Order of the President March 8, 1862. Announced March 13, 1862, General Orders, No. 101, Army of the Potomac, to consist of Couch's, Smith's, and Casey's divisions. Discontinued August 1, 1863, General Orders, No. 262, Adjutant-General's Office, the troops having been distributed to other corps.

  Commander: Brig. Gen. E. D. Keyes, March 13, 1862

Fourth Army Corps, Army of Cumberland: Created, September 28, 1863, General Orders, No. 322, Adjutant-General's Office. Order carried into effect, October 9, 1863, by the consolidation of the Twentieth and Twenty-first Army Corps, Army of the Cumberland. Discontinued, General Orders, No. 131, Adjutant-General's Office, August 1, 1865.

Commanders:
  Maj. Gen. Gordon Granger, October 10, 1863
  Maj. Gen. O. O. Howard, April 10, 1864
  Maj. Gen. D. S. Stanley, July 27, 1864
  Brig. Gen. T. J. Wood, December 1, 1864
  Maj. Gen. D. S. Stanley, January 30, 1865

Fifth Army Corps, Army of the Potomac: Created by order of the President, March 8, 1862, to consist of Bank's and Shield's divisions. Discontinued, General Orders, No. 34, Adjutant-General's Office, April

4, 1862. Merged into the Department of the Shenandoah. The divisions commanded by Generals F. J. Porter and George Sykes were designated the Fifth Provisional Army Corps, Army of the Potomac, by General Orders, No. 125, Army of the Potomac, May 18, 1862. Confirmed by General Orders, No. 84, Adjutant-General's Office, July 22, 1862. Discontinued, General Orders, No. 35, Army of the Potomac, June 28, 1865.

Commanders:

Maj. Gen. N. P. Banks, March 20, 1862
Maj. Gen. F. J. Porter, May 18, 1862
Maj. Gen. Joseph Hooker, November 10, 1862
Brig. Gen. D. Butterfield, November 16, 1862
Maj. Gen. George G. Meade, December 25, 1862
Maj. Gen. George Sykes, January —, 1863
Maj. Gen. George G. Meade, February 5, 1863
Maj. Gen. George Sykes, June 28, 1863
Maj. Gen. G. K. Warren, March 23, 1864
Brevet Maj. Gen. S. W. Crawford, January 2, 1865
Maj. Gen. G. K. Warren, January 27, 1865
Brevet Maj. Gen. Charles Griffin, April 1, 1865

Sixth Army Corps, Army of the Potomac: Created by General Orders, No. 125, Army of the Potomac, May 18, 1862, to consist of Franklin's and Smith's divisions. Confirmed by General Orders, No. 84, Adjutant-General's Office, July 22, 1862. Discontinued by General Orders, No. 35, Army of the Potomac, June 28, 1865.

Commanders:

Maj. Gen. William B. Franklin, May 18, 1862
Maj. Gen. Williams M. Smith, November 16, 1862
Maj. Gen. John Sedgwick, February 4, 1863
Maj. Gen. H. G. Wright, May 9, 1864
Brevet Major Gen. George W. Getty, January 17, 1865
Maj. Gen. H. G. Wright, February 11, 1865

Seventh Army Corps, Department of Virginia: Created by General Orders, No. 84, Adjutant-General's Office, July 22, 1862, to consist of the forces under Maj. Gen. Dix. Discontinued by General Orders, No. 262, Adjutant-General's Office, August 1, 1863, and the troops transferred to the Eighteenth Army Corps, Department of Virginia and North Carolina.

Commanders:

Maj. Gen. John A. Dix, July 22, 1862
Maj. Gen. H. M. Naglee, July 25, 1863

Seventh Army Corps, Department of Arkansas: Created by General Order No. 14, Adjutant-General's Office, January 6, 1864, to consist of the troops in the Department of Arkansas. Discontinued by General Orders No. 131, Adjutant-General's Office, August 1, 1865.

Commanders:

Maj. Gen. Frederick Steele, January 20, 1864
Maj. Gen. J. J. Reynolds, December 22, 1864

Eighth Army Corps, Middle Department: The troops in the Middle Department, under Major-General Wool, were designated the Eighth Army Corps, by General Orders, No. 84, Adjutant-General's Office, July 22, 1862. Discontinued by General Orders, No. 131, Adjutant-General's Office, August 1, 1865.

Commanders:

Maj. Gen. John E. Wool, July 22, 1862
Maj. Gen. Robert C. Schenck, December 22, 1862
Brevet Brig. Gen. William W. Morris, August 10, 1863
Maj. Gen. Robert C. Schenck, August 31, 1863
Brig. Gen. Erastus B. Tyler, September 28, 1863
Maj. Gen. Robert C. Schenck, October 10, 1863
Brig. Gen. Henry H. Lockwood, December 5, 1863
Maj. Gen. Lew Wallace, March 22, 1864
Brevet Brig. Gen. William W. Morris, February 1, 1865
Maj. Gen. Lew Wallace, April 19, 1865

Ninth Army Corps: Created by General Orders, No. 84, Adjutant-General's Office, July 22, 1862, to consist of the troops under Major-General Burnside, belonging to the Department of North Carolina. Discontinued by General Orders, No. 131, Adjutant-General's Office, August 1, 1865. The Ninth Army Corps served in the Department of North Carolina until Aug. —, 1862; Army of the Potomac until Feb. —, 1863; Department of Virginia until March —, 1863; Department of the Ohio until June —, 1863; Department of the Tennessee until Aug. —, 1863; Department of the Ohio until March —, 1864; under the direct orders of General Grant until May 1864; Army of the Potomac until April 1865; and in the Department of Washington until July 1865.

Commanders:

Maj. Gen. A. E. Burnside, July 22, 1862
Maj. Gen. J. L. Reno, September 3, 1862
Brig. Gen. J. D. Cox, September 14, 1862
Brig. Gen. O. B. Willcox, October 8, 1862
Maj. Gen. John Sedgwick, January 16, 1863
Maj. Gen. William F. Smith, February 5, 1863
Maj. Gen. A. E. Burnside, March 17, 1863
Maj. Gen. J. G. Parke, March 19, 1863
Brig. Gen. O. B. Willcox, April 4, 1863
Maj. Gen. J. G. Parke, June 5, 1863
Brig. Gen. R. B. Potter, August 21, 1863
Brig. Gen. O. B. Willcox, January 18, 1864
Maj. Gen. J. G. Parke, January 26, 1864
Brig. Gen. O. B. Willcox, March 16, 1864
Maj. Gen. A. E. Burnside, April 13, 1864
Maj. Gen. J. G. Parke, August 15, 1864
Brig. Gen. O. B. Willcox, December 31, 1864
Maj. Gen. J. G. Parke, January 12, 1865
Brevet Maj. Gen. O. B. Willcox, January 24, 1865
Maj. Gen. J. G. Parke, February 2, 1865
Brevet Maj. Gen. O. B. Willcox, June 17, 1865
Maj. Gen. J. G. Parke, July 2, 1865

Tenth Army Corps: Created by General Orders, No. 123, Adjutant-General's Office, September 3, 1862, to consist of the forces in the Department of the South. Reorganized, April 28, 1864. Discontinued, by General Orders, No. 297, Adjutant-General's Office, December 3, 1864. White troops transferred to the Twenty-fourth Army Corps, and the colored troops to the Twenty-fifth Army Corps. Reorganized, by General Orders, No. 49, Adjutant-General's Office, March 27, 1865, to consist of all troops in North Carolina not belonging to General Sherman's army. Discontinued by General Orders, No. 131, Adjutant-General's Office, August 1, 1865. The Tenth Army Corps served in the Department of the South until May 1864, and in the Department of Virginia and North Carolina until December 3, 1864. The reorganized corps served in the Department of North Carolina.

Commanders:
Maj. Gen. O. M. Mitchell, September 15, 1862
Brig. Gen. J. M. Brannan, October 27, 1862
Maj. Gen. David Hunter, January 20, 1863
Maj. Gen. Q. A. Gillmore, June 12, 1863
Brig. Gen. A. H. Terry, June 15, 1864
Brig. Gen. W. T. H. Brooks, June 19, 1864
Brig. Gen. A. H. Terry, July 18, 1864
Maj. Gen. D. B. Birney, July 23, 1864
Brig. Gen. A. H. Terry, October 11, 1864
Maj. Gen. A. H. Terry, March 27, 1865. (Reorganized corps.)
Brig. Gen. A. Ames, May 12, 1865

Eleventh Army Corps, Army of the Potomac, until September 25, 1863, and Department of the Cumberland until April 18, 1864: Created by General Orders, No. 129, Adjutant-General's Office, September 12, 1862 by changing the designation of the First Army Corps, Army of Virginia. Merged into the Twentieth Army Corps, Army of the Cumberland, by General Orders No. 144, Adjutant-General's Office, April 4, 1864.

Commanders:
Maj. Gen. F. Sigel, September 12, 1862
Brig. Gen. J. Stahel, December 9, 1862
Maj. Gen. F. Siegel, February 5, 1863
Brig. Gen. A. Von Steinwehr, February 23, 1863
Maj. Gen. C. Schurz, March 29, 1863
Maj. Gen. O. O. Howard, April 2, 1863
Maj. Gen. C. Schurz, January 21, 1864
Maj. Gen. O. O. Howard, February 25, 1864

Twelfth Army Corps, Army of the Potomac, until September 25, 1863 and Department of the Cumberland until April 18, 1864: Created by General Orders, No. 129, Adjutant-General's Office, September 12, 1862, by changing the designation of the Second Army Corps, Army of Virginia. Merged into the Twentieth Army Corps, Army of the Cumberland, by General Orders No. 144, Adjutant-General's Office, April 4, 1864.

Commanders:
Brig. Gen. A. S. Williams, September 18, 1862
Maj. Gen. H. W. Slocum, October 20, 1862
Brig. Gen. A. S. Williams, August 31, 1863
Maj. Gen. H. W. Slocum, September 13, 1863

Thirteenth Army Corps, Department of the Tennessee, until August 7, 1863, and Department of the Gulf until June 11, 1864: Created by General Orders, No. 168, Adjutant-General's Office, October 24, 1862, to consist of the troops under the command of General Grant (Department of the Tennessee). Reorganized by General Orders, No. 210, Adjutant-General's Office, December 18, 1862. Discontinued by General Orders, No. 210, Adjutant-General's Office, June 11, 1864.

Commanders:
Maj. Gen. U. S. Grant, October 25, 1862
Maj. Gen. J. A. McClernand, January 31, 1863
Maj. Gen. E. O. C. Ord, September 15, 1863
Maj. Gen. C. C. Washburne, August 7, 1863
Maj. Gen. E. O. C. Ord, September 15, 1863
Maj. Gen. C. C. Washburne, October 20, 1863
Maj. Gen. N. J. T. Dana, October 26, 1863
Maj. Gen. E. O. C. Ord, January 9, 1864
Maj. Gen. J. A. McClernand, February 23, 1864
Brig. Gen. W. P. Benton, June 1, 1864

Thirteenth Army Corps, Military Division, West Mississippi: Created by General Orders, No. 20, Military Division of West Mississippi February 18, 1865, to consist of the reserve of that military division. Confirmed by General Orders No. 28, Adjutant-General's Office, February 26, 1865. Discontinued by General Orders, No. 124, Adjutant-General's Office, July 20, 1865.

Commander: Maj. Gen. Gordon Granger, February 18, 1865

Fourteenth Army Corps, Department of the Cumberland: Created by General Orders, No. 168, Adjutant-General's Office, October 24, 1862, to consist of the troops under Major-General Rosecrans (Department of the Cumberland). Reorganized by General Orders, No. 9, Adjutant-General's Office, January 9, 1863. Discontinued by General Orders, No. 131, Adjutant-General's Office, August 1, 1865.

Commanders:
Maj. Gen. W. S. Rosecrans, October 27, 1862
Maj. Gen. George H. Thomas, January 9, 1863
Maj. Gen. J. M. Palmer, October 28, 1863
Brig. Gen. R. W. Johnson, August 6, 1864
Brevet Maj. Gen. J. C. Davis, August 9, 1864

Fifteenth Army Corps, Department of the Tennessee: Created by General Orders, No. 210, Adjutant-General's Office, December 18, 1862, consisting of troops in the Department of the Tennessee and Department of the Missouri, operating on the Mississippi River. Discontinued by General Orders, No. 131, Adjutant-General's Office, August 1, 1865.

Commanders:

Maj. Gen. W. T. Sherman, January 5, 1863
Maj. Gen. F. P. Blair, Jr., October 29, 1863
Maj. Gen. John A. Logan, December 11, 1863
Maj. Gen. P. J. Osterhaus, September 23, 1864
Maj. Gen. John A. Logan, January 2, 1865
Maj. Gen. W. B. Hazen, May 23, 1865

Sixteenth Army Corps, Department of the Tennessee: Created by General Orders, No. 210, Adjutant-General's Office, December 18, 1862, consisting of troops in the Department of the Tennessee and Department of the Missouri, operating on the Mississippi River. Discontinued by General Orders, No. 277, Adjutant-General's Office November 7, 1864.

Commanders:

Maj. Gen. S. A. Hurlbut, February 5, 1863 to April 17, 1864 (Corps had no commander from then until October 15, 1864)
Maj. Gen. N. J. T. Dana, October 15, 1864

Sixteenth Army Corps, Military Division of West Mississippi: Organized by General Orders, No. 20, Military Division of West Mississippi February 18, 1865, to consist of the infantry divisions from the Army of the Cumberland. Confirmed by General Orders, No. 28, Adjutant-General's Office, February 26, 1865. Discontinued by General Orders, No. 124, Adjutant-General's Office, July 20, 1865.

Commanders: Maj. Gen. A. J. Smith, February 18, 1865

Seventeenth Army Corps, Department of the Tennessee: Created by General Orders, No. 210, Adjutant-General's Office December 18, 1862, to consist of troops in the Department of the Tennessee and Department of the Missouri operating on the Mississippi River. Discontinued by General Orders No. 131, Adjutant-General's Office, August 1, 1865.

Commanders:

Maj. Gen. J. B. McPherson, January 11, 1863
Maj. Gen. F. P. Blair, Jr., May 4, 1864
Brig. Gen. T. E. G. Ransom, September 22, 1864
Brig. Gen. M. D. Leggett, October 10, 1864
Maj. Gen. J. A. Mower, October 24, 1864
Maj. Gen. F. P. Blair, Jr., October 31, 1864
Brig. Gen. W. W. Belknap, July 19, 1865

Eighteenth Army Corps, Department of North Carolina, until August —, 1863, and Department of Virginia and North Carolina (Army of the James) to December 3, 1864: Created by General Orders, No. 214, Adjutant-General's Office, December 24, 1862, to consist of troops in North Carolina, Reorganized, April 28, 1864. Discontinued by General Orders, No. 297, Adjutant-General's Office, December 3, 1864. White troops transferred to the Twenty-fourth Army Corps, and the colored troops to the Twenty-fifth Army Corps.

Commanders:

Maj. Gen. J. G. Foster, December 24, 1862
Brig. Gen. I. N. Palmer, July 2, 1863
Maj. Gen. J. G. Foster, August 8, 1863
Maj. Gen. B. F. Butler, October 28, 1863
Maj. Gen. W. F. Smith, May 2, 1864
Brig. Gen. J. H. Martindale, July 19, 1864
Maj. Gen. E. O. C. Ord, July 21, 1864
Maj. Gen. John Gibbon, September 4, 1864
Maj. Gen. E. O. C. Ord, September 22, 1864
Brevet Maj. Gen. G. Weitzel, October 1, 1864

Nineteenth Army Corps, Department of the Gulf until July —, 1864, and Middle Military Division until March —, 1865: Created by General Orders No. 5, Adjutant-General's Office, January 5, 1863, to consist of the troops in the Department of the Gulf, to date from December 14, 1862. Discontinued by General Orders, No. 4, Adjutant-General's Office, March 20, 1865.

Commanders:

Maj. Gen. N. P. Banks, December 16, 1862
Maj. Gen. William B. Franklin, August 20, 1863
Brig. Gen. William H. Emory, May 2, 1864
Brig. Gen. B. S. Roberts, July 2, 1864
Brig. Gen. M. K. Lawler, July 6, 1864
Maj. Gen. J. J. Reynolds, July 7, 1864
Brevet Maj. Gen. William H. Emory, November 7, 1864
Brig. Gen. C. Grover, December 10, 1864
Brev. Maj. Gen. William H. Emory, December 28, 1864

Twentieth Army Corps, Department of the Cumberland: Created by General Orders, No. 9, Adjutant-General's Office, January 9, 1863, to consist of troops in the Army of the Cumberland. Discontinued October 9, 1863, in compliance with General Orders, No. 322, Adjutant-General's Office, September 28, 1863. Merged into the Fourth Army Corps, Army of the Cumberland. Reorganized by General Orders No. 144, Adjutant-General's Office, April 4, 1864, by the consolidation of the Eleventh and Twelfth Army Corps, Army of the Cumberland. Discontinued, June 1, 1865, by General Orders, No. 131, Adjutant-General's Office, July 28, 1865.

Commanders:

Maj. Gen. A. McD. McCook, January 9, 1863
Maj. Gen. Joseph Hooker, April 4, 1864
Brig. Gen. A. S. Williams, July 27, 1864
Maj. Gen. H. W. Slocum, August 27, 1864
Brig. Gen. A. S. Williams, November 11, 1864
Maj. Gen. J. A. Mower, April 1, 1865

Twenty-first Army Corps, Department of the Cumberland: Created by General Orders, No. 9, Adjutant-General's Office, January 9, 1863, to consist of troops in the Army of the Cumberland. Merged into the

Fourth Army Corps, Army of the Cumberland, October 9, 1863, in compliance with General Orders, No. 322, Adjutant-General's Office, September 28, 1863.

Commanders:

Maj. Gen. T. L. Crittenden, January 9, 1863
Brig. Gen. T. J. Wood, February 18, 1863
Maj. Gen. T. L. Crittenden, March 4, 1863
Maj. Gen. J. M. Palmer, July 18, 1863
Maj. Gen. T. L. Crittenden, August 11, 1863

Twenty-second Army Corps, Department of Washington: Created by General Orders, No. 26, Adjutant-General's Office, February 2, 1863, to consist of troops in the Department of Washington. Discontinued, June 11, 1866.

Commanders:

Maj. Gen. S. P. Heintzelman, February 7, 1863
Maj. Gen. C. C. Augur, October 13, 1863
Maj. Gen. J. G. Parke, June 7, 1865
Maj. Gen. C. C. Augur, June 26, 1865

Twenty-third Army Corps, Department of the Ohio, until January —, 1865, and Department of North Carolina until August 1865: Created by General Orders No. 103, Adjutant-General's Office, April 27, 1863, to consist of the troops in Kentucky, not belonging to the Ninth Army Corps. Reorganized by Special Orders, No. 101, Department of the Ohio, April 10, 1864. Discontinued by General Orders, No. 131, Adjutant-General's Office, August 1, 1865.

Commanders:

Maj. Gen. G. L. Hartsuff, May 28, 1863
Brig. Gen. M. D. Manson, September 24, 1863
Brig. Gen. J. D. Cox, December 8, 1863
Maj. Gen. George Stoneman, January 28, 1864
Maj. Gen. J. M. Schofield, April 4, 1864
Maj. Gen. J. D. Cox, April 2, 1865
Brig. Gen. S. P. Carter, June 8, 1865

Twenty-fourth Army Corps, Department of Virginia: Created by General Orders, No. 297, Adjutant-General's Office, December 3, 1864, to consist of the white troops of the Tenth and Eighteenth Army Corps. Discontinued by General Orders, No. 131, Adjutant-General's Office, August 1, 1865.

Commanders:

Maj. Gen. E. O. C. Ord, December 3, 1864
Brevet Maj. Gen. A. H. Terry, December 8, 1864
Brig. Gen. C. Devens, January 2, 1865
Maj. Gen. John Gibbon, January 15, 1865
Brevet Maj. Gen. J. W. Turner, July 1, 1865

Twenty-fifth Army Corps, Department of Virginia, until June 1865, and Department of Texas until January 1866: Created by General Orders, No. 297, Ad-

jutant-General's Office, December 3, 1864, to consist of the colored troops of the Tenth and Eighteenth Army Corps. Discontinued by General Orders, No. 2, Adjutant-General's Office, January 8, 1866.

Commanders:

Maj. Gen. G. Weitzel, December 4, 1864
Brig. Gen. C. A. Heckman, January 12, 1865
Maj. Gen. G. Weitzel, February 17, 1865

Cavalry Corps, Army of the Potomac: Created by General Orders, No. 6, Army of the Potomac, February 5, 1863, to consist of the cavalry of the Army of the Potomac. Discontinued, June 28, 1865.

Commanders:

Brig. Gen. George Stoneman, February 7, 1863
Brig. Gen. Alfred Pleasonton, June 7, 1863
Brig. Gen. D. McM. Gregg, March 26, 1864
Maj. Gen. P. H. Sheridan, April 6, 1864
Brevet Maj. Gen. D. McM. Gregg, August 4, 1864
Maj. Gen. P. H. Sheridan, March 28, 1865

THE NAVY

Navy Department

Office of Secretary of Navy:
Secretary of the Navy—Gideon Welles
Assistant Secretary—Gustavus V. Fox
Chief Clerk—William Faxon

Chiefs of Bureaus:

Yards and Docks—Joseph Smith
Navigation—Charles Henry Davis
Ordnance—Henry A. Wise
Equipment and Recruiting—Albert N. Smith
Medicine and Surgery—William Whelan
Provisions and Clothing—Horatio Bridge
Construction and Repair—John Lenthall
Steam Engineering—B. F. Isherwood

Naval Commanders
(From Navy Register, Jan. 1, 1865)

Admirals:
Vice Admiral—David G. Farragut
Rear Admiral—L. M. Goldsborough
            Samuel F. DuPont
            Charles H. Davis
            John A. Dahlgren
            David D. Porter

Commodores:
Theodorus Bailey
Thomas T. Craven
Henry K. Hoff
Henry H. Bell
William Smith
John W. Livingston
Henry K. Thatcher
John S. Missroon

Robert B. Hitchcock
Stephen C. Rowan
Joseph Lanman
Thomas Turner
Charles H. Poor
James F. Schenck
Timothy A. Hunt
Sylvanus W. Godon
James S. Palmer
William Radford
John Rodgers

(An additional 30 are listed on the Retired List).

Other Officers:

Captains—35 active, 14 retired
Commanders—67 active, 22 retired
Lt. Commanders—139 active, 1 retired
Lieutenants—113 active, 11 retired, 10 reserved
Ensigns—55 all classes
Midshipmen—32 all classes

MARINE CORPS COMMANDERS
(Navy Register, January 1, 1865)

Colonel Commandant—Jacob Zeilen

General Staff:

Quartermaster—Major William B. Slack
Adjutant and Inspector—Major A. S. Nicholson
Paymaster—Major John C. Cash
Asst. Quartermaster—Captain W. A. T. Maddox
    Captain James Wiley
Colonel—William L. Shuttleworth
Lieutenant Colonel—Mathew R. Kintzing
    James H. Jones
Major—Thomas Y. Field
    Charles G. McCawley
    George R. Graham
    John L. Broome
Captains—19
First Lieutenants—30
Second Lieutenants—22

CONGRESSIONAL CITATIONS

The following are honors conferred by the Congress of the United States in Public Acts, together with dates of approval.

ARMY

Joint Resolution:

"To the gallant and patriotic services of the late Brigadier-General Nathaniel Lyon, and the officers and soldiers under his command at the battle of Springfield, Missouri."

December 24, 1861

———

"To the officers, soldiers, and seamen of the Army and Navy of the United States, for the heroic gal-lantry that . . . has won the recent series of brilliant victories over the enemies of the Union and constitution."

February 22, 1862

———

"To Major-General William S. Rosecrans, and the officers and men under his command, for their gallantry and good conduct in the battle of Murfreesboro, Tennessee."

March 3, 1863

———

"To Major-General Ulysses S. Grant, and the officers and soldiers who have fought under his command during the rebellion; and providing that the President shall cause a medal to be struck, to be presented to Major-General Grant in the name of the people of the United States of America."

December 17, 1863

———

"To Major-General Nathaniel P. Banks, and the officers and soldiers under his command at Port Hudson."

January 28, 1864

———

"To Major-General Ambrose E. Burnside, and the officers and men who have fought under his command, for their gallantry, good conduct, and soldier-like endurance."

January 28, 1864

———

"To Major-General Joseph Hooker, Major-General Geo. G. Meade, Major-General Oliver O. Howard, and the officers and soldiers of the Army of the Potomac, for the skill, energy, and endurance in covering Washington and Baltimore, and for the skill and heroic valor displayed at Gettysburg, Pa."

January 28, 1864

———

"To Major-General W. T. Sherman, and the officers and soldiers who served under him, for their gallant and arduous services in marching to the relief of the Army of the Cumberland and at the battle of Chattanooga."

February 19, 1864

———

"To the Volunteer Soldiers who have re-enlisted in the army."

March 3, 1864

———

"To Lieutenant-Colonel Joseph Bailey, Fourth Wisconsin Volunteers, for distinguished services in the recent campaign on the Red River, by which the gunboat flotilla under Rear-Admiral David D. Porter was rescued from imminent peril."

June 11, 1864

———

"To Major-General William T. Sherman, and the officers and soldiers of his command, for their gallant conduct in their late brilliant movement through Georgia."

January 10, 1865

————

"To Brevet Major-General Alfred H. Terry, and to the officers and men under his command, for the unsurpassed gallantry and skill exhibited by them in the attack upon Fort Fisher, and for their long and faithful services and unwavering devotion to the cause of the Country.

January 24, 1865

————

"To Major-General Geo. H. Thomas, and the army under his command, for the signal defeat of the rebel army under General Hood."

March 3, 1865

————

"To Major-General Winfield S. Hancock for his services with the Army of the Potomac in 1863."

April 21, 1866

————

"To the officers, soldiers, and seamen of the United States, by whose valor and endurance, on land and on sea, the rebellion has been crushed."

May 30, 1866

NAVY

Joint Resolution:

"To Captain Samuel F. DuPont, and through him to the officers, petty officers, seamen, and marines attached to the squadron under his command, for the decisive and splendid victory achieved at Port Royal on the seventh day of November last.

February 22, 1862

————

"To Captain A. H. Foote of the United States Navy, and to the officers and men of the western flotilla under his command, for the great gallantry exhibited by them in the attack upon Forts Henry and Donelson, for their efficiency in opening the Tennessee, Cumberland, and Mississippi rivers to the pursuits of lawful commerce, and for their unwavering devotion to the cause of the Country in the midst of the greatest difficulties and dangers."

March 19, 1862

————

"To Lieutenant John L. Worden, of the United States Navy, and to the officers and men of the iron-clad gunboat *Monitor*, under his command, for the skill and gallantry exhibited by them in the late remarkable battle between the *Monitor* and the rebel iron-clad steamer *Merrimac*.

July 11, 1862

————

"To Captain David G. Farragut, of the United States Navy, and to the officers and men under his command, composing his squadron in the Gulf of Mexico, for their successful operations on the lower Mississippi river, and for their gallantry displayed in the capture of Forts Jackson and St. Philip and the city of New Orleans, and the destruction of the enemy's gunboats and armed flotilla."

July 11, 1862

————

"To Captain Louis M. Goldsborough, and through him to the officers, petty officers, seamen, and marines attached to the squadron under his command, for the brilliant and decisive victory achieved at Roanoke Island on the seventh, eighth, and tenth days of February last."

July 11, 1862

————

"To Captain Andrew H. Foote, of the United States Navy, for his eminent services and gallantry at Fort Henry, Fort Donelson, and Island Number Ten, while in command of the naval forces of the United States."

July 16, 1862

————

"To Commander John L. Worden for highly distinguished conduct in conflict with the enemy in the remarkable battle between the United States iron-clad steamer *Monitor*, under his command, and the rebel iron-clad frigate *Merrimac*, in March, eighteen hundred and sixty-two."

February 3, 1863

————

"To Commodore Charles Henry Davis, for distinguished services in conflict with the enemy at Fort Pillow, at Memphis, and for successful operations at other points in the waters of the Mississippi river; Captain John A. Dahlgren, for distinguished service in the line of his profession, improvements in ordnance, and zealous and efficient labors in the ordnance branch of the service; Captain Stephen C. Rowan, for distinguished services in the waters of North Carolina and particularly in the capture of Newbern, being in chief command of the naval forces; Commander David D. Porter, for the bravery and skill displayed in the attack on the post of Arkansas, which surrendered to the combined military and naval forces on the tenth of January, eighteen hundred and sixty-three; Rear Admiral Silas H. Stringham, now on the retired list, for distinguished services in the capture of Forts Hatteras and Clark."

February 7, 1863

————

"To Captain John Rodgers for the eminent skill and gallantry exhibited by him in the engagement with the rebel armed iron-clad steamer *Fingal*, alias *Atlanta*, whilst in command of the United States iron-clad steamer *Weehawken*, which led to her capture on June seventeenth, eighteen hundred and sixty-three; and also for the zeal, bravery, and general good conduct shown by this officer on many occasions."

December 23, 1863

"To Commodore Ringgold, the officers, petty officers, and men of the United States ship *Sabine,* for the daring and skill displayed in rescuing the crew of the steam transport *Governor* wrecked in a gale on the first day of November, eighteen hundred and sixty-one, having on board a battalion of United States marines under the command of Major John G. Reynolds, and in the search for, and rescue of, the United States line-of-battle ship *Vermont,* disabled in a gale upon the twenty-sixth day of February last, with her crew and freight."

March 7, 1864

"To Admiral David D. Porter, commanding the Mississippi squadron, for the eminent skill, endurance and gallantry, exhibited by him and his squadron, in cooperation with the Army, in opening the Mississippi River."

April 19, 1864

"To Captain John A. Winslow, of the United States Navy, and to the officers, petty officers, seamen and marines of the United States steamer *Kearsage,* for the skill and gallantry exhibited by him and the officers and men under his command in the brilliant action on the nineteenth of June, eighteen hundred and sixty-four, between that ship and the piratical craft *Alabama,* a vessel superior to his own in tonnage, in guns, and in the number of her crew."

December 20, 1864

"To Lieutenant William B. Cushing, of the United States Navy, and to the officers and men under his command, for the skill and gallantry exhibited by them in the destruction of the rebel iron-clad steamer *Albemarle* at Plymouth, North Carolina, on the night

of the twenty-seventh of October, eighteen hundred and sixty-four."

December 20, 1864

"To Rear-Admiral David D. Porter, and to the officers, petty officers, seamen and marines under his command, for the unsurpassed gallantry and skill exhibited by them in the attacks upon Fort Fisher and the brilliant and decisive victory by which that important work has been captured from the rebel forces and placed in the possession and under the authority of the United States, and for their long and faithful services and unwavering devotion to the cause of the country in the midst of the greatest difficulties and dangers."

January 24, 1865

"To Vice-Admiral David G. Farragut, of the United States Navy, and to the officers, petty officers, seamen, and marines under his command, for the unsurpassed gallantry and skill exhibited by them in the engagement in Mobile Bay on the fifth day of August, eighteen hundred and sixty-four, and for their long and faithful services and unwavering devotion to the cause of the country in the midst of the greatest difficulties and dangers."

February 10, 1866

CIVIL WAR OFFICERS WHO BECAME PRESIDENT
Brigadier General Andrew Johnson 1865-1869
Lieutenant General U. S. Grant 1869-1877
Bvt. Maj. Gen. R. B. Hays 1877-1881
Maj. Gen. James A. Garfield 1881
Bvt. Brig. Gen. Benjamin Harrison 1889-1893
Bvt. Maj. William McKinley 1897-1901

To this list could be added Chester A. Arthur (1881-1885) who rendered valuable service during the Civil War as Quartermaster-General of the State of New York.

CHAPTER 22

Civil War Bibliography

ALMOST A quarter of a century ago one of the foremost American historians pointed out that the sources and literature of the Civil War are of enormous proportions. This historian, James G. Randall, has left one of the best general bibliographies on the war which has yet appeared. It covers some forty pages of his excellent *Civil War and Reconstruction*, which appeared in 1937. Owing to the plethora of books and articles on the Civil War published during the last two decades, the problem of drawing up a selective list is even more complicated than when Randall wrote.

Accordingly, the approach has been, first of all, to list at the end of each chapter the specific works consulted in the preparation of that chapter. The second step has been to select for each field of interest (e.g. the Navy) those works which extensive study and cross-checking of reference material have indicated as being the most critical and informative. No attempt has been made to cover the rich sources available in unpublished manuscripts, graduate theses, or in Federal and local archives. Such Government publications as the *Congressional Globe* and the "Congressional Documents" are indexed in Benjamin P. Poore's indispensable *Descriptive Catalogue of Government Publications, 1774-1881.* The *United States Statutes at Large* have been of very real value in preparation of various sections of this book. The student of the Civil War period will get contemporary flavor by consulting newspapers which appeared from 1861 to 1865; lists of newspapers are given in *A Check List of Newspapers in the Library of Congress* (1901), and in various other depositories. Many libraries have valuable guides to periodical literature. A good general introduction to Northern writing on the Civil War is found in the "notes" and annotations of Edward Channing's *History of the United States,* Volume VI. For references on all biographical subjects the reader should consult the *Dictionary of American Biography.* A list of training manuals, with annotations is given in Chapter III.

A good source of information on the attitudes and mores of the war period is the historical novel. Although, in general, historians tend to be patronizing about this form of war literature, some of these novels are excellent for getting the spirit of the times; and, in fact, many are fictionalized accounts of personal experiences and actual events. A very worthwhile beginning in the field of Civil War fiction is Robert A. Lively's *Fiction Fights the Civil War* (Chapel Hill, 1957). Personal experiences of individuals appear in such published sources as regimental histories; published diaries, journals, and reminiscences; and Loyal Legion publications. The author has cited all unpublished letters and diaries which he has used in the preparation of this work. With the renewed interest in the war which has been heightened by the approaching centennial celebration, it is anticipated that many diaries and letters, heretofore unpublished, will be made available to the public in published form. It is to be regretted that so little was done to record the anecdotes and experiences of the "Boys in Blue" while they were still with us. But we were young then and much more concerned with the Argonne Forest or the Normandy beachhead.

Material on the Federal Navy and Marine Corps is disappointingly meager. Practically no personal reminiscences of enlisted personnel in either the Navy or Marine Corps are available. The situation with respect to officers of the Navy is somewhat better. Some of the Loyal Legion papers, for example, were given by officers of the Federal Navy.

However, in contrast with the commanders of the armies, many of whom wrote and published memoirs, such as Grant, Sherman, Sheridan, and others—comparatively few of the chief naval commanders left behind their memoirs, formal histories, or autobiographies. Foote died during the war, and DuPont two months after it ended. Farragut kept a journal and wrote numerous family letters, the most important of which are found in the biography written by his son. Admiral Porter wrote a naval history of the war and also an inaccurate but interesting book of personal recollections. There are extremely few personal accounts by subordinate officers or ordinary seamen.

The reader is referred to the *Official Records, Battles and Leaders,* the Gideon Welles *Diary,* and the *Confidential Correspondence of Gustavus Vasa Fox,* Welles' assistant in the Navy Department. One of the best bibliographies is to be found in Macartney's

Mr. Lincoln's Admirals. The list of works cited in this chapter, although by no means complete, is a beginning for the student of naval operations during the war. Technical naval literature of the war period is listed in the appropriate place in the chapter on training manuals. Volume 6 of *Photographic History* is invaluable, while personal accounts in the various Loyal Legion publications contain much personal reminiscence of considerable interest. See also the various articles of Civil War interest in issues of *U. S. Naval Institute Proceedings*.

SELECTED BIBLIOGRAPHY

The works have been selected with the purpose of introducing the reader to many of the books already published in his particular field of interest. In some cases, letters, diaries, and Government publications, already cited earlier in this book, have not been listed in this bibliography. But in such cases the reader will find the citation included in the footnotes in the chapter in which the work was used.

1. *Civil War Bibliographies*

Bartlett, John R. (Compiler), *The Literature of the Rebellion. A Catalogue of Books and Pamphlets Relating to the Civil War . . .*, Boston, 1866.

Coulter, E. Merton, *Travels in the Confederate States*, Norman, Oklahoma, 1948.

Nicholson, John P., *Catalogue of Library of Brevet Lieutenant Nicholson . . . Relating to the War of Rebellion 1861-1866*, Philadelphia, 1914.

Ryan, Daniel J., *The Civil War Literature of Ohio*, Cleveland, 1911. U. S. War Department, *Bibliography of State Participation in the Civil War . . .*, 3rd Edition, Washington, D. C., 1913.

2. *Primary Sources*

A. National Government Documents

Barnes, Joseph K. ed. *Medical and Surgical History of the War of the Rebellion.* 6 volumes. Washington, 1870-1888.

Committee on the Conduct of the War. *Report.* 8 volumes. Washington, 1863-1866.

House Executive Documents

37 Congress, 2 Session, Documents 60, 65, 96, 114, 116, 136.

37 Congress, 3 Session, Document 1.
38 Congress, 1 Session, Document 1.
38 Congress, 2 Session, Document 83.
39 Congress, 1 Session, Document 1.

House Miscellaneous Documents

37 Congress, 2 Session, Document 73.

House Reports

37 Congress, 2 Session, Report 43.
37 Congress, 3 Session, Report 5.
38 Congress, 1 Session, Reports 37, 65, 67.
38 Congress, 2 Session, Report 23.

Official Records of the Union and Confederate Navies in the War of the Rebellion. 28 volumes, 1894-1927.

Peters, Richard, (ed.) *The Public Statutes at Large of the United States of America.* Volume I (1789-1799), Boston, 1854, Volume II (1800-1813), Boston, 1848.

Senate Executive Documents

36 Congress, 1 Session, Document 60.
37 Congress, 2 Session, Documents 7, 16, 26, 64, 67, 72.

Senate Miscellaneous Documents

38 Congress, 2 Session, Documents 13, 47.

Senate Rep. Com.

37 Congress, 3 Session, Report 82.

U. S. War Department, *Memorandum Relative to Probable Number and Ages of Federal Veterans*

War of the Rebellion: A Compilation of the Official Records of the Union and Confederate Armies. 128 serial volumes and 3 volumes of atlases, Washington, 1880-1901.

B. Manuscript Material

(1) Diaries

Boston, William, Corporal, 20th Michigan Infantry. Michigan Historical Collections, University of Michigan, Ann Arbor.

Buffum, Francis H., Color Sergeant, 14th New Hampshire Infantry. Owned by author.

Frank, Frederick, First Lieutenant, 11th Indiana Infantry. Owned by author.

Goodman. R. S., Delegate, United States Christian Commission. William L. Clements Library, University of Michigan, Ann Arbor.

Haines, David H., 4th Michigan Cavalry. Burton Historical Collection, Detroit Public Library.

Ladies Soldier's Aid Society of Grand Haven. Michigan Historical Collections, University of Michigan, Ann Arbor.

Soule, Harrison, Major, 6th Michigan Heavy Artillery. Michigan Historical Collections, University of Michigan, Ann Arbor.

Spaulding, Oliver L., Colonel, 23d Michigan Infantry. Michigan Historical Collections, University of Michigan, Ann Arbor.

Stearns, Frederick, Private, 1st New York Engineers. Owned by author.

Vanderpool, George, Private, 3rd Michigan Infantry. Burton Historical Collection, Detroit Public Library.

C. Letters

(Manuscript letters found in Burton Historical Collection, Detroit Public Library, will be designated as BHC; manuscript letters found in William L. Clements Library, University of Michigan, will be designated as Clements; manuscript letters found in Michigan Historical Collections, University of Michigan, will be designated as MHC.)

Alger, Russell A., Colonel, 5th Michigan Cavalry. Official letters endorsed by Meade, Sheridan, Merritt, Custer, and Torbert. Alger Papers, Clements.

Bailey, Franklin H., 4th Michigan Cavalry, to his mother. Franklin H. Bailey Papers, MHC.

Barnes, Clet, 104th New York Infantry. Owned by author.

Billings, George M., 8th Michigan Infantry, to Governor Austin Blair. Blair Papers, BHC.

Bowerman, Stephen to Governor Austin Blair. Blair Papers, BHC.

Brearley, William H., 17th Michigan Infantry. Brearley Paper, BHC.

Buck, Henry A., 51st Illinois Infantry. Buck Papers, BHC.

Chamberlin, David P., Surgeon, 4th Michigan Infantry, to T. H. Hinchman. Hinchman Papers, BHC.

Clark, Thomas S., Lieutenant Colonel, 6th Michigan Infantry, to Governor Austin Blair. Blair Papers, BHC.

Custer, George A. to Captain A. E. Dana, with endorsements by Merritt, Torbert, and Sheridan. Transcript of Alger Papers, Clements. The original letter is in the possession of the Alger family.

Detroit Liberty Guards, to Governor Austin Blair. Blair Papers, BHC.

Fish, Benjamin P., Lieutenant, Union Home Guard (Missouri). Smith Papers, BHC.

Fomtam, H. H., Quartermaster General, Michigan Militia, to Colonel Dwight A. Woodbury. Dwight A. Woodbury Papers, MHC.

Giroux, Benjamin, Captain, 1st United States Sharpshooters, to Colonel Hiram Berdan. Blair Papers, BHC.

Halleck, H. W., to Governor Austin Blair. Blair Papers, BHC.

Haxford, Frederick, Lieutenant, 19th Michigan Infantry, to Governor Austin Blair. Blair Papers, BHC.

Hutchins, Charles H., Lieutenant, 5th Michigan Infantry. Clements Papers, BHC.

Jewett, Moses W., Corporal, 6th Connecticut Infantry. Owned by author.

Kinneman, John Walter, Corporal, 100th Ohio Infantry. Kinneman Papers, BHC.

Parkhurst, John G., Colonel, 9th Michigan Infantry. John G. Parkhurst Papers, MHC.

Prey, Gilbert G., 104th New York Infantry. Owned by author.

Rosecrans, W. S., to Governor Austin Blair. Blair Papers, BHC.

Salter, Charles H., Lieutenant, 16th Michigan Infantry, Duffield Papers, BHC.

Sherman, Adelbert C., Captain, 28th United States Colored Troops. Owned by author.

Stanton, Edwin M., to Governor Austin Blair. Blair Papers, BHC.

Stevens, William C., Lieutenant, 3rd Michigan Cavalry (later, Major, 9th Michigan Cavalry). William C. Stevens Papers, MHC.

Stewart, William C., Lieutenant, 23d Michigan Infantry, to Governor Austin Blair. Blair Papers, BHC.

Tower, John A., to Governor Austin Blair. Blair Papers, BHC.

Vernor, James, Hospital Steward, 4th Michigan Cavalry. De Graff Papers, BHC.

Vincent, Thomas M., Assistant Adjutant General, United States Army, to Governor Austin Blair. Blair Papers, BHC.

Walker, H. A., Captain, 27th Massachusetts Infantry. Owned by author.

Westervelt, William H., 1st New York Engineers, to William Porter. Reilly Papers, BHC.

Wiley, Henry A., Major, 104th New York Infantry. Owned by author.

Willcox, O. B., General, to Governor Austin Blair. Blair Papers, BHC.

Wood, W. S., Secretary, Republican State Central Committee, Detroit, Michigan, to Governor Austin Blair. Blair Papers, BHC.

Woodbury, Dwight A., Colonel, 4th Michigan Infantry, to Governor Austin Blair. Blair Papers, BHC.

3. *Published Diaries, Letters, Autobiographies, Reminiscences*

A. Northern Observers

Abbott, A. O., *Prison Life in the South.* New York, 1865.

Adams, C. F., *A Cycle of Adams Letters*, 2 vols., Boston, 1920.

Adams, John G. B., *Reminiscences of the Nineteenth Massachusetts Regiment*, Boston, 1899.

Agassiz, George, (ed.) *Meade's Headquarters 1863-1865. Letters of Colonel Theodore Lyman from the Wilderness to Appomattox.* Boston, 1922.

Alcott, Louisa M., *Hospital Sketches.* Boston, 1892.

Andrews, E. Benjamin, *A Private's Reminiscences of the First Year of the War.* Providence, 1886.

[Anonymous] *The United States Sanitary Commission.* Boston, 1863.

[Anonymous] *Notes on Hospital Life*, Philadelphia, 1864.

Bardeen, C. W., *A Little Fifer's War Diary.* Syracuse, 1910.

Billings, John D., *Hardtack and Coffee.* Boston, 1888.

Blanding, Stephen F., *In the Defences of Washington*, Providence, 1889.

Blegen, T. C., *The Civil War Letters of Colonel H. C. Heg*, Northfield, Minnesota, 1936.

Brinton, John H., *Personal Memoirs.* New York, 1914.

Brown, Augustus C., *The Diary of a Line Officer.* 1906.

Browne, Junius Henri, *Four Years in Seccesia.* Hartford, 1865.

Buell, August, *The Cannoneer.* Washington, 1890.

Burt, Silas W., *My Memoirs of the Military History of the State of New York . . . 1861-1865.*

Butler, Benjamin F., *Butler's Book.* Boston, 1892.

Calvert, Henry Murray, *Reminiscences of a Boy in Blue.* New York, 1920.

Clark, Olynthus, (ed.), *Downing's Civil War Diary.* Des Moines, 1916.

Coffin, Charles Carleton, (Coffin also wrote under the pen name of "Carleton.") *Boys of '61.* Boston, 1896.

Coffin, Charles Carleton, *Following the Flag.* Boston, 1865.

Coffin, Charles Carleton, *My Days and Nights on the Battlefield.* Boston, 1864.

Collis, Septima M., *A Woman's War Record.* New York, 1889.

Cooper, A., *In and Out of Rebel Prisons.* Oswego, New York, 1888.

Copp, Elbridge J., *Reminiscences of the War of the Rebellion.* Nashua, 1911.

Cox, Jacob Dolson, *Military Reminiscences of the Civil War.* 2 vol., New York, 1900.

Croffut, W. A. (ed.), *Fifty Years in Camp and Field.* (Dairy of Major Ethan Allen Hitchcock), New York, 1909.

Croushore, James H., (ed.), *A Volunteer's Adventures.* (Letters of Captain John William DeForest, 12th Connecticut Infantry), New Haven, 1946.

Curtis, Newton Martin. *From Bull Run to Chancellorsville.* New York, 1906.

Dana, Charles A., *Recollections of the Civil War.* New York, 1898.

Doster, William E., *Lincoln and Episodes of the Civil War.* New York, 1915.

Du Pont, H. A., *The Campaign of 1864 in the Valley of Virginia and the Expedition to Lynchburg.* New York, 1925.

Ellis, Thomas T., *Leaves from the Diary of an Army Surgeon.* New York, 1863.

Fleming, George Thornton, (ed.), *Life and Letters of Alexander Hays.*

Flinn, Frank M., *Campaigning with Banks and Sheridan.* Lynn, 1887.

Ford, Harvey S., (ed.), *Memoirs of a Volunteer.* (John Beatty, 3 Ohio Infantry), New York, 1946.

Fry, James B., *Military Miscellanies.* New York, 1889.

Geer, J. J., *Beyond the Lines: Or a Yankee Loose in Dixie*, Philadelphia, 1864.

Gibbon, John, *Personal Recollections of the Civil War*, New York, 1928.

Gilmore, James R., (ed.) *Letters of a War Correspondent*, (Charles A. Page, correspondent for New York *Tribune*) Boston, 1899.

Glazier, Willard, *Three Years in the Federal Cavalry*, New York, 1873.

Grant, U. S., *Personal Memoirs*, 2 vol., New York, 1885.

Greely, Horace, *Recollections of a Busy Life*, New York, 1869.

Harris, Samuel, *Personal Reminiscences of Samuel Harris*, Chicago, 1897.

Harris, William, *Prison-Life in the Tobacco Warehouse at Richmond*, Philadelphia, 1862.

Haupt, Herman, *Reminiscences*, Privately printed, 1901.

Hedley, F. Y., *Marching Through Georgia*, Chicago, 1885.

Higginson, Thomas Wentworth, *Army Life in a Black Regiment*, Boston, 1900.

Hoffman, Wickham, Camp, Court and Siege, New York, 1877.

Holstein, M., Three Years in Field Hospitals, Philadelphia, 1867.

Hosmer, James K., The Color Guard, Boston, 1864.

Howard, O. O., Autobiography, 2 vol., New York, 1908.

Howe, Daniel, Civil War Times, Indianapolis, 1902.

Howe, Julia Ward, Reminiscences, Boston, 1899.

Howe, M. A. De Wolfe (ed.) Marching With Sherman, (Letters and diaries of Major Henry Hitchcock) New Haven, 1927.

Howe, Mark De Wolfe (ed.) Touched with Fire, (Letters and Diary of Oliver Wendell Holmes, Jr. 1861-1864), Cambridge, 1946.

Humphreys, Charles A., Field, Camp, Hospital and Prison in the Civil War 1863-1865, Boston, 1918.

Huyette, M. C., Reminiscences of a Soldier in the American Civil War, Buffalo, 1908.

Hyde, Thomas W., Following the Greek Cross or Memories of the Sixth Army Corps, Boston, 1897.

Jaquette, H. S. (ed.) South after Gettysburg, (Letters of Cornelia Hancock from the Army of the Potomac 1863-1865) Philadelphia, 1937.

Johnson, Robert Underwood, Remembered Yesterdays, Boston, 1923.

Jones, Evan, Four Years in the Army of the Potomac, London, (N. D.).

Jones, Jenkin L., An Artilleryman's Diary, Madison, Wisconsin, 1914.

Keeler, Francis D., War Letters Written During the Rebellion, Saginaw, Michigan, 1895.

Keifer, Joseph Warren, Slavery and Four Years of War, 2 vols, New York, 1900.

Kerner, Robert J. (ed.) The Diary of Edward W. Crippen, Private, 27 Illinois Volunteers, War of the Rebellion, August 7, 1861 to September 19, 1863, (N. Imp.)

Kidd, J. H., Personal Recollections of a Cavalryman, Ionia, Michigan, 1908.

Kieffer, Harry M., Recollections of a Drummer Boy, Boston, 1881.

[Lane, David] A Soldier's Diary: The Story of a Volunteer, 1862-1865. Jackson (?), Michigan, 1905.

Langworthy, Daniel Avery, Reminiscences of a Prisoner of War and His Escape, Minneapolis, 1915.

Livermore, Mary, My Story of the War, Hartford, 1890.

Livermore, Thomas L., Days and Events (1860-1866), Boston, 1920.

Lusk, William Chittenden (ed.) War Letters of William Thompson Lusk, New York, 1911.

Lynch, Charles H., The Civil War Diary of Charles H. Lynch, 18th Conn. Vol's, Privately printed, 1915.

Marks, J. J., The Peninsular Campaign in Virginia, Philadelphia, 1864.

McClellan, George B., McClellan's Own Story, New York, 1887.

McClure, Alexander K., Recollections of Half a Century, Salem, Massachusetts, 1902.

Meade, George Gordon (ed.) The Life and Letters of George Gordon Meade, 2 vols, New York, 1913.

Miles, Nelson A., Serving the Republic, New York, 1911.

Nichols, George, The Story of the Great March, (From the diary of a staff officer) New York, 1865.

Norton, O. W., Army Letters (1861-1865), Chicago, 1903.

Parker, David, A Chautauqua Boy in '61 and Afterward, Boston, 1912.

Perry, Martha Derby, Letters from a Surgeon in the Civil War, (Surgeon John G. Perry, 20th Massachusetts Infantry) Boston, 1906.

Porter, Horace, Campaigning with Grant, New York, 1897.

Putnam, George Haven, A Prisoner of War in Virginia 1864-1865, New York, 1912.

Putnam, George Haven, Some Memories of the Civil War, New York, 1924.

Reed, William Howell, Hospital Life in the Army of the Potomac, Boston, 1866.

Richardson, Albert D., The Secret Service, the Field, the Dungeon, and the Escape, Hartford, 1865.

Riddle, Albert, Recollections of War Times, New York, 1895.

Schofield, John M., Forty-Six Years in the Army, New York, 1897.

Schurz, Carl, Reminiscences, 3 vols., New York, 1907.

Sedgwick, Henry D. (compiler) Correspondence of John Sedgwick, Major-General, 2 vols, 1902.

Shannon, F. A., (ed.) The Civil War Letters of Sergeant Onley Andrus, Urbana, 1947.

Sheridan, P. H., Personal Memoirs, 2 vols., New York, 1888.

Sherman, W. T., Personal Memoirs, 2 vols., New York, 1891.

Small, Harold Adams (ed.), The Road to Richmond, (Civil War Memoirs and diary of Major Abner R. Small, 16th Maine Infantry), Berkeley, California, 1939.

Smith, W. B., On Wheels and How I Came There, New York, 1892.

Smith, William Farrar, From Chattanooga to Petersburg Under Generals Grant and Butler, New York, 1893.

Stevens, George T., Three Years in the 6th Corps, Albany, 1866.

Stillwell, Leander, The Story of a Common Soldier of Army Life in the Civil War 1861-1865. Second edition, Erie, Kansas, 1920.

Sturgis, Thomas, Prisoners of War 1861-1865, New York, 1912.

Thorndike, Rachel Sherman (ed.) The Sherman Letters, New York, 1894.

Tremain, Henry, Two Days of War, New York, 1905.

Trobriand, Regis de, Quatre Ans de Campagne a l'Armee du Potomac, 2 vols, Paris, 1867.

Trumbull, H. Clay, War Memories of an Army Chaplain, New York, 1898.

Tyler, William S. (ed.) Recollections of the Civil War, (Letters and diaries of Lieutenant Colonel Mason Whiting Tyler, 37th Massachusetts Infantry), New York, 1912.

[United States Sanitary Commission] Hospital Transports, Boston, 1863.

Vail, Enos B., Reminiscences of a Boy in the Civil War, Privately printed, 1915.

Van Alstyne, Lawrence, Diary of an Enlisted Man, New Haven, 1910.

Wallace, Lew, Autobiography, 2 vols, New York, 1906.

Wells, Seth J., The Diary of Seth J. Wells, Detroit, 1915.

Wheelock, Julia S., The Boys in White, New York, 1870.

Wilkeson, Frank, Recollections of a Private Soldier in the Army of the Potomac, New York, 1887.

Williams, Charles Richard, (ed.) Diary and Letters of Rutherford Birchard Hayes, 5 vols., Columbus, Ohio, 1922-1926.

Wilson, James H., Under the Old Flag, 2 vols, New York, 1912.

Winther, Oscar Osburn (ed.) With Sherman to the Sea, (Letters, diaries, and reminiscences of Theodore F. Upson), Baton Rouge, 1943.

Wormeley, Katharine Prescott, The Other Side of War with the Army of the Potomac, (Letters from Katharine Prescott Wormeley, United States Sanitary Commission), Boston, 1889.

B. Southern Observers

Alexander, E. P., Military Memoirs of a Confederate, New York, 1907.

Allan, William, The Army of Northern Virginia in 1862, Boston, 1892.

Baylor, George, *Bull Run to Bull Run*, Richmond, 1900.

Beale, George William, *A Lieutenant of Cavalry in Lee's Army*, Boston, 1918.

Bernard, George S. (ed.) *War Talks of Conferedate Veterans*, Petersburg, 1892.

Blackford, Charles Minor, (ed.) *Letters from Lee's Army*, New York, 1947.

Blackford, William W., *War Years with Jeb Stuart*, New York, 1945.

Clark, Walter, (ed.) *Histories of the Several Regiments and Battalions from North Carolina in the Great War 1861-'65*, 5 vols., Raleigh, 1901.

Dame, William Meade, *From the Rapidan to Richmond and the Spottsylvania Campaign*, Baltimore, 1920.

Dawson, Warrington, (ed.) *A Confederate Girl's Diary*, (Sarah Dawson), Boston, 1913.

Douglas, Henry Kyd, *I Rode with Stonewall*, Chapel Hill, 1940.

Dunaway, Wayland Fuller. *Reminiscences of a Rebel*. New York, 1913.

Durkin, Joseph T. (ed.) *John Dooley Confederate Soldier*. Georgetown, 1945.

Early, R. H. (ed.) *Lieutenant General Jubal Anderson Early C. S. A.* Philadelphia, 1912.

Eggleston, George Cary. *A Rebel's Recollections*. New York, 1875.

French, Samuel G. *Two Wars—Mexican, Confederate*. Nashville, 1901.

Gilmor, Harry. *Four Years in the Saddle*. New York, 1866.

Goodloe, Albert Theodore. *Confederate Echoes*. Nashville, 1907.

Gordon, John B. *Reminiscences of the Civil War*. New York, 1903.

Hagood, Johnson. *Memoirs of the War of Secession*. Columbia, South Carolina, 1910.

Harrison, Burton (Mrs.) *Recollections Grave and Gay*. New York, 1911.

Hood, John. *Advance and Retreat*. New Orleans, 1880.

Hopkins, Luther. *Bull Run to Appomattox. Baltimore*, 1908.

Howard, McHenry. *Recollections of a Maryland Confederate Soldier and Staff Officer Under Johnston, Jackson and Lee*. Baltimore, 1914.

Johnson, Adam. *The Partisan Rangers of the Confederate States Army*. Louisville, 1904.

Johnston, Joseph E. *Narrative of Military Operations Directed, during the Late War Between the States*. New York, 1874.

Jones, J. B. *A Rebel War Clerk's Diary*. Philadelphia, 1866.

Longstreet, James. *From Manassas to Appomattox*. Philadelphia, 1896.

Martin, Isabella and Myrta Lockett Avary, (editors) *A Diary from Dixie* (Mary Boykin Chesnut). New York, 1905.

Maury, Dabney. *Recollections of a Virginian*. London, 1894.

McCarthy, Carlton. *Detailed Minutiae of Soldier Life in the Army of Northern Virginia*. Richmond, 1882.

Owen, William Miller. *In Camp and Battle with the Washington Artillery of New Orleans*. Boston, 1885.

Palley, J. B. *A Soldier's Letters to Charming Nellie*. New York, 1908.

Pryor, Roger, (Mrs.). *Reminiscences of Peace and War*. New York, 1905.

Smith, Gustavus W. *Confederate War Papers*. New York, 1884.

Stevenson, William. *Thirteen Months in the Rebel Army*. New York, 1863.

Stiles, Robert. *Four Years Under Marse Robert*. New York, 1903.

Taylor, Richard. *Destruction and Reconstruction*. New York, 1879.

Welch, Spencer Glasgow. *A Confederate Surgeon's Letters to His Wife*. New York, 1911.

Wise, John S. *The End of an Era*. New York, 1899.

Wright, Geraud D. (Mrs.). *A Southern Girl in '61*. New York, 1905.

Wyeth, John Allan. *With Sabre and Scalpel*. New York, 1914.

C. Foreign Observers

[An English Combatant]. *Battlefields of the South, from Bull Run to Fredericksburg*. New York, 1864.

Chanal, Francois Adolphe Victor de. *L'Armée Américaine*. Paris, 1872.

Chesney, Charles C. *A Military View of Recent Campaigns in Virginia and Maryland*. London, 1863.

Estaván, B. *War Pictures from the South*. New York, 1863.

Gasparin, Agenor. *The Uprising of a Great People*. New York, 1861.

Gurowski, Adam. *Diary from March 4, 1861 to November 12, 1862*. Boston, 1862.

Lawrence, George Alfred. *Border and Bastille*. Second edition. London, 1863.

Lecomte, Ferdinand. *The War in the United States*. New York, 1863.

Paris, Louis Philippe Albert D'Orléans, Comte De. *History of the Civil War in America*. 4 volumes. (Translated by L. F. Tasistro) Philadelphia, 1875-1888.

Russell, William Howard. *My Diary North and South*. 2 volumes. London, 1863.

Salm-Salm, Felix Princess. *Ten Years of My Life*. Detroit, 1877.

Schalk, Emil. *Campaigns of 1862 and 1863*. Philadelphia, 1863.

Struve, Gustav. *Diesseits und Jenseits des Oceans*. Coburg, 1863.

Trognon, A. (LePrince de Joinville). *Campagne de L'Armée du Potomac Mars-Juillet 1862*. New York, 1862.

4. *Veterans' Societies, Reunions, and Battlefield Tours*

[Anonymous] *Report of the Select Committee Relative to the Soldiers' National Cemetery . . .* March 1864, Harrisburg, Pa., 1864.

[Anonymous] *History of Battle-Flag Day, September 17, 1879*, Hartford, 1879.

[Anonymous] *Fiftieth Anniversary of the Battle of Gettysburg*, Harrisburg, Pa., 1913.

[Anonymous] *Pennsylvania at Gettysburg*, 4 vols., Harrisburg, Pa., 1904-1939.

[Anonymous] *Stories of Our Soldiers*, 2 vols., Boston, 1893.

Beath, Robert B., *History of the Grand Army of the Republic*, New York, 1889.

Buffum, Francis H., *Sheridan's Veterans*, 2 vols., Boston, 1883, 1886.

Cowan, John F., *A New Invasion of the South*, New York, 1881.

District of Columbia Commandery, Military Order of the Loyal Legion of the United States, *War Papers*, No. 1-98, Washington, 1887-1916.

Hanson, Joseph Mills, *Bull Run Remembers*, Manassas, Va., 1953.

Illinois Commandery, Military Order of the Loyal Legion of the United States, *Military Essays and Recollections*, 2 vols., Chicago, 1891, 1894.

Iowa Commandery, Military Order of the Loyal Legion of the United States, *War Sketches and Incidents*, 2 vols., Des Moines, 1893, 1898.

Kansas Commandery, Military Order of the Loyal Legion of the United States. Paper read by H. Seymour Hall. *Personal Experience of a Staff Officer at Mine Run and Albermarle County Raid, and as Commander of the 43rd Regiment U. S. Colored Troops, Through the Wilderness Campaign, and at the Mine Before Petersburg, Virginia, from November 7, 1863 to July 30, 1864.* Publication XIV (1894).

Kansas Commandery, Military Order of the Loyal Legion of the United States, *War Talks in Kansas*, Kansas City, Missouri, 1906.

King, W. C. and Derby, W. P. *Camp-Fire Sketches and Battlefield Echoes.*

Maine Commandery, Military Order of the Loyal Legion of the United States, *War Papers*, 3 vols., Portland, 1898-1908.

Massachusetts Commandery, Military Order of the Loyal Legion of the United States, *Civil War Papers*, 2 vols., Boston, 1900.

Michigan Commandery, Military Order of the Loyal Legion of the United States, *War Papers*, 2 vols., Detroit, 1893, 1898.

Minnesota Commandery, Military Order of the Loyal Legion of the United States, *Glimpses of the Nation's Struggle*, 6 vols., St. Paul, 1887-1909.

New York Commandery, Military Order of the Loyal Legion of the United States, *Personal Recollections of the War of the Rebellion*, First series, James Grant Wilson and Titus Munson Coan (editors), New York, 1891; Second series, A. Noel Blakeman (ed.), New York, 1897.

Ohio Commandery, Military Order of the Loyal Legion of the United States, Paper read by Henry M. Neil. *A Battery at Close Quarters*, Columbus, 1909.

Rathbun, Julius G., *Trip of the First Regiment, C.N.G. to Yorktown, Va., and Charleston, S. C.*, Hartford, 1882.

Trowbridge, J. T., *The South: A Tour of its Battle-Fields and Ruined Cities*, Hartford, 1866.

Wisconsin Commandery, Military Order of the Loyal Legion of the United States, *War Papers*, 4 vols., Milwaukee, 1903-1914.

5. Miscellaneous Sources

Adjutant General of the Commonwealth of Massachusetts. *Annual Report for the Year Ending December 31, 1861*, Boston, 1861.

American Annual Cyclopaedia and Register of Important Events of the Year/s/ 1861-1865. 5 vols., New York, 1861-1865.

Fry, James B., *New York and the conscription of 1863*, New York, 1885.

Jacobs, M., *Notes on the Rebel Invasion of Maryland and Pennsylvania*, Philadelphia, 1864.

Moore, Frank B. (ed.) *The Rebellion Record; A Diary of American Events with Documents, Narratives, Illustrative Incidents, Poetry, etc.*, New York, 1861-1868.

Richardson, James D., *A Compilation of the Messages and Papers of the Confederacy*, 2 vols., Nashville, 1905.

Schneck, B., *The Burning of Chambersburg*, Philadelphia, 1864.

Wiley, Bell Irvin, *The Life of Billy Yank*, Indianapolis, 1951.

Woman's Central Association of Relief (A branch of the United States Sanitary Commission.) *Annual Reports for 1863-1865.*

Wright, E. N., *Conscientious Objectors in the Civil War*, Philadelphia, 1931.

6. Periodicals

A. Contemporary Periodicals

Abbott, S. C. "The Military Hospitals at Fortress Monroe," *Harper's New Monthly Magazine*, XXIX (August 1864), 306-322.

[Anonymous]. Illustration, *Frank Leslie's Illustrated Newspaper*, XII (July 6, 1861), 117.

[Anonymous]. Advertisement, *Frank Leslie's Illustrated Newspaper*, XIII (April 26, 1862), 416.

[Anonymous]. "Miscellaneous," *Frank Leslie's Illustrated Newpaper*, XIV (May 3, 1862), 30.

[Anonymous]. "Common Sense to the Rescue!" *Frank Leslie's Illustrated Newspaper*, XIV (August 16, 1862), 321.

[Anonymous]. "Impedimenta," *Frank Leslie's Illustrated Newspaper*, XV (October 4, 1862), 18.

[Anonymous]. Advertisement, *Frank Leslie's Illustrated Newspaper*, XV (October 18, 1862), 63.

[Anonymous]. "Items for Soldiers," *Frank Leslie's Illustrated Newspaper*, XVI (April 18, 1863), 50.

[Anonymous]. "The Opera in the 2d Corps," *Frank Leslie's Illustrated Newspaper*, XVIII (March 26, 1864), 7.

[Anonymous]. "An English Officer," "A Month's Visit to the Confederate Headquarters," *Blackwood's Edinburg Magazine*, XCIII (January 1863), 1-29.

[Anonymous]. "Regulars and Volunteers," *Fraser's Magazine for Town and Country*, LXXI (April 1865), 421-433.

[Anonymous]. "A Visit to General Butler and the Army of the James," *Fraser's Magazine for Town and Country*, LXXI (April 1865), 434-448.

[Anonymous]. Cartoon, *Harper's Weekly: A Journal of Civilization*, V (September 7, 1861), 576.

[Anonymous]. "Health in the Camp," *The Atlantic Monthly*, VIII (November 1861), 571-580.

[Anonymous]. "The Contest in America," *The Illustrated London News*, XL (June 14, 1862), 599-600.

[Anonymous]. "The Confederate Struggle and Recognition," *The London Quarterly Review*, CCXXIV (October 1862), 281-300.

[Anonymous]. "The American Aristocracy," *The Spectator*, XXXIV (July 27, 1861), 806.

(The following unsigned articles were mainly from officers and men in the field and appeared in *The United States Army and Navy Journal and Gazette of the Regular and Volunteer Forces.*)

"What We have Neglected. A Reserve Corps—Incompetent Officers." I (August 29, 1863), 11.

"Waste of Ammunition," I (August 29, 1863), 11-12.

"The Cavalry Bureau," I (August 29, 1863), 3.

"Simple Hints on Marches of Infantry," I (September 5, 1863), 26-27.

Article on Rosecran's Corps Flags. I (September 5, 1863), 31.

"System in Promotions," I (September 12, 1863), 35.

"Artillery in the United States. Its Changes and Present Condition," I (September 12, 1863), 39.

"Re-organize the Militia," I (September 19, 1863), 51-52.

"Artillery in the United States. No. II. Siege Artillery," I (September 19, 1863), 51.

"Artillery in the United States Army. No. III. Sea-Coast Artillery," I (September 26, 1863), 68-69.

Article on Staff Work. I (October 3, 1863), 89.

"System in Promotions," I (October 10, 1863), 99.

"Military Training," I (October 10, 1863), 98-99.

"Coups d'Armée," I (October 24, 1863), 136-137.

"Infantry Clothing," I (November 14, 1863), 180-181.

"Lancers and Dragoons," I (November 14, 1863), 185.

"Infantry Equipments," I (November 28, 1863), 213.

"Improvement in Cavalry Accoutrements," I (December 5, 1863), 229.

"Chaplains," I (December 19, 1863), 261.

"An Ambulance System," I (December 26, 1863), 280-281.

"Soldier's Tricks," I (January 9, 1864), 314.

"Gen. Casey's Board and How to Pass It," I (January 30, 1864), 363.

"The Second Army Corps," I (February 6, 1864), 371.

"Responsibilities of the Staff," I (February 13, 1864) 392-393.

"The Ball of the Second Corps," I (March 12, 1864), 484.

"General Courts-Martial," I (March 19, 1864), 507-508.

"Spots on the Uniform," I (April 9, 1864), 547.

"Battles Between Officers," I (April 16, 1864), 564.

"The March of the Brigade," I (April 23, 1864), 582-583.
Article on Patents for Breech-loading Weapons. I (May 7, 1864), 617.
"The Examination of Officers," I (May 7, 1864), 614.
"Negro Troops," I (July 2, 1864), 741.
"Negro Troops," I (July 9, 1864), 758.
"A Uniform for Hot Climates," I (July 9, 1864), 758.
"The Pay of Officers," II (September 10, 1864), 35-36.
Advertisement, II (September 24, 1864), 79.
"The Pay of Army Officers," II (October 1, 1864), 85-86.
"A Glance at the Bayonet," II (November 12, 1864), 180-181.
"Officers' Pay," II (November 19, 1864), 196.
"Officers' Pay and Allowances," II (December 3, 1864), 228.
"Medals for Soldiers," II (December 17, 1864), 262.
"Breech-loading Rifles," II (December 24, 1864), 278.
"Music in the Army," II (December 31, 1864), 292.
"Officers' Pay—Still Another Point," II (January 14, 1865), 326.
"Whiskey in the Army," II (February 11, 1865), 391.
"The Fighting of Troops. No. III," II (February 25, 1865), 419-420.
"The Fighting of Troops. No. IV," II (March 4, 1865), 435-436.
"The Fighting of Troops. No. VI," II (March 18, 1865), 467-468.
"The Fighting of Troops. No. VII," II (March 25, 1865), 483-484.
"Whiskey in the Army," II (March 25, 1865), 486.
"A Badge for the Regular Officers," II (March 25, 1865), 486.
"Whiskey in the Army," II (April 15, 1865), 534-535.
Advertisement, II (April 29, 1865), 572.
"Carleton" [Charles Carleton Coffin]. "The May Campaign in Virginia," The Atlantic Monthly, XIV (July 1864), 124-132.
Casey, Silas to Thomas Webster. (Letter dated September 26, 1863.) "The Competency of Our Officers," The United States Army and Navy Journal and Gazette of the Regular and Volunteer Forces. I (October 10, 1863), 99.
Cleveland, H. W. S. "The Use of the Rifle," The Atlantic Monthly, IX (March 1862), 300-306.
Dwight, Henry O. "How We Fight at Atlanta," Harper's New Monthly Magazine, XXIX (October 1864), 663-666.
"Editor's Drawer," Article on the 25 Indiana Infantry, Harper's New Monthly Magazine, XXX (December 1864), 128.
"Editor's Easy Chair," Article on the United States Sanitary Commission Fair in New York City, Harper's New Monthly Magazine, XXIX (June 1864), 131-132.
Hannaford, Eben. "In Hospital after Stone River," Harper's New Monthly Magazine, XXVIII (January 1864), 260-265.
Higginson, Thomas Wentworth. "Regular and Volunteer Officers," The Atlantic Monthly, XIV (September 1864), 348-357.
Higginson, Thomas Wentworth. "Leaves from an Officer's Journal," The Atlantic Monthly, XIV (November 1864), 521-529 and 740-748.
Jarvis, Edward. "Sanitary Condition of the Army," The Atlantic Monthly, X (October 1862), 463-497.
Prescott, G. B. "The United States Armory," The Atlantic Monthly, XII (October 1863), 436-451.
Sherman, William T. to John A. Spooner, Recruiting Agent for the Commonwealth of Massachusetts. (Letter of July 30, 1864), "Major-General Sherman on Recruiting Negroes," The United States Army and Navy Journal and Gazette of the Regular and Volunteer Forces, II (August 27, 1864), 7.
Tomes, Robert. "The Fortunes of War," Harper's New Monthly Magazine, XXIX (July 1864), 227-231.

B. Periodicals

Barnard, George S. "The Battle of the Crater," Southern Historical Society Papers (R. A. Brock, ed.), XVIII (1890), 1-38.
Featherston, John C. "Graphic Account of Battle of Crater," Southern Historical Society Papers (R. A. Brock, ed.), XXXIII (1905), 358-374.
Fish, Carl Russell. "The Northern Railroads, April, 1861," American Historical Review, XXII (July 1917), 778-793.
Gibbon, John. "Personal Recollections of Appomattox," The Century Illustrated Monthly Magazine, LXIII (April 1902). 936-943.
Haskell, Fritz (ed.). "Diary of Colonel William Camm, 1861 to 1865," Journal of the Illinois State Historical Society, XVIII (January 1926), 793-969.
Illinois Historical Records Survey (Compiler). Calendar of the Robert Weidensall Correspondence 1861-1865. (George Williams College, Chicago, Illinois), 1940.
Kilmer, George Langdon. "Boys in the Union Army," The Century Illustrated Monthly Magazine, LXX (June 1905), 269-275.
McKelvey, Blake (ed.). "Civil War Letters of Samuel S. Partridge of the 'Rochester Regiment,'" Rochester in the Civil War. Rochester Historical Society Publications XXII (1944), 77-90.
McKelvey, Blake (ed.). "Civil War Letters of Francis Edwin Pierce of the 108th New York Volunteer Infantry," Rochester in the Civil War. Rochester Historical Society Publications XXII (1944), 150-173.
Meigs, M. C. (document). "General M. C. Meigs on the Conduct of the Civil War," American Historical Review, XXVI (January 1921), 285-303.
Parks, Leighton. "What a Boy Saw of the Civil War," The Century Illustrated Monthly Magazine, LXX (June, 1905) 258-264.
Prentice, W. R. "On the Dry Tortugas," McClure's Magazine, XVIII (April 1902), 564-570.
Randall, James G. "The Newspaper Problem in Its Bearing Upon Military Secrecy During the Civil War," American Historical Review, XXIII (January 1918), 303-323.
Robinson, Charles. "My Experiences in the Civil War," Michigan History Magazine, XXIV (Winter number, 1940), 23-50.
Stewart, Wm. H. "The Charge of the Crater," Southern Historical Society Papers (R. A. Brock, ed.), XXV (1897), 77-90.
Volwiler, A. T. (ed.) "Letters from a Civil War Officer," Mississippi Valley Historical Review, XIV (March 1928), 508-529.

7. General Works

Adams, Charles Francis. Studies Military and Diplomatic, 1775-1865. New York, 1911.
(Anonymous). The Light and Dark of the Rebellion. Philadelphia, 1863.
(Anonymous). The Union Army. 8 Vols. Madison, Wisconsin, 1908.
Barnard, J. G. and W. F. Barry. Report of the Engineer and Artillery Operations of the Army of the Potomac From Its Organizations to the Close of the Peninsular Campaign. New York, 1863.
Battine, Cecil. The Crisis of the Confederacy. London, 1905.
Beale, James. Battle Flags of the Army of the Potomac at Gettysburg, Penna. Philadelphia, 1885.
Benton, Josiah. Voting in the Field: A Forgotten Chapter of the Civil War. Boston, 1915.
Beyer, Walter F. and Oscar F. Keydel. Deeds of Valor. 2 Volumes. Detroit, 1901-1902.

Bigelow, John Jr. *The Campaign of the Chancellorsville.* New Haven, 1910.

Brownlow, William Gannanway. *Sketches of the Rise, Progress, and Decline of Secession; with a Narrative of Personal Adventures Among the Rebels.* Philadelphia, 1862.

Buel, Clarence Clough and Robert Underwood Johnson (editors). *Battles and Leaders of the Civil War.* 4 volumes. New York, 1887.

Cox, Jacob Dolson. *The March to the Sea: Franklin and Nashville.* New York, 1882.

Cox, Jacob Dolson. *The Second Battle of Bull Run as Connected with the Fitz-John Porter Case.* Cincinnati, 1882.

Crawford, Samuel Wylie. *The Genesis of the Civil War.* New York, 1887.

Davis, Jefferson. *The Rise and Fall of the Confederate Government. 2 volumes.* New York, 1881.

Dwight, Theodore F. *Campaigns in Va.* 1861-1862. Boston, 1895.

Eliot, Ellsworth Jr. *West Point in the Confederacy.* New York, 1941.

Evans, Clement A. (ed.) *Confederate Military History.* 12 volumes, Atlanta, 1899.

Fox, William F. *Regimental Losses in the American Civil War.* Fourth Edition. Albany, 1898.

Fry, James B. *McDowell and Tyler in the Campaign of Bull Run.* New York, 1884.

Freytag-Loringhoven, Hugo F. P. J. *Studien ueber Kriegfuehrung auf Grundlage des Nordamerikanischen Sezessionskrieges.* 3 volumes. Berlin, 1903.

Ganoe, William Addleman. *The History of the United States Army.* New York, 1942.

Gillmore, Q. A. *Engineer and Artillery Operations Against the Defences of Charleston Harbor in 1863.* New York, 1865.

Goldsborough, W. W. *The Maryland Line in the Confederate States Army.* Baltimore, 1869.

Henry, Robert Selph. *The Story of the Confederacy.* Indianapolis, 1931.

Hepworth, George H. *The Whip, Hoe, and Sword.* Boston, 1864.

Hesseltine, William B. *Civil War Prisons: A Study in War Psychology.* Columbus, Ohio, 1930.

Hosmer, James K. *The Appeal to Arms.* New York, 1907.

Hosmer, James K. *Outcome of the Civil War.* New York, 1907.

Humphrey, Willis C. *The Great Contest.* Detroit, 1886.

Humphreys, Andrew A. *From Gettysburg to the Rapidan.* New York, 1883.

Johnston, R. M. *Bull Run—Its Strategy and Tactics.* Boston, 1913.

Kaufmann, Wilhelm. *Die Deutschen im Amerikanischen Buergerkriege.* Munich and Berlin, 1911.

Leech, Margaret. *Reveille in Washington.* New York, 1941.

Livermore, Thomas L. *Numbers and Losses in the Civil War in America 1861-1865.* Boston. 1900.

Logan, John. *The Volunteer Soldier of America.* Chicago, 1887.

Lonn, Ella. *Desertion During the Civil War.* New York, 1928.

Lonn, Ella. *Foreigners in the Confederacy.* Chapel Hill, 1940.

Lossing, Benson J. *Pictorial History of the Civil War in the United States of America.* 3 volumes. Philadelphia, 1866.

Meredith, Roy. *Mr. Lincoln's Camera Man—Mathew B. Brady.* New York, 1946.

Miller, Francis Trevelyan. (ed.) *Photographic History of the Civil War.* New York, 1911.

Moore, Frank B. *The Civil War in Song and Story.* 1889.

Palfrey, Francis Winthrop. *The Antietam and Fredericksburg.* New York, 1882. (this is one of 13 volumes entitled, *Campaigns of the Civil War.*)

Phisterer, Frederick. *Statistical Record of the Armies of the United States.* New York. 1883.

Pollard, Edward A. *The Lost Cause.* New York, 1866.

Pollard, Edward A. *First Year of the War.* Richmond, 1862.

Pollard, Edward A. *Second Year of the War.* New York, 1863.

Pollard, Edward A. *Third Year of the War.* New York, 1865.

Quartermaster General, United States Army. (Director of Compilation) *Flags of the Army of the United States Earned During the War of the Rebellion.* Washington, 1887.

Randall, James G. *The Civil War and Reconstruction.* Boston, 1937.

Reed, John C. *The Brother's War.* Boston, 1905.

Rodenbough, Theo. F. *The Bravest Five Hundred of '61.* New York, 1891.

Ropes, John Codman and William R. Livermore. *The Story of the Civil War.* 4 volumes. New York, 1894-1913.

Schaff, Morris. *The Battle of the Wilderness.* Boston, 1910.

Scott, Robert N. *An Analytical Digest of the Military Laws of the U. S.* Philadelphia, 1873.

Shannon, Fred Albert. *The Organization and Administration of the Union Army 1861-1865.* 2 volumes. Cleveland, 1928.

Stackpole, Edward J. *Drama on the Rappahannock: The Fredericksburg Campaign.* Harrisburg, 1957.

————. *Chancellorsville: Lee's Greatest Battle.* Harrisburg, 1958.

————. *From Cedar Mountain to Antietam.* Harrisburg, 1959.

————. *They Met at Gettysburg.* Harrisburg, 1956.

Stafford, F. H. *Medals of Honor Awarded for Distinguished Service during the War of the Rebellion.* Washington, 1886.

The Navy in the Civil War. 3 volumes. (each by a separate author). New York, 1883.

(United States Sanitary Commission). *Narrative of Privations and Sufferings of the United States Officers and Soldiers while Prisoners of War in the Hands of the Rebel Authorities.* Philadelphia, 1864.

Victor, Orville J. *A History Civil, Political, and Military, of the Southern Rebellion.* 4 volumes. New York, 1861-1865.

Victor, Orville J. *Incidents and Anecdotes of the War.* New York, 1862.

Webb, Alexander S. *The Peninsula: McClellan's Campaign of 1862.* New York, 1881.

Wiley, Bell Irvin. *The Life of Johnny Reb.* New York, 1943.

8. *Biographies*

A. Northern

Bowman, S. M. and R. B. Irwin. *Sherman and His Campaigns.* New York, 1865.

Bradford, Gamaliel. *Union Portraits.*

Burne, Alfred H. *Lee, Grant, and Sherman.* Aldershot, England, 1938.

Butterfield, Julia L. *A Biographical Memoir of Gen. Daniel Butterfield.* New York, 1904.

Butts, Joseph Tyler. (ed.) *A Gallant Captain of the Civil War.* (Frederick Otto Baron Von Fritsch). New York, 1902.

Coppee, Henry. *Life and Services of Gen. U. S. Grant.* New York, 1866.

Dana, Charles A. *The Life of Ulysses S. Grant.* Springfield, Massachusetts, 1868.

Fuller, J. F. C. *The Generalship of Ulysses S. Grant.* London. 1929.

Hancock, A. F. *Reminiscences of Winfield Scott Hancock.* New York, 1929.

Humphreys, Henry H. *Andrew Atkinson Humphreys.* Philadelphia, 1924.

Kamm, Samuel R. *The Civil War Career of Thomas A. Scott.* Philadelphia, 1940.

Larke, Julian K. *General Grant and His Campaigns.* New York, 1864.

Lewis, Lloyd, *Sherman—Fighting Prophet.* New York, 1932.

Nicolay, John and John Hay. Abraham Lincoln. 10 volumes. New York, 1890-1904.

Palfrey, Francis Winthrop. *Memoirs of William Francis Bartlett.* Boston, 1878.

Perkins, Jacob R. *Trails, Rails, and War! The Life of General G. M. Dodge.* Indianapolis, 1929.

Remlap, L. T. *The Life of General U. S. Grant.* Chicago, 1885.

Stevens, Hazard, *The Life of Isaac Ingalls Stevens,* 2 vols., Boston, 1900.

B. Southern

Freeman, Douglas Southall. *R. E. Lee.* 4 volumes. New York, 1941.

Henderson, G. F. R. *Stonewall Jackson and The American Civil War.* 2 volumes. London, 1898.

Jones, Virgil Carrington. *Ranger Mosby.* Chapel Hill, 1944.

Lytle, Andrew. *Bedford Forest.* London, 1939.

McClellan, H. B. *The Life and Campaigns of Major-General J. E. B. Stuart.* Boston, 1885.

Sigaud, Louis. *Belle Boyd.* Richmond, 1944.

9. *Races and Creeds in the War*

Abel, Annie. *The American Indian as Participant in the Civil War.* 1919.

Blied, Benjamin J., The Reverend. *Catholics and the Civil War.* Milwaukee, 1945.

Britton, Wiley. *The Union Indian Brigade in the Civil War.* Kansas City, Mo. 1922.

Brown, William Wells. *The Negro in the American Rebellion.* Boston, 1867.

Fredman, J. G. and Folk, L. A. *Jews in American Wars.* New York, 1942.

Korn, Bertram Wallace. *American Jewry and the Civil War.* Philadelphia, 1951.

Lonn, Ella. *Foreigners in the Union Army and Navy.* Baton Rouge, 1951.

Pivany, Eugene. *Hungarians in the American Civil War.* Cleveland, 1913.

Quarles, Benjamin. *The Negro in the Civil War.* Boston, 1953.

Rosengarten, J. G. *The German Soldier in the Wars of the United States.* 2nd edition. Philadelphia, 1890.

Williams, George W. *A History of Negro Troops in the War of the Rebellion.* New York, 1888.

Wilson, Joseph T. *The Black Phalanx.* Hartford, 1890.

Wolf, Simon. *The American Jew as Patriot, Soldier, and Citizen.* Philadelphia, 1895.

10. *Unit Histories*

A. State Histories

Adams, Henry C. *Indiana at Vicksburg.* Indianapolis, 1910.

Belknap, Charles E. *History of the Michigan Organizations at Chickamauga, Chattanooga, and Missionary Ridge 1863.* Lansing, 1899.

Benedick, G. G. *Vermont in the Civil War.* 2 volumes. Burlington, 1886.

Byers, S. H. M. *Iowa in War Times.* Des Moines, 1888.

(Commission of Indiana). *Indiana at Chickamauga.* Indianapolis, 1901.

(Commision of Michigan). *Michigan at Gettysburg.* Detroit, 1889.

(Commission of Maine). *Maine at Gettysburg.* Portland, 1898.

Coons, John W. *Indiana at Shiloh.* 1904.

Croffutt, W. A. and John M. Morris. *The Military and Civil History of Connecticut During the War of 1861-5.* New York, 1869.

Cunningham, D. and Miller, W. W. *Report of the Ohio Antietam Battlefield Commission.* Springfield, Ohio, 1904.

Fisher, Margaret M. *Utah and the Civil War.* 1929.

Foster, John Y. *New Jersey and the Rebellion.* Newark, 1868.

Fox, William F. *New York at Gettysburg.* 3 volumes. Albany, 1900.

Gault, W. P. *Ohio at Vicksburg.* 1906.

Ingersoll, L. D. *Iowa and the Rebellion.* Philadelphia, 1866.

Lindsey, T. J. *Ohio at Shiloh.* 1903.

Magdeburg, F. H. *Wisconsin at Shiloh.* Milwaukee, 1909.

Mason, George. *Illinois at Shiloh.* 1905.

McElroy, Joseph. *Ohio at Chickamauga.* Cincinnati, 1896.

Nason, George W. *Minute Men of '61.* (Massachusetts). Boston, 1910.

Pennsylvania Antietam Battlefield Memorial Commission. *Report.* 1906.

Pennsylvania Gettysburg Battlefield Commission. *Pennsylvania at Gettysburg.* 4 volumes. 1893-1939.

Pennsylvania at Andersonville, Georgia. 1905.

Pennsylvania at Salisbury, North Carolina. 1910.

Pennsylvania at Cold Harbor, Virginia. 1912.

Reed, D. W. *The Battle of Shiloh.* (A summary of State participation in the Battle of Shiloh.) Washington, 1903.

Report of the Culpeper Virginia Monument Commission of Pennsylvania. Harrisburg, 1914.

Reid, Whitelaw. *Ohio in the War.* 2 volumes. Cincinnati, 1895.

Robertson, Jno. *Michigan in the War.* Lansing, 1880.

Schouler, William. *A History of Massachusetts in the Civil War.* 2 volumes. Boston, 1868, 1871.

Toombs, Samuel. *New Jersey Troops in the Gettysburg Campaign.* Orange, N. J. 1888.

Waite, Otis. *New Hampshire in the War.* Norwich, Connecticut, 1873.

B. The High Command

Ballard, Colin R. *The Military Genius of Abraham Lincoln.* Cleveland, 1952.

Hendrick, Burton J. *Lincoln's War Cabinet.* Boston, 1946.

Huidekoper, Frederic Louis. *The Military Unpreparedness of the United States.* New York, 1915.

Ingersoll, L. B. *History of the War Department of the United States.* Washington, 1879.

Meneely, A. Howard. *The War Department, 1861.* New York, 1928.

Pratt, Fletcher. *Stanton: Lincoln's Secretary of War.* New York, 1953.

Thian, Raphail P. *Legislative History of the General Staff of the Army of the United States . . . 1775 to 1901.* Washington, 1901.

Upton, Emory. *The Military Policy of the United States.* (third impression), Washington, 1911.

Weeden, William B. *War, Government, Federal, and State.* Boston, 1906.

Williams, T. Harry. *Lincoln and His Generals,* New York, 1952.

C. Army Histories

Fitch, John. *Annals of the Army of the Cumberland.* Philadelphia, 1864.

French, Samuel L. *The Army of the Potomac from 1861 to 1863,* New York, 1906.

Stine, J. H. *History of the Army of the Potomac.* (second edition), Washington, D. C., 1893.

Swinton, William. *Campaigns of the Army of the Potomac.* New York, 1866.

Van Horne, Thomas. *History of the Army of the Cumberland.* 2 volumes and atlas. Cincinnati, 1875.

D. Corps Histories

Bickham, W. D. *Rosecrans' Campaign with the Fourteenth Army Corps.* Cincinnati, 1863.

Fox, William F. *Slocum and His Men: A History of the Twelfth and Twentieth Army Corps.* Albany, 1904.

Irwin, Richard B. *History of the Nineteenth Army Corps.* New York, 1892.

Powell, William H. *The Fifth Army Corps.* New York, 1896.

Shreve, William P. *The Story of the Third Army Corps Union.* Boston, 1910.

Walker, Francis. *History of the Second Army Corps.* New York, 1887.

Woodbury, Augustus. *Major General Ambrose E. Burnside and the Ninth Army Corps.* Providence, 1867.

E. Division Histories

Dodge, Wm. Sumner. *History of the Old Second Division Army of the Cumberland.* Chicago, 1864.

Embick, Milton A. *Military History of the Third Division, Ninth Corps.* Pennsylvania, 1913.

Sypher, J. R. *History of the Pennsylvania Reserve Corps.* Lancaster, Pa., 1865.

Wister, Francis. *Recollections of the 12th U. S. Infantry and Regular Division 1861-1865.* Philadelphia, 1887.

F. Brigade Histories

(Anonymous). *History of the Ram Fleet and the Mississippi Marine Brigade in the War for the Union.* St. Louis, 1907.

(Anonymous). *Proceedings of Crocker's Iowa Brigade at the Second Annual Reunion.* Muscatine, Iowa, 1883.

(Anonymous). *Shaler's Brigade.* Philadelphia, 1888.

(Anonymous). *Second Brigade of the Pennsylvania Reserves at Antietam.* Harrisburg, 1908.

Banes, Charles H. *History of the Philadelphia Brigade.* Philadelphia, 1876.

Baquet, Camille. *History of the First Brigade, New Jersey Volunteers.* Trenton, 1910.

Bradley, G. S. *The Star Corps.* (2nd Brigade, 3rd Division, 20th Army Corps) Milwaukee, 1865.

Conyngham, D. P. *History of the Irish Brigade and Its Campaigns.* New York, 1867.

Hinman, Wilbur F. *The Story of the Sherman Brigade.* 1897.

Hough, Franklin B. *History of Duree's Brigade.* Albany, 1864.

Norton, Oliver W. *Strong Vincent and His Brigade at Gettysburg.* Chicago, 1909.

Smith, Charles H. *The History of Fuller's Ohio Brigade.* Cleveland, 1909.

Vale, Joseph G. *Minty and the Cavalry.* Harrisburg, 1886.

Walker, Aldace F. *The Vermont Brigade in the Shenandoah Valley, 1864.* Burlington, Vt., 1869.

G. Regimental Histories

Abbott, Stephen G. *The First Regiment New Hampshire Volunteers in the Great Rebellion.* Keene, 1890.

(Anonymous). *Story of the Service of Company E . . . Twelfth Wisconsin . . . Infantry.* Milwaukee, 1893.

(Anonymous). *The Story of One Regiment: The Eleventh Maine Infantry Volunteers in the War of the Rebellion.* New York, 1896.

(Anonymous). *A brief History of the Twenty-Eighth Regiment New York State Volunteers.* Buffalo, 1896.

Avery, P. O. *History of the Fourth Illinois Cavalry.* Humboldt, Nebraska, 1903.

Baker, Levi W., *History of the Ninth Mass. Battery.* South Framingham, 1888.

Bartlett, A. W. *History of the Twelfth Regiment New Hampshire Volunteers in the War of the Rebellion.* Concord, 1897.

Beach, William H. *The First New York (Lincoln) Cavalry.* New York, 1902.

Bidwell, Frederick David. *History of the Forty-Ninth New York Volunteers.* Albany, 1916.

Billings, John D. *The History of the Tenth Massachusetts Battery of Light Artillery in the War of the Rebellion.* Boston, 1909.

Bowen, James L. *History of the Thirty-seventh Regiment Mass. Volunteers in the Civil War of 1861-1865.* Holyoke, 1884.

Brainard, Mary Genevieve Green, *Campaigns of the One Hundred and Forty-sixth Regiment New York State Volunteers.* New York, 1915.

Brown, Alonzo L. *History of the Fourth Regiment of Minnesota Infantry Volunteers During the Great Rebellion, 1861-1865.* Saint Paul, 1892.

Bryant, Edwin E. *History of the Third Regiment of Wisconsin Veteran Volunteer Infantry 1861-1865.* Madison, 1891.

Buffum, Francis H. *A Memorial of the Great Rebellion: Being a History of the Fourteenth Regiment New Hampshire Volunteers.* Boston, 1882.

Burlingame, John K. *History of the Fifth Regiment of Rhode Island Heavy Artillery.* Providence, 1892.

Carpenter, Geo. N. *History of the Eighth Regiment Vermont Volunteers 1861-1865.* Boston, 1886.

Chamberlin, Thomas. *History of the 150th Pennsylvania Volunteers.* Philadelphia, 1905.

Cheek, Philip and Pointon, Mair. *History of the Sauk County Riflemen . . . Company "A" Sixth Wisconsin . . . Infantry.* 1909.

Cheyney, Newel, *History of the Ninth Regiment, New York Volunteers Cavalry.* Poland Center, New York, 1901.

Child, William. *A History of the Fifth Regiment New Hampshire Volunteers in the American Civil War 1861-1865.* Bristol, New Hampshire, 1893.

Clark, Orton S. *The One Hundred and Sixteenth Regiment of New York State Volunteers.* Buffalo, 1868.

Cogswell, Leander W. *A History of the Eleventh New Hampshire Regiment Volunteer Infantry in the Rebellion War.* Concord, 1891.

Cowles, Luther E. *History of the Fifth Massachusetts Battery.* Boston, 1902.

Cowtan, Charles W. *Services of the Tenth New York Volunteers (National Zouaves) in the War of the Rebellion.* New York, 1882.

Crowninshield, B. W. *A History of the First Regiment of Massachusetts Cavalry Volunteers.* Boston, 1891.

Curtis, O. B. *History of the Twenty-fourth Michigan of the Iron Brigade.* Detroit, 1891.

Cutcheon, Byron M. *The Story of the Twentieth Michigan Infantry.* Lansing, 1904.

Denison, Frederic. *Sabres and Spurs: The First Regiment Rhode Island Cavalry in the Civil War.* Central Falls, Rhode Island, 1876.

Denison, Frederic. *Shot and Shell: The Third Rhode Island Heavy Artillery Regiment in the Rebellion,* Providence, 1879.

Dornblaser, T. F. *Sabre Strokes of the Penn, Dragoons.* (7th Pennsylvania Cavalry) Philadelphia, 1884.

Eldredge, D. *The Third New Hampshire (Infantry)* Boston, 1893.

Elliott, Isaac H. *History of the Thirty-third Regiment Illinois Veteran Volunteer Infantry.* Gibson City, Illinois, 1902.

Ewer, James K. *The Third Massachusetts Cavalry in the War for the Union.* Maplewood, Mass. 1903.

Fenner, Earl. *The Story of Battery "H," First Regiment Rhode Island Light Artillery in the War to Preserve the Union.* Providence, 1894.

Fleharty, S. F. *Our Regiment. A History of the 102d Illinois Infantry Volunteers.* Chicago, 1865.

Gammons, John G. *The Third Massachusetts Regiment Volunteers Militia in the War of the Rebellion.* Providence, 1906.

Gates, Theodore B. *The "Ulster Guard" (20th N. Y. State Militia) and the War of the Rebellion.* New York, 1879.

Gibson, J. T. (ed.) *History of the Seventy-eighth Pennsylvania Volunteer Infantry.* Pittsburgh, 1905.

Gould, Joseph. *The Story of the Forty-eighth.* Philadelphia, 1908.

Graham, Mathew J. *The Ninth Regiment New York Volunteers (Hawkins' Zouaves).* New York, 1900.

Haines, A. A. *History of the Fifteenth Regiment New Jersey Volunteers.* New York, 1883.

Haynes, Martin A. *A History of the Second Regiment New Hampshire Volunteer Infantry in the War of the Rebellion.* Lakeport, New Hampshire, 1896.

Hays, Gilbert Adams. *Under the Red Patch.* (63rd Pennsylvania Infantry). Pittsburgh, 1908.

Holbrook, Wm. C. *A Narrative of the Services of the Officers and Enlisted Men of the 7th Regiment of Vermont Volunteers.* New York, 1882.

Hopkins, William P. *The Seventh Regiment Rhode Island Volunteers in the Civil War 1862-1865.* Providence, 1903.

Horton and Teverbaugh. *A History of the Eleventh Regiment (Ohio Volunteers Infantry).* Dayton, 1866.

Hubert, Charles F. *History of the Fiftieth Regiment Illinois Volunteers Infantry.* Kansas City, Mo., 1894.

Isham, Asa B. *An Historical Sketch of the Seventh Regiment Michigan Volunteer Cavalry.* New York, 1894.

Jackman, Lyman. *History of the Sixth New Hampshire Regiment in the War for the Union.* Concord, 1891.

Jenkins, Luke E. *First Regiment of Infantry Massachusetts Volunteer Militia.* Boston, 1903.

Keil, F. W. *Thirty-Fifth Ohio (Infantry).* Fort Wayne, Ind., 1894.

Kent, Charles N. *History of the Seventeenth Regiment New Hampshire Volunteer Infantry. 1862-1863.* Concord, 1898.

Kiefer, William R. *History of the One Hundred and Fifty-third Regiment Pennsylvania Volunteers Infantry.* Easton, Pennsylvania, 1909.

Kirk, Hyland C. *Heavy Guns and Light* (4th New York Heavy Artillery). New York, 1890.

Kreutzer, William. *Service with the Ninety-Eighth N. Y. Volunteers.* Philadelphia, 1878.

Lee, William O. *Personal and Historical Sketches and Facial History of . . . the Seventh Regiment Michigan Volunteer Cavalry 1862-1865.* Detroit, 1902.

Lincoln, W. S. *Life with the Thirty-fourth Mass. Infantry in the War of the Rebellion.* Worcester, 1879.

Little, Henry F. W. *The Seventh Regiment New Hampshire Volunteers in the War of the Rebellion.* Concord, 1896.

Lord, Edward O. *History of the Ninth Regiment New Hampshire Volunteers in the War of the Rebellion.* Concord, 1895.

Macnamara, Daniel G. *The History of the Ninth Regiment Massachusetts Volunteer Infantry.* Boston, 1889.

Marbaker, Thos. D. *History of the Eleventh New Jersey Volunteers.* Trenton, 1898.

McGregor, Charles. *History of the Fifteenth Regiment New Hampshire Volunteers 1862-1863.* 1900.

Mills, John Harrison. *Chronicles of the Twenty-first Regiment New York State Volunteers.* Buffalo, 1887.

Moors, J. F. *History of the Fifty-second Regiment Massachusetts Volunteers.* Boston, 1893.

Morris, W. S. *History 31st Regiment Illinois Volunteers.* Evansville, Indiana, 1902.

Muffly, J. W. *The Story of Our Regiment. A History of the 148th Pennsylvania Vols.* Des Moines, Iowa, 1904.

Murray, Thomas Hamilton. *History of the Ninth Regiment Connecticut Volunteer Infantry.* New Haven, 1903.

Page, Charles D. *History of the Fourteenth Regiment Connecticut Vol. Infantry.* Meriden, 1906.

Pettengill, S. B. *College Cavaliers.* (A troop of New Hampshire Cavalry.) Chicago, 1883.

Powers, George W. *The Story of the Thirty-eighth Regiment of Massachusetts Volunteers.* Cambridge, 1866.

Preston, N. D. *History of the Tenth Regiment of Cavalry New York State Volunteers.* New York, 1892.

Rawling, C. J. *History of the First Regiment Virginia Infantry. (Federal).* Philadelphia, 1887.

(Regimental Association). *History of the Eighteenth Regiment of Cavalry Pennsylvania Volunteers.* New York, 1909.

(Regimental Committee). *History of the Third Pennsylvania Cavalry . . . in the American Civil War 1861-1865.* Philadelphia, 1905.

Rhodes, John H. *The History of Battery "B," First Regiment, Rhode Island Light Artillery.* Providence, 1894.

Roe, Alfred S. *The Fifth Regiment Massachusetts Volunteer Infantry.* Boston, 1911.

Roe, Alfred S. *The Tenth Regiment Massachusetts Volunteer Infantry, 1861-1864.* Springfield, 1909.

Roe, Alfred S. *The Thirty-ninth Regiment Massachusetts Volunteers 1862-1865.* Worcester, 1914.

Royse, Isaac H. C. *History of the 115th Regiment Illinois Volunteer Infantry.* Terre Haute, Indiana, 1900.

Scott, R. B. *The History of the 67th Regiment Indiana Infantry Volunteers.* Bedford, Indiana, 1892.

Small, A. R. *The Sixteenth Maine Regiment in the War of the Rebellion.* Portland, 1886.

Stanyan, John M. *A History of the Eighth Regiment of New Hampshire Volunteers.* Concord, 1892.

Stevens, C. A. *Berdan's United States Sharpshooters in the Army of the Potomac.* St. Paul, Minnesota, 1892.

Sumner, George C. *Battery "D" First Rhode Island Light Artillery in the Civil War.* Providence, 1897.

(Survivors' Association). *History of the 118th Pennsylvania Volunteers.* Philadelphia, 1905.

Thatcher, Marshall P. *A Hundred Battles in the West.* (2nd Michigan Cavalry). Detroit, 1884.

Thompson, Gilbert, *The Engineer Battalion in the Civil War.* Washington, D. C., 1910.

Thompson, S. Millett. *Thirteenth Regiment of New Hampshire Volunteer Infantry.* Boston, 1888.

Thompson, O. R. Howard, and William N. Rauch. *History of the "Bucktails."* (42nd Pennsylvania Infantry or 13th Pennsylvania Reserves). Philadelphia, 1906.

Thorpe, Sheldon B. *The History of the Fifteenth Connecticut Volunteers.* New Haven, 1893.

Tobie, Edward P. *History of the First Maine Cavalry 1861-1865.* Boston, 1887.

Todd, William. *The Seventy-ninth Highlanders New York Volunteers in the War of the Rebellion 1861-1865.* Albany, 1886.

Townsend, Luther T. *History of the Sixteenth Regiment New Hampshire Volunteers.* Washington, 1897.

Waitt, Ernest Linden. *History of the Nineteenth Regiment Massachusetts Volunteer Infantry 1861-1865.* Salem, 1906.

Ward, George W. *History of the Second Pennsylvania Veteran Heavy Artillery.* Philadelphia, 1904.

Ward, Joseph R. C. *History of the One Hundred and Sixth Regiment Pennsylvania Volunteers.* Philadelphia, 1906.

Westbrook, R. S. *History of the 49th Pennsylvania Volunteers.* Altoona, 1898.

Whitcomb, Caroline. *A History of the Second Massachusetts Battery of Light Artillery.* Concord, New Hampshre, 1912.

Williams, John M. *The Eagle Regiment.* (8th Wisconsin Inf.) Belleville, Wisconsin, 1890.

Woodbury, Augustus. *The Second Rhode Island Regiment (Infantry).* Providence, 1875.

Wray, William J. *History of the Twenty-third Pennsylvania Volunteer Infantry. 1903-1904.*

Wulsin, Lucien. *The Story of the Fourth Regiment Ohio Veteran Volunteer Cavalry.* Cincinnati, 1912.

11. Arms of the Federal Army

A. Infantry

(There is no one work denoted exclusively to the Infantry of the Federal Army.)

B. Sharpshooters

Barker, "Ren". *Military History . . . Company "D" 66th Illinois Birge's Sharpshooters in the Civil War 1861-1865.*

Ripley, Wm. Y. W. *Vermont Riflemen in the War for the Union 1861-1865. A History of Company "F" First United States Sharpshooters.* Portland, 1883.

Stevens, C. A. *Berdan's United States Sharpshooters in the Army of the Potomac 1861-1865.* St. Paul, Minn. 1892.

C. Artillery

Birkheimer, William B. *Historical Sketch of the Organization, Administration, Material, and Tactics of the Artillery United States Army.* Washington, D. C. 1884.

D. Cavalry

Brackett, Albert G. *History of the United States Cavalry.* New York, 1865.

Gray, Alonzo, *Cavalry Tactics as Illustrated by the War of the Rebellion.* Fort Leavenworth, Kansas, 1910.

Wagner, Arthur L. (editor). *Cavalry Studies from Two Great Wars.* Kansas City, Missouri, 1896.

E. Signal Corps

Brown, J. Willard. *The Signal Corps, U. S. A. in the War of the Rebellion.* Boston, 1896.

The U. S. Veteran Signal Corps Association including a Partial Roster . . . with a Brief Resume of its Operations from August 14, 1861 to March 14, 1862. 1884.

F. Telegraph

Bates, David Homer. *Lincoln in the Telegraph Office.* New York, 1907.

O'Brien, J. E. *Telegraphing in Battle.* Scranton, Pa. 1910.

Plum, William R. *The Military Telegraph during the Civil War in the United States.* Chicago, 1882.

G. Aeronautics

Haydon, F. Stansbury. *Aeronautics in the Union and Confederate Armies.* Vol. 1 (only one published) Baltimore, 1941.

H. Railroads

Starr, John W. Jr. *Lincoln and the Railroads.* New York, 1927.

Summers, Festus P. *The Baltimore and Ohio in the Civil War,* New York, 1939.

Weber, Thomas. *The Northern Railroads in the Civil War 1861-1865.* New York, 1952.

12. Services of the Federal Army

The best single source for the services in:
Raphael P. Thian. *Legislative History of the General Staff of the Army of the United States . . . 1775-1901.* (Already cited under "High Command.")
Much additional information is contained in the following special accounts.

A. Subsistence Department

Barriger, John W. *Legislative History of the Subsistence Department of the United States Army from June 16, 1775 to August 15, 1876.* (2nd Edition). Washington, D. C. 1877.

Symonds, H. C. *Report of a Commissary of Subsistence 1861-1865.* Sing Sing, New York. 1888.

B. Quartermaster Department

Leib, Charles. *Nine Months in the Quartermaster's Departmen or the Chance of Making A Million.* Cincinnati, 1862.

Major, Duncan K. and Fitch, Roger S. *Supply of Sherman's Army During the Atlantic Campaign.* Fort Leavenworth, Kansas, 1911.

C. Medical Department

Adams, George Worthington. *Doctors in Blue.* New York, 1952.

Bowditch, Henry I. *A Brief Plea for an Ambulance System for the Army of the United States.* 1863.

Duncan, Louis C. *The Medical Department of the United States Army in the Civil War.*

Garrison, Fielding H. *John Shaw Billings: A Memoir.* New York, 1915.

Greenbie, Marjorie Barstow. *Lincoln's Daughters of Mercy.* New York, 1944.

Holland, Mary M. Gardner. *Our Army Nurses . . . 1861-1865.* Boston, 1897.

Johnson, Charles Beneulyn. *Muskets and Medicine or Army Life in the Sixties.* Philadelphia, 1917.

MacFarlane, C. *Reminiscences of an Army Surgeon.* Oswego, New York, 1912.

Otis, George A. *A Report on a Plan for Transporting Wounded Soldiers by Railway in Time of War.* Washington, D. C. 1875.

Palmer, S. A. *The Story of Aunt Becky's Army-Life.* New York, 1868.

Powers, Elvira J. *Hospital Pencillings.* Boston, 1866.

Robinson, Victor. *White Caps: The Story of Nursing.* Philadelphia, 1946.

Smith, Adelaide W. *Reminiscences of an Army Nurse during the Civil War.* New York, 1911.

D. Ordnance Department

(See "Munitions of War")

E. Intelligence Agencies

Baker, L. C. *History of the United States Secret Service.* Philadelphia, 1867.

Beymer, William. *On Hazardous Service: Scouts and Spies of the North and South.* New York, 1912.

Bryan, George S. *The Spy in America.* Philadelphia, 1943.

Edmonds, S. Emma E. *Nurse and Spy in the Union Army.* Hartford, 1866.

Gray, Wood. *The Hidden Civil War: The Story of the Copperheads.* New York, 1942.

Kane, Harnett T. *Spies for the Blue and Gray.* New York, 1954.

Kerbey, J. O. *The Boy Spy.* Chicago, 1889.

Pinkerton, Allan. *The Spy of the Rebellion.* New York, 1885.

F. Non-Military Agencies

(1) Loyal Publication Society
Tracts (various authors). No. 1-76. New York, 1863-1865.
(2) United States Christian Commission
Annual Reports, 1863-1865
Cross, Andrew B. *The War and the Christian Commission.* 1865.

Moss, Lemuel. *Annals of the United States Christian Commission.* Philadelphia, 1868.

Smith, Edward P. *Incidents of the United States Christian Commission.* Philadelphia, 1871.

(3) United States Sanitary Commission
Hamilton, F. H. (editor). *Surgical Memoirs of the War of the Rebellion.* 3 volumes, New York, 1870-1871.

Maxwell, William Quentin. *Lincoln's Fifth Wheel: The United States Sanitary Commission.* New York, 1956.

Stille, Charles J. *History of the United States Sanitary Commission.* Philadelphia, 1866.

U. S. Sanitary Commission Bulletins. 3 volumes. No. 1-40 November 1, 1863 to August 1, 1865. New York, 1866.

U. S. Sanitary Commission Documents. 2 volumes. New York, 1866.

13. The Federal Navy

Ammen, Daniel. *The Atlantic Coast.* New York, 1883.

Ammen, Daniel. *The Old Navy and the New.* Philadelphia, 1891.

Benjamin, Park. *The United Naval Academy.* New York, 1900.

Bodder, Charles H. *Under Fire with Farragut.* New York, 1919.

Boynton, Charles B. *The History of the Navy during the Rebellion.* 2 volumes. New York, 1867-1868.

Dahlgren, M. V. *Memoirs of John A. Dahlgren.* New York, 1891.

Davis, Charles H. *Life of Charles Henry Davis, Rear Admiral.* Boston, 1899.

Dewey, George. *Autobiography.* New York, 1913.

Dupont, H. A. *Rear-Admiral Samuel Francis Dupont, United States Navy.* New York, 1926.

Ellicott, John M. *The Life of John Ancrum Winslow Rear-Admiral, United States Navy.* New York, 1905.

Franklin, S. R. *Memoirs of a Rear-Admiral.* New York, 1898.

Hamersly, Thomas H. S. *General Register of the United States Navy and Marine Corps.* Washington, 1882.

Hoppin James Mason. *Life of Andrew Hull Foote, Rear-Admiral, United States Navy.* New York, 1874.

Lewis, Charles Lee. *David Glasgow Farragut, Our First Admiral.* Annapolis, 1943.

Macartney, Clarence Edward. *Mr. Lincoln's Adimrals.* 1956.

Mahan, A. T. *The Gulf and Island Waters.* New York, 1883.

Morse, John T. Jr. *Dairy of Gideon Welles.* 3 volumes, Boston, 1911.

Paine, Albert B. *A Sailor of Fortune.* (personal memoirs of Captain B. S. Osbon). New York, 1906.

Porter, David D. *The Naval History of the Civil War.* New York, 1886.

Porter, David D. *Incidents and Anecdotes of the Civil War.* New York, 1885.

Pratt, Fletcher. *Civil War on Western Waters.* New York, 1956.

Sands, Benjamin F. *From Reefer to Rear-Admiral.* New York, 1899.

Schley, Winfield Scott. *Forty-Five Years under the Flag.* New York, 1904.

Selfridge, Thomas O. *Memoirs.* New York, 1924.

Soley, James Russell. *The Blockade and the Cruisers.* New York, 1883.

Thompson, R. M. and Wainwright, R. *Confidential Correspondence of Gustavus Vasa Fox.* 2 volumes, New York, 1920.

United States Navy Department. *Register of the Commisioned and Warrant Officers of the Navy of the United States including Officers of the Marine Corps.* Washington, 1861-1865.

Regulations for the Government of the United States Navy. Washington, 1865.

Laws Relating to the Navy and Marine Corps and the Navy Department. Washington, 1865.

Reports of Secretary of the Navy, 1861-1865. Washington, 1861-1865.

West, Richard S. *The Second Admiral: A Life of David Dixon Porter 1813-1891.* New York, 1937.

14. The Federal Marine Corps

Aldrich, M. Almy. *History of the United States Marine Corps.* Boston, 1875.

15. Munitions of War

37 Congress, 2nd Session. *House Executive Document* No. 67 ("Purchase of Arms").

37 Congress, 2nd Session. *House Report* No. 2 ("Government Contracts").

42 Congress, 2nd Session. *Senate Report* No. 183 ("Sale of Arms").

45 Congress, 3rd Session. *Senate Executive Document* No. 16.

Bruce, Robert V. *Lincoln and the Tools of War.* Indianapolis, 1956.

Buckeridge, J. O. *Lincoln's Choice.* Harrisburg, 1956.

Catalog, Francis Bannerman, Sons. (501 Broadway, N. Y.) 1955.

Chinn, George M. *The Machine Gun.* Vol. 1, Washington, 1951.

Fuller, Claud. *The Whitney Firearms.* Huntington, W. Va. 1946.

Fuller, Claud. *The Rifled Musket,* Harrisburg, Pa., 1958.

Fuller, Claud. and Steuart, Richard D. *Firearms of the Confederacy.* Huntington, W. Va., 1944.

Gluckman, Arcadi. *United States Martial Pistols and Revolvers.* Buffalo, 1944.

United States Muskets, Rifles, and Carbines. Buffalo, 1948.

Satterlee, L. D. *American Gun Makers.* 1953.

Hicks, J. E. *Notes on United States Ordnance.* 2 volumes, Mount Vernon, New York, 1940.

Manucy, Albert. *Artillery through the Ages.* Washington, 1949.

Peterson, Harold L. *The American Sword 1775-1945.* New Hope, Pa., 1954.

American Knives. New York, 1958.

Notes on Ordnance of the American Civil War, Washington, 1959.

Sawyer, Charles Winthrop. *Our Rifles.* Boston, 1941. (First Edition, 1920).

Smith, Winston O. *The Sharps Rifle.* New York, 1943.

16. Northern Press Correspondents

Bullard, F. Lauristin. *Famous War Correspondents.* Boston, 1914.

Crozier, Emmet. *Yankee Reporters 1861-65.* New York, 1956.

Cutler, Andrews Jr. *The North Reports the Civil War.* Pittsburgh, 1955.

Starr, Louis M. *Bohemian Brigade: Civil War Newsmen in Action.* New York, 1954.

Weisberger, Bernard A. *Reporters for the Union,* Boston, 1953.

17. Northern Clergy and the War

Dunham, Chester F. *The Attitude of the Northern Clergy toward the South 1860-1865.* Toledo, Ohio, 1942.

Stanton, R. L. *The Church and the Rebellion.* New York, 1864.

CHAPTER 23

Comments and Conclusions

A S THE YEARS went by, the average Federal veteran came to look back on the war as the greatest event of his life. No experience struck so deep into the lives of the Americans of the last century as the War for the Union. For the descendants of early colonists, the Civil War was a re-affirmation of the principles for which their forebears had fought at Bunker Hill and Lundy's Lane. For the immigrants it was the precipitate which accelerated their absorption into the American melting pot of democracy. German immigrants, in contrast with Irish and English, felt a national consciousness, a participation in the common effort to defend the unity of America, their new home. With the Irish, loyalty to America did not diminish loyalty to Ireland; Irishmen never ceased to try to use America to forward Irish independence. Hence they organized "circles" during the Civil War in the armed forces to take advantage of the strained relations between the United States and England to launch at the close of the war a movement for Irish freedom. It culminated in the so-called "Fenian Invasion of Canada." Scandinavians were helped in effecting the transition from immigrant to American. For the immigrant and native born, the war was a liberal education for many men who had never left their farms or provincial towns. Even some wives visited their husbands in far away states.

Probably the finest result that flowed from this heterogeneous assemblage of various nationalities was the creation of a truly American army, composed of native sons and adopted sons, all animated by a genuine devotion to the Union. All the various racial groups in the population of the North presented to the world a striking example of devotion and loyalty to the Government which had welcomed the exiles of the world.

Possessing greater resources in materials and manpower, the North eventually won the war which very probably could have been terminated much sooner had several mistakes been avoided at the beginning, or at all events, corrected as their effects were realized. At the outbreak of war the Government shared in the prevalent belief that the struggle would be of short duration and permitted short term enlistments.

This policy was partially amended in the later acceptance of three-year volunteers but throughout the entire war Federal commanders were forced to modify their strategy due to the loss of thousands of veterans whose terms of service had expired. A draft was put into execution in the middle of the war but was too long deferred and too discriminatory. The system of bounties and substitutes gave foundation to the not unreasonable claim that it was a poor man's fight. Instead of having an out-and-out draft of the nation's manpower, the Government provided decimated regiments with as "vice-hardened and desperate set of human beings" as ever disgraced an army. Not only was it an insult to the original volunteers who continued to do the fighting but was also the cause of many failures due to the defection of the mercenary riff-raff. The employment of Negroes was a political measure but their presence was resented by both sides while their contribution on the battlefield was of little value. The services of many experienced officers were lost when they were assigned to colored regiments that never saw action. Just how much racial prejudice influenced the volunteer soldier in his opinion of the fighting ability of Negroes and foreigners is difficult to state, but unquestionably it played a part. The dislike for soldiers of Irish extraction would seem to have been less, possibly because of the admittedly fine record such units as the Irish Brigade made.

The training of the volunteer units should have been entrusted to the Regular Army. This was not done, however, and the majority of Federal regiments received little training before going into combat. The training which they did receive consisted in the main of the simplest drill maneuvers exercises in extended order and marksmanship were surprisingly few.

Federal armies were well organized according to the accepted mode into armies, corps, divisions, brigades, and regiments. The great asset of training and experience possessed by officers of the Regular Army was taken advantage of in making assignments on the higher echelon level, but the high rank given to certain political leaders and foreigners can only be justified on the grounds of political expediency. Similar motivation prompted the raising of new regiments instead of keeping the old units up to strength. In general, the artillery units were the best of the Federal arms. Federal guns slowed up and halted enemy attacks when often their supporting infantry had disappeared completely. The cavalry was admittedly inferior to the hard-riding and hunting gentry of the South until the enemy's supply of good mounts was depleted and the Federal horse had acquired an adequate esprit de corps under Hooker. Federal cavalry and infantry suffered from too much impedimenta and inflexibility of movement in the early years of the war. Federal engineer, signal, telegraph, and railroad units gave a good account of themselves; it is unfortunate that the balloon branch of the Federal Army was abolished in view of the potentialities it possessed.

The forces in the field were well supplied by the Quartermaster's Department despite some inferior supplies resulting from early contracts under Cameron. The Ordnance Department provided an ever-increasing supply of weapons and munitions, supplemented in the early months by foreign purchases. General Ripley's refusal to give breech-loading and repeating arms a fair trial very possibly lengthened the war to some degree. Care of the sick and wounded improved after the rejuvenation of the Medical Department which received considerable assistance from civilian agencies. Simultaneously with the inception of the draft appeared the Provost Marshal General's Department which, under excellent leadership, performed invaluable service in checking desertion and administering the draft itself. Intelligence and counterintelligence work was only mediocre.

There was too much spirit of individual independence, especially in the West, to have rendered the enforcement of discipline an easy matter for experienced leaders, but the problem was greatly aggravated by the unusually high proportion of inefficient officers. Natural leaders were lacking in a country where all possessed a keen sense of equality. Soldiers' letters and diaries are filled with criticisms of their officers' intelligence, ability, and morals. Discipline appears to have been better in the East, where a larger number of West Point graduates were assigned. Mutinies were rare but absenteeism and desertion were commonplace with men who exercised their individual judgment as to the immediate need for service and the relative calls of home and Army. Desertion was not adequately punished, but punishments for other offenses weighed much more heavily on

COMBAT VETERANS

A company of the 6th Maine Infantry shortly after their successful bayonet charge against the stone wall and Marye's Heights on May 3, 1863. These men were real fighters, not parade-ground or garrison soldiers. Note how few men remain in this heroic unit.

the men than on their officers, who found solution to their misdemeanors ridiculously easy by resigning.

The individuality of the Federal volunteer stood him in good stead in combat; he was rarely routed even after a severe defeat. Lost battles did not destroy armies. Morale fluctuated less in the West where the armies early acquired the habit of victory; in the East the volunteers displayed remarkable resiliency in recovering from one defeat after another resulting mainly from a succession of poor leaders. Although promotions were fairly rapid for both officers and men the former received leaves of absence much more frequently than their men were granted furloughs. This was partially equalized in the conferring of Medals of Honor to enlisted men only.

Whether in camp, hospital, prison pen, or at the front, the Federal volunteer retained his belief that the cause for which he was fighting was just and would triumph. Those regiments that saw action demonstrated their ability in aggressive, hard, stand-up fighting; over forty Federal regiments lost more than two hundred in killed and mortally wounded alone. The North lacked enthusiastic sentiment for a military life; it considered the war a rebellion which had to be crushed. Until the end the enemy continued to be the brave soldier who was fighting for a wrong cause, but it was the cause which had to be destroyed, not the gallant antagonist. There was little of local hatred or personal antipathy in the attitude of the Federal soldiers toward "Johnny Reb." Northern troops fought under the great handicap of being invaders, as ones who had come to free the slaves, and as destroyers of homes and property. The added incentive possessed by their antagonists, of standing to gain more both politically and materially by the war, was denied to them. Captured "Rebels" yielded little in food and equipment; captured "Yanks" yielded much. Despite these handicaps, despite inferior leadership until 1864, and heavy casualties necessarily resulting from his usually being the aggressor in battle, the Federal volunteer displayed courage and persistency in winning the war. These qualities deserved to be remembered and honored.

INDEX

NOTE: Consult the appropriate chapters for subjects, individuals, and places not listed in the index.

HQ II Corps

1st Div IV Corps

2d Div I Corps

FULL DRESS
*Sergeant Major
Artillery*

UNDRESS
Lt. General

FATIGUE
*Marching Order
Private, Infantry*

2d Div IV Corps

2d Div II Corps

2d Div XXI Corps